PRAISE FOR *JUDGMENT DAYS*

....

Books by Nick Kotz

WILD BLUE YONDER
Money, Politics, and the B-1 Bomber

A PASSION FOR EQUALITY
George Wiley and the Movement
with Mary Lynn Kotz

THE UNIONS
with Haynes Johnson

LET THEM EAT PROMISES
The Politics of Hunger in America

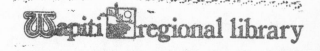

Judgment Days

Lyndon Baines Johnson,
Martin Luther King Jr.,
and the Laws
That Changed America

Nick Kotz

A MARINER BOOK
HOUGHTON MIFFLIN COMPANY
Boston • New York

First Mariner Books edition 2006

Visit our Web site: www.houghtonmifflinbooks.com.

Library of Congress Cataloging-in-Publication Data
Kotz, Nick.
Judgment days : Lyndon Baines Johnson, Martin Luther King Jr.,
and the laws that changed America / Nick Kotz.
p. cm.
Includes bibliographical references (p.   ) and index.
ISBN-13: 978-0-618-08825-6   ISBN-10: 0-618-08825-3
ISBN-13: 978-0-618-64183-3 (pbk.)   ISBN-10: 0-618-64183-1 (pbk.)
1. Johnson, Lyndon B. (Lyndon Baines), 1908–1973 — Friends and associates.
2. King, Martin Luther, Jr., 1929–1968 — Friends and associates. 3. Johnson,
Lyndon B. (Lyndon Baines), 1908–1973 — Relations with African Americans.
4. African Americans — Civil rights — History — 20th century. 5. African
Americans — Legal status, laws, etc. 6. United States. Civil Rights Act of
1964. 7. United States. Voting Rights Act of 1965. 8. United States — Politics
and government — 1963–1969. 9. United States — Race relations — Political
aspects. I. Title.
E847.2.K67 2005 323'.092'2 — dc22 2004059852

Printed in the United States of America

Book design by Robert Overholtzer

MP 10 9 8 7 6 5 4 3 2 1

For Mary Lynn Kotz

Once more the method of nonviolent resistance was unsheathed from its scabbard and once again an entire community was mobilized to confront the adversary. And ... Selma, Alabama, became a shining moment in the conscience of man.

—MARTIN LUTHER KING JR.
March 25, 1965

Their cause must be our cause too. Because it is not just Negroes, but really it is all of us, who must overcome the crippling legacy of bigotry and injustice. And we shall overcome.

—LYNDON BAINES JOHNSON
March 15, 1965

Can the liberties of a nation be thought secure when we have removed their only firm basis, a conviction in the minds of the people that these liberties are the gift of God? That they are not to be violated but with his wrath. Indeed, I tremble for my country when I reflect that God is just: that his justice cannot sleep forever.

—THOMAS JEFFERSON
"Notes on the State of Virginia," 1787

The mystic chords of memory, stretching from every battlefield and patriot grave to every living heart and hearthstone all over this broad land, will yet swell the chorus of the Union, when again touched, as surely they will be, by the better angels of our nature.

—ABRAHAM LINCOLN
March 4, 1861

Fondly do we hope, fervently do we pray, that this mighty scourge of war may speedily pass away. Yet, if God wills that it continue until all the wealth piled by the bondsman's two hundred and fifty years of unrequited toil shall be sunk, and until every drop of blood drawn with the lash shall be paid by another drawn with the sword, as was said three thousand years ago, so still it must be said "the judgments of the Lord are true and righteous altogether."

—ABRAHAM LINCOLN
March 4, 1865

CONTENTS

INTRODUCTION:
SECOND EMANCIPATION

THEY WERE UNLIKELY PARTNERS, the master politician who became president and the eloquent minister who led a revolution. They were suspicious of each other: the president, a rough-talking Texas white man who had lived through a time of rampant racism in the South; the preacher, a southern black visionary who inspired the nation by fighting a nonviolent war.

Yet they came to work together, in a political pas de deux of immense complexity and fragility, to produce the most dramatic social change in America since the Emancipation Proclamation. When it happened, with the passage of the 1964 and 1965 civil rights acts, the Reverend Martin Luther King Jr. told the president of the United States, "You have created a Second Emancipation."

"The real hero is the American Negro," replied Lyndon Baines Johnson.

These two were the indispensable leaders, in the right place at the right time to effect the end of legal apartheid in America. Without the synergy they created together, the outcome of the civil rights revolution would have been very different. That brief moment in the 1960s, a time of jolting social and political turbulence, created significant consequences for all of its citizens. Inspired by the hopes, the dreams, and the acts of courage performed by countless African Americans, along with their white allies, the revolutionaries believed that America ought to be a more just society, a country more firmly anchored to the words the Founding Fathers inscribed in the Declaration of Independence and the Constitution. It so happened that the president of the United States shared those beliefs, to the surprise of many, especially his fellow white southerners. Out of the leadership of Johnson and King came strong new federal laws that erased the indignities of being denied the right to vote, to eat in a restaurant, to use a public restroom, to hold a job, and to choose one's dwelling place strictly because of the color of one's skin, the origin of one's ancestors, or one's gender.

The changes in the status of African Americans and other minorities empowered by the laws emerged from a long history of men and women striving for equality over many generations, dating from appeals to the first Congress in 1789. But those who stood up for change in the 1960s have a special place in that history. A panoply of events and circumstances converged then to create a unique opportunity for the nation to move closer to its ideals. Without tens of thousands of demonstrators demanding change as they transformed restaurant counters into venues for sit-ins, bus trips into Freedom Rides, and voter registration lines into bloody battlefields, the shining moment of the 1960s never would have become even a possibility. Yet for the revolution to succeed, it required extraordinary political leadership from individuals who felt the pressure of the civil rights movement, responded to it, and seized the moment, leaders with sufficient vision, skill, and courage to realize concrete achievements during a brief opportunity for change.

The alliance between Johnson and King was critical in turning opportunity into a realized American dream. They played their roles brilliantly. The dynamic interaction between the two men was remarkable, as were their willingness and their ability to overcome differences, accommodate each other's political needs, and work in complementary ways.

Without both Johnson and King, the civil rights revolution might have ended with fewer accomplishments and even greater trauma. Both had transcended their time and place, even before becoming players on a larger stage. Both had lived through experiences that caused them to see the world a little differently from their peers. Both were men of extraordinary ambition, southerners who shared an understanding of the agony and the promise of their native region. Each was proud, profoundly bold and courageous, and yet privately fearful. King was afraid of going to jail or even of being killed, and was tormented by a sense that he was unworthy and undeserving of his accolades. Johnson was a big man afraid of being laughed at and belittled, insecure about his background and his upbringing. They were never likely to become friends, but they learned to understand each other. Each saw the other as a man with an agenda. Once they learned to let the other's pride prevail, to yield to each other, they worked in powerful tandem. King knew that he had to hold back — to give Johnson time. Johnson knew that he had to support King's marches — up to a point. They were like two forces of nature. It was only when their paths were forced together that they accomplished, in a very brief time, what people thought could not be done.

The partnership between Johnson and King was never easy. Their massive egos and equally massive vulnerabilities made cooperation difficult. Most devastating to their relationship was the insidious role played by another powerful man, J. Edgar Hoover, sole director of the Federal Bureau of Investigation from its inception in 1924 until his death in 1972. His hatred of King, fueled by racism, drove Hoover's relentless five-year campaign to destroy the minister as a respected national leader by constantly whispering poison about King into the president's ear. After Johnson and King split irrevocably over the war in Vietnam, the poison finally did its ugly work.

In the end there was tragedy, as both Johnson and King belatedly realized, with broken hearts, that neither had the power to tame the rage arising from a disastrous war, or to persuade a reluctant nation to take the next necessary steps to repair the residual damage from four hundred years of slavery, racism, and inequality.

At a critical moment in history, however, Johnson and King were united by one uncommon belief. They shared a passion for equality and a dedication to improving the lives of those left out of America's affluent society.

The first rough drafts of this remarkable history were shaped by the traumatic period in which those events were recorded. The brief time span between the assassinations of President John F. Kennedy, the Reverend Martin Luther King Jr., and Senator Robert F. Kennedy — with the instant martyrdom bestowed on each — has made it difficult to see them clearly in all their humanity, much less to judge their effectiveness as leaders. At the same time, the tragedy of the war in Vietnam has obscured a more complete picture of Lyndon Johnson as a national leader. At present, popular memory has fixed King principally as an inspiring orator with a dream of brotherhood and hope. He is joined by the Kennedys, John and Robert, in the popular imagination as the trilogy of heroes who produced the civil rights triumphs of the 1960s. In sharp contrast, Johnson is often perceived as a crude, self-seeking wheeler-dealer who recklessly plunged his country into a Vietnam quagmire and promised grandiose domestic social programs that mostly failed. In the nation's fading recollection, Johnson merely completed in civil rights what John F. Kennedy had already largely accomplished.

What is missing from the popular concept of Lyndon Johnson's presidency is a more complete, balanced picture of his historic record. Against Johnson's devious handling of and tragic miscalculations in Vietnam, other chapters of his administration must be measured. After President Kennedy's assassination, Johnson swiftly united the nation at a time of grievous national tragedy and peril. With masterly skill he persuaded Congress to take the most important action on civil rights since Abraham Lincoln's Emancipation Proclamation. And he expanded the rights and expectations of Americans to include medical care for the elderly and the poor; scholarships and loans to help ensure that any American youth could attend college; federal aid to foster elementary and secondary public education; federal responsibility to protect the quality of the air we breathe and the water we drink; as well as a host of other measures to make life fairer for our poorest citizens and safer and more fulfilling for all Americans.

What is too often missing from our celebrations of Martin Luther King is an appreciation of his skills as a tough, effective, and pragmatic politician, and as an extraordinary healer of factional disputes within the movement. Seldom mentioned is Martin Luther King the prophetic radical who sadly came to believe that the country and its institutions were unwilling to address the issues of economic justice at home and the struggle for freedom by people of color abroad.

Fortunately, a continuing study of history always provides opportunities for reconsideration and revision. Now, such an opportunity presents itself as voluminous new records have become available, and as we move farther from the intense heat and passion of the decade of the 1960s, with its civil rights battles, urban riots, and rancorous discord over the Vietnam War. As we continue the endless search to understand the events that have shaped us — even hoping to glean wisdom for the future — this book seeks to present another view of these men and those times.

Lyndon Johnson's and Martin Luther King's lives intersected at the moment of the assassination of President John Fitzgerald Kennedy on November 22, 1963. At the time of Kennedy's death, his legislative program was deadlocked, the civil rights movement was losing its critical momentum, and public opinion polls suggested that a majority of white Americans believed that black Americans were moving "too fast" in their quest for equality. It was against this background of great uncertainty that Johnson became president and King sought to recharge the energy of the civil rights movement. Both men invoked the memory of the assassinated president as they sought to inspire the nation to a higher purpose.

Even as he took firm and reassuring command of the federal government, Johnson began to recast the civil rights struggle from a legal question to a ringing moral issue.* With a credibility that no northerner could claim, Johnson took his case for equal rights directly to the South. When advisers cautioned him in the earliest days not to deplete his initial store of goodwill on such a divisive issue, Johnson replied, "Well, what the hell's the presidency for?" Instead of husbanding his political capital, Johnson pushed furiously ahead, intent on overcoming the inertia of a deadlocked Congress. He emboldened his supporters with a favorite gambling metaphor, "Let's push in our stack." All the while, the new president wielded legislative skills that earlier had earned him a reputation as the most powerful Senate leader in American history. He had mastered the Senate, it was said, with a dazzling array of tactics collectively known as "the treatment."

King operated most effectively in a different arena, one fraught with uncertainty, volatility, and great personal danger. He sought out the most promising settings for creating dramatic confrontations that would serve as moral passion plays. A successful performance would reveal to the nation the stark contrast between peaceful African American demonstrators and brutal southern racists. King, too, was a gambler and provocateur. Whenever he challenged segregationist power in the Deep South, he knew that he risked his own life and the lives of others. When his campaigns stumbled, he could act with cool ruthlessness to attract national media attention.

As a minister, King wanted to save souls — especially his own — but he measured success only in terms of how effectively he had aroused common American decency to demand an end to the official racism of the South. From church pulpits in Montgomery and Birmingham, and in their streets, King succeeded brilliantly in creating a tableau of good versus evil, justice versus injustice. At the time of President Kennedy's death, King was seeking a new venue for keeping the pressure on the government.

As the fortunes of Johnson and King intertwined in the sad autumn of 1963, each saw ample reason for pessimism about whether they could

---

* On June 11, 1963, President Kennedy, with Vice President Johnson's counsel, first propounded the question of civil rights in terms of moral rights.

work together. Johnson, the consummate Washington insider, was most comfortable working with lobbyists from well-established interest groups, including the polished representatives from the venerable National Association for the Advancement of Colored People. King, by contrast, knew little about Washington's corridors of power. He was a classic outsider, one whose methods of confrontation Lyndon Johnson deplored. In Johnson's universe, the place to write legislation and settle disputes was in the Senate, not in the streets. Yet Johnson recognized at the outset of King's public career that the young southern minister was a force to be reckoned with. From his own political roots in the rural South, Johnson well understood the power of gifted black preachers.[1]

In the events that followed, Johnson and King were both master political jugglers performing a tenuous high-wire act before a national audience. To govern effectively, Johnson had to balance shaky coalitions of unlikely allies, even enemies. King faced a similar challenge to hold together a fractious movement. And the juggling made their cooperation even more difficult. A Johnson-King meeting was guaranteed to produce volumes of hate mail to the president from segregationists and archconservatives. Meanwhile, stinging rebukes would be slung at King by radical young blacks, who would accuse the man who had promised victory through nonviolence of having "sold out." Critical moments of cooperation between Johnson and King therefore needed their own disguises in order to succeed.

The monumental complexity of Lyndon Johnson presented a daunting challenge for Martin Luther King. Johnson was indeed, as others often described him, "a larger-than-life figure," a man of stunning contradictions, enormous abilities, and deep flaws. At his best, Johnson could command forcefully, pouring immense talent and inexhaustible energy into making government work better for its citizens. At other times, Johnson was a driven man, tormented and unpredictably volatile. He was hampered by his tremendous ego, his deeply rooted insecurities, and a personal neediness that no accomplishment could ever completely satisfy. At his eloquent best, Johnson could move a nation with clarion calls for justice, then wield his exceptional ability to persuade others to work with him toward common goals. He could be a caring, generous friend and associate. But at his worst, Johnson was a crude, overbearing bully. When he felt thwarted from getting his way, Johnson sometimes would sink into mournful depression or throw childish tantrums. At such times, Johnson would insist that he was quitting whatever job he held, including the presidency.

As the Vietnam crisis deepened, with mounting American casualties in Southeast Asia and vociferous opposition at home, Johnson graphically displayed that lifelong predisposition toward periods of dark self-doubts and depression. At those times of despair, he spoke of conspiracies against him, and seemed to mistrust the motives of all who opposed his policy. Anyone who disagreed with him, Johnson insisted, was either a Communist or a Communist dupe.*

Johnson's wife, Lady Bird, and his close White House aide Bill Moyers worried about what they described as the president's deep bouts of depression. Moyers, the White House press secretary, whom Johnson treated at times like a son, fretted over what he saw as Johnson's "paranoia," with symptoms that made him "irascible, suspicious, and inconsistent," and combined to create "a very uneven persona."[2]

For Johnson, Vietnam represented a double disaster. From the outset, his instincts told him that the war was not winnable. He feared that he was sinking deeper into a morass with no end in sight. But he did not know how to extricate his nation while still maintaining its credibility and prestige, as well as his own pride and political career. And as the cost of the conflict soared, Johnson sadly realized that the war in Southeast Asia was draining vital resources from the war he most cared about — the one he had declared against poverty. Although Lyndon Johnson was secretive by nature, his repeated deceptions of the American public about his plans for and actions in Vietnam cloaked his self-deceit, the belief that he could somehow preserve his antipoverty programs, his dreams for creating a Great Society.

"There's no chance the ordinary person in the future will ever remember me," Johnson lamented to his biographer Doris Kearns Goodwin, in a telephone conversation just days before he died. "No chance. I would have been better off looking for immortality through my wife and children, and their children in turn, instead of seeking all that love and affection from the American people. They're just too fickle."[3]

Unrealistically, he had wanted to be recognized by African Americans as the champion of civil rights. When black leaders opposed him in a political fight, Johnson was crushed to the point of threatening to resign as

---

* This book cannot devote the space necessary for more than a cursory summary of President Johnson's decision-making process on Vietnam, even though those decisions had important consequences for civil rights and poverty programs. The endnotes and bibliography list the numerous books and records consulted in the attempt to understand Johnson's motivations and actions concerning Vietnam. Of particular importance are the several hundred recorded telephone conversations and notes of national security meetings in which the president spoke at length about Vietnam.

president. "They say I want great power," he confided to an aide. "All I want is a little love." His hunger for public affection was compounded by his perception that "the people" worshiped John F. Kennedy and Martin Luther King Jr. but denied him the same honor.

The glamorous Kennedys touched another raw nerve in Lyndon Johnson, a feeling of inferiority about his rural Texas roots. Although he took fierce pride in his origins, Johnson brooded obsessively that the "Eastern Establishment" scoffed at him as a country bumpkin with only a degree from a small South Texas teachers' college. Johnson believed — with good reason — that he was smarter than "those Harvards," but he also was in awe of the knowledge and polish he imagined the easterners possessed.

Martin Luther King Jr. also wrestled with demons he could neither slay nor tame. He drove himself unmercifully, often ending up in the hospital with physical and mental exhaustion and depression. He would bounce back, just as Johnson did, but his resilience ebbed — as Johnson's did — as the enormous task ahead came to seem overwhelming. King was tormented by feelings of unworthiness as honors were heaped on him, including the Nobel Peace Prize. He did not seek martyrdom, but wanted to lead a normal and prayerful life. He accepted his fate as the movement leader who could not quit, but he longed for the tranquillity of a campus and a life far away from the always dangerous struggle.

As a minister, he prayed daily, with an unwavering faith. King felt guilty, however, about the brief pleasures he experienced in the time he spent with his few close friends, associates in the Southern Christian Leadership Conference with whom he could relax. But he also was riddled with guilt that his personal life was not consistent with his sermons on morality. And he was fearful that J. Edgar Hoover's vendetta against him would finally succeed in exposing his repeated marital infidelities and knock him off his righteous pedestal. King worried about his transgressions as a sinner, but he could not change his chaotic life.

Whatever their differences, Johnson and King were united by their most closely held values. Foremost, both men believed passionately in the promise of American democracy. Each was certain of his own place in that history. Perhaps of equal importance, they shared an affection and genuine affinity for the South, consciously having chosen to base their lives and careers there. They held the same understanding of basic human hopes, of the bitter fruits of grinding poverty and racial conflict, and of the deep longing to live in peace, away from the violence that lurked beneath the façade of southern politeness. In the end, the two men realized, and acknowledged to each other, that only a southern minister could have stirred the movement of southern blacks — and only a president from the South could have moved the federal government and the nation at large in the mid-1960s. It took both the preacher and the president to end the state-sanctioned cruelties and injustices that prevailed in the South.

By the end of the 1960s, the civil rights movement was shattered, and counterrevolutionaries were in the ascendancy. Johnson and King's relationship ended badly. Divided over the Vietnam War, they set out to destroy each other. In the process, they weakened their common pursuit of civil rights. Each man's life ended in frustration and sorrow. But they shared a shining moment, a story that Americans would do well to remember.

Judgment Days

1

✦ ✦ ✦ ✦ ✦ ✦

The Cataclysm

THE DAY BEGAN in triumph for John Fitzgerald Kennedy. Riding through the sunny streets of downtown Dallas in an open convertible, his young wife, Jacqueline, beside him, the president of the United States beamed at the cheering crowds. Two cars back in the motorcade, Lyndon Baines Johnson, who knew he had been Kennedy's choice for vice president principally to keep the South in the Democratic fold, felt vindicated by the warm reception in his home state. Both men had been apprehensive about open hostility from angry southerners in the wake of Kennedy's call for a new civil rights law.

Instead, thousands of ebullient Texans applauded and waved at their handsome young president and at their own Lyndon Johnson. In the front car, Nellie Connally, wife of Texas governor John Connally, turned back toward John Kennedy. "You can't say Dallas doesn't love you," she beamed.[1]

An instant later, Nellie Connally heard a loud noise, followed rapidly by several more explosions. She saw President Kennedy grip his throat with both hands and heard her husband moan, "Oh, no, no, no," and then, "My God, they are going to kill us all!" Kennedy was slumped over, bleeding, as was Governor Connally, whom she cradled in her arms as the convertible sped away.[2]

Two cars behind them, Secret Service agent Rufus Youngblood yelled, "Get down!" and shoved Lyndon Johnson to the floorboard. The agent threw his own two hundred–pound body across Johnson to protect the vice president. Pinned down and unable to see, Johnson heard tires screeching as he felt the car accelerate. He heard the radioed voice of agent Roy Kellerman from Kennedy's car shouting, "Let's get the heck out of here!" Then he heard still another agent's voice: "The President has been shot. We don't know who else they are after."

Moments later, Secret Service men rushed Johnson and his wife, Lady Bird, into Parkland Memorial Hospital, where they huddled silently together in an examining room with the shades drawn. In an adjoining room, Secret Service agent Henry Roberts spoke into his radio to headquarters in Washington. "We don't know what the full scope of this thing is," he said. "It could be a conspiracy to try to kill the president, vice president — try to kill everybody."[3]

Less than an hour after the shots were fired, at 1:22 P.M. Central Standard Time, November 22, 1963, White House aide Kenneth O'Donnell came into the Johnsons' room. "He's gone," he told them. At that moment, fifty-five-year-old Lyndon Baines Johnson became the thirty-sixth president of the United States.[4]

In his two-story frame home on Auburn Avenue in Atlanta, the Reverend Dr. Martin Luther King Jr. struggled awake late that November morning, physically and mentally exhausted from too much travel and too little sleep. During the previous seven days, King had been constantly on the road, first for a rally at Danville, Virginia, where the sparse turnout of supporters suggested that the civil rights leader would have trouble launching a planned major campaign there. The young minister was deeply worried that the civil rights movement was losing momentum and perplexed about where he should now direct the energies of his Southern Christian Leadership Conference (SCLC) to pressure Congress into approving civil rights legislation. If not Danville, where should King go next? With conflicting advice coming from his aides, King did not know what to do.

After Danville, he had flown to New York to meet privately at Idlewild Airport with two key advisers, attorneys Clarence Jones and Stanley David Levison, who both urged him to launch a new campaign, lest the mantle of civil rights leadership pass to younger, more radical men. He then stopped off at a resort in New York's Catskill Mountains at the national convention of United Synagogues of America to receive its annual leadership award. Next, he flew to Chicago to speak to the annual convention of the Union of American Hebrew Congregations, representing Reform Jews. Such speeches, more than 150 a year, left him constantly tired. They were necessary to build support and raise the funds needed to keep the SCLC afloat, yet aides constantly reminded King that those activities were no substitute for the kinds of direct-action demonstrations that had catapulted him to prominence. It had been just such an action in Birmingham, Alabama, six months earlier that had prompted President Kennedy to introduce a civil rights bill, after two years of urging from movement leaders. His proposed bill would outlaw segregation in public accommodations, forbid discrimination in employment, and withdraw federal aid from state and local governments that discriminated against anyone because of race, national origin, or religion. But now the legislation faced poor prospects in Congress, and King feared that Kennedy's enthusiasm for the bill had waned as his 1964 reelection campaign drew nearer.

A television set flickered in the background as King tried to rest in his upstairs bedroom. At the first news bulletin, he shouted downstairs to his wife, "Corrie, I just heard that Kennedy has been shot, maybe killed!" Coretta Scott King, who had been writing notes at her desk, rushed upstairs to her husband's side. Horrified, the couple stared at scenes of the Dallas motorcade and the vigil at Parkland Memorial Hospital.

"This is just terrible," cried King. Death threats had become a constant in the King home. "I hope he will live. . . . I think if he lives — if he pulls through this, it will help him to understand better what we go through." Moments later, the television news anchor announced that the president was dead.

"This is what's going to happen to me," an agonized King told his wife. "This is such a sick society."[5]

Lyndon Johnson's first fear was that the Soviet Union might have unleashed an attack against the United States. If the Soviets had shot the president, he thought, who would they shoot next? And what was going on in Washington? And when were the missiles coming? With these thoughts racing through his mind, Johnson ordered the Secret Service to delay public announcement of Kennedy's death until he and Lady Bird had left Parkland Hospital.[6]

As they prepared to leave, Johnson urged his wife to go see "Jackie and Nellie." In a narrow hallway outside the main operating room, Mrs. Johnson found Jacqueline Kennedy standing alone, her face frozen in horror, her pink suit spattered with her husband's blood. "God help us all!" Lady Bird said, embracing John F. Kennedy's young widow. Lady Bird next went to her old friend Nellie Connally, who was being reassured by doctors that her husband would live.[7]

The Johnsons then were rushed out a side door of the hospital and into separate unmarked police cars. Eight minutes later they arrived at Love

Field. Scrambling up the ramp into Air Force One, Lyndon Johnson faced his first decisions as president. General Godfrey McHugh and other White House aides had been urging that the president's official plane take off for Washington the moment the Johnsons came on board, but Lyndon Johnson countermanded the general's order.[8]

He would not leave Dallas without Jacqueline Kennedy and the body of her husband — then en route to Love Field — nor without first taking the oath of office as president. With that ceremony, he meant to show the world that the government of the United States was still functioning in an orderly manner. U.S. district judge Sarah Hughes, an old Johnson friend and supporter, was summoned from her office in Dallas. Hughes boarded the Boeing 707, and as Lyndon Baines Johnson placed his hand on a Catholic prayer book, she administered the oath of office. Lady Bird Johnson and Jacqueline Kennedy stood at his side. After kissing each woman on the cheek, President Johnson commanded Colonel James Swindall, the pilot of Air Force One, "Let's be airborne!"[9]

As the plane sped toward Washington, Johnson telephoned Rose Kennedy, mother of the murdered president. "I wish to God there was something I could do," he said. "I wanted to tell you that we were grieving with you." Choked with emotion, Johnson handed the telephone to Lady Bird to try to console Mrs. Kennedy.[10]

Over the jet's sophisticated communications system, Johnson then arranged for congressional leaders and national security advisers to meet at the White House upon his arrival in Washington.[11] And he instructed six members of the Cabinet aboard an airplane bound for Japan to change course and return to the capital. A few minutes earlier, Secretary of State Dean Rusk had informed that planeload of Cabinet members, reporters, and their party that President Kennedy had been shot, but they had not been told his condition. The delegation sat in stunned silence. When the airplane began to make a slow U-turn over the Pacific and head back toward the United States, they knew that their president was dead.[12]

Two hours and ten minutes after leaving Dallas, Johnson stood in darkness on the tarmac at Andrews Air Force Base outside Washington. His craggy face illuminated by klieg lights, the new president spoke to the nation: "This is a sad time for all people. We have suffered a loss that cannot be weighed. For me it is a deep personal tragedy. I know the world shares the sorrow that Mrs. Kennedy and her family bear. I will do my best. That is all I can do. I ask for your help and God's."[13]

Touching down on the South Lawn of the White House after a ten-minute helicopter ride from Andrews, Johnson strode deliberately toward the entrance of the Oval Office. Then, abruptly changing his mind, he walked through the White House basement to his vice presidential suite in the Executive Office Building. There he asked the assembled congressional leaders for their support.[14] He approached each member of Kennedy's Cabinet and staff and asked them all to stay on. "I need you more than the President needed you," Johnson told them.[15] He called Keith Funston, chairman of the New York Stock Exchange, to thank him for shutting down the market as soon as news broke of the assassination.[16] He phoned Richard Maguire, treasurer of the Democratic National Committee and chief fundraiser for the expected 1964 Kennedy presidential campaign, and asked him to continue his work.[17] He contacted former presidents Harry Truman and Dwight Eisenhower to request their advice.* He arranged to meet Eisenhower in Washington the following morning.[18]

FBI director J. Edgar Hoover called the new president with disquieting information about Lee Harvey Oswald, who had just been arrested and charged with Kennedy's murder, a story that hinted at Cold War conspiracy. A former U.S. Marine, Oswald had lived for several years in the Soviet Union, where he had married a Russian woman and tried to become a Soviet citizen. Oswald had worked for a group supporting Cuban Communist leader Fidel Castro and recently had visited the Soviet consulate in Mexico City.[19]

The news could hardly have been more ominous. The Cold War between the United States and the Soviet Union was raging across the world — from the divided city of Berlin to Vietnam. Only thirteen months had passed since the United States and the Soviet Union had come within an eyelash of nuclear war over the presence of Soviet missiles on the island of Cuba, ninety-two miles from the American shore. After a nerve-wracking thirteen-day standoff, the crisis had ended when the Soviets agreed to remove the missiles.

Despite his own fears about Soviet involvement in the assassination, Johnson knew that the nation needed his reassurance. Concerned that Dallas district attorney Henry Wade might rush to a public judgment involving Oswald in a Communist plot, the new president asked his longtime adviser Horace Busby to assign Texas attorney general Waggoner Carr to take command of the assassination investigation.[20]

For most of his life, Lyndon Johnson had dreamed of becoming president. Now, under nightmarish circumstances, his wish had been fulfilled, and he faced a nation stunned by sorrow, fear, and troubling questions:

---

* Johnson also tried to reach the oldest living ex-president, eighty-nine-year-old Herbert Hoover, but was unable to do so and instead left a message with Hoover's son.

Who had killed Jack Kennedy and why? And who was this hulking Texan with the deep southwestern twang who had suddenly taken Kennedy's place as president of the United States?

Congressman Hale Boggs of Louisiana, the deputy majority leader of the House of Representatives, raced toward the Capitol from his office across the street in the Cannon House Office Building as soon as he heard the news, nearly crashing into Representative William Colmer, a Mississippi Democrat and diehard segregationist. "Your people killed that man!" Boggs shouted at a startled Colmer. "Your Ross Barnetts!"[21]

The grief-stricken Boggs was not the only person to leap to the conclusion that Kennedy's murder was related in some way to racial strife in the South. In late September 1962, Governor Ross Barnett of Mississippi had fueled a deadly riot by defying President Kennedy's order making James Meredith the first African American admitted to the University of Mississippi.[22] Barnett's Mississippi had produced more civil rights–related violence than any other state. Civil rights activists had been beaten and murdered, black churches had been burned, and Ku Klux Klansmen had waged a campaign of terror with virtual immunity from state and local law enforcement.

Senator Richard Russell, a Georgia Democrat and leader of the southern segregationist forces in the Senate, stood in his usual spot in the Senate Marble Room reading the news wires as they came out of a ticker tape machine. Russell's eyes welled with tears as he read of the "dastardly crime . . . which had stricken a brilliant, dedicated statesman at the very height of his powers." Russell took solace in knowing that his friend and protégé Lyndon Johnson would be taking over the reins — a man he had long believed had "all the talents and abilities to be a strong president."[23]

Senator Hubert Humphrey, a Minnesota Democrat and deputy majority leader of the Senate, heard the news as he was attending a luncheon at the Chilean embassy in Washington. Overcome by emotion, Humphrey wept openly, then steadied himself to announce the sad news to the assembled guests. As he left the embassy, Humphrey worried about the health of his friend Lyndon Johnson — about his earlier heart attack and how he might have been shaken emotionally by the trauma of the day. But that evening Humphrey felt reassured by Johnson's measured calm when he saw Johnson in his office. Putting his arm around Humphrey, Johnson told him that he desperately needed the help of his friend from Minnesota — who had been the Democrats' point man on civil rights since 1948.

Most Americans, regardless of their political beliefs, reacted to the assassination with a profound sense of shock and grief. The attractive young president and his glamorous wife had charmed the nation, and indeed people throughout the world, with their vitality, graciousness, and style. But race had become a dominant, divisive issue in American public life. In disturbing ways, feelings about race influenced immediate reactions to Kennedy's murder. Some hard-core racists, bitter about the president's proposals to outlaw segregation and forbid discrimination against Negroes, actually cheered the news of his death. In a dormitory at Mississippi State College, cowbells rang in celebration.[24] A young man from Alabama proclaimed on an Atlanta radio call-in show that night that "Kennedy got exactly what he deserved — that any white man who did what he did for niggers should be shot!"[25]

A large majority of America's 22 million African Americans admired John F. Kennedy and considered him a sympathetic friend. Many assumed at first that his assassin had been motivated by racial hatred. That assumption proved unfounded, but it reflected the highly charged political and social climate of the times. After four years of increasingly potent civil rights protests, the White House and Congress finally had begun to respond to black citizens' demands for legislation forbidding segregation and discrimination in public accommodations, voting, employment, and schools. As the civil rights forces led by Martin Luther King and other black leaders increased pressure for change, southern vigilantes from the Ku Klux Klan and White Citizens Councils retaliated with increased violence. Only two months earlier, four young black girls, wearing their white Sunday dresses, had died in a fiery blast when Klan members dynamited their Birmingham, Alabama, church as parishioners gathered for morning worship.

In a Cleveland, Ohio, hotel ballroom, Leslie Dunbar, director of the Southern Regional Council, a moderate voice for improved race relations, was preparing to address a luncheon meeting of civil rights leaders. When he heard about the president's assassination, he tore his prepared speech into pieces and dropped it into a wastebasket just before his scheduled presentation. Dunbar had intended to excoriate President Kennedy and his brother, Attorney General Robert Kennedy, for moving too slowly on civil rights. Instead, the meeting abruptly broke up as the attendees raced to the telephones and television set in the hotel lobby.

Dunbar's complaints about the Kennedy administration were widely shared among the civil rights leaders present at that meeting of the National Association of Inter-group Relations Officials (NAIRO). They were critical of Kennedy for his hesitation in advocating new civil rights laws and for the government's failure to protect peaceful black demonstrators who were being brutalized in the South. Even though Kennedy was widely admired by the black masses, many civil rights leaders had come to see him as a white politician who had initially shown great promise but who seemed to respond only to constant prodding and political pressure.[26]

The assessment was harsh but not far off the mark. Two days earlier, on November 20, Robert Kennedy had celebrated his thirty-eighth birthday at an office party in which he stood on his desk and satirically described how his work on civil rights as attorney general had made President Kennedy much more popular in the South. He joked that "the administration would have floundered without him — he'd captured the South, labor would be committed to Democrats forever," and that he had made the Democrats the "law-and-order party." As Assistant Attorney General Ramsey Clark left the celebration, he reflected that with the attorney general about to resign to run his brother's reelection campaign, the civil rights bill was dead until after the 1964 election.[27]

Leslie Dunbar's speech was not the only one discarded that Friday afternoon. Senate Majority Leader Mike Mansfield, a Montana Democrat, had prepared a speech defending Congress from criticism that it was moving too slowly on civil rights legislation. In an earlier civil rights fight, he planned to tell his colleagues, haste had only helped the bill's segregationist opponents. At news of the assassination, Mansfield hurried to the Senate dais to comfort Senator Edward Kennedy, the slain president's youngest brother, who was presiding. At a loss for words, Mansfield adjourned the Senate.

The Reverend Walter Fauntroy, Washington director of King's Southern Christian Leadership Conference, heard news of the assassination on his car radio as he was leaving a restaurant in downtown Washington, D.C. He too thought at first that the violence directed against black civil rights demonstrators "has now reached the White House. They hate Kennedy the way they hate us!" As for Lyndon Johnson, Fauntroy dismissed the new president as "a 'wheeler-dealer' from the South."[28]

Twenty-three-year-old Julian Bond, an officer of the Student Nonviolent Coordinating Committee (SNCC), the most militant national civil rights organization, was having lunch with a columnist from the *Atlanta Journal* when he heard the news. Bond wondered first "whether Kennedy's assassin was a left-winger, and would people like us be blamed?" Bond then called a friend in Texas to ask, "Who is this guy Lyndon Johnson?" His friend warned him that Johnson was "a tool of the oil interests with a mixed civil rights record" and that "we should be wary and suspicious."[29]

In Atlanta, eight-year-old Yolanda King arrived home from school in tears. Rushing into her father's arms, she cried, "Oh, Daddy, now we will never get our freedom." Martin Luther King responded softly, "Now don't you worry, baby. It's going to be all right."[30]

King spent the afternoon at home on the telephone gathering information and advice from his aides and preparing a statement about the assassination. He found that the SCLC's leaders were spread out around the South. In St. Helena Island, South Carolina, the Reverend Andrew Young, Dorothy Cotton, and Septima Clark were conducting an SCLC workshop training new local leaders for upcoming demonstrations. Upon hearing the news, Young led the group in prayers for the country; then, for the rest of the day, the activists sang movement spirituals.[31]

In Danville, Virginia, the Reverend C. T. Vivian, an official of King's Southern Christian Leadership Conference, was briefing a group of new civil rights workers who would fan out across the southwestern Virginia town to inform its citizens why Martin Luther King Jr. had chosen it as the next target in his campaign for racial equality. After a messenger whispered news of the assassination, Vivian told the recruits to go home. They would demonstrate another day. Vivian himself was stoic, dry-eyed about the president's murder. The movement was used to murder. Kennedy's death was one more event to be tallied in Vivian's deep belief that "everything done to destroy us, develops us."[32]

By late afternoon, Martin Luther King had reached Clarence Jones and Stanley Levison, his two closest advisers outside the SCLC staff. Together they agreed on a statement which stressed that an atmosphere of violence and hatred in the country had contributed to President Kennedy's assassination. "I am shocked and grief stricken at the tragic assassination of President Kennedy," King's statement read. "He was a great and dedicated President. His death is a great loss to America and the world. The finest tribute that the American people can pay to the late President Kennedy is to implement the progressive policies that he sought to initiate in foreign and domestic relations."[33]

Tension is expected anytime power is transferred from one group to another, but the normal tension accompanying a presidential transition was compounded by the upheaval of November 22, 1963. Grief and resentment led to emotional outbursts from people close to both Jack Kennedy and Lyndon Johnson. It began in the rear of Air Force One on the sad flight back to Washington as JFK's closest aides huddled with Jacqueline Kennedy around the coffin of the late president. The Kennedy men seethed, feeling that Johnson was grasping power too quickly. They thought that he should have used Air Force Two, the vice presidential plane, to return to Washington.[34] Lawrence O'Brien, Kennedy's chief of congressional relations, was disturbed that Johnson had begun imploring him to stay on in his job at a time when O'Brien wanted only to mourn beside his friend's coffin.[35]

As soon as Air Force One came to a stop at Andrews, Robert Kennedy charged onto the plane, shouting, "Where is Jackie? I want to be with Jackie." As he pushed through the plane, he brushed past Lyndon Johnson without saying a word to the new president. Johnson ignored the snub, but Congressman Jack Brooks of Texas, also on the plane, declared that Johnson should fire Kennedy immediately "because he never will be loyal."[36]

Standing on the tarmac watching Jack Kennedy's coffin being lowered from the airplane, John F. Bailey, the burly chairman of the Democratic National Committee, muttered, "Now that son-of-a-bitch Lyndon Johnson is going to be President."[37]

As Johnson and Kennedy staff members worked side by side that night in the Executive Office Building, grief occasionally exploded into anger. When Johnson aide Cliff Carter asked a Kennedy secretary to bring him some sheets of White House notepaper for President Johnson, she burst into tears. "He can't even let the body get cold before he starts using his stationery," she complained.[38]

Johnson used the stationery that night to write notes to President Kennedy's children, Caroline and John Jr. "It will be many years before you understand fully what a great man your father was," he wrote to the late president's little son. "His loss is a deep personal tragedy for all of us, but I wanted you particularly to know that I share your grief. You can always be proud of him."[39]

That the assassination had occurred in Johnson's native state heightened the tensions surrounding his sudden ascension to the presidency. Even before Kennedy and Johnson had embarked on their fateful trip, Dallas was notorious for its nasty political climate. Less than a month earlier, a mob of right-wing zealots in Dallas had jeered and spat at Adlai E. Stevenson, Kennedy's ambassador to the United Nations and himself a former Democratic presidential candidate. In the 1960 presidential campaign, even Johnson, then Senate majority leader, and Lady Bird had been heckled and shoved as they campaigned in Dallas for the Kennedy–Johnson ticket.

On the helicopter ride from Andrews Air Force Base to the White House, animosity toward Texas poured out. Kennedy aide Theodore Sorensen exploded at George Reedy, the Johnson aide seated beside him. "George, I hate that goddamned state of Texas of yours," Sorensen shouted above the roar of helicopter engines. "I wish it never had existed!"[40] Other Kennedy aides would acknowledge later that in their first blinding emotions of shock, grief, and anger, the thought had even crossed their minds that Lyndon Johnson was somehow involved in the assassination.

The special burden of being a Texan on November 22 occurred to Lady Bird Johnson almost immediately. Overwhelmed by her own feelings as she tried to comfort Jacqueline Kennedy on board Air Force One, Lady Bird almost pleaded for understanding. "Oh, Mrs. Kennedy," she said, "you know we never even wanted to be vice president, and now, dear God, it's come to this." She was horrified that the assassination had taken place in Texas.[41] "There is that sense of shame over the violence and hatred that has gripped our land," she later wrote in her diary. "Shame for America! Shame for Texas!"[42]

When the helicopter landed at the White House, Lady Bird stepped into a limousine to drive to the Johnson home in northwest Washington, where friends and advisers were gathering. Riding through the darkened streets, she and her longtime friend Elizabeth Carpenter talked about the difficult days ahead. After closing the window separating them from the driver, Carpenter said, "It's a terrible thing to say, but the salvation of Texas is that the governor of Texas was hit."

"Don't think I haven't thought of that," Lady Bird replied. "I only wish it could have been me."

Searching for a positive thought, the new first lady said quietly, "Lyndon is a good man to have in a crisis." Carpenter nodded. Both women also knew that, without a crisis or major undertaking to challenge his enormous talents, Lyndon Johnson could behave abysmally. He could be arrogant, crude, overbearing, spoiled, petulant, and brooding, with mood swings into deep depression and pessimism. They had seen that Lyndon Johnson far too often during the nearly three years he had served loyally but unhappily as vice president.[43]

As he had set out with President Kennedy on the trip to Dallas, Lyndon Johnson felt burdened with the frustrations of his largely ceremonial office. Having been the most powerful majority leader in the history of the

U.S. Senate, Johnson had to endure the ignominy of powerlessness in the vice presidency — his role reduced to cutting ribbons and making good-will tours around the world. He was ignored at important administration meetings — or not even invited. He worried about recurrent rumors that Kennedy would dump him from the ticket in the 1964 campaign.

The vice president's misery was compounded by the disrespect shown him by some of the younger New Frontiersmen, especially the president's brother, Attorney General Robert Kennedy, who in meetings either ignored Johnson or treated him with contempt. Carried away by the hubris of their first taste of political power — and blinded by their inexperience — the young Kennedy men saw none of Johnson's complexities and effectiveness as a leader, but saw him as the caricature of a crude, irrelevant frontier westerner, a throwback to a bygone era. At a White House reception two young Kennedy appointees had rudely ignored Johnson's effort to join their conversation. "Fuck Lyndon Johnson," one muttered — an imprecation heard clearly by the vice president, a man of great pride and surprisingly thin skin to such slights.[44]

The man who had just become president of the United States stood just over six feet, four inches tall. Eyes fixed in a piercing squint, a long nose, and even longer ears, his was a mien that made an easy target for political cartoonists. With both an ego and insecurities as outsized as his extraordinary talent, an intense desire to be loved by everyone, and a burning need to be in control of the action, Johnson had brooded constantly about his future in the Kennedy administration. In the months before the assassination, his aides had been shocked to see the vice president grossly overweight, depressed, and drinking too much whisky — dangerous indulgences for a man who eight years earlier had barely survived a massive heart attack. Bathing himself in maudlin self-pity, Johnson had poured out his unhappiness to his closest associates. He talked of retiring from politics — giving up his ambition to become president — and turning again to teaching.[45] At times he claimed he would quit — go into business and make a lot of money. Now, after the gunfire in Dallas, his situation had changed dramatically.

Jack Kennedy and Lyndon Johnson had gone to Texas to raise campaign funds. Kennedy feared that feuding Democratic factions in the state, locked in a mean-spirited internecine battle, could cost him Texas — and the upcoming presidential election. After almost three years in office, Kennedy was gaining popularity and self-confidence. He had just achieved a major agreement with the Soviet Union to halt nuclear testing in the atmosphere. He was admired for his youthful energy, his pledge "to get the country moving again," and his idealistic call for Americans to volunteer for public service — to "ask what you can do for your country."[46] Thousands had responded, joining the Peace Corps and other new government initiatives. Elected president at age forty-three, Kennedy represented a new generation of leaders, tested in battle in World War II and optimistic that their day to govern the country had come.

But Kennedy faced legislative gridlock with a Congress that had failed to succumb to his considerable charm, refusing to approve the major proposals of his New Frontier: tax relief to stimulate a lethargic economy, medical care for the elderly, and education aid for the young. Now, in November 1963, even the routine appropriations bills were stalled, threatening a shutdown of government services. Kennedy had been neither a leader nor an insider in Congress. He had few deep relationships with his former colleagues to rely on, and he lacked the temperament to push them hard on behalf of his programs.

Beyond question, the most critical issue facing the country was civil rights. Black civil rights activists, along with their white allies, were marching in the South, confronting officials who denied them the right to vote, to eat in restaurants, to attend integrated schools, and to win jobs reserved for "whites only." Clashes between civil rights demonstrators and southern law enforcement officers, and violence directed at blacks by sheriffs and police chiefs as well as by the Ku Klux Klan and White Citizens Councils, had created a crisis atmosphere.

For most of his three years in office, Kennedy had disappointed black leaders who had expected him to champion their cause. After he had promised in the 1960 campaign to end housing discrimination "with the stroke of a pen," it had taken Kennedy more than two years to sign a limited executive order forbidding government-backed financial institutions from discriminating against blacks in housing loans.* Kennedy had defeated Vice President Richard Nixon in 1960 by the narrowest of margins. Facing a coalition of southern Democrats and conservative Republicans who could block his programs in Congress, he hesitated to introduce strong civil rights legislation that might anger the powerful southerners who chaired the major committees in the Senate and could block his other legislative initiatives. To Kennedy's dismay, the southern congressional barons had stalled his domestic programs even though he hadn't pushed civil rights until circumstances had forced him to act.

In June 1963, Kennedy finally had proposed comprehensive legislation

---

* A number of civil rights supporters across the country, frustrated with Kennedy's slow progress in delivering his pledged executive order, began sending pens to the White House, hoping to help along the promised "stroke of a pen."

to help the nation's Negroes, who faced blatant discrimination in every realm of American society from the workplace to the voting booth. His hand had been forced by the Reverend Martin Luther King Jr. When television news showed King's demonstrators in Birmingham, including children, being attacked by police dogs and bowled over by high-pressure fire hoses, the nation reacted with outrage. As demonstrations spread to dozens of cities, the southern civil rights crisis threatened to become a national crisis of law and order. Prodded by these events, Kennedy finally delivered his first passionate speech calling for civil rights legislation. "We are confronted primarily with a moral issue," Kennedy said in a televised address from the Oval Office. "The heart of the question is whether all Americans are to be afforded equal rights and equal opportunities." One hundred years after Abraham Lincoln had emancipated the slaves, Kennedy said, "their grandsons are not fully free. They are not yet freed from the bonds of injustice. They are not yet freed from social and economic oppression. And this Nation, for all its hopes and boasts, will not be fully free until all of its citizens are free."[47]

But as summer had passed into autumn, public opinion polls, which Kennedy followed avidly, showed that half the nation thought he was pushing too fast on civil rights.[48] Observing that the president was mentioning civil rights less often in speeches — including those given during the first two days of his trip to Texas — King suspected that Kennedy would not be unhappy if the issue were held over in Congress until after the election.[49] Now Kennedy was gone, and black leaders faced a new question: How would Lyndon Johnson, a southerner with a mixed record on civil rights, respond to their pressing needs?

Lyndon Baines Johnson reached The Elms, his three-story, twelve-room brick-and-stucco Norman chateau in Spring Valley, an upper-class enclave in northwest Washington, just after 9 P.M. on November 22. As her father entered the foyer, daughter Luci, age seventeen, thought "he looked like he had been run over by a truck, and yet very strong."[50]

Johnson settled in the den. Close friends, including former aide Horace Busby and his wife, Mary Beth, had gathered at the house and now surrounded the new president as they watched the television news replay scenes of the nightmare in Dallas. A film clip showed the young Kennedy family in happier times, with the president and his wife watching their daughter, Caroline, riding Macaroni, a pony given to her several months earlier by Vice President Johnson.[51] "It's all too fresh. I can't watch it," Johnson said.[52]

Above the television set hung a portrait of the late Sam Rayburn,

Speaker of the House of Representatives, a Texas Democrat and mentor to Johnson from the time he had come to Congress in 1937. The president raised a glass of soda to Rayburn's picture. "Oh, Mr. Sam, I wish you were here now," he said. "How I need you."[53]

Shortly after 11 P.M. Johnson went upstairs, put on a pair of gray pajamas, and climbed into bed.[54] Dr. Willis Hurst, Johnson's cardiologist since his heart attack in 1956, urged him to take a sleeping pill and rest. Instead, Johnson summoned Bill Moyers, Jack Valenti, and Cliff Carter, three aides who had ridden back from Dallas with him aboard Air Force One.* For the next four hours, sitting in his bed, propped up on pillows, Johnson talked virtually nonstop. As Moyers listened while Johnson switched from one subject to another, he thought that the president "seemed to have several chambers of his mind operating simultaneously."[55]

Eighteen hours earlier, Johnson had begun the day having breakfast with Jack Kennedy in Fort Worth. Now, with Moyers sitting on one side of his bed and Valenti and Carter in chairs on the other, the new president began ticking off assignments to be carried out the next morning: calls to members of the Kennedy family, arrangements for the funeral, and meetings with members of Congress, with former president Eisenhower, with national security advisers, and with the Cabinet.[56]

As Johnson weighed and made decisions about the coming days, Cliff Carter, his chief political aide, was struck by how carefully he was walking a "chalk line." On the one hand, Johnson wanted the country to have "confidence that he could do the job." On the other, he wanted to avoid giving the impression that he was rushing to take power. Johnson had to demonstrate leadership while showing sensitivity to the bereaved Kennedys and their devoted followers, whose help he would need immediately.[57]

In a telephone conversation earlier that night with Arthur Goldberg, an associate justice of the U.S. Supreme Court, Johnson revealed just how aware he was of having to balance many sensitivities and concerns as he took his first steps as president. "I want you to be thinking about what I ought to do," he told Goldberg, "to try to bring all these elements together and unite the country to maintain and preserve our system in the world, because — if it starts falling to pieces — why, we could deteriorate pretty quickly."

Johnson asked Goldberg whether he should speak to a joint session of

---

* On hearing that President Kennedy had been shot, Moyers, a twenty-nine-year-old former Johnson Senate aide from Texas and at the time deputy director of the Peace Corps, chartered a plane from Austin to Dallas to be at President Johnson's side when Air Force One took off for Washington. He immediately joined Johnson's presidential staff, as did Valenti.

Congress soon after Kennedy's funeral. Goldberg thought that he should, and Johnson asked him to help prepare the speech. Johnson wanted to address the nation "with dignity and reserve and without being down on my knees but, at the same time, letting them know of my respect and confidence."[58]

As Johnson talked through the early-morning hours, Jack Valenti observed that he already seemed to know what he wanted to accomplish with his presidency. Valenti listened with surprise as Johnson spelled out ambitions that added up to a sweeping agenda for social change in the United States.[59]

"Well, I'm going to tell you," Johnson said, "I'm going to pass the civil rights bill and not change one word of it. I'm not going to cavil, and I'm not going to compromise. I'm going to fix it so everyone can vote, so everyone can get all the education they can get. I'm going to pass Harry Truman's health care bill."[60]

Valenti, a Houston advertising man by profession, had helped Johnson organize political events in Texas, but he had never heard him talk so expansively about how he would run the country. It seemed to Valenti that Lyndon Johnson, president of the United States for little more than twelve hours, already had resolved "to radically change the social environment of the nation" so that the "poor, the aged, the blacks, those denied an education . . . would have a new opportunity . . . absolutely essential to an equitable America."[61]

No president since Franklin Delano Roosevelt in the 1930s had attempted such a broad assault on social and economic inequality. Now Lyndon Johnson, in his first hours as president, apparently aspired to match FDR, his hero and mentor when Johnson first came to Washington thirty years earlier. In the past Johnson had demonstrated gargantuan ambition, a populist philosophy about government helping those with the least, and a shrewd ability to wield political power. Thrust into the presidency, Johnson faced formidable immediate challenges: to reassure a shocked nation and to move a paralyzed and deadlocked federal government to action at a time of crisis.

2

✦ ✦ ✦ ✦ ✦ ✦

Let Us Continue

T HE CHALLENGE WAS immediate and immense. From the
moment the rifle shots in Dallas catapulted Lyndon Baines
Johnson into the presidency, he knew he must convince a grief-stricken
nation that he could unite the country and lead it through the crisis. Although Johnson had served as Senate majority leader beginning in the
1950s and as vice president for almost three years, his public image was
hazy at best. The first opinion surveys after the assassination showed that
many Americans had doubts about whether he was up to the job. A Louis
Harris poll on November 24 reported that one-third of the population
believed that the southerner would slow down action on civil rights.[1]
Other polls showed that 70 percent doubted Johnson could carry on as
well as Kennedy, and 67 percent claimed to know "next to nothing" about
the new president.[2] But Johnson didn't wait for polls to tell him that he
had to move swiftly to win the confidence of Americans who mistrusted,
disliked, or simply didn't know him.

From his first moments as president, Johnson reached out to leaders of
the nation's diverse interests — governors and members of Congress, corporate executives and organized labor, church and religious leaders, and
perhaps most important, liberals and civil rights organizers. With many
liberals, Johnson had to overcome suspicions, feuds, and misunderstand-
ings that had been decades in the making. He knew that no Democrat
could govern effectively, much less win the presidency in his own right,
without the support of the party's large and powerful liberal wing. With
the 1964 election less than a year away, he had little time to spare.

The new president worked from sunrise until late into the night — taking part in ceremonies for President Kennedy, meeting with governors
and foreign leaders arriving in Washington for the funeral, shaping the

budget headed for Congress, urging the Kennedy Cabinet and White House staff to stay on, while reaching out by telephone to dozens of influential Americans. To all of them Johnson's message was clear: The country faced a crisis that required national unity and continuity. As president, he personally needed and welcomed their advice.

Johnson began November 25, 1963, his third full day as president, by walking in the funeral procession from the White House to St. Matthew's Cathedral with the late president's widow and brother Robert. He did so over the strenuous objections of the Secret Service, whose leaders, fearing yet another assassination, wanted him to ride in an armored car.[3]

Watching the procession from a crowded sidewalk, anonymous among the weeping thousands, was a dispirited Martin Luther King. King had flown to Washington from Atlanta the previous evening for the funeral. He was deeply disappointed that the Kennedy family had not invited him as an official guest.* The battle-scarred minister came anyway, standing unnoticed among the throngs watching the funeral cortege with its riderless black horse, the veiled widow, and the new president pass by.[4]

On the day after the assassination, King had issued a statement saying that he believed that "President Johnson will follow the path charted by President Kennedy in civil rights. . . . It does not at all mean a setback." King felt that Johnson, with his "statesmanlike grasp of the problem and great political sagacity," was "equipped to be affirmative in getting congressional results" on civil rights.[5] The statement clearly delivered a compliment and at the same time issued a challenge.

Turning to the Reverend Walter Fauntroy, the SCLC associate who stood beside him on the sidewalk, King remarked, "If they can take out a president, they can take us out, too." At least, the two ministers agreed, "Lyndon Johnson was no George Wallace." They speculated hopefully that Johnson might have "freed himself from the racism of his region." But King could not overcome his own despair. "We're still a ten-day nation, Walter," he said gloomily, referring to his sense that the country seemed unable to focus on a single issue such as civil rights for more than ten days.[6] Three months had passed since the heralded March on Washington and King's dramatic "I Have a Dream" speech. Now civil rights legislation was again stalled, black children had been killed in a Birmingham church bombing, and a president who had just started to show promising signs of support for their cause had been assassinated.

---

* King might have felt less slighted if he had known that Roy Wilkins of the National Association for the Advancement of Colored People (NAACP) and Whitney Young of the National Urban League were guests only because President Johnson had intervened with the Kennedys at Young's request.

President Johnson telephoned King the evening of the funeral, reaching him at 9:40 P.M. at the Waldorf-Astoria in New York City, where he and other civil rights leaders had gathered to decide how they should deal with the new president.[7] They were comparing their opinions of — and experiences with — Lyndon Johnson, debating how the assassination would affect the pace and direction of their movement, and discussing whether to call off scheduled demonstrations or convert them into memorials for the slain president.

Most of the leaders had been impressed by Johnson's support for civil rights as vice president. Yet they still had reservations about how committed the tall Texan was to their cause. They had not forgotten that during his first twenty years in Congress, Johnson had opposed every civil rights bill. Civil rights veterans still remembered candidate Johnson in the 1948 Senate race, his career hanging in the balance, shouting at audiences, "I voted against the so-called and misnamed civil rights bills, and I expect to continue fighting them in my six years as senator."[8] Johnson's position on civil rights had evolved over time, but his reputation was that of a political wheeler-dealer without ideological bearings and a fierce defender of the Southwest's oil and gas interests.

Johnson began his telephone call to King by thanking the minister for his public expression of confidence. In his folksy, intimate style, the new president immediately engaged King as a confidant and partner in his effort to get results from Congress. "It's just an impossible period," the president explained. "We've got a budget coming out that's practically already made, and we've got a civil rights bill. . . . We've got to just not give up on any of them. . . . I'm going to call on Congress Wednesday to just stay here until they pass them all. They won't do it, but we'll just keep them here next year until they do, and we just won't give up an inch."

"Well, this is mighty fine," replied King. "I think one of the great tributes we can pay in memory of President Kennedy is to try to enact some of the great progressive policies that he sought to initiate."

"I'm going to support 'em all!" Johnson replied. "And I'm going to do my best to get other men to do likewise, and I'll have to have you-all's help. I never needed it more than I do now." ·

"Well, you know you have it. And just feel free to call us for anything," said King, speaking for the group. "Regards to the family," he added.

"Thank you so much, Martin," Johnson replied. "Call me when you're down here next time and let's get together — and any suggestions you have, bring them in."[9]

In that brief telephone exchange, King politely hinted at what the civil rights movement wanted most from Lyndon Johnson: his commitment to pass the bill formally proposed by the late president five months earlier.[10] The legislation had not yet been approved either by the House or by the Senate, where it faced a certain filibuster from opponents in the all-white southern delegation.

Independently, Johnson and King had reached the same judgment: the outpouring of admiration and affection for the late president — along with widespread feelings of grief, remorse, and guilt — had created a compelling opportunity for action. Both men were instinctive masters at seizing unexpected openings and turning them into victories. "Now's the time to shove in our stack, boys," Johnson would exhort his allies when they held the high political cards.[11] In similar fashion, King pressed his demonstrators relentlessly when he sensed the possibility of a decisive victory.

Martin Luther King, the minister and passionate orator, expressed surprisingly little public emotion at Kennedy's death. In his Thanksgiving Day sermon six days afterward, King mentioned the assassination only perfunctorily, preaching instead on the black experience of slavery in America.[12] Meeting privately the next day with Donald H. Smith, a graduate student at the University of Wisconsin, King suggested coolly and pragmatically that Kennedy's death might actually improve prospects for civil rights legislation. "I think that we still have the possibility for a strong civil rights bill," King told him. "It may well be that the president's death will speed this up. Because I'm convinced that, had he lived, there would have been continual delays and attempts to evade it at every point and water it down at every point. But I think his memory . . . will cause many people to see the necessity for working passionately and unrelentingly to get this legislation approved."[13]

Although he admired and even envied Kennedy's easy, graceful political style, King judged him strictly on the way he responded to the plight of black Americans. In King's view, the late president had repeatedly been slow to deliver on grand promises. At the time of Kennedy's death, King was furious at the way the president and the attorney general were handling a civil rights confrontation in Albany, Georgia.[14] Curtly rejecting King's fervent appeals, Robert Kennedy had insisted on prosecuting nine black demonstrators for picketing a store owned by an unfriendly white merchant, but did nothing to punish white mobs that were terrorizing the demonstrators. Not a single white attacker had been arrested.[15] Meeting with the attorney general about the case, King had erupted in a rare display of anger. He found ludicrous Robert Kennedy's claim that he was only dispensing "even-handed justice."[16]

*   *   *

Lyndon Johnson immediately focused on gaining a mastery of civil rights and other critical domestic issues, but he could not ignore a nagging problem nine thousand miles away. In a visit to Washington, Henry Cabot Lodge, the U.S. ambassador to South Vietnam, had told Johnson, as the president put it, that "it's going to hell in a hand basket out there." Three weeks before President Kennedy's assassination, the United States had sanctioned a coup that resulted in the assassination of Vietnamese president Ngo Dinh Diem. Now there was continuing chaos, Lodge told Johnson. The new president expressed his considerable "misgivings" about "whether we took the right course in upsetting the Diem regime," and about influential members of Congress "who felt we should get out of Vietnam." But then Johnson came to a quick, firm conclusion.

"I am not going to lose Vietnam," he told Lodge. "I am not going to be the president who saw Southeast Asia go the way China went." Two days later Johnson signed a National Security Action Memorandum reaffirming U.S. determination to assist the people and government of Vietnam "to win their contest against the externally directed and supported Communist conspiracy." The United States would maintain its level of financial support and of "advisers" — whose numbers had risen from 685 to 16,700 during John Kennedy's nearly three years in office.

After meeting with Lodge, Johnson revealed his underlying motives in a conversation with aide Bill Moyers. "I told [Lodge] to go back and tell those generals in Saigon that Lyndon Johnson intends to stand by our word, but by God I want something for our money. I want 'em to get off their butts and get out in those jungles and whip hell out of some Communists. And then I want them to leave me alone, because *I got some bigger things to do right here at home.*" From the outset, Johnson drew a connection between success in Vietnam and achieving his goals for overarching social reform at home. If he were going to equal or exceed Roosevelt's New Deal, Johnson believed, he had to satisfy conservatives in Congress by bringing Vietnam to a successful conclusion.[17]

Not all of President Johnson's friends agreed that he should wrap himself in the cloak of the martyred president. Senator George Smathers, a Florida Democrat, told Johnson in a telephone call that he had the opportunity and freedom to chart his own course. Smathers suggested that Johnson start by dropping Kennedy's tax cut plan, which had the Senate tied up, blocking other important legislation.

"No, no, I can't do that," Johnson replied. "That would destroy the party and destroy the election and destroy everything. We've got to carry on. We can't abandon this fellow's program, because he is a national hero and people want his program passed, and we've got to keep this Kennedy aura around us through this election."[18]

Speaking with the conservative Smathers, Johnson talked the tough, pragmatic politics of necessity. With others he sounded sincere in his desire to pursue civil rights vigorously on moral grounds.* At a long meeting at The Elms that first week, Johnson's advisers debated how he should handle civil rights. When one veteran insider cautioned the president against expending his early goodwill on the controversial legislation, Johnson loudly retorted, "Well, what the hell's the Presidency for?"[19]

Was LBJ acting out of political necessity or out of conviction? If political necessity, how long would it last? Those questions were on the mind of James Farmer, executive director of the Congress of Racial Equality, as he met with the president in the Oval Office. Farmer thought that Johnson radiated an optimism bordering on euphoria as he described his plans to fight for civil rights legislation. Farmer listened, fascinated, as Johnson periodically interrupted their conversation to take telephone calls in which he vigorously lobbied senators to support the civil rights bill.

"Mr. President," asked Farmer, "why are you doing this?" Johnson answered by describing the humiliations experienced by his college-educated cook, Zephyr Wright, and her husband whenever they traveled in the segregated South. In Johnson's vivid story, Mrs. Wright, denied the use of "whites only" restrooms, would have to "go squat in the middle of a field to pee." A key feature of the proposed civil rights law called for eliminating segregated public accommodations, including motels, restaurants, restrooms, movie theaters, parks, and swimming pools.

Then, with a twinkle in his eye, Johnson gave Farmer another explanation for his civil rights advocacy. "To quote a friend of yours," he said, "free at last. Thank God almighty, I'm free at last!"[20]

In quoting Martin Luther King's "I Have a Dream" speech, Johnson intimated that now that he had reached the presidency, he was free of the political constraints that had bound him during twenty-seven years as a representative and senator and even as vice president. In his first years in Congress, Johnson had told civil rights advocates that his vote for a civil rights bill would only guarantee his defeat in the next election. By 1957, as a Senate majority leader who hungered for national office, Johnson had begun to change his position on civil rights. Demonstrating extraordinary political and parliamentary skills, he had steered through Congress

---

* After his presidency had ended, Johnson told his biographer Doris Kearns, "I knew that if I didn't get out in front on this issue [civil rights], the liberals would get me!"

the first civil rights law enacted since Reconstruction.* For his efforts he was condemned by southerners as a traitor to his region and race and by liberals for pushing through a toothless piece of legislation. Now Johnson had to win over those who had scorned his performance in 1957, including Roy Wilkins, who had called the 1957 law "soup made from the bones of an emaciated chicken which had died from starvation."[21] Wilkins also compared Johnson's next civil rights bill, three years later — which sought to guarantee black voting rights — to prescribing "liniment to cure a tumor."[22]

Now Wilkins, sixty-two years old and in his ninth year as the NAACP's executive director,[23] was the first civil rights leader President Johnson summoned to the Oval Office. A slim, immaculately dressed man, Wilkins spoke with the dignity and authority of the leader of the nation's largest and best-known civil rights organization. Despite his contempt for Johnson's handling of the earlier civil rights bills, Wilkins had been impressed by Johnson's performance as vice president, particularly his work chairing the President's Committee on Equal Employment Opportunity, which sought to end job discrimination and segregation by government contractors. When Wilkins had complained to Johnson about racial discrimination at the Lockheed Corporation's Georgia airplane plant, the vice president had acted quickly to remedy the problems. Over the years, Wilkins had judged Johnson to be not a "visceral segregationist" but a product of his political circumstances.[24]

When the NAACP leader entered the Oval Office, the president pulled his own chair up to Wilkins's so their knees almost touched. Johnson poked his finger in Wilkins's chest, thrust his nose within an inch of Wilkins's, and declared, "I want that bill passed!" Moreover, Johnson said, he wanted the legislation approved intact — without compromise or weakening amendments. In 1957 and 1960, Majority Leader Johnson had watered down stronger bills passed by the House in order to get them through the Senate, and black leaders feared that he would follow the same tactic as president. Johnson spent the rest of their forty-five-minute meeting telling Wilkins how he expected him and other civil rights leaders to lobby Congress to pass the bill.[25]

Wilkins's doubts about the president's intentions were largely dispelled by the meeting. In past dealings with Johnson, even though they often disagreed, Wilkins had found him forthright, a man of his word. Now he

---

* The 1957 Civil Rights Act established a Commission on Civil Rights and a civil rights division in the Justice Department, and made it a crime to interfere with a person's right to vote in federal elections.

believed that Johnson had committed himself to go much further on civil rights than ever before. Leaving the meeting, Wilkins told White House reporters that the president would push the civil rights bill both out of "his own convictions" and because of "political necessity."[26]

Wilkins's experiences with Lyndon Johnson were quite different from his dealings in the Oval Office with John F. Kennedy. Kennedy had been "polite and sympathetic on all matters of basic principle, but too often evasive when it came to action." Although Kennedy portrayed himself as "dry-eyed and realistic," Wilkins had thought that the young president was too "green," lacking in understanding of "what was possible in Congress, and in his knowledge of the South." In contrast, Wilkins believed that "Johnson knew exactly what was possible" in dealing with Congress, and was more forthright in saying what he would do. Whereas Kennedy had been reluctant to pressure members of Congress to support his program, Johnson was a master of persuasion. Kennedy's greatest contribution was to help change "the moral climate of the country, the first step before civil rights legislation could be passed," Wilkins decided.[27] But it would take an entirely different kind of president — a Lyndon Johnson — to get a strong civil rights bill enacted into law.

Even as they worried about Johnson's deep ties to the South, black leaders based their hopes to some extent on a story from black folklore. Blacks would finally gain their freedom, the story went, after the arrival of an enlightened white southern leader. The folktale received new attention as black leaders discussed what they could expect from Johnson and how they should deal with him.

There was something else about Johnson's southern roots that the black leaders found significant: any southern white politician who dared take up the cause of civil rights did so knowing full well that his commitment would expose him to rejection by his closest white southern friends and allies. Advocating civil rights could spell defeat in the next election. There was a real cost, politically and personally, for a southerner that the northern white politician did not face. Therefore the southerner's commitment demonstrated true courage.

As Johnson sought the support of a succession of black leaders, he reached back to his past and passionately described the populist roots that had animated his early political career. Meeting with Dorothy Height, president of the National Council of Negro Women (NCNW), Johnson reminisced about how "Mary McLeod Bethune put my integration diapers on me during my NYA days." Bethune, an intimate of Eleanor Roosevelt and founder of the NCNW, served as deputy director of the National Youth Administration, one of Franklin Roosevelt's New Deal programs. At age twenty-six, Lyndon Johnson had been the youngest state director of the NYA, which funded jobs for unemployed youths during the Great Depression. Bethune had lectured an initially reluctant Johnson that "you represent the federal government, and the NYA is a federal program" — and that therefore the program must serve all youths, not just whites. "From that point on," Johnson told Height, "I never questioned. I was an agent of the federal government."* The reminiscence created an important connection for Johnson: as a young woman, Dorothy Height had served as Bethune's personal assistant.[28]

Johnson also reminded black leaders of his experiences in the late 1930s as a young Texas congressman who proudly marched under the banner of President Franklin Delano Roosevelt and his progressive New Deal. As a freshman congressman, Johnson had gone to the White House to protest to the president that Agriculture Department programs grossly discriminated against black farmers in his congressional district. Johnson had been one of only three representatives from the South who dared to support Roosevelt's bill to establish a minimum wage. As a freshman, he had brought one of the nation's first public housing grants to Austin — and directed part of the funds to housing for blacks and Mexican Americans. Critics noted that the housing was segregated and that Johnson often did more for whites than for blacks. Still, he was among the rare southern politicians who risked white disapproval by openly supporting measures to help his black constituents. In return, blacks in Texas supported Johnson, even knowing that in the 1930s and 1940s he had voted against civil rights legislation that would have eliminated the poll tax† and made lynching a federal crime.[29]

Johnson's ambitions were tied to another populist influence that he seldom talked about out of political caution. It was all right to acknowledge Franklin Roosevelt as a personal mentor. But Johnson also was an admirer

---

* Johnson did not follow Bethune's instruction in 1936 to integrate his state advisory board. If he did so, Johnson wrote Washington, whites would not cooperate, and the program would be killed. His solution was to form separate white and black advisory boards. At the same time, Johnson doubled the number of jobs at two black colleges despite warnings from his mentor, Texas governor James Allred, about the political consequences of placing *any* jobs in black colleges.

† Blacks in Texas won the right to vote after the Supreme Court of the United States in 1944 ruled unconstitutional the "all-white Democratic primary," the winning of which was tantamount at the time to election.

of Huey Long, the legendary "Kingfish," who built a huge populist following as governor of Louisiana, as a senator advocating a radical and highly controversial "Share the Wealth" plan, and as a politician ambitious enough to challenge FDR himself for the presidency.

Horace Busby, who had joined Johnson's staff in 1948 and served as an idea man and speechwriter, recalled Johnson's enduring fascination with Long as he listened to the president discuss his plans and ambitions for the second night running, and into the morning of November 24.[30] After dinner at The Elms, Johnson got a rubdown from his masseur Olaf Anderson and then slipped into a pair of white silk pajamas — the kind LBJ believed had been worn by Huey Long. As a young congressional aide to Representative Richard Kleberg of Texas in the early 1930s, Johnson had studied everything he could about Long. He seldom missed an opportunity to hear Long speak in the Senate. He and a friend from Oklahoma took one of Long's secretaries out to dinner and questioned her about her boss's interests and habits — including how he dressed and what he liked to eat. What most fascinated Johnson was how Long had amassed political power and then won adoration from his constituents by using that power to secure government services for them. Long had paved Louisiana's muddy network of rural roads and helped the poor, while avoiding the virulent racism then virtually universal among southern politicians.[31]

Johnson talked with Busby until 3 A.M. about all the things he wanted to accomplish — pass strong civil rights legislation, reform immigration laws so they didn't discriminate against immigrants who were not from England and western Europe, build up the Social Security system, and complete the agenda of the New Deal. Most important, he wanted to provide health care for the elderly and guarantee federal support so that no American would be denied an education for lack of funds. In Busby's view, Johnson not only wanted to accomplish great things but also yearned to be loved by the people, as he imagined Huey Long had been. Long's rambunctious, outsized personality may not have been cut to fit the image of the successful politician in the age of television, but Lyndon Johnson still identified with the Louisianan as much as he did with Franklin Roosevelt.

As her husband spoke with Busby, Lady Bird Johnson sat at her dressing table nearby, getting ready for bed. Listening to her husband talk endlessly about his White House plans, she said, "Thank God there's only ten months of this to go." The new first lady was counting the months until someone else would be elected president. "No, Mrs. Johnson, it's going to be more like nine years," replied Busby, adding to the remaining time in

Kennedy's term the two four-year terms Johnson could serve in his own right. "Don't say that," Lady Bird protested as she adjusted an eye mask and went to bed.[32]

In a meeting earlier that same evening at Johnson's office in the Executive Office Building across from the White House, Walter Heller, chairman of the President's Council of Economic Advisers, told Johnson about a program to fight poverty that he had been designing for President Kennedy's consideration. Johnson seized upon the idea. "That's my kind of program," he said. "We should push ahead full tilt." Johnson instructed Heller, an economist from the University of Minnesota, to spread the word to his liberal friends that the president was not a "conservative budget slasher." "If you look at my record," Johnson told him, "you would know that I'm a Roosevelt New Dealer. As a matter of fact, John F. Kennedy was a little too conservative to suit my taste."[33]

Continuing his exploration of the poverty issue and reconnecting with his liberal past, Johnson invited two of his oldest friends from his New Deal days, social worker Elizabeth Wickendon and her husband, Arthur Goldschmidt, to The Elms for Sunday supper. "I have a very difficult problem," Johnson confided to them. "I feel a moral obligation to carry on the things that Kennedy proposed, but I have to have issues I can take on as my own. I have to get reelected in a year."[34] Johnson told them that he was considering making poverty his issue.

Less than two weeks after becoming president, Johnson wrote a public letter to the National Welfare Association promising "a national assault on the causes of poverty."[35] Suddenly a complex political dynamic was transforming a proposed modest investigation into the causes of poverty into a full-blown "War on Poverty," though the strategy and the weapons to fight the war had yet to be chosen. Competition between the new president and Kennedy aides carrying their fallen leader's banner quickly drove up the political stakes. The expansion of Johnson's agenda from securing civil rights to fighting poverty was propelled by multiple forces: his old populist instincts, his desire to find his own issues, his need to heal old quarrels with the liberal wing of the Democratic Party, and his competition with the Kennedys. Although he publicly praised the fallen president at every turn, Johnson would begin privately pointing out that he was succeeding with Congress where Kennedy had failed.

As Senate majority leader, Johnson often had scorned liberal senators as impractical — more interested in rhetoric than in results, hidebound against compromise, and devoid of political savvy.* One of his favorite jokes was, "You know the difference between cannibals and liberals? Cannibals eat only their enemies!"[36]

To achieve results in an ideologically divided Senate, Johnson had had to perform a constant juggling act — seeking courses of action that would command the votes of both liberal northern Democrats and conservative Democrats from the South. Had he failed, a coalition of conservative Republicans and southern Democrats could have controlled the Senate. Johnson had achieved legislative results, including the 1957 and 1960 civil rights laws, however much they might be criticized by liberals who believed that his compromises better served the interests of President Eisenhower and the Republicans than their own.

Blinded by their passion and their personal dislike of Johnson, the liberals denied their majority leader any credit, even for two remarkable accomplishments: Johnson had succeeded in getting the Senate to censure Senator Joseph McCarthy of Wisconsin for recklessly slandering political opponents as Communists,† and he had defeated an effort by the body's right-wing conservatives to strip power from the Supreme Court after its 1954 decision declaring school segregation unconstitutional. In those fights, the liberals had made the fiery speeches while Johnson worked behind the scenes, employing shrewdness, guile, and a knowledge both of Senate rules and of the members themselves to win victories. Other senators shared conservative Iowa Republican Bourke Hickenlooper's view that the wheeler-dealer majority leader was a man whose partisanship was exceeded only by his "personal opportunism."[37]

Most politicians, whether friend or foe of Lyndon Johnson, struggled to comprehend the complexity of this leader, with his huge ambition and extravagant personality. Former representative Helen Gahagan Douglas, a liberal California Democrat, onetime actress, and intimate Johnson friend, thought she knew what the nation was in for when Johnson be-

---

* Ironically, John F. Kennedy and his brother Robert shared much of Johnson's jaundiced view of the politics of liberals. The Kennedys prided themselves on their pragmatism and scorned the high-minded idealism of liberals whose rhetoric was not coupled with results. Attorney General Robert Kennedy, in a conversation with two aides, said he'd rather deal with Senator James Eastland of Mississippi than with some of the Senate liberals. At the time, Eastland, a plantation owner and unyielding segregationist, chaired the Senate Judiciary Committee, from whose doors no civil rights legislation had ever emerged.

† Johnson defeated McCarthy by waiting until the Wisconsin demagogue overplayed his hand. When McCarthy attacked the Episcopal bishop G. Bromley Oxnam as a Communist, Johnson told an ally that "McCarthy just made a fatal mistake." Oxnam was a close friend of Senator Harry Byrd, the conservative southern patriarch, who then joined the fight and brought with him the votes needed to censure McCarthy.

came president. She catalogued his contradictory qualities: "Ambitious, driving, alert, careful, calculating, secretive, seemingly with inexhaustible energy, sensitive to criticism, vain, an explosive temper that could erupt over the smallest details, a natural talent for organization, a listener — not a reader, a legislative director, organizer — not a legislative designer, an activist — not a planner. LBJ perfected the plans of others. He was an operator, and I say that in the best sense, not a creator."[38]

With key members of the liberal establishment, Johnson tried with words and deeds to assuage the bitter feelings left over from old political feuds. To that end, Johnson did something that had been virtually unthinkable in the past: he apologized. He admitted that he had been wrong.

No telephone call Johnson made in the early days of his presidency was more difficult than his conversation November 23 with Senator Ralph Yarborough, a Texas Democrat who led a liberal faction in the Lone Star State that often opposed Johnson. The division between liberal and conservative Democrats in Texas ran bitter and deep. Only the day before in Dallas, Yarborough had ridden in the same car as the vice president only because President Kennedy had insisted. The day before the shots rang out in Dallas, Johnson was still pressing several of his Texas congressional allies to challenge Yarborough in the 1964 Senate primary.[39] Now everything had changed. Johnson told Yarborough he needed his support and Yarborough pledged to give it.[40] In return, Johnson asked the conservative Democratic faction not to oppose Yarborough's bid for reelection.[41]

On his second Sunday in the White House, Johnson called in James Rowe, a liberal Washington insider who had begun his political career as a clerk to Supreme Court justice Oliver Wendell Holmes and then as an aide to Franklin Roosevelt. It was Rowe who had pushed Johnson to support civil rights legislation in 1957, arguing that the Democratic Party could not regain the presidency without proving its dedication to the interests of black voters in the big cities. Rowe's tolerance of Johnson's petulant tirades had run out during the 1960 campaign. When the vice presidential candidate made one petty demand too many, Rowe quit. The two had parted angrily and had barely spoken in three years.

Now Johnson admitted to Rowe that he had been out of line during the campaign. He wanted to mend their relationship and needed Rowe's support. Rowe, ever the gentleman, tried to take the blame for their quarrel, to which Johnson responded, "Damn it, can't you be content to be the first man the thirty-sixth president of the United States has apologized to?"[42]

Next Johnson reached out to Joseph Rauh, chairman of Americans for

Democratic Action and a key strategist and lobbyist for the Leadership Conference on Civil Rights. Rauh had denounced Johnson as majority leader for selling out to his Deep South friends on the 1957 civil rights bill. At the 1960 Democratic convention, Rauh had taken the floor to denounce Kennedy's choice of Johnson as his running mate.[43] Now Johnson asked Rauh to fly with him to the funeral of former New York senator Herbert Lehman, a liberal hero.[44] The president then brought his former detractor to the White House, where the two men agreed to work together to pass the new civil rights bill.[45]

Johnson then sought to make peace with Senator Paul Douglas of Illinois, whom Johnson had humiliated during a civil rights debate in the 1950s. Douglas, a white-maned liberal orator, had distinguished himself as a professor of economics at the University of Chicago and then as a fifty-year-old marine enlistee in World War II. Of all the Senate liberals, Douglas had been the most determined opponent of Johnson's high-handed leadership style and his temporizing on civil rights. Now Johnson invited Douglas to his Texas ranch, where he apologized for his rude treatment of the Illinois senator. "He said we'd had many disputes," Douglas later recalled, "but in looking back, he felt that it was mostly his own fault — which I thought was very handsome of him."[46]

As Johnson drove Douglas and others around his ranch in the heart of the Texas hill country, he talked of growing up there in the early years of the century. From those central Texas hills, with their thin soil, mesquite trees, and struggling farmers came the rural populism that shaped Johnson's early political career. He often recited for guests his family history — how he had started out in the political footsteps of his father and grandfather, both of whom had served in the Texas state legislature, where they had opposed the Ku Klux Klan and championed the rights of the workingman.[47]

There were few blacks in Blanco County, so Johnson never experienced anything like the stratified and segregated plantation society of the Deep South. But there were lots of poor white people who tried to scrape by farming. Johnson's father had failed as a farmer, and money was scarce as Johnson grew up. He vowed never to fail as his father had. Johnson identified with underdogs, even after he had become a rich and powerful senator backed by and often serving the interests of the state's wealthy oil and business men.

At his ranch, Johnson entertained visitors in his swimming pool and on harrowing rides in which he would startle unsuspecting guests by driving his amphibious car straight into the middle of Lake Lyndon Baines Johnson. He told them of the upbringing that had shaped his character and influenced his ideas, including the story of how his grandmother and her children had hidden in a cellar under a trapdoor while marauding Indians ransacked their house.

Born in 1908, Johnson was the last president to have experienced the final vestiges of the American frontier. He would show visitors the one-room schoolhouse where he had begun his education and tell them of his heart-rending experiences as principal of a dilapidated school attended by poor Mexican American children in rural Cotulla. From his own meager salary Johnson had bought school supplies and paid for extracurricular activities. Later, when he served as debate coach at a high school in Houston, he again used his own money to help poor Mexican American children.*[48]

Johnson would tell his visitors about his proudest accomplishment: bringing electricity to the farmers and ranchers in his sparsely settled congressional district. Before he was elected to Congress in 1937, there had been no electric power in the thousands of square miles of the hill country. First Johnson persuaded President Roosevelt to approve dams on the Colorado River to generate power. Next he won special approval from the Rural Electrification Administration to install power lines through vast stretches of country with a population density of less than one person per square mile. The project, built between 1937 and 1948, brought the hill country people into the twentieth century. For the first time, they could listen to the radio, draw water by electric pump instead of by hand, wash clothes without backbreaking labor, and light their homes. The grateful voters remained loyal to Lyndon Johnson all their lives.

By the time guests such as Senator Douglas left the LBJ Ranch, they had a better understanding of their old adversary: Lyndon Johnson was more than a political operator with slicked-back hair, hand-tailored suits, and a domineering personality. Douglas decided that Johnson was sincere, and that securing civil rights was more important than nursing old political grievances.[49]

From a small sitting room on the second floor of the White House where she recorded her daily diary, Lady Bird Johnson could see the procession of leaders arriving to meet with the president. She found it painful to watch Johnson's relentless courtship of men like Joe Rauh, who she felt had unfairly excoriated her husband and his native region. She was particularly upset when the president virtually ordered conservative Texas con-

---

* In Cotulla, Johnson would buy an ice cream cone for a different child every day from the ice cream vendor who came by the school since he didn't have enough money to buy cones for all of them.

gressman Joe Kilgore, the Johnsons' close friend, not to challenge Johnson's political foe Ralph Yarborough for reelection. Lady Bird feared that Lyndon's wooing of the liberals and the intensity of the civil rights struggle would damage her relationships with members of Congress from the Deep South and their wives, who had been the Johnsons' closest friends in Washington. She understood and agreed with her husband's push for civil rights,* but it still angered her that the South's most strident critics never acknowledged the region she loved for its beautiful land and its gracious people.[50]

She had grown up Claudia Alta Taylor, nicknamed Lady Bird as a child, in the town of Karnack in East Texas, where her father, Thomas Jefferson Taylor, a prosperous merchant, landowner, and community leader, was called "Boss" Taylor by the black sharecroppers. It was an environment vastly different from Lyndon Johnson's hill country, which was more a part of the Southwest. Karnack belonged in Deep South plantation country, and Lady Bird Taylor was raised in the manner of a southern gentlewoman. She was bright and well educated, with a master's degree in journalism from the University of Texas. Lyndon Johnson, still a congressional aide at the time they met, had swept her off her feet in a cross-country courtship that he pursued as relentlessly as any political campaign. After eight weeks of impassioned letters, roses, and exhortations to her father, she agreed to marry him.[51] He called her "Bird." She became the anchor in his life, radiating serenity in the most difficult times. On the afternoon of November 22 it was she who had made the telephone call to their daughter Lynda Bird, an eighteen-year-old student at the University of Texas. "Lynda, the president has been shot and killed," Lady Bird told her calmly. "We are fine, on the plane flying back to Washington. You go over to the governor's mansion and be with Johnnie Connally. You'll be safe there." Lynda was struck by how self-controlled her mother always was, in contrast with her tempestuous father.[52] With patience and inner strength, Lady Bird Johnson constantly saved her husband from his worst excesses. Lyndon Johnson depended on and trusted his wife's judgment like no one else's.

His whirlwind round of meetings was important, but the acid test came on November 27, 1963, at 12:30 P.M., as Lyndon Baines Johnson entered

---

* Like her husband, Lady Bird Johnson was first sensitized to the cruelties of discrimination by the experiences of their servents. In the 1950s Mrs. Johnson was horrified when ambulance companies in Washington, D.C., refused to pick up Zephyr Wright, the Johnson's black cook, after she fell on an icy sidewalk and broke her leg. Senator Johnson finally demanded and got help for Mrs. Wright.

the chamber of the House of Representatives. Johnson knew that this address to a joint session of Congress would be the most important speech of his life. All of the private entreaties he had made to leaders of government, business, labor, churches, the news media, and the civil rights movement would be for naught if he did not connect with the American people. Dressed in a dark blue suit, speaking in a quiet and controlled voice, Johnson began his speech: "Mr. Speaker, Mr. President, Members of the House, Members of the Senate, my fellow Americans — all I have I would give gladly not to be standing here today. The greatest leader of our time has been struck down by the foulest deed of our time."

In uttering those few words, Johnson identified with the grief felt by millions of Americans. His central theme was that he would continue the policies and maintain the spirit of John F. Kennedy. After quoting the 1961 inaugural address in which Kennedy had declared, "Let us begin," Johnson now affirmed, "Let us continue."

Then Johnson boldly seized the moment: "No memorial oration or eulogy could more eloquently honor President Kennedy's memory than the earliest possible passage of the civil rights bill for which he fought so long. We have talked long enough in this country about civil rights. We have talked for one hundred years or more. It is time now to write the next chapter, and to write it in a book of law."

No president from the South had ever uttered such words — much less a president who had opposed every civil rights bill offered during his six terms as a Texas congressman in that very House chamber. Now, Johnson left no doubt about his meaning, or about his commitment.

"I urge you again, as I did in 1957 and again in 1960, to enact a civil rights law so that we can move forward and eliminate from this nation every vestige of discrimination and oppression that is based upon race or color. There could be no greater source of strength to this nation both at home and abroad. . . . The time has come for Americans of all races and creeds and political beliefs to understand and respect each other. So let us put an end to the teaching and preaching of hate and violence. Let us turn away from the fanatics of the far left and the far right, from the apostles of bitterness and bigotry, from those defiant of law, and those who pour venom into the nation's bloodstream."[53]

Johnson's speech was interrupted thirty-four times by applause. It struck a positive chord around the nation, spawning widespread public sentiment that Johnson was indeed up to the job of succeeding Jack Kennedy as president. The response from the civil rights community was immediate and generous. Martin Luther King Jr. called the speech "a heroic and courageous affirmation of our democratic ideals." Roy Wilkins said that Johnson had provided "a profound sense of new hope."[54] But the political importance of what Johnson had just done was summed up best by black comedian and activist Dick Gregory. "When Lyndon Johnson finished his speech," cracked Gregory, "twenty million American Negroes unpacked."[55]

The impact of Johnson's first presidential address came in part from where he chose to make it. He rejected the idea of a televised speech from his desk in the Oval Office, choosing instead the halls of Congress, where he reminded his former colleagues that "for 32 years Capitol Hill has been my home. I have shared many moments of pride with you, pride in the ability of the Congress of the United States to act, to meet any crisis, to distill from our differences strong programs of national action."[56] He knew most of the people there well. Many were his friends. Some were enemies. But all appreciated his declaration that he respected the independence of the legislative branch and his vow to govern with Congress as an equal partner.

Although civil rights was his most dramatic theme, Johnson addressed other issues, too. He committed himself to the major proposals of the Kennedy–Johnson administration: medical care for the elderly, federal aid to elementary and secondary education, commitment to a strong national defense, loyalty to the nation's allies, maintenance of a stable economy, prudence in government spending — themes that were reassuring to a wide range of Americans, including those who did not support the president's passionately declared commitment to civil rights. In historical terms, Johnson had described the major unfulfilled promises made by a series of Democratic presidents, from Franklin Roosevelt's New Deal to Harry Truman's Fair Deal to Jack Kennedy's New Frontier. Few in the audience realized just how long Johnson had dreamed of gaining the power to fulfill those promises, and to compete with Roosevelt in accomplishments and in winning the love of an appreciative people.

In the first critical days, Johnson used all the techniques of persuasion — known collectively as "the Johnson treatment" — that he had used to dominate the Senate as its majority leader from 1955 until his inauguration as vice president in 1961. He knew the intricate details of the most complex legislation. He possessed an encyclopedic knowledge of each senator's interests, strengths, and weaknesses. He knew which senators to flatter, which to promise favors — and, when necessary, which to threaten. Most often, though, Johnson's appeal of last resort was to urge a senator to put the national interest above his own. Almost from the first moments of his presidency, Johnson employed the "treatment" toward achieving his greatest priority: passage of the civil rights bill.

The Johnson treatment was highly physical. He would stand nose to nose with another senator and literally press the flesh of a hand, an arm, a shoulder. At six foot four, Johnson loomed over most men and women, and he employed his size as another resource for dominating others. "He'd get right up on you," Hubert Humphrey recalled. "He'd just lean right in on you. . . . He was so big and tall he'd be kind of looking down on you, then he'd be pulling your lapels, and he'd be grabbing you."[57]

Johnson also outworked the other ninety-nine senators with an energy and intensity few could match. "Let us reason together," he would say as he reached for consensus. Not every senator liked Johnson. Some resented his ceaseless hunger for power and his arrogance. Yet most admired his ability to make the Senate work effectively on the public's business.[58]

Now, on an even larger political stage, Johnson sought to persuade men and women from a broad range of interest groups to follow his leadership. Courting the liberals and civil rights activists was essential. But Johnson also needed support from conservative Democrats and Republicans, including those opposed to granting equality to 20 million black Americans. Perhaps no consensus could be reached with diehard southerners on civil rights. But that issue aside, he still sought consensus.

In those first days of his presidency, Johnson reached out with extraordinary gestures to a wide range of Washington power brokers. Early one morning, he stopped his limousine at the home of George Meany, president of the AFL-CIO, and rode with him to the White House. Over breakfast the president pledged his commitment to Meany's top priority: passage of the civil rights bill.[59] The next morning, he repeated the same limousine-and-breakfast routine with Charles Halleck, the Republican leader of the House. Normally cantankerous and highly partisan, Halleck left the White House clearly charmed and pleased by his visit — and pledging to cooperate with the new president.[60]

With the conservative Senate barons — the powerful committee chairmen — he offered a menu of enticements. For John McClellan, the crusty Arkansas scourge of wasteful government spending and corruption, Johnson promised to attack fraud and waste in defense contracts. And he followed up on his words with action, instructing Defense Secretary Robert McNamara to cut Pentagon spending even by the politically sensitive method of closing unneeded military bases.[61]

*   *   *

As an essential part of his legislative strategy, Lyndon Johnson set out to break the coalition of southern Democrats and conservative Republicans that had held up President Kennedy's top legislative priorities, civil rights and tax reduction. The tax bill was needed to stimulate a sluggish economy. The civil rights bill was a response to legitimate grievances long ignored and to the growing wave of black demonstrations, which both Kennedy and Johnson feared could escalate into rebellion. The southerners' strategy — planned by Richard Russell of Georgia, the most powerful member of the Senate — was to stall the tax bill as long as possible in order to delay and defeat the civil rights bill. With the start of a presidential election campaign only months away, the southerners hoped to drag their feet on civil rights until the summer political conventions forced adjournment of Congress.

Revising Kennedy's legislative strategy, Johnson decided to concentrate first on the tax bill — the less difficult fight to win. Once the tax legislation was out of the way, Johnson planned to bring the civil rights bill to the Senate floor for a fight to the finish against the segregationist bloc. The key to passing the tax bill was to overcome the opposition of Virginia's Harry Byrd, chairman of the Senate Finance Committee and an ardent opponent of government spending.* Byrd had held the tax bill hostage in his committee, refusing even to hold hearings.

Johnson speculated with his advisers that Byrd might be persuaded to release the bill if Johnson could cut the proposed federal budget, which was expected for the first time to exceed $100 billion, a number with great symbolic significance for opponents of government spending like Harry Byrd. Johnson told his aides to find ways to reduce the budget. "Unless you get that budget down around $100 billion," said Johnson, "you won't pee one drop."[62] Then Johnson personally arranged all the details — including a menu of potato soup, salad, and vanilla ice cream — for a private lunch with Byrd in a small room next to Johnson's office.

Harry Byrd was a proud southern aristocrat, patriarch of a political machine that ruled the Commonwealth of Virginia and, as he saw it, guardian of the U.S. Treasury against reckless spending. At Byrd's command, Virginia had defied the U.S. Supreme Court by closing its public schools rather than integrate them. From their Senate years together, Johnson liked Byrd and had found ways to work with him. Now, over dessert, Johnson maneuvered the strong-willed Virginian toward a budget figure he would accept. If he could bring the budget below $107 billion,

---

* In *Lyndon,* his oral biography of President Johnson, Merle Miller describes Senator Byrd as a "steadfast opponent of most of the twentieth century."

the president asked, would Byrd permit the tax bill to come to the Senate floor? "Too big, Mr. President, too big," Byrd replied. Johnson asked the same question with successively lower totals. Repeatedly Byrd shook his head "no." Finally Johnson asked, "Just suppose I could get the budget somewhere under $100 billion. What would you say then?"* Reluctantly, Byrd agreed that he would allow the bill to come up for a vote in the full Senate.[63]

At his first legislative breakfast with Democratic congressional leaders on December 3, President Johnson laid out his strategy for passing the civil rights bill. Over scrambled eggs and bacon, he discussed the obstacles facing the bill with Senate Majority Leader Mike Mansfield of Montana, House Speaker John McCormack of Massachusetts, and House Majority Leader Carl Albert of Oklahoma. Ahead loomed the immense task of breaking the filibuster that would be mounted by the determined segregationists from the Deep South.[64] But the first roadblock was the House Rules Committee, where chairman Howard Worth Smith, an ardent segregationist from Virginia, had kept the bill bottled up. Smith, who ruled northern Virginia as his personal duchy within the political empire of Senator Harry Byrd, refused to call committee meetings whenever his dictatorial power was threatened. When "Judge" Smith, as he was called, wanted to block a bill, he simply retired to his farm outside Washington.[65]

To get the bill to the House floor, Johnson and the legislative leaders agreed to employ a seldom-used parliamentary procedure called a discharge petition. The leaders would file a petition to strip the bill from Smith's committee and bring it before the full House for consideration. A majority of the House — 218 members — would have to sign the petition. The tactic seldom succeeded because the committee chairmen and other senior members would band together to repel any threat to their power. In taking on Judge Smith, however, Johnson hoped to do more than bring a successful discharge petition; he was sending a message to Congress and the country. In the drive to overrule Smith's power, Johnson would use the bully pulpit of the White House to demonstrate his determination to move the stalemated Congress forward.

In a series of meetings, telephone calls, and public statements, Johnson

---

* The budget gambit with Byrd was Johnson at his manipulative best. But there was a cost to Johnson's credibility. Both Byrd and the White House press corps felt later that Johnson had deceived them by first suggesting that the budget would far exceed $100 billion so he could claim a great triumph.

hammered at the message that he was going to push a strong civil rights bill through Congress. He knew he had to convince friend and foe alike that he would not bargain away provisions to gain its approval, as he had done in 1957 and 1960. "I want that bill passed without one word changed," the president repeated to Americans for Democratic Action lobbyist Joseph Rauh and Clarence Mitchell of the NAACP.[66] Next he delivered an important message to Senator Richard Russell, leader of the southern opposition — and a Johnson mentor, benefactor, and friend.

Lyndon Johnson's rise to power had been aided by a knack for cultivating mentors who helped advance his career. Johnson had made himself useful to a series of powerful men and women, beginning with the president of Southwest Texas State Teachers' College, where he received his degree in education, and going on to include President Franklin Roosevelt, House Majority Leader (later Speaker) Sam Rayburn, and Richard Russell. In Rayburn and Russell, Johnson befriended aging, lonely bachelors. He not only served as their loyal lieutenant but also brought them into his home, where Lady Bird cooked their favorite foods and the Johnson daughters, Lynda and Luci, affectionately called them "Mr. Sam" and "Uncle Dick." Johnson was unstinting in his devotion to the senior legislators, who recognized his promise and assisted his rise in Congress. With Russell's support, Johnson had become assistant minority leader, minority leader, and then, at age forty-six, majority leader of the Senate. Johnson's critics saw his courting of Rayburn and Russell as the actions of a sycophant. But Johnson had apprenticed himself to masters of the art of politics, much as an ambitious young carpenter might seek to learn his trade from a master craftsman.

On December 7, Johnson invited Russell to the White House for a swim and a leisurely lunch. Afterward, in the Oval Office, he delivered a firm message to his old friend. The subject was civil rights. "Dick, you've got to get out of my way," Johnson said. "If you don't, I'm going to roll over you. I don't intend to cavil or compromise."

"You may do that," Russell replied. "But it's going to cost you the South, and cost you the election."

"If that's the price I have to pay," Johnson answered, "I'll pay it gladly."[67]

For decades, the Democratic Party's ability to win the presidency and to control Congress had depended on the "solid South." What Russell was warning — and Johnson clearly understood — was that his advocacy of civil rights would likely precipitate a southern political realignment to the Republican Party.

As Johnson had expected, Russell carried the president's message back to the other southerners in the Senate: the South should not expect any more compromises on civil rights from Lyndon Johnson. Asked whether Johnson would weaken the bill, Russell replied, "No. The way that fellow operates, he'll get the whole bill, every last bit of it."[68] The die was cast. No quarter would be given — by either side. Either Russell and his lieutenants would stop the bill with a monumental filibuster, or the nation would get its strongest civil rights law since Lincoln.[69]

Johnson sent another signal to his fellow southerners. "You've got a southern president," he told them. "If you want to blow him out of the water, go right ahead and do it, but you boys will never see another one again. We're friends on the q.t. Would you rather have me administering the civil rights bill, or do you want to have Nixon or [Pennsylvania governor William] Scranton? You have to make up your mind."[70]

Demonstrating his usefulness to the South, Johnson pushed through the House cotton legislation that provided several billion dollars in aid to southern farmers. To win that vote, he lobbied House Speaker McCormack and Chicago mayor Richard Daley, who controlled the eleven votes of the Chicago delegation,[71] to back the farm supports. McCormack and Daley opposed helping southern members of Congress who voted against civil rights and other social legislation, but they responded to Johnson's appeal.[72] By passing farm relief, Johnson demonstrated to the southerners and to conservative midwestern Republicans that he had the power to see that their needs were met — or not.

Using his support for the cotton bill as a lever, Johnson got a few southerners to sign the civil rights discharge petition. In a telephone call to Harry Provence, a Waco, Texas, newspaper editor and Johnson supporter, the president told him to ask if Texas Democrat William Robert Poage, chairman of the House Agriculture Committee, would also sign the petition — after first reminding Poage of Johnson's help on the farm bill.[73] Poage refused, but half a dozen Texas congressmen did sign — out of loyalty to Johnson and at risk to their political careers.

For the civil rights legislation to prevail in Congress, strong Republican support was required, and from his first days in office Johnson sought GOP votes. He had to have at least seventy Republican signatures on the House discharge petition, and he would need most of the Senate Republicans to defeat a filibuster there. He asked the Republican leaders for support, but he also sent them a tough political message. His chosen messenger was conservative Texas banker Robert Anderson, Treasury secretary in the Eisenhower administration and a close Johnson friend. The president told Anderson that if Rules Committee chairman Smith succeeded in stalling the bill until March, it would not pass in 1964. "Now, this country is not in any condition to take that kind of stuff. . . . Roy Wilkins told me yesterday that Negroes will be out in the streets again if we don't make some little progress."

Johnson told Anderson he wanted the Republicans to know that "you're either for civil rights or you're not. You're either the party of Lincoln or you ain't. By God, put up or shut up. This is it. If you are, you sign the [discharge] petition to consider it. If you're not, why, just get over there, by God, with Jim Eastland* and Howard Smith, and stay [there]."

If Republicans opposed the civil rights bill, Johnson told Anderson, "I believe we can dramatize it enough that we can wreck them. But I don't want to do it that way, but when a man won't even give you a hearing . . . that is just getting too damn rough."[74]

Johnson reached out to all the centers of power in America on civil rights. He called the executives who ran the television networks, national newsmagazines, and major newspapers. On December 2 he phoned Katharine Graham, publisher of the *Washington Post,* to ask for her newspaper's editorial support for the petition to bring the civil rights bill to the House floor. Johnson had been a close friend of Kay Graham and her late husband, Philip, for years, and he now turned on the Johnson treatment full-throttle. He flirted mischievously: "I hear that sweet voice on the telephone, and I'd like to break out of here and be like one of those young animals on my ranch — jump a fence." He told her how much he missed Phil Graham's wise advice. He tried flattery, saying that the commission to investigate President Kennedy's assassination should be called the "Kay Graham Commission" because it was her newspaper that had suggested the idea. As a personal favor to her, he agreed to speak at an upcoming meeting of the American Book Publishers Association. Finally, he chided the *Post* for writing about sex scandals on Capitol Hill rather than about the civil rights crisis. "Whether [a Senate official] had a girl or whether he didn't is not a matter that is going to settle this country," Johnson said, "but whether we have equality or justice is pretty damn important." He asked Graham to publicize as "anti–civil rights" the name of any member of Congress unwilling to permit the bill to get a hearing on the floor of the House.[75] The *Post* supported the discharge petition, running strong editorials for three consecutive days after the president's conversation with Mrs. Graham.[76]

---

* James Eastland had blocked consideration of the bill in the Senate from his position as chairman of the Judiciary Committee.

In his first twelve days as president, Johnson pushed every lever of power he could reach to create a tide of public sentiment that Congress should move forward on civil rights. On December 3, the day after speaking with Katharine Graham, he held his first meeting as president with Martin Luther King Jr., the civil rights leader who Johnson knew could exert the greatest influence on American public opinion.[77]

3

✦ ✦ ✦ ✦ ✦ ✦

"A Fellow Southerner in the White House"

I N ATLANTA, MARTIN LUTHER KING JR. and his advisers watched anxiously as other civil rights leaders were called to the White House. In his first ten days in office, President Johnson had held well-publicized meetings with both Roy Wilkins, executive director of the NAACP, and Whitney Young, president of the National Urban League. With the fate of a historic law at stake, each civil rights advocate sought to press his case with the president. Dr. King and his associates speculated that he was being intentionally ignored. "Send Johnson a message," King's counselors urged. If Johnson did not give King "a play," argued Stanley Levison, the New York lawyer and businessman who advised King on strategy, the president would lose votes in the next election. The civil rights movement "can't rely on Roy Wilkins alone" to carry its message to the White House, Levison told King. The other advisers agreed.[1] A call from King's lawyer Clarence Jones to Louis Martin, a friendly black official at the Democratic National Committee in Washington, quickly remedied the perceived slight.[2] King was invited to meet with Lyndon Johnson in the Oval Office at 11:30 A.M. the following Tuesday, December 3.[3]

The meeting held special meaning for King, who had felt excluded from the Kennedy White House. Indeed, Jack Kennedy had viewed King warily. At the height of the demonstrations King led in the spring of 1963, Kennedy had joked nervously that an upcoming appointment with King was akin to "inviting Karl Marx to the White House."[4] Kennedy's handlers had tried to play down his meeting with King by sandwiching it between a conversation with Roy Wilkins and a joint meeting with all the major civil rights leaders. The NAACP under Wilkins was a highly structured national organization that tried to influence policy through lawsuits and lobbying. The National Urban League, led by Young, worked with the business establishment to end employment discrimination and open up better jobs for black Americans. Kennedy felt comfortable dealing with Wilkins and Whitney Young, who represented the two oldest, most established civil rights organizations, but dealing with King was another matter.

King's Southern Christian Leadership Conference and other civil rights groups that sprang up in the late 1950s represented a new brand of advocacy. They challenged racial discrimination not only with lobbying and lawsuits but also with demonstrations in the streets. These new groups — King's SCLC, James Farmer's Congress of Racial Equality (CORE), and the Student Nonviolent Coordinating Committee (SNCC) — injected energy, and volatility, into the civil rights struggle. The new acronyms* were confusing to the nation's leaders, and came to imply a feared militancy. An NAACP lawsuit to desegregate public schools would follow a predictable route through the court system. But SCLC street protests aroused far more controversy and often led to unpredictable results, ranging from bursts of public support for civil rights to violent attacks on demonstrators by law enforcement officers and white vigilantes.

As the movement's best-known leader, King inspired both whites and blacks to the civil rights cause, but he also ignited anger and hatred among segregationists. President Kennedy and his brother, the attorney general, had feared that black riots could spread and grow into a general uprising. A White House meeting with King always brought a deluge of hate mail. So Kennedy had proceeded cautiously, trying to satisfy the increasing demand for civil rights legislation while retaining enough support among southern Democrats in Congress to pass other parts of his program. From Kennedy's perspective, the few meetings he'd held with King had only raised political temperatures and complicated his quest for compromise. Now Lyndon Johnson faced the same dilemma as he embraced the deadlocked legislative program he had inherited. Indeed, George Reedy, a longtime Johnson aide who became White House press secretary, warned Johnson early on that he should try to spotlight Roy Wilkins as the preeminent black leader and play down the controversial King.

* Opponents called them "Snick, Slick, and Core" in one breath.

"Stand Up for Justice. Stand Up for Truth"

The modern civil rights era had opened as the nation prepared for World War II. To avoid a threatened black protest march on Washington in 1941,[5] President Franklin Delano Roosevelt had acceded to the demands of black leader A. Philip Randolph, founder of the Brotherhood of Sleeping Car Porters, and issued an executive order banning racial discrimination in war production plants.[6] At war's end, African American soldiers, as well as Mexican Americans and Asian Americans, returned from military service determined to secure full citizenship in the nation they had risked their lives to defend.* Responding to black veterans and civil rights leaders, President Harry S. Truman desegregated the armed services in 1948.[7]

That same year, after the Democratic National Convention approved a progressive civil rights platform,[8] southern Democrats rebelled, forming the segregationist "Dixiecrat" Party, which proclaimed the doctrine of states' rights. Headed by Governor Strom Thurmond of South Carolina, the Dixiecrat ticket carried his state along with Mississippi, Louisiana, and Alabama in the 1948 election. With strong black support in the North, Truman won the election despite the loss of these southern states and another challenge from the left, by Progressive Party candidate Henry Wallace. A split had begun to form within the Democratic Party, however, between the northern progressive integrationists and the southern conservative segregationists. Democratic Party leaders, including Senate Majority Leader Lyndon Johnson, found it increasingly difficult to maintain party unity in the face of ideological schism over civil rights.[9]

In 1954 the U.S. Supreme Court, in a case involving a black Kansas student named Linda Brown, ruled unanimously that racially segregated school systems were unconstitutional.[10] Their order to desegregate "with all deliberate speed"[11] inspired increased activism for civil rights — and the beginning of massive resistance by white southerners. In 1955 the brutal slaying of Emmett Till, a fourteen-year-old black youth visiting Mississippi, allegedly for daring to whistle at a white woman, stirred outrage, reminding the nation of the continued shame of violence and other degradations afflicting blacks in the South.[12] At the same time, in response to the Supreme Court's *Brown* ruling, southerners organized resistance, forming White Citizens Councils and expanding the Ku Klux Klan. In the

---

* When a Mexican American soldier killed in the Pacific campaign was denied burial in 1949 in a cemetery in his hometown in Texas, Senator Lyndon Johnson responded to the outrage of Mexican Americans by arranging for the soldier to be buried at Arlington National Cemetery.

heated racial politics of 1956, every southern senator save three signed a "Southern Manifesto" vowing to defy the Court's school desegregation decision. The holdouts were Majority Leader Lyndon Johnson of Texas and Senators Albert Gore and Estes Kefauver of Tennessee, each of whom had ambitions for the presidency.[13]

The civil rights movement was transforming mid-twentieth-century America, building political pressure for change. John Kennedy and Lyndon Johnson — indeed, any Democrat aspiring to run for national office — would now need to respond to the rising tide of black protest against inequalities that belied the nation's most cherished ideals if they hoped to be elected.

A new kind of civil rights activism had first caught fire — and gained national attention — in Montgomery, Alabama, in December 1955, when Rosa Parks, a black seamstress and civil rights activist, weary after a long workday, refused to give up her seat to a white passenger and move to the back of a city bus. When she was convicted of violating a city segregation ordinance, a spirited protest movement sprang into action. For more than a year, the black citizens of Montgomery maintained a boycott of the city's bus system. Walking, car-pooling, and bicycling, they braved economic reprisals, arrests, assaults, the firebombing of their homes and churches, and threats against their lives.[14] In the end, they won in the U.S. Supreme Court, which ruled in November 1956 that the city ordinance mandating racial segregation on buses was unconstitutional.[15]

The Montgomery bus boycott captured the attention of the country and thrust a twenty-six-year-old minister onto the national stage. Martin Luther King had taken the pulpit of the Dexter Avenue Baptist Church little more than a year earlier with no intention of becoming a civil rights leader. He had just received his doctorate in systematic theology from Boston University and had chosen a pastorate at the prominent black church in Montgomery rather than follow his inclination to become a university professor or honor the request of his father, Martin Luther King Sr., to return to Atlanta and become his assistant at the Ebenezer Baptist Church.[16] (King's plan was to gain practical experience for a few years as a minister, and then teach philosophy and theology at a university.) Montgomery's black leaders had chosen King to lead the bus boycott knowing little more about him than that he was an eloquent speaker and that, as a newcomer, he was unencumbered by ties to either the white power structure or any of the various factions within the city's black community.

Until he became president of the hastily formed Montgomery Improvement Association, King's chief concerns had been his family and his church. Just months before, he had turned down the presidency of the local chapter of the NAACP because he already felt overwhelmed starting a career and a family at the same time. His wife, Coretta, was pregnant with their first child, and King was consumed with building and reviving Dexter Avenue Baptist, whose middle- and upper-middle-class members had not pursued their church duties with the diligence he expected. King urged his congregation to participate in the NAACP, but he had no plans to become a leader in the struggle.[17]

Growing up in Atlanta the son of a prominent minister, King had never known poverty and was shielded by his parents from many of the blows of a segregated society. Even so, he endured humiliations. He and his high school debate coach had been forced to give up their seats to white passengers and stand throughout a long cross-country bus trip. This and similar experiences were etched into King's memory, as was the character of his father, who never tolerated a racial slight without protest. When a store clerk once informed his father that young Martin would have to try on a pair of shoes in a back room, the senior King stormed out, his son in tow.[18]

As an undergraduate at Morehouse College in Atlanta, King had made mediocre grades at first and had not taken academics very seriously.[19] He was a "sharp dresser," recognizable by his sport coat and brimmed hat.[20] Although, urged on by his father, he felt a call to preach, he considered becoming a lawyer instead. In the end, however, he decided on the ministry and entered Crozer Theological Seminary in Pennsylvania, where he became a serious scholar, graduating first in his class,[21] and was elected president of the student body his final year.

Pursuing his doctorate at Boston University, King continued his intellectual growth, studying a broad range of theologians and philosophers as he sought a meaningful philosophy to guide his life. He was attracted to the teachings of Reinhold Niebuhr, with their emphasis on the power of collective evil, but could not accept Niebuhr's ultimate pessimism about man's fate. In the German philosopher G.W.F. Hegel, with his analysis of the dialectical process, King found a structure of thinking with which he could feel comfortable. King adopted Hegel's view that a higher truth emerged as a synthesis between seemingly contradictory views — a thesis and an antithesis. In the context of King's own concerns, he reached for a synthesis between the economic theories of capitalism and Marxism and between conceptions of good and evil. He decided that men and women had the personal power to seek God and to choose good over evil. Harold DeWolf, King's academic adviser, called him "a scholar's scholar" of great promise, and considered King one of the half-dozen best graduate students he had taught in more than three decades at Boston University.[22]

King enjoyed debating politics and public affairs with his friends, yet he still managed a lively social life. He dated both black women and white women, and at one time seriously considered marrying a young white woman whose father was an employee at Crozer. His friends convinced him, however, that an interracial marriage would make the couple's lives miserable, especially if they returned to the South.[23] Then an old friend set him up with her classmate Coretta Scott, a talented concert singer from Alabama who was working toward her master's degree at the New England Conservatory of Music. On their first date, King told Coretta that she had all the qualities he sought in a wife — character, intelligence, personality, and beauty. Fifteen months later they were married at her parents' Alabama farm, with Martin's father officiating.[24] In their union, both had made hard choices. Coretta had agreed to set aside her professional career and accepted Martin's condition that he wanted a wife who would stay at home and raise a family. After experiencing their freedom as students in the North, both accepted with eyes wide open that they were returning to a rigid world of segregation and discrimination. Against that grim reality they weighed their opportunity as well-educated blacks to contribute, to be of service, and both of them felt genuine affection for their home region despite its racial oppression. And so the Kings moved into the parsonage of Dexter Avenue Baptist. Fifteen months later, they found themselves in the national spotlight.

As the Montgomery bus boycott held strong going into its third month, the white resistance turned violent. By late January 1956, King was receiving thirty to forty hate letters a day, many of them threatening his impending murder. On the night of January 30, a bomb was ignited on the porch of the King home, blowing the porch apart and scattering glass into the living room. A frightened King rushed home from a mass meeting to find that Coretta and their baby, Yolanda, were unharmed. Other bombings followed at the churches and homes of leaders of the Montgomery Improvement Association. Only in the violence of Montgomery did Martin Luther King find his own deep commitment to serve and lead in the movement to achieve equal rights for African Americans. One night, after enduring dozens of telephone calls threatening his life and the lives of his family, King underwent a transforming experience. About midnight he picked up the ringing telephone to hear a menacing voice: "Nigger, we are tired of you and your mess now. If you aren't out of this town in three days, we're going to blow your brains out and blow up your house."

Trembling with fear, King sat at the kitchen table holding a cup of coffee and imagining horrifying images of his infant daughter being killed by racists. In desperation he prayed out loud, "Lord, I'm down here trying to do what's right. . . . But Lord, I must confess that I'm weak now. I'm faltering. I'm losing my courage."

At that moment, King later wrote, "I could hear an inner voice saying to me: 'Martin Luther, stand up for righteousness. Stand up for justice. Stand up for truth. And, lo, I will be with you even until the end of the world.' I heard Jesus saying still to fight on. He promised never to leave me, never to leave me alone." The epiphany deepened King's resolve to commit himself fully to the struggle for equal rights.[25] He would continue to fear violent death; he would never relinquish his longing to enjoy a full, normal life; and he always would harbor doubts about his worthiness to lead the movement. Yet during the bus boycott it became clear to King and others that he possessed leadership skills beyond his natural abilities as an inspiring speaker. He was deft at organizing people and managing complex logistics. During the twelve-month boycott, King's followers had created and operated an alternative transportation system of private cars and taxis to ferry Montgomery's forty thousand black workers to and from work.[26] The young preacher also had shown skill in mediating disputes between quarrelsome factions within the black community. Most important, King became the eloquent voice of the Montgomery movement. First reporters, then national television audiences responded to his effortless blend of passion, scholarly knowledge, common sense, and the best ideals of the American tradition.

The impression quickly developed across the nation that King was the spokesman not just for the Montgomery Improvement Association but for the movement itself, that he was personally responsible for its creation and its success. King was critically important in giving voice to the protest and drawing political and national support to it, but he was moved along by its irresistible grassroots force. "The amazing thing about our movement is that it is a protest of the people," Montgomery teacher Jo Ann Robinson told a reporter. "It is not a one-man show. It is not a preachers' show. It's the people. The masses of this town, who are tired of being trampled on, are responsible. The leaders couldn't stop it if they wanted."[27] In the years that followed, King continued to symbolize the aspirations of the entire civil rights movement, but he almost always was being pulled or pushed forward by other black leaders and by widespread protests and demonstrations from blacks demanding change.

King's experience in the bus boycott dovetailed with his earlier philosophical studies — and particularly his examination of Mahatma Gandhi's passive resistance to British rule in India. In adopting Gandhi's methods, King believed that true pacifism represented "a courageous confrontation of evil by the power of love." He stressed that pacifist techniques represented not passivity but an "active non-violent resistance to evil." What emerged was an effective new weapon in the war against segregation. King called it "nonviolent direct action resistance."[28] Making up only 10 percent of the population of the United States, blacks could not expect to win equal rights through violent rebellion, which was abhorrent to King's religious beliefs in any case. Demonstrations of nonviolent resistance dramatized both the rightness and the righteousness of the cause, as well as the wrongness of its opponents. When whites in Montgomery used dynamite against the peaceful demonstrators, they created a tableau that underscored the stark reality of racism. The confrontations between unyielding white officials or violent white thugs and the peaceful bus boycotters belied the ideals of American equality and brought to light the laws and practices of the segregated South. And when scenes were shown on national television of black protesters kneeling, praying, and singing while whites yelled, spat, and threw objects or beat them, the movement gained sympathy and support from fair-minded citizens across the country. The bus boycott spurred blacks in communities throughout the South to initiate their own protests against segregated bus systems, schools, restaurants, and hotels, and against the widespread denial of the right to vote.

After the victory in Montgomery, King reached out to his fellow black ministers to form the Southern Christian Leadership Conference, a loose coalition of clergy who vowed from their pulpits to fight segregation throughout the South. But both the impetus to expand on the Montgomery victory and the ideas for forming the SCLC came from three northerners: Bayard Rustin, a black intellectual, organizer, longtime advocate of nonviolent protest, and key adviser to King in Montgomery; Ella Baker, an influential black organizer and activist; and Stanley David Levison, a New York lawyer and activist. These three leaders drafted the documents and position papers and encouraged King to initiate an effort beyond Montgomery. "Until the Negro votes on a large scale," Rustin wrote, "we will have to rely more and more on mass direct action as the one realistic political weapon." From Montgomery, wrote Rustin, came the realization that "the center of gravity has shifted from the courts to community action."[29] On February 10, 1957, ninety-seven people, mostly southern black ministers, meeting in New Orleans created the SCLC and elected King its president.

The Movement Spreads

The new voices of protest out of the South had a profound effect on politics in Washington. In 1956, Senate Majority Leader Lyndon Johnson had helped kill civil rights legislation in Congress. But after Adlai Stevenson lost the 1956 presidential election to Dwight Eisenhower, Democratic leaders realized that they were also losing their hold on northern black voters — an integral part of the eclectic Democratic coalition of organized labor, minorities, and the "solid South." Black citizens in the North were questioning their allegiance to a party represented by southern segregationists in Congress. The party's 1960 presidential candidate would have even greater difficulty winning if the Democrats lost their monopoly on the urban black vote. Johnson had realized that if he were to have any chance of fulfilling his ambition to be elected president, he had better start supporting civil rights.[30]

In 1957, for the first time in his twenty-year congressional career, Johnson not only backed a civil rights bill but also used his formidable legislative skills to secure its passage. The Civil Rights Act of 1957 was not a strong measure, but it created the U.S. Commission on Civil Rights, established a civil rights division in the Justice Department, and made a first effort to stop state and local officials from preventing voting by blacks in the Deep South. Significantly, it was the first civil rights legislation adopted since Reconstruction almost a century earlier. From 1957 on, the evolving political career of Lyndon Johnson became inextricably intertwined with the rise of the civil rights movement and of Martin Luther King Jr.

On February 1, 1960, four young black men, students from North Carolina A&I, sat down at an F. W. Woolworth's lunch counter in Greensboro, North Carolina. When they were refused service, they in turn refused to leave and were arrested. First by word of mouth, then through news coverage, hundreds of black youths learned about and then spontaneously followed the example of the Greensboro sit-in. In the days and weeks that followed, thousands of other black youths were arrested as lunch counter sit-ins spread throughout the South. The students — mostly from traditionally black colleges — inspired one another to action. They were influenced as well by the words and actions of emerging leaders like Martin Luther King Jr., who had reached a national television audience, and the Reverend James Lawson of Nashville, another disciple of Gandhi's strategy of nonviolent passive resistance. From the outset, however, the students insisted on running their own show. Recognizing their potential, King had initially tried to recruit the student groups to serve as a youth arm of his SCLC, but had pulled back in response to objections from Roy Wilkins, who did not want the SCLC in competition with his NAACP as a membership organization. Even though she was executive director of King's SCLC, the ever-independent Ella Baker urged the students to maintain their autonomy. She believed that King and the other SCLC ministers were too authoritarian, that they spent too little time helping poor blacks organize at the grassroots level.[31] Baker felt, "to be very honest, the movement made Martin rather than Martin making the movement."[32] On April 15, 1960, two hundred students met at Shaw University in Raleigh, North Carolina, and formally created the Student Nonviolent Coordinating Committee, known as SNCC, which quickly became an important force in the movement.

To devote more time to building the SCLC, King resigned his pulpit at Dexter Avenue Baptist in 1960 and returned to Atlanta to become his father's co-pastor at Ebenezer Baptist Church. Soon afterward, SNCC's Atlanta leaders asked King to join them at a sit-in planned for Rich's, Atlanta's leading department store. The students wanted the publicity the nationally known King would bring to their demonstration. King was reluctant to offend his father, who believed that he and his contemporaries alone should make decisions affecting Atlanta's black community. The students pressed their case. "Martin, you've got to come with us," said Lonnie King, a student at Morehouse College. When Martin again demurred, Lonnie pressed harder, telling the SCLC leader that "he was going to have to go to jail if he intended to maintain his position as one of the leaders in the civil rights struggle." Lonnie challenged Martin to explain how he could advocate "jail, not bail" if he were unwilling to risk being arrested himself. The argument was persuasive. Martin went with the students to Rich's the next morning, October 19, was arrested with them, and spent his first night ever in a jail cell.[33] After six months of sit-ins, Atlanta's business leaders capitulated, worried about national publicity tarnishing their self-proclaimed motto as "the city too busy to hate." Lunch counters, restrooms, and other facilities in the downtown department stores were desegregated.

The sit-ins provided a jolt of youthful energy to the movement and helped to energize the SCLC, which still had not launched a major campaign, and CORE, which was seeking to revive itself after a period of activism twenty years earlier. SNCC also trained a coterie of new leaders. From 1960 on, the young SNCC organizers constantly pushed King's

SCLC and the other older civil rights organizations to take more radical action.

The Kennedys Face the Civil Rights Issue

The drama of the sit-ins and the continuing fight over school integration, six years after the Supreme Court's decision in *Brown v. Board of Education*, kept civil rights in the spotlight during the 1960 presidential election campaign, which pitted the young Senator John F. Kennedy against Vice President Richard M. Nixon. By being jailed in Atlanta, King had inadvertently violated the terms of his probation resulting from a minor traffic incident in DeKalb County, Georgia, a few weeks earlier. So when the students were released four days after their arrest, King was kept in custody in a state prison. A week into King's incarceration, on October 26, Kennedy campaign aide Harris Wofford persuaded the candidate to call Coretta King to express his concern. The same day, campaign manager Robert Kennedy called a DeKalb County judge to ask for King's release. The judge released King on $2,000 bond on October 27. On the Sunday before the election, November 6, 1960, the Democratic National Committee distributed tens of thousands of flyers in black churches around the country publicizing the Kennedys' intercession — and Martin Luther King Sr.'s last-minute decision to switch his support from Nixon to Kennedy.[34] The Kennedys' phone calls never became a major national news story, but the flyers made an impact in black urban precincts. No one can say for certain how many people were moved to cast their ballots for the Democratic ticket because of the Kennedys' calls, but with only forty thousand fewer votes in three key states, Jack Kennedy would have lost to Richard Nixon.

While the newly elected President Kennedy tried to regain his balance in the spring of 1961 after a bungled U.S.-led effort to overthrow Fidel Castro at the Bay of Pigs in Cuba, civil rights activists at home launched a new offensive. Members of the Congress of Racial Equality, led by James Farmer, set out to integrate the interstate bus system in the South.[35] An urbane intellectual who spoke in a deep bass voice, Farmer had pioneered passive resistance techniques in the 1940s by staging restaurant sit-ins at segregated northern restaurants, and now sought to revive CORE after having worked for the NAACP. CORE members, along with volunteers from SNCC and other groups, formed two integrated bus-riding teams to challenge segregation on interstate Greyhound and Trailways buses and at bus stations in southern cities.

The thirteen original Freedom Riders departed from Washington, D.C., on May 4, 1961, divided between Greyhound and Trailways buses, with a planned itinerary that would take them through Virginia, the Carolinas, Mississippi, and Alabama, arriving in New Orleans on May 17. The trip through Virginia and North Carolina was uneventful, as local authorities chose momentarily to forgo enforcing their laws governing segregated eating and restroom facilities at bus stations. At Rock Hill, South Carolina, violence first broke out when white thugs beat up two Freedom Riders who attempted to integrate the whites-only bus station waiting room. As the buses crossed the state line from Georgia into Alabama, the violence escalated. A group of white toughs boarded one bus, armed with pieces of chain, brass knuckles, blackjacks, and pistols. They attacked the riders, causing one man a cerebral hemorrhage. At the bus station in Birmingham, another rider, Jim Peck, was accosted by a white mob and suffered permanent injuries. Outside Anniston, Alabama, a bus was hijacked by white rioters who blocked the exits and tossed a firebomb through a window. The Freedom Riders managed to escape before the bus was completely burned out, but not before they were overcome by severe smoke inhalation. On their arrival in Montgomery, the Freedom Riders again were set upon by a white mob and beaten unmercifully as state and local police withdrew from the scene and an FBI agent passively took notes on the bloodshed. Among those knocked unconscious were twenty-one-year old John Lewis, already a veteran leader of the SNCC sit-ins, and John Seigenthaler, Attorney General Robert Kennedy's assistant, sent down as an observer, who was attacked while trying to rescue a young woman Freedom Rider.[36]

That night a mob surrounded Montgomery's First Baptist Church, where the Freedom Riders had taken refuge and their supporters had gathered for a meeting. Among those trapped inside were Martin Luther King Jr. and James Farmer, both of whom had come to address the rally. Throughout the night, King spoke by telephone with Attorney General Kennedy, pleading for federal officers to protect the group.[37] After one call, King told Farmer that the attorney general had requested a "cooling-off period to give him time to work things out." King seconded Kennedy's recommendation, telling Farmer that perhaps the Freedom Ride "had made its point." But after consulting with the riders, Farmer replied, "Please tell the attorney general we have been cooling off for 350 years. If we cool off any more, we'll be in a deep freeze. The Freedom Ride will go on."[38]

After another conversation with Robert Kennedy, King reported to the riders that the Kennedys seemed completely unaware that the Freedom Rides were "part of the social revolution going on in the world." Incredibly, Robert Kennedy claimed not to have known about the Freedom Rides until violence erupted — despite the fact that CORE had publicized its plans and James Farmer had written to inform the Justice Department exactly what the group intended to do. In fact, Kennedy's attention was elsewhere. At that point civil rights was just one of many issues preoccupying the new administration — and a prickly issue at that because it irritated the powerful southern congressional committee chairmen the administration was trying to do business with. Robert Kennedy's single priority was to protect the interests of his brother, and the demonstrations were a source of embarrassment to the president as he was about to depart for his first meeting with Soviet leader Nikita Khrushchev. Despite his annoyance with King and the Freedom Riders, the attorney general worked frantically to avoid a bloodbath at the Montgomery church. Just as the white mob battered down a basement door and surged into the church basement, U.S. marshals arrived and, with reinforcements from the Alabama National Guard, led the Freedom Riders to safety.[39]

The next day the riders prepared to depart on the most perilous leg of their trip — through Mississippi, a state where law enforcement officers were known to collaborate with the Ku Klux Klan and the White Citizens Council. Although the young activists from SNCC had set up beachheads in rural Mississippi, King and the minister-led SCLC rarely had ventured into the state, seeing great dangers and few hopeful venues for waging a high-profile nonviolent campaign. Before the Freedom Riders boarded the bus for Jackson, several SNCC leaders challenged King to join them on the ride.[40]

"No, I can't go," King said. "I'm on probation from my arrest in Atlanta."

"We're all on probation," scoffed a SNCC rider. "That doesn't stop us. We're in a war. Probation can't keep us from doing what we have to do."

"What's your real reason?" they challenged King. "Why can't you go? You're the leader of this nonviolent movement. How can you stay home?"

"Well, now," King said slowly. "I think I should pick the time and place of my Golgotha."*[41]

As the meeting broke up, some of the students left the room mocking King as "De Lawd." Accounts of the incident quickly made their way through the movement, feeding the increasing sense of competition with which SNCC's twenty-year-olds viewed King, himself only thirty-two. As the best-known figure in the movement, King received the most media at-

---

* Golgotha (Calvary) was the hill outside Jerusalem where Jesus was crucified.

tention. As a result, he and the SCLC sometimes got credit — and financial contributions — for accomplishments the students felt belonged to SNCC. The leaders of SNCC saw themselves as the new vanguard, the shock troops of the movement. Ironically, southern lawmakers attributed the surge in protests by the upstart young to Martin Luther King.

"Project C"

Unlike other SCLC demonstrations, the one planned at a meeting in Dorchester, Georgia, in January 1963 was cloaked in secrecy. Its code name, "Project C," stood for confrontation. In the code names assigned SCLC leaders, King was "JFK," the Reverend Ralph David Abernathy "Dean Rusk," key local leader the Reverend Fred C. Shuttlesworth "Mac" (for Robert McNamara), and SCLC executive director Wyatt Tee Walker "RFK."[42] The target was Birmingham, Alabama, considered by many the most segregated big city in the South. The goal was to jar the Kennedy administration into introducing civil rights legislation outlawing segregation and to force the administration to protect civil rights workers from the Ku Klux Klan and racist local and state officials. For King and the Southern Christian Leadership Conference, the stakes were high. Seven years had passed since the Montgomery bus boycott; since then, King and the SCLC had led no successful action. The organization had a skeleton staff and was plagued by constant money problems. King's reputation rested far more on his oratorical power on the speakers' circuit than on concrete accomplishments since Montgomery. Younger leaders viewed him as a fading hero of the 1950s. His two-year effort to mount a major campaign against segregation in Albany, Georgia, had recently ended in failure. For the third consecutive year, President Kennedy had refused to announce major civil rights proposals in his State of the Union speech, and again he had ignored King's pleas to bypass Congress and strike down segregation in the South by executive order — a second Emancipation Proclamation. Instead, Kennedy had offered only a quiet, unpublicized reception for black luminaries at the White House, an event so devoid of substance that King and other activists boycotted it. For King and his lieutenants, Birmingham was a make-or-break effort. If successful, it would dramatize the evils of segregation so forcefully that the government would be compelled to act. If it failed, King felt, he would be out of business as a civil rights leader.[43]

The Montgomery bus boycott in 1955–56 had proved that nonviolent demonstrations could win public sympathy and generate political support. King's most ambitious effort to repeat that success had been mounted in Albany, the principal town in southwest Georgia, where the SCLC and other groups demonstrated against segregation, employment discrimination, and efforts to prevent blacks from voting. But there he had been outmaneuvered by a shrewd opponent. Instead of allowing the heavy-handed law enforcement tactics and uncontrolled violence by white mobs that were revealed on national television during the bus boycott, the student sit-ins, and the Freedom Rides, Laurie Pritchett, the police chief in Albany, had smothered the King effort with restraint. Pritchett had made arrests without violence — and usually outside the range of television cameras. He had played to the news media with reasonable talk and a polite manner. Without dramatic scenes to photograph, the national media had left Albany, declaring that King had failed.

In planning Project C, King had vowed not to repeat the mistakes of Albany. He would not again target local officials, who were able to ignore demonstrators' demands because blacks could not register to vote against them. Instead King would target Birmingham's white business establishment, which could be hurt if the large black population boycotted its stores. Timing would be important. Project C's sit-ins and economic boycott were aimed at disrupting the lucrative Easter shopping season. Birmingham also offered the right villain. In hulking Eugene "Bull" Connor, the Birmingham police commissioner, King knew that he would be confronting a hotheaded bully who craved the spotlight and believed that violence stirred support from his white working-class followers as well as his secret big-business backers.

King realized that he was playing with fire. "If [violence] comes," he declared grimly, "we will surface it for all to see." To stage a passion play that would stir the nation by Easter Sunday, he would have to provoke a major confrontation. Yet he trembled at the possible consequences. Making final plans with his closest aides, King warned them: "I have to tell you, in my judgment, some of us sitting here today will not come back alive from this campaign. I want you to think about it."[44]

The Birmingham campaign would be initiated and led by King and the Reverend Fred Shuttlesworth, a fiery activist who led the SCLC's local affiliate, the Alabama Christian Movement for Human Rights. Unlike in the sit-ins, the Freedom Rides, and the Albany protests, King would not be entering a fray started by others. The NAACP, CORE, and SNCC all were weak in Birmingham, so squabbling among the rival organizations might be avoided. But despite meticulous planning, as Project C got under way a potentially ruinous fact became apparent: except for the courageous Shuttlesworth, whose home had been dynamited by the Ku Klux

Klan, King and the SCLC had limited support within the black leadership of Birmingham. (Even Shuttlesworth, out of concern for the safety of his family, lived in exile in Cincinnati.) Most black business leaders and ministers in Birmingham did not want King fomenting trouble in their city. To garner the attention of the television networks and federal authorities, King needed wave upon wave of demonstrators willing to fill the Birmingham jail. Instead, in the first eight days, fewer than 150 demonstrators had been arrested. Project C was not producing the kind of conflict that made news. Its message had not reached Washington. Three weeks into the project, reporters ignored the demonstrations in Birmingham as they questioned President Kennedy at a White House press conference. The political and business leaders of Birmingham also ignored the demonstrators' demands for the integration of lunch counters, department store dressing rooms, toilets, and water fountains, and the hiring of black store clerks. The retailers were doing business as usual; Project C, it seemed, had fizzled. So dim were its prospects that Wyatt Walker informed the Justice Department that the SCLC would soon switch its campaign from confrontation in Birmingham to voter registration in other southern and northern cities.

On Good Friday, King decided that only desperate measures would stave off failure. For the first time in his civil rights career, he donned dungarees and work shoes — rather than his customary blue suit — and went to jail in Birmingham for violating a court order against further demonstrations. Once again, it was a decision he made reluctantly and fearfully. Initially hesitant to go to Birmingham, he finally responded to the fervent pleas of Fred Shuttlesworth, who had never ducked a battle. Now King pleaded with Ralph Abernathy, his best friend and closest aide, to accompany him to jail, and Abernathy answered his call.

From his jail cell, King was both angered and inspired after he read a letter in the *Birmingham News* in which relatively moderate local white clergy called his protests "unwise and untimely." On the newspaper itself, King scribbled what would become his famous response. "I cannot sit idly by in Atlanta and not be concerned about what happens in Birmingham," he wrote. "Injustice anywhere is a threat to justice everywhere." As for their call for patience, King replied, "Perhaps it is easy for those who have never felt the stinging dart of segregation to say, 'Wait.'" In a passionate recitation of reasons why African Americans could not wait, King wrote:

> When you have seen vicious mobs lynch your mothers and fathers at will and drown your sisters and brothers at whim; when you have seen hate-filled policemen curse, kick and even kill your black brothers and sisters;

when you see the vast majority of your twenty million Negro brothers smothering in an airtight cage of poverty in the midst of an affluent society; when you suddenly find your tongue twisted and your speech stammering as you seek to explain to your six-year-old daughter why she can't go to the public amusement park that has just been advertised on television, and see tears welling up in her eyes when she is told that Funtown is closed to colored children . . . when you are forever fighting a degenerating sense of "nobodiness" then you will understand why we find it difficult to wait.[45]

King's arrest put Birmingham back in the news. To turn up the heat, King made the excruciating decision to approve the Reverend James L. Bevel's plan to throw children into the battle. As a twenty-three-year-old theology student in Nashville, Jim Bevel emerged as a leader of the 1960 sit-ins, and then became a SNCC organizer, venturing into hostile rural areas in his native Mississippi. In April 1963, King summoned Bevel to Birmingham to help train demonstrators. As the demonstrations ran out of adult volunteers, Bevel and Dorothy Cotton, a veteran King aide, began recruiting and training high school students, and then children from junior high and elementary schools. Easily distinguishable by the yarmulke he wore on his shaved head,* Baptist minister Jim Bevel looked and acted like an eccentric, messianic preacher. He was a captivating speaker, an imaginative tactician, and, in the eyes of other SCLC staff, a "loose cannon." When reckless courage was needed, King called on Bevel, whom he called "one of my wild men." Over the heated objections of Birmingham ministers and parents, on May 2, 1963, King unleashed Bevel and his "children's crusade." They marched into downtown Birmingham to protest segregation and discrimination by the city's merchants.

That day more than six hundred children were arrested and locked up, filling the Birmingham jail and spilling over into outdoor pens at the cold and damp state fairgrounds. The arrests continued. By May 6, when almost eight hundred more children were arrested, the total came to more than three thousand. King resolutely resisted when SNCC executive director James Forman wanted parents summoned to take blankets and warm clothing to the makeshift jail. King feared that once parents saw the miserable conditions at the fairgrounds, they would stop their children from demonstrating. As he and Bevel had hoped, the courage shown by the children inspired — and shamed — Birmingham's adults into joining the protests.[46]

Project C reached its zenith as police commissioner Bull Connor unleashed high-pressure fire hoses and police attack dogs against the on-

---

* Although Bevel was a Baptist, he wore the Jewish skullcap.

coming waves of demonstrators, both children and adults. Television networks interrupted prime-time programs to show scenes of children being bowled over by the hoses and bitten by snarling police dogs. Viewers were horrified. As the confrontation escalated, King refused the Kennedy administration's appeal for a truce. He deflected the attorney general's criticism of the use of children. "When I was growing up, I was dog-bitten for nothing," said King, "so I don't mind being bitten by a dog for standing up for freedom." Coolly and with tough-minded pragmatism, King pushed his children's army. The nation was shaken, and the White House had to respond.

King had maintained a clear and intense focus on his objective even when the civil rights battlefield was obscured by what the military strategist Carl von Clausewitz called the "fog of war." When his plans went awry, as plans always do in battle, he seized the opportunities that presented themselves and pressed them to advantage. With critical support from Walker, Bevel, Shuttlesworth, and other talented lieutenants, King finally had demonstrated once again the skills of a great tactician.

Only when angry Birmingham blacks started pelting their tormentors with rocks and the orderly protests began disintegrating into riots did King decide the time had come for a truce. Meeting in secret with white business leaders, he negotiated a timetable for ending segregation in their stores. By then, President Kennedy had told an audience that he was "sickened" by the picture of a policeman unleashing a dog to bite a black teenager in the stomach. The Birmingham protests quickly spread across the country. Within six weeks, 758 demonstrations in 178 cities had resulted in nearly fifteen thousand arrests. Even Roy Wilkins felt compelled to go to jail for the first time in many years as he launched a Birmingham-type campaign in Jackson, Mississippi. As Jack and Bobby Kennedy heard reports from around the country, they feared that the nation's cities might be engulfed in race riots.

Suddenly, the politics of civil rights had been transformed in the nation's capital. Public support for a strong civil rights law soared. The president and attorney general decided that the threat of riots meant they could no longer postpone legislation to dismantle segregation in the South. "This is a terribly difficult situation," Robert Kennedy said at a White House meeting on the crisis. "We will need new legislation."[47]

LBJ Seizes the Day

The events in Birmingham had whetted Lyndon Johnson's immense political appetite. Suddenly the vice president saw an opportunity to emerge from the backwaters of his office, where he had languished unhappily for two and a half years. Jack Kennedy had chosen Johnson as his running mate in 1960 after defeating him for the presidential nomination. The choice angered liberals, but Kennedy thought Johnson's presence on the ticket would help him carry the South. As chairman of the President's Committee on Equal Employment Opportunity — one of his few actual responsibilities — the vice president had achieved only modest success in persuading government contractors to hire more black workers and eliminate segregated facilities. Yet in the process, he learned more about the problems and politics of civil rights than either of the Kennedys. Suddenly Johnson was under fire from an aroused Robert Kennedy. As Birmingham focused his attention on the civil rights struggle, the attorney general learned that black Americans held only low-wage or menial jobs, not just in the private sector but in the federal government as well. In Birmingham, where 37 percent of the population was black, African Americans held fewer than 1 percent of non-menial federal jobs, Kennedy was told by the Census Bureau. The numbers were an embarrassment to a White House asking businessmen to integrate their stores and to hire blacks. Suddenly, the attorney general was enraged.

At a President's Committee meeting on May 29, 1963, he blasted Johnson's staff for not having detailed statistics on black employment at their fingertips. He demanded information by city, by occupation, and by region. When the staff couldn't respond immediately, the attorney general stormed out. Johnson, glumly chairing the meeting, was humiliated. Bobby Kennedy had been his nemesis ever since he had opposed Johnson's selection as Jack's running mate in 1960. Johnson was still steaming when he arrived home at The Elms that afternoon. Sitting beside his swimming pool with a lone aide, he decided that he would raise his own banner in the civil rights revolution and — at the same time — strike back at Robert Kennedy. Johnson too could practice one-upmanship.[48]

The next day the vice president was scheduled to make the one hundredth anniversary Memorial Day speech on the historic Gettysburg battlefield. With his speechwriter, Horace Busby, Johnson crafted a speech recalling the cadence and spirit of Lincoln's Gettysburg Address a century earlier. Before taking the short helicopter ride to Gettysburg, Johnson paused to hand-deliver a copy of his remarks to his friend Philip Graham, publisher of the *Washington Post*. In Gettysburg the vice president looked out across the battleground and spoke: "One hundred years ago the slave was freed. One hundred years later, the Negro remains in bondage to the color of his skin. Until justice is blind to color, until education is unaware of race, until opportunity is unaware of the color of men's skins, emancipation will be a proclamation but not a fact. The Negro today asks justice. We do not answer him — we do not answer those who lie beneath this soil — when we answer 'Patience.' "[49]

The speech appeared the next day on the front page of the *Washington Post* and in dozens of other newspapers. Whatever position President Kennedy finally chose to take on civil rights legislation, Johnson had emancipated himself on the issue of race in America. Having been ignored by the White House on legislative issues, Johnson was suddenly in demand. Now that he needed to tackle civil rights legislation, President Kennedy turned to the former Senate majority leader for advice. In White House meetings and telephone calls, Johnson lectured Kennedy and his aides on pragmatic politics, including the need to consult congressional leaders, win pledges of Republican support, and ferret out the strategy of southern opponents.[50] More important, he urged Kennedy to transform civil rights from a legal issue to a moral one. "I know these risks are great, and we might lose the South [in 1964], but those sorts of states may be lost anyway," he told Kennedy aide Theodore Sorensen. "The difference is, if your president just goes down there and enforces court decrees, the South will feel it's yielded to force. But if he goes down there and looks them in the eye and states the moral issue and the Christian issue, and he does it face to face, these southerners will at least respect his courage." Johnson continued, "Now the whites think we're just playing politics to carry New York. The Negroes feel we're just doing what we got to do. Until that's put to rest, I don't think you're going to have much of a solution." If Kennedy decided to look the South in the eye, Johnson guaranteed Sorensen, the vice president would be at his side.[51]

Kennedy listened, absorbed, as Vice President Johnson described how he had persuaded the National Aeronautics and Space Administration (NASA) to obey a Defense Department order not to let its astronauts and other employees live in segregated housing off base in Houston. Johnson had simply called Albert Thomas, the Texas congressman in whose district the NASA facility was located, and warned him that NASA would comply or else further grants would dry up. Kennedy considered himself a tough politician, but as president he had never strong-armed a powerful appropriations subcommittee chairman like Thomas. Such tactics were necessary, Johnson instructed, in order to get Congress to pass a civil rights law.[52]

Six days after Johnson had given his counsel to the White House, the president received strikingly similar advice from Martin Luther King. A front-page article in the June 10 *New York Times* quoted King as saying that the president must begin to address race as a moral issue, in terms "we seldom if ever hear" from the White House.[53] The following evening, with little preparation and against the advice of his staff, the president went before television cameras with a sketchily drafted text and committed himself to the main issues of the civil rights struggle. "We are confronted primarily with a moral issue," he declared. "It is as old as the Scriptures and is as clear as the American Constitution. The heart of the question is whether all Americans are to be afforded equal rights and equal opportunities, whether we are going to treat our fellow Americans as we want to be treated." It was the first time Kennedy had spoken of a political issue in moral and religious terms.[54] An elated King called the speech "one of the most profound pleas ever made by a president" and declared that the proposed legislation, if implemented, would "move our nation considerably closer to the American Dream."[55] The Kennedys were expected to back a bill that would outlaw segregation and discrimination in public accommodations, but other details were as yet unclear.

The president's message that night was answered by a single rifle shot. Shortly after Kennedy had finished speaking from the White House, Mississippi NAACP leader Medgar Evers was gunned down by an assassin* lying in ambush outside Evers's home in Jackson.[56] A decorated veteran of World War II, Evers had braved death threats for years. Together, Kennedy's speech and Evers's murder steeled the resolve of King and every element in the movement from Roy Wilkins to the fire-eaters in SNCC.

Less than a week after his speech, President Kennedy sent comprehensive civil rights legislation to Congress. The proposed legislation outlawed segregation and discrimination in public accommodations, empowered the federal government to cut off federal funds to state and local governments that discriminated on the basis of race, strengthened federal laws protecting voting rights, supported school desegregation, and reauthorized the Civil Rights Commission. At this point, the proposal contained no prohibition on employment discrimination.

Through the summer and fall, however, as the 1964 election drew closer, Kennedy seemed less eager. As it became clear that Senator Barry Goldwater, a conservative Arizonan, probably would be the Republican presidential nominee, King sensed that Kennedy was less inclined to push for civil rights. But the die was cast. The Kennedys had committed themselves to civil rights legislation.

The vice president, meanwhile, missed no opportunity to broadcast his own commitment. At a White House meeting he chaired in the absence of

---

* Only thirty-one years later was his assassin, Byron de la Beckwith, convicted of the murder.

the president, Johnson assured civil rights leaders that they could add measures to strengthen the administration's bill, including one against employment discrimination. And in a display of the old Johnson exuberance and ego, he swept up half a dozen liberal Democratic senators, took them to his ornate vice presidential office off the Senate floor, and told them how he would steer the civil rights legislation through the paralyzed Congress if he were still in charge.[57]

After Kennedy sent the civil rights bill to Congress in June, Johnson even needled Senator John Stennis, arch-segregationist and southern Democratic oligarch, about supporting the bill's prohibition against segregated public accommodations. In mid-June, as he sat presiding over the Senate, Johnson privately questioned Stennis, who was standing beside him. When Stennis said that he couldn't possibly support desegregating restaurants, restrooms, and other public facilities, Johnson recounted his favorite story about how his cook Zephyr Wright, while driving through the South, "would have to squat in the road to pee." He told Stennis, "You know, John, that's just bad. That's wrong. And there ought to be something to change that. And it seems to me that if the people in Mississippi don't change it voluntarily, that it's just going to be necessary to change it by law."[58]

At the National Governors' Conference in Miami in July, Johnson departed from the White House playbook and pushed civil rights on his own. Hoping to avoid an embarrassing fight on the subject among Democratic governors at the conference, the White House had cleverly eliminated the conference's resolutions committee. Johnson, disregarding White House orders to tone down references to civil rights, instead asked speechwriter Horace Busby to add more. In a stirring address, Johnson told the governors, "We must strip away slogans such as 'states' rights.' . . . We must attack the 'wrongs' in our society," which he named: segregated schools and public accommodations, employment discrimination, and denying blacks the right to vote.[59]

For all his passion, it was hard for Johnson — or for any vice president — to attract much notice. So it was unusual when, in late August, a popular syndicated column in the *Washington Post* quoted an anonymous southern senator as saying, "I don't know what's got into Lyndon, but he's out-talking Bobby Kennedy on civil rights."[60]

Robert Kennedy was not amused. He complained that Johnson was advocating civil rights at a time "when it was not useful."[61] The Kennedys expected Johnson to help hold at least some of the South in the next election — the main reason he had been put on the ticket in 1960 — not to antagonize southerners further over civil rights. The White House even considered sending Johnson to Scandinavia so he would not be present for the March on Washington by civil rights advocates slated for August 28.

The march was conceived by King and other national civil rights leaders as a means of expanding on the momentum of Birmingham and persuading Congress to act on the civil rights bill and address a broad range of other issues, including black unemployment. President Kennedy feared that the planned march, officially the March for Jobs and Justice, would spark disorder and create a congressional backlash against the civil rights bill. At a White House meeting on June 22, both Kennedy and Johnson urged King and the other leaders to call off the demonstration, which they said would alienate key members of Congress.

But the march on August 28 surpassed even the hopes of its organizers. The spectacle of 200,000 Americans of all races marching peacefully, joined in prayer and singing freedom songs as they filled every square yard of space on the Ellipse from the Washington Monument to the Lincoln Memorial, had a powerful impact on the nation and on Congress. In the final speech of the day, Martin Luther King Jr. spoke of his dream for an America that lived up to its ideals, but he also laid out a detailed indictment against racism throughout the country and its institutions:

> There are those who are asking the devotees of civil rights, "When will you be satisfied?" We can never be satisfied as long as the Negro is the victim of the unspeakable horrors of police brutality. We can never be satisfied as long as our bodies, heavy with the fatigue of travel, cannot gain lodging in the motels of the highways and hotels of the cities. We cannot be satisfied as long as the Negro's basic mobility is from a smaller ghetto to a larger one.
>
> We can never be satisfied as long as our children are stripped of their selfhood and robbed of their dignity by signs saying "for white only." We cannot be satisfied as long as a Negro in Mississippi cannot vote and a Negro in New York believes he has nothing for which to vote.

King concluded powerfully with his repeated incantation of "I have a dream" followed by a recitation of the highest ideals of America — a nation where all citizens could come together in a society of equal opportunity, in which differences of race, religion, national origin, and region were no longer barriers to brotherhood and peace. He spoke of his dream of a place "where little black boys and black girls will be able to join hands with little white boys and white girls and walk together as sisters and brothers." The speech resonated throughout the country and the world.[62]

*   *   *

Less than three weeks after the triumphant March on Washington, an explosion rocked the Sixteenth Street Baptist Church in Birmingham, killing four young black girls dressed in their Sunday finery for the church service that was about to begin. The bloody act of Ku Klux Klan terrorists brought home the stark extremes of race relations in Birmingham and beyond. The bombing — the fiftieth in Birmingham since World War II[63] — along with the failure of Birmingham merchants to fulfill their pledge to end segregation and the slow pace of action on the legislation in Congress reduced King to despair. In their sorrow and fury, the Reverend James Bevel and his wife, Diane Nash, committed advocates of nonviolence, contemplated taking vigilante action against the Birmingham bombers.

By the end of the SCLC's annual convention in Richmond, Virginia, on September 27, King's hopes for the Kennedys had been dashed. "I was naïve enough to believe that proof of good faith would emerge," said King of the emissaries Kennedy had sent to Birmingham, who failed to produce results. "Today we are faced with the midnight of oppression which we had believed to be the dawn of redemption. . . . We are faced with an extreme situation, and therefore our remedies must be extreme." Yet King vacillated on which remedies to pursue. Under his leadership, he confessed, the movement was "standing still, doing nothing, going nowhere." King could not decide whether to resume his campaign in Birmingham, start a new effort in Danville, Virginia, begin a hunger strike, or leave the South and concentrate on voter registration in the North.[64] Not two months later, rifle shots in Dallas would bring Martin Luther King face to face with Lyndon Johnson.

The Meeting

As Dr. King prepared to meet with President Johnson on December 3, 1963, his adviser Clarence Jones implored King to stress their shared southern roots. "You've got more in common with Lyndon Johnson than you do with John F. Kennedy or with me," Jones told him. Despite the wall of segregation and racism separating them, "white and black people in the South share the same culture — food, music, religion, speech. You need to talk with him like no one else can."[65]

Jones was right. Apart from the critical matter of race, Johnson and King shared a sensibility born of their southern roots — an understanding of basic human hopes, grinding poverty, and racial conflict, of the deep longing to live beyond the violence that lurked beneath the façade of southern politeness. They shared a genuine affection for the South. And both knew how the South's stubborn clinging to its past kept the region down.[66]

As they shook hands in the Oval Office, King was struck by how much bigger the president was than he appeared on television. Lyndon Johnson towered over King, who stood five foot seven. With Johnson seated behind his desk and King in a chair beside him, the men quickly moved past pleasantries. They agreed on the need to increase job opportunities and training for black Americans. And, like Kennedy, Johnson urged King to stop holding demonstrations, which he said only antagonized Congress and hurt the prospects for civil rights legislation. Johnson advised him to concentrate instead on registering voters and lobbying Congress. King agreed about the need for voter registration; in fact, he had met several weeks earlier with Louis Martin, deputy chairman of the Democratic National Committee, to discuss a registration campaign.[67]

The president dominated the rest of the forty-five-minute meeting with an exuberant description of the tactics required to win strong civil rights legislation. The first step was to get the bill quickly out of the segregationist grip of Howard Smith, chairman of the House Rules Committee. If they couldn't get the bill out of committee before Congress recessed for Christmas, Johnson feared that time would run out, and the southerners in the Senate could filibuster the bill to death in 1964. Proponents needed the support of 218 members, a majority of the House of Representatives, for a discharge petition taking the bill away from Smith. Johnson showed King a list of members who had not yet agreed to sign and asked him to work on them, particularly the Republicans.[68]

During the conversation, Johnson took a telephone call from David McDonald, president of the United Steelworkers, who reported on his own efforts to line up support. McDonald had thirty-three steelworkers combing Capitol Hill and had already collected 108 signatures with the possibility of 13 more. But he hadn't yet contacted any of the southern legislators. "Well, you won't get many there," said the president. McDonald replied, "Well, we can put the muscle on them."

Johnson then thrust the telephone into the hands of a startled Martin Luther King, saying, "Here's Dr. King, who's talking to me about it right now!" King listened as McDonald rattled off more statistics and urged King to tell the president what a great job the steelworkers were doing.[69]

King knew little about legislative tactics, and lobbying was not the SCLC's strong suit, but he appreciated the new president's energy and determination. Leaving the Oval Office, King descended into a swarm of reporters. "I was very impressed by the president's awareness of the need of civil rights and the depth of his concern," he told them. "As a southerner, I am happy to know that a fellow southerner is in the White House who is concerned about civil rights.

"He made it very clear he wants the civil rights bill out of the Rules Committee before Christmas. He means business. I think we can expect even more from him than we have had up to now."

King assured the reporters, "I have implicit confidence in the man, and unless he betrays his past actions, we will proceed on the basis that we have in the White House a man who is deeply committed to help us."

King said that he and the president had discussed his plans to tour the country in 1964 to encourage voter registration. "Getting people to vote is the only way to break this tragic coalition in Congress," said King, referring to the partnership between southern Democrats and conservative Republicans that had stymied President Kennedy's program.[70]

When President Johnson read King's public statements about their meeting, he was pleased — except for one thing. King had told the news media that he had made clear to the president that "we will have demonstrations until the injustices that have caused them are eliminated."[71] Johnson thought that King had nodded in agreement to his request for a cessation of demonstrations — which had been curtailed for thirty days during the official mourning period for President Kennedy. For Lee White, Johnson's civil rights aide, who had attended the meeting, the incident raised doubts about King's reliability.[72] In a larger sense, the disagreement was a continuation of an argument that had started with the Kennedys. Like Jack Kennedy, Lyndon Johnson hated the swirling pressures that erupted out of King's confrontations with segregationists in the Deep South — pressures to move faster on legislation, to intervene with federal forces to protect demonstrators from lawless mobs. Like Kennedy, Johnson wanted to see orderly government processes exercised in the traditional manner. But the marchers of the SCLC, SNCC, and CORE believed that traditional methods alone would never win them equality.

After he left the White House, King told Clarence Jones and his SCLC aide Andrew Young, "LBJ is a man of great ego and great power. He is a pragmatist and a man of pragmatic compassion. It just may be that he's going to go where John Kennedy couldn't." Johnson had done most of the talking, King told them, in contrast to Kennedy, who had mostly asked questions and in the end made few commitments. King, who had admired Kennedy's ease and grace, found Johnson a little too rough and brusque. But Johnson had committed himself to action, King said. And he had not mentioned the name Stanley David Levison.[73]

4

✦ ✦ ✦ ✦ ✦ ✦

Hoover, King, and Two Presidents

MARTIN LUTHER KING JR. left his first meeting with President Lyndon Johnson relieved that the new president had not raised a troubling subject that had preoccupied his predecessor. Johnson seemed focused on describing the tactics he thought necessary to pass a strong civil rights bill. The discussion stood in stark contrast to the last private conversation King had with President Kennedy.

At that meeting, on June 22, 1963, Kennedy had taken King by the arm and led him from the Oval Office into the Rose Garden to warn him that two "agents of a foreign power" had penetrated the civil rights leader's inner circle. The men were Stanley David Levison, whom the president described as "a secret Communist agent," and Hunter Pitts "Jack" O'Dell, whom Kennedy referred to as the fifth-ranking member of the Communist Party in the United States. "They're Communists; you've got to get rid of them," Kennedy demanded, repeating warnings that Robert Kennedy and his assistant Burke Marshall had passed along to King that morning. Even more disturbing to King were the president's next words, spoken almost in a whisper: "I assume you know you're under very close surveillance."[1] King's associations, Kennedy suggested, could bring the civil rights leader to ruin, just as the sex scandal in England involving Minister of War John Profumo was threatening to bring down the British government.* Kennedy emphasized how much was at stake: any scandal or

---

* In 1963, Prime Minister Harold Macmillan's government was shaken when Profumo was accused of having an affair with a nineteen-year-old prostitute. The scandal led to the resignation of both Profumo and Macmillan.

exposé about Communists in King's organization could defeat the civil rights bill and perhaps even destroy Kennedy's presidency. "If they shoot you down, they'll shoot us down, too," the president cautioned, "so we're asking you to be careful."[2]

After his meeting with Kennedy, King joked with his aides that the whispered warnings in the Rose Garden must have meant the president feared that even his own Oval Office was bugged.[3] But banter aside, King was deeply worried. The attorney general and other administration officials had been pressuring him for many months to break with Levison and O'Dell, though they refused to produce evidence against them.[4] Newspaper articles, apparently based on leaks from the government, had spread charges about Communists in King's organization. After some hesitation and subterfuge that further exasperated the Kennedys, a regretful King fired O'Dell and sent the attorney general a copy of the dismissal letter.[5] Levison, however, was too valuable an adviser and friend to give up, and King continued to communicate with him frequently, albeit indirectly.

Stanley David Levison, a white New York lawyer and businessman, had befriended King in December 1956 at the outset of King's career as a civil rights leader. Bayard Rustin, the gifted black organizer and strategist, had brought the mild-mannered, self-effacing Levison to a King speech in Baltimore. Rustin told King that Levison wanted to help their cause. After World War II, Levison had purchased a Ford dealership in New Jersey, then built with his brother Roy Bennett a variety of businesses, including real estate management and investment, that provided a substantial income.[6] Along with his second wife, Beatrice, and his teenage son, Levison lived comfortably in an apartment on New York City's Upper West Side.

After their first meeting, the forty-four-year-old Levison devoted much of his time to helping King, turning down repeated offers to pay for his services. He had made money "in the commercial jungle," Levison wrote King, using "practices [that] to me were always abhorrent."[7] Now he wanted to "use these skills not for myself but for socially constructive ends. . . . The liberation struggle is the most positive and rewarding area of work anyone could experience." King appreciated that Levison appeared to seek nothing from their relationship but to serve him and the cause of civil rights.[8]

Over time, Levison had become King's most valued adviser outside of the SCLC staff. Along with Rustin and activist Ella Baker, Levison helped King capitalize on the Montgomery bus boycott victory by creating the

SCLC. Levison introduced King to his friends from the American Jewish Congress, labor unions, and various liberal causes. He helped King write books and articles, and he worked on fundraising, personnel decisions, and political strategy. King made few major decisions without first seeking Levison's advice. At meetings with government officials or movement leaders, Levison, wearing a bow tie and thick horn-rimmed glasses, usually sat quietly and garnered little attention. Only in King's inner circle did he give advice freely. Insiders saw him as a typical liberal Jewish social activist from New York: tough, pragmatic, sophisticated, knowledgeable about the personalities and dynamics of contemporary American politics.[9]

As a longtime activist in anti-McCarthyism campaigns as well as Jewish, labor, and civil liberties causes, Levison had associated closely with members of the Communist Party. Few in the SCLC were put off by the company he kept. Andrew Young understood that Levison had numerous contacts with the "old left" and remained "philosophically a Socialist," though he believed Levison's claim that he had never been a Communist Party member.[10] Levison had testified in 1962 before a Senate committee, "I am a loyal American and am not now and never have been a member of the Communist Party," but then cited the Fifth Amendment in refusing to answer their detailed questions about his knowledge of the party, its finances, and its leaders.[11]

Almost a decade earlier, the FBI had come to a different conclusion regarding Levison's background. The bureau's information came from its top secret "Operation Solo."[12] "Solo" was the code name for the double-agent team of brothers Jack and Morris Childs, disenchanted Communists whom the FBI had sought to "reactivate" in the early 1950s to keep an eye on the Communist Party USA (CPUSA) and its finances. Before the CPUSA would welcome the Childs brothers back into the fold, party officials wanted to know more about the men and their several years of distance and disaffection. As a result, they sent out a high-level emissary to ask their questions for them: Stanley Levison.[13]

In September 1952 Levison arrived in Chicago and spent two days meeting with Morris Childs, who apparently satisfied both Levison and the CPUSA with his responses and expressions of party loyalty. As a result, the Childs brothers were reintegrated into the upper reaches of the CPUSA, on their way to more than a quarter-century as key undercover agents for the FBI. Jack and Morris Childs provided intelligence not only about the CPUSA but also about how it was financed and directed by the Soviet Union. Based in New York, Jack Childs was the courier who secretly picked up the Soviet funds that kept the CPUSA afloat.[14]

For much of the 1950s, the FBI monitored Levison's activities through the Childs brothers. Their "Solo" reports detailed Levison's role as a key manager of the party's finances and as a fundraiser. The brothers described how a stream of money passed through Levison's hands and into secret CPUSA accounts, such as the emergency "Reserve Fund." Levison was also suspected of funneling money to party fugitives.[15] As it struggled to understand the Levison brothers' tangle of business entities and finances,* the FBI came to see Stanley Levison as a secret captain of Communist industry, setting up front companies that would earn the CPUSA needed cash.[16] Although discrepancies suggested that the party's accounting left something to be desired, the Childs brothers reported that the Levisons had made secret annual contributions of $12,000 to $41,000 from 1955 to 1961. The sums declined over this period, though the Levisons were reportedly still pledging contributions as late as November 1962 — almost six years after Stanley began working for Martin Luther King.[17]

Money and contributions were not the whole story, however. In late 1956 the FBI began to receive reports that the Levisons were dissatisfied with the CPUSA.[18] A sketchy account of a December meeting suggested that the Levisons and others close to them were "frustrated" and "politically confused." Over the next year the Childs brothers reported that these former stalwarts were becoming "politically unstable"; while the Levisons continued their work for the party, "some of their political questions had not been answered." Offstage, FBI officials watched CPUSA leaders grow increasingly wary as the Levisons gradually turned off the financial spigot in the later 1950s. As Stanley Levison appeared to step away from the party's high-level finances, the FBI responded by removing his name from its list of "key figures" in the CPUSA in March 1957. Sensing that he might be disillusioned with the party, the FBI even approached Levison in 1960 to recruit him to help with their secret struggle against the CPUSA.[19]

The FBI backtracked from its downgrading of Levison's importance as a Communist when it learned in the early 1960s of the depth of his relationship with Martin Luther King. In January 1962 a CPUSA official told Jack

---

* Over time the FBI determined that Levison and his brother had been connected to twenty-six separate businesses since roughly the Second World War, from construction to the tool and die industry, and from tanneries to Hollywood films. These business interests, the FBI alleged, were often founded with CPUSA funds. Their successful ventures funneled sizable profits to the Communist Party's coffers; in 1954 the Levisons' busy Ford dealership alone was said to generate approximately $15,000 per year for the CPUSA.

Childs that Levison had written a speech for King to deliver at an AFL-CIO convention in Miami.[20] With this revelation, FBI director J. Edgar Hoover thought that he had evidence proving his strongly held theory that the Communist Party had infiltrated the civil rights movement and exercised influence with its most prominent leader. Levison's friendship with King prompted the FBI to promulgate a new theory: Levison had gone underground to become an "agent of influence" whose mission was to manipulate King and the civil rights movement for Communist purposes. Hoover alerted Attorney General Robert Kennedy about the King–Levison connection.* More menacingly, Hoover also observed that "our source also said that Levison, through his association with King, reportedly has access to the White House and has been in contact with the President and you."[21]

The FBI continued to sound alarm bells over the next several weeks. In February 1962 a CPUSA official reported to Communist leader Gus Hall that Stanley Levison had a message for him: "King is a wholehearted Marxist who has studied it [Marxism], believes in it, and agrees with it, but because of his being a minister of religion does not dare to espouse it publicly."[22] This report later found its way into FBI boilerplate and, through repetition, came to underpin the bureau's conventional wisdom on King. Within two months of the discovery of Levison's connection with King, Robert Kennedy approved Hoover's request to install wiretaps on Levison's office telephones.[23]

At first the taps revealed little more than Levison's steady assistance and advice to King.[24] But in the summer of 1962, the FBI was listening in when Levison spoke with Jack O'Dell, a black former labor organizer working in the New York SCLC office. Levison had floated the idea of promoting O'Dell to serve as King's new executive assistant. Both men knew that O'Dell's previous public affiliation with the Communist Party presented a complication. But Levison noted that King was aware of O'Dell's work for the party in the past and apparently was not concerned. "No matter what a man was," King reportedly had said, "if he could stand up now and say he is not connected, then as far as I am concerned, he is eligible to work for me."[25]

The FBI made no such distinctions. Although O'Dell never formally as-

---

* The friendship between King and Levinson was at first totally transparent. King once attended a conference at the Justice Department with a coterie of aides that included Levison. After the meeting, Harris Wofford, then an assistant to Attorney General Robert Kennedy, pointed out to his surprised boss that the man seated next to him was none other than Stanley David Levison (Harris Wofford, *Of Kennedys and Kings*, p. 216).

sumed the position Levison proposed, the conversation provided the rationale for the FBI to escalate its probe into the "Communist infiltration" (or COMINFIL) of the SCLC in October 1962.[26]

Throughout the winter, the FBI geared up its new COMINFIL investigation of Levison, King, and the SCLC. But on March 20, 1963, "Solo" agent Jack Childs reported on an unusual and confrontational meeting the previous day between Levison and his CPUSA colleague Lem Harris.[27] Levison, apparently speaking for a group of eleven former party stalwarts, blamed business problems for the group's declining financial support of the party. But Levison also indicated that the group had become "disenchanted." Some members had found fault with a number of the party's positions, including its encouragement of "adventurism" in Latin America. Levison also was reportedly critical of the CPUSA for giving up its "vanguard leadership" in a number of areas, particularly in civil rights. According to Levison, the group had determined that the party was "irrelevant" and "ineffective." Levison suggested that it was merely "habit and sentiment" that had caused the group to continue its financial support up to that point, and Harris noted that even "token support" of the CPUSA appeared unlikely in the future.

In June 1963 Jack Childs recounted for his FBI handlers another conversation with Lem Harris. The Levisons, according to Harris, continued to feel "that the Party has done little, if anything, to assist the fight for Civil Rights for Negroes" and that its "do nothing" attitude had caused the party to lose prestige. Harris claimed that the Levisons were not renouncing their party membership but still did not "desire to be openly 'linked up' with the Party." They were "severing themselves, financially and in a disciplinary way, from the Party. . . . With respect to the Martin Luther King movement, they will act on their own initiative, and will not accept instructions from the Party."[28]

Signs of a serious breach between the Levisons and the Communist Party USA developed over the next several months. In July 1963 General Secretary Gus Hall told Jack Childs that the party had come to terms with "the fact that Stanley Levison and Roy Bennett have severed themselves from Party discipline." Another high-level official told Childs that the Levisons were "definitely working their way out from under Party discipline." By mid-September the FBI had heard through "Solo's" contacts with Hall that "the CP is not happy with Stan Levison," who was rebuffing direct party orders and other efforts to reestablish contact. In an irony the FBI apparently chose to ignore, in late October 1963 Gus Hall denounced the Levisons as "anti-Communist" and accused them of influencing Martin Luther King to criticize anti-Semitism in the Soviet Union.[29]

Apparently seeking some clarity, in November 1963 FBI officials asked Jack Childs to analyze the relationship between Levison and the CPUSA. The portrait Childs painted was hardly one of Communist zealotry. He believed that the Levison brothers had "used" the party and its funds to build their own business empire and line their own pockets. Even Levison's criticism of the party's "ineptness" in the civil rights field was merely an excuse for breaking with the CPUSA.[30]

While the FBI put great stock in the information passed along by the "unimpeachable" Childs brothers, this view — and any suggestion that Levison might be anything other than a calculating, concealed party operative — was pointedly omitted from the ominous reports the FBI continued to send to the White House and the attorney general.

Unencumbered by the ambiguities in the "Solo" reports, which the FBI had never shown them, the Kennedys repeatedly sent their emissaries to King, warning him to get rid of Jack O'Dell and his purported party "handler," Stanley Levison. When the president's words of caution to King in the Rose Garden on June 22 came to naught, the FBI renewed its pressure on King through leaks to the press charging that the Communist Jack O'Dell was working for King.[31] The whisper campaign succeeded where the president's warnings had not. In early July, King broke off the relationship with O'Dell, though the SCLC continued to assert that charges of Communist connections were baseless.

King found it more difficult to separate himself from Stanley Levison. In early July the pair stopped meeting openly, but in a move that fooled no one — especially not the Kennedys or the eavesdropping FBI — King and Levison began to communicate through New York lawyer Clarence Jones. King clearly regretted the distance, and as the months passed, he sought reassurance from Jones that Levison understood why the two could not be in touch directly.[32]

The political problem of King's reported Communist Party ties became clear as the congressional debate on Kennedy's 1963 civil rights bill heated up. Opponents of the bill declared that it was part of a Communist conspiracy to undermine the United States. In testimony before the Senate Commerce Committee on July 15, Alabama governor George Wallace raised the O'Dell issue, noting the "fawning and pawing" of administration officials over King and his entourage — including, Wallace charged, a "known Communist" who had remained on the SCLC payroll despite King's public statements to the contrary.[33]

Publicly the Kennedys defended King and the SCLC. At a press conference two days after Wallace testified, the president offered the first of two carefully nuanced statements. The government had "no evidence that any of the leaders of the civil rights movement in the United States are Communists" or that the demonstrations were Communist inspired, he said. "It is a convenient scapegoat to suggest that all of the difficulties are Communist," he continued, "and that if the Communist movement would only disappear that we would end this [effort]."[34]

Privately, however, the Kennedys took a different view. The attorney general had already urged and approved a wiretap on Clarence Jones, Levison's intermediary with King. And only after reflection did he back away from another, potentially more explosive proposal: to wiretap King's home and office telephones.[35]

As the summer of 1963 heated up, the FBI watched and listened while preparations for the March on Washington intensified. In mid-July the FBI sent a top secret memo to the White House again alerting the president and his brother to the role of the Communist Party in the "current Negro revolution."[36]

A week before the March on Washington, top FBI officials sought to sort out conflicting information they were receiving regarding the Communist Party and the march. In internal memos, agents in the Domestic Intelligence Division working under William Sullivan evaluated the evidence of Communist involvement in the march and, by extension, in the civil rights movement. On the one hand, they concluded that Levison "does not consider himself to be under the control of the Party with respect to his dealings with King." On the other hand, FBI officials acknowledged that the Communist Party was targeting America's 19 million blacks, and "it would be foolhardy on anybody's part to ignore this very significant truth." The United States was involved in a "racial revolution," and "the time has never been so right for exploitation of the Negroes by communist propaganda." These memos ended on an ambiguous note, concluding that the Communist Party "may fail dismally with the American Negro as it has in the past" or "may make prodigious strides and great successes with the American Negroes, to the serious detriment of our national security. Time alone will tell."[37]

The fence-straddling irked Hoover, who excoriated his subordinates for what he saw as their wrongheaded conclusion that Communists were exercising little influence over the March on Washington and the civil rights movement in general. In a heated rejoinder Hoover wrote, "This memo reminds me vividly of those I received when Castro took over Cuba. . . . I for one can't ignore the memos re King, O'Dell, Levison, Rustin, Hall et al. . . . as having an infinitesimal effect on the efforts to exploit the American Negro by the Communists."[38] Hoover's rebuke reverberated throughout the bureau as more than a quarter-million protesters gathered in Washington.

Two days after the march ended and the National Mall had been cleared, Sullivan responded to Hoover's message by reversing his position. "We regret greatly," Sullivan wrote, "that the memorandum did not measure up to what the Director has a right to expect from our analysis." Highlighting the "demagogic speech" King had given from the steps of the Lincoln Memorial — the "I Have a Dream" speech — Sullivan warned, "We must mark him now, if we have not done so before, as the most dangerous Negro of the future in this Nation from the standpoint of communism, the Negro, and national security."[39]

Hoover's message to Sullivan and his colleagues had come through loud and clear. Debates on the finer points of Levison's Communist affiliations were now beside the point. As Sullivan understood it, no longer would the FBI limit itself to seeking out "legalistic proofs or definitively conclusive evidence that would stand up in testimony in court or before Congressional committees." Instead the bureau would intensify its surveillance and develop "imaginative and aggressive tactics" to be used against King and his Communist advisers. Shaken and fearful that he would be fired, Sullivan became the most zealous champion of a plan to destroy King — a plan so audacious that even Hoover would have to applaud it.

Insisting that he was Communist influenced, the bureau began to view King as a counterintelligence target in the fall of 1963. With the operation placed in Sullivan's intelligence division, the FBI campaign against King freed itself from the bureau's more conventional responsibility: investigating crimes and arresting lawbreakers. The idea had never been to investigate whether King or Levison had broken the law, but to harass and cripple King, using all the dirty tricks and hardball tactics employed in the espionage trade.

Within the bureau, this tougher approach became quickly apparent. Beginning in November 1963, when the FBI received word of a plot against King, Hoover ordered that his agents should no longer follow the bureau's standard operating procedure, and should not warn King about threats against his life.[40]

The rise of Martin Luther King Jr. as both leader and symbol of the civil rights campaign sparked fear and resentment within the FBI's upper echelons. Hoover in particular seemed to take it as a personal affront.[41]

John Edgar Hoover had grown up in Washington, D.C. He attended the city's segregated public schools, then worked as a government clerk while attending law school at night. A lifelong bachelor, he lived with his mother until her death when he was forty-three years old.[42] For the remainder of Hoover's life his constant companion was Clyde Tolson, another bachelor whom Hoover appointed the FBI's second-ranking official. The two men were virtually inseparable.[43]

After World War I, Hoover served as an assistant to President Woodrow Wilson's attorney general, A. Mitchell Palmer, who led the notorious "Red raids" against Americans suspected of leftist views. Palmer was impressed by Hoover's ability and loyalty, as was Calvin Coolidge's attorney general Harlan Fiske Stone, who in 1924 appointed Hoover to head up the Justice Department agency that in 1935 became the Federal Bureau of Investigation.[44] Hoover brought needed reform to federal law enforcement, which prior to his appointment had often been ineffective and laced with corruption. But Hoover made his reputation in the 1930s as the intrepid square-jawed "G-man" who captured notorious bank robbers like John Dillinger and "Baby Face" Nelson. Hoover had a flair for publicity; he carried out his exploits with a masterly command of public relations aimed at promoting a gleaming image of the FBI and its director. During World War II, Hoover shifted his focus from nabbing bank robbers to unmasking German spies, and in the postwar years he turned his attention back to the threat he had begun fighting in 1919: Communism. Hoover's FBI found a new and urgent purpose in tracking Soviet spies and investigating the activities of the Communist Party USA.[45]

Hoover's feelings about King and his connections to Communism were clear from the beginning of the FBI's investigation in January 1962, when he noted on one internal memo, "King is no good anyway."[46] When *Time* magazine named King its "Man of the Year" for 1963, a furious Hoover wrote on a memo that circulated at FBI headquarters, "[*Time*] really had to reach deep into the garbage for this one."[47]

Hoover harbored negative feelings about African Americans that were fairly typical of the racial prejudices prevalent throughout American society — North as well as South — in the 1960s. "The colored people," Hoover later told a conference of newspaper editors, "are quite ignorant, mostly uneducated, and I doubt if they would seek an education if they had the opportunity. . . . They can proceed in time to gain the acceptance which is necessary and rights equal to those of the white citizens in their community."[48] These prejudices spilled over into the operation of the bureau. When an embarrassed Kennedy administration looked into the near-absence of blacks in non-menial federal jobs, the FBI could count only five black agents — and this number consisted entirely of Hoover's drivers and stewards.[49]

Nothing infuriated Hoover more than criticism of the bureau, whose reputation he had burnished carefully for four decades. His animosity toward King increased in January 1962 when the SCLC leader publicly criticized the FBI for failing to protect civil rights activists.[50] King alleged that FBI agents in the South had cozy relationships with local law enforcement officers who brutalized peaceful demonstrators. Hoover's anger intensified when King failed to return a telephone call from assistant director Cartha "Deke" DeLoach, who had been instructed to set King straight about the FBI's role in the South.

Exchanges between Hoover and DeLoach regarding King's failure to break with Levison and O'Dell reveal the FBI leaders' anger and imperatives. After King met with Levison at a secret SCLC meeting outside Savannah, Georgia, in defiance of President Kennedy's advice that King break with the suspected Communist, DeLoach wrote in a memo that King had used "deceit, lies, and treachery as propaganda to further his own causes." DeLoach recommended that the bureau cease all contact with King, "a vicious liar" beyond hope and unworthy of redemption. At the bottom of the memo Hoover wrote, "I concur."[51]

The FBI wiretap on the telephone at the suburban New York home of Clarence Jones provided Hoover with additional ammunition.[52] Agents heard King, in what he believed was the privacy of Jones's home, engage in conversations with women that were full of lusty language and sexual allusions — language that stood in marked contrast to the soaring rhetoric of his "I Have a Dream" speech. Bureau officials noted that "King's extramarital affairs while posing as a minister of the gospel leave him highly susceptible to coercion and possible blackmail . . . in view of his continued close association . . . [with] Levison and O'Dell."[53]

Armed with these new reports, the bureau renewed its push for wiretaps on King's home and offices. After five months of indecision, Robert Kennedy signed an order authorizing the wiretaps on October 10, 1963.[54]

The president and the attorney general no doubt agreed to the wiretaps out of genuine concern about possible Communist influence on King. Moreover, the taps would provide intelligence about King's plans at a volatile moment when it seemed that the civil rights struggle might explode into riots all over the South.

By July 1963, Robert Kennedy's anger at King had become nearly equal to Hoover's. The attorney general was furious that King not only had defied the president by not breaking with Levison but also was dissembling about the matter.

On June 22, before King met with President Kennedy for their walk in the Rose Garden, he first had a meeting with Attorney General Robert Kennedy. "You haven't broken with Levison," asserted the attorney general. When King replied, "Yes, I have," Kennedy declared icily, "I have a tape of a conference call* that you and three others had with Levison."[55] In his various meetings with King, Robert Kennedy was further irritated by the manner in which King seemingly dismissed the government's concerns. Whenever Kennedy raised the Levison issue, King would respond with a deep chuckle, as if he were amused at the fuss being made about his loyal friend.[56] Personally, the strait-laced Robert Kennedy had little use for King. After the FBI wiretaps recorded King's intimate calls made from Clarence Jones's home telephones, the attorney general forwarded the FBI memo describing the conversations on to the president with the notation, "I thought you would be interested in the attached memorandum."[57] Robert Kennedy's personal distaste for King was conveyed in a dinner table conversation with Marietta Tree, a U.S. representative to the United Nations, who had come to Washington in August 1963 to participate with King in the March on Washington. "He's not a serious person," Kennedy told Tree. "If the country knew what we know about King's goings on, he'd be finished."[58]

Robert Kennedy also may have authorized the King wiretap out of a growing fear that Hoover intended to make his allegations about King public, leaving the president vulnerable to charges that he had failed to act against a national security threat. Hoover's intention to publicize King's alleged Communist connections and his marital infidelities became clearer when he distributed an explosive and salacious profile of King not just to the White House and the attorney general, but also to the secretary of state, the secretary of defense, the secretary of the army, the Defense Intelligence Agency, and the CIA.[59] The attorney general demanded that Hoover recall the reports — and Hoover complied, but not before they had been read by top officials throughout the government.[60] It

---

* Kennedy was referring to a June 10 conference call, recorded by the FBI, in which Levison, King, Clarence Jones, and SCLC executive director Wyatt Tee Walker discussed plans for the forthcoming March on Washington. In that conversation, Levison urged King to praise President Kennedy, who the following day declared his support for a sweeping civil rights law. The march should be directed at the inaction of Congress, not the president, Levison argued.

was now only a matter of time, Kennedy believed, before Hoover would succeed in smearing King's reputation.

Robert Kennedy's decision to approve the King wiretaps may have been influenced, too, by Hoover's knowledge of embarrassing secrets concerning the president's private life. Hoover learned about and warned President Kennedy to break off two sexual liaisons, affairs that could have destroyed his presidency. Kennedy had shared a mistress, Judith Campbell Exner, with Chicago mob boss Sam "Momo" Giancana — a man whom Attorney General Kennedy was trying to prosecute and the CIA had enlisted to help assassinate Cuban leader Fidel Castro.[61] The other affair was with Ellen Rometsch, a Capitol Hill party girl the FBI suspected of being an East German agent. With FBI and Justice Department help, Robert Kennedy succeeded in hustling Rometsch back to Communist East Germany in August 1963 just as a Senate investigation was on the verge of exposing her affair with the president, as well as sexual liaisons with senators of both political parties. The inquiry was halted only after Robert Kennedy persuaded Hoover to intervene with Senate leaders Mike Mansfield and Everett Dirksen.[62]

Helping the Kennedys with one hand, Hoover had placed the renewed wiretap request before them with the other, and the Kennedys were in a weak position to deny him. Hoover had succeeded in shutting down King's access to the Kennedy White House. Now the FBI director focused on the new occupant of 1600 Pennsylvania Avenue.

Poisoning the Well at the Johnson White House

Martin Luther King hoped that Lyndon Johnson might put an end to the government's obsessive interest in his associates and his private life. As he walked out of his first meeting with the new president, he failed to realize that Johnson's decision not to confront him as Kennedy had done represented only a difference in presidential style, a different approach to dealing with troublesome problems — and with the FBI.

One of Johnson's first calls after returning from Dallas was to J. Edgar Hoover. "You're more than the head of the bureau," Johnson told Hoover. "You're my brother and personal friend. . . . You have been for twenty-five to thirty years. . . . I have more confidence in your judgment than anybody in town."[63]

Hoover answered Johnson's flattery with a flurry of activity. In short order he began inundating the new president with letters and telephone alerts about the activities of Martin Luther King and Stanley Levison. Two days after JFK's funeral, Hoover told the White House that a statement prepared under King's name for the *New York Herald Tribune* actually had been penned by Levison's intermediary Clarence Jones, whose alleged past Communist-related affiliations were diligently noted.[64] Then, after Hoover learned through an FBI wiretap that King would meet with the president on December 3, he sent an aide to warn Johnson about the grave implications that King's association with Levison posed for national security. Johnson took note of the warnings but, much to Hoover's chagrin, did not cancel the meeting.[65]

Instead, Johnson took advantage of Hoover's spying in order to prepare for the encounter. Hoover reported King's movements from New York to a hotel room at Washington's Statler Hilton Hotel, where King conferred at 9:30 A.M. on December 3 with Clarence Jones and Harry Wachtel before taking a taxi to the White House for his 11:30 A.M. appointment. Hoover told Johnson that in the 1950s Jones and Wachtel had been members of organizations the FBI considered to be Communist fronts. In Hoover's voluminous files were the names of virtually everyone who had ever belonged to an organization branded "Communist related" by the FBI or a congressional committee. It was standard procedure in FBI reports to identify people by citing their affiliations — however distant or vague — with suspected leftist groups.

As he received Hoover's reports, Johnson expressed no outward concern about King's alleged Communist connections, but he eagerly absorbed the information — impressed by the FBI's ability to describe the civil rights leader's private conversations, plans, and meetings.

A story in the *Long Island Press* by conservative columnists suggested how the FBI was wielding its power. Robert Allen and Paul Scott reported that President Johnson and Attorney General Kennedy soon would have to confront "evidence obtained by tapping telephones" which showed that an unnamed civil rights leader had been linked to a Soviet agent. The writers warned that "if this close association isn't ended, the new administration faces public disclosures about this individual's Red ties in the midst of the coming congressional debate on civil rights legislation."[66] Johnson had no doubt where the information had come from. And he knew that the FBI would be listening in as King expressed his frightened reaction to the column. It was as though the FBI was playing mind games with King — leaking the story and then observing its handiwork. The column also contained a not-so-veiled threat against Johnson: if he did not deal with King and his Communist adviser, the ensuing scandal might sink the civil rights bill and embarrass the president.

Johnson did not need any heavy-handed signals from the FBI to understand the importance of maintaining a good relationship with J. Edgar Hoover. The two men had traded favors over the years as both advanced their careers in Washington. Johnson and Hoover had been neighbors for almost twenty years on the same block of Thirtieth Place in an affluent, all-white neighborhood in northwest Washington. They chatted across the backyard fence; Hoover had befriended the young Johnson daughters; occasionally the two men would share a cocktail at Johnson's home. Hoover liked to joke about how Johnson would come over every few nights and say, "Edgar, Little Beagle Johnson's gone again — let's go find him," and the two men would search the neighborhood for the senator's dog.[67]

Above all, both men understood that secret information, skillfully employed, was an instrument of power. As veteran Washington infighters, Johnson and Hoover shared an interest in collecting information about people — including their friends, their foes, and any potential rivals. Johnson believed that Hoover was hoarding in his personal files enough information to destroy anyone in the public arena who had not led a perfect life. From his Senate days onward, Johnson had cultivated Hoover as a friend and ally.

Soon after he became president, Johnson called the FBI director with a request. He wanted Deke DeLoach assigned to be the FBI's special liaison to the White House. Hoover readily agreed.[68] DeLoach, an assistant FBI director, had served both Johnson's and Hoover's interests when Johnson was Senate majority leader and DeLoach was the FBI's primary contact with Congress. On one occasion, as Hoover planned ahead for his own financial security should he be forced to retire at age sixty-five or seventy, his deputy Clyde Tolson had dispatched DeLoach to seek Johnson's help in getting Congress to pass special legislation guaranteeing Hoover his full salary in retirement. The director got his wish.[69]

When Johnson became vice president, Hoover and DeLoach returned the favor. Johnson feared being implicated in a scandal involving Texas con man Billie Sol Estes.* A secret witness in the case told the Justice Department that Estes, in return for government favors, had once paid for the purchase of an airplane that Johnson used for campaigning. DeLoach came up with a solution: he and Johnson's top assistant, Walter Jenkins, confronted the witness in an interview, the witness recanted his accusations against Johnson, and the Estes problem evaporated.[70]

The Johnson–Hoover bond was further strengthened by their shared

---

* Billie Sol Estes was a prominent cotton broker accused of fraudulent business dealings and influence peddling.

dislike and mistrust of Robert Kennedy. With the Cold War still a dominant national concern, Hoover was convinced that the principal internal threat to national security came from the Communist Party USA. The attorney general scoffed at Hoover's concern, joking that there were more undercover FBI agents in the ranks of the party than there were actual Communists. He wanted the FBI to focus on his chief interest: fighting organized crime, represented by the Mafia, an organization whose importance Hoover at first had dismissed.[71] The moment Jack Kennedy died, Hoover felt liberated from the unwanted authority of Bobby Kennedy. Almost immediately, Hoover started bypassing him and dealing directly with the new president.

As for Johnson, in mid-January White House aide Jenkins confided to DeLoach that "the President was not yet quite ready to take on Bobby," but that Johnson was planning to oust some of his close associates soon.[72] This gave Hoover confidence that he could ignore the attorney general. By feeding Johnson rumors about Kennedy's disloyalty to him, Hoover increased his own standing.

Hoover exercised his new freedom by escalating the FBI's investigation of Martin Luther King. A month after Johnson took office, on December 23, 1963, seven FBI officials held an extraordinary nine-hour conference at FBI headquarters in Washington to address King's "unholy alliance with the Communist Party, USA." They claimed that King was "knowingly, willingly, and regularly cooperating with and taking guidance from communists" whose long-term strategy was the creation of a "Negro-labor" coalition that would endanger national security.[73]

William Sullivan, the FBI's chief of domestic intelligence, chaired the meeting. He reported to Hoover that the agents had "gathered for the purpose of neutralizing King as an effective Negro leader."[74] Participants, including field agents from Atlanta, discussed more than twenty tactics for undermining King's stature as a public leader. They discussed ways to exploit any "shady financial dealings" King was engaged in and proposed introducing a "good looking female plant" into the SCLC offices. They might seek assistance from other ministers, as well as disgruntled employees or acquaintances.[75]

The participants knew that by intensifying their campaign against King they risked "extreme embarrassment to the Bureau" — a danger Sullivan noted five times in his two-and-a-half-page report to Hoover.[76] As a result, their chief tactic remained the use of wiretaps and other discreet forms of "technical coverage," which continued to produce "excellent information," Sullivan reported. FBI taps had already recorded King in conference with people the FBI believed had Communist connections. Moreover, the taps "had gathered information concerning weaknesses in [King's] character which are of such a nature to make him unfit to serve as a minister of the Gospel." Sullivan declared that agents would "expose King for the clerical fraud and Marxist he is at the first opportunity." Because King's status as a minister accounted for much of his moral authority, Sullivan felt that the civil rights leader could not survive revelations that he was "an immoral opportunist who is not a sincere person but is exploiting the racial situation for personal gain."[77]

Once Hoover approved the elaborate undertaking, FBI agents in Atlanta and elsewhere moved into action. Officials asked the Internal Revenue Service to scrutinize King's personal income tax returns, as well as those filed by the SCLC and other nonprofit organizations that supported his movement's activities. Agents also began recruiting an SCLC employee in Atlanta to become an informant. Electronic surveillance remained the highest priority. Agents hoped to plant microphones in the hotels King used in his almost continuous travel in the hope of gaining evidence of his "immorality" and "hypocrisy."[78]

When agents learned through wiretaps that King planned to stay at the Willard Hotel in Washington on the nights of January 6 and 7, 1964, assistant director Sullivan got Hoover's permission to install microphones for the first time in a hotel room occupied by King. With cooperation from the hotel's management, FBI technicians installed listening devices in King's suite, which they monitored in an adjacent room. King was in town to hear oral arguments before the Supreme Court in *New York Times v. Sullivan* — a landmark free speech case focused on whether an advertisement critical of King's treatment in Montgomery was protected under the First Amendment. After King returned to his hotel room early in the evening of January 6, the FBI technicians recorded nineteen reels of tape.[79]

What the FBI tapes depicted remains a matter of dispute. FBI officials claimed that the tapes revealed King and his associates engaged in a night of revelry with two women from the Philadelphia Navy Yard. Technicians reported hearing clinking glasses and laughter at bawdy jokes about "scared Negro preachers and stiff white bosses." They claimed that they could identify "the sounds of courtship and sex with distinctive verbal accompaniment." Three technicians later told King's biographer Taylor Branch that they had "heard King's distinctive voice ring out above others, with pulsating abandon, saying 'I'm fucking for God!' and 'I'm not a Negro tonight!' "[80] Aides to King who later heard what they believed to be portions of the Willard Hotel tapes disputed the FBI's account, claiming that the scratchy sounds were indistinct and difficult to comprehend.*

Officials believed that the tapes held conclusive proof of King's personal failings. At FBI headquarters on Pennsylvania Avenue, the intelligence division prepared a "highlights" tape and an eight-page memorandum summarizing the evidence, which Sullivan sent to Hoover on January 13.[81]

"They will destroy the burrhead!" Hoover exclaimed triumphantly regarding the Willard tapes.[82] Hoover urged his agents to capitalize on King's supposed indiscretions in subsequent hotels and cities, noting that "King is a 'tom cat' with obsessive, degenerate sexual urges."[83]

Buoyant over the Willard Hotel spying, Sullivan wrote to Hoover that he was determined "to [take] King off his pedestal and reduce him completely in influence."[84] He recommended that the memorandum summarizing the tapes be shown to Walter Jenkins at the White House "inasmuch as Dr. King is seeking an appointment with President Johnson." The task of taking the document to the White House was assigned to Deke DeLoach, the FBI liaison between Hoover and Johnson.[85]

A big man with a Georgia drawl, DeLoach had joined the FBI after serving in the navy during World War II and graduating from Stetson Law School in Florida. He had caught Hoover's eye early in his career and risen to be the fourth-ranking official in the bureau. Among his skills was the ability to read Hoover's moods and whims. DeLoach's title, assistant director for the Crime Records Division, was misleading; his most important duty was serving as Hoover's personal public relations emissary. In this role DeLoach developed power of his own as he befriended government officials and important private citizens — from top businessmen to church leaders — and they in turn sought his counsel and help. Now his friends included the president of the United States and his most trusted aide, Walter Jenkins.[86]

DeLoach and Jenkins were close. Both headed large Catholic families. They played golf together, attended parties at each other's homes, and spent a weekend with their wives as President Johnson's guests at Camp David. DeLoach and Jenkins had learned to work together as each served the interests of his powerful boss.

* The accuracy of the tapes, including identification of King's voice in various segments, has never been documented by independent analysts and remains a matter of dispute. The tapes were sealed by a federal court order and will remain closed until 2027.

In the first days of the Johnson presidency, DeLoach was a familiar presence in the White House. Johnson instructed that he be issued a White House pass and granted access to the president on request, and a White House telephone line was installed in DeLoach's home so President Johnson could contact him at any time. DeLoach typically arrived at the White House late in the afternoon and went straight to Jenkins's office, one door away from the Oval Office. There he delivered to Jenkins — or the president himself — the latest FBI reports.[87]

On January 14, DeLoach presented to the White House the eight-page summary of the recordings of the party in King's room at the Willard Hotel. In his official report to Hoover, DeLoach wrote: "I told Jenkins that the Director indicated I should leave this attachment with him if he desired to let the President personally read it. Jenkins mentioned that he was personally aware of the facts [and] that he could verbally advise the President of the matter. Jenkins was of the opinion that the FBI could perform a good service to the country if this matter could somehow be confidentially given to members of the press. I told him the Director had this in mind, however, he also believed we should obtain additional information prior to discussing it with certain friends."[88]

DeLoach's carefully worded note to Hoover allowed Johnson to deny that he had ever seen or read the report. On a related internal memo, however, DeLoach noted that this matter had been "handled with Jenkins *and the President*"* on January 14, 1964.[89] Read between the lines, DeLoach's report signaled that the president would not object if Hoover used the material from the tapes to attack King. The Kennedys had never ordered Hoover to stop harassing King. Now, in his first encounter with Hoover's campaign to smear King, neither did Lyndon Baines Johnson.

---

* Emphasis added. In an interview with the author, DeLoach said that he personally delivered the report to President Johnson, who received it without comment.

5

◆ ◆ ◆ ◆ ◆ ◆

A Fire That No Water
Could Put Out

T HE FORTY ACRES CLUB, a University of Texas faculty retreat in downtown Austin, still sparkled with Christmas
lights as it geared up for a special New Year's Eve party. Secret Service
agents had combed the building as well as the guest list of the all-white
private club, which ironically shared its name with the "forty acres and a
mule" supposedly promised every freed slave after the Civil War. Nearly a
hundred years later, to ring in 1964, the president of the United States
walked into the club with a broad smile on his face and a black woman on
his arm. She was Gerri Whittington, a tall, attractive woman Johnson had
recently hired as his secretary, integrating his personal staff — as he was
now breaking the color barrier at the faculty club. As vice president, Johnson had tried with only limited success to integrate his home state's largest
and most prestigious university, whose few black students lived in segregated housing and were barred from participating in intercollegiate ath-
letics, drama clubs, and other extracurricular activities. Many public facilities were still segregated in Austin, the capital of Texas and a supposed
bastion of liberalism.* Now, with Gerri Whittington as his symbolic first
strike, Johnson vowed to assert the power of the presidency to tear down
the walls of official racial discrimination in American society.[1]

* LBJ was concerned by the fact that his daughter Lynda was living in a segregated dormitory
at the university. After the semester ended, she transferred to George Washington University
and lived at the White House. On January 2, 1964, a University of Texas professor who earlier
had resigned from the Forty Acres Club in protest of its segregation policy called the club to
ask whether it really was integrated. "Yes," he was told, "the president of the United States integrated us on New Year's Eve."

After a working holiday at the LBJ Ranch, Johnson returned to Washington in the new year charged with energy and filled with optimism about what he could accomplish as president. "I've never felt freer in my life,"* he told White House reporters.[2] A man of towering — and mercurial — emotions, Johnson was ebullient. With remarkable speed, the new president had taken charge of the government and reassured a shaken nation. His deft handling of Congress, his calm public presence, his empathetic outreach to virtually every major sector of America all contributed to widespread public support. In early January 1964, the Gallup Poll reported that 80 percent of Americans approved of Johnson's handling of the presidency; only 5 percent expressed disapproval.[3] Another poll showed Johnson favored by 75 percent of voters in the upcoming presidential election, compared to only 20 percent for the leading Republican candidate, Senator Barry Goldwater of Arizona.[4] Johnson, who watched polls closely, found the results exhilarating, even though he knew that popularity and power in America were ephemeral.

Determined to seize the moment, Johnson stood before a joint session of Congress on January 8, 1964, to deliver his first State of the Union address. "Let this session of Congress be known as the session which did more for civil rights than the last hundred sessions combined," he began. "As far as the writ of Federal law will run, we must abolish not some, but all racial discrimination, for this is not merely an economic issue or a social, political or international issue. It is a moral issue — and it must be met by the passage this session of the [civil rights] bill now pending in the House."

Addressing the injustices that the proposed Civil Rights Act sought to remedy, Johnson declared: "All members of the public should have equal access to facilities open to the public. All members of the public should be equally eligible for federal benefits that are financed by the public. All members of the public should have an equal chance to vote for public officials and to send their children to good public schools and to contribute their talents to the public good. . . . Today, Americans of all races stand side by side in Vietnam and Berlin. They died side by side in Korea. Surely they can work and eat and travel side by side in their own country."

Johnson urged Congress to approve the late President Kennedy's unfinished legislative agenda, which included federal aid to education, medical care for the elderly, and a tax cut. He appealed to fiscal conservatives by

* LBJ's sense of freedom was in contrast to the experience of President Dwight Eisenhower, who was quoted as saying that he had felt as if he were in prison during his eight years in the White House.

requesting $500 million less than in the previous year's budget. Then Johnson placed his own imprint on the program: "This administration today, here and now, declares unconditional war on poverty in America. . . . It will not be a short or easy struggle, no single weapon or strategy will suffice, but we shall not rest until the war is won. The richest nation on earth can afford to win it. We cannot afford to lose it."[5]

The speech was interrupted by applause seventy-nine times and praised throughout the country. Johnson's prowess as a behind-the-scenes political operator was legendary. But his friends, listening to the State of the Union address, were surprised by his emergence as a powerful public speaker. They were familiar with Lyndon the stump speaker — shouting until he was hoarse, gesturing with his long arms in a manner that often detracted from his message, his style especially ill suited to the cool medium of television. But in his first weeks in office, the public had seen a more restrained Johnson. He spoke calmly but intensely, with a dignity, conviction, and passion that many citizens found inspiring. His State of the Union address was a landmark.

Johnson's quest to conquer poverty — soon couched as part of creating a Great Society — went far beyond what any president had ever suggested as a goal for government action. But Johnson's grand vision of eliminating poverty and promoting excellence was in keeping with an extraordinary moment in American history.

However much Johnson craved power and used it to his own ends, he had always believed that the purpose of government was to benefit ordinary people. He pursued this goal as Texas director of the National Youth Administration in the 1930s and, later, as a full-fledged New Deal supporter in Congress. At the heart of his drive was his intense competitiveness, his conscious reaching for his own place in history, and his desire to be appreciated, even loved. From the beginning, he aimed to match the accomplishments of his hero and mentor, Franklin Roosevelt. He wanted to complete the unfinished New Deal agenda with Medicare and aid to education, but then go beyond it — not just with poverty programs but with federal efforts to protect the environment, promote the arts, and rebuild the cities. In time he would speak of his desire to "out-Roosevelt Roosevelt" and to "out-Lincoln Lincoln."[6]

Johnson's sweeping ambitions suited the times. The early 1960s were marked by a heady optimism about what government could accomplish. John F. Kennedy had inspired thousands of citizens to serve their country in ventures such as the Peace Corps. Confident from victory in World War II and buoyed by a flourishing economy, a new generation of American leaders believed in the notion propounded in 1962 by economist John Kenneth Galbraith that the United States was truly an "affluent society,"[7] one with enough wealth to lift up the poor without unduly burdening the already prosperous. At the same time, books such as Michael Harrington's *The Other America* stirred the public's conscience by focusing a rare spotlight on poverty in the land of prosperity.[8] Americans took seriously Johnson's desire to conquer poverty in the United States. And the civil rights movement finally was forcing the nation to confront the glaring racial inequalities in American life.

Intellectuals, liberal politicians, and many ordinary citizens believed — along with Johnson — that there was a renewed opportunity now for major social change. For years, progressive legislation had been blocked in Congress by a coalition of conservative Republicans and southern Democrats, and by an electorate that rarely favored radical change. Conservatives warned that a larger role for the federal government would carry the nation down the road to socialism. Southerners also feared that government programs — open to all — threatened their segregated society. If a moment for historic change was indeed at hand, it would take a gifted national leader to overcome the conservative alliance in Congress.

At a White House breakfast meeting on January 7, 1964, a day before his address to Congress, Johnson and Democratic congressional leaders had set demanding legislative goals and timetables. They would try to enact tax cut legislation and win House approval of the civil rights bill by the end of February, then make an all-out push to pass the bill in the Senate before the summer's political conventions. If necessary, the president would reconvene Congress after the conventions to finish the job.[9] The president's address the next day, and the positive public reaction to it, strengthened their resolve.

As the Eighty-eighth Congress reconvened for its second session, Johnson embarked on his strategy to split the conservative alliance blocking civil rights in the Senate. He also set out to persuade southern Democrats in both houses to work with northern liberals to pass a tax cut and the rest of the administration's agenda. Time was of the essence. Unless the House acted quickly on civil rights and the Senate on the tax bill, Johnson knew that there would not be enough time left before the election to overcome a Senate filibuster against civil rights or to pass major legislation addressing medical care, education, and poverty.

Lyndon Johnson's hardball tactics for dividing and conquering the conservative alliance were supplemented by a "charm and dance" campaign. Starting on January 17, the president invited members of Congress and their spouses in groups of about fifty to a twice-a-week series of evenings at the White House. After cocktails, he would take the members down to the projection room, where administration officials briefed them on issues of special interest to them while Lady Bird took the spouses on a tour of the White House living quarters. The couples then would gather for dinner and dancing in the East Room. Johnson danced with every congressional wife and recruited his aides to do so, too. (Before the last dinner, Johnson joked with his legislative aide Lawrence O'Brien, "I want you to get a good afternoon nap so you can dance with the big fat women."[10]) The president was a graceful ballroom dancer, and the receptions were just one more piece of a life devoted almost 100 percent to politics. At one reception, Johnson waltzed past Claude Desautels, a White House aide assigned to congressional relations, and shouted, "Dance, Claude!"[11] By early spring, Johnson had entertained virtually every member of the House and Senate at a White House dinner dance.

The evenings worked. Even right-wing Republicans were pleased to be wined and dined and shown areas of the White House they had never visited. Many remarked that Lyndon and Lady Bird's White House entertaining contrasted sharply with that of Jack and Jackie Kennedy. Members of Congress, few of whom were Kennedy's close friends, had been invited only to large ceremonial events. More intimate Kennedy evenings were devoted to dinners upstairs with people prominent in the arts and society whom Jackie found interesting, as well as authors and reporters who were the president's friends. Kennedy, like Johnson, was a master politician, but he did not study or court Congress with Johnson's intensity.[12]

On Saturday morning, January 18, Johnson summoned to the Oval Office the leaders of the four largest civil rights organizations: the NAACP's Roy Wilkins, the National Urban League's Whitney Young, CORE national director James Farmer, and the Reverend Martin Luther King Jr., president of the SCLC.

As the president met with the black leaders, the civil rights bill that the House Judiciary Committee had passed the day before President Kennedy was killed still was stalled in Howard Smith's House Rules Committee. When Smith's authority had appeared threatened in December by the petition to remove the bill from his committee, the cagey chairman had agreed to hold hearings, which he convened on January 9, the day after Johnson's speech. But he was moving them along at a snail's pace. Johnson remembered how Smith had stalled the 1957 civil rights bill by claiming that he had to go home to Virginia to inspect a barn that had burned down, a ruse that had prompted House Speaker Sam Rayburn to quip, "I knew Howard Smith would do most anything to block a civil rights bill, but I never thought he would resort to arson."[13]

Johnson was taking no chances. As he and the four civil rights leaders were discussing the details of the legislation, the president suddenly picked up the telephone and dialed Lawrence O'Brien, his chief of congressional relations. O'Brien, a cheerful and effective politician from Springfield, Massachusetts, had stayed on in the job after Kennedy's assassination, quickly establishing the same easy rapport with Johnson that he had shared with his predecessor. "Larry, how many names do we have on this [discharge] petition?" Johnson asked. "I believe 178," O'Brien replied. An additional forty signers would be needed to strip the bill from the Rules Committee. "I've got some leaders down here," said Johnson, naming his guests. He instructed O'Brien to bring him a list of the twenty-five additional Republicans and fifteen Democrats most likely to sign.[14] If Smith continued to stall, Johnson told his guests, he would need them to round up the signatures.

The civil rights leaders, having met previously to coordinate their own agendas, had expected to hear the president explain why he needed to compromise on the bill. He declared instead that he wanted the bill approved "without a word or comma changed." The black leaders also were surprised to learn that Johnson had another purpose for calling them to the White House. The president asked them to "join him" as partners "to help find the ways and means to mobilize support for the war on poverty,"[15] legislation for which he planned to send to Congress soon. As the discussion traveled around the table, all agreed that the problems of civil rights and poverty were inextricably connected. James Farmer emphasized the debilitating handicaps caused by illiteracy and pointed out that combating it was a "vital part of the fight on discrimination."[16] Whitney Young called the high level of black unemployment, particularly among young black men, "a national disgrace."[17] Martin Luther King called poverty "a real catastrophe for Negroes" and declared an "urgent need for action in education, remedial education, vocational training, and illiteracy." If poor blacks and whites alike were to enjoy their rights as Americans, the group agreed, help on a massive scale was needed.[18]

When the leaders left the Oval Office and spoke to waiting reporters, it was clear that Johnson had skillfully broadened the civil rights agenda to include an attack on root problems suffered not just by racial minorities but by the poor of all races. There would be a dual war — against both poverty and racial discrimination — and Johnson had enlisted the nation's best-known black leaders as his allies. Each one had pledged his support for Johnson's agenda. "I'm sure the President will go all out in this program to meet the enormity of the problem," King said.[19] The poverty problem, he added "affects the whole nation in general, and the Negro in particular."[20]

King emphasized to reporters that the president had not asked for compromise on civil rights. "We feel this bill should not be watered down any further. We are not prepared to compromise in any form," he said.[21] In another interview King cautioned, "It's better to have no bill at all than one without fair employment practices and public accommodations" — the two provisions that faced the greatest opposition.[22] The showdown had begun.

In the nine weeks since the assassination, the black leaders had tried to honor Johnson's plea that demonstrations be curtailed to prevent a backlash against the civil rights bill. But as months passed and racial tensions built, demonstrations and clashes with segregationists and police were increasing. King went on television to assert that "the Negro's gains have only whetted his appetite for more." If the civil rights bill were blocked in Congress, he warned, "the nation should fasten its seatbelt."[23]

Indeed, even as he and his colleagues sat in the White House that Saturday, clashes were erupting in Atlanta and New York City, where activists were boycotting public schools to protest de facto segregation. King was particularly worried about Atlanta, "the city too busy to hate." Even as he was meeting with Johnson in the Oval Office, SNCC activists were confronting police and Ku Klux Klan members who were trying to prevent a sit-in at a segregated Atlanta restaurant. King knew that even if he had been there, he would not have been able to stop the demonstrators, several of whom abandoned the tactics of passive resistance and fought back against police.[24]

On that same Saturday, Barry Goldwater, campaigning in Fayetteville, North Carolina, spoke out against the civil rights bill, especially the section calling for an end to segregation in public accommodations. Goldwater hoped that the "white backlash" against the bill would fuel his campaign, especially in the Deep South, which traditionally had voted solidly Democratic.

Lyndon Johnson launched the "War on Poverty" with great fanfare — and before many details had been filled in. This much he knew: he did not want the kind of small, experimental programs envisioned by Jack Kennedy's advisers. This president was determined to seize the opportunity for radical change. He had been waiting for such a moment his entire career.

Johnson's views about race and poverty were shaped by the experiences of his youth and by his climb to power. His passion for helping the under-dog stemmed from his own deep feeling of being an outsider, excluded and looked down upon in the dusty hill country town where he grew up — a victim, he felt, of his father's economic failure. Nevertheless, as he re-flected in private on the root causes of poverty among minorities, John-son at times echoed the prejudices and crude stereotypes of his time and place.

Speaking on the telephone on January 6, 1964, to Walker Stone, the Texas-bred editor of *U.S. News & World Report* and a longtime friend, Johnson said: "I'm going to try to teach these niggers that don't know anything how to work for themselves instead of just breeding. I'm going to try to teach these Mexicans that can't talk English to learn it so they can work for themselves. I'm going to try to build a road in eastern Kentucky and West Virginia . . . so they can get to school and get off the taxpayers' backs." Stone replied enthusiastically, "You've made the God-damnedest impact on this country imaginable. . . . I know I'm going to like [your budget message, and] I'll support you on poverty too!"[25]

In private conversations, especially with southerners, Johnson still oc-casionally used the term "nigger" or "nigra," and even admiring civil rights leaders wished that he would learn to pronounce "Negro" with less of a southwestern drawl: "Nee-grow." Racial epithets and jokes were still part of his vernacular speech, but Johnson's stereotyping of blacks and Mexican Americans had little effect on his determination to help them. For Johnson, the war against poverty could be won with programs he be-lieved in deeply — with education and job training, with better health care and housing. He disliked welfare programs, believing in a "hand up, not a handout."

As he pushed the War on Poverty, Johnson was equally passionate about moving qualified African Americans, Mexican Americans, and women of all races into the higher-level government jobs from which they had been excluded. After he finished speaking with Walker Stone, John-son's next telephone conversation was with Whitney Young, in whom the president placed special trust. Johnson heartily endorsed Young's recom-mendations that he should appoint black lawyers A. Leon Higginbotham Jr. and Constance Baker Motley to federal judgeships. But the president remained thin-skinned about liberal easterners' portrayal of him as a southern bigot and their refusal to give him the credit he craved for his pathbreaking actions on behalf of minorities. With exaggerated petu-lance, Johnson told Young that he didn't want to make the appointments "unless the whole Negro community knows that I'm doing it, and the

Democrats are doing it, and this damn *Jet* [magazine] and the rest of them quit cutting us up and saying that we hate the Negroes."[26]

In the next few days, Johnson worked the telephone promoting the appointment of blacks, Mexican Americans, and women to highly visible public posts. He called Richard Russell to head off southern senators' opposition to Carl Rowan, a respected black newspaper columnist whom he planned to name director of the United States Information Agency (USIA). Johnson had been impressed with Rowan when he served as Kennedy's ambassador to Finland. "I'm going to appoint Carl Rowan," Johnson told Russell. "I want you to hold your hat. . . . He's the best man that's available anywhere." When Russell noted that Rowan had written stories critical of the South, Johnson replied, "He's a Tennessee boy and he's born and raised there," assuring Russell that Rowan would "lean over backwards" to be fair.[27] The president then called Senator John McClellan of Arkansas, chairman of the appropriations subcommittee responsible for USIA's funds: "USIA is in your department under Appropriations, and I don't want you to cut his guts out 'cause he's a Nigra. . . . I've seen you operate with a knife, and I've seen a few people get de-nutted."[28] Rowan not only got the job; he was confirmed unanimously by the Senate.

A few days later Johnson called Assistant Secretary of State Thomas Mann to urge appointment of a Mexican American as ambassador to Mexico and suggested Daniel Luevano, finance commissioner for the state of California. When Mann argued that "the Mexicans don't like what they call 'pochan,' " a derisive term for those born in the United States but who call themselves Mexican Americans, the president replied, "I don't goddamned think I understand that. . . . Go get me a good one. I want to help 'em. We've been miserable to the Mexicans."[29]

Johnson found a more sympathetic ear in Secretary of Defense Robert McNamara, whom he urged to appoint Luevano to a prominent post in the Pentagon. "He's a Mexican boy and we got 'em dying all over the world as privates but we never do put any of them in any of these top jobs," Johnson complained. "The Mexicans just are all raising hell that you've got Negroes all over the government but you haven't got any Mexicans, and California's got 23 percent of all the Mexicans in the United States."[30] Luevano was sworn in as an assistant secretary of defense on July 1, 1964.[31]

Johnson met in January with his old friend Anna Rosenberg Hoffman, a renowned management expert who in the early 1950s had become the first woman to serve as an assistant secretary of defense. She convinced the president that highly qualified women were being denied promotion to top government positions. Johnson immediately called White House assistant Elizabeth Carpenter and Assistant Secretary of Labor Esther Peterson to a Cabinet meeting at ten o'clock the following morning. Carpenter and Peterson stayed up all night preparing information on the status of women in the federal government. At the meeting on January 17, Johnson declared to his Cabinet appointees: "I'm sure there are plenty of high-level positions available for qualified women in your departments. And I'm sure there are many women already on your payrolls who have been waiting for promotions for a long time. So go back to your departments and see what you can do. Then report to me next Friday how many you have placed." The startled Cabinet secretaries managed to come up with fifty-eight recommended promotions, which President Johnson announced the following weekend at a dinner meeting of the National Women's Press Club.[32]

Whether hiring members of minority groups or white males, Johnson always sought talented people he could trust. With women, he had special requirements. Dissatisfied with the inefficiency of the White House secretarial pool, Johnson called Civil Service Commission chairman John Macy. "I want the five smartest, best-educated, fastest, prettiest secretaries in Washington," he said. "I don't want any old, broken-down old maids. I want them from twenty-five to forty. I want them that can work Saturday and Sunday, I want them that can work at night. . . . I've got to have some people that I can trust."[33]

After his White House meeting on January 18, Martin Luther King left for a troubled three-day retreat with his closest SCLC advisers at the former site of Black Mountain College outside Asheville, North Carolina. They debated night and day whether they should mount demonstrations in a new location or again in Birmingham — where their dramatic protests had moved public opinion — or whether to try to build political power instead by focusing on northern voter registration for the 1964 election.

As the sometimes stormy meeting unfolded, King's staff was divided over where to mount the next campaign. SCLC demonstration tactics aside, Johnson had influenced the civil rights agenda. The SCLC, at King's urging, had broadened its stance from focusing only on rights for African Americans and endorsed the president's War on Poverty program for people of all races. King even changed the ending of his forthcoming book, *Why We Can't Wait*, to reflect the new poverty message.* "Today,

* Thanks to FBI wiretaps on the telephones of King, Levison, and Clarence Jones, Johnson received advance notice from J. Edgar Hoover that King's book would praise him and his poverty program.

the dimensions of Johnson's leadership have spread from a region to a nation," King wrote. "His recent expressions, public and private, indicate to me that he has a comprehensive grasp of contemporary problems. He has seen that poverty and unemployment are grave and growing catastrophes, and he is aware that those caught most fiercely in the grip of this economic holocaust are Negroes. Therefore, he has set the twin goal of a battle against discrimination within the war against poverty." He added, "I do not doubt that the President is approaching the solution with sincerity, with realism and, thus far, with wisdom."[34] At Johnson's request the SCLC leaders had agreed to make his agenda their own, but they rejected his calls to cease their demonstrations. After all, they knew that the political action was in the White House and in the Congress, an arena in which the SCLC barely had a presence.

Yet King remained the best-known and most inspiring voice of the movement, a voice heard over and over as he stumped the nation, calling for enactment of the civil rights bill. In early 1964 King maintained a frenetic schedule, with speaking and fundraising events in Milwaukee, San Francisco, Los Angeles, and Honolulu, interspersed with brief stops at SCLC headquarters in Atlanta, and in New York, where he met with Clarence Jones, Stanley Levison, and Bayard Rustin in an effort to plan future demonstrations and to cope with the SCLC's constant money problems.

In the president's speeches, interviews, and private conversations in January 1964, he tried to create an aura of political inevitability about a strong new civil rights law. Senator Richard Russell, leader of the southern opposition, immediately understood the president's strategy. This would be a fight to the finish, with Johnson giving no quarter, his old friend knew. "We would have beaten President Kennedy, but now I won't predict [the outcome]," Russell told a reporter. "Now it will be three times harder. President Kennedy didn't have to pass a strong bill to prove anything on civil rights. President Johnson does."[35] To another reporter Russell noted that Johnson was a much tougher opponent than Kennedy. "He knows more about the uses of power than any man," Russell said. As majority leader, he added dryly, "Johnson could get three votes when all he had to offer was one office room the [three] senators [all] wanted to use."[36]

Although Johnson was now locked in battle with Russell, his mentor and closest friend in the Senate, LBJ made certain that he maintained his friendship with the Georgian and other southerners, working with them on matters of common interest. The president already had saved a cotton price-support bill important primarily to the southern states. Now he asked Defense Secretary Robert McNamara "to give credit to Russell [chairman of the Senate Armed Services Committee] for everything you can without being too sappy."[37]

Three days after his meeting with the "Big Four" civil rights leaders, Johnson called in Clarence Mitchell and Joseph Rauh Jr., who represented the Leadership Conference on Civil Rights, a coalition of civil rights, labor, church, and civic organizations. Mitchell, a black attorney for the NAACP and the group's chief lobbyist, sometimes was called "the 101st senator" for the respect he commanded from members of Congress, both Democrats and Republicans. They admired his civility and his encyclopedic knowledge of their institution. Rauh, a white lawyer and the Leadership Conference's legislative counsel, was a relentless advocate and a superb legislative craftsman. The two men were an effective team.

In the civil rights fights of the 1950s, both Mitchell and Rauh had bitterly criticized Johnson for watering down bills advocated by the Leadership Conference. With hindsight, both had decided that Johnson's pragmatic wheeling and dealing had perhaps achieved a useful first step, paving the way for much more sweeping legislation now.

The president first told Mitchell and Rauh what they had hoped to hear — that he was not intimidated by the prospect of a Senate filibuster. "I don't care how long it takes," Johnson said. "I don't care if the Senate doesn't do one other piece of business this year. You've got to keep this bill on the floor. You can tell [Senate Majority Leader] Mansfield — you can tell anybody — the president of the United States doesn't care if this bill is there forever. We are not going to have anything else hit the floor until this bill is passed!" Rauh realized immediately that Johnson's declaration neutralized the filibusterers' strongest weapon — "that they could hold out until other important legislation required that the Senate put aside the civil rights bill."[38]

As he listened to the president, Mitchell was reminded of Johnson's uncanny knowledge about each member of the Senate. At a meeting with the vice president in the summer of 1963, Mitchell had heard Johnson explain why he thought the southerners could no longer sustain a filibuster. With their command of the Senate's key committees, they had appeared invincible. But Johnson had dealt with the oligarchs for years and studied them closely. These were sick old men, Johnson had said, describing the weaknesses of each, starting with Richard Russell's worsening emphysema and Mississippian James Eastland's drinking problem.[39]

Now, however, President Johnson laid down a constraint that disappointed Rauh and Mitchell. He reiterated that he didn't want any "weakening amendments" to HR 7152, the bill reported out of the House Judiciary Committee in October 1963, but he also opposed adding any "strengthening amendments" to the bill. Mitchell and Rauh already had plans to beef up the legislation on the House floor. Now Johnson's admonition gave them pause. Mitchell reflected on a lesson he had learned as a young firebrand in the 1950s from then majority leader Johnson. "Clarence, you can get anything you want if you have the votes," Johnson had told him during a civil rights debate. "How many votes have you got?"[40] Although Johnson's assertion of raw power rankled at the time, Mitchell had come to appreciate its simple logic. In the end, legislative victories required winning votes — and accurately counting them. Now, in 1964, they needed Lyndon Johnson to help them get those votes. They handed him a list of eight senators they thought the president might sway. The idealistic crusaders decided to restrain their natural impulse to seek a perfect civil rights law and, convinced of Johnson's commitment to the cause of racial justice, agreed to do it his way.[41] Mitchell knew that Johnson, always trying to keep his options open, did not easily make firm commitments, but once he did, "he would work tirelessly to see that his commitment was fulfilled."[42]

Johnson was worried about attempts to add "strengthening" changes to the civil rights bill for good reason. The bill that had emerged from the House Judiciary Committee on October 29, 1963, was a fragile compromise stitched together by the Kennedy administration and Republican and Democratic House leaders. Seventy-year-old William McCulloch of Ohio, the ranking Republican on the committee, was the key to the agreement. A fiscal conservative who believed in government action to eliminate discrimination, McCulloch had sought an ironclad commitment that Kennedy and the Democratic House leaders would defend their agreed-upon compromise. In the past, McCulloch had put his Republican troops on the line for strong civil rights legislation, only to see Majority Leader Johnson weaken it in the Senate. If the Democrats betrayed him again, McCulloch swore, he would withdraw his support and sink the bill.

In his State of the Union speech, Johnson had stressed the need for national unity. "If we fail," he declared, "if we fritter and fumble away our opportunity in needless, senseless quarrels between Democrats and Republicans, or between the House and the Senate, or between the South and the North, or between the Congress and the administration, then history will rightfully judge us harshly."[43] Seven weeks into his presidency, Johnson knew that enactment of an effective civil rights law hinged on an extraordinary degree of cooperation between natural adversaries. If the legislation failed, Johnson feared more chaos in the streets, a deepening schism between North and South — and a devastating blow to his chances of being elected president in his own right in November.

At their weekly legislative breakfast on January 22, Johnson told House Democratic leaders that the time had come to take the civil rights bill away from Howard Smith. In eight days of hearings, the Rules Committee had heard testimony from only eight of thirty members of Congress — mostly opponents of the bill — who had asked to testify. In theory, the committee's function was only procedural: to set the terms and time of legislative debate on the House floor. In practice, the wily Smith used his committee to block or stall progressive legislation.[44]

The next day, January 23, the president, Speaker John McCormack, and other House Democratic leaders made a deal with Republican leader Charles Halleck and Congressman William McCulloch. Together they would defeat Smith in his own committee, forcing the bill to the House floor on January 31, with a final vote scheduled for February 10.* Then the House would recess for six days, allowing Republicans their traditional week of Lincoln's birthday speeches and dinners, at which they could boast of their contribution toward passing historic civil rights legislation. Johnson's timetable was politically astute.†

Taking no chances, Johnson decided to remind the Republicans publicly of their agreement to act in the Rules Committee. Calling an impromptu press conference on Saturday, January 25, the president casually remarked, "We are very happy about the progress being made in civil rights. I have said to the [congressional] leadership that I thought that it would be rather unbecoming to go out and talk about Lincoln when we still had the civil rights bill, that Lincoln would be so interested in, locked up in a committee that couldn't act on it."[45]

On January 30, 1964, the House Rules Committee unlocked the civil rights bill, voting 11 to 4 — the dissenters being Smith and three other southern Democrats — to schedule the measure for floor debate the following day. The final vote by the full House was scheduled for February 10.[46]

At the same time that he pushed the House on civil rights, President Johnson had been pressing the Senate to end a year of delay in voting on tax

---

* A bipartisan majority on the House Rules Committee informed Smith that they would schedule a meeting three days hence, at which they would formally vote out the civil rights bill. They chose this procedure over the more difficult discharge petition, which would have required 218 signatures.

† In a telephone conversation with Roy Wilkins on February 6, LBJ claimed he had told House Republican leader Charles Halleck that if he couldn't get the civil rights bill passed before the Lincoln's birthday speeches, people "ought to laugh him off the platform because he and Howard Smith had their foot on Lincoln's neck."

cut legislation. Now that he was beginning to see daylight on civil rights, he realized that the tax legislation was in trouble. The proposed $11 billion tax cut was designed to spur the economy by cutting personal and corporate taxes and encouraging consumer spending by reducing the withholding rate on salaries from 18 to 14 percent.

The tax cut turned out to be politically more difficult than Johnson had foreseen. Liberal Democrats feared that reduced revenues would result in cuts in social programs. Conservatives worried that higher deficits would drive up inflation. To win enough Senate votes, Johnson went to work on his former colleagues. With rigorous budget cutting and the masterly exercise of public relations, Johnson thought he had secured the votes needed to pass the bill. He convinced liberals that any spending cuts would come from eliminating waste in the Defense Department. He impressed conservatives with his fiscal prudence by holding the new budget below $100 billion — even lower than President Kennedy's budget of the previous year.

The logjam appeared to have been broken, and the measure was moving smoothly through the Senate Finance Committee. But on the morning of January 23, the White House suddenly lost control when Republican leader Everett Dirksen won adoption of a measure that would reduce federal excise taxes on a variety of "luxury items," including jewelry, furs, and musical instruments. Dirksen prevailed in the committee 10 to 7 by garnering support from Democrats representing states with industries that would benefit. The new luxury tax cuts would add $445 million to the cost of the bill. Worse still, Johnson feared, the Dirksen amendment might open the floodgates on the Senate floor to cutting other excise taxes — on telephone equipment and service, on automobiles. Johnson was afraid that the weight of more than $2 billion in additional tax cuts — and lost government revenue — would sink the entire measure.[47]

When the Finance Committee recessed for lunch, he sprang into action. Over the next two hours, the president telephoned most of the seventeen members of the committee. Johnson pleaded with Senator Vance Hartke, a Democrat from Indiana, "Can't you help me on this excise tax thing? You're going to wreck this damn bill." When Hartke replied that manufacturers of musical instruments in his state would benefit from the cut, the president retorted, "The goddammed band and musical instruments . . . they won't be talking about it next November. What they are going to be judging us by . . . is whether we pass a tax bill or not, and whether we got prosperity. . . . So get in there and try to help me on this thing!"[48]

Next, Johnson called Senator Abraham Ribicoff, a Connecticut Democrat who had already announced that he had just won a tax cut for jewelry manufacturers in his state. The president reminded Ribicoff that it had been Johnson himself, as Senate majority leader, who had placed Ribicoff on the prestigious committee; now it was critically important that he serve the national interest. "Well, let me see how I can save my face," said Ribicoff. "You save my face this afternoon," replied Johnson, "and I'll save your face tomorrow. . . . I don't give a damn about the details. . . . I just want you to work it out."[49]

At 2 P.M. the Finance Committee reconvened. On a 9–8 party line vote — with Ribicoff and Hartke on board — the Democratic majority restored the original tax proposal. The president had applied the "Johnson treatment" — cajoling, demanding, but in this case never threatening. Until Lyndon Johnson, it was unthinkable that a president of the United States would, in the space of two hours, personally lobby the entire membership of a committee. Only with trepidation and caution had presidents ignored the separation of powers dictum, "Presidents propose, Congress disposes."

Johnson knew well the dangers of alienating Congress, but he plunged ahead. With the Democrats back in line, he hoped to get the tax bill through the full House before the Lincoln's birthday recess. The way would then be clear for civil rights.

After his early 1964 speaking tour, King took a brief vacation in Puerto Rico. On his return, he resumed discussions with his advisers on how to play a bigger role in helping to pass the civil rights bill. With this goal in mind, King promoted his friend Walter Fauntroy to head up a new SCLC lobbying office in Washington, D.C. Each of these activities was duly noted by the Federal Bureau of Investigation.[50]

The FBI wiretap on King's home telephone in Atlanta gave J. Edgar Hoover advance notice that King would be meeting with President Johnson on January 18. The director was surprised — and furious. Hoover thought he had effectively blocked King's access to the president just four days earlier, when he had sent Johnson the microphone surveillance summary of the "wild party" in King's Washington hotel room. Deke DeLoach had returned from the White House and told Hoover that Walter Jenkins, Johnson's top assistant, had approved the FBI's plan to leak details of King's extramarital sex life to the news media. Yet on January 19 the Sunday *New York Times* featured on its front page a large photograph of King seated in the Oval Office next to President Johnson.[51]

Hoover's response to the White House meeting was to order additional bugs placed in King's hotel rooms and to flood the White House with salacious reports of Stanley Levison's "Communist" influence on King and the latter's alleged love affairs.[52] In an eleven-page document marked "Top Secret," Hoover reported: "King has shown not only a willingness but even an eagerness to accept communist aid, to support communist causes, to associate and confer with prominent communist leaders, and to work closely with and rely upon the advice and guidance of dedicated communists with concealed affiliations, despite the fact they have been identified reliably to him." Within the Communist Party, Hoover reported, King was described "as a true Marxist-Leninist from the top of his head to the tips of his toes."[53]

Whether Johnson believed the FBI's reports or not, he read them eagerly and discussed their contents with aides and Cabinet members, including Secretary of Defense McNamara. Johnson — like Kennedy before him — enjoyed gossip and reports of scandalous behavior by people in public life. Hoover's reports were chock-full of both. Johnson did not yet seem worried by the Levison–King relationship, but in the tense atmosphere of the Cold War, Hoover's insistent campaign was beginning to sow seeds of doubt in high places about King's loyalty and judgment, as well as his moral values.[54]

On January 29, 1964 — two days before the House was to begin debate on the civil rights bill — Hoover testified before a closed hearing of a House appropriations subcommittee, many of whose members were his staunch allies, that the Communist Party had penetrated King's organization and was influencing his actions.[55] Speaking off the record, he also told the committee about King's purported sexual indiscretions, including the January 6 Willard Hotel party. With subcommittee chairman John Rooney of Brooklyn, Hoover had shared tapes and transcripts of the bugging of King's hotel suite.[56]

Predictably, committee members quickly whispered Hoover's charges to their colleagues. When Howard Smith learned about Hoover's testimony, he called DeLoach and told him he wanted to "inform the public about this matter" in a speech on the House floor. The Virginia congressman clearly thought he had found the "smoking gun" that would cut King down and cripple the civil rights bill.

DeLoach parried that if the FBI were to make public information about King's Communist connections, other bureau operations would be compromised. DeLoach agreed with Smith "that King obviously needed to be exposed" and that the objective might be accomplished soon with the information about King's personal life. But when DeLoach proposed a limited exposé to Hoover, the director shot it down. "I do not want anything on King given to Smith or anyone else at this time," he wrote DeLoach.[57]

The last thing Hoover wanted was for the FBI to put its information about Levison or King on the public record. That could lead to unwanted questions. When a Justice Department official in the internal security division sought to prosecute Levison, Hoover opposed the idea. He was worried about exposing Jack and Morris Childs, the FBI's valuable counterspies, who were the source of most FBI information about Levison. And he had another reason to avoid open disclosure. The FBI had compelling evidence that Levison had been an active Communist Party member until the late 1950s but could not verify Levison's Communist ties after he started working with King. Despite the FBI's wiretapping, its bugging of offices and hotel rooms, its informants and undercover agents, and its constant physical surveillance of Levison and King, the bureau lacked any hard evidence that Levison still worked for the Communist Party or had given King any advice from the party. Nor did it have any way of authenticating the voices on the so-called "sex tapes" from the hotel rooms. For Hoover's purposes, it was better for King to remain the target of a hidden counterintelligence campaign. Hoover's goal was to break the King–Levison tie and discredit King, not to prosecute Levison. Meanwhile, Hoover was playing fast and loose with the facts, confident that no one would challenge him.

Neither Lyndon Johnson nor the Kennedys before him made an independent effort to evaluate the FBI's information about Levison and King or to examine its relevance to national security. Nor did they ever make more than a token effort to stop Hoover from leaking salacious personal information and charges of Communist influence against King. Through the years a succession of presidents had found it easier simply to accept Hoover's defamatory reports than to challenge his power. After all, who knew what he could leak about them?

King, however, did want to learn more about the Levison accusations. He assigned their friend Clarence Jones the task of questioning Levison about his relationship with the Communist Party. Levison admitted that he had been a member of CPUSA until the late 1950s but told Jones that he had broken completely with the party after he started working with King. The explanation was enough to satisfy King.[58]

At the stroke of noon on Friday, January 31, 1964, seventy-five-year-old John McCormack, Speaker of the House of Representatives, called the

House to order to consider civil rights legislation that John F. Kennedy had sent to Congress more than seven months earlier. In his zeal to move quickly and smoothly, President Johnson had urged that the House approve the bill "without a word or comma changed" — good rhetoric but hardly a realistic possibility in a body of 435 legislators. Under the rules agreed on for the debate, each member could offer an unlimited number of amendments. Southern Democratic opponents could be expected to try to attack the bill with dozens of amendments designed to cripple the legislation if not defeat it outright. They expected support from conservative northern Republicans, who saw the legislation as a federal usurpation of states' rights.

The strength of the final bill would depend on the skill and discipline of a bipartisan leadership team headed by Representative Emanuel Celler, chairman of the House Judiciary Committee, and William McCulloch, the committee's ranking Republican. Celler, a feisty seventy-four-year-old liberal Democrat from Brooklyn, and McCulloch, a gentle conservative Republican from Piqua, Ohio, were a study in contrasts, but they shared a determination to hold together the fragile coalition in favor of the legislation.

Though Celler's serious-minded approach won him the respect of his colleagues, it was his sense of humor that endeared him to them, regardless of party. A young Maryland Republican congressman, Charles Mathias, was impressed by Celler's ability to defuse tense moments by reciting verse. (His favorite was: "King David and King Solomon lived very merry lives / With very many concubines and very many wives. / Old age came upon them with its very many qualms, / Solomon wrote the Proverbs, and David wrote the Psalms.")

For Celler, the challenge was to prevent liberal Democrats from adding amendments that would break the compromise and drive away McCulloch's Republicans. McCulloch could count on liberal Republicans and those who identified with the tradition of Abraham Lincoln; but he had to win the support of fellow conservatives who felt little political pressure to vote for civil rights. They came mainly from small towns and rural areas in the Midwest where there were few African Americans and whites were not necessarily free of racial prejudice. With Republicans divided on civil rights, McCulloch could count on little help from the party's leadership. In fact, the cautious House GOP leaders did not establish a party position on the bill. Republican civil rights supporters knew that their minority leader, Charles Abraham Halleck, generally took his cues from the ranking Republican on each committee, and they believed that he would eventually support the bill, since he had been given his middle name in honor of the antislavery father of the party, Abraham Lincoln.[59]

In the ten hours of opening debate, southerners argued that the bill represented an unconstitutional usurpation by the federal government of both individual liberties and the rights of states to govern themselves. Whom a restaurant owner chose to hire or serve were rights protected by the Constitution, they argued, as was the right of each state to adopt segregation laws. Civil rights advocates responded that Congress had not only the constitutional power but also the moral responsibility to grant equal rights long denied African Americans and other minorities.

Throughout the 1950s and 1960s, white southern politicians contended that civil rights protests were the handiwork of outside agitators, not of local blacks; now the White House and Congress were yielding to violence and lawlessness provoked by these "outsiders." "What is the rush?" challenged Democrat William Colmer of Mississippi. "Is all of this done out of fear? Is the Congress of the United States to yield to threats of further demonstrations by minority group leaders — blackmail if you will? . . . Is the Congress to comply by legislation with the demands and even riots of every organized minority group in the country?"[60]

Colmer's speech touched a nerve with many members of Congress, who not only resented the pressure of demonstrators but also were afraid of being accused by their constituents of acting under duress. Bill McCulloch, the Republican floor leader for the bill, bluntly replied to Colmer that "not force or fear, but belief in the inherent equality of man induces me to support this legislation." As a conservative, McCulloch said, he too believed that "state authority should not be needlessly usurped by a centralized government. But I also believe that an obligation rests with the national government to see that the citizens of every state are treated equally without regard to their race or color or religion or national origin. The Constitution doesn't say that whites alone shall have our basic rights, but that we all shall have them."[61]

In reality, both the White House and Congress were responding in part to the effects of civil rights demonstrations on public opinion and to the fear that racial tensions could spin out of control if Congress did not act. The Kennedy administration had proposed the bill in 1963 only after the televised brutality of Birmingham police against peaceful black demonstrators had pricked the conscience of Americans and spawned demonstrations all over the South. President Johnson constantly warned members of Congress that legislation was needed to avoid a deeper racial crisis.

Even as the House debate began, the president faced almost daily decisions about whether to intervene in racial crises in the South. In early February federal marshals were dispatched to Tuskegee, Alabama, after Governor George Wallace and local authorities refused to protect black children trying to attend a school newly integrated by federal court order. Johnson prepared orders to nationalize the Alabama National Guard if the marshals could not handle the situation.[62]

On Wednesday, February 3, the House took up the most controversial provision of the bill. Title II provided that no individual could be denied the use of "public accommodations" because of "race, color, religion, or national origin." The student sit-ins at lunch counters had focused a spotlight on segregated facilities throughout the South. The proposed law would end segregation not only in publicly owned facilities such as courthouses, parks, and swimming pools, but also in privately owned businesses such as restaurants, hotels, and motels.

House opponents first tried to cripple the public accommodations section by limiting its application to "interstate travelers." Edward Willis, a Democrat from Louisiana, argued that the commerce clause of the U.S. Constitution permitted the federal government to regulate commerce between the states, not businesses within a state. Judiciary Committee chairman Celler replied that Willis's amendment would prevent enforcement of the law. "You cannot expect inns, hotels, and motels to advertise that they are — or they are not — catering to interstate travelers," he said. Furthermore, Celler argued, "how can the interstate traveler or any traveler know that he would be safe in seeking lodging? He would never know."[63] Willis's amendment was defeated decisively, as was a similar one by Michigan Republican George Meader that sought to limit the law to public accommodations located along interstate or primary highways.*

As the segregationists lost vote after vote, the initially moderate tone of the House debate became harsher. On February 4, Howard Smith introduced an amendment that he said would apply, for instance, to a chiropodist whose office, if located in a hotel, would be covered by the public accommodations law. "If I were cutting corns," said Smith, "I would want to know whose feet I would have to be monkeying around with. I would want to know whether they smelled good or bad."[64]

To protect the rights of chiropodists (now called podiatrists), Smith

---

* From the 1930s on, the U.S. Supreme Court began to interpret the commerce clause more broadly to cover activities affecting interstate commerce. The court would do so again in upholding the 1964 Civil Rights Act in *Heart of Atlanta Motel, Inc. v. United States*, 379 U.S. 241 (1964).

cited the Thirteenth Amendment's prohibition against slavery or involuntary servitude and proposed that no one be required by the law to contribute a labor or service "without his consent." Lamenting that the Constitution "doesn't mean much around here anymore," Smith challenged his colleagues: "See if you can vote against it. I defy you to do so!" After Celler pointed out that Smith's "innocent" proposal would nullify court enforcement of the public accommodations law, the House defeated it 149 to 107.[65]

The southerners' frustration grew as expected support from conservative midwestern Republicans failed to materialize. The coalition of southern Democrats and conservative Republicans that had blocked so much progressive legislation over the years was not holding. After Clark MacGregor, a Republican from Minnesota, spoke in favor of the bill, an angry Howard Smith followed him off the House floor. "That's all right for you, MacGregor," he said. "You don't have any Negroes in your district." To which MacGregor jokingly replied, "Oh, that's not true, Judge Smith — we have seventeen."[66]

The following day, William Colmer of Mississippi tried to exclude beauticians and barbers from coverage under the public accommodations provision. Citing Abraham Lincoln in describing the physical differences between the races, Colmer said that white barbers were not properly trained to cut the hair of black customers. "You should give some thought about these barbers," he said, "when they get that razor to operating around your throat. They might get a little too enthusiastic in their opposition to the fact that you required them to perform a service for which they were not trained."

Infuriated by the comments of Smith and Colmer, California Democrat James Corman announced that he was fed up with amendments that would "subtly or blatantly" defeat the purpose of the law. Referring to Smith's chiropodist example, Corman retorted, "If you are going to trim the stinking, sweaty white corns, you must do the same with the black ones." Colmer's amendment was defeated 114 to 69.[67]

Tensions rose again as the House considered Title VI, which would forbid the use of federal funds in any program in which discrimination was practiced. Virtually every segregated school and hospital in the South could lose federal funding. Albert Rains, an Alabama Democrat, argued that poor blacks would suffer most from fund cutoffs, and then made a thinly veiled threat: "Do you realize who sits on the Committee on Appropriations in this Congress? Are they going to give money — and I am looking at them — to any bill that will not give aid to every city and municipality in the Union?"[68] Many of the powerful appropriations subcommittee chairmen, entrenched in office through seniority, were southerners opposed to the civil rights bill. Three days earlier the southerners on the House Agriculture Committee had signaled their displeasure with the civil rights bill by rejecting larger benefits in the food stamp program requested by President Johnson to help the poor.[69] Chairman Celler gave an impassioned response, pointing out that from the moment of birth in inadequate, segregated hospitals, segregation took its toll on black children.

When Louisiana's Hale Boggs, the Democratic whip, rose to support an amendment that would make the federal fund cutoffs a discretionary authority of the president, the Republican civil rights supporters suspected a sellout. Boggs was not only the third-ranking Democratic official in the House but also an intimate friend of Lyndon Johnson. Republican John Lindsay of New York rose to challenge Boggs: "I might ask who else the gentleman speaks for when he takes the floor and asks us to throw in the ashcan Title VI of this bill?" A red-faced Bill McCulloch, also suspecting that the president was offering a concession to southern Democrats, proclaimed that if the amendment were adopted, "I regret to say that my individual support for this legislation will come to an end!" Chairman Celler backed McCulloch, and the weakening amendment was defeated 206 to 80.

The bill's managers defeated dozens of hostile amendments, partly because they were more disciplined than their opponents in drawing supporters to the House floor for key votes. The effort was directed by the Democratic Study Group, a coalition of 125 liberal House members, and by the Leadership Conference on Civil Rights, particularly civil rights lawyer Joseph Rauh and NAACP lobbyist Clarence Mitchell, with support from volunteers led by Jane O'Grady, a young lobbyist for the Amalgamated Clothing Workers. Lawrence O'Brien directed a contingent of Justice Department lawyers and White House staffers. On occasion, O'Brien, monitoring every word and nuance in the Capitol, would ask the president to call wavering members to reinforce their support.

On February 8, the eighth day of debate, crafty old Howard Smith had one more surprise. Title VII banned discrimination by employers and labor unions on the basis of race, religion, and national origin. Smith offered an amendment forbidding discrimination based on sex — an amendment he assumed would make the bill harder to pass. When Chairman Celler shouted his opposition, Smith, feigning shock, retorted, "Oh, no!" A debate ensued between the two elderly men about the biological differences between men and women that was punctuated by laughter on the floor and in the galleries. In an odd role reversal, it became clear that the liberal Celler was opposed to equal rights for women, whereas Smith had supported an Equal Rights Amendment dating back to 1945.* A number of southern segregationists rose to support Smith and to proclaim their chivalrous concern that white, Christian, Anglo-Saxon women not be the only group left unprotected.[70]

The seriousness of what was happening on the House floor became clear after five of the House's eleven women spoke passionately for the amendment, citing examples of discrimination against women in hiring practices and in pay.[71] New York Republican Katharine St. George, hearing Celler proclaim that he did not recall that sex had ever been an issue in the civil rights bill, quipped that sex might be "just a distant memory" for the Judiciary chairman.[72] Civil rights advocates suddenly realized the political hazard of opposing Smith's amendment. Despite concern in the Johnson administration and among House leaders that Smith's amendment would sabotage the bill, it was adopted 168 to 133 with the backing of both segregationists and civil rights supporters who heard the message of their female colleagues. Labor Secretary W. Willard Wirtz, who had initially thought the amendment would sink the bill, realized that it only strengthened it. He said of Smith's gambit, "We and he were wrong. More people had sense than we thought."[73]

Smith next tried to add age discrimination to the law, citing himself (age eighty) and Celler (nearly seventy-five) as "Exhibit A" and "Exhibit B." Although many civil rights supporters were sympathetic to the amendment's aim, they argued that racial and age discrimination were different problems and required different solutions, with age meriting separate legislation.† The amendment was defeated 123 to 94.[74]

On February 10, after sixty-six hours and thirty-seven minutes of debate over nine days, the House of Representatives passed the 1964 Civil Rights Act by a vote of 290 to 130. A large majority of Democrats (152 yeas, 96 nays) and an even larger majority of Republicans (138 yeas, 32 nays) backed final passage. Civil rights advocates had defeated more than one hundred hostile amendments. A jubilant President Johnson called House leaders to praise their efforts. Next he tracked down Clarence Mitchell and Joe Rauh, who were summoned to a pay phone in a Capitol corridor.

---

* Smith's sister Lucy Smith Price had been one of the first female state legislators in West Virginia history.

† A law against age discrimination in the workplace, the Age Discrimination in Employment Act, was enacted by Congress and signed by President Johnson in 1967.

"All right, you fellows, get on over there to the Senate and get busy!" Johnson told them.[75]

Late into the night, Johnson pressed White House telephone operators to find Jake Pickle, a Texas Democrat who had won a special election to fill Johnson's old seat in the House.* Finally, at 2 A.M., Johnson reached Pickle at the Rotunda, a restaurant and bar near the House Office Building. "Jake," the president said, "I can get hold of the pope a lot quicker than I can find you." He then got to the point: "Well, I ought to have known you'd have been out somewhere trying to drown that vote, but you ought to be celebrating. As long as you live, you'll be proud of that vote. I couldn't go to sleep tonight until I had a chance to tell you as my congressman, I was proud of what you did today. . . . I don't think I would have had the courage to do it."[76]

During his twelve years in the House of Representatives, from 1937 through 1948, Lyndon Johnson had never cast a vote for civil rights. But Johnson had changed, and so, he hoped, would his native region. Ahead lay a much tougher fight in the Senate, where the southerners wielded a weapon unavailable to their colleagues in the House.

---

* Pickle was one of only seven representatives from the South — three of them from Texas — who voted for the bill. Pickle had been elected in December 1963 to fill the seat of Homer Thornberry, who had resigned to accept appointment as a federal judge.

6

✦ ✦ ✦ ✦ ✦ ✦

An Idea Whose Time Has Come

AFTER LYNDON JOHNSON had formally greeted each of the 150 ambassadors and their wives who braved a foot of snow to attend the White House's annual diplomatic reception — their first with the new president — he spotted Deputy Attorney General Nicholas Katzenbach across the crowded room. It was the day following the House's passage of the civil rights bill. While the Marine Band was playing, and with the ambassadors milling around them, Johnson pulled up two chairs (in the middle of the room) and engaged Katzenbach in intense conversation. With Panama peaceful again after a brief but deadly anti-American riot in the Canal Zone, and Vietnam not yet a burning issue, the president's attention was focused not on diplomacy but on his most urgent domestic issue.

"How are you going to get the civil rights bill through the Senate?" Johnson asked Katzenbach, the Justice Department official responsible for shepherding the legislation through Congress.

"Well, we're going to have to get cloture,"* Katzenbach volunteered, reopening a heated discussion with the president that had begun several hours earlier in the Oval Office. At that late-afternoon meeting, surrounded by White House and Justice Department officials, Johnson had

---

* In 1919 the Senate adopted Rule 22, providing that two-thirds of the Senate could, on any given bill, end its traditional unlimited debate by voting cloture. In 1975 the Senate modified Rule 22 to allow sixty senators to shut off a filibuster. America's founders had intended for the Senate to be an "impediment" against "improper acts of legislation," as Hamilton, Madison, and Jay wrote in *Federalist Paper* 62. The filibuster rule helped ensure such an impediment.

argued that the only path to victory would be to wear out the aging southern senators certain to filibuster the bill by staging grueling twenty-four-hour sessions. Justice Department lawyers, however, thought a better strategy would be to get enough votes to cut off the filibuster by invoking cloture. Now, in the midst of his diplomatic debut, Johnson was demanding that Katzenbach prove his case.

"How the hell are you going to get cloture?" Johnson demanded. "I don't think you can do that." Skeptical that they could ever win the sixty-seven votes needed to end a filibuster, he was challenging his deputy attorney general to accomplish that difficult mission. Katzenbach pulled from his jacket pocket a list of the one hundred members of the Senate. A majority, they agreed, were clearly committed to the civil rights legislation. Johnson had already spoken with many of them. But a two-thirds majority was needed to invoke cloture and end the diehard resistance already rehearsed by the men who represented the ten states of the Old Confederacy. In the previous thirty-seven years the Senate had stopped a filibuster only once, and in the body's entire history no filibuster on a civil rights issue had ever been defeated.[1] Moreover, the nineteen or twenty southern opponents would find additional support from conservative Republicans and from senators of both parties who represented small and sparsely populated western states — states that fiercely defended the filibuster as their ultimate weapon against being overwhelmed by the larger states.

In writing the Constitution in 1789, America's Founding Fathers designed a system of "checks and balances" among the three branches of government and within the legislative branch itself. The Senate would represent the "States," with each state electing two senators. The House, with membership based on population, would represent the "People." The right of unlimited debate in the Senate — the filibuster — was the last defense for states about to be overrun by the majority.

As Katzenbach and Johnson worked through the list of senators, they counted fifty-eight they thought would eventually vote to cut off a filibuster. "Where are you going to get the other nine votes?" Johnson asked.

"We're going to have to pull the votes from a group of about fourteen senators," explained Katzenbach. As he ticked off their names, Johnson shook his head in doubt. One critical group included conservative Republicans from the Midwest and West: Roman Hruska and Carl Curtis from Nebraska, Bourke Hickenlooper and Jack Miller from Iowa, Karl Mundt from South Dakota, Frank Carlson from Kansas, Milton Young from North Dakota, and Clifford Hanson from Wyoming. The conservative and cantankerous Democrat Frank Lausche of Ohio also was a concern. The others were Democrats from small western states, senators who on principle never voted against filibusters, and Democrats from border states where sympathies on civil rights were closely divided. These were Alan Bible and Howard Cannon of Nevada, Frank Moss of Utah, Carl Trumbull Hayden of Arizona, J. Howard Edmondson from Oklahoma, Ralph Yarborough from Texas, and Tennesseans Albert Gore Sr. and Herbert Walters. "Hayden's never going to vote for cloture," insisted Johnson.[2] The eighty-six-year-old president pro tempore of the Senate, a member of Congress ever since Arizona was admitted to the Union in 1912, Hayden had always been a zealous defender of the filibuster.*

Nick Katzenbach, a balding, barrel-chested man and a match in size for the president, had been skeptical about Johnson's commitment to civil rights. A former University of Chicago Law School professor, Katzenbach admired the way Johnson, as vice president, had run the President's Committee on Equal Opportunity and had spoken out for Kennedy's civil rights bill. He wondered, however, whether Johnson's stance was just a matter of loyalty to President Kennedy. He knew also that Johnson was an endlessly complex person who didn't always mean what he said or reveal his true purposes. Now that Johnson was president, Katzenbach feared that he might again become the agile compromiser of the 1957 civil rights law. Unless the Senate invoked cloture, Katzenbach believed, no legislation would be possible without major concessions to the bill's opponents. In that case, civil rights leaders, including Martin Luther King and Roy Wilkins, had served notice that they would denounce a sellout. With racial tensions high, there surely would be chaos.

Yet as he worked with Johnson during the first twelve weeks of his presidency, Katzenbach, a product of eastern prep schools and Ivy League colleges tempered by a term as a prisoner of war during World War II, began to discover that the often crude, overbearing southwestern politician held more passionate views on civil rights than his predecessor, the cerebral and cautious Jack Kennedy.[3] After Johnson again publicly emphasized his commitment to the House-passed bill, Katzenbach decided that the president would fight fiercely to crack the filibuster and win a strong civil rights law. The administration would not compromise to appease the southerners in the Senate. They would win this fight — or lose it — on

---

* Arizona's statehood had been made possible by the filibuster rule. President Theodore Roosevelt and the Republican Congress, concerned that Arizona was too Democratic, had sought to merge New Mexico and Arizona into one state. A Democratic filibuster killed this effort, and both states achieved separate statehood in 1912.

the Senate floor. Johnson agreed to concentrate on Katzenbach's list of fourteen.

From the outset, Lyndon Johnson was convinced that one man — Senator Everett Dirksen of Illinois, the Republican minority leader — held the key to victory. The Democrats needed at least twenty-five Republican votes, and Johnson knew that they could not get them without Dirksen's help. After the Democratic congressional leaders' weekly strategy breakfast at the White House on February 18 — a week after his conversation with Katzenbach — Johnson took aside Senator Hubert Humphrey, the Minnesota Democrat who would manage the legislation on the Senate floor. "The bill can't pass unless you get Ev Dirksen," Johnson told him. "You and I are going to get Ev. It's going to take time. But we're going to *get* him. You make up your mind now that you've got to spend time with Ev Dirksen. You've got to let him have a piece of the action. He's got to look good all the time. Don't let those bomb throwers now, talk you out of seeing Dirksen. You get in there to see Dirksen. You drink with Dirksen! You talk with Dirksen! You listen to Dirksen!"[4]

Humphrey, the majority whip, was the ideal leader for the Senate fight. Civil rights had been his deepest concern since 1948, when, as the young mayor of Minneapolis, he had inspired the Democratic National Convention to adopt its strongest civil rights platform to date. Humphrey and Johnson were old allies: Johnson had helped liberal "bomb thrower" Humphrey into the Senate's inner circle, while Humphrey had given the majority leader entrée to the body's liberals. With his gregarious personality, he was a perfect suitor for Everett Dirksen.

The relationship between Johnson and Dirksen reached back to the 1930s, their days in the House of Representatives, and their connection grew stronger in the Senate. They shared a love for the profession of politics — the partisan combat, the deal making, the oratory, the craft of legislation, and not least a patriotic dedication to the national interest. An old-style pro, Dirksen had started out a right-wing isolationist from rural Illinois but had gradually moderated his views. With his thatch of silver curls and a deep rumbling voice that he lubricated daily by gargling with a solution of Ponds cold cream and warm water, Dirksen was the Senate's most ambitious orator. Dirksen's voice was "like the froth on a warm pail of milk just extracted from a fat Jersey cow," wrote Brooks Atkinson, drama critic for the *New York Times*.[5] Indeed, Senator Dirksen's melodramatic efforts earned him the title "the Wizard of Ooze." But liberals who dismissed Dirksen as a failed Shakespearean actor badly underestimated him. As Lyndon Johnson well knew, Everett Dirksen was the one man who could bring together the Senate's Republicans, who were sharply divided between liberals from the East and hard-core conservatives from the Midwest and West.

At the outset of the civil rights debate, Dirksen had signaled his opposition to the two most important provisions of the proposed law: federally enforced equal access to public accommodations, and a federal ban on discrimination in employment. Like his conservative, pro-business constituents, he regarded those provisions as an invasion of individual and property rights. Dirksen reliably represented the concerns of the U.S. Chamber of Commerce and the National Association of Manufacturers.

As the Senate leader of an almost perpetual minority party,* Dirksen also was remarkably adept at — and unabashed in — seeking power wherever he could find it. On December 3, 1963, Dirksen had personally delivered a turkey to Johnson at the White House, compliments of the National Turkey Growers' Association. Along with the bird, Dirksen handed Johnson a note asking the new president to help a radio station owner from Illinois who was about to have his station's license revoked by the Federal Communications Commission.†[6]

Dirksen's appetite for political favors was boundless, and Johnson wanted Dirksen obligated to him. Two weeks later, on December 20, Dirksen telephoned Johnson to encourage the appointment of William McComber as an ambassador.

"Do *you* want him appointed ambassador?" asked Johnson.

"Well, he's a good man," replied Dirksen.

"I don't care if he's a good guy," Johnson shot back. "There are a million Johnson men that are good guys, but he's a Republican, and if we're appointing a Republican ambassador, it better be *your* Republican ambassador. Do you want this guy appointed?"

"Yeah," replied Dirksen.[7]

Johnson wanted to make certain Dirksen knew that he was keeping count of every political favor he granted, and that the Republican would be indebted to him for the McComber appointment. Dirksen often came over to the White House at day's end to sip Cutty Sark with Johnson. White House aide Jack Valenti observed that the Republican leader al-

---

* Between 1932 and 1964, the Republicans controlled the Senate for only four years and the House for only four years.

† A White House aide subsequently discussed the radio station owner's problem with FCC commissioner Kenneth Cox, who suggested a solution (LBJL, Manatos to O'Brien, 12/16/63, Office Files of Larry O'Brien, box 27).

ways arrived with "a laundry list" of favors he wanted — especially federal projects for Illinois or appointments to federal regulatory commissions, which were required by law to have commissioners from both parties. Dirksen wanted to seat at least one of his own appointees on each commission. Johnson, like Kennedy before him, granted Dirksen judicial appointments in Illinois that by custom would have come under the patronage of Paul Douglas, Illinois's Democratic senator. So long as Dirksen's candidates were qualified and could pass an FBI character check, Johnson was ready to help. In return, he wanted Dirksen's support on legislation — with civil rights at the top of the list.[8]

But Johnson knew that patronage and friendship alone would not win Dirksen's vote on civil rights. The men were partisan rivals, and Dirksen was furious when Johnson, on a 48–45 vote on February 24, defeated the Republican leader's effort to add more tax breaks for business to the tax bill. Dirksen complained afterward that his tax proposals were "victims of that new White House telephonic half Nelson known as the 'Texas Twist.'"[9] With civil rights, the wily Illinois senator would consider every element in a complex political equation: his own political standing in Illinois, his leadership role with the other thirty-two Republican senators, his devotion to the craft of legislation, and, not least, his own pride. Johnson understood that Dirksen, too, longed to be remembered as a statesmanlike "great man."*

Johnson recruited every possible ally to help win the critically needed votes of Dirksen and other Senate Republicans. "They say I'm an armtwister," the president told the NAACP's Roy Wilkins, "but I can't any more make a southerner change his spots than I can make a leopard change 'em. . . . I'm no magician." Therefore, Johnson pressed Wilkins, "unless you get twenty-five Republicans, you're not going to get cloture. . . . I think you all are going to have to sit down and persuade Dirksen that this is in the interest of the Republican Party. . . . If the Republican goes along with you on cloture, that you're going to go along with him and help him. . . . If we lose this fight, Roy, we're going back ten years."[10]

After the House passed the civil rights bill, Martin Luther King also directed his attention to the Senate. In an article in the *Nation* magazine, King wrote: "There are men in the Senate who now plan to perpetuate the injustices Bull Connor so ignobly defended. His weapons were the high-

---

* Dirksen described himself as "a legislator, not a moralist." Riding home to his farm at night in his chauffeured limousine and to the Capitol in the morning, Dirksen studied the fine print of the civil rights bill, marking changes he wanted in the legislation.

pressure hose, the club and the snarling dog; theirs is the filibuster. If America is as revolted by them as it was by Bull Connor, we shall emerge with a victory."[11] Johnson saw King as most effective in stirring grassroots support with his eloquence, but he believed Wilkins to be more effective in lobbying senators.

The intricate maneuvering on the civil rights bill began on February 17, as the House-passed bill was delivered to the Senate. Normally, the legislation would have been assigned to the Judiciary Committee, but Judiciary — under longtime chairman James Eastland of Mississippi — was known as "the graveyard" of civil rights legislation: 121 such bills had been buried there in the previous ten years alone. So at the president's urging, Majority Leader Mike Mansfield intercepted the bill instead.[12] On February 26, civil rights advocates won their first procedural victory. By a vote of 54 to 37, they succeeded in placing the civil rights bill on the Senate calendar, bypassing Eastland's committee. For the civil rights forces, it was a cautionary victory. Their fifty-four solid liberal votes were thirteen short of the number they ultimately would need to crack a filibuster.

Mansfield, a mild-mannered Montanan dedicated above all to fairness and decorum in his beloved Senate, asked his colleagues to put aside partisanship and sectionalism and to approve legislation not too different from the House-approved measure. He appealed personally to Richard Russell, leader of the southerners, to let the Senate come to a decision, but Russell made no such promise. The Georgian called the legislation "a massive assault on the constitutional system . . . a bill far more drastic than any bill ever presented even during the days of Reconstruction." Russell charged that the proposed legislation gave "such vast governmental control over free enterprise in the country so as to commence the process of socialism." Minority Leader Dirksen then expressed his opposition to a federal public accommodations law but told his colleagues he would cooperate while maintaining his independence. The debate was officially under way.[13]

Meanwhile, President Johnson maneuvered behind the scenes to break the yearlong legislative gridlock and win passage of the program he had inherited from Kennedy, as well as his own poverty program. Toward that end he improvised, taking calculated risks. He helped slip a farm subsidy bill through the Senate, with an eye on carrying midwestern farm states in the fall and winning support from conservative Republicans for civil rights. He instructed Humphrey to tell Republican Milton Young of North Dakota — a key senator in the vote for cloture — "that you don't want him fighting you [on civil rights] if you get up this wheat bill." As Johnson had wanted, the Senate took up the farm bill and quickly approved it.[14]

In the early months of Johnson's presidency, the legend of his previous achievements as majority leader contributed to an aura of political omnipotence which in itself shook the Republican opposition. After Johnson had united the Democrats and moved the stalled tax bill through Congress on February 26, Republican senators Hugh Scott of Pennsylvania and Thruston Morton of Kentucky charged that Johnson had won the votes of southern Democrats by promising to weaken the civil rights legislation. Johnson had made no such deal. At a press conference three days after the tax bill had passed, he refuted their charge and reiterated his no-compromise position on the bill. "I am in favor of it passing the Senate exactly in its present form," he stated. "So far as this administration is concerned, its position is firm and we stand on the House bill." To the consternation of the Republican opposition, Johnson seemed unbeatable both in Congress and in public opinion polls as he completed his first one hundred days in the White House.[15]

Yet Johnson's power in the Senate was finite. The president could not force Majority Leader Mansfield to adopt the tough tactics he wanted to use on the civil rights bill. Johnson kept urging Mansfield to keep the Senate in continuous session while enforcing the rule that a senator could make no more than two speeches in a legislative day on a single topic. By extending the legislative day indefinitely — never recessing — Johnson thought that his forces could wear out the eighteen hard-core southern Democratic opponents. Complaining about Mansfield's slow pace as the debate began, the president told Larry O'Brien to keep pushing the Senate leaders. "I'm for civil rights, period. Just as it passed the House, period," he told his congressional liaison. "And if that means all-night sessions, I'll stay here all night, every night, to do it myself. I've passed two [civil rights bills] and I never did it on any nine-to-four schedule."[16]

Aside from his own skepticism about the likely success of cracking a filibuster, Johnson was concerned about the rest of his program. If, indeed, it took all summer to pass civil rights, there wouldn't be time left before the August conventions and the November election for the president to win his poverty program or his medical program for the elderly.

But Mansfield, the pipe-smoking former college professor, refused to be persuaded — or bullied — by the president. Mansfield feared that a twenty-four-hour schedule might kill Carl Hayden or one of the other older senators. He thought that the same exhaustion tactic had failed Johnson himself in the 1960 civil rights fight, and he would not jeopardize the dignity of the Senate.* "This is not a circus or a sideshow," Mansfield declared. "We are not operating a pit with spectators coming into the gallery late at night to see senators of the Republic come out in bedroom slippers, without neckties, with their hair uncombed, and pajama tops sticking out of their necks."[17] When a pro–civil rights religious leader argued that Johnson and NAACP lobbyist Clarence Mitchell favored around-the-clock sessions, Mansfield snapped, "When Johnson was majority leader, he ran things the way he wanted them. Now *I* am majority leader and will run things the way *I* want them."[18]

The southerners, led by Richard Russell, realized that they faced probable defeat — unless public support for civil rights slackened in the North. So the Georgia senator played for time, hoping for a break in events that would swing voter sentiment against the bill. Russell realized that there was a growing backlash in the North against civil rights, in reaction to the increasingly militant protests of SNCC and CORE. He hoped it would gain momentum with the presidential campaigns of conservative Republican Barry Goldwater and Alabama governor George Wallace, who was challenging President Johnson in three northern Democratic primaries — and stating that his main purpose was to defeat the civil rights bill.[19] If Wallace — whose battle cry in Alabama was "Segregation now! Segregation tomorrow! Segregation forever!" — were to rack up a substantial protest vote in the Wisconsin, Indiana, and Maryland primaries, and if Goldwater were to trounce liberal governor Nelson Rockefeller of New York in the Republican primaries, then Russell hoped that conservative Republican senators might join Goldwater in opposing the bill — or at least in demanding weakening amendments as their price for supporting cloture. Russell also held out hopes that the pro–civil rights Republicans and their Democratic allies, ever suspicious of each other, would fall out, damaging their coalition. He knew that he needed only thirty-four votes to stop the civil rights bill: his solid nineteen Deep South senators and fifteen others who would refuse to vote cloture. Dividing his southern filibuster forces into three six-man teams to conserve their strength, Russell vowed that they would go down fighting "with our boots on to the last ditch."[20] A

---

* During the 1960 filibuster, exhausted senators had slept on cots in their offices. Lady Bird Johnson delivered meals to her husband, and Mrs. Paul Douglas pleaded with Senate secretary Bobby Baker that the all-night sessions were killing her husband. Johnson kept the Senate in session twenty-four hours a day for nine days before agreement was reached to consider a more limited bill. The liberals, needing to keep fifty-one senators present at all times for quorum calls, had worn out before the southerners did.

wary Hubert Humphrey did not underestimate Russell, warning his allies that "Russell runs a war of nerves. He will yell, 'Benedict Arnold,' 'traitor,' and 'lynch law!' He is like the French general who always said, 'Attack, attack, attack.'"[21]

Russell's hopes were based on more than wishful dreams. As Johnson gained popularity with northern liberals by supporting civil rights, he was losing political support in the South and among white blue-collar workers in the industrial North who felt threatened by African American gains. Two historic and contradictory political trends were gaining momentum and heading toward an inevitable collision. In the wake of President Kennedy's assassination and Johnson's masterly start as chief executive, the forces of American liberalism were winning popular support for civil rights and progressive social welfare legislation. At the same time, however, a grassroots conservative movement was beginning to take over the Republican Party, and southern opposition to civil rights was hardening into a potent political force that no longer felt at home in the Democratic Party. The resulting turmoil created a volatile political climate in which only the most agile and resourceful politicians might triumph.

The most reliable supporters of civil rights legislation were a group of forty-two to forty-five Democrats and twelve to fifteen Republicans, liberal giants such as Humphrey of Minnesota, Philip Hart of Michigan, Paul Douglas of Illinois, Jacob Javits of New York, and Clifford Case of New Jersey who had fought resolutely for years on behalf of civil rights. Their efforts had often gone unappreciated or been ignored by Presidents Eisenhower and Kennedy — and by Lyndon Johnson as Senate majority leader. Previous civil rights battles were lost in part because the liberals had lacked shrewd political leadership and organizational skill, a fact much on Lyndon Johnson's mind. In the past, Johnson had been unmerciful in his scorn for impractical liberals — especially those who disliked and opposed him.

"You have this opportunity now, Hubert, but you liberals will never deliver," Johnson scolded Humphrey. "You don't know the rules of the Senate, and you liberals will be off making speeches when they ought to be present in the Senate. I know you've got a great opportunity here, but I'm afraid it's going to fall between the boards."[22]

Humphrey agreed with Johnson's assessment of liberal weaknesses and this time took his familiar admonition to heart. As the two men parted, Johnson's tone grew gentler. "Call me whenever there's trouble or anything you want me to do," he said.[23] Later Humphrey told friends, "I knew he was goading me and I kind of enjoyed it." Like most proud men who worked with Lyndon Johnson, Humphrey could not admit that he also feared him. Humphrey had observed — and endured — the cruelty with which Johnson as majority leader had punished senators who crossed him, cutting off political largess and torturing the disfavored with his famous "silent treatment." But Johnson could also lavish generosity and rewards, and Humphrey wanted desperately for the president to choose him as his vice presidential running mate in the upcoming election. As Humphrey took on the greatest challenge of his career, the Minnesota liberal was driven by his own idealism, his ambition, and his fear of Lyndon Johnson. The president was watching him "like a hawk," Humphrey warned his legislative assistant John Stewart. "We can't let it get out of hand because he will come in and take over."*[24]

For the first time in a civil rights fight, Humphrey welded the liberal senators into a cohesive political force as disciplined as the southerners. Three teams of four senators each, soon known as "the corporal's guard," alternated duty on the Senate floor. Two-person teams were assigned to study and defend each section of the bill. Two groups of twenty-five Democrats each would take turns being instantly available to answer quorum calls, keeping the Senate in session. Without those preparations, Johnson and Humphrey feared that the liberals might again be tied into knots by the southerners' mastery of the labyrinthine rules of the Senate and by their zealous determination.

King Goes to St. Augustine

The Montgomery bus boycott of 1956, the sit-ins of 1960, the Freedom Rides of 1961, the Birmingham demonstrations of 1963, and the March on Washington later that year — these and dozens of other protests had dramatized the inequities and the violence of the segregated South, aroused the public to demand change, and convinced political leaders that the alternative to reform might be rebellion. Now that legislation was before Congress, however, the diverse civil rights organizations disagreed with one another about the continuing role of demonstrations. Roy Wilkins and Clarence Mitchell of the NAACP wanted the civil rights groups to focus on lobbying Congress, as Johnson had requested, holding demonstrations in reserve only as a threat if Congress did not act. But the SCLC, SNCC, and CORE refused to stop their direct-action demonstrations.

---

* Johnson had always driven his own staffers to the limits of their ability and endurance. As a result, many tolerated his unlikable qualities and came away from Johnson's service confident that they could accomplish more than they had ever imagined.

Day-to-day lobbying of senators was carried out primarily by the Leadership Conference on Civil Rights — particularly lobbyists from the major unions affiliated with the AFL-CIO, the NAACP, and a recently organized coalition of Protestant, Catholic, and Jewish organizations. But apart from the NAACP and its superlobbyist Clarence Mitchell, the civil rights groups played only limited roles in trying to shape the legislation and guide it through Congress. The Reverend Walter Fauntroy, appointed by Martin Luther King as the SCLC's Washington representative, felt frustrated at weekly strategy meetings of the Leadership Conference.[25] There were no senators from the nation's capital. While others busily assigned their members to lobby senators from their home states, Fauntroy lamented that he didn't have anyone to lobby.[26]

The strength of the SCLC, SNCC, and CORE was primarily manifested in the streets, not in the legislative maze of Washington. Their role was to dramatize and expose injustice, thereby building popular support for change. Civil rights protests — long confined to the segregated South — spread to the North in the spring of 1964, as blacks began protesting against de facto school segregation in New York, Chicago, Philadelphia, and other northern cities, as well as against segregated housing and employment discrimination. In Cleveland a civil rights demonstrator was accidentally killed when he and other protesters lay down in front of a tractor to block construction of a new school in a white neighborhood. A renegade CORE chapter in Brooklyn gained notoriety when it announced a "stall-in" — a plan to create gridlock on major highways leading to New York's World's Fair just as President Johnson arrived to speak there.

Publicity about the protest alienated white voters across the country. As the protests grew more strident, the congressional managers, as well as leaders of the NAACP and the Urban League, feared that further demonstrations would alienate the swing senators needed for cloture. William McCulloch, the key Republican civil rights advocate in the House of Representatives, warned Senate colleagues that he had lost the support of 25 percent of the Republican congressmen who had voted for the bill six weeks earlier. Humphrey complained to Clarence Mitchell about CORE's picketing outside Everett Dirksen's house after Dirksen had voted to send the bill to James Eastland's Judiciary Committee.[27]

Alarmed that the public's rising anger at disruptive demonstrations would cost them Senate votes, Humphrey and the Republican floor leader for the bill, Thomas Kuchel of California, issued a warning: "Civil wrongs do not bring civil rights. Civil disobedience does not bring equal protection under the law. Disorder does not bring law and order. . . . Unruly demonstrations are hurting our efforts in Congress to pass an effective civil rights bill." At the same time,[28] President Johnson declared at a press conference that violence and threats "do the civil rights cause no good." Passing the bill, he said, is "the key to bringing demonstrations from the streets and alleys into the courts where they belong."[29]

For Martin Luther King Jr., the tumult within the movement in 1964 raised difficult issues. Always skeptical when politicians called demonstrations counterproductive, King refused to join the NAACP, the National Urban League, and CORE executive director James Farmer in criticizing the Brooklyn CORE chapter's stall-in. In private, however, King criticized the World's Fair protest as a tactical mistake, and he worried that SNCC and CORE were moving away from his own nonviolent tactics, which had yielded hard-won sympathy and support for the movement in the South. Yet he was equally concerned about keeping pressure on Congress. He resented Humphrey and Kuchel for presuming to dictate movement tactics to black Americans. "Which is worse," King wrote in a letter to his fellow civil rights leaders, "a 'stall-in' at the World's Fair, or a 'stall-in' in the United States Senate? The former merely ties up the traffic of a single city. But the latter seeks to tie up the traffic of history, and endanger the psychological lives of 20 million people."[30]

No one else in the movement was as successful as King in bridging the differences between establishment leaders such as Roy Wilkins and Whitney Young, in their business suits, and the angry young militants of SNCC and CORE, in their jeans and overalls. He understood the value of both approaches and the importance of giving the appearance of unity. The only group that King avoided was the Black Muslim movement of Elijah Muhammad and his errant disciple Malcolm X. At this stage, King believed in integration and conciliation — and saw the Black Muslims' separatism as a threat to racial progress.

In the spring of 1964, King had not yet found a city in which to mount demonstrations that would both influence Congress and prove that his Gandhian nonviolent tactics were still effective. He weighed creating a voter registration campaign throughout Alabama. He considered returning to Birmingham, where city officials had already reneged on promises to desegregate. He threatened to bring protests to Washington if the Senate filibuster continued past May 1. He then considered throwing the SCLC into a national voter registration campaign and taking his first partisan stand, opposing Goldwater. Yet despite the president's words, he was not yet ready to endorse Johnson "until I see how he acts in a crisis, like Kennedy did."[31] He threatened to go on a hunger strike. "I have made the decision," he told his board at a mid-April meeting in Washington, "that if there is a determined filibuster to water down the civil rights bill, that I will engage in a fast and refuse to eat, but I have not decided how far I will go — whether unto death. But this is a decision I have not made."[32] If the civil rights bill did not pass, King said in a Detroit speech to a religious group, "I'm afraid our many pleas of nonviolence in fighting segregation will fall on deaf ears." King still steadfastly proclaimed an integrated society as his goal. He criticized heavyweight boxing champion Cassius Clay for becoming a Black Muslim and changing his name to Muhammad Ali, charging that in doing so Clay "became a champion of racial segregation, and that is what we are fighting against." Unable to decide on a course of action himself, King felt that he was floundering, losing the initiative to the more radical SNCC and CORE, and that a white backlash was gaining force. The lack of activity by the SCLC also contributed to money woes. "We're about to go out of business," King told Clarence Jones in early April. The SCLC had a payroll of $50,000 a month that it could not meet.[33]

Just as King was feeling most desperate, a black dentist from Florida appeared with precisely the venue he needed. Dr. Robert Hayling, a fiery civil rights activist from St. Augustine, Florida, appeared at the SCLC's state convention in Orlando to plead for King to help his beleaguered community. Hayling told a tale of horrors in the oldest community in America.* On the surface, St. Augustine — 23 percent of whose 14,700 residents were black — seemed a sleepy seaside town whose principal activity was catering to elderly tourists visiting the old slave market and the fountain where Ponce de León was said to have discovered the purported Fountain of Youth. But beneath the surface tranquillity, black activists confronted an unyielding city government and a hostile county sheriff aligned with a mob of Ku Klux Klan vigilantes. The Klan was terrorizing black citizens, shooting up their homes, and its members had beaten Hayling almost to death at a cross-burning rally. The city council adamantly refused even to speak with civil rights groups about desegregating restaurants and motels or hiring blacks as policemen and firemen. Of the six black families who dared to enroll their children in all-white schools, two had seen their houses firebombed and a third its car burned.[34] A local judge had ordered that student demonstrators be confined indefinitely in a juvenile detention home.[35]

Listening to Hayling's story, the Reverend C. T. Vivian, the SCLC's di-

---

* St. Augustine was founded in 1565 by the Spanish explorer Ponce de León.

rector of affiliates, decided that St. Augustine offered the ideal ingredients for a successful direct-action protest campaign: strong local black leadership, unyielding white officials, and an atmosphere of violence.[36] Seizing an opportunity both to revitalize the SCLC and to put pressure on the U.S. Senate, King and the SCLC board accepted Hayling's invitation to come to St. Augustine. The leaders decided to capitalize on the upcoming college spring break and Easter week, which would bring many visitors to the city. King hoped that the town's business community, fearful of losing Easter business and tarnishing St. Augustine's reputation on the eve of its four hundredth anniversary celebration, would capitulate to demonstrators attempting to integrate restaurants and motels. With no time left for advance planning, the SCLC improvised, recruiting students, professors, and chaplains from New England colleges to travel to St. Augustine. King himself called faculty supporters and ministers in the Boston area. To Attorney General Robert Kennedy he wrote that "400 years of local control and states' rights have not led to the betterment of relations but to a denial of basic human rights."[37]

President Johnson watched the developing demonstrations in St. Augustine warily. Just a year earlier, as vice president, he had attended a dinner in preparation for the upcoming anniversary — but only after insisting that the city desegregate the hotel dining room where the event was held. Integration, it turned out, lasted only for that night. Now, Assistant Attorney General Burke Marshall advised the president not to act on King's request for federal intervention in St. Augustine. White House aide Lee White noted hopefully that the "situation could be used in showing the need for the civil rights bill."[38]

The spring break demonstrations received an unexpected boost when it was learned that the visiting protesters from New England included three distinguished septuagenarians: Mrs. Malcolm Peabody, wife of an Episcopal bishop and mother of Massachusetts governor Endicott Peabody; Mrs. John Burgess, wife of a prominent black Episcopal bishop; and Mrs. Donald J. Campbell, wife of a retired Episcopal bishop. Arriving in St. Augustine, the women set out with a group of African Americans to integrate Tuesday morning services at Trinity Episcopal Church. They found the doors locked and their path blocked by the church's vestrymen. When one vestryman complained about "do-gooders," Mrs. Peabody replied, "That's exactly what we are — or hope we are."

The bishops' wives had traveled to St. Augustine only after promising their husbands that they would not go to jail. They stuck to their pledge for several days, even though the Reverend Hosea Williams, the SCLC leader for the St. Augustine protest, repeatedly implored them, "Ladies, you need to make your witness!" If the SCLC's Easter ploy were to influence the national civil rights debate, Williams insisted, gray-haired Mary Peabody had to go to jail. After they saw black youths being beaten, the women's resolve to accede to their husbands' requests weakened. An angry Esther Burgess was arrested on March 29 as she tried to integrate a restaurant. Upon seeing her being carried off in a police car with a German shepherd attack dog, Mary Peabody called her minister husband to announce, "I'm sorry, dear, but I must go to jail." Newspapers across the country published front-page photographs of Mrs. Peabody — mother of a governor, wife of a bishop, and grandmother of seven, wearing a muted pink suit with a necklace of pearls — being hauled off to jail by the sheriff after she attempted to have lunch at the Ponce de León Motor Lodge in an integrated group. Stunned by the black eye to his town's tourist industry, St. Augustine mayor Joseph Shelley railed against the women, calling them hypocrites from exclusive suburbs who "don't practice what they preach."[39] The bishops' wives served their purpose well, however. As Hosea Williams had well understood, the arrests of a prominent white woman received far more publicity than the arrests of two hundred young black activists. In St. Augustine itself, though, the flurry of national attention only hardened white resistance.[40]

J. Edgar Hoover's Campaign

In early March, as King prepared to campaign in St. Augustine, J. Edgar Hoover stepped up his own anti-King campaign. Hoover and his top aides were perplexed that President Johnson was continuing to receive King. Hoover had sent the president ten different FBI reports describing King's association with "Communist" Stanley Levison and detailing the minister's alleged promiscuous behavior.[41] "It is shocking indeed that King continues to increase his influence and status in government circles notwithstanding the information which the White House has concerning his communist connections" and personal conduct, an FBI official wrote Hoover on March 3. The FBI hierarchy could not fathom how Johnson could meet with "an individual so fraught with evil as King."[42]

The continuous bugging of King's hotel rooms scored what the bureau regarded as its most promising haul since the Willard Hotel eavesdropping in January. After King spent two nights in late February at the Los Angeles Hyatt House Motel, Hoover sent Deke DeLoach to the White House on March 6 with an eight-page report summarizing what purported to be the latest surveillance. It described conversations between King and his aides that were allegedly raucous, sacrilegious, and sexually explicit, including lewd remarks supposedly uttered by King as he watched a television rerun of Jacqueline Kennedy kneeling at her husband's casket.* What some listeners might dismiss as humorous, off-color conversations between friends after a few drinks, Hoover reported as shocking, hypocritical revelations that would knock the Reverend King off his lofty pedestal.[43]

Three days after he received this latest FBI "exposé" about King, Johnson summoned Hoover and DeLoach to the White House. During a leisurely two-hour lunch in the second-floor living quarters, Hoover brought up the subject of the King surveillance, but the president's immediate interests lay elsewhere. What he wanted was intelligence about Attorney General Robert Kennedy and his allies who were still in Johnson's administration. Johnson was concerned that Kennedy, his longtime adversary, was trying to implicate him in a criminal investigation of Johnson's former Senate aide Bobby Baker. The president also wanted to know what the FBI had found out about Democratic National Committee official Paul Corbin, who was promoting Kennedy as Johnson's vice presidential running mate — a prospect Johnson abhorred. The Baker investigation was soon shut down without implicating Johnson, and two days later a member of Congress friendly to the FBI made a speech in the House attacking Kennedy supporter Corbin for alleged Communist associations earlier in his life.†[44]

The relationship between the new president and the FBI director was serving the interests of both men, who shared an intense dislike of Robert Kennedy. In exchange for useful political information about Kennedy and other political foes, Johnson refrained from requiring Hoover to obey the attorney general — his nominal boss — or restraining the director's war against Martin Luther King. For the moment, Johnson apparently was not worried that a few leaked stories harmful to King might impede passage of the civil rights bill. As he discussed the FBI reports about King's alleged sex life, Johnson apparently regarded them as nothing more than amusing gossip — even entertainment.[45] At times Johnson, to his aides, called King the "sex-mad preacher."[46] But the president showed no appar-

* After having excluded Robert Kennedy from receiving other memos about King's bedroom activities, Hoover pointedly sent the attorney general the memo with King's alleged comments about his assassinated brother's widow.

† Johnson first asked the FBI to investigate Corbin in late January, at which time DeLoach informed the president of information about Corbin's alleged Communist connections, which the FBI and the House Un-American Activities Committee had once investigated. Only after Johnson pressed the issue with the FBI did the House committee renew its interest in Corbin.

ent interest in King's relationship with the alleged secret Communist Stanley Levison.[47]

Johnson kept Hoover on a long leash, not only because he feared Hoover's ability to bring down even a president with his files, but also because of his own ambivalent feelings toward King. He felt an acute sense of competition with King, as with every other major figure on the political scene. The president wanted to be recognized as a civil rights leader, and he craved recognition of his accomplishments on behalf of racial justice. He did not hesitate to remind Whitney Young and other civil rights leaders that he expected to receive credit for his efforts. As he told House Majority Leader Carl Albert, "If Martin Luther King wants to catch up with me, he is going to have to get up early and march fast!"[48]

But Johnson was taking no chances that Hoover — with his conservatism, his zeal to ferret out subversives, and his own racism — might undermine the realization of his poverty program, not to mention civil rights. As they lunched on March 9, Johnson surprised Hoover by asking for his appraisal of the final recommendations for the War on Poverty. Hoover responded enthusiastically, praising Johnson's mission to help the poor.[49] Johnson, of course, was less interested in Hoover's views on social programs than in letting the director know how important the program was to him. Hoover and DeLoach got the message.[50]

Thus unrestrained in pursuing King, Hoover fired off another set of attacks. The *Washington Post* and other newspapers printed a syndicated column by Joseph Alsop charging that King had lied to the government about his association with Jack O'Dell and with an even more important unnamed adviser "who is known to be a key figure in the covert apparatus of the Communist Party."[51] The next day, a House appropriations subcommittee made public Hoover's earlier accusations of Communist influence on the civil rights movement. The day after that, George Wallace opened his campaign in Wisconsin for the Democratic presidential nomination with an attack on the civil rights bill and an allusion to Communist Party infiltration of the civil rights movement.[52]

King had known of Hoover's antipathy toward him but naturally had been reluctant to take on the director of the FBI. Finally his anger erupted. "He makes me hot!" King told his attorney Clarence Jones in a telephone conversation carefully monitored by the FBI. "I want to hit him hard."[53] At a press conference on April 23, King denied Communist influence on the civil rights movement. "It would be encouraging to us," King said, "if Mr. Hoover and the FBI would be as diligent in apprehending those responsible for bombing churches and killing little children as they are in seeking out alleged Communist infiltration of the civil rights movement. . . . Our struggle each day is to achieve the American dream, a concept which is alien to those who espouse the cause of the Communist Party."[54]

The latest attacks came while King was in Washington meeting with two dozen black ministers to decide how the SCLC could help pass the civil rights bill. He went to Capitol Hill to discuss strategy with Senators Humphrey and Thomas Kuchel. As Humphrey explained one provision of the bill, King commented, "Mighty complicated, isn't it?"[55] King was less interested in the fine points than in getting a strong law on the books. After his meeting King told reporters that the SCLC would organize demonstrations, both in Washington and around the country, should the Senate take more than a month to debate the bill. "If there is a prolonged filibuster," he threatened, "it will be necessary to engage in a creative direct action program to dramatize the blatant injustice to Negroes." Should the Senate kill the bill, King warned, America would see a "dark night of social disruption."

As he left the Capitol, King unexpectedly encountered Malcolm X in a Senate reception room. King exchanged pleasantries and posed for photographers with the controversial Black Muslim leader. Although they had never before met in person, King was particularly sensitive to Malcolm's taunts about his "being soft" on white people and "being sort of a polished Uncle Tom." From King's viewpoint, philosophical differences aside, Malcolm's advocacy of black separatism and references to "white devils" was the worst kind of publicity for a movement desperately fighting to pass a civil rights bill. Still, in their cordial chance encounter Malcolm X joked innocently that King, too, would be investigated by the FBI if they were seen together.[56]

Calling for Prophets in Our Time

On March 26, after weeks of parliamentary shadowboxing with the southerners, Mike Mansfield, the ever-patient majority leader, finally won a procedural victory as the Senate defeated, 50 to 34, another effort to send the civil rights bill to the "graveyard" of James Eastland's Judiciary Committee. Then the Senate voted 60 to 17 — with only the southerners dissenting — to make civil rights legislation the immediate business of the Senate. After caucusing with his southern colleagues, a grim Richard Russell told reporters that "we intend to fight this bill with all the vigor at our command."[57]

"We have lost a skirmish," he said. "Now the real war will begin!"[58]

To win the "real war," the civil rights forces first needed enough support to end the threatened southern filibuster. Kuchel's assistant Steven Horn estimated that the civil rights allies were at least ten votes short — exactly where they had stood six weeks earlier. But floor leaders Humphrey and Kuchel, watching for even subtle changes in senatorial attitudes, were heartened that Republicans Roman Hruska of Nebraska and Karl Mundt of South Dakota had voted against sending the bill to Eastland's committee. The conservative Republicans would be prizes among the swing votes needed for cloture. A clue to their ultimate disposition came shortly afterward when both Hruska and Mundt complained about pressure from religious leaders. Mundt muttered to his colleagues, "I hope that satisfied those two goddamned bishops who called me last night."[59]

Hruska's and Mundt's irritation signaled the influence of an emerging new force in the civil rights battle — the armies of God — an organized coalition of churches and synagogues, rabbis, ministers, and congregants. Motivated by dramatic demonstrations and by King's powerful oratory, white church activists had quickly built a sophisticated lobbying campaign to win civil rights legislation. The National Council of Churches (NCC), the National Conference of Catholic Bishops, and various Jewish organizations established a Washington presence and nationwide networks to lobby members of Congress. The church people, working through the Leadership Conference and with Senate leaders, zeroed in on conservative Republicans from midwestern states with few African American voters.

In 1963 the NCC had created the National Commission on Religion and Race, which, with its Catholic and Jewish allies, had convened a nine-state legislative conference in Lincoln, Nebraska, followed by a series of civil rights workshops throughout the Midwest. The commission then dispatched four-member teams to every state and congressional district where members of Congress needed persuading. The effort was aided by Senate strategist Steve Horn, who supplied a list of target senators. Beside each name Horn wrote the senator's religion.[60]

Each morning the Commission on Religion and Race held a "Church Assembly on Civil Rights" at the Lutheran Church of the Reformation, just across the street from the Capitol. At 9 A.M., Monday through Saturday, for the duration of the filibuster, groups from across the country gathered in the church for an interfaith religious service led by a religious leader, usually from their hometown. The diverse clergy leaders included black and white men and women from many denominations across the country, including a Syracuse Presbyterian pastor, an Indianapolis Methodist bishop, and the SCLC's Andrew Young of Atlanta. After a sermon on civil rights issues, the visitors were instructed on how to lobby their senators to support cloture and final passage. Constituents and others were especially encouraged to lobby targeted undecided senators of the same denomination.

One visiting clergyman, Methodist bishop Newell S. Booth (a missionary to central Africa since 1930), spoke to the assembled civil rights supporters about the impact the racial problems in the United States were having abroad. As nearby Cambridge, Maryland, erupted in racial violence relating to a campaign appearance by Governor Wallace, Booth reminded his audience, "A transistor radio in the Congo village just under the equator is tuned to the Swahili broadcast from Peking" telling "of the disturbances between the races" in Cambridge. "Tomorrow they will report the big Wallace vote. And on the television screens in Kitwe, Northern Rhodesia — the police dogs rear at the students in Cambridge. Literally, the eyes of the world look into our windows; their ears are at our back doors." In the end, dozens of groups of clergymen and women from across the nation had come and made their voices heard.

The religious campaigns were effective. Whenever Roman Hruska, a Unitarian, flew home to Omaha, he would "accidentally" be greeted at the airport by an important Nebraska church leader. Those seemingly chance encounters were engineered with the complicity of Robert Kutak, Hruska's administrative assistant, who wanted his boss to support the civil rights bill. Kutak would alert Nebraska church officials whenever Hruska headed for home.[61] Senator Mundt was skillfully lobbied by Father John Cronin, a staff member of the National Conference of Catholic Bishops, who called the bishops in South Dakota. A priest who had been a high school classmate of Mundt's was asked to work on the senator.[62]

From his own bully pulpit, President Johnson preached to the churches. Reaching straight to the heart of the South's segregated society, he summoned 150 leaders of the Southern Baptist Convention — the most influential white church in the South — to the Rose Garden on March 25. There Johnson spoke proudly about his deep Southern Baptist roots: his great-grandfather George Washington Baines Sr. had been president of Baylor University, an important Southern Baptist institution, as well as minister to Texas pioneer hero Sam Houston. Then the president spoke bluntly about the power of Baptist ministers in the South. "No group of Christians has a greater responsibility in civil rights than Southern Baptists," the president said. "Your people are part of the power structure in many communities of our land. The leaders of states and cities and towns are in your congregations, and they sit there on your boards. Their attitudes are confirmed or changed by the sermons you preach and by the lessons you write and by the examples you set. . . . The cause of human rights demands prophets in our time, men of compassion and truth, unafraid of the consequences of fulfilling their faith."

Johnson confronted head-on the ministers' passivity and even their active support of segregation. "There are preachers and there are teachers of injustice and dissension and distrust at work in America this very hour," he declared. "They are attempting to thwart the realization of our highest ideals. There are those who seek to turn back the rising tide of human hope by sowing half-truths and untruths wherever they find root. There are voices calling peace, peace, peace, when there is no peace."[63]

Heartened by Johnson's bold truth-telling, Martin Luther King, in Washington at the time, immediately praised the president's "passionate and eloquent [plea] for the church to live out its ethical commitment in the field of race relations."[64]

Lyndon Johnson was now practicing what he had earlier preached to Jack Kennedy — taking the moral issue of civil rights directly to the South. Southerners may not like what you say, Johnson had advised Kennedy, but they will respect you for stating where you stand. Johnson left no doubt where he stood. In a speech at a Democratic Party dinner in Miami on February 27, the president had pledged to "press forward with legislation and with education — and, yes, with action — until we have eliminated the last barrier of intolerance."[65] Speaking before the Georgia state legislature on May 8, Johnson told lawmakers "not to heed those who would come waving the tattered and discredited banners of the past, who seek to stir old hostilities and kindle old hatreds, who preach battle between neighbors and bitterness between states." The president summoned a vision of a new South that would cast off its legacy of poverty and racism and join "the entire nation to insure that every man enjoys all the rights secured him by the American Constitution." The Georgia legislators gave the president a standing ovation.[66]

Even in Richard Russell's segregated Georgia, the assertion of moral leadership by the president and by church leaders seemed to move public opinion. In early 1964 the Georgia state senate surprisingly ratified the constitutional amendment outlawing the poll tax that long had been used to keep poor blacks from voting.* Russell described the Georgia vote as personally "humiliating." The senator was embarrassed again when his nephew, the Reverend William D. Russell of Decatur, Georgia, joined more than four hundred southern Presbyterian ministers, educators, and laymen in a petition calling for passage of the civil rights bill. "The voice of the filibuster has for too long been regarded as the most authentic

---

* In 1964 only five states — Alabama, Arkansas, Mississippi, Texas, and Virginia — still used the poll tax as a prerequisite for voting.

southern voice," the petitioners declared. "It is not. The South's most authentic voice is the voice of conscience and faith."[67] Russell attributed such aberrant views on race among Georgians to their having been brainwashed by northern propaganda. After he again introduced his favored civil rights remedy — a plan in which the federal government would spend $1.5 billion to "relocate" African Americans from the South equally among the fifty states — the Atlanta Constitution said in an editorial that the senator had exposed the South to ridicule "by callously suggesting that Negroes can be moved about like chess pawns." (Clarence Mitchell, the NAACP lobbyist, joked that he supported Russell's plan and couldn't wait to get his free airplane ticket to move from Baltimore to Hawaii.[68])

As the filibuster dragged on, the southern senators' genteel oratory and legal arguments about constitutional principles gave way to raw emotion and demagoguery. On March 24, James Eastland told the Senate that the civil rights bill "takes us back to Stalin, Khrushchev, Nasser, Hitler, and a dictatorship." To which Hubert Humphrey quickly retorted, "What is closer to Stalin and Hitler and Khrushchev is discrimination on the basis of race."[69]

Democrat Sam Ervin of North Carolina, a self-proclaimed constitutional scholar, denounced the House-passed bill as "a monstrous blueprint as full of legal tricks as a mangy hound dog is of fleas."[70]

"I'm not an anthropologist," said Richard Russell, "but I've studied history. And there is no case in history of a mongrel race preserving a civilization, much less creating one."[71] On April 20 Russell declared to the Senate, "This is mere socialism. . . . Every Socialist and Communist in this country has been supporting the proposed legislation since it was first dreamed up and submitted to Congress."[72] Senator John McClellan, the crusty Arkansas Democrat, baited Lyndon Johnson by contrasting the president's ardent support for banning employment discrimination in 1964 with his stand as a freshman Texas senator in 1949, when Johnson had proclaimed that "such a law would necessitate a system of federal police officers as we have never seen before."*[73]

*   *   *

---

* McClellan was quoting from Johnson's maiden speech in the Senate after his eighty-seven-vote "landslide" victory over Texas governor Coke Stevenson in a race in which both men had opposed civil rights. Johnson was defending the filibuster as a means to block civil rights laws, which he said allowed the federal government to usurp states' rights. After the speech, Johnson went to the Senate gallery and told Horace Busby, his legislative assistant, "That's the last time you'll hear me make that speech." It may not have been the last time, but the ambitious Johnson already realized that the politics of race would not carry him or his region very far (Author's interview [AI], Horace Busby).

While he fought to pass a strong civil rights bill in the Senate, President Johnson nimbly worked behind the scenes with the segregationist southerners, supporting their issues when he could. Just as he had pushed the farm bill through the Senate in February, the president pressed Speaker McCormack in March to line up reluctant northern urban Democrats to help win House approval. "We'll tell the northern Democrats we just finished civil rights for you," he prompted the Speaker. "Now the president wants you to stay with him on this 'cause we've got to do some little something for the farmer."[74] Next Johnson persuaded Chicago mayor Richard Daley to conscript his congressional delegation to vote for the bill. Finally, with a barrage of phone calls from the White House on the night of April 7, Johnson persuaded seven liberal House Democrats to provide the margin of victory for the farm bill. It was classic Lyndon Johnson.

Such legislative successes influenced a lot more than the price of cotton. The president again had cracked the conservative coalition in Congress, as northern and southern Democrats united on still another issue. In subtle but significant ways, Johnson also was making it easier to pass the civil rights bill. He had maintained the goodwill of his former southern colleagues, especially opposition leader Richard Russell.* Most of them accepted the political reality that Johnson would push hard for civil rights while otherwise remaining a loyal and reliable friend.

An Idea Whose Time Has Come

As the cherry blossoms along the Tidal Basin announced the arrival of spring in the capital, Hubert Humphrey dogged the footsteps of the elusive Everett Dirksen, who held the key to Republican support. For weeks Dirksen had evaded Humphrey's persistent question, "When are we going to talk about civil rights?" So on a bipartisan social cruise down the Potomac River aboard the presidential yacht *Sequoia*, Lyndon Johnson said to Dirksen, "Everett, goddammit, we've got to pass the civil rights bill. We know how many we've got — how many will we get from your side?"

"Well, that's damn difficult," replied Dirksen. "I have a hell of a problem with my side. But I think it will work out."[75]

* In the midst of the 1964 civil rights fight, Russell instructed the Democratic Senate Campaign Committee to take $25,000 designated for his campaign and give it to Hubert Humphrey. Russell told Senator Gaylord Nelson over lunch in the Senate dining room, "I did something yesterday that my people would throw me out if they knew — and so would Hubert Humphrey's people." Although he would not say so publicly, Russell told Nelson, "Humphrey is good for the institution" (AI, Gaylord Nelson).

Finally, on April 7, Dirksen made his first move, presenting his Republican colleagues a package of forty amendments that would gut the equal employment section of the legislation. "I would like to strike [equal employment] altogether," Dirksen told reporters. Another Dirksen proposal called for a year of voluntary compliance before the public accommodations provisions would become law. Liberal Senate Republicans denounced Dirksen's proposals, as did civil rights leaders. With Dirksen threatening to cripple the bill, Representative William McCulloch, the Republican civil rights floor leader in the House, walked across the Capitol to warn the Illinois senator that House Republicans would not accept his weakening the bill they had helped pass.[76]

Dirksen was playing a complex and potentially dangerous game. On the one hand, he and his conservative business constituency felt strongly that the House-passed bill permitted too much unchecked federal enforcement power. But Dirksen also was putting on a theatrical performance — for the conservative Republican senators who demanded a Republican imprint on the bill, and for President Johnson and the liberal coalition from whom Dirksen needed some semblance of concessions. In what amounted to a high-stakes game of political poker, Humphrey and Johnson surmised that Dirksen had only limited room to maneuver; the Republican leader also needed politically to achieve a respectable civil rights measure. In fact, Dirksen thought it would be disastrous for the party of Abraham Lincoln to be tarred with having blocked a civil rights bill in an election year — especially as Senator Barry Goldwater, its presumptive presidential candidate, seemed certain to oppose the legislation.

In the volatile and fragmented Senate, the outcome was very much in doubt. The danger of political posturing was risky. Heightened tensions between civil rights activists and white segregation extremists had created a tinderbox in the South, and a conflagration could spread to northern ghettoes. Based on ominous warnings from the Justice Department, Lyndon Johnson warned Russell that there was going to be "a bunch of killings" in the coming summer as hundreds of volunteer civil rights workers flooded Mississippi, where the Ku Klux Klan operated largely unrestrained.[77] If Dirksen pushed too hard and somehow succeeded too well, Martin Luther King and his allies would disown the bill.

When Dirksen formally introduced his amendments, a fight erupted behind closed doors between the civil rights organizations and Humphrey. The Johnson–Humphrey tactic of wooing Dirksen publicly had irritated liberal Democrats earlier; now that Dirksen was openly threatening the bill, the issue of how to deal with him became even more contentious.

"If we let the Dirksen amendments prevail," argued Clarence Mitchell, "it will be a disaster. There will be a Negro revolution around the country!" Mitchell worried that "the Dirksen amendments are being offered as a way out for the South. We need to let the country know that we are willing to fight to the end!"

"We don't plan on letting them pass," Humphrey replied. "Don't you break out in a sweat, Clarence."

Humphrey assured Mitchell that he could control Dirksen — he already "had talked Dirksen down from seventy amendments to fifteen." He urged Mitchell and Leadership Conference counsel Joseph Rauh not to criticize or antagonize the Republican leader. "Our theory is that Dirksen will go through his public acting process, take a licking, and then be with us," said Steve Horn, assistant to Senator Kuchel.[78]

As Justice Department officials began to meet privately with Dirksen, Clarence Mitchell grew even more suspicious. "Is our side caving in?" Mitchell asked his Senate allies at an April 16 meeting. With the filibuster in its third month, Mitchell urged Humphrey to adopt President Johnson's strategy of wearing out the southerners with around-the-clock sessions. Mitchell argued that the sergeant at arms should arrest southern senators, if necessary, to maintain a quorum and keep the Senate in session.* "I don't want to be tiresome," said Mitchell, his voice choking with emotion, "but I haven't spent twenty years here [on the Hill] for nothing. If you don't get round-the-clock sessions, our side will get tired and give up something. I don't care whether it's one leader or a combination of leaders who do it. I will rise up and object to any compromise. Who is Senator Russell that he can't be arrested when that might save lives in Mississippi!"

"Nobody won a war starving the enemy," Humphrey replied. "We must shoot them on the battlefield."

"You are shooting your friends if you trade with Dirksen," countered Mitchell.

"We don't have 65 votes for cloture," Humphrey said. "Unless we are ready to move in our clothes and our shavers and turn the Senate into a dormitory — which Mansfield won't have — we've got to do something else. The President grabbed me by the shoulder and damn near broke my arm. He said, 'I'd run the show around the clock.' I told the President he

---

* Rule VI of the Standing Rules of the Senate dictates that should a quorum ("a majority of the Senators duly chosen and sworn") not be present during a call of the roll, "a majority of those Senators present may direct the sergeant at arms to request, and, when necessary, to compel the attendance of the absent Senators." While this technically allows the sergeant at arms to arrest absent senators, the procedure has very rarely been used.

grabbed the wrong arm. . . . The President says, 'What about the pay bill? What about poverty? What about food stamps?' Clarence, we aren't going to sell out, and if we do, it will be for a hell of a price!"[79]

The next day Humphrey bristled at the constant pressure from Mitchell and the Leadership Conference on Civil Rights. "The worst thing they can do is tell me what to do," he told colleagues. "I want a bill. I think I'm smarter than they are. It's a matter of trust and confidence. You can't give people blood tests for [civil rights purity] every fifteen minutes." Yet Humphrey realized that the civil rights leaders could blow apart any agreement the moment they decided that their allies had given away the heart of the legislation: effective prohibitions against a segregated and discriminatory society.[80]

If there were any doubts about the movement's resolve, King made the point clearly when he declared on Face the Nation on May 10 that he "would rather have no bill at all" than one without provisions ending discrimination in employment and public accommodations. King criticized Justice Department officials and senators for negotiating with Dirksen on "crippling amendments" that would "emasculate the bill [so] that it will have no meaning." Those who were doing business with Dirksen, he added, were "really playing with dynamite and playing with the health of our nation."[81]

Chastened by Mitchell's criticism and King's warning, the liberal coalition and Justice Department lawyers stiffened their negotiating stance with Dirksen. In the face of stronger resistance, Dirksen abruptly decided to circumvent Humphrey and Kuchel and negotiate directly with his deal-making friend in the White House. Before meeting with the president, however, Dirksen blundered badly. First, he told reporters exactly what he planned to say to Johnson — an almost certain prescription for infuriating the secretive, keep-all-options-open president. In addition, Dirksen had joined a public chorus of dog owners who were criticizing the president for lifting his two beagles by their ears for White House photographers.

As Johnson consulted with Majority Leader Mansfield about Dirksen's visit, he expressed puzzlement over Dirksen's behavior. "He [Dirksen] gave out a long interview of what he's going to tell me today . . . which is not like him. . . . He's acting like a shit-ass. It's none of his damn business how I treat my dogs," Johnson ranted. "I'm a hell of a lot better with dogs and humans, too, than he is."[82]

Sweeping into the Oval Office at noon on April 29, Dirksen confidently declared that the southern filibuster could not be defeated unless Johnson agreed to substantial changes in the bill. If he did, Dirksen said, he could deliver twenty-five Republican votes for cloture. "Now, it's your play," said Dirksen. "What do you have to say?"[83]

Johnson was prepared. He flatly refused to negotiate, sending the disappointed minority leader back to Humphrey and Kuchel, whose hand was now strengthened. Johnson had stuck to his strategy of maintaining presidential leverage by staying above the fray — publicly committed only to passing the House-approved bill. Privately, he would keep pressure on everyone — the southerners, Dirksen, the liberal coalition, Robert Kennedy and his Justice Department lawyers, the Congress itself. When reporters asked his view of an amendment that Dirksen and Mansfield had agreed on, Johnson pleaded ignorance: "I haven't seen it. All I know is what I read in the newspapers." In fact, Kennedy had just briefed him on a compromise "jury trial amendment."* Johnson had replied, "If it's okay by you, it's fine by me."[84]

For the first seven months of 1964, President Johnson and his attorney general had worked harmoniously together on civil rights legislation and racial flare-ups in the South. Nicholas Katzenbach did most of the work on Capitol Hill, but Kennedy was very much involved. Just beneath the surface of their civility, however, lurked a powerful animosity between Johnson and Kennedy. Kennedy, for instance, believed that Johnson had assigned responsibility for the civil rights bill to the Justice Department so that he, Kennedy, would be blamed if it failed. An intense, mutual personal dislike dated from at least 1960, when Kennedy had opposed giving Johnson the vice presidential nomination. Kennedy, the flinty, ironic New Englander, was contemptuous of Johnson, with his outlandish, sometimes crude southern style — and Johnson returned the sentiment.

Now Kennedy, searching for a way to reclaim national power, badly wanted Johnson to offer him the vice presidency. Johnson had become nearly paranoid, suspecting Kennedy and his allies of plotting behind the scenes to undermine him — or even steal the presidential nomination.[85]

When the exuberant, often indiscreet Humphrey departed from Johnson's script by telling reporters that some of Dirksen's amendments might be acceptable to the White House, the president exploded: "I'm against any amendments, and I'm going to be against them right up until the moment I sign them!" He warned Humphrey that any talk of presidential compromise would be interpreted as a sign of weakness by Russell and the

---

* Southern senators and conservative Republicans were pushing hard for a provision requiring that defendants accused of violating provisions of the proposed law be guaranteed the right to a jury trial.

southerners. Two days later, Johnson was incredulous to read a *New York Times* report on how he had chewed Humphrey out for suggesting that amendments were possible.[86] Given Humphrey's liberal reputation, Johnson told him, "I think *you* can get by with repealing the goddamn [civil rights] bill." But Johnson knew that if he, a southerner, "changed a comma," he would be accused of selling out the cause. "The only bill that I am going to sign is one that you and the attorney general recommend in writing."[87]

Turning up the pressure, Johnson threatened to call Congress back into session after the Republican and Democratic nominating conventions unless the legislators quickly enacted his top-priority programs: the civil rights bill, the poverty program, medical care for the elderly, food stamps for the poor, relief for Appalachia. "The people's business must come first," Johnson told reporters gathered on the South Lawn on May 6. "And I think that the people of this country are entitled to have a vote on these important measures."[88]

Johnson's strategy was working. Dirksen started giving ground in daily negotiations with the Senate liberals and with Attorney General Kennedy. Humphrey's legislative assistant John Stewart recorded in his diary, "Dirksen is beginning to swallow the great man hook and, when it is fully digested, we will have ourselves a civil rights bill."[89]

On May 13 the negotiators — Humphrey, Kuchel, and Kennedy — finally reached a tentative agreement with Dirksen. His package of amendments limited arbitrary federal power to some degree by slightly restricting the circumstances in which the government could sue to cut off funds to state and local governments. It also gave effective state antidiscrimination laws an initial precedence over federal law. It delayed for one year the effective date of the employment discrimination provisions. It provided that persons charged with criminal contempt of court for violating the new law would be entitled to a jury trial if the penalty were more severe than a brief jail term.* And it forbade the use of school busing to correct de facto school segregation.

Emerging from the meeting to announce the agreement — which still had to be accepted by his Republican colleagues — Dirksen paraphrased Victor Hugo: "No army is stronger than an idea whose time has come." It was one of Dirksen's finest moments on the Senate stage.[90] Everett

---

* The civil rights coalition knew that the jury trial provision left a loophole in enforcement because the typical all-white southern jury in 1964 was not likely to convict a white person accused of violating the civil rights of a black person. The coalition nevertheless decided that the issue would have to be dealt with later. A 1968 law, as well as several U.S. Supreme Court decisions, subsequently eliminated the worst abuses of all-white juries.

Dirksen had created drama and mystery around his intentions through many weeks of filibuster. Mansfield ignored complaints from Democrats about his having allowed Dirksen to steal the spotlight. "Six months from now," he said, "what people will remember is that a Democratic president and Democratic Congress had passed a historic civil rights bill — or failed in that effort."[91] Lyndon Johnson's plan to overwhelm Dirksen with flattery had worked.

Humphrey called Lyndon Johnson with news of the agreement: "Mr. President, we've got a much better bill than anyone ever dreamed possible. We haven't weakened the bill one damn bit. In fact, in some places, we've improved it." Humphrey reported that the meeting had gone smoothly, except that the Leadership Conference lobbyists were griping and had not yet endorsed the agreement. Johnson urged Humphrey to stress to the Leadership Conference why winning Dirksen's and other bipartisan support was essential: "Unless we have the Republicans joining us and helping us . . . we'll have a mutiny in this goddamn country, so we've got to make this an *American* bill and not just a Democratic bill. And they [the civil rights leaders] have got to be glad that the Republicans have participated, like William McCulloch from Ohio and Dirksen, because it doesn't do any good to have a law like the Volstead Act if you can't enforce it."*

Robert Kennedy also was annoyed that the civil rights leaders hadn't yet signed off on the agreement. "They're not going to be happy," he told Johnson, "but nothing makes them happy." Then Kennedy added wistfully, "Who would have thought a year ago that this could happen?"

Johnson next called Dirksen again to warn of urban unrest "when schools let out at the end of the month if we don't have a bill" — and to praise his cooperation. "We don't want this to be a Democratic bill," the president said. "We want it to be an American bill. It is going to be worthy of the 'Land of Lincoln,' and the man from Illinois is going to pass the bill, and I'm going to see that he gets proper credit."[92]

Even without knowing the details of the agreement, Martin Luther King decided to keep the heat on. In a statement released that day, King said he was appalled by the trading away of vital sections of the bill. He accused pro–civil rights senators and the Department of Justice of "resigning themselves to the view that there can be no civil rights bill without compromise." Again King warned, "I hate to think of the dire consequences if a strong civil rights bill doesn't pass soon."

* The 1919 Volstead Act unsuccessfully attempted to enforce the Eighteenth Amendment's prohibition on alcohol.

Stirring the White Backlash

The agreement with Dirksen was crucial, but it did not guarantee victory. The southerners were not appeased; Russell compared Dirksen's amendments to putting a "plaster on a cancer" and accused him of "selling out" the once reliable coalition of southern Democrats and conservative Republicans. Dirksen's amendments made the bill even worse, Russell claimed, calling it "a punitive expedition into the South. It is clearer than ever that this bill is directed at the South and no other part of the country."*

Even with Dirksen's pledge to vote for cloture, it was uncertain how many conservative Republicans would follow him. After three months of sporadic debate, the coalition still was at least half a dozen votes short. The first votes taken on an amendment revealed confusion and weakness: it took the bipartisan coalition four separate votes to prevail, 46 to 45, on its version of the jury trial amendment. And the fallout from George Wallace's racist presidential campaign was spreading to the North.

A key element of Russell's strategy was to avoid any cloture votes until after the Democratic presidential primaries, in which the Alabama governor was challenging President Johnson on the issue of civil rights.[93] Russell was heartened — and civil rights advocates were shaken — as primary election returns came in from Wisconsin, long a bastion of liberalism. Wallace received a surprising 264,000 votes — 34 percent of the total — against Governor John Reynolds, Johnson's stand-in in the April primary. In Indiana the following week, Wallace won 170,000 votes — 30 percent of the total — against Johnson's stand-in there, Governor Matthew Welch.

Russell hoped that a Wallace victory in Maryland would persuade enough conservative Republican senators to vote with the southerners against cloture. Wallace's Maryland campaign drew fervent support from ethnic working-class neighborhoods in Baltimore, where angry whites shouted down Johnson surrogate Senator Daniel Brewster's efforts to

---

* One Dirksen amendment required the Justice Department to show "a pattern or practice of discrimination" before it could initiate a suit for violations of the public accommodations or employment discrimination sections of the bill. In the South, the pattern and practice of discrimination was obvious. In the North, individuals denied access to a restaurant or motel might have to file their own action unless they could show that the practice was widespread. The prohibition against using busing to combat de facto school segregation meant that the federal government would be restrained from pursuing school desegregation in the North unless it could prove that schools were segregated by government action and not just by neighborhood residential patterns.

speak, calling him "a race-mixing socialist."* A Wallace campaign appearance in Cambridge on Maryland's rural Eastern Shore ignited a three-day riot in which civil rights activists intent on desegregating the town battled Wallace supporters and then took on state police and National Guardsmen. Shaken by the prospect of a Wallace victory, Johnson hastily arranged last-minute financial aid for Brewster's campaign and accompanied him on a helicopter tour to review poverty problems in western Maryland's Catoctin Mountains.[94] In a telephone conversation with Hubert Humphrey, Johnson complained about Brewster's campaign — "I didn't know that boy was as dumb as he is," the president said — and suggested that Humphrey put a new spin on the southern refrain about "outsiders" coming into their states to cause trouble: Humphrey should leak a story claiming that Wallace was the real carpetbagger, with "Alabama coming into Maryland . . . stirring up the struggle and these tear gases."[95] Johnson was concerned about white backlash, but he was equally sensitive to criticism from Gloria Richardson, the black civil rights leader in Cambridge, who had declared in an interview that she "had no confidence" in the president.[96]

On primary election day, Brewster defeated Wallace 54 to 43 percent. Wallace claimed victory nonetheless: "If it hadn't been for the nigger block vote, we would have won it all," he said. "We have a majority of the white vote." Indeed, Brewster had won only because of solid support from inner-city blacks in Baltimore and equality-minded whites from the affluent Baltimore and Washington suburbs. The Maryland results underscored a sharp polarization on issues of race. Polls showed that 70 percent of Americans supported passage of the civil rights bill, yet opponents of black demands for equal rights, including thousands of working-class Democrats, threatened to become a new political force. In the words of Democratic senator Abraham Ribicoff of Connecticut, Wallace's primary votes foretold that "the next 20 years will be years of strife and turmoil in the field of civil rights, with the troubles primarily in the North." Richard Russell declared that a "groundswell" of opposition was building up as people learned what the "misnamed bill" would "do to their government and to their heritage." Russell told reporters he had warned President

---

* Johnson used stand-ins in the primaries to spare him potential embarrassment in running against Wallace. The forty-year-old Brewster, a decorated World War II marine, entered the primary at the president's request after Governor Millard Tawes refused. In Wisconsin, the popular senator Gaylord Nelson had turned down Johnson's request. "The pot of gold at the end of the rainbow was a bunch of horse turds," Nelson explained later of his unwillingness to take on the hate-mongering Wallace (AI, Gaylord Nelson).

Johnson that "he may pass this bill, but he will have more new faces in Congress in the next four to six years than any President ever had without regard to party."

The New Crusaders

As a showdown on the filibuster drew closer, the religious organizations escalated their campaign. Wave after wave of church delegations poured into Washington to lobby their senators. On April 28 an interfaith rally at Georgetown University drew 6,500 people.[97] The following day nearly two hundred ministers, rabbis, and priests gathered in the East Room of the White House to hear President Johnson exhort their efforts. "It is your job as prophets in our time," Johnson told them with evangelical fervor, "to direct the immense power of religion in shaping the conduct and the thoughts of men toward their brothers in a manner consistent with compassion and love. So help us in this hour. Help us to see and do what must be done."[98] Seminary students held continuous vigils at a site on the Mall near the Lincoln Memorial. President Johnson congratulated the vigil organizers on their initiative, writing to them that "*this particular type* of demonstration can be a constructive influence."[99]

Working closely with the White House, the Senate coalition, and the Leadership Conference, the religious leaders began to hit hard. One target was Senator Carl Curtis, a conservative Nebraska Republican. James Hamilton, deputy director of the Commission on Religion and Race's Washington office, persuaded a local Omaha businessman to enlist his minister at Omaha's First Methodist Church to ask the state's most important banker to lobby the senator. Then J. Irwin Miller, president of the National Council of Churches and chief executive of the Cummins Engine Company of Columbus, Indiana, provided Dirksen and other midwestern senators with free transportation in his corporate jet to and from their home states. Once airborne, Miller not only spoke to the senators about the moral and religious issues involved in equal rights, but also emphasized that segregation was giving the United States a black eye overseas and hurting American businesses.[100] In Iowa, businessmen joined church leaders to lobby Senator Bourke Hickenlooper, who opposed the civil rights bill's expansion of federal power. B'nai B'rith recruited all the Iowa Jewish lawyers in its membership, including one of Hickenlooper's former law partners, to lobby the senator. Hubert Humphrey prevailed on the Most Reverend James Byrne, the Catholic archbishop of Dubuque, to seek Iowa senator Jack Miller's vote.[101]

*   *   *

President Johnson, too, began to lobby other senators to help break the filibuster. At Mike Mansfield's suggestion, Johnson sent Secretary of State Dean Rusk to see Hickenlooper with instructions "to kiss his ass." If Hickenlooper would vote for cloture, three or four other midwestern Republicans might follow. But as the ranking Republican on the Foreign Relations Committee, Hickenlooper was miffed that Johnson had not appointed an ambassador he had recommended.[102]

Since a pro–civil rights vote could spell political disaster for Arkansas Democrat William Fulbright, Johnson sought only to get him out of the Senate during the filibuster vote.* Johnson urged Fulbright, chairman of the Foreign Relations Committee, to travel overseas on a presidential mission at the time of the vote. But Fulbright replied that he had a commitment to Russell to vote against cloture.[103]

With West Virginia Democrat Robert Byrd, a former member of the Ku Klux Klan, Johnson dangled appointment to the federal bench of a nominee Byrd had recommended. Byrd refused. He also turned down Johnson's entreaty that he "not fight too hard" and the suggestion that the president might send Byrd "off on a tour somewhere." But Johnson refused to be discouraged by the rebuffs. Single-minded in pursuit of victory, he likened political lobbying to propositioning women. "You get slapped a lot of times," he would say, "but then you get some 'yeses' as well."[104]

The most important target on Johnson's cloture list was Carl Hayden of Arizona, the oldest member of the Senate and a strong advocate of the filibuster. If Johnson could win Hayden's support for cloture, the two Democrats from neighboring Nevada, Howard Cannon and Alan Bible, might be brought along with him. After the president's weekly breakfast with Democratic congressional leaders on May 5, he asked Hayden to stay behind. If Hayden would consider voting for cloture, Johnson told him, he would consider approving the long-delayed Central Arizona Project, a multibillion-dollar plan to bring water to Phoenix and Tucson from California, a project Hayden had been pushing for decades. On May 11, White House congressional liaison aide Mike Manatos reported to Johnson that he had scored "a ten-strike" with Hayden. The next day Johnson and Hayden reached a secret agreement: if his vote were needed, Hayden would vote for cloture; in return, Johnson would support the water project.[105]

---

* Because cloture required approval by two-thirds of those senators "present and voting," the absence of one senator reduced the required number from sixty-seven of one hundred to sixty-six of ninety-nine.

Trapped in St. Augustine

As Senate leaders were debating when to schedule the cloture vote, in St. Augustine Martin Luther King was purposefully trying to crank up the pressure on Congress and the White House. On May 28 violence erupted. As King's lieutenants Andrew Young and Hosea Williams led a nighttime march of 400 demonstrators from St. Paul AME Church to the old slave market in the town square, they were attacked by a mob of some 250 Klansmen and other white extremists wielding chains, tire irons, and fists. As police stood by observing the melee, Klansmen beat up not only marchers but also Associated Press photographer James Kerlin and NBC television cameraman Irving Gans, smashing their cameras. Gans was taken to the hospital, his neck cut open by a bicycle chain. Shouting, "There's that nigger lover," a deputy sheriff unleashed his German shepherd on Harry Boyte, a white King aide, then pummeled him as he lay entangled in the dog's leash. Before the night ended, vigilantes fired fourteen rifle shots into King's rented house — fortunately empty at the time — at St. Augustine Beach.[106]

Hosea Williams, a former U.S. Department of Agriculture chemist in Savannah, Georgia, had initiated the night marches as a deliberate provocation to the Klan and to hard-pressed local law enforcement agencies. With violence almost certain under cover of darkness, Williams sought to draw television news coverage and force federal protection for the civil rights demonstrators. The plan was the kind of action for which King said he needed his "wild men," among them Williams and James Bevel, who were courageous, reckless, and possessed by a zeal bordering on fanaticism.[107] Williams thought a good day in St. Augustine was one that began with integrating beaches in the morning, moved on to staging restaurant sit-ins at noon, and ended with a march to the old slave market square at night. As St. Augustine became engulfed in a nightly war, the SCLC organizers tried to laugh away their fears. "We aren't going to allow the segregationists to get any sleep," joked SCLC secretary Fred Shuttlesworth.[108]

Despite their bravado, the SCLC leaders — including King — were conflicted about their venture in St. Augustine, which Andrew Young soon realized would be the most violent confrontation in the history of the movement. Young was beaten twice by Klansmen, leaving him wounded and angry. With his first blooding, he vowed not to desert the people who suffered violence and humiliation daily in St. Augustine. But he didn't want King there. "[They'll] kill all of us as they're aiming at you," he told his leader. King was torn about whether the St. Augustine action would help or hurt passage of the civil rights bill, and he was frightened by the prospect of marching at night into a mob of Klansmen. King, whom Young considered totally rational in his religious and intellectual commitment to the movement, confided to his lieutenant, "I don't mind bearing the cross, but I'll be damned if I am going to go looking for it." King felt trapped in the historic town, unable to win concessions from city and county officials. Yet he didn't know how to get out without suffering a painful public defeat.[109]

Seeking help from Washington, King wired President Johnson on May 29: "All semblance of law and order has broken down at St. Augustine . . . with raw and rampant violence even beyond much of what we have experienced in Alabama and Mississippi." King pleaded with the president "to immediately provide federal protection . . . to restrict the violent onslaught of the racist opposition."[110] Johnson worried that use of federal force would heighten the backlash against the civil rights bill and cost him southern votes in the November election. Worse, the federal government could be drawn into struggles throughout the South and be left to take over law enforcement duties as state and local authorities abdicated their responsibilities. In Johnson's worst nightmare, the rest of the nation could again be engaged in warfare with the South.

"They're giving me unshirted hell on [St. Augustine]," Johnson told Florida senator George Smathers on June 1. "They say they're shooting into King's 'white man's house.'* . . . He's demanding we go in." In a familiar southern response to charges of racist violence, Smathers told Johnson he believed the shooting into King's house was a "damn plant" carried out by the movement itself while King was out of town. "King is — naturally he loves the headlines," said Smathers, warning Johnson not to send in federal marshals or troops. "Is St. Augustine a pretty bad place?" the president probed. "No," Smathers replied. "St. Augustine is a typically rural place." What was happening, he explained confidently, was that King "was trying to squeeze St. Augustine," a segregated town, by threatening to spoil the city's anniversary celebrations, which were partially financed by federal funds that Johnson could cut off. Instead of dispatching federal troops, Johnson quietly sought assurances from Governor Farris Bryant that he would maintain order. He then directed White House aide Lee White and Assistant Attorney General Burke Marshall to try to satisfy King's complaints.[111]

King reported to Marshall that he had received death threats and that

* King was leasing a beach house from a white owner who lived in the Northeast.

the local authorities were refusing to protect him and the SCLC demonstrators. He charged that local law enforcement officers were in collusion with the Ku Klux Klan, prompting Marshall to order the FBI to investigate. While protests still raged, the FBI confirmed King's complaints, as did U.S. district judge Bryan Simpson in Jacksonville. In a court hearing, Simpson established that a large gathering of Klansmen were threatening civil rights workers and committing violent acts against the demonstrators. Their leader was Halstead "Hoss" Manucy, a hog farmer who headed a thousand-member vigilante group called the Ancient City Hunting Club. The FBI reported that Manucy was the Exalted Cyclops of the Klan in St. Augustine and that he and other Klansmen served as special deputies to St. Johns County sheriff W. O. Davis, who had bragged that he would use Klansmen to control civil rights demonstrators.[112] Earlier, Manucy had been convicted of a felony in Simpson's court.

Originally unsympathetic to the demonstrations, Judge Simpson was repelled by the police-assisted violence and by conditions at the county jail. "More than cruel and inhuman punishment is shown," he declared as he rescinded the ban on demonstrations, ordered protection for the demonstrators, and forbade such practices as confining prisoners in chicken coops and concrete sweatboxes and requiring exorbitant bonds for minor offenses. "Here is exposed in its raw ugliness, studied and cynical brutality, deliberately contrived to break men physically and mentally," he wrote in a court opinion in early June.[113]

Despite efforts by the governor and the Florida Highway Patrol to maintain order, however, the clashes continued. Officials still refused to negotiate, and the SCLC dreamed up new ways to dramatize the city's intransigence. An effort to integrate St. Augustine's Atlantic Ocean beaches provided front-page pictures showing Hoss Manucy's henchmen trying to drown several of the demonstrators, including the Reverend C. T. Vivian, the SCLC secretary. "Come on out and swim," taunted Manucy's men, standing a hundred yards out in the water. In response, Fred Shuttlesworth carefully waded in close to the shore and shouted back, "Come on in."[114]

The FBI's actions during the crisis demonstrated a very different set of priorities from those pursued by the White House, the Justice Department, and Judge Simpson. On the one hand, while the federal government was trying to pressure the state to restore order and ensure the safety of King and the demonstrators, Hoover and his agents seemed preoccupied with harassing King and anyone who expressed concern about his well-being. FBI agents conceived a scheme to give Florida lawmen a copy of a wiretapped telephone conversation in which Martin and Coretta

King had engaged in a heated argument. The bureau theorized that King, confronted with embarrassing revelations about his marital life, would retreat from St. Augustine. Florida state police, however, showed little interest in the tape.[115]

J. Edgar Hoover did not want the bureau involved in protecting the civil rights demonstrators, and he tried to derail any attempts by the government to help them. When news stories reported that the bureau would investigate violence against "King and other Negroes," an angry Hoover instructed his agents, "Be certain that we do not yield on our basic stand against doing guard duty." After Lee White at the White House promised publicly that the FBI "would keep an eye" on the violence against the demonstrators, Hoover sent a memo to his subordinates asking, "What do we know about Lee White?" The director then ordered a full file search for derogatory information about the president's top assistant for civil rights.[116] Hoover also remained addicted to purveying stories about King's alleged extramarital activities. On June 1 he sent Johnson a memorandum claiming that he had learned from Las Vegas police that King had taken a prostitute to his hotel room during a recent visit there and, according to the prostitute, had treated her roughly.[117]

The Countdown

In a Washington, D.C., hospital, California Democrat Clair Engle, a fifty-three-year-old liberal nearing the end of his first term in the Senate, was in critical condition. He had undergone surgery for a malignant brain tumor on April 24,[118] and he was not expected to recover. His chances of returning to the Senate chamber were minimal at best; without him, civil rights forces would certainly lose one vote.

As the last days of May slid by, Johnson and the civil rights coalition intensified their campaign to end the filibuster. Their tally showed them six votes short of the sixty-seven needed. On Tuesday morning, May 26, the president summoned Senator Howard Cannon of Nevada to the White House. In that sparsely settled state, the filibuster was considered an important weapon for warding off legislative threats to legalized gambling, on which Nevada depended for tourism and tax revenue. As majority leader, Johnson had given the freshman Cannon two coveted committee assignments. Now, Johnson appealed to Cannon's gratitude and to his sense of patriotism in an attempt to win his vote. In another secret lobbying effort, the president garnered the vote of J. Howard Edmondson of Oklahoma. He leaned on Humphrey and Dirksen to find more votes.[119]

On June 1, as demonstrations continued in St. Augustine, Majority

Leader Mansfield and Minority Leader Dirksen filed a petition for cloture and scheduled a vote for 10 A.M. on June 9. On June 4, Jack Miller of Iowa became the first conservative midwestern Republican to announce his intention to vote for cloture. Miller admitted that Iowa's church groups had convinced him of the need for the bill. As a former professor of law at Notre Dame, Miller had paid special attention to the pleas of Dubuque's archbishop James J. Byrne, a key leader of the Catholic Church's civil rights lobbying team.[120]

Unfortunately for the civil rights supporters, Dirksen fell ill and was hospitalized with stomach ulcers. In his absence, Bourke Hickenlooper led a Republican revolt, charging that the legislation granted "gargantuan" new powers to the attorney general. At a Republican caucus, other senators echoed Hickenlooper's complaints that Dirksen had ignored their amendments. Taken aback, Dirksen reported to his Democratic allies that he was no longer certain he could deliver the promised twenty-five Republican votes for cloture.

On June 5 Hickenlooper issued his demands: that the vote be postponed until June 10 and that the Senate grant unanimous consent for three new limiting amendments to be voted on *before* the cloture vote. The White House and Humphrey agreed. In return, they received cloture commitments from Hickenlooper, Cotton, Hruska, and Curtis.[121]

The president spent the day before the showdown alternating between last-minute efforts to win cloture and dealing with a new crisis — in Vietnam. Several days earlier, two U.S. fighter planes had been shot down over North Vietnam by artillery batteries located inside neutral Laos. The United States had just retaliated by knocking out the batteries in Laos. Johnson debated how much to tell Congress and the American public. In briefing Mike Mansfield he confided, "I don't want to give any indication we're getting involved in a war. I'm playing it down."

The president received a welcome call from Karl Mundt of South Dakota. Even though civil rights "was a very ticklish issue" in his state, Mundt said, "I'm going to vote for your doggone cloture motion. I appreciate the fact that you didn't call me up and give me the old Texas twist."

"I haven't called a human, Karl," Johnson said innocently. "I don't do that."

What Johnson and the civil rights coalition had done was to arrange for Mundt to be barraged by South Dakota churches. In fact, Clarence Mitchell of the NAACP had even enlisted Mundt's wife, Mary, as a covert ally. Mitchell would call her after Mundt left for work, find out the senator's whereabouts, and then direct prominent South Dakotans to meet him.

Early in the afternoon of June 9, Robert Kennedy called the president to tell him it looked as though they had enough votes. "It's just a miracle," Kennedy said.

"It's wonderful," Johnson replied. "Now, are you making your plans on who to call in to follow through on it for us?" He directed Kennedy and other Cabinet officials to ask influential Americans to help implement the sweeping new law swiftly and peacefully.[122]

Before the night was over, Johnson had checked in twice with Humphrey, questioning him closely about individual senators, pressing to confirm that he had the necessary sixty-seven votes. Humphrey believed that he did, but — responsive to Johnson's demand for 100 percent certainty — he stayed up most of the night to make sure.

Shortly after 10 A.M. on Wednesday, June 10, the Senate clerk began to call the roll of a hundred names. Hubert Humphrey, Everett Dirksen, now out of the hospital, and Richard Russell all sat at their desks, marking the votes as they were announced. The civil rights forces got hopeful news early in the roll call as Howard Cannon voted aye, and again as Howard Edmondson voted for cloture. Just before his name was due to be called, Clair Engle was wheeled into the Senate chamber, attended by a nurse. When his effort to speak failed, Engle slowly lifted his hand and pointed to his own eye. "Senator Engle votes aye," said the Senate clerk, prompting a standing ovation from Engle's colleagues.* When John Williams of Delaware cast the sixty-seventh vote for cloture, Humphrey raised his hands over his head in triumph.

Waiting in the wings, ready to cast his first-ever vote for cloture — if it were needed — was President Pro Tempore Carl Hayden, who finally emerged from the Democratic cloakroom and walked slowly onto the Senate floor. "It's all right, Carl," Mansfield whispered. "We've got the votes." With that, Hayden voted no.[123]

---

* Engle's act was reminiscent of a similar display at the founding of the republic. Almost two hundred years earlier, the Continental Congress had sat in Philadelphia deliberating on the question of independence. Adopting the Declaration of Independence required a unanimous vote of all thirteen colonies, and the delegation from Delaware was deadlocked. Thomas McKean supported independence, George Read opposed it, and Caesar Rodney, who supported it, was at home in Delaware, weakened by cancer. Determined that Delaware would not be the vote that blocked the declaration of freedom from England, McKean sent a messenger to retrieve Rodney, who arrived on horseback just as the vote was being taken. He broke the tie, allowing Delaware and the Continental Congress to give birth to a new nation. In 1964 Clair Engle was similarly determined to make his presence count in behalf of the cause of civil rights. Lyndon Johnson played a role in the drama. After consultation with doctors and Engle's wife, Lucretia, the president arranged to transport the cancer-stricken Engle to the Senate floor.

The final vote for cloture on the bill was 71 to 29. All one hundred senators voted, ending a seventy-five-day talkathon, the longest filibuster since the adoption of the cloture rule in 1917.

"A Good Day"

One day after the cloture vote, Martin Luther King kept the pressure on with a noontime visit to the segregated restaurant at St. Augustine's Monson Motor Lodge. Before a herd of news cameras and reporters, owner James Brock informed the visitors, "We can't serve you here. We're not integrated." King responded that he would wait there until they were.

On charges of breach of peace, conspiracy, and trespassing, King and eight allies were hauled off to the county jail. As the supporters of the civil rights bill celebrated their victory, King struggled to keep the focus on the SCLC's efforts, pleading for reinforcements. Few came. A day later King posted bail to travel to Springfield, Massachusetts, and New Haven, Connecticut, where he delivered commencement addresses at Springfield College and Yale University.[124]

The following week, the Senate voted 73 to 27 to pass the Civil Rights Act of 1964. Once again, the courageous Clair Engle was rolled in his wheelchair to the Senate floor and pointed to his eye, signifying his yes vote. Barry Goldwater of Arizona, two weeks away from becoming the Republican presidential nominee, voted no, rejecting Everett Dirksen's plea that he support the bill for the good of the Republican Party.* Goldwater replied that the civil rights bill was unconstitutional — advice he had received from a little-known Arizona lawyer named William Rehnquist and a young Yale law professor named Robert Bork. He stressed his personal opposition to segregation, but opposed the bill.[125] Three western senators who had opposed cloture — Young of North Dakota, Bible of Nevada, and Hayden of Arizona — voted for the bill. Hickenlooper, who reluctantly had supported cloture, voted no.

In the House, both Judiciary Committee chairman Emanuel Celler and ranking Republican William McCulloch announced that they would accept the Senate version of the bill. One more obstacle remained: a partisan struggle between President Johnson and House Minority Leader Charles Halleck. Johnson wanted the House to recess for only one week for each of the national political conventions, giving him more time to ram through the poverty bill and other legislation prior to the fall elections.

---

* A few days earlier, Goldwater had flown to see former president Eisenhower at his Gettysburg farm and asked for his support in his decision to oppose the bill. Goldwater was angered and disappointed when Eisenhower declined to give it to him.

Halleck wanted two weeks off for the Republican convention, a move that would also serve to slow Johnson's legislative juggernaut. Halleck offered the president a deal: if Johnson approved a two-week recess, Halleck would not hold up final passage of the civil rights bill.

"You want civil rights as much as we do," Johnson told Halleck. "I believe it's a nonpartisan bill and don't think it's a Johnson bill."

"No! No! No!" shouted Halleck. "You're going to get all the political advantage. We aren't going to get a goddamn thing."

"I should be entitled to get my program voted on," insisted Johnson. Halleck would not relent. The Republicans would get their two-week recess, and the country would get a historic new law before the Fourth of July.

On July 2 the Senate's version of the bill was passed by the House of Representatives 289 to 126. Charles Weltner, a thirty-six-year-old Democrat from Atlanta, was the only southerner to switch his vote to aye. After casting that vote, the Georgian declared, "I would urge that we at home now move on to the unfinished task of building a new South. We must not forever be bound to another lost cause."

That evening, in the crowded East Room of the White House, President Johnson hailed the 1964 Civil Rights Act as further fulfillment of the ideals of the Declaration of Independence, which "a small band of valiant men" had signed 188 years earlier. Surrounded by the men who had been instrumental in passing the new law, Johnson called on all Americans to help "eliminate the last vestiges of injustice in America." The reasons for racial discrimination, he said, "are deeply embedded in history, tradition, and the nature of man. . . . But it cannot continue. The Constitution, the principles of freedom and morality all forbid such unequal treatment. And the law I will sign tonight forbids it." Johnson then announced that he already had "directed the agencies of this government to fully discharge the new responsibilities imposed upon them by the [civil rights] law and to continue to do it without delay, and to keep me personally informed of their progress."

With seventy-five pens, President Johnson signed the bill. He handed the first pen to Everett Dirksen, the second to Hubert Humphrey, and others to Emanuel Celler and William McCulloch. He gave six pens to Robert Kennedy, recognizing the contributions of his Justice Department team. He handed pens to the leaders of the major civil rights organizations, without whose efforts there would have been no law. Martin Luther King Jr., Roy Wilkins, James Farmer, Whitney Young, and A. Philip Randolph each came forward to shake Johnson's hand and receive a pen.

As Lady Bird Johnson stepped up to congratulate him, Johnson smiled.

"Did you remember that nine years ago today, I had a heart attack?" he asked. Lady Bird laughed. "Happy anniversary," she said. From his own near brush with death, Johnson was taking the kinds of strides that he always hoped would win him the hearts — and votes — of the American public.[126]

But Lyndon Johnson never stopped to relish his victories. A few days earlier he had discussed with Lady Bird using the occasion of the bill signing to announce that he would not be a candidate for election in November. Johnson felt that he had lost his base of support in the South, and never would win the loyalty of blacks and of Democrats as a whole, whose loyalty was to Robert Kennedy. In the Oval Office after the bill-signing ceremony, Johnson met with White House aide Bill Moyers. Puzzled by the expression of gloom on Johnson's face, Moyers asked why he was not celebrating. "It is an important gain," the president replied, "but I think we just delivered the South to the Republican Party for a long time to come."[127] Johnson, who had deep feelings for his native South, fully understood the political consequences of this victory.

Over the next two days Johnson was relieved to learn that several of his old southern friends from the Senate were speaking out about the new law. He had asked them to appeal for compliance and calm. Richard Russell encouraged his Georgia constituents to obey the law "as long as it is there," as did Allen J. Ellender in Louisiana. William Fulbright of Arkansas urged "calmness, reflection."

Good news also came from St. Augustine, where restaurant and motel owners had voted overwhelmingly to obey the law and integrate. After their prolonged and bitter struggle, the black citizens of what Martin Luther King had called the most violent city in America had taken their first steps into a new society — one in which they were served by apprehensive but polite waitresses. King and his SCLC staff integrated a restaurant in Birmingham, where one nervous waitress spilled coffee at King's table and then apologized profusely.

On the evening of July 4, Attorney General Kennedy called President Johnson at his Texas ranch. Johnson had spent most of the day on his boat soaking up sunshine on Lake Lyndon Baines Johnson. Kennedy was at his desk in Washington, nervously monitoring compliance with the two-day-old public accommodations law, which King had vowed to test throughout the South. Johnson and Kennedy were fearful that Independence Day celebrations, fueled by alcohol, would add to the tensions of a radical new legal challenge to the southern way of life, producing more lethal explosions than mere Fourth of July fireworks. So Kennedy was eager to share some positive news with his boss.

"Well, listen, we had a good day!" Kennedy reported.

"Good," said the president.

"I think that the most significant thing is that the Chamber of Commerce in Jackson, Mississippi, voted last night to abide by the law," Kennedy said. "And the vote was 16 to 1."

"Good. That's wonderful!" Johnson said.

"Yeah, and then . . . Savannah, Atlanta, and all these cities went along. Birmingham, Montgomery, and a lot of the cities went along very, very well."

Johnson proudly reported that the cafés in his hometown of Johnson City were now peacefully serving black customers.

"Oh, that's good," said Kennedy. "It's been very, very good."[128]

Johnson and Kennedy soon would face other crises arising out of the racial violence in America. But for a brief moment, the two often bitter rivals could share the satisfaction of reaching a goal that both of them had worked so hard to achieve.

7

✦ ✦ ✦ ✦ ✦ ✦

Lyndon Johnson
and the Ku Klux Klan

ETERMINED BUT APPREHENSIVE, three young men drove south from Oxford, Ohio, through the early-morning darkness of Saturday, June 20, 1964, members of an advance guard bound for the civil rights wars in Mississippi. Late that afternoon they arrived in Meridian, a city of 49,000 people located in east central Mississippi, a rolling land of small farms, red clay soil, and a reputation for racial violence. On the edge of the hill country, Meridian would serve as their home base during a massive effort jointly sponsored by the nation's major civil rights organizations to help the state's African Americans obtain their rights of citizenship — rights long denied them by state and local laws, established customs, the unyielding resistance of state officials, and the terror tactics of a newly resurgent Ku Klux Klan.

Nearly seven hundred Mississippi Summer Project volunteers, mostly white students from elite northern colleges, had started the trek to Mississippi, where they would join local civil rights workers to establish and run "Freedom Schools." The volunteers would teach Mississippi blacks about their constitutional rights and then assist them in attempting to register to vote. In the summer of 1964, fewer than 5 percent of Mississippi's 500,000 adult black citizens were registered. Some who had tried to register had paid a heavy price: driven off the plantations where they lived as sharecroppers, cut off from food aid and other federal assistance, fired from their jobs, burned out of their homes and churches, beaten and jailed — and, on occasion, murdered.

The three civil rights workers slept for only a few hours. They had hurried to Mississippi from a Summer Project training session in Ohio after learning that the Mount Zion Methodist Church in Longdale, an all-black community near Philadelphia, the Neshoba County seat, had been burned to the ground four nights earlier. Several of its members had been severely beaten. After a quick breakfast in Meridian, the three men set out for the thirty-five-mile drive to the church in a 1963 blue Ford Fairlane station wagon owned by the Congress of Racial Equality.

Driving the station wagon was twenty-one-year-old James E. Chaney, a black native of Meridian and newly appointed staff member of CORE. A part-time plasterer who had attended school only through the tenth grade, "J. E." Chaney had eagerly volunteered at CORE's Meridian office the previous year, and quickly became invaluable because of his courage, his widespread contacts in the black community, and his skills as a driver and navigator of the hill country's narrow, twisting roads.

Beside Chaney sat Michael Schwerner, at twenty-four the leader of the Summer Project in the Meridian area, where he and his wife, Rita, had opened a community center for the black residents. After six months in Mississippi, Mickey Schwerner already was considered a veteran of the movement. A native of Brooklyn and graduate of Cornell University, Schwerner had started out as a social worker on New York's Lower East Side. Drawn to the civil rights movement, he had joined CORE in Mississippi, where he impressed CORE leaders as a superb organizer, able to persuade poor blacks like those in Longdale to stand up and fight for their rights. With his prominent nose, well-trimmed goatee, New York Mets baseball cap, and standard movement uniform of T-shirt and blue overalls, Schwerner had become much noticed in Meridian and the surrounding countryside. As white "foreigners," Mickey and Rita Schwerner attracted the attention not only of the black community but also of local white citizens, who bitterly resented their presence. In that close-knit white community, suspicious of all strangers — especially northerners — the Schwerners carried the multiple stigmas of being outsiders, civil rights workers, and Jews.

Twenty-year-old Andrew Goodman, a second-year anthropology student at Queens College in New York, rode in the back seat of the station wagon. Like Schwerner, Andy Goodman was white, from a New York Jewish family involved in progressive political causes. Only a week earlier he had joined the first wave of volunteers attending the Summer Project's training center on the campus of Western College for Women in Oxford, Ohio. Before leaving his home on Manhattan's cosmopolitan Upper West Side, Goodman had told his mother that he wanted to be in Mississippi "because it's the most important thing going on in the country."[1] Impressed by the young student's political awareness and composure — he had participated in CORE's protests in late spring at the New York World's Fair — Schwerner had recruited Goodman to run the Freedom School he planned to hold in the Mount Zion Methodist Church in Longdale.

Now, Schwerner anxiously hurried toward Philadelphia, Mississippi, to learn firsthand what had happened to the church and the brave congregants he so recently had befriended. Arriving at the torched church site, Schwerner and his companions found in the ashes the church bell, a few blackened hymnals, and the twisted remains of the metal roof. Nothing else was left. Nearby were several empty kerosene cans, the apparent cause of the fire. Just three weeks earlier on Memorial Day, Schwerner had spoken from the pulpit of the sixty-five-year-old church. "You have been slaves too long," he told the congregants. "We can help you help yourselves. Meet us here and we'll train you so you can qualify to vote."[2] In response, the church leadership had voted to hold a Freedom School at Mount Zion.

Leaving the church ruins, the three civil rights workers drove to the homes of church members who had been present at Mount Zion on June 16, the night of the fire. From Junior Roosevelt "Bud" Cole and his wife, Beatrice, the trio heard a tale of brutality and terror. As the Coles and eight other church leaders left their regular Tuesday night business meeting at Mount Zion, the church exit was blocked by a group of about thirty masked white men armed with rifles and pistols. With a blunt instrument, they had beaten Bud Cole unconscious, then kicked him as he lay motionless on the ground, breaking his jaw and bruising most of his body. With Beatrice on her knees praying fervently for mercy, the men suddenly departed.

When Schwerner pieced together the stories he heard from Roosevelt and Beatrice Cole and from several other church members he interviewed that Sunday, one chilling fact emerged. Cole and two other church members had been beaten because they could not answer satisfactorily a single question demanded of them by the armed white men: "Where are those white boys? Where is 'Jew Boy?'"

As Schwerner, Chaney, and Goodman pulled away from Longdale at 3 P.M., headed back toward Meridian, Schwerner realized that the church had been burned and its members attacked because of their involvement with him and his planned Freedom School. Beyond any question, the white men had come specifically looking for the man whom some of them called "Goatee" or "Jew Boy."

When Schwerner, Chaney, and Goodman failed to arrive back at their Meridian office by the scheduled time or call in to say that they would be late, emergency alarms went off throughout the network of civil rights outposts in the South. A fundamental operating procedure — one rigidly observed by the movement in Mississippi — required civil rights workers out on a mission to keep their home office informed of their every move. Too many workers had been arrested, beaten, and held incommunicado in Mississippi jails for days without the knowledge of their coworkers. When Schwerner had not contacted her by 4 P.M., Louise Hermey, a new volunteer from Drew University in her first day at the Meridian Community Center, followed the instructions Schwerner had given her that morning. She called the Mississippi Summer Project office in Jackson. By 5 P.M. Hermey and Summer Project workers in Jackson were methodically calling all their civil rights contacts, as well as every jail and hospital in a four-county area of east central Mississippi. Their concerns escalated into fear as the hours lengthened with no sign of the three men, who seemed to have vanished.

On Monday morning, June 22, Robert Moses of SNCC, director of the Mississippi Summer Project, was lecturing to the second group of volunteers at the Ohio training center when an aide interrupted him to whisper a message: the CORE office in Jackson had just learned that the three missing men had been arrested by Neshoba County deputy sheriff Cecil Price at about 3:30 P.M. the previous afternoon and released at 10 P.M. from the county jail in Philadelphia.[3]

Already desperately worried, Moses now feared the worst, knowing Neshoba County's reputation for close ties between its law enforcement officers and the Mississippi White Knights of the Ku Klux Klan. Over the objections of some of SNCC's other black staffers, Moses had argued successfully for bringing hundreds of white student volunteers to Mississippi. A dedicated pacifist and believer in nonviolence, the idealistic Moses envisioned blacks and whites working together toward a more just society. But Moses's clearly stated and overriding motive for involving northern white students in the deadly southern struggle was to produce a confrontation between federal and state authorities that could not be ignored, precipitating a crisis that finally would force the federal government to protect civil rights workers and Mississippi's black citizens who were trying to register to vote.

Moses had not minced his words. "No administration in this country is going to commit political suicide over the rights of Negroes," he had said the previous week to the first group of student volunteers, including the now missing Andy Goodman. "This is part of what we are doing . . . getting the country involved through yourselves. . . . Get pressure, continual, mounting, steady public pressure on all the agencies of the federal government. That's the only way we'll get any kind of creative solution to what's going on down here."[4] Along with David Dennis, the director for CORE in Mississippi, it was Moses who had assigned the Schwerners to Meridian, the first white workers they had dared station outside the relative safety of Jackson.

Now, Moses's grim prediction had come true. As John Lewis, the national chairman of SNCC, and other organizers arrived in Philadelphia to help search for their missing colleagues, Lewis told a press conference, "It is a shame that national concern is aroused only after two white boys are missing!"[5]

Officially the Summer Project was a joint undertaking of the Conference of Federated Organizations (COFO), the umbrella group under which CORE, SNCC, the NAACP, and the SCLC were participating in voter registration activities in Mississippi. Because SNCC had the most organizers in Mississippi, the young activists dominated the project. The SNCC organizers, mostly young southern blacks, lived on bare subsistence salaries not only in the cities but also in the rural towns and hamlets and the long stretches of red clay farmland, piney woods, and vast wetlands that dominated Mississippi's lush, beautiful landscape. In Meridian, Mickey Schwerner was attempting to carry out the SNCC organizers' overriding mission as defined by the philosophy of Robert Moses: work with poor blacks at the grass roots, seeking to empower them to fight for and win their own rights.

Like Martin Luther King Jr. facing Bull Connor's police dogs in Birmingham in 1963, Bob Moses now strove to create a highly visible confrontation that would focus the nation's attention on the unyielding brutality of segregation in Mississippi. A native of Harlem with a master's degree in philosophy from Harvard, Moses, now twenty-nine, had quit his job as a high school teacher in New York and come to Mississippi in 1961, inspired by the student sit-ins. A quiet, soft-spoken black man with a burning intensity, Moses built SNCC in Mississippi, recruiting more than a dozen talented young black activists and sending them into the field as organizers. From the outset Moses believed that the answer to injustice in Mississippi was political power — which he felt blacks could achieve if their 40 percent of the state's population were permitted to register and vote. Moses and his organizers had endured beatings, jail, and death threats, yet their unrelenting efforts had resulted in the registration of only a few new African American voters. Even worse, two black Mississippians who dared to help Moses with voter registration had been gunned down. Herbert Lee, a fifty-two-year-old farmer in Amite County, the father of nine children, was killed by a white state representative in September 1961.[6] More than two years later, Louis Allen, a logger who had witnessed the Lee shooting and whom Moses had persuaded to testify before a grand jury, also was killed. No one ever was charged in either killing, nor did the two men's deaths produce either national indignation or federal action.[*] After Allen's death, Moses became even more determined to use the Summer Project volunteers to expose the lawlessness against blacks in Mississippi. Now, with three young men missing — two of them white northerners — civil rights officials and the missing men's families began calling Washington, D.C., demanding help from members of Congress, the FBI, the Justice Department, and the White House.

At an impromptu press conference late Tuesday morning, June 23, a reporter asked President Johnson, "Do you have any information about those three kids who disappeared in Mississippi?" The president replied that he hadn't received any new information since breakfast, but that the FBI was "making every effort to locate them." Then Johnson added, "Several weeks ago I asked [the FBI] to anticipate the problems that would come from this [Mississippi Summer Project] and to send extra FBI personnel into the area. They have substantially augmented their personnel in the last few hours."[7]

In fact, no extra FBI personnel had been sent to Mississippi in earlier weeks. That possibility had been discussed between the president and the attorney general, but FBI officials had decided that none were needed. The role of the federal government in protecting civil rights workers in the South had been debated at the White House and Justice Department since the beginning of the Kennedy administration. Like John F. Kennedy before him, President Johnson saw extraordinary perils in the federal government assuming law enforcement functions that are normally the responsibility of state and local governments. Both the president and the attorney general worried that, in addition to raising difficult questions of when federal intervention is legally justified, introducing federal marshals, FBI agents, or troops could escalate into a situation akin to the occupation of the South by federal troops after the Civil War. And so President Johnson, like President Kennedy, resisted using federal law enforcers

---

[*] A state grand jury ruled that state representative E. H. Hurst had shot Lee in self-defense.

except in the extraordinary circumstances of a violation of a federal court order accompanied by a breakdown in public order, as had happened in the lethal riots over desegregation at the University of Mississippi in 1962.

Nevertheless, as the time approached for the students to head south, Robert Moses and the parents of the Mississippi Summer Project volunteers had pressed hard for federal protection. "We're asking that the federal government move before the fact," Moses declared in a June 14 wire to the president. Lee White, President Johnson's special assistant for civil rights, was stunned by the barrage of appeals from Moses and the parents of the volunteers. In a June 17 memorandum to the president White reported: "Although on the surface it is nearly incredible that those people who are voluntarily sticking their heads into the lion's mouth would ask somebody to come down and shoot the lion, we now have a request from the parents group to meet with you and their insistence on federal protection 'before a tragic incident takes place.'"[8] Johnson did not respond to the requests.

Johnson, Attorney General Kennedy, and White had not been unmindful of or unconcerned about the strong possibility of increased violence in Mississippi. Throughout the spring they had received disturbing reports of trouble brewing, especially from the Mississippi White Knights of the Ku Klux Klan. The newly organized Klan in Mississippi had grown rapidly to ten thousand members in 1964, and had dramatized its strength on April 24 with sixty-one simultaneous cross burnings across the state.[9] But Kennedy and Johnson remained perplexed about what to do. A military force was out of the question. The six hundred–man force of federal marshals was too small and not trained for such a mission. And J. Edgar Hoover, increasingly an independent power in Washington, was dead set against using his FBI agents to protect civil rights workers or even to investigate crimes against them. Twenty-four hours after the three men disappeared, however, Kennedy ordered an FBI investigation under the provisions of the Lindbergh kidnapping statute. The theoretical question of how to deal with racial violence in Mississippi was rapidly becoming a real political crisis.

Shortly after noon Lee White informed President Johnson that James Farmer, the national director of CORE, had called asking to speak with the president, as had Congressman William Fitts Ryan of New York, who called White at midnight demanding federal action. Ryan was now on his way to Washington, along with Representative Ogden Reid of New York and their constituents — the parents of Andrew Goodman and the father of Michael Schwerner. The congressmen wanted to bring the parents to see the president.

In the midst of a whirlwind morning devoted to a crisis in Cyprus and a change of American leadership in Vietnam, Johnson was irritated by White's report, perhaps because this new civil rights problem had emerged just as a huge victory was at hand. The Senate had passed the 1964 Civil Rights Act four days earlier, on June 19, and the House was expected to concur soon in the Senate's version of the bill. On the eve of this presidential triumph, the radical young organizers of SNCC and CORE, whose direct-action demonstrations Johnson opposed, had apparently precipitated a new crisis.

"I'm shoving in as much [in the way of FBI agents] as I can," Johnson told White. "I didn't ask [the civil rights volunteers] to go, and I can't control the actions of Mississippi people. The only weapon I have to find them is the FBI. . . . I can't find them myself."[10]

Trying to stay detached from the immediate political situation, Johnson then called Speaker John McCormack, asking him to reassure Congressmen Ryan and Reid that the president already was doing "everything humanly possible" to find the missing men. Johnson hoped that McCormack could help him ward off a visit from the congressmen, the Goodmans, and Schwerner.[11]

That afternoon the situation evolved rapidly. Attorney General Kennedy called the White House at 3:23 P.M. to report that he had just met with Robert and Carolyn Goodman and Nathan Schwerner. Even though the president had already made a press conference statement about the FBI search for the men, Kennedy now urged White House aide Jack Valenti to have Johnson deliver a statement on television "about his concern on this thing. It's the human element that's damn important — for everything."[12]

A few minutes later, President Johnson tried to return Kennedy's call but instead reached Deputy Attorney General Nicholas Katzenbach. "I'm afraid," Johnson said, "that if I start house-mothering each kid that's gone down there and didn't show up, that we'll have this White House filled with people every day asking for sympathy, and congressmen too, 'cause they want their pictures made and to be on TV. I don't know whether the president of the United States ought to be doing that or not."

Johnson's manner softened considerably, however, after Katzenbach speculated that Schwerner, Chaney, and Goodman had been "picked up by some of these Klan people" and probably had already been murdered.

"How old are these kids?" asked the president.

"Twenty, twenty-four, and twenty-two," replied Katzenbach.

Suddenly changing his mind about the political protocol, Johnson instructed Katzenbach to send the Goodmans and Schwerner straight to the

White House, where Lee White would see them — "and I just may drop in to his office and say a word or two to them."[13]

A few minutes later, J. Edgar Hoover called the president to report that FBI agents had just found the burning hulk of the missing men's car in a swampy area outside Philadelphia. They didn't yet know whether there were bodies inside because of the intense heat, yet Hoover was certain that the men had been killed.

"Why won't an agent be able to look at a car and see if any bones are in it?" asked Johnson, as he pressed Hoover repeatedly to find out whether the men had died in the car.

"Well, the reason for that," replied Hoover, "is that the car is so burned and charred with heat that you can't get close to it."

"You mean the car is still burning?" Johnson asked, starting a relentless cross-examination of the FBI director.[14] Two hours later, when Hoover still had no answers about whether there were bodies in the car, the president exploded, "Why in the hell can't they take a crowbar and break into the car?"[15]

In contrast to his earlier reticence, the president suddenly was totally engaged in directing a search for the bodies, for he now assumed that the men had been murdered. He was unimpressed when Senator James Eastland of Mississippi called a few minutes later to suggest that the disappearance was a hoax. The CORE office had reported the men missing "in advance" on Sunday, Eastland claimed, before they had even set out on their trip to the Longdale church. The president listened to Eastland's assurances that Governor Paul Johnson fully expected the men to turn up "claiming that someone had whipped them, when he didn't believe a word of it."

"Okay, now here's the problem, Jim," the president responded. "Hoover just called me one minute ago" with news of the burned-out car.[16]

The president learned of another problem — this one political — when he was handed a wire service story from the news ticker in his office. Earlier in the day he had agreed enthusiastically to meet privately on Wednesday afternoon with his cooperative friend Roy Wilkins and thirty members of his NAACP board of directors who, along with two thousand NAACP members, were in Washington attending the organization's annual meeting. With the news report in his hand, Johnson called Hoover at 5:35 P.M.

"Edgar," Johnson began, then started reading rapidly from the wire: "The NAACP votes to demonstrate in front of the White House tomorrow to protest the worsening civil rights situation in Mississippi. In a unanimous vote, during a special meeting of the NAACP, members voted unanimously to stage demonstrations . . . to urge stronger federal action."

"What can I tell the parents?" the president asked Hoover.[17]

Lee White ushered Robert and Carolyn Goodman and Nathan Schwerner into the Oval Office while the president was still on the telephone with Hoover. "I'm sorry to give you this news," Johnson said. Telling the parents about the burned-out hulk of their sons' car was painful. He saw the agony in their eyes. The president then called Defense Secretary Robert McNamara so he could ascertain, and his visitors could hear, that he had made navy helicopters and personnel available for the search.

Robert and Carolyn Goodman and Nathan Schwerner fought back tears as they told the president that they "were proud of their sons, and that if it had to be done over again, they would still authorize the trip to Mississippi." Ever since their college years together at Cornell, the Goodmans had been committed to causes of "progressive politics" — from the Spanish civil war against fascism to the antinuclear movement to civil rights. The Goodmans earned a good living from a family-owned heavy construction business. At their fashionable art-filled apartment on West Eighty-sixth Street they had hosted many luminaries of the political left, including the actor Zero Mostel and the novelist Howard Fast, both of whom had been blacklisted after refusing to testify before the House Un-American Activities Committee. Because Andy Goodman was following in his parents' political footsteps, they fearfully and reluctantly had given him their permission to go to Mississippi.

Devastated as they were, the Goodmans and Schwerner steeled their resolve to maintain self-control and remain true to their values. They urged the president not only to find their sons but also to provide federal protection for other civil rights workers in Mississippi. Anne Schwerner, who did not make the trip to Washington, described her son Mickey's relationship with James Chaney as that of "brothers," as she offered her prayers to his mother, Fannie Lee Chaney, a day worker in Meridian's white homes.

As the twenty-minute meeting in the Oval Office drew to a close, Lyndon Johnson took the hand of Carolyn Goodman. "Ma'am," he said, "we'll do everything we can." Goodman, whose background as a cosmopolitan New Yorker seemed worlds apart from that of this towering southwestern politician, felt that at that moment, Johnson "changed from a public figure . . . to a human being genuinely concerned about the life of my son. I could tell. There is no fooling a mother about this."[18]

For the next three hours Lyndon Johnson worked the telephones in the

Oval Office trying to contain the growing racial crisis in Mississippi, which now was being reported on national television and in front-page headlines across the country. With Justice Department officials Robert Kennedy, Nicholas Katzenbach, and Burke Marshall at his side, the president spelled out a plan to challenge the tide of terror that the Ku Klux Klan had unleashed.

Weeks earlier, Attorney General Kennedy had recommended — and the president had agreed — that the best way to counter growing Klan violence in the South was to mobilize the FBI to infiltrate and undermine the secretive hate group, just as the bureau had done so effectively in its twenty-year disruptive counterintelligence campaign against the Communist Party USA.[19] The challenge was daunting. As Johnson spoke with Kennedy and his aides, he described the great political obstacles they would have to overcome.

"There are three sovereignties involved," Johnson said. "There's the United States, and there's the state of Mississippi — and there's J. Edgar Hoover."[20]

The president would have to convince each of the "sovereignties" to assume responsibility for enforcing federal and state laws, for taking on the Klan, and for cooperating with one another. If he failed, and if the Klan's terrorism continued — burning churches and homes, assaulting and killing civil rights activists — pressure would mount for a massive federal intervention, which would be opposed by hostile state and local officials, along with many Mississippi citizens.

The Justice Department traditionally had insisted that it lacked the legal authority to combat violence against participants in civil rights activities. An assault against — or even the murder of — a civil rights worker was never considered a federal crime, except in rare instances in which prosecutors relied on the authority of an 1860s Reconstruction era law.* As narrowly interpreted by the courts, this statute made it illegal for anyone to interfere with a person attempting to exercise his or her civil rights. If state and local authorities refused to enforce state laws against violent crimes committed against civil rights activists, Johnson and Kennedy agreed, they would prosecute Klansmen, using whatever limited federal authority they had.

Another huge roadblock to effective action against the Klan was the hostility of the sovereign state of Mississippi. State and local officials from

---

* In the 1945 *Screws* decision dealing with police brutality, the Supreme Court had held that when the "color of law" is used by police, even in their "unofficial" conduct, they are as responsible as if they were acting in an official capacity.

Governor Johnson on down had defied the U.S. Supreme Court's 1954 school desegregation decision and promised similar resistance to the pending 1964 civil rights law, which was only days away from final passage. Neither the Mississippi state government nor local jurisdictions had prosecuted Klansmen for attacks against civil rights activists. In fact, a state agency, the Mississippi State Sovereignty Commission, set up to resist integration, was supplying information on civil rights workers to help state and local law enforcement officers, as well as the omnipresent White Citizens Councils.* Even more ominously, more than a few county sheriff and police departments — and even the Mississippi State Highway Patrol — had Klan members on their payrolls.

The FBI suspected almost immediately that Neshoba County sheriff Lawrence Rainey and his deputy Cecil Price were involved in whatever foul play may have befallen the three missing men after Price first arrested them Sunday afternoon. As Hoover acknowledged to the president in a telephone call on Wednesday, "That sheriff is a pretty bad fellow."[21] Yet Klansmen and local police alike felt secure from the reach of federal power.

When FBI agent John Proctor of Meridian went to question Price on Monday afternoon, the deputy casually dismissed the disappearance as "a hoax." In his uniform, wearing cowboy boots and a western hat, Price exuded confidence in his close relationship with local FBI agents. After Proctor had finished questioning him, Price popped open the trunk of his police cruiser, pulled out a fifth of confiscated bootleg whisky, and said, "Hell, John, let's have a drink."[22]

Director Hoover, the president's stubbornly independent third "sovereign" power, had adamantly refused to involve the FBI in any law enforcement efforts having to do with civil rights workers. No one in the federal government felt that it might be possible to provide advance protection, as all the civil rights organizations had demanded. But Hoover's barely disguised racism and his antagonism toward the movement went further — especially his contempt for CORE, SNCC, and the SCLC, organizations whose leaders he denigrated as "rabble rousers" and "outside agitators" and whom he accused of being under the influence of the Communist Party. Despite the level of racial violence in the state, Hoover refused to send additional FBI agents to Mississippi — the only state in which the

---

* The Sovereignty Commission, which gathered and distributed intelligence about the civil rights movement, had obtained a description and the license plate number of the CORE-owned blue station wagon, and passed this information on to state and local law enforcement agencies and the White Citizens Councils (John Dittmer, *Local People*, p. 251).

FBI did not maintain even a central office. FBI resident agents scattered around the state spent entire careers in a single town, working out of their own homes or a small office in a federal building and reporting to FBI offices in New Orleans and Memphis.

What most infuriated civil rights leaders was the studied detachment of FBI agents amidst the racial turmoil in the Deep South. Following Hoover's orders, agents customarily stood by passively taking notes while white mobs viciously beat nonviolent demonstrators. And their FBI reports very seldom led to any filing of charges.

As the president began to make a rapid succession of telephone calls Tuesday afternoon, he maneuvered Governor Johnson and FBI director Hoover into accepting responsibility for enforcing whatever laws were available to stop the Klan. In approaching the Mississippi governor, the president acted as warily as he would have in dealing with the leader of a hostile foreign power. Having seen how President Kennedy's trust was betrayed by former governor Ross Barnett during the University of Mississippi integration crisis in 1962, the president first cautiously tested the Mississippi political temperature, using Senator James Eastland as his thermometer.

"Jim, we got three kids missing down there," Johnson said. "What can I do about it?"

The president discussed various options, including sending an impartial observer to Mississippi. When Eastland casually volunteered that it wouldn't do any harm for him to call the governor to pass along the president's concerns, Johnson seized the opening. "You just do that," the president said. "And I'll say I've communicated with the proper people."[23]

Twenty-five minutes later Eastland called back to report on his conversation. "The governor said for you to send some *impartial* guy down here and that you'll get the surprise of your life. . . . There's just nothing, no violence, no friction of any kind."[24]

"Well, much obliged," replied the president.

With Kennedy and his aides as his audience, Johnson suggested Allen Dulles, former head of the CIA under President Eisenhower, as the ideal "impartial observer" to send to archconservative, patriotic Mississippi. Dulles's credentials as an acceptable envoy, Johnson suggested, would be his reputation as a highly respected and conservative Republican leader of the Cold War. Furthermore, Johnson thought that Dulles would be the perfect foil to force Hoover into action, since Dulles had been a bitter bureaucratic rival who in 1953 had won the CIA job that Hoover coveted.[25]

"We got the ox in the ditch and we need help," President Johnson began after he reached Allen Dulles on the telephone at 7:05 P.M. Governor Johnson had requested the dispatch to Mississippi of an impartial observer, the president said, and he wanted Dulles to take the assignment.

After Dulles raised doubts about whether he was the best person for the job, Attorney General Kennedy came on the line. "I think this could be awfully important," said Kennedy. "The situation is explosive in Mississippi — very little contact for the last few years between federal and local authorities. The governor said he'd accept this. It would give us some breathing room."

Sweeping aside Dulles's further objections that he was "no expert in the field" and was already busy working on the Warren Commission investigation of the assassination of President Kennedy, Johnson said, "I'll get you assistance. [Tom] Finney would be good.* I'll talk to the governor and give you a ring and we can get together in the morning."[26]

Even before they asked Dulles to go on the mission, Johnson and Kennedy knew exactly what they planned for their impartial observer to recommend to the White House: a massive increase in the FBI's presence in Mississippi. With the Dulles arrangement in place, the president called Governor Johnson to tell him that the observer he had requested earlier in the day through Senator Eastland would be Allen Dulles, who would fly to Mississippi the very next afternoon. Even though the governor still insisted that the disappearance was a hoax, he pledged to cooperate in the search, and agreed with the president that they needed to work together in what promised to be "a long summer." As the governor complained about his problems in trying to cope with civil rights demonstrators "with long police records that are professional agitators," the president expressed understanding.

"They're picketing us tomorrow," said Lyndon Johnson.†[27]

Before leaving the Oval Office Tuesday night, the president made two more calls — updating Robert and Carolyn Goodman and Nathan Schwerner on developments since their meeting. He assured them that more FBI agents were flying into Mississippi that night and that the governor had promised to help.

In the space of a few hours, Lyndon Johnson had moved from distracted avoidance to total commitment to coping with a major chapter of

---

* Johnson and Attorney General Kennedy already had decided to send attorney Tom Finney, a former CIA agent and law partner of White House adviser Clark Clifford, along with Dulles. Finney would provide background to Dulles on the situation and see that the president's wishes were carried out.

† Johnson was referring to the NAACP demonstration.

the civil rights crisis. It was classic Johnson — reacting quickly to events in order to seize an issue and then exerting his strong-willed leadership to find a solution. At 11 P.M. the president finally responded to Lady Bird's pleas that he join her for dinner upstairs in the family dining room.

The next day, Wednesday, June 24, before Dulles had departed for Mississippi, Hoover predictably objected to the arrangement, relaying his displeasure through his aide Deke DeLoach, who spoke with presidential aide Walter Jenkins. Johnson immediately called Hoover.

"Walter told me that Deke was upset . . . that Dulles was supposed to go down there and be an FBI inspector," said the president. "That's the furthest thing from my mind. . . . Now, I feel like if the governor asked me to send an impartial observer, and I didn't send it, I'd be in bad shape later on if I had to do something."

"Certainly would," said Hoover.

"I haven't got a better friend in the government than you," said Johnson soothingly. "Ain't nobody gonna take our thirty-year friendship and mess it up one bit. . . . God bless you."[28]

Traveling with the prestige of Air Force One, Dulles flew into Jackson, the Mississippi state capital, late Wednesday afternoon, accompanied by undercover White House representative Tom Finney and by Burke Marshall, assistant attorney general for civil rights. Marshall remained incognito aboard the airplane, where he could serve as a private adviser to Dulles yet not stand out as a federal symbol of integration to Mississippi's diehard segregationists.[29]

In a twenty-four-hour stay in Jackson, Dulles fulfilled his diplomatic mission perfectly, listening to all sides, publicly proclaiming cooperation between Governor Johnson and the federal government, pretending that his visit had nothing to do with the missing civil rights workers. The only interruption to the smoothly scripted trip came when Rita Schwerner confronted Dulles, who tried to beg off, claiming he was late for an appointment. "I want to offer you my deepest sympathy," Dulles said. "I don't want sympathy," replied Schwerner. "I want my husband back."[30]

By Friday morning, June 26, Dulles was back in the Oval Office, where administration officials helped him quickly draft a brief summary report. That done, the president put his emissary on the telephone to sell his recommendations to both Governor Johnson and J. Edgar Hoover.*

---

* By the day after Dulles's visit, Governor Johnson had resumed his jovial mood of denial, saying that the missing activists probably would show up in Fidel Castro's Communist Cuba. In a joint appearance with Alabama governor George Wallace, as they pledged their defiance against integration, Paul Johnson joked with reporters about the missing men. "Governor Wallace and I are the only two people who know where they are," Governor Johnson said, "and we're not telling" (Seth Cagin and Philip Dray, *We Are Not Afraid*, p. 356).

With the president, Deputy Attorney General Katzenbach, and attorney Tom Finney at his elbow, Dulles called the Mississippi governor. Point one, Dulles told him, was for the president and governor to work together "to control and punish terroristic activities, particularly activities of clandestine groups in the state." Point two was "to see if security could be improved by beefing up the [FBI] staff" in Mississippi. Point three — suggested earlier by the governor — was for Dulles to urge National Council of Churches officials to warn students of the dangers of the Mississippi Summer Project, in hopes of discouraging them from going.*

President Johnson then picked up the phone to explain to the governor how Dulles's suggested actions would well serve his and his state's interests. The presence of more FBI agents working with state authorities in Mississippi would help the president to resist the pressure of lawyers "telling me . . . I got to have marshals and troops [in Mississippi]. I want to show 'em we're going to have a state-federal relationship like we have."[31]

As soon as he finished speaking with the governor, Johnson called Hoover to tell the FBI chief that he wanted Dulles to go over his recommendations with him before Dulles announced them at a press conference and "you read about 'em [in the newspapers]."

"I realize it's difficult for you," Dulles began, "but you ought to review the number of agents you have in that state. They're not really going to enforce this business unless they have someone looking over their shoulder, and I think you're the only fellow who can do it."

Hoover replied that it would be an "almost superhuman task" to prevent violence against "a thousand of these youngsters going down there . . . living in the homes of the colored population." To prevent more volunteers from being killed, Hoover said, "you almost have got to keep an agent with them as they come into the state, because the Klan crowd, members of the Mississippi Highway Patrol — some of those are Klansmen, a number of the chiefs of police and the sheriffs are, and therefore you can't count upon local people to really extend any protection."

Despite Hoover's bleak assessment of the scale of the problem, Dulles told him that "if you [the FBI] have a few more people down there, it is going to make a tremendous difference."

Realizing that the decision to send in more federal officers had already been made, Hoover switched to arguing that U.S. marshals would be

---

* Dulles had close connections with leaders of the National Council of Churches, which had just played a major role in lobbying in favor of the 1964 Civil Rights Act. The NCC had been a major financial participant in the Mississippi Summer Project, funding the Ohio training program and assigning a number of NCC staff members to work in Mississippi over the summer.

more suitable than FBI agents. "U.S. marshals are a symbol of authority," said Hoover, "and at the same time, they don't have to conduct any investigative work, which we have to do." Demonstrating the FBI's willingness to provide a new "deterrent" against the Klan, Hoover noted that his agents were ready to arrest some "hoodlums" who, the previous day in Itta Bena (which Hoover called "Teeny Weenie"), had briefly kidnapped two summer volunteers, telling them, "If you don't get out of town, the same thing's gonna happen to you that happened up in Philadelphia."

At this point, President Johnson picked up the telephone to assure Hoover that the Justice Department would give him the authority to bring charges against perpetrators of the mini-kidnapping in Itta Bena. Then Johnson settled the matter of marshals versus FBI agents. "Edgar," said Johnson, "what he is saying there in substance is we want to avoid the marshals thing and the troops thing. I rather think we ought to send more of your people in. Maybe we can prevent acts of terror by the very presence of your people. . . . I'd rather you sent another fifteen people or twenty people."*

Johnson ended the call by describing what the White House would announce: "We'll say we've asked for additional men and you're going to send them."

"Yes, that's right," replied Hoover.[32]

In successive conversations with Hoover over the next six days, Johnson kept increasing the number of agents he wanted assigned to Mississippi. Finally, on July 2, Johnson called Hoover to put the finishing touches on his plan to fight the Ku Klux Klan in Mississippi and throughout the South. Despite his own reservations, Hoover agreed with the president's request that he would go to Jackson the following week and personally open a major new FBI state headquarters there, one that would have nearly two hundred agents assigned by the end of the summer. Then, describing the FBI's newly expanded mission, Johnson said, "I think you ought to put five thousand people after this Klan and study this from one county to another. . . . You ought to have the best intelligence system, better than you've got on the Communists. I read a dozen of your reports last night till one o'clock, and they can't open their mouths without your knowing what they're saying."

Unless they could stop the Klan in Mississippi, the president warned

---

* Listening to the conversation in the Oval Office along with Allen Dulles and Nicholas Katzenbach, attorney Tom Finney signaled to the president how many more agents he should request from Hoover by up holding up his hands and flexing his fingers to indicate twenty (AI, David Busby).

Hoover, the violent hate group would spread throughout the eleven southern states, gathering the kind of power it had exerted in the 1920s, "when they were electing senators in Texas." Ever proud that both his grandfather and father, as members of the Texas state legislature, had fought against the Klan, Lyndon Johnson now seized the opportunity to follow in their footsteps.

As always, Johnson handled Hoover with flattery — telling him, "No one in the country has the respect you do" — and with suggestions rather than direct orders. Flattery and gentle persuasion were important elements of the "Johnson treatment," but in Hoover's case, Johnson considered them the safest methods of winning cooperation from a man who had the capacity to destroy any politician. Observing Johnson's maneuvers with Hoover, Governor Johnson, and others over that ten-day period, Robert Kennedy, Nicholas Katzenbach, and Burke Marshall were fascinated. Yes, they agreed, he was a master wheeler-dealer, a manipulator, a sleight-of-hand artist who operated by indirection and who shaded the truth. To their astonishment, however, he had achieved the desired results, which earlier had seemed impossible.[33]

Hoover was not averse to fighting the Klan. He considered the Klansmen "a group of sadistic, vicious white trash" who had no respect for the law.[34] He simply did not want to assist the civil rights activists, whom he disliked equally. In an act worthy of an absurdist play, Hoover had agreed to launch a counterintelligence campaign to undermine the Klan at the same time that he was pressing a similar effort to destroy the character and political effectiveness of the nation's most prominent civil rights leader.

The new pledge of cooperation between the United States and Mississippi governments and Hoover's reluctant commitment on the part of the FBI to deal with racial turmoil in Mississippi bore immediate results. Inspector Maynard King of the Mississippi Highway Patrol handed FBI agent John Proctor a list of the names of seven men he suspected of being involved in the disappearance of Schwerner, Chaney, and Goodman. To Proctor's surprise, the names of Sheriff Rainey and Deputy Price were on the list.[35] While in Jackson to open the new FBI office, Hoover gave Governor Johnson the names of Klan members who worked for the Mississippi Highway Patrol, and Johnson promptly fired them. The Hoover trip — President Johnson's shrewd dispatch of the federal official most respected and liked in Mississippi — accomplished its purpose. As one source told a *New York Times* reporter, "For all the talk of magnolias, an awful lot of federal feet got in the door." The newly empowered and greatly expanded FBI team in Mississippi immediately arrested and filed charges against two groups of Klansmen — those who had tried to kidnap the two summer volunteers in Itta Bena and three others who had beaten Silas McGee, a young black Mississippian, after he had successfully integrated a movie theater in Greenwood.

But even with the FBI involved, the tide had by no means turned against either the Klan or resistance to integration in the South. While restaurants and motels had peacefully integrated in many southern cities, defiance was struck in others, including Atlanta, where restaurateur Lester Maddox wielded an ax handle as he turned away black customers from his Pickrick Restaurant. Maddox became the defendant in one of the Justice Department's first actions as the 1964 Civil Rights Act became effective on July 2.* On July 11, U.S. Army lieutenant colonel Lemuel Penn was killed in a random Klan attack as he drove through Georgia on his way home from summer reserve training with two other black reserve officers. J. Edgar Hoover got news of the bushwhacking as he flew back from opening the new FBI headquarters in Jackson. After another flurry of calls from the president, Hoover's agents quickly identified five prime suspects, all Klan members, but struggled to bring charges against them, given the lack of cooperation of state and local law enforcement officials.

The stark realities of the situation remained grim for civil rights activists in Mississippi. As federal and state lawmen dragged rivers and lakes looking for the bodies of Goodman, Chaney, and Schwerner, they found instead the bodies of three other civil rights participants. The bodies of Charles Moore and Henry Dee, both nineteen and activists at Alcorn A&M, a black college, were found in the Pearl River.† The headless body of another black youth, his legs tied together, was recovered in the Old River near Natchez. Freedom House, headquarters for the summer volunteers in Macomb, was dynamited.[36]

On Friday, June 26, five days after Schwerner, Chaney, and Goodman had disappeared, Robert Moses solemnly told the second group of trainees in Ohio that "the kids are dead." He gravely acknowledged that his effort to engage the federal government by bringing middle-class white youths to Mississippi had contributed to the deaths of three young men. Nevertheless, beyond any question, it was the disappearance of Schwerner

---

* With the notoriety he gained in his resistance to the new law, Maddox was elected governor of Georgia in 1966.

† FBI agents later arrested two Klansmen who admitted kidnapping Moore and Dee in Meadville, beating them to death, and dumping their bodies in the river, weighted down with an automobile motor block. State officials declined to prosecute them.

and Goodman — the white northerners — that created the national stir which propelled the president into action.

"There may be more deaths," Moses told the volunteers. "I justify myself because I'm taking risks myself, and I'm not asking people to do things that I'm unwilling to do. And the other thing is, people were being killed already, the Negroes of Mississippi, and I feel responsible for their deaths. Herbert Lee killed. Louis Allen killed. Five others killed this year. In some way, you have to come to grips with that, know what it means. If you are going to do anything about it, other people are going to be killed," Moses reflected. "The way some people characterize this project is that it is an attempt to get some people killed so the federal government will move into Mississippi. And the way some of us feel about it is that in our country we have some real evil, and the attempt to do something about it, involves enormous effort — and therefore tremendous risks."[37]

Summoning Dr. King

The next stage of Robert Moses's strategy for the 1964 Mississippi Summer Project required Martin Luther King Jr. to share "the tremendous risk" of challenging the "closed society" of Mississippi. On July 10 Moses urged King to come to Mississippi to help promote the recently created Mississippi Freedom Democratic Party (MFDP), which planned to challenge the state's "lily white" delegation at the 1964 Democratic National Convention in Atlantic City. With voter registration efforts so discouragingly unproductive, Moses and his allies in the Conference of Federated Organizations had decided to dramatize the constitutional denial of black voting rights by organizing a separate election system — parallel to the existing one, so entrenched in segregation. In their first effort, the Freedom Vote Campaign for governor in 1963, COFO had set up its own polling places in black churches, businesses, and community centers. Despite two hundred instances of violent harassment by Klansmen and trumped-up arrests by white officials, 83,000 black citizens and a few sympathetic whites cast their unofficial votes for governor. Their candidate was Aaron Henry, an African American Clarksdale pharmacist and Mississippi president of the NAACP. His running mate for lieutenant governor was the Reverend Edwin King, the white chaplain at Tougaloo, a predominantly black college outside Jackson. In the official election, Paul Johnson, then lieutenant governor and a perennial candidate, was elected governor. The COFO campaign, however, had stimulated black political participation throughout the state.[38]

In midsummer 1964, with the grievous cost of voter registration efforts mounting — six killed, five hundred beaten or arrested, thirty-five churches burned — Moses decided to switch the emphasis of the Summer Project from voter registration to selecting delegates from the newly created Freedom Democratic Party for the national convention in August. Paralleling the regular Democratic Party procedure, the MFDP planned to hold caucuses at the precinct, county, and state levels to select delegates. To publicize and add credibility to this campaign, Moses believed Dr. King's help was essential.

The urgent request from Moses provoked a strenuous debate between King and his lieutenants, already in disagreement about where the SCLC should launch its next campaign. In early July, the SCLC was still mired in St. Augustine, where unyielding city officials refused to reach an agreement with King, and "Hoss" Manucy's Klansmen still terrorized local blacks who dared to participate in the SCLC's night marches to the old slave market downtown or the "swim-ins" at segregated beaches. When the new civil rights law went into effect on July 3, many St. Augustine motels and restaurants briefly integrated, then backed off quickly when Klansmen picketed and threatened them.

As King searched for a face-saving agreement to get out of St. Augustine, his aides debated the options of continuing the Florida campaign, as Hosea Williams wanted, or opening a voter registration campaign in Alabama, as Jim Bevel strongly urged. At a July 16 meeting in St. Augustine, King and his staff weighed those choices and another contentious issue: the plea for King to come to Mississippi to help the embryonic Freedom Democratic Party effort. The SCLC had stimulated little activity in Mississippi, and King had not been in the state since the funeral of assassinated NAACP leader Medgar Evers more than a year earlier. Some of King's aides strongly opposed allowing him to become an assassination target in a state already awash in the blood of civil rights workers. Others, including SCLC executive director Andrew Young, argued that King must answer the summons of the embattled COFO workers, especially with the national spotlight focused on Mississippi. Already dreading the risks of the trip, King walked out of the meeting. An hour later, though, he returned — and agreed that he could not avoid Mississippi. He told John Gibson, the SCLC assistant program director, "I want to live a normal life." But the assembled staff members insisted, "'You have no normal life. You are not an ordinary man.'" At that moment, Gibson thought, King "gave himself to the movement as he never had before that."[39]

On the morning of July 21, as King prepared to leave for Mississippi, his aides made a final plea that he cancel the trip. Assistant Attorney General Burke Marshall had warned King the previous day about credible reports of plans to assassinate him. To dissuade King, his aides sought the help of Harold DeWolf, King's principal professor at Boston University, who was visiting the King family in Atlanta. "It's just suicidal for you to go there at the present time," pleaded DeWolf. "You must let some people who are not so clearly labeled for destruction carry the load." King was unwavering, and DeWolf watched with concern and awe as his friend calmly read Bible stories to his four young children at breakfast, then matter-of-factly told Coretta what to do "if I don't come back." He wanted her to know precisely what his plans were, so that she could advise "the movement" during the transition to a new leader.[40]

As King headed for the Atlanta airport, Attorney General Kennedy urgently called President Johnson at the White House at 12:35 P.M. to express concern for King's safety that afternoon when he would arrive in Greenwood, a bastion of violent Klan activity in the Mississippi Delta. Moreover, Kennedy reported that the Mississippi Highway Patrol had refused the suggestion of Justice Department officials that it provide protection to King as he traveled by car through the state.

"It's a ticklish problem," said Kennedy, "because if he gets killed — uh — it creates all kinds of problems — not just being dead, but also all kinds of other problems."

"Can we have FBI people down there, and have them keep their eyes and ears open and preceding him and following him?" suggested the president.

Kennedy agreed with Johnson's plan for FBI protection, then — in embarrassment — asked that the president himself give Hoover the orders, since Kennedy's office "had no dealings with the FBI anymore." Kennedy also said he understood that Hoover now was sending the president reports "about me plotting and planning things." After Johnson feigned ignorance that Hoover was regularly bypassing the attorney general or submitting to the Oval Office intelligence reports about Kennedy's political ambitions, Kennedy added with wry sarcasm, "Well, I had understood that they send reports over about me plotting the overthrow of the government by force and violence, leading a coup."[41]

Given that they were political rivals — Kennedy was now trying to impose himself on an unwilling Johnson as his vice presidential running mate — the two men nevertheless worked with surprising cooperation in their efforts to pass the civil rights bill, to contain the Klan, and to implement the new Civil Rights Act peacefully and effectively. Neither permitted his dislike for the other to interfere with a shared commitment to the civil rights effort.

Seconds after his conversation with Kennedy, the president phoned

Hoover to tell him, "We got another problem that you ought to give some thought to. Martin Luther King is going to speak tonight in [Greenwood]."

"I understand," replied Hoover. "And there are threats they're going to kill him."

"I think it would be the better part of wisdom and national interest that [the FBI] work out some arrangements where somebody's in front of him and behind him when he goes over there," said Johnson. "It's a hell of a lot easier to watch a situation like that before it happens . . . so we don't find another burning car." Johnson stressed that even if Mississippi authorities refused to cooperate with the FBI, "you don't want to be looking for bodies after the fact."

"I'll take care of that," said Hoover.

In his conversation with the president, the FBI director agreed to take on two assignments that he earlier had avoided and abhorred: having the FBI provide protection to King, and involving the FBI in law enforcement efforts that would help civil rights activists. In 1963 Hoover had even ordered the FBI not to notify King about death threats against him. Now he was simultaneously pursuing three diverse agendas: a new mission to restrict and punish Klan violence, a continuing effort in frequent memos to the president to smear King as an immoral, Communist-influenced leader, and an ongoing counterintelligence campaign to destroy King's public credibility. In the spring, Hoover blocked King from receiving honorary degrees from Marquette University and Springfield College by having FBI officials give the institutions derogatory information about him. Hoover also routinely sent the president whatever defamatory material the FBI possessed on others involved with civil rights activities in which Johnson was interested. For instance, he sent the president FBI reports claiming that both Michael Schwerner's and Andrew Goodman's parents had been Communist Party members in 1944, as was the lawyer representing the Schwerners in the disappearance of their son. He even informed the president that the now missing — and presumed murdered — Michael Schwerner had recently subscribed to *Freedomways*, a magazine that Hoover claimed was financed by the Communist Party.

While Hoover held a deeply bigoted personal animus toward King, President Johnson now was developing highly conflicted views of his own about the civil rights leader. From the outset of his presidency, Johnson had worked with King, recognizing his importance as a political leader who could help achieve their common goal of racial equality. At the same time, Johnson realized, as had Kennedy, that his association with King produced a reflexive backlash from conservative white voters. Also, as a traditional politician, Johnson strongly disliked the tactics used by King and other movement activists, who continued to demonstrate in the streets of Birmingham and St. Augustine to achieve their aims rather than lobbying Congress like Roy Wilkins of the NAACP. Now, after eight months as president, Johnson was growing even more cautious in dealing with King.

Two days after Johnson and King were photographed shaking hands at the historic signing of the Civil Rights Act, the president unmercifully berated White House press secretary George Reedy for having suggested at a press briefing that "the president had been in continuous touch with (King)." In a telephone call on July 4, Johnson shouted at Reedy, "I haven't been in touch with him at all. . . . You know his record!"[42] As Johnson read Hoover's continuous stream of memos defaming King and recognized Hoover's eagerness to discredit him, the president grew even more worried about the political repercussions if those reports were made public. Over a period of time, Hoover's reports had colored the thinking of Johnson and some White House aides — even those who discounted the relevance or accuracy of Hoover's information.

Yet the president wasn't about to stand by — as Hoover apparently was — while someone tried to assassinate the nation's best-known and most revered civil rights leader. In fact, he reemphasized to Hoover several times the importance of providing adequate FBI protection for King. When King's plane arrived in Jackson, he was greeted by an entourage of FBI agents, who accompanied him on the drive to Greenwood.

With the agents surrounding him, Martin Luther King walked through the black neighborhood of Greenwood that Tuesday afternoon, gathering a crowd along the way as he poked his head into the Van Pool Room and the Red Rooster juke joint, then spoke to the onlookers while standing on a wooden bench in front of the Savoy Café. "Every Negro has worth and dignity," King told them. "Mississippi has treated the Negro as if he is a thing, instead of a person. Above all things, they have denied us the right to vote. We have got to show the world we are determined to be free."[43]

The following night in Jackson, speaking to one thousand people at the Elks Lodge, King called on President Johnson to send federal marshals to Mississippi to protect the rights of blacks to register and vote. While he spoke, a small plane circled overhead, dropping leaflets warning that the Klan would take charge of law and order if local authorities were incapable of handling "outside interference" by the "Rt. Rev. Inciter King" and his agitators. The leaflets were signed "The White Knights of the Ku Klux Klan of Mississippi."[44]

Meanwhile, on the Senate floor, James Eastland charged that there was "a Communist conspiracy to further or participate in the invasion of Mississippi." He reeled off a list of alleged Communist agitators in his state — utilizing the identical information that Hoover had supplied in his daily reports to President Johnson. Responding to Eastland the next day King declared, "There are as many Communists in this movement as there are Eskimos in Florida."[45]

As King and his SCLC staff made their way on Friday morning through the small towns and byways of Mississippi on their way through the hill country for their dreaded visit to Philadelphia, they fought back fear — as they often did — with kidding and rollicking down-home humor. At a little country store with a single gas pump, King bought a two-gallon jar of pig's feet for his hungry entourage of Southern Baptist black ministers, then jokingly chided Andrew Young for being too much a New Orleans sophisticate to join in the feast. As at other moments of extraordinary danger, King sustained his companions with both prayer and biting satiric humor about their eccentricities and vanities, to relax them and get them through their ordeal. On this trip they were also amused — and relieved — at the unexpected protective detail of FBI men who hovered about them.[46]

Arriving in Philadelphia, King visited the ruins of the Mount Zion Methodist Church, then met with farmer Bud Cole, who had been beaten unconscious by the Klansmen before they had burned the church five weeks earlier. While expressing sorrow for the parishioners' suffering, King rejoiced that they had lost their church "because [they] took a stand." In the black community center in Philadelphia atop a hill of red gravel, King played — and lost — a game of eight ball with teenager Robert Hudson, then stood on a bench to say, "Three young men came here to help set you free. . . . I know what you have suffered in this state — lynching and murders. But things are going to get better. Walk together, children, don't you get weary."[47] King struck his most responsive chord when he addressed the fear that had seized the community with foreboding that the three missing men had already been murdered. "But if we are going to be free as a people, we've got to shed ourselves of fear," King said, "and we've got to say to those who opposed us with violence that you can't stop us by burning a church. You can't stop us by shooting at us. You can't stop us by brutalizing us, because we're going to keep on keeping on until we're free."[48] King and his SCLC group got through their five-day Mississippi trip without incident.

Riots, Backlash, and the War on Poverty

With the political attention of the nation focused on racial injustice and conflict in the South, it came as a surprise to both Lyndon Johnson and Martin Luther King Jr. when Harlem exploded in a race riot on July 18, followed quickly by other racial disturbances in Rochester, Newark, and Jersey City. The politics of race had suddenly become an even more complex and acute national issue. Black northerners raised issues not readily addressed in the new civil rights law: police brutality, de facto school segregation, and joblessness in overcrowded urban ghettoes. And white anger against the northern black rioters also intensified a political backlash against politicians who supported the civil rights cause.

The precipitating event in New York City was an altercation on the city's Upper East Side on June 26, when a white apartment building engineer cursed at and then sprayed his cleaning hose on a group of rambunctious black teenagers from Harlem who were taking remedial summer classes in this affluent Manhattan neighborhood. After the teenagers retaliated by tossing bottles and trash can lids, an off-duty police lieutenant came on the scene. He shot and killed one of the students, fifteen-year-old James Powell. Within twenty-four hours, peaceful black demonstrations against the shooting erupted into a riot in the streets of Harlem and Bedford-Stuyvesant. Black neighborhoods experienced looting, arson, and shootings. By the time order was restored three days later, fifteen people had been shot and two hundred arrested. A dozen police officers and more than one hundred citizens were injured.[49]

Defensive New York authorities, supported by J. Edgar Hoover, quickly blamed the riot on Communist agitators, a view also conjectured by President Johnson, who was bewildered that the black population should riot only days after passage of the Civil Rights Act.* Protecting his political flank, the president sent the FBI to check on the situation in New York, as he had just done to investigate Klan terror in Mississippi and Georgia. With the 1964 election less than four months away, the president refocused his political energy on winning approval of poverty legislation — which he knew would help poor blacks in Harlem as well as in Mississippi. He implored black leaders to declare a moratorium on demonstrations, hoping that this would reduce the inflammatory rhetoric and the

---

* In October 1964 the FBI report on the riots failed to find evidence that Communists or any other single cause had precipitated the riots. A common denominator was that each riot had been preceded by an incident involving police officers and black citizens.

clashes that were leading resentful whites to support newly nominated Republican presidential candidate Barry Goldwater.

At the Republican National Convention at the Cow Palace in San Francisco in mid-July, Goldwater easily trounced two moderate governors, Nelson Rockefeller of New York and last-minute candidate William Scranton of Pennsylvania. Even more significant politically, a tough new breed of radical conservatives from across the country — including the Deep South — captured control of the party. The new GOP leaders ran roughshod over Rockefeller, liberals and moderates, and the very few black delegates, thereby shattering the long-held civil rights tradition of the party of Abraham Lincoln.

As the riots were quickly brought to an end, President Johnson quickly regained his political equilibrium. Although he believed Hoover's contentions about Communist agitation, Johnson realized that the roots of unrest in northern ghettoes, as in southern towns, were discrimination and deep, grinding poverty. While sternly admonishing those who took the law into their own hands, the president called for action against the problems of discrimination and poverty in the inner city. National concern over urban unrest gave the president another motivation to push his War on Poverty legislation — his unique contribution to the Kennedy–Johnson administration.

The 1964 economic opportunity bill exemplified Lyndon Johnson's belief in the power of education and training, and his philosophy of offering a "hand up, not a handout." The new law would focus on education and job training for underprivileged children and youths, with programs such as Head Start, the Job Corps, the Neighborhood Youth Corps, Volunteers in Service to America (which would be a kind of domestic Peace Corps), and Community Action (in which local agencies would coordinate resources and include representatives of the poor in program governance).

After the relatively smooth Senate approval of the "poverty bill" in mid-July, Johnson faced almost solid Republican opposition in the House, as well as strong resistance from conservative southern Democrats, many of whom feared that the poverty programs would be perceived by their white constituents as another boon for the black population. House Republican leader Charles Halleck was determined to defeat the president, who had rolled over him with an imposing string of legislative victories. With the Republican and southern Democratic alliance now revitalized, Johnson knew that he faced an uphill battle.

Again wielding his skills at legislation and persuasion, the president worked the phones. First, he demanded that Minority Leader Halleck support his effort to force the poverty bill out of the ironclad grip of Howard Smith, the Rules Committee chairman. "You ought not hold up my poverty bill," Johnson told Halleck. "That's a good bill and there's no reason you ought to keep a majority from voting on it. If you can beat it, go on and beat it, but you ought to give me a fair shake."⁵⁰ It took Johnson five weeks, but he finally embarrassed the Republicans into allowing the bill to reach the House floor.

With the House showdown fast approaching, Johnson called George Meany, president of the AFL-CIO, to ask for the help of his labor federation. "We're within a hair's breadth of being able to put 150,000 young men to work in the next ninety days," said Johnson, "but it looks like we're going to get beat by five to ten votes unless we can get some liberal Republicans." Meany promised to get right to work.⁵¹

In a similar appeal to Walter Reuther, president of the United Automobile Workers union, Johnson pleaded that his presidency — and all the social legislation favored by Reuther — was on the line. "They're going to beat our poverty bill, and we can stand that, we can survive it. But one thing we can't survive is just getting beat this time of the year, because it's like Roosevelt's Supreme Court. They're going to say 'the king's dead.'"* He continued, "'If Johnson can't pass a little $900 million poverty bill, he damn sure can't pass anything else. And that's what's bad. . . . It's going to de-nut him.' . . . This is just going to lose me my leadership in the House to Charlie Halleck." From the New York congressional delegation, Johnson asked Reuther to get him the votes of liberal Republicans John Lindsay and Ogden Reid and conservative Democrat Otis Pike. Finally, invoking the recent racial violence in New York City, Johnson said, "Tell these folks that if there's a place in the world that needs this poverty allocation . . . they need it bad in New York."⁵² He promised aid to New York within ten days after the bill passed.

Johnson then called reluctant Democratic House members to make a similar pitch. His rhetoric was loaded with hyperbole about looming political disaster, but his arguments were backed by the political coin of the realm — rewards for cooperation and collection of IOUs already owed to him. In talking to George Mahon, a fellow Texas Democrat, Johnson pleaded that this was the first piece of legislation of his own he'd offered as president. "If the headlines say . . . forty Democrats joined Halleck to defeat it," he predicted, "I think it will hurt every bill I recommend."⁵³ He invoked earlier favors in reminding North Carolina Democrat Harold

---

* President Franklin Roosevelt lost momentum for his New Deal social legislation after his plan to pack the U.S. Supreme Court was defeated by Congress in 1937.

Cooley that his first act as president had been to pass an agriculture bill that had helped him with farmers in his state.[54] He promised future favors, pledging to Florida Democrat Don Fuqua, "If you'll do a little talkin' for me I'll try to repay you with interest."[55] He even promised a federal appointment to Alabama Democrat Robert Jones should voting for the bill cost the congressman reelection: "I'll give you anything including creating a new judgeship if it's necessary for you . . . 'cause I'm going to be here awhile."[56]

The bill passed on August 8 by a 226–184 vote. Lindsay, Reid, Pike, Cooley, Jones, Fuqua, and Mahon all voted in favor. President Johnson emerged victorious in part because many Americans at the time shared his optimism that the nation possessed the resources, the know-how, and the will to solve the problems of poverty. Only later would come the realization of the immense difficulty and cost of overcoming deeply ingrained poverty in the United States.

The quid pro quos involved in passing the Economic Opportunity Act were not all pristine to behold. To win Cooley and other Democrats in the North Carolina delegation, Johnson pledged to jettison Adam Yarmolinsky, a brilliant aide to Secretary of Defense McNamara who had helped design the legislation and had been promised the deputy directorship of the new poverty agency.* Like German leader Otto von Bismarck in Germany a century earlier, Johnson would have argued that passing legislation is like making sausage — not a sight for those with queasy stomachs.

With riots now springing up in northern cities and Goldwater the Republican presidential nominee, Roy Wilkins called together the civil rights leadership for an emergency strategy meeting at his NAACP office in New York City. The impetus for the July 29 meeting came from President Johnson. The subject — not revealed in advance to the participants — was a moratorium on demonstrations until after the presidential election on November 3. Three weeks earlier, Johnson had urged such a pause on the same group of leaders, meeting with them after he signed the civil rights law. After the riots he pressed Wilkins again for a halt to demonstrations. Those gathered around Wilkins at his conference table included the so-called "Big Six" leaders of national organizations: Martin Luther King Jr.

---

* Yarmolinsky's downfall was precipitated by a J. Edgar Hoover report to his southern allies concerning Yarmolinsky's alleged radical background. Yarmolinsky kept his job in the Defense Department, but President Johnson's support with liberals was damaged, as was his credibility with the news media, to which Johnson had lied, saying that Yarmolinsky was never offered the job and in fact had never left the Defense Department.

of the SCLC, James Farmer of CORE, Whitney Young of the National Urban League, John Lewis of SNCC, movement patriarch A. Philip Randolph, and strategist Bayard Rustin.

Wilkins argued that continued demonstrations would only help Goldwater, whose victory over Johnson would represent a disaster for the civil rights movement. Wilkins's call for a moratorium until after the election won enthusiastic support from Young, Randolph, and Rustin. With Farmer and Lewis vigorously dissenting, a contentious debate ensued. "Demonstrations are CORE's only weapons," argued Farmer. "If we talk to wrongdoers and ask them to change their ways, they'll laugh at us if they know we've given up our weapon. If we try to negotiate, we become an amateur Urban League. If we file suit, we become an amateur NAACP or Legal Defense and Education Fund. For CORE to give up demonstrations, even for six months, would be to give up its genius, its raison d'être. It might sound our death knell." John Lewis joined Farmer in opposing a moratorium, saying that "the right to demonstrate was . . . something that must never be compromised."

Challenged by Randolph as to whether he wanted a Goldwater victory on his conscience, Farmer replied, "No I don't, but CORE people are politically motivated and activated. We're going to be out there getting people registered and turning out the vote for Johnson. Johnson will win the election."[57]

With the exception of CORE and SNCC, all the groups, including King and his SCLC, agreed to a statement. The resolution called for the organizations "voluntarily to observe a broad curtailment, if not a total moratorium, of all mass marches, mass picketing and mass demonstrations until after Election Day, next Nov. 3."[58]

After having initiated the moratorium idea to begin with, President Johnson now publicly endorsed the statement with diplomatic restraint. Choosing his words carefully, Johnson told reporters on July 30 that he "would not argue with anyone who chose to pursue a policy of registration in lieu of demonstration." He was quick to add, however, that "it is understandable that those who are aggrieved will take to the streets, whether rightly or wrongly. . . . Their judgments might be wrong as to how justice could be obtained, but they would be less or more than human if they did not seek justice."[59]

In this case, as in others, Lyndon Johnson and Martin Luther King were men who positioned themselves in the middle in political disputes. King thought that the moratorium made sense, but he did not want to alienate Farmer and Lewis and their activist followers. As he often did, King listened to the debate, then agreed with the validity of points made by both sides. In the end, he helped to tone down the statement. Instead of an absolute moratorium, it called only for "a broad curtailment, if not a total moratorium," on demonstrations. After the meeting both Farmer and Rustin privately commented on what they considered King's "ineptness" at the craft of political infighting. King's aides, however, saw another dynamic at work. Whether with his diverse, contentious SCLC staff or with his equally self-centered national civil rights colleagues, King believed that his success as a leader depended on his maintaining credibility with a large, diverse constituency. He would sit quietly through long arguments, and then seek a middle way.

Lyndon Johnson faced a similar challenge — whether in the election booth or with the Congress. He too needed to satisfy the interests of a majority of members of Congress or of the electorate in a large, diverse nation.

In their goals, both Johnson and King were seeking radical change in the equities of social justice in America. They both spoke passionately about the need for a more just society. King and Johnson disagreed strongly about the role of the nonviolent demonstration. In action, however, they both revealed a belief that change is achieved most effectively by pragmatic, conciliatory leaders. At this point in his evolving career, King still believed strongly in the possibilities of reform in American society. As in his trademark "I Have a Dream" speech, he continued to call for the country to achieve its highest ideals, just as Johnson had appealed to Congress to fulfill the fallen John F. Kennedy's noble legacy by approving his civil rights legislation. Now, Johnson and King were both focused on the 1964 election and the possibilities for change that a Johnson victory might make possible.

Damning the Souls of the Indifferent

On August 4, 1964, an FBI agent in Mississippi called FBI headquarters in Washington to deliver a cryptic message. "We have uncapped one well," the agent reported. The FBI had just excavated the body of the first missing CORE worker from a newly built earthen dam on a farm southwest of Philadelphia. Before the day was over, two more "wells" were reported uncapped. With a payment of $30,000, the FBI had learned from a Klansmen where their murderers had buried James E. Chaney, Andrew Goodman, and Michael Schwerner.

With FBI agents now swarming the state and infiltrating the Klan, Justice Department officials put together the evidence by which they would eventually charge the murderers. After releasing the CORE organizers from the county jail at about 10 P.M. on June 21, Neshoba County deputy sheriff Cecil Price had again followed their blue station wagon and stopped the men outside Philadelphia. What occurred over the next two hours was a horror story of inhumanity and racism in its most primitive form. Joined by two carloads of Klansmen who had been summoned from Meridian and Philadelphia, Price took the civil rights workers to a deserted clay road, where they were summarily executed. Before Schwerner was shot, his executioner asked, "Are you the nigger lover?" Schwerner replied, "Sir, I know just how you feel." Schwerner and Goodman each had been killed with a single pistol shot. Chaney had been shot three times, and apparently also had been badly beaten. Their bodies were then taken to the Owen Burrage farm and buried by the same equipment operator who was building the dam. The Klansmen doused the station wagon with gasoline and destroyed it. Schwerner had been executed on the direct orders of Sam Bowers, the Imperial Wizard of the Mississippi White Knights of the Ku Klux Klan.

In December 1964 charges would be brought against nineteen men, all Klan members, including Sheriff Rainey, Deputy Price, a Meridian police officer, and Imperial Wizard Bowers.*[60] But justice would be difficult to achieve. As FBI major case inspector Joseph Sullivan explained, "They owned the place. In spirit, everyone belonged to the Klan."[61]

James E. Chaney was buried on Friday, August 7, in a new black cemetery on top of Mount Baron, a few miles outside Meridian. Michael Schwerner was to have been buried beside him, but no funeral director — black or white — dared to administer an integrated funeral. The black funeral home operator who buried Chaney told the Schwerner family that if he buried their son, he would lose his Mississippi funeral license — or worse.

---

* The men were charged on December 4, 1964, not with murder, a state crime, but with "conspiring to violate the civil rights of citizens" under provisions of the Reconstruction era federal law. The original case was thrown out of court by federal district judge Harold Cox, a law school classmate of Senator Eastland, appointed in 1961 by President Kennedy and soon reprimanded by a higher court for calling black plaintiffs in a voting rights case "a bunch of chimpanzees." In a 1967 trial, with Judge Cox again presiding, seven men were convicted, including Price, Bowers, and triggerman Wayne Roberts. Eight other defendants, including Sheriff Rainey, were acquitted. The jury failed to reach a verdict with three other defendants. Roberts and Bowers received ten-year sentences, the other men three to five years. Judge Cox later said, "They killed one nigger, one Jew, and a white man. I gave them all what I thought they deserved." As of August 2004 the Mississippi attorney general still was seeking to bring murder charges against the surviving defendants.

After the Chaney funeral, seven hundred people squeezed into the First Union Baptist Church in Meridian for a memorial service. David Dennis, the leader of CORE in Mississippi, spoke angrily and bitterly about the racial violence that had now added one more name to the list of black martyrs who had died fighting for equality in Mississippi. "As I stand here, I not only blame the people who pulled the trigger or did the beating or dug the hole with a shovel," Dennis said. "I blame the people in Washington, D.C., and on down in the state of Mississippi for what happened."

With tears running down his face, Dennis continued: "I'm sick and tired of going to the funerals of black men who have been murdered by white men. I've got vengeance in my heart tonight, and I ask you to feel angry with me. I'm sick and tired, and I ask you to be sick and tired with me. The white men who murdered James Chaney are never going to be punished. I ask you to be sick and tired of that. I'm tired of people in this country allowing that to continue to happen.

"We've got to stand up. The best way we can remember James Chaney is to demand our rights. Don't just look at me and go back and tell folks you've been to a nice service. Your work is just beginning. If you go back home and sit down and take what these white men in Mississippi are doing to us. If you take it, and don't do something about it — then God damn your souls!"[62]

Out of J. E. Chaney's memorial service flowed an angry and passionate political energy that would propel the delegates of the Mississippi Freedom Democratic Party to the Democratic National Convention in Atlantic City. Seasoned by their battles with implacable racism, the foot soldiers of the Mississippi Summer Project were determined to test the values of President Lyndon Johnson, the Democratic Party, and the nation.

President Johnson takes the oath of office on Air Force One following the assassination of President Kennedy. Judge Sarah Hughes administers the oath as (*from left to right*) Mac Kilduff, Jack Valenti, Congressman Albert Thomas, Mrs. Johnson, Mrs. Kennedy, and Congressman Jack Brooks watch.

Dr. King's first meeting with President Johnson at the White House, December 1963.

President Johnson, in January 1964, seeking the support of civil rights leaders for his War on Poverty programs. Pictured are Dr. King, Whitney Young, and James Farmer.

President and Mrs. Johnson visit the Tom Fletcher family of Inez, Kentucky, during a 1964 poverty tour.

Dr. King and the Reverend Ralph Abernathy in jail in St. Augustine, Florida, during the SCLC's 1964 demonstrations.

CENTER: Dr. King shakes hands with President Johnson following the signing of the 1964 Civil Rights Act.

BOTTOM: Senate Republican leader Everett Dirksen gets the "Johnson treatment" in the Oval Office.

With pictures of slain civil rights workers Michael Schwerner, James Chaney, and Andrew Goodman in the background, Dr. King speaks at a rally outside the 1964 Democratic National Convention in Atlantic City, New Jersey, in support of the Mississippi Freedom Democratic Party delegation.

As Mrs. King looks on, Dr. King is congratulated on his Nobel Prize by Vice President–elect Hubert Humphrey in Harlem, December 1964.

ABOVE LEFT: After J. Edgar Hoover called him the "most notorious liar in America," Dr. King went to FBI headquarters in December 1964 to discuss his differences with the director.

ABOVE RIGHT: Stanley David Levison, King's controversial adviser.

LEFT: President Johnson embraces J. Edgar Hoover at a 1965 meeting. The president knew the importance of a good relationship with the powerful FBI director.

A billboard, erected by King's detractors along the 1965 Selma march route and across the South, attempts to smear Dr. King for having appeared at a movement leadership training program that they branded a "Communist training school."

Chairman John Lewis
of SNCC is pounded
by a state trooper's club
during the March 7, 1965,
attempted Selma-to-
Montgomery march.

Dr. and Mrs. King
march in Selma with
SNCC's John Lewis.

Dr. King receives from
President Johnson one of
the pens used to sign the
1965 Voting Rights Act.

President Johnson calls the shots during the July 1967 Detroit riots, with the advice of Marvin Watson, J. Edgar Hoover, Robert McNamara, Harold Johnson, Joseph Califano, and Stanley Resor.

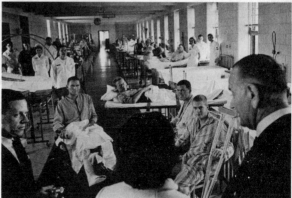

The National Guard patrols a Detroit neighborhood devastated by the riots.

After escalating U.S. involvement in Vietnam in 1965, President Johnson visits injured servicemen at the National Naval Medical Center in Bethesda, Maryland.

BELOW: Mrs. King with Dr. Benjamin Spock (behind her) and others at a 1967 anti–Vietnam War protest outside the White House gates.

A tense moment as Dr. King and President Johnson discuss the proposed open housing bill.

BELOW LEFT: A relieved President and Mrs. Johnson talk with friends on the telephone following the president's March 31, 1968, announcement that he would not seek reelection.

BELOW RIGHT: The Reverend Ralph Abernathy, the Reverend Jesse Jackson, and others on the balcony of the Lorraine Motel in Memphis point in the direction of a gunshot following the April 4, 1968, assassination of Dr. King, who lies at their feet.

Spurred by Dr. King's assassination one week earlier, President Johnson signs the just-passed 1968 Open Housing Act. Watching are (*from left*) Senator Edward Brooke, Speaker John McCormack, Congressman Emanuel Celler, Senator Walter Mondale, and Justice Thurgood Marshall.

8

✦ ✦ ✦ ✦ ✦ ✦

A Political Revolution

DELEGATES POURED INTO THE Masonic Hall in downtown Jackson, Mississippi, from county after county. They waved banners proclaiming "LBJ for President" and "One Man, One Vote." They pledged their support to the Democratic Party and to Lyndon Baines Johnson for president of the United States. But this was no ordinary political convention. The delegates, nearly 2,500 African Americans and a handful of whites, were risking their lives to be there. Denied access to the state's official "lily white" Democratic Party, Mississippi's black citizens had suffered humiliation, threats, beatings — even murder — to create their own political party to challenge the regular delegates for the right to represent their state at the Democratic National Convention.

Now, on August 6, 1964, they were jammed into an auditorium at the first statewide convention of the Mississippi Freedom Democratic Party. Dressed in their Sunday best, fanning themselves in the oppressive summer heat, they gathered under placards naming the counties they represented — including Neshoba, Sunflower, Tallahatchie, and Hinds, where intense violence had met their every attempt at voter registration — and elected their own sixty-eight-member delegation, sixty-four blacks and four whites, to the Democratic National Convention in Atlantic City. There, declared keynote speaker Ella Baker, a veteran civil rights organizer, they would "demand to be let into America." As the convention drew to a close, with pride overcoming fear, they joined hands to sing "We Shall Overcome."[1]

The convention in Jackson was the latest step in a three-year grassroots organizing campaign aimed at winning Mississippi's more than 915,000 black citizens — approximately 42 percent of the population[2] — the power of the ballot box. Civil rights organizers from SNCC, CORE, the SCLC, and the NAACP had helped to dramatize the discrimination faced daily by blacks in the Deep South — and the terror often visited upon those who demanded equal rights. After a black barber in Greenwood permitted Freedom Democrat precinct voting in his barbershop, a brick was hurled through the plate glass window; two days later he was evicted from the premises. Bob Masters, a local organizer in the same town, was beaten by whites as he walked down the street — and then was charged with assaulting his assailant.[3] Lawrence Guyot, the newly elected state chairman of the MFDP, would be jailed on trumped-up charges to prevent him from attending the Democratic National Convention. The Mississippi attorney general would charge the Mississippi Freedom Democratic Party itself with "conspiring" unlawfully to use the name "Democratic Party."

The 1964 Civil Rights Act was only the first door to open. Now, the Freedom Democrats were heading for a showdown on August 22 in Atlantic City, where the integrated delegation would ask the national party to choose between them and the regular Democratic Party of Mississippi — which had just passed a resolution at its state convention declaring, "We believe in the separation of the races in all phases of life."[4]

That same Sunday afternoon, while the Freedom Democrats were choosing their delegates in Jackson, President Johnson and his advisers were looking for ways to prevent the black Mississippians from disrupting party unity at the national convention. If the delegate challenge were not settled soon, predicted White House aide Jack Valenti, it would "surface like a ticking time bomb on the convention floor . . . where the conflict could be aired for all the country to see . . . to the delight of the Republican party."

In the Oval Office meeting, President Johnson realized that his advisers had not found a solution to "the Mississippi problem."* He demanded nothing less than a magical compromise — one that would satisfy the aspirations of disenfranchised black citizens without driving the white Mississippi regulars and their neighboring southern sympathizers from the convention. "Get those problems settled," he demanded, angrily dismissing his aides. "Organize yourselves, get a sensible plan, and then come back and talk to me!"[5]

Newsweek magazine posed Johnson's dilemma: "To disregard the Ne-

---

* Present at the meeting on August 6, 1964, were the president, White House aides Jack Valenti, Walter Jenkins, Bill Moyers, Kenneth O'Donnell, and Lawrence O'Brien, as well as Democratic national chairman John Bailey and attorney James Rowe.

gro's demands would be to repudiate the moral drive of the Negro revolution; to satisfy them would mean a floor fight almost certain to trigger a southern walkout."[6] One observer noted that the Freedom Democrats lacked "legal standing," while the Mississippi regulars lacked "moral standing."[7] A *New York Times* editorial advised Johnson to split the state's delegate votes between the Freedom Democrats and the regulars. If Johnson did not respond positively to the MFDP cause, the *Times* warned, "he remains open to the charge [that] he chose silence as a way to compete for white racist votes in the South."[8]

For years, Lyndon Johnson had striven to achieve a united Democratic Party. As Senate majority leader, he had forged his great congressional successes by uniting southern and northern Democrats to overcome the conservative coalition. He had recently won enactment of his poverty program by persuading many southern Democrats to vote for it. With a united party, Johnson hoped to win sweeping new legislative initiatives in his push for a Great Society. Passing laws. Making the machinery of government work for the people. These were Lyndon Johnson's imperatives. He didn't understand symbolic struggles such as the Freedom Democrats' challenge. He saw this one not as a battle over right and wrong but as an unnessary provocation to the South.[9]

Johnson felt pressured from all directions. The Reverend Martin Luther King Jr. publicly demanded that the president support the MFDP. On the eve of the convention, King sent a wire to Johnson declaring that the Freedom Democrats should be seated "as the only democratically constituted delegation from Mississippi."[10] If the president did not respond to the Mississippi challenge, King adviser Bayard Rustin told White House aide Lee White, then black voters might "sit on their hands" instead of supporting Johnson in the November election.*[11] At the same time, politicians from the Deep South were threatening to boycott the convention if the black Mississippians displaced the regular delegation. Governor John Connally of Texas, a former Johnson aide and protégé, bluntly warned the president, "If you seat those black buggers, the whole South will walk out!"[12]

The turbulent civil rights revolution, in which the presidential election of 1964 was taking place, had profound consequences for both the Repub-

---

* By virtue of the FBI wiretaps on King's telephones, the president knew in advance what Rustin would say. The FBI reported to the White House on August 14 King's instructions to Rustin for his conversation with Lee White. What King told Rustin to say was "Lyndon Johnson needs the Negro vote. He feels we have no way to go, but we can certainly stay home" ("Communist Influence in Racial Matters," FBI Bufile 100-3-116).

lican and the Democratic party. At stake was nothing less than the balance of political power in the United States. Lyndon Johnson felt the undercurrents of change. His seven-month campaign to win approval of the Civil Rights Act had won him popularity with many voters, especially blacks and northern white liberals and moderates, but — as he had predicted — his stand inevitably had begun to alienate voters representing other sections and interests. "The governor of my own state won't even introduce me [at the convention]," Johnson complained to Roy Wilkins. "John Connally's got a popularity of 82 percent right now, and I've got 41 percent. The difference is that I was for public accommodations, and he wasn't. That's all."*

Wilkins sympathized with Johnson but cautioned that "finding the bodies [of civil rights workers Schwerner, Chaney, and Goodman] means there is nothing any organization can do except endorse the seating [of the MFDP]." Civil rights groups and northern liberals would not vote against the cause of black Mississippians for which the three young men had died.[13]

Johnson realized that he would lose Alabama and Mississippi — the most intransigently segregated states in the Deep South — to Senator Barry Goldwater, the Republican presidential nominee, who had voted against the 1964 civil rights bill. But Johnson was now afraid that the Goldwater-led Republicans would carve even deeper inroads into the once solidly Democratic South. In July the Republican National Convention in San Francisco had produced a seismic shift in the racial politics of the party founded by Abraham Lincoln. The fast-growing Republican parties now emerging in virtually every southern state were systematically purging blacks, who traditionally had been included at national conventions. Even some northern delegations followed suit, as did California's Republicans. "Negro Delegates to GOP Convention Suffer Week of Humiliation" headlined the wire story from the Associated Negro Press news agency. According to a black delegate from New Jersey, Negro delegates "had been shoved, pushed, spat on, and cursed with a liberal sprinkling of racial epithets." "I now believe I know how it felt to be a Jew in Hitler's Germany," declared liberal Republican Jackie Robinson, the legendary Hall of Famer who had integrated major league baseball in 1947.†[14] Goldwater's acceptance speech — proclaiming "that extremism in defense of

---

* Connally had broken with Johnson to oppose the 1964 civil rights bill, but Connally eventually did nominate Johnson for president at the convention.

† Robinson was one of several black Republicans to cross party lines and endorse President Johnson.

liberty is no vice" — was received as a thinly veiled message of encouragement to the radical right and also to southern segregationists. The Goldwater banner became a new rallying point for southern Democrats who refused to accept the sweeping Civil Rights Act of 1964 and its southern-born champion, Lyndon Johnson.

The desertion by southern Democrats distressed Johnson. His rise to political power had been based in part on the strong support he had received from political leaders throughout the South. Even beyond basic political calculations, Johnson was deeply hurt that he was being disowned by his own region, which he revered, celebrated, and still strongly identified as home. When Senator James Eastland of Mississippi called to ask whether his state's delegation would be seated, the president poured out his inner turmoil. "Here are people who murdered folks who were trying to help people get a chance to vote," Johnson pleaded, "and you're coming up here to recognize them as members of the Democratic Party when they won't even say they will support the nominee. . . . I am anathema to the South. And a lot of them feel that they can't be associated with me in any way. On the other hand, I am a white southerner!"

As a minimum condition for being seated at the convention, Johnson wanted members of the Mississippi delegation to pledge in writing that they would support him as the party's presidential nominee. But Eastland provided little comfort to his longtime Senate colleague. He knew that fewer than a handful of Mississippi delegates would back the president.[15] Neither Eastland nor Mississippi's other Democratic congressional barons attended the convention, and they had limited influence with which to help Johnson in any case. Their power came from their seniority as chairmen of Senate and House committees, not from playing a role in the national politics of a liberal, pro–civil rights Democratic Party. Supporting Johnson in Atlantic City could only antagonize voters at home.

There were limits to what President Johnson could do to mollify the Deep South. He had ordered immediate enforcement of the new civil rights laws and pressed for peaceful implementation of school desegregation orders. In mid-August he called Governor John McKeithen of Louisiana and urged him to guarantee peaceful integration of schools in St. Helena Parish, a segregationist stronghold. If the governor did not comply, the president said, the federal government would enforce school integration. In response, McKeithen huddled with his fellow segregationist governors George Wallace of Alabama, Paul Johnson of Mississippi, and Orval Faubus of Arkansas and complained that the president had threatened him. After hearing reports from the governors' meeting, Congressman Hale Boggs advised Johnson that Florida, Arkansas, and his own state of Louisiana would walk out of the convention if the Mississippi regulars were not seated.[16]

The desertion of Texas Democrats wounded Johnson most of all. Hearing that forty to fifty Democratic precinct chairmen in Houston planned to support Goldwater, the president phoned Governor Connally. "If I don't carry but one state in the Union, it's got to be this one," Johnson told him. "I think we ought to get our [campaign] manager to say, 'Come on boys, if Texas doesn't want this presidency, we can turn it over to Bobby Kennedy.' And I imagine that's what's to happen if I withdraw."[17]

Johnson's deepest concern about the delegate challenge was not about losing Mississippi itself but about the effect on other states. He planned to seat the Alabama and Mississippi delegations "near the exits so they can leave voluntarily whenever they want."[18] But he feared that if the convention officially booted out the Mississippi regulars and replaced them with the mostly black MFDP delegation, other southern delegations would walk out in protest. The states most likely to do so were Louisiana and Arkansas, yet the president could foresee as many as ten delegations leaving in protest. Beyond the convention, his concern went as well to the fall election results in southern and border states, where the backlash against his civil rights record was strongest. Most worrisome to the president were the pleas of Governors Connally of Texas and Carl Sanders of Georgia, who repeatedly insisted that he must seat the Mississippi regulars. With thirty-seven electoral votes between them, Johnson knew that losing Texas and Georgia in November would be a serious political blow.[19]

As the convention approached, the president grew increasingly agitated. The Mississippi delegate dispute threatened to undermine his crowning moment — his nomination as the Democratic candidate for the nation's highest office, his lifelong goal. He wanted to prove that he was more than just an "accidental president," in office only because of an assassin's bullet. The Mississippi fight also exacerbated other Johnson insecurities. Even though he had publicly ruled out Attorney General Robert Kennedy as a possible running mate, Johnson still feared that some untoward event at the convention could stampede the delegates into nominating Kennedy for vice president — or even president. He confided to friends his fear that a wide-open floor fight over the seating of the Freedom Democrats might trigger a pro-Kennedy uprising. Johnson also fretted that a planned memorial celebration for the late President Kennedy, featuring his widow, Jacqueline, and brother Robert, might unleash the delegates' pent-up loyalty to their fallen leader. To diminish the chances of a groundswell of Kennedy support, Johnson moved the Kennedy salute to the last night of the convention — by which time he and his vice presidential choice would be safely nominated — but he still could not shake his fear of the Kennedys' legendary charisma and their command of public affection, which Johnson felt he could never equal.[20]

Johnson also felt resentment toward the national civil rights leaders, who seemed to him ungrateful for his hard-won accomplishments. He could not understand, he said, why elements within the civil rights movement would want to hurt him politically after he had done so much for their cause — winning the Civil Rights Act and his beloved antipoverty program, the newly enacted Economic Opportunity Act — and was ready to do more. "If the liberals weren't in charge, and didn't have the president, and didn't have the vice president,* and didn't have the platform, and didn't have everything they want, they ought to do this [Freedom Democrats challenge]," Johnson complained to Labor Secretary Willard Wirtz, "but they do [have all of those things]."[21]

Although Johnson identified emotionally with the basic civil rights struggle for legal equality, he had difficulty relating to the feelings and experiences that drove the young black SNCC organizers or the sharecroppers and day laborers who were coming to Atlantic City. Johnson was more than a generation older than SNCC leaders like Robert Moses and John Lewis, and his views of African American behavior were at times paternalistic and condescending. He was comfortable with Roy Wilkins, who knew the game of national politics, but not with the insurgents who were redefining political struggle through demonstrations combined with passionate grassroots organizing of the poorest, most disenfranchised African Americans. Wilkins, experienced in dealing with Washington politicians, accepted Johnson's good intentions when the president told him, "I'd let the [official] Mississippi delegation sit, and I'd salute the S.O.B.'s, and in the next four years I'd see the Promised Land."[22] For young black organizers, fresh from the deadly struggle in Mississippi, such a rationalization was unacceptable, even incomprehensible.

Johnson's distrust of the militants' tactics made him receptive to J. Edgar Hoover's constant barrage of FBI memoranda insisting that civil rights agitation was the result of Communist influence on Martin Luther King. Hoover stimulated and fed the president's sense that conspiracies

---

* In saying that the liberals had "the vice president," Johnson was referring to his anticipated choice of Senator Hubert Humphrey as his running mate. Humphrey was the first choice of most liberals and of civil rights leaders.

were forming against him. As Johnson grew more anxious about his ability to control the Mississippi outcome, he became depressed, pessimistic, and gripped by paranoia. Whether or not Johnson actually believed Hoover's sweeping accusations of Communist influence, he nevertheless used the charges as a weapon in the fight.*

"Those Communists are moving in on King, and King's moving in on Rauh," Johnson complained to Secretary Wirtz.[23] Washington attorney Joseph Rauh, a key Johnson ally and brilliant legislative strategist in passing the recently won civil rights bill, now was serving as the MFDP's lawyer at the convention. Johnson's sources were the FBI wiretaps of what King and Rauh had thought were private telephone conversations.

When Mayor Richard Daley of Chicago questioned whether there was "someone behind" the MFDP challenge, Johnson replied, "Oh, yes, Dick. The Communist Party is the leader!"[24] Complaining to Walter Reuther, president of the United Automobile Workers, about King's seeking a White House meeting to discuss the Mississippi situation, Johnson said, "I tell you, Walter, on my word of honor, every [move] is led primarily by members of the Communist Party."[25] In an August 14 conversation with Senator Humphrey, Johnson charged that Communists were behind King's support for the MFDP: "You've got Martin Luther King, the Communists have got hold of him, and they're managing and directing him every day. . . . [M]embers of [his] organization are calling up here and asking us to do things for them and their Mississippi Freedom Party every day!"[26]

With NAACP leader Roy Wilkins, King's sometime rival, Johnson didn't have to initiate the Communist charge. Wilkins, who had received his own briefings from Hoover about King, told the president in a conspiratorial tone, "The motivation of King is known to you. You know some of the forces behind it." Replied Johnson, "Yes, I do!"[27]

The Mississippi delegate fight brought out the worst in Lyndon Johnson: anger laced with self-pity. Johnson was a person whose moods fluctuated from self-confidence and ebullience to deep despair and a sense of defeat. This dispute brought him to a definite low point. Other factors also were at play. In his civil rights advocacy, Johnson was cutting himself off from his home region, his natural base of political support. He knew that his actions were setting in motion a historic realignment — that the Democrats were about to lose the South, on his watch.

---

* A number of White House aides believed that in 1964 Johnson was still skeptical of Hoover's charges of Communist influence on the civil rights movement.

Ironically, the convention should have been the celebratory crowning point of his career. He had just passed the Civil Rights Act, the tax bill was now on the books, and the War on Poverty was under way. His popularity had reached an all-time high. Yet he felt that those whose gratitude he most expected were spoiling his convention. Rather than praising his successful efforts on behalf of civil rights, black leaders were demanding reform of the Democratic Party. Rather than being grateful for the first southern president in a century, the white southerners were threatening to walk out. Johnson, who believed that reasonable compromise could bridge any gap, could not get them to come reason together. He had done the right thing, yet the complex, fickle citizenry did not appreciate it. In his depression, Johnson perceived this to be an even greater threat than it was.

In contrast to the president's concerns about him, Martin Luther King was in fact trying to maintain a cautious and moderate position on the delegate seating fight. The civil rights leader wanted to support the Freedom Democrats, but in a manner least likely to antagonize President Johnson or to contribute to backlash support for Barry Goldwater. As he weighed his options with Bayard Rustin, King hoped to limit his involvement in the convention fight. He already had defied death threats in traveling through Mississippi to support the Freedom Democrats' cause. Now he planned to testify for the MFDP before the credentials committee, but he hoped to avoid the rest of the convention. Seeing King limping from a recently sprained ankle, Rustin suggested that the injury provided a ready excuse for King's limited participation. "You should demonstrate this handicap by taking your crutch with you to the credentials committee hearing," Rustin advised.[28]

Besides thinking the MFDP effort was worthwhile because it dramatically illustrated the exclusion of blacks from southern Democratic politics, King also felt a need to demonstrate his support of the young SNCC leaders, who, jealous of his fame, were disparaging him for "lacking adequate militancy." But King viewed the convention fight as a potentially hazardous distraction from his primary goals for the latter half of 1964. He was afraid that the MFDP effort might devolve into violent demonstrations, which would hurt the civil rights movement, Johnson's campaign, and his own broader objectives. King told Clarence Jones, his New York attorney, that the civil rights leaders' agreed-upon moratorium on demonstrations "was a wise thing, because change occurs in the North through political power and nothing else." Jones agreed, adding, "There are some black Negroes who are acting as if they are paid agents to disrupt the movement. . . . We have to be careful of people who urge extreme action."[29]

King wanted to see Goldwater defeated decisively, and wished to help ensure a big Johnson victory by conducting a vigorous campaign to register black voters. The political reward, he hoped, would be presidential support for new voting rights legislation in 1965 — legislation that would empower millions of African American voters in the South. It was a time, King felt, to put direct action aside and concentrate on traditional electoral politics. In their private conversations, King and SCLC executive director Andrew Young dismissed the MFDP's tactics "as a game, not the real politics." They saw the Freedom Democrats as a parallel effort to their endeavor of "build[ing] black strength in the real politics." They wanted to work with Lyndon Johnson; they knew he could get a bill passed.[30]

With the Mississippi issue foremost in his mind, Johnson sought to nail down the loyalty of the officials he would name to run the convention. Asking House Speaker John McCormack to serve as permanent chairman of the convention, Johnson focused on his primary concern. "With the Mississippi delegate challenge coming up," he told McCormack, "I think it's important that I have a man that loves me and that I can trust."[31] Approaching Representative Hale Boggs, the Democratic whip, to serve as convention parliamentarian, he instructed him "to try to anticipate Mississippi," adding, "I've got to have somebody I can depend on — day or night, right or wrong." Replied Boggs, "Mr. President, I just rule for Johnson. Period!"[32]

To political observers, the president's intense preoccupation with the Mississippi delegate fight and the threats posed by Robert Kennedy and Barry Goldwater seemed out of proportion, given the basic political realities. Opinion polls showed Johnson leading Goldwater by a two-to-one margin, with commanding majorities in all parts of the country except the South. Although the civil rights backlash appeared to be costing Johnson 10 percent of the Democratic vote, the president knew that Goldwater's extreme rhetoric, threatening the use of nuclear weapons and calling for an end to popular federal programs such as Social Security, had frightened 30 percent of Republicans into supporting Johnson — a phenomenon the president dubbed "the frontlash." Politicians knew that Johnson could wield a totally free hand to select anyone he wanted as a running mate. The Kennedy for vice president issue seemed settled, with Robert Kennedy now planning to run for the Senate from New York. And the Mississippi delegate fight, though troublesome politically, was not an unfamiliar occurrence at Democratic conventions. Civil rights had been an explosive issue since the 1948 convention, when several southern states walked out to protest a strong civil rights platform.*

Friends knew that Johnson often exaggerated the desperation of political situations as a means of motivating his followers or winning their sympathy. Whatever his reasons, Lyndon Johnson was sufficiently agitated about the convention that in late July he issued an order to unleash in Atlantic City an unprecedented program of illegal political espionage designed to further his own political interests.

Unleashing the FBI

Walter Jenkins, the president's most trusted aide, called his close friend Deke DeLoach, fourth-ranking official in the FBI, on August 1. "Deke," Jenkins began, "the President is very concerned about his personal safety and that of his staff while they're at the convention. Would you head a team to keep us advised of any potential threats? We want to make sure the President is safe — and that there aren't any disruptions at the convention."

Reading between the lines of Jenkins's unusual request, DeLoach immediately went to FBI director J. Edgar Hoover. "Lyndon is way out of line," was Hoover's first reaction. Nonetheless, he instructed DeLoach to "tell Walter we will give him whatever help he wants."[33] What President Johnson wanted, the FBI officials understood, was not protection for his "personal safety" — an assignment handled by the Secret Service — but an expanded version of the political spying they had already performed on Attorney General Robert Kennedy and others.[34]

Jenkins soon spelled out his instructions. The president wanted all the information the FBI could gather about the Mississippi Freedom Democratic Party, its sixty-eight delegates to Atlantic City, and its allies from SNCC, CORE, and the SCLC. He wanted to know the details of the Freedom Democrats' strategy and tactics as they presented their case to the convention's credentials committee. Six weeks earlier, the president had persuaded the reluctant FBI chief to investigate the Ku Klux Klan's murderous rampage against black civil rights activists in Mississippi. Now he

* In protest of the 1948 Democratic Party platform supporting civil rights legislation, a number of southern delegates, mostly from Mississippi and Alabama, walked out of the convention, formed their own States' Rights, or "Dixiecrat," Party, and carried four southern states for Strom Thurmond, governor of South Carolina. The election was won by President Harry S. Truman despite the southern defection.

intended to use the FBI to thwart the political aims of those same black Americans — if their political ambitions interfered with his own.

Even before the convention opened, the FBI was supplying useful intelligence on convention maneuvering. Its wiretaps on King's office and home telephones, as well as on those of Stanley Levison, Clarence Jones, and Bayard Rustin, brought FBI reports directly to the president. Over dinner at the White House on August 20, President Johnson complained to Senator Richard Russell that it took him "hours each night" to read all the wiretap reports he was receiving, including those of Martin Luther King speaking with Joseph Rauh about Rauh's Mississippi clients. "Hoover apparently has been turned loose and is tapping everything," Russell noted in his diary. He also observed that, despite Johnson's complaints about spending hours reading FBI reports, "he loves it."[35]

Now, with only three weeks' advance notice before the credentials committee hearings on the Mississippi delegate dispute were to begin on Saturday, August 22, Deke DeLoach began to assemble a team of FBI agents, wiretappers, and informers who would try to supply the president with a continuous stream of information about what the Mississippi Freedom Democrats and their supporters were saying and planning.

Rauh described the Freedom Democrats' political strategy simply as "11 and 8." Their goal was to present their case to the entire national convention, where they felt certain they would win the support of a majority of delegates. To reach the full convention, they needed only 11 members of the 122-member credentials committee to file a minority report on their behalf. Once in front of the convention, the fledgling party would require the support of only 8 states or territories to demand a recorded vote. Both Rauh and President Johnson expected that northern liberal delegations would support the cause of the Freedom Democrats in an on-the-record vote. For Johnson, the political challenge was to find an acceptable compromise — one that would satisfy enough southern delegates to keep the South in the convention and enough northern liberals to keep the Freedom Democrats' petition from reaching the convention floor. Or Johnson could simply try to exert enough political power to prevent the Mississippi case from reaching its magic numbers of "11 and 8."

Johnson used his trademark political shrewdness in taking into account the ambitions, strengths, and vulnerabilities of others. He placed primary responsibility for settling the delegate fight on Senator Hubert Humphrey and labor leader Walter Reuther. Humphrey desperately wanted Johnson to choose him as his running mate, and Reuther, president of the largest labor union in the country, was Humphrey's most powerful supporter. Longtime champions of civil rights, both men would be credible advocates for any proposals Johnson might make. And Joseph Rauh, a close Humphrey friend and admirer, earned his living as the highly paid Washington general counsel of Reuther's United Automobile Workers union.

Rauh already was fielding favorable publicity for the MFDP cause. "If you and Hubert Humphrey have any influence, you'll get Rauh off of TV," Johnson told Reuther on August 9. "If [the MFDP and its supporters] will give us four years, I'll guarantee the Freedom delegation somebody representing views like that will be seated four years from now. But we can't do it all before breakfast."[36]

Johnson's message was even more explicit when he called Reuther on August 17, five days before the credentials committee hearings. "You better talk to Hubert Humphrey, because I'm telling you he's got no future in this party at all if this big war comes off here and the South all walks out and we all get in a helluva mess. Number one," he said bluntly. "Number two: if you two can't control Joseph Rauh and get this settled without him making an ass out of himself, then I'm not much of a leader."[37]

On August 20 the president tried to impress on Humphrey the urgency of his assignment. "You need to stop Joe Rauh before this goes too far," Johnson told him. "[James] Farmer and King are out of control. . . . Let them have a modest demonstration like at San Francisco.* . . . If you and Reuther and Joe Rauh don't step in now and say, 'This is going to elect Goldwater,' it will be too late."[38]

Johnson called Reuther again the next day to describe his plan for settling the Mississippi dispute: Each of the Mississippi regulars would have to take a party loyalty oath in order to be seated. The Freedom delegates would be seated as honored guests — but without voting privileges. And the convention would pass a resolution that, beginning in 1968, the Democratic Party would never seat another delegation that excluded people because of race.[39]

Johnson then tried to sell his compromise plan to Mississippi's James Eastland. He told Senator Eastland that he knew Mississippi and Alabama were already lost to the Democrats no matter what happened at the convention, "so all I'm trying to do is just keep my friends from being battered around and run over, if I can without losing my own tail." Eastland was noncommittal, promising only that he would pass the proposal on to Governor Paul Johnson.[40]

"We're having trouble up in Atlantic City with your man Rauh," said

* The major civil rights organizations had staged little-noticed demonstrations at the Republican convention.

Johnson in yet another call to Reuther. "I sure wish you'd make them behave."

"He's going to behave, I assure you," replied Reuther. "I'm going to disown him if he doesn't."

"I don't mind if he puts on a little show," said Johnson, "so long as he doesn't wreck us."

"If he doesn't come through on this, he won't be my lawyer," promised Reuther.[41]

Quite apart from representing Reuther's labor union, Rauh was an influential figure in liberal Democratic politics. The big barrel-chested lawyer in his trademark bow tie was a familiar presence in meetings to advance civil liberties, civil rights, and economic and social justice. He served as legislative counsel with the Leadership Conference on Civil Rights, as national chairman of Americans for Democratic Action — which had endorsed the MFDP challenge — and as a Washington, D.C., representative to the Democratic National Committee. At the Atlantic City convention he also was a member of the credentials committee. To sway Rauh, Reuther reported that the president had told him "that the Hubert [Humphrey] vice presidency rode on the settling of the Mississippi thing to the satisfaction of the president." If Rauh didn't cooperate, Reuther threatened, "he would have Humphrey's blood on his conscience for the rest of his life." In their next conversation, Reuther said that the president believed — and Reuther agreed — that if the Mississippi dispute could not be settled with the president's plan, "the South would walk out of the convention" and "Goldwater would win the presidential election." Rauh called Johnson's claim preposterous: the president would decisively defeat Goldwater, irrespective of what happened with Mississippi at the convention.[42]

One Woman's Power

After a thirty-hour journey north from Jackson, Mississippi, the delegates from the Mississippi Freedom Democratic Party gingerly stepped out of their two chartered buses onto the fabled Atlantic City boardwalk for a look — the first for many — at the Atlantic Ocean. Alongside the boardwalk rose the sprawling gray Convention Center, where they hoped to be included within the national Democratic Party. They checked in to the Gem Motel, a cheap accommodation in a black neighborhood. The delegates then hurried back to the fancier hotels along the boardwalk a mile away. There, they would buttonhole delegates to support their cause.

The road-weary contingent was encouraged by news that a group of twenty-five liberal Democratic members of the House of Representatives had just issued a statement declaring that "elementary justice" demanded seating the Freedom Democrats. The congressmen had rejected the regular Mississippi Democrats for their "repugnant principles" — opposition to blacks, the Supreme Court, labor unions, and the platform of the national Democratic Party.[43] As he prepared his clients for their credentials committee hearing the next day, Joe Rauh felt confident that the challengers had won the support of more than enough committee members and state delegations to take their case before the entire convention.

What Rauh and his clients did not know was how deeply engaged President Johnson was in the most minute details of the fight. Back and forth with White House political advisers Kenneth O'Donnell and James Rowe, the president had identified eleven MFDP "supporters" on the credentials committee and was directing efforts to persuade them to change their votes.[44] In a phone call Johnson methodically steered O'Donnell down a list of each delegate — and each state delegation — considered a "problem." Even as the president was consumed with trying to persuade members of Congress to pass his poverty plan and approve the Tonkin Gulf Resolution endorsing his authority to wage war in Vietnam, he wrestled obsessively with the issues he thought were undermining him in Atlantic City.

When the credentials committee convened its hearing in the Convention Center on Saturday afternoon, August 22, the two rival Mississippi delegations eyed each other warily across the ballroom. The Mississippi regulars represented the state's white establishment — its lawyers, bankers, cotton planters, state and county officeholders, and major campaign contributors. In stark contrast, the Freedom Democrats were mostly poor, rural African Americans — ministers and undertakers, barbers and beauticians, carpenters and painters, cleaning ladies and maids, small farmers and sharecroppers, teachers and shopkeepers. SNCC's Bob Moses had worked hard to ensure that the delegation represented a cross section of the state's black population. The cadre of SNCC organizers also had sought out strong, independent people, unafraid to speak their minds and assert their rights despite their limited education and experience. The success of SNCC's three-year effort to develop grassroots leadership was being tested as Fannie Lou Hamer, vice chairman of the delegation, began to testify before the committee on national television.

Speaking in a strong, resonant voice, Hamer, age forty-six, a large black woman in an inexpensive cotton dress, described her life. As the twentieth and youngest child of Mississippi sharecroppers, she had been born on a large Delta plantation, started picking cotton at age six, and dropped out of school in the eighth grade to work full-time in the fields. After her marriage in 1944, she moved with her husband to another plantation nearby, where they and their young children sharecropped for eighteen years — until August 31, 1962, the day she first tried to register to vote.

After she and a busload of other black people were turned away by the voting registrar at the county courthouse in Indianola and then harassed by police, Hamer told the credentials committee, she returned home to find her husband and children anxiously awaiting her.

"My husband came and said the plantation owner was raising Cain because I had tried to register, and before he quit talking, the plantation owner came and said, 'Fannie Lou, did Pap tell you what I said?'

"I said, 'Yes, sir.'

"He said, 'I mean that. . . . If you don't go down and withdraw your registration, you will have to leave. Then, if you do withdraw,' he said, 'you might have to go [anyway] because we are not ready for that in Mississippi.'

"And I addressed him and told him and said, 'I didn't try to register for you. I tried to register for myself.' I had to leave that same night."[45]

Hamer then described what happened to her and four traveling companions on June 9, 1963, as they rode home in a bus from a voting rights seminar. At the Continental Trailways bus station in Winona, Mississippi, four of the women — but not Hamer — had gone inside to buy food and use the bathroom. They were confronted by the Winona police chief and a Mississippi highway patrolman, who arrested all of the women, including Hamer, and took them to the county jail.

"After I was placed in the cell," Hamer testified, "I began to hear sounds of licks and screams . . . and I could hear somebody say, 'Can you say, yes sir? Nigger, can you say, yes sir?'

"And they would say other horrible names. She would say, 'Yes, I can say, yes sir.'

"'So, say it.'

"She says, 'I don't know you well enough [to call you 'sir'].'"

Then, Hamer testified, a state highway patrolman ordered her to lie facedown on the bunk bed in a jail cell, saying, "You are going to wish you were dead." He ordered two male Negro prisoners to beat her with a blackjack.

"The first Negro began to beat, and I was beat by the first Negro until he was exhausted. . . . The state highway patrolman ordered the second Negro to take the blackjack. The second Negro began to beat me and I began to work my feet, and the state highway patrolman ordered the first Negro who had beat to set on my feet to keep me from working my feet. I began to scream and one white man got up and began to beat me in my head and tell me to hush. One white man — my dress had worked up high, he walked over and pulled my dress down — and he pulled my dress back up.

"All of this on account we want to register, to become first-class citizens. And if the Freedom Democratic Party is not seated now, I question America. Is this America the land of the free and the home of the brave where we have to sleep with our telephones off the hooks because our lives be threatened daily because we want to live as decent human beings in America?"[46]

Hamer's raw, dramatic testimony brought tears to the eyes of credentials committee members and television viewers across the country, but it incensed President Johnson, who broke away from a White House meeting with thirty Democratic governors to stage an impromptu press conference.* His ploy knocked the latter part of Hamer's testimony off the air. That evening, however, the television networks replayed Hamer's graphic account in prime time. Following Hamer's testimony, the White House received 417 telegrams — all but one in favor of seating the Freedom Democrats.[47]

Roy Wilkins, James Farmer, and Joseph Rauh also spoke on behalf of the Mississippi Freedom Democratic Party, as did Aaron Henry, the delegation chairman, and the Reverend Edwin King, the vice chairman.† Dr. Martin Luther King Jr. brought his eloquence to bear. "If you value your party, if you value your nation, if you value the democratic process, then you must recognize the Freedom Party delegation," King testified, "for it is in these saints in ordinary life that the true spirit of democracy finds its most profound and abiding expression." King went on to contrast the MFDP's party loyalty with that of the Mississippi regulars, who were "already pledged to defy the candidate and the platform of this great party."[48] For the regulars, Mississippi state senator E. K. Collins argued to the skeptical committee that the Mississippi Democratic Party was open to all, including black citizens. A lawyer from Jones County, Collins failed to dispel the notion that most of his Democratic delegation, on their re-

---

* Johnson told reporters that he still had not decided on a vice presidential running mate, discussed some of the criteria he considered important for a vice president, and then returned to his leisurely meeting with the governors.

† King, chaplain at Tougaloo College, a predominantly black institution located outside Jackson, was one of the four white MFDP delegates. The others were A. D. "Dan" Beittel, president of Tougaloo; Lois Chaffee, a professor of English at Tougaloo; and a labor union official from Gulfport. Beittel did not attend the convention.

turn to Mississippi, planned to endorse Republican Barry Goldwater for president.

The next morning, an optimistic Rauh counted seventeen committee members who would support the Freedom Party, as well as ten state delegations willing to call for a vote on the convention floor. Fannie Lou Hamer and her fellow Freedom Democrats were now celebrities, mobbed by reporters and welcomed as they presented their case at various state delegation meetings. On the boardwalk in front of the convention center, crowds gathered at MFDP rallies to hear Hamer, in her strong alto voice, lead the delegates in singing "This Little Light of Mine." In an outdoor diorama the MFDP and its allies displayed powerful symbols: photographs of the shacks in which MFDP members and other black Mississippians lived, notarized stories of violence and racism, and the lists and locations of Ku Klux Klan bombings. The centerpiece was a replica of a charred Ford station wagon, delivered by flatbed truck from Mississippi; three poles beside it bore photographs of James Chaney, Andrew Goodman, and Michael Schwerner, a reminder of the murders committed only nine weeks earlier.[49]

The Freedom Democrats' excitement over their growing support was tempered by the reality of the president's ironclad control of the convention. Despite Hamer's testimony, the veteran Rauh knew that most of the 112 credentials committee members would follow the lead of chairman David Lawrence, former governor of Pennsylvania, and support whatever proposal the White House wanted. Maintaining the loyalty of their few supporters on the credentials committee was critical.

Political Espionage in Atlantic City

While Martin Luther King was testifying for the Freedom Democrats on Saturday afternoon, a team of FBI agents placed wiretaps on the telephones in his Claridge Hotel suite, rooms 1901, 1902, and 1923. Next they installed wiretaps and hidden microphones in the storefront offices at 2414 Atlantic Avenue, a shared headquarters rented by SNCC and CORE, the primary organizations supporting the Freedom Democrats.* Meanwhile, a team of four other FBI agents set up electronic equipment in room 1821 of the Claridge — directly below King's suite — from which they monitored and recorded King's calls and those from the SNCC–CORE headquarters.

On Sunday, August 23, assistant FBI director Deke DeLoach drove from

---

* The FBI agents were unable to place bugs for overhearing conversations within King's suite itself because King's aides returned before the installation could be completed.

Washington to Atlantic City to command a team of twenty-seven agents, one technical assistant, two secretaries, and a group of black informers assigned to infiltrate the MFDP delegation and its SNCC and CORE allies, all to help the president thwart the Freedom Democrats' challenge.

The agents set up an elaborate communications system to relay information almost instantly to President Johnson in the Oval Office. They made contact nearby with Walter Jenkins and Bill Moyers, the president's two most trusted aides at the convention center. From a special command post on the second floor of the old Atlantic City Post Office building, the FBI installed a direct telephone line to the president. The agents used walkie-talkies to speak directly to one another. Carrying a walkie-talkie, FBI agent Robert Tagg accompanied Jenkins and Moyers. To maintain strict security, key participants were assigned code names. Moyers, an ordained minister, was called "Bishop." The undercover informants identified themselves by saying, "This is Elmer." Posing as an NBC correspondent, FBI agent Ben Hale "interviewed" Freedom Party delegates and supporters on his walkie-talkie. His interviews were transmitted not to the broadcast network but to the FBI command post manned by DeLoach and four agents. FBI agent Lloyd Nelson, also using NBC credentials, posed as a news photographer.* A radio console monitor installed at the command post allowed agents to overhear SNCC–CORE communications. FBI informants — including one who became a driver for SNCC leaders — submitted reports.

DeLoach called the president frequently over the secure FBI line and sent him a stream of written messages. The agents monitoring King's telephone called in reports to the command post, where they were transmitted immediately to FBI headquarters in Washington, then sped to the White House by courier.

This FBI spy network produced instant results. Delegates Fannie Lou Hamer and Victoria Gray were observed conferring at breakfast Saturday morning with Verna Canson, a black activist from Sacramento, California, and a member of the credentials committee. The president and his operatives had counted on Canson as a supporter. The FBI report on her breakfast meeting with Hamer now heightened White House concern about her vote.

After debating the Mississippi delegate dispute all Sunday afternoon, the credentials committee was deadlocked. The Freedom Democrats rejected the president's three-point plan: to seat those "regulars" willing to take a

---

* NBC officials acknowledged to congressional investigators that they had supplied the FBI with official news credentials and badges for admission to the convention hall.

loyalty oath to the Democratic Party, its platform, and its presidential candidate; to make the Freedom Democrats honored guests at the convention; and to pledge an end to discrimination at future conventions. The delegation instead endorsed Oregon representative Edith Green's proposal, which would have seated both delegations, then divided the votes among delegates willing to take the loyalty oath. President Johnson immediately rejected Green's attempt at a compromise. "We'd have more damn wars than you ever saw," he warned. His concern was that any plan to seat the Freedom Democrats would trigger a walkout not only by Mississippi but by other southern delegations as well.[50]

With no solution in sight, the president told credentials committee chairman David Lawrence "to procrastinate." Lawrence promptly did just that, appointing a five-member subcommittee to study the problem. For subcommittee chairman he picked Minnesota attorney general Walter Mondale, a thirty-seven-year-old protégé of vice presidential aspirant Humphrey, who was working feverishly to satisfy Lyndon Johnson.

That Sunday evening Walter Jenkins called the president with more bad news. The Freedom Democrats had recruited more than enough votes on the credentials committee for Rauh to lead a floor fight. "Tell Rauh if he plans to play with us in this administration, he better not let that [Mississippi dispute] get out on the floor," Johnson instructed his aide. "Tell him the president said he watched you on TV, and you didn't do anything but hurt us."[51]

If the Mississippi issue reached the convention floor, Johnson knew, the deep schism already dividing the Democratic Party would be exposed — in all of its bitterness — to a national television audience, as would the conflicting loyalties within the president himself. The large northern delegations from states with substantial black populations would surely back the Freedom Democrats. Even Chicago's Mayor Daley, the last of the tough big-city bosses, warned Johnson that there would be an unacceptable stench of hypocrisy if Democrats who had just championed the greatest advance in civil rights since Lincoln now rejected courageous Mississippi blacks and embraced bitter-end segregationists who wouldn't even pledge loyalty to their own party's presidential candidate. Johnson realized that delegates such as Pittsburgh mayor Joe Barr, up for reelection in a city that was 20 percent black, would never vote for Mississippians perceived to have the blood of Chaney, Goodman, and Schwerner on their hands. But Johnson also knew that more was involved than just power politics. One faction of the party wanted to stand up proudly in support of its accomplishments in civil rights; another part, led by the president, didn't want to abandon its southern wing — segregation baggage and all — and tilt the country toward a Republican majority.

Johnson was as frustrated by the southerners who refused to give up their lost segregationist cause as he was with the MFDP. He demanded of Senator Eastland whether the Mississippi regulars had come to the convention "as traitors to the party — or are they going to try to be helpful?" After a half-dozen telephone pleas had produced only evasions, Johnson turned to threats. On Sunday evening he warned Eastland that he "might cut out your goddamn subsidies and cut out your $6 billion cotton program." Since he wouldn't carry Mississippi anyway, Johnson joked, he might as well "save about $6 billion I'm spending on agriculture."

Although Johnson laughed as he threatened the budget cuts, cotton subsidies were a serious matter for Mississippi, and for Eastland personally. The senator received thousands of dollars in federal payments on his own plantation in Sunflower County.* Twenty minutes later Eastland reported back that Governor Johnson had decided to let the individual delegates "use their own judgments" on whether or not to sign a loyalty oath.[52]

Martin Luther King Jr. and Lyndon Baines Johnson were shadowboxing — each seeking to influence the outcome of the Mississippi delegate fight, yet neither daring to score a public knockout. Personal feelings aside, they needed each other as allies against Barry Goldwater — and to win further civil rights victories in Congress. Now King jabbed again with a 1 A.M. telegram to the president.

"Only you are in a position to make clear the Democratic Party's position on the basic issues involved in this case," King wrote. "A great number of members of the credentials committee have made clear their wishes to follow you in helping the Mississippi Freedom Democratic Party's cause. Indeed, these delegates have also made clear their intention to wage a fight for the MFDP on the floor of the convention. . . . We urge you to join with these delegates in seating the only Mississippi Party chosen democratically and which is representative of the people in Mississippi."[53]

The FBI quickly informed the president that King and Robert Moses had drafted the telegram to register "a mild protest over what they considered a violated pledge" to stay neutral. According to the FBI report, "King

---

* The federal farm price support program tried to balance supply and demand by paying farmers to withhold part of their land from production. Mississippi and California planters received more cotton payments than those in any other state.

and Moses wanted to draft the telegram most carefully so as not to offend the President."

However "mild" King's intentions, Johnson woke on Tuesday morning, August 24, perceiving the King message — which had also been made public — as a major challenge to his authority. In a long telephone conversation with Senator Russell, Johnson saw terrible portent in the telegram: "What do you do when they [King and the Freedom Democrats] are getting ready to take charge of the convention . . . and they run over you — which they will — then what do you do?"

Sensing that Johnson was overreacting, Russell calmly advised, "You don't do a thing, but say you're sorry. You think they are ill-advised. And let it go." Simply ignore the telegram, Russell said. But Johnson would not let it go. He told Russell the country would conclude that "the Negroes have more power in the Democratic Party than the president has . . . and to hell with the Democratic Party." The president then speculated that King's telegram was part of a plot hatched by the attorney general. "This is Bobby's trap," Johnson insisted. Russell tried to convince his former protégé that he would win the election handily, that Robert Kennedy had no interest in helping Barry Goldwater, and that Negro voters would support him overwhelmingly regardless of what happened with the Mississippi challenge at the convention. The senator, however, could not budge the president.

Senator Hubert Humphrey, fearing that the vice presidency might be slipping from his grasp, scheduled a meeting in his suite at the Pageant Motel at 1:40 P.M. on Tuesday, August 24. He had invited a small cadre of national civil rights leaders: Martin Luther King and his lieutenant Andrew Young, King adviser Bayard Rustin, James Farmer of CORE, and Roy Wilkins of the NAACP. Humphrey hoped to persuade Dr. Aaron Henry, chairman of the Mississippi Freedom Democratic Party delegation, the Reverend Edwin King, the most prominent white member of the MFDP delegation, and their lawyer, Joseph Rauh, to accept the president's compromise. But Henry and Edwin King brought with them two uninvited guests — SNCC organizer Bob Moses and the imposing Fannie Lou Hamer, vice chairman of the Freedom Democrats' delegation. Also crowding into the suite — some participants had to sit on the floor — were several credentials committee members who supported the MFDP, among them Verna Canson, central California field secretary for the NAACP, and Representative Edith Green from Oregon.

The meeting did not go smoothly. Bob Moses at once challenged the justice of Humphrey's offer, which included only honorary status for the MFDP delegates. "The time has come for Negroes to speak for Negroes, for Negroes to represent Negroes," Moses insisted. "The Freedom Democrats can accept no less than equal votes at the convention."

"I have to disagree with you," Humphrey replied. "If your position is true, then democracy is not real; this cannot be a society in which we all live in peace as brothers." Then, turning to King, Humphrey said, "Doctor, if this is true, you may as well throw away your book and stop preaching love and brotherhood." King nodded agreement.

Humphrey appealed to the Freedom Democrats, reminding them of not only his own lifelong support for civil rights but also his hopes of being chosen as the vice presidential candidate. "Senator Humphrey, I've been praying about you," Fannie Lou Hamer told him, "and you're a good man, and you know what's right. The trouble is you're afraid to do what you know is right." How could Humphrey regard his own political ambitions as more important than "400,000 black people's lives?" she asked.[54]

The meeting disintegrated into further accusations. Rauh requested that the credentials committee meeting scheduled for 2 P.M. — twenty minutes later — be postponed. Humphrey replied testily, "Well, I don't see what all the people from the credentials committee are doing here anyway," at which point Representative Green, who had proposed splitting the delegation between the rival groups, stormed out to announce to waiting journalists, "Humphrey is trying to force the Freedom Party to sell out!"[55]

After the meeting an exasperated Humphrey reported back to the president: "I walked into the lion's den. I listened patiently. I argued fervently. I used all the heartstrings that I had, and I made no headway. The least — the very minimum they would accept — would be something that would involve giving them some votes, perhaps the Ullman proposal that gives them two."* Johnson and Humphrey agreed that Humphrey should test the idea of allowing the MFDP several votes in the convention.[56]

Grasping at straws, Johnson briefly explored an idea suggested by his secretary, Juanita Roberts: one or two of the friendly Mississippi regulars could relinquish their convention seats and be replaced by Freedom Democrats. But he soon turned his attention to machinations aimed at reducing the MFDP's support. From the White House he instructed Jenkins in Atlantic City to ask former governor Mennen Williams of Michigan to work on his state's committee members, for former New York governor

---

* Representative Al Ullman of Oregon had proposed to the credentials committee on Sunday that the MFDP be given two votes, a suggestion that at the time satisfied nobody.

Averell Harriman to lobby his members, and for his own commerce secretary, Luther Hodges, a former governor of North Carolina, to appeal to the southern delegates. To dissuade the two Colorado credentials committee members from backing a minority report, Johnson called Palmer Hoyt, publisher of the *Denver Post*, who was thoroughly puzzled by Johnson's complex instructions about what the Colorado delegates must do to keep "Goldwater from becoming president."[57]

With his penchant for maintaining secrecy while keeping his options open, Johnson repeatedly enjoined his aides to deny his involvement even as he tried to orchestrate every political detail in Atlantic City. "My name's Joe Glutz and you haven't talked down here," he cautioned Humphrey.[58]

That Tuesday evening the convention opened with a stem-winding keynote address from Senator John Pastore of Rhode Island. He roused the 5,200 delegates and alternates by declaring the Republican Party captive to "reactionaries and extremists" and calling Senator Goldwater's candidacy a "Trojan horse" that would threaten American security and prosperity. The delegate dispute was postponed for another day while the president continued, in a telephone call with Walter Reuther in Detroit, to fret over it. Even though he was engaged in tense contract negotiations with Detroit's major auto manufacturers, Reuther succumbed to Johnson's arm-twisting. The UAW president agreed to fly by chartered jet into Atlantic City at 3 A.M. to try to help the president of the United States.[59]

Voices and Moods

Lyndon Johnson awoke Wednesday morning, August 25, depressed and bitter. It was the sort of mood he had displayed at earlier critical moments in his political career — the final days of his first run for Congress in 1937, or when he was debating whether to run for the Senate in 1948. On those occasions Johnson had sounded like a man filled with self-doubt; even on the eve of victory, he seemed ready to give up whatever political prize he had worked so tirelessly to achieve.

At 8:15 A.M. Johnson called Senator Richard Russell at his home in Winder, Georgia. He had "reached a decision" he would not discuss "with anyone," he said, except with Russell and A. W. Moursund, Johnson's close Texas friend and fellow rancher. He told Russell that he "had tried to get harmony and unity [in the Democratic Party] and had failed," and that his "enemies and the Negro leaders had taken over the convention." He was going to Atlantic City at about 7:30 that night, and there he would serve notice that he had incurred "too many scars and could not unite the country in today's troubled world." He would tell the convention "to get some fresh figure to nominate and elect." Then he would try to hold the country together until January. He told Russell that he was "especially bitter towards the Massachusetts members of the credentials committee [presumably Kennedy followers who supported the Freedom Democrats' challenge] and Martin Luther King." The "Freedom Party has control of the convention," Johnson again lamented.

Russell listened patiently to the stream of complaints until Johnson told him that he had "only accepted the vice presidential nomination in 1960 to avoid dropping dead on the Senate floor as majority leader" and was "looking for the peace and quiet of the vice president's job." That disclaimer was too much for Russell, who had endured Johnson's voracious ambition for sixteen years. Russell interrupted the president's monologue. Asking forgiveness for his frankness, Russell told Johnson that he was "speaking like a child — and a spoiled one at that." The senator said that he knew Johnson was not serious. He advised him to "take a tranquilizer and get a couple of hours' sleep."

After the telephone call ended, Russell wrote in his diary that Johnson's self-pitying conversation reminded him of a time years earlier when Johnson, as Senate minority leader, had "wept for a half-hour over something I had said on the [Senate] floor. . . . This complex and usually ruthless man was as bitter in his disappointment as a child and had to cry on someone's shoulder. He knew or should have known that I knew he was as likely to try to swim the Atlantic Ocean as he was to retire." Russell concluded, "If he had been at Atlantic City to work with people and issues, he would never have had this depressed and bitter mood."[60]

In four more conversations Wednesday morning, however, each with someone he trusted, Johnson vowed to step down as president. With press secretary George Reedy, Johnson read from his draft of a speech he said he would give at the convention: "Our country faces grave dangers. These dangers must be faced and met by a united people under a leader they do not doubt. The times require leadership and a voice that men of all parties, sections, and color can follow. I have learned after trying very hard that I am not that voice or that leader." The president's conversations that morning followed several themes. One was his hypersensitivity to criticism. "I do not have the hide of a rhinoceros," he told Reedy. Another was the extraordinarily high value he placed on national unity — or perhaps on his own authority. "I have a desire to unite people," he told Reedy, "and the South is against me, and the North is against me, and the Negroes are against me, and the press really doesn't have any affection for me." He was hurt, he said, when British journalist Henry Brandon wrote that "people respected [Johnson's] ability," but "he has not aroused any excitement as a person or any emotion or enthusiasm as a human being."

Johnson's deep longing for appreciation came through in his conversation with longtime friend and loyal employee Walter Jenkins. "Here, at the crowning point of my life, when I need people's help, I haven't even got the loyalty here," he complained. "People, I think, have a mistaken judgment. They think I want great power. What I want is great solace, a little love. That is all I want."[61]

Lady Bird Johnson lamented in her diary, "I do not remember hours I ever found harder." When Johnson was not on the telephone or at meetings, she observed a depressed husband crawling into his bed with the covers drawn and window shades lowered. Lady Bird, who had lived with Johnson through all of his mercurial moods, responded in the way she thought would be most reassuring: "Beloved — you are as brave a man as Harry Truman — or FDR — or Lincoln. You can go on to find some peace, some achievement amidst all the pain. . . . To step out now would be wrong for your country, and I see nothing but a lonely wasteland for your future. Your friends would be frozen in embarrassed silence and your enemies jeering. . . . I know it's only your choice. I love you always, Bird."[62]

Lady Bird had expressed the same thoughts in a much longer note to her husband just three months earlier when he was in similarly downcast spirits. His mood seemed to consist of a mixture of self-pity and self-doubt, or else — as some of his close associates thought — it was a manipulative attempt to win sympathy and get his own way. Although Johnson ultimately may have had no intention of quitting, his close friend Abe Fortas believed that the president "wasn't just playing games with his intimates" but "was constantly rearguing the question with himself . . . saying to himself, 'This is not the right thing to do. . . . Maybe the convention really won't want me, and even if they do want me . . . I shouldn't do it.'"[63]

Johnson's personality, his actions, and his motives confounded even those closest to him. In this situation, when Johnson said he was going to quit, some thought he was only seeking attention and reassurance . . . or that he was having a childish temper tantrum. Others felt that he was genuinely conflicted about his ability to unify and lead the nation . . . or that he was limitlessly manipulative. In truth, Lyndon Johnson was a highly complex human being whose behavior defied a simple explanation.

Arriving in Atlantic City at three o'clock Wednesday morning, Walter Reuther huddled with Hubert Humphrey and Walter Mondale, now the credentials subcommittee chairman, charting a new proposal to settle the Mississippi delegate dispute. They decided to sweeten the president's earlier plan by offering the Freedom Democrats two at-large seats with full voting rights. They assigned the seats to delegation chairman Aaron Henry, the black pharmacist from Clarksdale, and the Reverend Edwin King, the white chaplain of historically black Tougaloo College and vice chairman of the Freedom Democratic Party.

With the two at-large seats and the establishment of a commission to prevent discrimination at future Democratic conventions, Reuther and Humphrey hoped to win over the Freedom Democrats. Failing that, they wanted at least to satisfy enough credentials committee members to avoid a floor fight. At two o'clock that afternoon, Mondale presented the plan to the full credentials committee. Meanwhile, across the street at the Pageant Motel, Humphrey and Reuther were still trying to win cooperation from the Freedom Democrats and national civil rights leaders.

Minutes before the credentials committee convened, Joseph Rauh answered an urgent summons to call Walter Reuther. From a pay phone outside the committee room, Rauh listened as Reuther, calling from Humphrey's hotel room, described the two at-large seats "as a tremendous victory" for the Freedom Democrats. "It is a great proposal," agreed Rauh, but he told Reuther he needed time to consult with delegation chairman Henry. "I want you to go to the credentials committee meeting [now] and accept this proposal," Reuther insisted. Rauh again said he needed his client's approval. The UAW president informed his union's general counsel in no uncertain terms that he would either follow orders or be fired. Now desperate, Rauh hurried into the committee meeting, hoping to stall a vote until he could find the Freedom Party leaders.[64]

In Humphrey's crowded hotel suite, Humphrey and Reuther presented the new plan to Martin Luther King Jr., Andrew Young, Bayard Rustin, Roy Wilkins, and Robert Moses, and to MFDP leaders Aaron Henry and Edwin King. Reuther wasted little time on pleasantries. "Your funding is on the line," he told Martin Luther King. If King would help the president settle the Mississippi dispute, the UAW would help underwrite King's civil rights work in Mississippi, as it had earlier in Birmingham. If King didn't help the president, Reuther warned, there would be no more union money.[65] King then urged Aaron Henry and Ed King to accept the agreement, arguing that it would be wonderful for Negro people all over America to see the Freedom Democrats recognized by having the two men seated at the convention.[66]

After conferring with the other leaders, Edwin King proposed several variations on Humphrey's two-delegate proposal: either he would give up his seat in favor of Fannie Lou Hamer, or the Freedom Democrats might ask for representation by four delegates, each with one-half vote. Humphrey said that the president was insisting on Edwin King "because he wants an inter-racial delegation."

"Well, I'm sure Mrs. Hamer has to be part of it," replied the white minister, who realized that his delegation would turn down any plan that omitted representation of its grassroots black leaders.

"The President has said that he will not let that illiterate woman speak on the floor of the Democratic convention," replied Humphrey.

When Moses accused Humphrey of being a racist, Humphrey defensively replied, "No, that's what the President said." Then, trying to soften his statement, Humphrey stumbled further, saying that surely the MFDP could find someone else to speak "who can handle themselves better." As Ed King interpreted Humphrey's comments, the president feared the backlash that would come from unsympathetic whites on hearing the raw emotional power of Hamer's unschooled speech.[67]

The discussion was interrupted when an aide rushed into Humphrey's room. "You must come look at the TV," he told Humphrey. A television set was rolled into the bedroom in time for the group to hear a newscaster announce that the credentials committee had approved the report, and the Mississippi Freedom Democratic Party had accepted its two seats.

"You cheated!" Moses shouted at Humphrey, convinced that he and the MFDP leaders had been lured to the meeting as a diversionary maneuver while the credentials committee approved the delegate plan. Moses rushed out of the room, slamming the door behind him.[68]

Across the street at the convention center, Rauh had implored the credentials committee to recess briefly so he could confer with his clients before the vote on the new plan. Mondale and Governor Lawrence were receptive to Rauh's plea, but the White House's orders were represented by delegate Sherwin Markman, a tough Iowa lawyer. Markman insisted on ramming the plan through for fear that delay would lead to a demand for more concessions. "A decision has been made," declared Markman. "There will be no further delay." The plan was approved by a voice vote, with Rauh and other MFDP supporters shouting their dissent.[69]

With the Mississippi delegate plan headed to the convention floor for a final vote, Rauh sought out MFDP supporters to sign a minority report. His heart sank as he realized that the Freedom Democrats' backing on the committee had plunged from seventeen votes to eight — not enough to compel a floor fight. Several committee members had been convinced by Mondale and Lawrence that the new proposal represented progress and a fair compromise. Others had yielded to pressure from politicians at home. The governors of California, Michigan, Washington, and Maryland, along with the mayors of New York and Chicago, were working with the president to change the votes of eight MFDP supporters from their states. Governor Edmund "Pat" Brown of California and Assembly Speaker Jesse Unruh leaned hard on black delegate Verna Canson. An assistant to the governor told her that the president had requested that she not sign a minority report. When she hesitated, California officials warned Canson that the state judgeship for which her husband was a candidate would be denied him if she continued to support the Freedom Democrats. Resisting the pressure, Canson stuck with the MFDP until the final compromise proposal, which she accepted as a fair solution.*[70] Victorine Adams, a black member of the Baltimore City Council, left the MFDP fold after relentless pressure from both the White House and state officials in Annapolis. Some committee members stood by the MFDP to the end, however. Even though he had been threatened with the loss of his federal job, a delegate from the Canal Zone said "to hell with the job" and joined Rauh's frantic efforts to round up enough signatures for a minority report.

President Johnson's mission to whittle away MFDP support was abetted by intelligence from Deke DeLoach and his FBI team. While the White House and MFDP were scrambling for votes on August 24 and 25, DeLoach kept the president informed of the minute-by-minute plans and tactics of the Freedom Democrats and their allies — especially those of Martin Luther King. First by telephone, then in written memos, DeLoach reported that the Freedom Democrats had implored King to ask the governors of California, Massachusetts, and New Hampshire and the mayors of New York and Chicago "to call the White House directly and put pressure on the White House in behalf of the MFDP." Later in the day, DeLoach reported that King also had been asked to enlist support for a floor fight from the governors of Alaska and Hawaii. The FBI wiretap on King's telephone in the Claridge Hotel produced more useful information Tuesday afternoon. A credentials committee member from Washington state called King to apologize that her state could no longer support the

* Her husband did not receive the judicial appointment. He and his family were convinced that his wife's show of independence, which he supported, had killed the appointment. In her diary, Verna Canson described the pressure she was under but claimed that she had approved the final compromise on its merits.

Freedom Democrats' challenge. Acting on information from those FBI reports, President Johnson had deployed his considerable forces to counter every MFDP move.

Johnson had acted ruthlessly, and recklessly as well. One slip-up by the FBI agents, and the president might have had his own Watergate in Atlantic City. Most of Johnson's strong-arm tactics were unknown to the convention delegates. But the president's obsession with crushing the MFDP challenge would cost him dearly with the young black idealists.

A Passion for the Underdog

President Johnson's mood soared Tuesday afternoon. With his victory in the credentials committee, his talk of resignation subsided, and his comments about the cause of the African Americans from Mississippi grew much more positive. Only the Mississippi and Alabama delegations walked out — as expected. The others all remained; Johnson had quashed the southern rebellion. His impatience was now redirected toward the segregationists — the Alabamans and Mississippians who had walked — and at other southerners who had insisted on further appeasement.

Learning of the credentials committee action, Governor Carl Sanders of Georgia called the president to argue against giving the MFDP even two seats at the convention. The agreement, he charged, made it appear that "the niggers took over the damn convention." He threatened a walkout himself.

Sanders's denunciation of the Freedom Democrats aroused in Johnson the same passion with which he had waged the ten-month battle to pass the Civil Rights Act of 1964. After complaining incessantly for ten days about how the black Mississippians and Martin Luther King were driving the South out of the party and helping to elect Barry Goldwater, the president now took the opposite side and defended the MFDP. "They're Democrats," he told Sanders, "and, by God, they tried to attend the convention and pistols kept them out. These people went in and begged to go and participate in the conventions — and they've got half the population [of Mississippi]. And they won't let them. They lock them out."

When Sanders complained that the Freedom Democrats were not registered to vote, the president countered, "The state of Mississippi wouldn't let them come in to their damn convention. They wouldn't let them vote. They wouldn't let them register — intimidated them. And by God they ought to be seated!

"Carl, you and I just can't survive our political modern life with these goddamn fellows down there that are eating them for breakfast every morning," he continued. "They've got to quit that. And they've got to let them vote, and they got to let them shave, and they got to let them eat . . . and things like that. And they don't do it."

In a period of several days in the MFDP fight, Lyndon Johnson had displayed each of the wildly contradictory aspects of his persona, his mixture of motives — from idealistic to base — and his insatiable thirst for control. Viewed in even limited historical perspective, Johnson's final compromise was a reasonable one, which acknowledged the legitimacy of the Freedom Democrats' complaint and provided a solution for future conventions.

On a voice vote, the official fight ended quickly. Acting chairman John Pastore, the senior senator from Rhode Island, pounded his final gavel on the credentials committee's proposal giving the Freedom Democrats two votes while charting the course for future reform. There would be no minority report. But the Freedom Democrats and their SNCC allies continued their resistance. In a meeting earlier Tuesday evening in the basement of the Union Temple Baptist Church, the MFDP had angrily voted against the compromise. Martin Luther King and Mississippi's Aaron Henry were shouted down as they tried to speak in favor of the plan. Before the meeting broke up, Ella Baker attacked the credentials committee delegates who had withdrawn their support for selling out "for $20,000 a year judgeships" and other material benefits. Joseph Rauh sadly returned to the convention chairman the official delegate badges that had just been awarded to Henry and Edwin King, both of whom had wanted to accept them.

The Freedom Democrats' four-month campaign to represent Mississippi at the Democratic National Convention now turned to protest. The two-day vigil SNCC and CORE organized outside the convention center swelled to more than two thousand demonstrators Tuesday evening, blocking the way of delegates trying to enter the building. After borrowing official badges from sympathetic delegates inside the convention, Robert Moses smuggled more than thirty members of the Freedom Party delegation through a basement door. They occupied the official Mississippi seats in the hall while the three Mississippi regulars who had signed Johnson's loyalty oath fled to a VIP delegate lounge.* President Johnson phoned the loyalists to praise their courage. "You saved your state," he told them.[71] Johnson assistant Bill Moyers then ordered the usurpers removed. Marvin Watson, another Johnson aide, asked a sergeant at arms to eject the delegates, but Walter Jenkins intervened, realizing that the televised presence of Fannie Lou Hamer and her colleagues was far less threatening to the president than the sight of guards trying to carry them out of the hall.[72]

* The three white Mississippi delegates were Doug Wynn, an attorney and Johnson family friend from Greenville; Fred Berger of Natchez; and Randy Holliday of Picayune.

When John Chancellor of NBC News questioned Moses about the compromise, the organizer replied, "What is the compromise? We are here for the people and the people want to represent themselves. They don't want symbolic token votes. They want to vote themselves." Moses and many of the delegates were not willing to settle for fewer than one-half of the seats. That the president had decided who would represent the Freedom Democrats in the two at-large seats added insult to injury. For Moses, Fannie Lou Hamer, and others, it was too much like the "white plantation boss making all the decisions for his black sharecroppers."[73]

The Freedom Democrats met again at the church on Saturday morning to reconsider whether to accept the convention's compromise. The issue now was how the delegation and the nation itself would perceive what had happened at Atlantic City. Would the outcome be viewed as a victory for the civil rights movement or as a defeat? An impressive array of national leaders from the movement, Congress, and the National Council of Churches urged the Freedom Democrats to accept the compromise as a significant victory in the long struggle for equal rights.

"We believe that a tremendous advance has been made," said MFDP attorney Rauh. "We succeeded in ousting the other group — they have taken the first available transportation home. We got the token representation in Aaron Henry and Reverend King. We have got the promise that this will never happen again."[74]

The civil rights movement was in transition "from protest to politics," argued Bayard Rustin, and in politics compromise was necessary. Rustin's argument did not persuade Robert Moses. "We're not here to bring politics to our morality," he said, "but to bring morality to our politics."[75]

The Rustin–Moses exchange captured the political and ideological divide emerging among the civil rights forces. On one side were leaders accustomed to working within the system, expecting to accept partial victories as they moved to their next objective. Martin Luther King concurred with Rustin that the civil rights forces were moving from protest to politics.

King spoke in favor of the agreement, but in the nuanced and balanced manner that characterized his efforts to mediate thorny issues within the movement and preserved his standing as a unifying leader. In what aides called King's "Hegelian" style, he presented arguments for supporting the agreement: the need to compromise, the help that could be expected from the president and the national government. But he also saw reasons to oppose it: the just cause and hard work of the MFDP delegates, the inadequacy of the compromise, the crude manner in which the White House had crushed the Freedom Democrats' petition. King told MFDP delegate

Ed King that he "wanted to see [the Freedom Democrats] take the agreement because it would mean strength for [him], help for [him] in Negro voter registration in both the North and South," and would encourage blacks in other southern states to initiate efforts similar to those in Mississippi.

"So, being a Negro leader, I want you to take this, but if I were a Mississippi Negro, I would vote against it," said Martin Luther King.[76]

The arguments of Dr. King and the other leaders, black and white, persuaded only a minority of the delegates and none of the SNCC organizers. Within the Freedom Democratic Party there was division as well along class lines: the professionals and more affluent delegates, including Aaron Henry and Ed King, argued for acceptance, while the lower-income rural delegates resented what they saw as condescension toward them. "You have made your point, but you don't know anything and should go home to Mississippi," Roy Wilkins told Hamer. Snapped Victoria Gray, another of the grassroots leaders, "You can't talk to Mrs. Hamer like that!" silencing Wilkins immediately.[77]

Both their passion and emotion and their political naïveté came into play as the Freedom Democrats again rejected the compromise. After risking death to reach Atlantic City, many considered the offer an insult. "We didn't come all this way for no two seats," insisted Hamer.

Even though the delegate battle ended inconclusively, with neither side accepting the compromise, the experience triggered dramatic changes within the civil rights movement. The disillusioned SNCC organizers and delegates were radicalized by what happened in Atlantic City. In their view, they had played by the rules only to see the liberal Democratic establishment participate in crushing their effort. As SNCC organizer Cleveland Sellers described the outcome, "Never again were we lulled into believing that our task was exposing injustices so that the 'good people' of America could eliminate them. We left Atlantic City with the knowledge that the movement had turned into something else. After Atlantic City, our struggle was not for civil rights, but for liberation."[78]

All the same, the convention had begun the process of opening up the Democratic Party to African Americans in the Deep South. More important, the MFDP effort sparked a surge in demand for federal voting rights legislation.

With the Mississippi delegate dispute settled, Lyndon Johnson emerged from his depression and enthusiastically chose Hubert Humphrey as his running mate. Both men were nominated by acclamation Wednesday evening to represent the Democratic Party in the November election. On

Thursday night the president celebrated his fifty-sixth birthday in Atlantic City with four thousand cheering convention guests. In his acceptance speech, greeted with thunderous applause from the partisan audience, Johnson reminded the nation: "Every American has the right to be treated as a person. He should be able to find a job. He should be able to educate his children, he should be able to vote in elections, and he should be judged on his merits as a person. Well, this is the fixed policy and the fixed determination of the Democratic Party and the United States of America."[79] The Johnson family then watched a parade on the boardwalk that ended with a gigantic fireworks display — a red, white, and blue portrait of Lyndon Baines Johnson spread across the sky.[80]

As the Freedom Party delegates boarded buses to return home to Mississippi, Martin Luther King and Andrew Young met with Walter Reuther to discuss King's role in the upcoming campaign. With Reuther providing the financing, King would campaign in northern cities to bring out the black vote for President Johnson. At the White House the next morning, Reuther gave the president a report on his efforts at the convention and his arrangements with King to aid the campaign.

As he thanked Reuther and others for their help in Atlantic City, Johnson wrote a letter of appreciation to J. Edgar Hoover for the FBI's work there: "Walter Jenkins and Bill Moyers have advised me that they were kept constantly alerted to the actions of certain personalities and groups who, if left unchecked, would certainly have proved far more disruptive. The presence of your men, although completely unobserved by all except my immediate assistants, contributed tremendously to the successful outcome of the convention." Anxious to avoid any public written record of the FBI undercover role, Johnson instructed Walter Jenkins not to mail the letter. Instead, the president scrawled on the bottom of the letter, "Walter, call Hoover and say this for me orally."*[81]

LBJ Confronts Southern Racism

The fall campaign took off in earnest at the end of September. Johnson drew large, enthusiastic crowds as he traveled through New England. From the outset, the polls consistently showed him with a two-to-one lead over Goldwater. The White House ran a tough, negative campaign, hammering at Goldwater as a political extremist who could not be en-

---

* Moyers also wrote a note to DeLoach thanking him and the FBI. In an effort to maintain secrecy, many of the FBI memos to Johnson were written on plain paper and handled only by Walter Jenkins and Mildred Stegall. After the president read them, Stegall locked them in a safe that also contained Johnson's personal and business papers. (AI, Mildred Stegall)

trusted with control of nuclear weapons and who would dismantle popular federal programs, including Social Security. The Democrats suggested that, in Vietnam, Goldwater would recklessly provoke a wider war with China or Russia. In contrast, Johnson sought to reassure the nation that he would not send "American boys" to do the fighting that the Vietnamese should be doing themselves. Goldwater cooperated in the negative portrayal by doing little to show himself as more moderate than his most outrageous statements suggested. Accusing Johnson of being a corrupt proponent of big government, Goldwater tried to focus his campaign on moral principles rather than programs, with slogans such as "In Your Heart, You Know He's Right" and "A Choice, Not an Echo." The Johnson advertising team responded with slogans of its own — "Yes, Far Right" and "In Your Guts, You Know He's Nuts."

Despite a public pledge by both candidates to avoid making race an issue, it remained an undercurrent throughout the campaign, with Goldwater courting a white backlash by associating Johnson with the past summer's riots and with rising crime rates in the cities. Still worried about the backlash, Johnson did not emphasize civil rights, though neither did he seek to avoid the question. The campaign reached an emotional peak in New Orleans on October 9 as the president again dramatically confronted the race issue in the heart of his native South.

Johnson went to the train station in New Orleans for a reunion with his wife, who was arriving there at the end of a whistle-stop tour in which she had ridden the "Lady Bird Special" for four days and made forty-seven speeches in six southern states. It was a brave effort to salvage some of the South, where the proud native of Texas hoped to draw support now denied to her husband and his running mate, Hubert Humphrey, the architects of the 1964 Civil Rights Act. She persevered despite refusals of help from many southern Democratic leaders — including Senator Willis Robertson of Virginia, who said that he would be away on an antelope-hunting trip, and a governor who claimed to be in mourning for his wife, who had died two years earlier. Klansmen burned a cross on the lawn of South Carolina governor Donald Russell's executive mansion to protest his welcoming the first lady to his state, and in Columbia an unruly crowd tried to drown out her speech with catcalls. In Charleston a mob chanted, "Johnson is a Communist. Johnson is a nigger lover." Mrs. Johnson won support from some southerners as she expressed affection for her native region, and respect for standing her ground against hostile crowds. "My friends, in this country, we are entitled to many viewpoints," she said in Charleston. "You are entitled to yours. But right now, I am entitled to mine."[82]

Lyndon Johnson proudly embraced his wife as the "Lady Bird Special" pulled into Union Station. Then he pointedly ignored political advice about what he should and shouldn't say in Louisiana, a strongly segregationist state. Although Barry Goldwater led in state polls, Johnson still had a chance to carry Louisiana on November 3. His White House briefing memo for New Orleans described civil rights as "the underlying campaign issue" and cautioned that "the less said about civil rights the better."[83] Yet it was civil rights and old-time southern populism that moved Johnson that night as he spoke to fifteen hundred Democrats at a $100-a-plate fundraiser in the ballroom of the Jung Hotel in downtown New Orleans. Thousands more saw the speech on a statewide television hookup.

Johnson departed from his prepared speech to describe how the political philosophy of "a young country kid from the poor hills of Texas" had been shaped during the depths of the Great Depression by Huey Long, the legendary Louisiana populist. Even though Long was "frequently harassed and criticized," Johnson said, "I became an admirer of his because I thought he had a heart for the people" and spoke out for those who couldn't make speeches for themselves.

Johnson then told the story of a U.S. senator from Texas who had grown up in another southern state.* The senator had once lamented to a friend how the South had been exploited by outside economic interests that maintained power by first dividing and conquering the South's people, then paying them poverty wages and shipping the South's resources to other regions. The old senator described what a great future the South could enjoy if it would just develop and benefit from its own resources. Finally, the senator said that he wished he could return to his birthplace to speak one last time.

"I would like to go back down there and make them one more Democratic speech," the old senator said. "I just feel like I have one in me. The poor old state, they haven't heard a Democratic speech in thirty years. All they ever hear at election time is 'Nigger, Nigger, Nigger.'"

The New Orleans audience sat in stunned silence, then slowly rose to give President Johnson an eight-minute standing ovation. Johnson, who had worked up a sweat, pulled off his suit jacket, loosened his tie, and rolled up his sleeves. The Lyndon Johnson now speaking in the Jung ballroom was the populist storyteller who had grown up poor in hardscrabble Texas hill country, taught even poorer Mexican children in a rural school, worked in the National Youth Administration, studied the Senate

---

* The unnamed senator was Joseph Bailey, who had grown up in Mississippi. Johnson had heard the story from Sam Rayburn, to whom Bailey had related it.

speeches of Huey Long, and come to Congress at age twenty-seven and voted down the line for Franklin Roosevelt's programs to lift the nation out of the depression. And this Lyndon Johnson believed that racism was the poison that was preventing the South from realizing its potential. Just as he had urged President Kennedy to do, he was confronting his fellow southerners honestly, to their face. As he had told Kennedy, that was the only way to win their respect, if not their agreement.

"I am not going to let them build up the hate and try to buy my people by appealing to their prejudice," Johnson continued. "Whatever your views are, we have a Constitution, and we have a Bill of Rights, and we have a law of the land [the Civil Rights Act], and two-thirds of the Democrats in the Senate voted for it, and three-fourths of the Republicans. I signed it, and I am going to enforce it, and I am going to observe it. And I think that anyone who is worthy of the high office of President is going to do the same thing."[84]

Columnist Mary McGrory, a Boston Irish Catholic with a soft spot in her heart for the Kennedys, wrote that Johnson's New Orleans address was the finest political speech she had ever heard. Other reporters said they finally understood Johnson's roots and motivations and admired his "show of deliberate courage."[85]

The Goldwater camp's hopes for a White House scandal touching Johnson were almost realized on October 12, when newspapers reported that Walter Jenkins, the president's aide and the father of six, had been arrested on October 7 in a YMCA men's room near the White House on a charge of indecent sexual behavior.* Jenkins, allegedly suffering from physical and mental exhaustion as a result of months of eighteen-hour workdays, was hospitalized and forced to resign immediately. Any possibility that the story might catch fire and hurt Johnson disappeared as the Jenkins case was overwhelmed by headlines from abroad: the resignation of Soviet premier Nikita Khrushchev, the Communist Chinese government's explosion of its first nuclear weapon, and the victory of a Labour government in Britain.

In mid-October, as a record Democratic victory looked possible, the president began to speak expansively about the possibilities of achieving a Great Society and of waging a triumphant War on Poverty.

---

* Goldwater did not personally seek to make the Jenkins arrest a campaign issue. As a general in a U.S. Air Force Reserve unit based at the Capitol, Goldwater consistently had given Colonel Walter Jenkins the highest fitness ratings. Johnson had the Pentagon retrieve these records in case Goldwater tried to bring it up.

Nobel Prize on the Hustings

Carrying out a plan he had conceived more than a year earlier, Martin Luther King Jr. also took to the political hustings. His style differed only in degree from that of the Johnson administration officials who were bashing Barry Goldwater as a danger to the American republic. With political advance men advertising his appearances, King barnstormed through key cities to bring out a maximum African American vote for "the most crucial and decisive election in our history." He began in the heart of a black Brooklyn neighborhood, telling 2,500 at the Antioch Baptist Church that a big Negro vote was essential "to insure not just a victory for President Johnson, but a telling blow against Goldwaterism."[86]

King waged what was, in effect, a shadow campaign targeted at black audiences in New York, Baltimore, Cleveland, Chicago, and Los Angeles — cities with the nation's largest concentrations of African American voters. The tour, planned by Louis Martin, vice chairman of the Democratic National Committee and the party's key black strategist, was designed without any effort to publicize King's appearances to the white community. Goldwater's candidacy made it "essential for us to turn all forces to areas where registration could be readily accomplished and where practical results were possible," King explained in Savannah.[87] Set aside for the moment was the difficult and dangerous work needed to call national attention to the suppression of black voting rights in the South. That effort would be redoubled once Goldwater was defeated and political credit was recognized.

Maintaining only a thin veneer of nonpartisanship, King usually spoke against Goldwater without overtly endorsing Johnson. His lieutenants Bayard Rustin, Ralph Abernathy, and Walter Fauntroy would start the chant "All the way . . ." and let the audiences provide the concluding "with LBJ." Asked in Cleveland whether blacks would vote for Johnson only "as the lesser of two evils," King responded, "Most Negroes take Johnson in good faith. The President has been strong on civil rights. His record shows it. And that is what the Negro is voting for."[88]

In the midst of the campaign, King received the momentous news that he had been selected to receive the 1964 Nobel Prize for Peace. At thirty-five, he was the youngest person ever to win the award, and only the second African American.* As congratulations poured in from all over the world, Coretta King was incensed at the lack of even a perfunctory acknowledgment from the White House.† With the election only two weeks

---

* The first was Ralph Bunche (1950), an undersecretary at the United Nations.

† Johnson had in fact sent a congratulatory telegram, but it had not yet been opened by King's busy SCLC office.

away, King told her, the president simply wanted to avoid irritating southern white voters.[89]

The Reverend Martin Luther King Jr., Nobel laureate, had time for neither celebration nor personal pique as he rose from a hospital bed — recovering from chronic exhaustion — to campaign at twenty street corner rallies in Chicago and then moved on to Detroit and Baltimore. King would ride in an open convertible through black neighborhoods where a crowd might be drawn, and then — after Rustin or Abernathy warmed up the audience — would speak from a flatbed truck. "To get rid of slums, ghettoes, poverty, unemployment, and segregation," King said in Baltimore on October 30, "we must recognize the power of the ballot — we must take a short walk to the voting booth on Tuesday."[90] If every registered black voter came out and voted for the same presidential candidate on Election Day, Johnson would carry every state in the union — except Mississippi and Alabama, King quipped, and "even the good Lord could not win there."[91]

A lost cause in Mississippi for Johnson and King in 1964 was still a challenge for some of the MFDP and SNCC veterans of Atlantic City. After the convention, MFDP chairman Lawrence Guyot led a concerted campaign for the Johnson–Humphrey ticket and fielded three MFDP candidates for Congress — spirited convention veterans Fannie Lou Hamer, Victoria Gray, and Annie Devine. Again denied entry into the official election process, the three women nevertheless polled sixty thousand votes at special MFDP polling places on Election Day.

The civil rights movement, never monolithic — not even during the inspired March on Washington — had developed new fractures. The cadre of SNCC organizers moved further to the left, and Martin Luther King struggled to maintain his position as the public voice of the movement. Robert Moses found few of his colleagues, already embittered by the convention experience, willing to stick with his idealistic but difficult vision of organizing the Mississippi poor to lead themselves. Eventually, Moses changed his name to Robert Paris and moved with his wife to Africa.*[92]

The election results on November 3 broke records and foretold enormous change. Lyndon Johnson defeated Barry Goldwater by 16 million votes — an unprecedented margin — winning an also unprecedented 61 percent of

---

* "Paris" was Moses's middle name. After seven years in Tanzania, where his first three children were born, he moved his family back to the United States. In 2003, once again as Robert Moses and back in Mississippi, he was running an innovative program called the Algebra Project.

the popular vote. Johnson carried forty-four states, with Goldwater taking only his own Arizona and five southern states: Alabama, Louisiana, Mississippi, South Carolina, and Georgia. The Democrats picked up forty-eight House seats in previously Republican districts and added two Senate seats: Robert Kennedy in New York and Joseph Montoya in New Mexico. With a record 96 percent of black voters casting ballots for Johnson and Humphrey, King's insistence on the significance of the black vote was affirmed. The election results also constituted a mandate for the 1964 Civil Rights Act. Southerners Charles Weltner of Georgia and Jake Pickle of Texas, who had courageously supported the law, were reelected. Not a single House member — Democrat or Republican — who had voted for the bill was defeated, while half of the northern Republicans who had opposed the legislation were swept out of office. With the largest Democratic majority in Congress since the one Franklin Roosevelt had enjoyed in 1938–39, the stage seemed set for Lyndon Johnson not just to complete the thirty-year-old agenda of the New Deal but to go well beyond it with his own vision of a Great Society.[93]

Yet the election results also contained portents of the Goldwater wing's takeover of the Republican Party and the white backlash against the civil rights movement. Four of the five southern states that Johnson lost had never gone Republican in a presidential contest before. And, for the first time since Reconstruction, the Deep South elected Republican members to the House of Representatives — twelve in all. And in California, voters by a two-to-one margin repealed a fair housing law against racial discrimination.

On November 5, two days after the election, Lyndon Johnson called Dr. King to thank him for his effective support in the campaign and for the tremendous turnout of black voters for Johnson. He even managed belated praise for King's Nobel Prize, saying that Negroes "take great pride in your great honor." More important to King, Johnson spoke enthusiastically about moving ahead with the poverty program and other efforts to help the underprivileged. "I'll be calling on you," the president said, "and we'll try to get our heads together on the things that are ahead. . . . We got this behind us. Now we got to move on the next four years and make some advances."

"It was a great victory for the forces of progress and a defeat for the forces of retrogress," replied King. "I think we have great challenges and opportunities ahead, and we're all with you. . . . We have some bright days ahead, I think."[94]

9

✦ ✦ ✦ ✦ ✦ ✦

Hoover Attacks

T HE REVEREND MARTIN LUTHER KING JR. received a personal blessing from Pope Paul VI at the Vatican on September 18, 1964. While King was in Rome, J. Edgar Hoover scrawled across a news report, "I am amazed that the Pope gave an audience to such a degenerate."* A month later, news that King had won the Nobel Prize for Peace angered Hoover further. "King could well qualify for the 'top alley cat' prize," he jotted on a news story. The prestigious award added new urgency to the FBI director's campaign to destroy King's stature as a national leader. Thus far Hoover had fought King stealthily, with top secret memos dispatched to high government officials and by innuendoes whispered in confidence to congressional, church, university, news, and business leaders. The Nobel Prize prompted the usually cautious master of counterintelligence to act out of character and charge into the open in his war against King.[1]

At an unusual three-hour press briefing with a group of eighteen women reporters in his office on November 18, he attacked. As stewards in white jackets served coffee from a silver service, Hoover catalogued his complaints against King. Two years earlier King had criticized the FBI for failing to investigate or prosecute repeated attacks against civil rights workers in Albany, Georgia. Now Hoover challenged King's criticisms. "I consider King to be the most notorious liar in the country," he

---

* The FBI had asked Cardinal Spellman of New York to forestall King's audience with the pope by informing the Vatican of King's personal failings and Communist ties. To Hoover's chagrin, the effort failed. One FBI motive for trying to block King's papal visit was that it would give King additional prestige as he was being considered for the Nobel Prize (FBI King file, Baumgardner to Sullivan, 8/31/64).

said.* "Off the record," Hoover then told his visitors that King was "one of the lowest characters in the country." He added knowingly that the Southern Christian Leadership Conference leader was "controlled" by Communist advisers.[2]

Martin Luther King was vacationing on the Bahamian resort island of Bimini when he learned of Hoover's accusations. The exhausted civil rights leader had been invited by Adam Clayton Powell to rest and work on his Nobel Prize acceptance speech. The colorful, controversial black congressman from Harlem and sometime critic of King owned a home on the island.

King wired Hoover immediately: "I was appalled and surprised at your reported statement maligning my integrity. What motivated such an irresponsible accusation is a mystery to me." Again King raised "the broader question of federal involvement in the protection of Negroes in the South and the seeming inability to gain convictions in even the most heinous crimes perpetrated against civil rights workers."[3]

Taking a different tack, the minister issued a press release. "I cannot conceive of Mr. Hoover making a statement like this without being under extreme pressure," he said. "He apparently has faltered under the awesome burden, complexities and responsibilities of his office. . . . I have nothing but sympathy for this man who has served his country so well."[4] In an interview in Bimini, he went even further. The FBI, under the direction of Hoover, King alleged, was "following the path of appeasement of political powers in the South. If this continues, the reign of terror in Mississippi, Alabama, and Georgia will increase rather than subside."[5]

As accusations flew back and forth, Hoover listened in on King's even angrier private comments. In a telephone call wiretapped by the FBI, King remarked to his aide the Reverend C. T. Vivian that Hoover was "old and getting senile" and needed to be "hit from all sides" so President Johnson would be forced to censure him.[6]

At the time, Lyndon Johnson was making plans to work with King and the civil rights leadership to achieve his Great Society programs. With Hoover and King dueling in the press, Johnson was caught in the crossfire. Here were King, the nation's most popular civil rights leader, and Hoover, a law enforcement legend and hero to millions of Americans, hurling accusations and insults at each other. The controversy came to a

---

* Hoover tailored his "most notorious liar" comment to a 1962 news story in which King's complaints about the FBI in Albany included the statement that one reason FBI agents empathized with local law enforcement officers was that most of the agents were from the South. Hoover made the point that four of the five agents assigned to Albany were natives of the North. But Hoover ignored the broader issues King raised about the FBI's failures.

head a day later, on November 19, when Johnson met with civil rights leaders to rally support for his initiatives. (King had declined, wiring Johnson that he needed time to rest and to write his Nobel acceptance speech, a move that annoyed the president.[7]) Despite King's absence, Roy Wilkins departed from the agenda and spoke forcefully about Hoover's "deplorable" comments. As the other leaders concurred, Johnson listened without comment.* After the meeting Wilkins told reporters, "We expressed our disagreement with Mr. Hoover's characterization of Dr. King. . . . We said we stood with Dr. King in his conviction that the FBI had not provided the protection colored people should receive from the federal government."[8]

Johnson attempted to ignore the issue, but it titillated the news media. Finally cornered at a press conference ten days later, he tried to pass off the exchange between Hoover and King as an unfortunate incident in which both men were exercising their freedom of speech. "My problem is to try to prevent the strong divisions that come to pass from time to time, instead of provoke them," the president said.[9]

To Johnson's dismay, the controversy continued to escalate. Hoover, speaking at Loyola University in Chicago, attacked "zealots or pressure groups" that were "spearheaded at times by Communists and moral degenerates," a thinly veiled reference to King and the SCLC.[10] The following day James Farmer, CORE's national director, fired back. Accusing Hoover of conducting a "vendetta" against civil rights groups, he called for the FBI director's resignation.

President Johnson finally decided to take steps to end the public feud. He requested help from assistant FBI director Deke DeLoach. "There's no use in trying to divide America," Johnson told him. "We need to try to pull them together now. And if I were you, I'd try to use your counsel with [Hoover] to let him know that the only way that anybody gets any advertisement that he's made any mistake is for him to advertise [it] himself."[11]

Johnson also was growing concerned about the scurrilous FBI reports on King's behavior. "What am I going to do about Martin Luther King

---

* Others at the meeting included A. Philip Randolph of the Brotherhood of Sleeping Car Porters, Whitney Young of the National Urban League, James Farmer of CORE, Dorothy Height of the National Council of Negro Women, and Jack Greenberg, head of the NAACP Legal Defense Fund. After the meeting Johnson asked Greenberg, "And what can I do for you?" Greenberg replied that civil rights lawyers' greatest problem in the South was trying to cope with segregationist federal judges appointed by President Kennedy. Johnson promised that henceforth he would clear all judicial appointments in the South with Greenberg and other civil rights leaders. Johnson followed through on his promise. On December 10 the FBI director was angered to learn via his wiretaps "the shocking information" that the White House had called King to get his views on an appointment to the U.S. circuit court in the South.

with all these reports that are coming in on him all the time?" he asked acting attorney general Nicholas Katzenbach.* "Can't someone tell him to watch his conduct?"

"It looks to me like [King's] too far gone on a lot of it — as far as his relationships with Communists are concerned," Katzenbach replied. "We've done that, Mr. President, so many times — told him to watch out."[12]

The president was most worried about the public fireworks. He advised Hoover — through Katzenbach — that he should accept King's request to meet and settle their differences. Hoover agreed and invited King to Washington; King readily accepted.[13]

At their meeting in Hoover's office on December 1, the two men pointedly avoided discussing their accusations against each other. Instead, King and the Reverend Ralph Abernathy, his deputy at the SCLC, praised Hoover and the FBI for its law enforcement work and expressed "the appreciation of the Negro race for the Director's fine work in the field of civil rights." King blamed news media inaccuracies for any stories suggesting that King had been critical of either Hoover or the FBI. Denying accounts of Communist influence on the movement, King said that he shared Hoover's concerns. "As a Christian," King said, he "could never accept Communism," which he recognized as "a crippling totalitarian disease."

For most of the hourlong meeting, the director talked about the FBI's recent accomplishments. The bureau had arrested several Ku Klux Klan members who had committed crimes against civil rights activists in the South, and had just apprehended two white supremacists who had murdered Henry Dee and Charlie Moore, young civil rights workers in Mississippi. Hoover won King's praise by telling him that the FBI would soon arrest the murderers of James Chaney, Michael Schwerner, and Andrew Goodman, though he cautioned that it would be difficult to convict the men. He expressed blistering contempt for the "redneck sheriffs" and "other trashy characters" who would not convict Klansmen the FBI had arrested.† Showing his empathy for black Americans facing discrimination, Hoover expressed shock that a young Howard University graduate he had recently met in Miami "could not get a job above the level of shoe-

* Katzenbach and Assistant Attorney General Burke Marshall accepted Hoover's accusations about Stanley Levison and the dangers of his closeness to King. Johnson, like the Kennedy brothers before him, also accepted the information. There is no record of any of these public officials' challenging Hoover to provide additional proof of his accusations about King and Levison, or of an examination of the hotel room tapes to authenticate identification.

† On December 4, 1964, the FBI charged nineteen men with the Mississippi murders on December 4, 1964. After numerous dismissals of charges by Mississippi state judges and juries, seven men finally were convicted on October 20, 1967, for violating the civil rights of Chaney, Goodman, and Schwerner, and sentenced to prison terms of three to ten years.

shine boy because of the color of his skin. . . . This was wrong," he said, adding that neither he nor anyone else at the FBI held "the opinion that the Negro, or any other race, should be kept down."

King emerged from the meeting to tell reporters that "the discussion was quite amicable. . . . I hope we can forget the confusion of the past and . . . get on with the job of . . . providing freedom and justice for all citizens of this nation."

Andrew Young, the SCLC executive director, left the meeting disgusted with both King and himself for failing to speak candidly about their complaints against the FBI. "It was a completely non-functioning meeting," Young said. King, however, had decided that he had little to gain — and much to lose — by confronting Hoover. He was shaken by Hoover's public outbursts and the intense whispering campaign Hoover had mounted about his personal life. He feared that confrontation would only further provoke Hoover, and since President Johnson had not come to his defense, King saw no other solution to his growing Hoover problem. So as he had done with great success in the past, King decided simply to turn the other cheek.[14]

Even though Hoover followed the president's request to tone down his public dispute with King, the FBI chief carefully tested how far Johnson would permit him to go in undermining the civil rights leader. On the very day of his peacemaking summit with King, he sent to the White House a thirteen-page FBI report titled "Communism and the Negro Movement — A Current Analysis," an updated version of the dossier he'd sent President Kennedy in October 1963. The report was a broadside against King. It provided detailed descriptions of his alleged "personal debauchery" and accusations of his association with Communists and Communism. "The information available about King," the report stated, "depicts an unprincipled, opportunistic individual, as well as a man considered and described within the Communist Party U.S.A. as a Marxist." King's relationship with Stanley Levison and his previous employment of Hunter Pitts O'Dell were cited as evidence that the SCLC leader "has shown not only a willingness but an eagerness to accept communist aid, to support communist causes, to associate and confer with prominent communist leaders, and to work closely with and rely upon the advice and guidance of dedicated communists with concealed affiliations, despite the fact that they have been identified reliably to him as such." According to Hoover, in 1962 Stanley Levison "had passed the word to [American Communist leader] Gus Hall that 'King is a wholehearted Marxist who has studied [Marxism], believes in it, and agrees with it, but because of his being a minister of religion, does not dare to espouse it publicly.'"

The report concluded that King "presents a security problem to this nation." The threat could be resolved, it suggested, by making 20 million unsuspecting American Negroes "aware of King's security liability" and "his personal debauchery."

In a letter accompanying the report, Hoover posed a critical question to the president: "Your advice is requested as to whether we should disseminate this document to responsible figures in the executive branch of government."

Two days later, on December 3, Hoover got his answer. Bill Moyers, who had replaced the departed Walter Jenkins as the president's chief liaison with the FBI,* told Deke DeLoach that Hoover should use his own judgment about sending out the report. After speaking with DeLoach on December 3,† Moyers carefully filed a "Note for the Record," saying, "I today informed Mr. DeLoach that we have confidence in Mr. Hoover's ability to decide who, on the basis of national security, should see the attached report. [DeLoach] replied that he would follow through accordingly."[15]

Lyndon Johnson, acting through Moyers, had now unambiguously given J. Edgar Hoover a green light to discredit King — so long as he did so quietly rather than in public proclamations.‡ Johnson was authorizing Hoover to spread defamatory information throughout the government, just as Hoover had done with the October 1963 report. In that case, however, then attorney general Robert Kennedy, learning of Hoover's action, had ordered him to retrieve all copies of the report. He feared that circulation of the attack on King within the administration was bound to produce a news leak, and that subsequent publication of the derogatory information about King would cripple President Kennedy's struggling efforts to pass a civil rights law. Johnson was less concerned than the Kennedys that disclosures about King would hurt civil rights legislation.

Four days after receiving Johnson's approval, with Senator-elect Robert

---

* Jenkins had resigned his White House position after his October arrest.

† DeLoach, in a December 7 memo, reported his understanding of the conversation with Moyers: "Bill Moyers called me to indicate that he and the President had read the Director's letter in connection with possible dissemination of the captioned monograph. He stated it was both his and the President's opinion that the FBI should disseminate this monograph if it was felt that dissemination would be in the best interests of internal security. I told Moyers that under the circumstances he appeared to be telling me that we should go ahead and disseminate. He answered in the affirmative." Hoover's sensitive memos to President Johnson always were addressed to an aide so Johnson could disclaim involvement. Walter Jenkins received the memos until his resignation in October. Moyers then received them until early in 1965, when a new aide, Marvin Watson, assumed the responsibility (FBIMLK, DeLoach to Mohr, 12/7/64, sec. 21).

‡ Ten months earlier, acting through Walter Jenkins, Johnson had given Hoover permission to disseminate secretly to the news media accounts of what the FBI had recorded during the January 7, 1964, party in King's suite at Washington's Willard Hotel.

Kennedy no longer at Justice to stand in his way, Hoover began circulating his inflammatory December 1, 1964, report on King. He sent copies to Secretary of State Dean Rusk, Secretary of Defense Robert McNamara, CIA director John McCone, acting attorney general Nicholas Katzenbach, U.S. Information Agency director Carl Rowan, the Office of Naval Intelligence, the Air Force Intelligence Agency, the Defense Intelligence Agency, and the director of the National Science Foundation. As the report was disseminated, its top secret contents became known to hundreds of federal employees. Whether or not anyone in government leaked the report to the press, it achieved Hoover's objective: to damage King's reputation within the most powerful agencies of the federal government. Information about King sent to the State Department and to the American embassies in London and Oslo immediately served its purpose. The FBI broadside and a telephone call from Bill Moyers contributed to deterring embassy officials from assisting King on his Nobel Prize trip, as custom and American interest usually dictated.*

An internal FBI discussion of the 1963 report recalled by President Kennedy showed that Hoover and his chief lieutenants were aware of problems within the document itself and of its potentially explosive impact on American politics and the civil rights movement. The principal difference between the 1963 and 1964 versions was that the latter contained several new pages of damaging detail about King's private life. FBI official Alan H. Belmont, author of the original 1963 study, had written a note to Hoover warning that it was "highly explosive" and "can be regarded as a personal attack on Martin Luther King." If the report leaked out, Belmont wrote, "it will add fuel to a matter which may already be in the cards as a political issue during the forthcoming [1964] presidential campaign." Although the FBI report "makes good reading and is based on information from reliable sources," Belmont had cautioned, "we may be charged with expressing opinions and conclusions, particularly with reference to some of the statements about King."[16] Johnson's aides, especially lawyers such as Joseph Califano, Harry McPherson, and Lee White, were well aware of the hearsay and conjecture in the reports.

Johnson's decision to give Hoover nearly free rein to conduct a counterintelligence campaign against King was motivated by several factors. Perhaps most important was the care with which Johnson handled his relationship with Hoover. Ever wary of Hoover's ability to destroy a career

---

* Hearing that the State Department was planning to pay for King's trip to Europe, Johnson asked Moyers to check on the matter. Moyers reported back that there would be no federal aid. The United States Information Agency had considered, but dropped, a plan to finance the trip in return for King's making several speeches abroad.

and reputation with information from his secret files, the president told aides that he had kept Hoover on beyond the mandatory retirement age of seventy because he would rather have him "inside the tent pissing out, than outside pissing in."[17] In his first year as president, Johnson had reached a cautious, tacit accommodation with Hoover: the FBI director would carry out extraordinary assignments for Johnson, including the covert spying campaign at the 1964 Democratic National Convention, and in return Johnson would not interfere with Hoover's pursuit of his own special interests. Even in ordering Hoover to fight the Ku Klux Klan in the summer of 1964, Johnson had handled the director gingerly. "How am I going to get 'the other country' [the autocratic FBI] involved down there [in Mississippi]?" he wondered to Assistant Attorney General Burke Marshall. "Dealing with the FBI is like dealing with France."[18]

Johnson's deference to Hoover regarding King also stemmed from the political climate of the times, including the ever-present and precarious tensions with the Soviet Union. Like John F. Kennedy, Johnson was a Cold Warrior who believed that the global dangers posed by the Soviet Union extended to Communist subversion at home. Also, as had been the case with Kennedy, Johnson never questioned the accuracy of the FBI's reports about Stanley Levison's Communist affiliation.* Both presidents found puzzling and disturbing King's failure to break with Levison and O'Dell — even after King had assured Justice Department officials that he had done so. With American involvement against Communism in faraway Vietnam growing deeper every day, even if Hoover's accusations about King's Communist connections proved inaccurate, Johnson — again like Kennedy — worried about his political vulnerability if he failed to address the FBI's concerns.[19] But even their fears about Communism did not provide a rationale for Johnson or the Kennedys to accept Hoover's efforts to publicize King's personal life.

Both Kennedy and Johnson also failed to recognize a significant historic reality. The Communist Party's fifty-year campaign to recruit African Americans to its cause had been a colossal failure, a point made by

---

* Had Kennedy or Johnson pressed the FBI for more detailed information about Levison and his relationship with King, a more complex picture might have emerged. The FBI had gathered impressive evidence about Levison's Communist ties prior to 1956 but little after that. What evidence the FBI did possess might have been interpreted as showing that Levison had severed his ties with the Communist Party in the late 1950s or early 1960s. But the FBI never shared with the White House information it had that cast doubt on its own thesis about Levison. Instead, the FBI adopted the hypothesis — with few supporting facts — that Levison had gone underground as an agent of influence targeted at King. Nor did the FBI provide convincing evidence that Levison was influencing King to follow any course other than that of the mainstream civil rights movement of the 1955–1965 period.

Robert Kennedy. Communist infiltration "couldn't be more feeble or less of a threat," he had found. Whenever Hoover warned of Communist infiltration of the civil rights movement, King would point to "the amazing lack of success that communism has met in attracting the Negro, who easily might be tempted to turn to some other discipline to gain respite from his desperate plight."[20] Furthermore, neither Kennedy nor Johnson questioned why the FBI was conducting a counterintelligence campaign against Martin Luther King rather than against Stanley Levison, the man the FBI claimed was the secret Communist agent.[21]

Johnson's acceptance of Hoover's animus toward King was prompted in part by the president's own mixed feelings about the civil rights leader. Johnson felt that King and other black leaders gave insufficient recognition to his civil rights accomplishments. He envied the public veneration King inspired, much as he still resented the public's adulation of John F. Kennedy. On a trip to Appalachia to gauge poverty in the mountain hollows there, the president emerged from one shack visibly shaken, not only by the miserable living conditions, including seven sick and malnourished children, but also by two photographs on the walls of the house — one of Jesus Christ and the other of John F. Kennedy. As he emerged, Johnson told his aide Richard Goodwin, "I felt as if I'd been slapped in the face."[22] As he had admitted to Jenkins months before, what Lyndon Johnson craved most was "a little love." He felt that he was not receiving it from either the poor, whose lives he had worked so hard to improve, or the civil rights leadership. If the black leaders were less than ebullient in their public praise of the president, it was because their own constituents expected them to keep the pressure on the White House for further progress.

Neither Lyndon Johnson nor Jack Kennedy before him shared Hoover's outrage about the dichotomy between King's high moral rhetoric and allegations of his adulterous conduct. Neither president, as later reports revealed, was a paragon of virtue himself. While Kennedy's womanizing received great notoriety after his death, Johnson was said to have carried on a less-publicized longtime affair with Alice Glass, wife of a Texas newspaper publisher, and had rumored encounters with other women, including several of his secretaries.[23] But Kennedy and Johnson each had worried about the impact a scandal involving King might have on his presidency. Lyndon Johnson enjoyed using stories about other men's weaknesses to make his points, advance his purposes, or simply tell a good tale. In the company of his aide Harry McPherson, a fellow Texan and an open admirer of the civil rights leader, the president enjoyed taking digs at King.

"Harry's so nice, he thinks these people are so fine," Johnson would say about McPherson's lack of concern about King's alleged peccadilloes. "He's so gullible and naïve."

"You can't believe all that stuff," McPherson replied.

"Don't you think it's terrible, Harry?" Johnson asked. "Men and women, men and men, women and women. Hoover's got tapes on those people."

"Well, don't knock it until you've tried it," McPherson replied wryly, to which Lyndon Johnson responded with what McPherson described as "an expression of mock horror, and a sly smile."

But McPherson also noted that there was no joking when Johnson used Hoover's information about King's alleged Communist ties to dismiss any King action that did not toe the Johnson administration line.[24] He would take Hoover's reports at face value and often said he was not going to be trapped, as President Truman had been, by accusations — based on information supplied by Hoover — that he was soft on Communism.[25]

Johnson was also irritated by King's constant maneuvering to seize the public spotlight and force his hand. Justice Department officials and White House aides shared the president's annoyance and encouraged him, as a matter of prudent politics, not to meet with King alone. By singling out King, they felt, Johnson would build him up at the expense of Roy Wilkins and Whitney Young in terms of recognition as the nation's foremost black leader.[26] Even though King clearly was the best-known and most respected figure in the civil rights movement, administration officials believed that the nation — and the Johnson presidency — would be better served if the venerable Wilkins were perceived as the chief spokesman for black Americans.

Although Johnson understood King's effectiveness, he had expected him to be a team player, as he had been in the campaign against Goldwater. The president's strategy was for the black leaders to appear together at the White House to promote his civil rights and antipoverty agendas. Roy Wilkins and Whitney Young accepted this role, but King felt it was in his interest, and that of his constituents, to maintain some independence from the White House.*

After the Nobel Peace Prize announcement, J. Edgar Hoover intensified his efforts to bring down Martin Luther King by focusing not on the min-

---

* Johnson's stated attitudes about King are derived from numerous published sources and from the author's interviews with more than twenty of Johnson's aides and administration officials, including Clifford Alexander, Horace Busby, Joseph Califano, George Christian, Warren Christopher, Ramsey Clark, Nicholas Katzenbach, Larry Temple, Lee White, Burke Marshall, Sherwin Markman, and Harry McPherson, as well as Lady Bird Johnson.

ister's alleged Communist connections but on his private life. The quickest way to discredit King, he believed, was to show that his personal behavior was at odds with his religious and moral rhetoric as a minister of God. Top FBI officials, as well as agents in the field, stepped up their visits to influential journalists and church leaders, offering information about King's alleged adulterous behavior. Even while King and Hoover were meeting on December 1, an FBI official showed James McCartney of the *Chicago Daily News,* as he waited outside Hoover's office, a picture of King leaving a motel with a white woman and implied that they had been engaging in sexual relations. If McCartney "wanted to get into the whole story of Martin Luther King's private sex life while he was posing as a highly moral civil rights leader," the official said, the FBI would give him the information. The only stipulation was that the FBI could not be identified as the source. McCartney rejected the offer.[27] David Kraslow, a Washington correspondent for the *Los Angeles Times,* received a similar offer: an FBI official telephoned Kraslow and read him a portion of what he said was a transcript of a King tape. Kraslow also declined the story, as did Louis Harris, editor of the *Augusta* (Georgia) *Chronicle,* a publication that supported segregation.

Even before King left on his Bimini vacation in mid-November, an FBI agent in Atlanta approached Eugene Patterson, editor of the *Atlanta Constitution.* The FBI, the agent said, wanted to convince the newspaper and its readers that King, whom the *Constitution* had portrayed "as a moral man and a Christian leader," actually was leading an immoral private life. The agent suggested that Patterson send a photographer and a reporter to a Florida airport the following Friday to catch King and a girlfriend departing for a weekend in the Caribbean. "Get a picture of this as well as a story on this man and expose him to the South and to the world," the agent urged. Patterson showed the agent the door and was amazed when the man returned for a second attempt to sell Patterson the story. Patterson told the agent that King's private life was not a story — "We're not a peephole journal," he told him — warning that "what *you're* doing is the story . . . the federal police force of the United States doing this to an individual citizen." A week later the agent received notice from Hoover that he was being transferred to New Orleans, punishment for being a few pounds overweight — or for failing in his mission with Patterson.*[28]

Meanwhile, Deke DeLoach sought out Ben Bradlee, then Washington bureau chief of *Newsweek,* to offer him transcripts of tapes allegedly of King engaged in sexual activities at a hotel party. Bradlee not only turned

---

* The punishment was rescinded three weeks later, and the agent remained in Atlanta.

down the offer but also told Justice Department officials Nicholas Katzenbach and Burke Marshall about the incident when they attended a *Newsweek* reception on November 25. Katzenbach confronted DeLoach, who denied having the conversation with Bradlee. Worried that Hoover's vendetta against King was about to become public, Katzenbach and Marshall decided to raise the issue with President Johnson that weekend at his Texas ranch.

After Johnson took the men for a tour of his cattle ranch and a boat ride on Lake Lyndon Baines Johnson, they settled in front of the fireplace in the living room. There Katzenbach and Marshall told the president about Hoover's effort to publicize King's personal behavior, including DeLoach's approach to Bradlee, as well as an "anti-King memorandum that Hoover was distributing with a diatribe about King, with an underlying emphasis on sex."*

"Terrible, terrible," was Johnson's only comment. "I've never heard of it."

"This is dynamite if it gets out," Katzenbach warned the president. "It is a very dangerous situation and should be stopped." Since Hoover would not listen to the attorney general, his Justice Department superior, Katzenbach hoped that the president would speak to him. Katzenbach and Marshall left the meeting, however, with a sinking feeling that Johnson knew more than he had let on.[29]

Back in Washington, Johnson instructed Bill Moyers to warn DeLoach that Bradlee could not be trusted — that he was spreading the story all over Washington of the FBI's effort to leak damaging information about Martin Luther King.†[30]

Hoover's campaign to discredit King had become so widespread by late 1964 that several civil rights leaders and friends of King spoke up, warning him about the FBI's activities and cautioning him about his personal behavior. James Farmer became concerned after a black reporter, Ted Poston, and his editor at the *New York Post* told Farmer that the newspaper, facing competitive pressures, was about to publish an FBI-leaked story on King's personal life, his Communist associations, and irregulari-

---

* Katzenbach was referring to the FBI report on King, which Johnson had given Hoover permission to distribute to government officials.

† Katzenbach believed that President Johnson, in telling Hoover that Bradlee had betrayed the FBI's confidence, was in his own Machiavellian way warning Hoover to stop leaking information about King's personal life. Moyers, testifying in 1976 before the Senate select committee investigating the FBI, said "it would be fair to conclude" that Johnson's complaint was about Bradlee's revealing that the FBI had offered him the tapes rather than about what the FBI was doing.

ties in SCLC finances. Farmer located King in Chicago. "Martin," he said, "I need to see you in person in the next forty-eight hours. It's a matter of life and death." King agreed to meet Farmer the next evening in the VIP lounge at JFK Airport in New York.

After the men embraced, they sat together on a couch. Farmer asked if King was aware that the "FBI was peddling stories about him."

"What kind of stories?" King asked. "About what?"

After Farmer described the allegations of financial corruption, Communist connections, and sexual liaisons, King denied the charges. He urged Farmer to keep an appointment the next day in Washington with Deke DeLoach to protest the bureau's treatment of King. Farmer met in an FBI limousine with DeLoach, who told Farmer that the stories about King were true but denied that the FBI was leaking them to the news media.[31] Roy Wilkins, also alarmed by conversations with newspaper reporters, had a similar meeting with DeLoach.[32]

FBI officials tried to leak information about King to leading church officials such as R. H. Edwin Espy, general secretary of the National Council of Churches, and Dr. Robert S. Denny, an official of the Baptist World Alliance. As the story traveled through Baptist Church circles, it reached a former White House staff member, former congressman Brooks Hays of Arkansas, a respected member of the church leadership. On December 14 a concerned Hays alerted Bill Moyers, himself a Baptist minister. In a memo Hays urgently requested a meeting to discuss the FBI's efforts to smear King to other prominent church leaders, such as Ted Adams, chairman of the Baptist World Alliance's program committee.[33]

John D. Maguire, then a professor of religion at Wesleyan University and a longtime King friend, feared that the FBI's whispering campaign not only threatened King's status as a civil rights leader but also was hurting him in the liberal church world, an important source of support for King and the civil rights movement. Maguire broached the subject with King on two occasions. At first King dismissed the stories, saying, "You shouldn't believe everything you hear." On the second visit, in late 1964, Maguire was more insistent.

"Martin, you are playing with fire," he told King. "It isn't a question of prudery. If the FBI gets this story out, it would be just terrible."

King replied by describing how he lived, traveling twenty-seven days out of every month, under constant anxiety and pressure. His extramarital affairs, he told Maguire, were just "fleeting exchange[s]" providing him comfort.[34]

That King engaged in extramarital affairs was no secret to the aides who traveled with him or to movement people in the cities he visited all over the United States.* Most took note but made no public judgment about King's personal life. Typical was Rabbi Richard Hirsch, director of the Union of American Hebrew Congregations' Religious Action Center, who provided King with office space during his frequent visits to Washington. Hirsch realized that "the tall, beautiful women who looked like models" who accompanied King were not really "secretaries," as King introduced them. Others, however, like John Maguire and Wiley Branton, director of the Council for United Civil Rights Leadership, feeling that too much was at stake to remain silent, gently confronted King in an effort to get him "to come to grips with whatever those problems were."[35]

The spotlight of fame as a result of the Nobel Prize, combined with Hoover's hot pursuit, caused King increased anxiety and depression even at his moment of triumph. Reporters from around the world clamored for interviews. Many were surprised to learn how modestly King lived. He drove a ten-year-old Pontiac, lived in a small rented house, and drew no salary from the Southern Christian Leadership Conference.† The money from his speaking engagements went back to the SCLC. The Kings and their three children lived frugally on his modest salary from the Ebenezer Baptist Church, where he still shared the pulpit with his father.[36]

What the reporters did not see was the tension within King's family, which the Nobel award only compounded. An intelligent, courageous woman, Coretta King already resented the role her husband insisted she play — that of housewife and mother. She had been an activist in the Women's Strike for Peace and wanted to participate in the movements for civil rights, social justice, and world peace. She resented her husband's spending so little time with her and the children, and his insistence that they live so frugally. The money issue arose, and not for the first time, when King ignored her wish that some of the Nobel Prize money be set aside for the education of their children.‡ Instead, he gave $37,000 to the SCLC and its affiliates and the other $17,000 to organizations in the Council for United Civil Rights Leadership.[37]

The FBI's effort to expose King's personal life caused further tension. Martin Luther King Sr. learned of the campaign to smear his son's name from his friend Atlanta police chief Herbert Jenkins, to whom the FBI had confided information about the younger King's personal life. Meanwhile,

---

* King had at least two long-term relationships with women over a period of years (David Garrow, *Bearing the Cross*, pp. 374–375).

† The SCLC paid King $1 annually so he would qualify for its health insurance plan.

‡ Entertainer Harry Belafonte, a major movement supporter, was so concerned about the King family's lack of resources that he set up a scholarship fund for each of the King children.

Martin Jr. was upset that his closest friend and associate at the SCLC, Ralph Abernathy — pressed by his wife, Juanita — was demanding that he be acknowledged as co-winner of the Nobel Prize.

Triumph and Turmoil

Even as he worried that the FBI's effort to bare his personal life was about to explode, King set out for Europe in early December. On the trip he would begin to expand his efforts beyond the battle for civil rights in the United States. In England, King called for a "massive economic boycott" of South Africa and its racist policy of apartheid. As he accepted the Nobel Prize in Oslo, King tied the American movement and its tactics of nonviolent resistance to the urgent need for disarmament and world peace. He accepted the award "on behalf of the civil rights movement — in recognition that nonviolence is the answer to the crucial political and moral questions of our time — the need for man to overcome oppression and violence without resorting to violence and oppression." And he expressed "his abiding faith in America and an audacious faith in the future of mankind."[38]

King returned to a hero's welcome in New York, honored by the mayor and governor in the presence of Vice President–elect Hubert Humphrey at a dinner at the Waldorf-Astoria Hotel.* Then King flew to Washington on Governor Nelson Rockefeller's private airplane to receive congratulations from President Johnson at the White House.

After considerable hesitation, Johnson finally had decided to see King, but he approached the visit warily. Lee White, Johnson's assistant for civil rights, arranged the December 18 meeting with King and his family to allow minimum news coverage. The meeting was choreographed so that, as it ended, the King entourage would be whisked out through a private exit with little time to spare to catch their flight home to Atlanta.

At the White House, Johnson warmly greeted Martin Luther and Coretta Scott King, Martin Sr. and Alberta King, SCLC executives Andrew Young, Walter Fauntroy, and Ralph Abernathy, and Abernathy's wife, Juanita. Meeting alone with King, the president stressed their common purposes. Johnson introduced King to Assistant Attorney General Ramsey Clark, a liberal Texan, son of Supreme Court justice Tom Clark, and an admirer of King. "I want you to meet this young fellow — his father just got nine

---

* Three days after participating in King's New York celebration, Humphrey received from Hoover the updated monograph on King's Communist connections and personal life, along with a separate memorandum titled "Martin Luther King, Jr.: His Personal Conduct" (Church, Final Report, bk. 3, p. 144).

votes for the constitutionality of the civil rights law and that just shows you what Texans are doing for [civil rights]. I signed it into law not long ago, and now this other Texan has [helped uphold its constitutionality]."*
The president proudly showed King a framed letter on his office wall from Texas hero Sam Houston to his minister, George Washington Baines, Lyndon Johnson's great-grandfather. King listened intently as Johnson described Baines's role in helping Texas win its independence from Mexico in 1836; the president promised to send King a copy of the letter.

After extolling the efforts of Texans for civil rights, Johnson asked King, "Now, what's Georgia doing? You ought to get back down there and get them to work."[39]

As they discussed the coming year, Johnson emphasized that King's leadership and that of other black leaders would be needed if the new War on Poverty programs were to succeed in helping African Americans. King informed the president that he would soon be launching a massive voting rights campaign in Selma, Alabama, to demonstrate that blacks could not register to vote in the Deep South without federal legislation.

"Martin, you are right about that," Johnson replied. "I'm going to do it eventually, but I can't get voting rights through in this session of Congress. . . . Now, there's some other bills that I have here that I want to get through in my Great Society program, and I think in the long run they'll help Negroes more, as much as a voting rights bill. And let's get those through and then the other."

King reminded the president, "Political reform is as necessary as anything if we're going to solve all these other problems."

Johnson responded, "I can't get it through, because I need the votes of the southern bloc to get these other things through. And if I present a voting rights bill, they will block the whole program. So it's just not the wise and the politically expedient thing to do."

King replied that his campaign for voting rights legislation would begin in Selma on January 2. He left the meeting pledging, "We'll just have to do the best we can."[40]

Later that day King received another triumphant reception in Atlanta. He hoped to rest there for ten days before opening his drive in Selma. Instead he faced continued turmoil.

On the subject of voting rights, as on most topics, Johnson's aides knew that one conversation with the president seldom revealed all that he was

---

* The Supreme Court unanimously upheld the Civil Rights Act of 1964 in the landmark case *Heart of Atlanta Motel, Inc. v. United States,* 379 U.S. 241.

thinking. Johnson liked to keep his options open. When he was at his best, Johnson's calculated strategy allowed him to be highly effective. Four days before letting King know that there could be no voting rights law in 1965, he had told Nicholas Katzenbach something quite different.

In a telephone conversation on December 14, Johnson surprised the acting attorney general by instructing him to start drafting a voting rights law: "I want you to undertake the greatest midnight legislative drafting that has happened since Corcoran and Cohen wrote the Holding Company Act."* Katzenbach groaned inwardly as the president discussed the various options by which federal registrars could be appointed to guarantee that black voters in the South were not denied their rights. Katzenbach would have much preferred to hear what Johnson told King — that Congress had just passed one civil rights bill and would not be amenable to taking up another one right away. Moreover, Katzenbach felt that the Justice Department lawyers needed time to work out the mechanics and enforcement procedures of the 1964 law before proposing a new one. Nevertheless, he and the president talked at length about how to register black voters in the South.

"I basically believe that we can have a simple, effective method of gettin' 'em registered," Johnson said. "Now, if the state laws are too high and they disqualify a bunch of them, maybe we can go into the Supreme Court and get them held unconstitutional." Johnson then suggested that "if the [local] registrars make them stand in line too long, maybe we can work that out where the [U.S.] postmasters can do it. Let's find some way." When Katzenbach suggested that it would take a constitutional amendment to approve federalizing voter registration, the president replied, "How can we beat it? Can we beat that some way?"

Lyndon Johnson was for the moment in a buoyant and optimistic mood, urging Katzenbach not only to draft a voting rights law, but also to find the best people he could to come up with other new legislative initiatives. "You've shown you can work with Congress," Johnson said. "Now try to get some of these thinkers to scratch their tail and let's see what we can do with the playgrounds, or the juveniles . . . or anything else you can propose. If you think we ought to have a constitutional amendment on voting, let's have it. Just get me some things you'd be proud of, to show your boy, and say, 'Here is what your daddy put through in nineteen sixty-four, -five, -six, -seven.'"

---

* The Public Utilities Holding Company Act, which provided regulation of utilities companies, was written by two young lawyers in the Franklin D. Roosevelt administration, Thomas Corcoran and Benjamin Cohen, and passed in 1935.

Did this conversation mean that President Johnson actually planned to seek voting rights legislation in 1965? Katzenbach wasn't certain, but he assigned a team of lawyers to start working on the legislation — both with a constitutional amendment and without. Johnson did not know when the right time would come, politically, for his next civil rights proposal — but he wanted to be prepared.[41]

The Poison-Pen Letter

The most diabolical FBI scheme to destroy Martin Luther King Jr. struck on January 5, 1965, just as the civil rights leader was launching his daring new campaign in Selma. Several months earlier, J. Edgar Hoover had directed his laboratory to assemble a composite of various tapes recorded by hidden microphones in King's hotel rooms during 1964. At first Hoover contemplated sending the tape to Coretta King in the expectation that she would become outraged and divorce her husband.* But the scheme took a new twist after the November exchange of charges between Hoover and King. When FBI officials advised Hoover not to dignify King's charges with a reply, Hoover scrawled his reactions across the bottom of the memo: "Ok. But I can't understand why we are not able to get the true facts before the public. We are never taking the aggressive [sic], but allow lies to remain unanswered."

Hoover's expression of frustration circulated among his top aides. The next day Deke DeLoach scribbled a response next to Hoover's: "Being handled." William C. Sullivan, FBI assistant director in charge of the King counterintelligence campaign, read the memo on November 20 and, following Hoover's suggestion, took aggressive action.[42]

It was Sullivan who directed the FBI laboratory to prepare the tape of "highlights" from microphone coverage of hotel rooms where King had stayed in Washington, D.C., San Francisco, and Los Angeles. Within a day, the lab delivered a tape to Sullivan's office. After asking an assistant to bring several sheets of plain paper (not watermarked so it could not be traced), Sullivan typed an anonymous letter. It read in part:

---

* Attempts to attack a target by creating marital discord was a common FBI ploy. One method was to have a woman call the target's wife on the telephone, creating the impression that she was a girlfriend looking for the husband. Both telephone calls and poison-pen letters were used not only against civil rights leaders such as King but also against Ku Klux Klan members, as the FBI tried to crack Klansmen suspected of crimes against civil rights activists. In terms of violating civil liberties, the FBI's war against the Klan was just as ruthless as its campaigns against targeted civil rights activists.

King, Look into your heart. You know you are a complete fraud and a great liability to all of us Negroes. White people in this country have enough frauds of their own but I'm sure they don't have one at this time that is anywhere near your equal. You are no clergyman and you know it. I repeat you are a colossal fraud and an evil, vicious one at that. You could not believe in God. . . . Clearly you don't believe in any personal moral principles.

King, like all frauds your end is approaching. You could have been our greatest leader. You, even at an early age have turned out to be not a leader but a dissolute, abnormal moral imbecile. . . . But you are done. Your "honorary degrees," your Nobel Prize (what a grim farce) and other awards will not save you. King, I repeat you are done.

The American public, the church organizations that have been helping — Protestant, Catholic and Jews will know you for what you are — an evil, abnormal beast. So will others who have backed you. You are done.

King, there is only one thing left for you to do. You know what it is. You have just 34 days in which to do (this exact number has been selected) for a specific reason, it has definite practical significant [*sic*]. You are done. There is but one way out for you. You better take it before your filthy, abnormal, fraudulent self is bared to the nation.

On November 21, Sullivan ordered Lish Whitson, an agent in his division, to fly to the Miami airport with a small, unmarked package containing the anonymous letter and the tape. Once there, Whitson called Sullivan, who instructed him to mail the package to King at his Atlanta office. Sullivan assumed that King would receive the package the next day.[43]

As it turned out, the package remained unopened in the SCLC offices for more than a month. It finally was sent to King's home, where Coretta King opened it on January 5, 1965. She listened to part of the tape, read the letter, and called her husband, stunned and horrified. King rushed home, listened closely to the tape several times, and then began assembling his most trusted associates. King, Ralph Abernathy, and Andrew Young listened to the tape. They recognized their own conversations and then heard what sounded like whispers and sighs from a bedroom.

"How dare they interfere with my private life," King exclaimed to Abernathy. "They have no right. It's nobody's business but my own."[44]

Much of the tape had been recorded a year earlier, when King and his SCLC associates were staying at the Willard Hotel in Washington, but there were conversations from other hotels, too. King and his aides quickly concluded that the tape had been prepared by the FBI. No one else had the capability. And, most chilling, King was convinced that the FBI was trying to drive him to commit suicide.[45]

King was devastated. In several telephone conversations the next day he expressed his despair. "They are out to get me, harass me, break my spirit," he said in one telephone call. In another conversation he said, "What I do is only between me and my God."[46]

Fully aware of King's distress as agents eavesdropped on his telephone calls, the FBI increased its pressure. In Atlanta, agents played at psychological warfare — dispatching fire trucks to a King hideaway known to only a few people. In Washington, Hoover sent letters to the president and Katzenbach describing King's emotional distress and fear of exposure.

The "suicide letter" prompted King and his lieutenants to try again to reason with the FBI. Andrew Young scheduled an appointment with DeLoach for the following Monday, January 11. Over the weekend the FBI listened via microphones planted in a room at New York's Park Sheraton Hotel as King, Young, and aide Bernard Lee discussed how Young should handle his meeting with DeLoach. King told Young and Lee that the anonymous hate letter was "a warning from God" that he was not living up to his responsibilities.[47]

On Monday morning, Young and Ralph Abernathy met at FBI headquarters with DeLoach and his assistant, Harold "Bud" Leinbaugh. When Young asked who the alleged Communists in the Southern Christian Leadership Conference were, DeLoach told him to contact the House Un-American Activities Committee, which many civil rights leaders and liberal activists considered a fount of dangerous misinformation. "These are the very racists we are fighting," replied Young. "I wouldn't respect anything that they've got to say."

When Young tried to discuss the bureau's efforts to expose King's affairs, DeLoach replied with a straight face that the FBI had not tried to leak stories and had no interest in King's personal life or in the SCLC's or King's finances. Afterward, a frustrated Young realized that he had gained nothing. He was dealing with people who, he felt, had "almost a fascist kind of mentality."[48]

Desperate to break out of what seemed like a hall of mirrors, Young met next with newsmen at the Washington bureau of the New York Times. One of DeLoach's assistants at FBI headquarters had offered to leak a story to Times correspondent Fred Graham about King's "immoral" personal life, including activities of the King party during his trip to Europe to receive the Nobel Prize. When a reporter called King to ask about the stories the FBI was whispering, King replied, "If John F. Kennedy had answered all the allegations made against him, he wouldn't have had time to run the country. And if I did, I wouldn't have time to do my work."

King referred the matter to Young, who met with Graham, John Herbers, and Robert Phelps at the *Times* Washington office. "You're being damaged by this whole underground movement [by the FBI]," said Herbers, "and we want to know what's going on — we want some guidance from you."

Young replied that King had done nothing wrong and asked the newspapermen to give him the names of the FBI officials who were trying to leak the stories. The reporters said that they could not reveal the identities of news sources who provided them with information "off the record" or "in confidence."[49]

Both King and the reporters seemed trapped. King could neither specifically identify his tormentors nor stop their cruel torture. And the correspondents could not — or would not — expose what the FBI was doing to King. By any measure of news judgment, the FBI's campaign to destroy King was a bigger story than whatever went on in King's hotel rooms. At least a dozen reporters from major news organizations had heard that sordid gossip when the FBI approached them seeking to leak the material. But the reporters would not expose the FBI because these contacts were "off the record." The reporters and editors apparently felt more strongly about observing the rules of the game — and keeping their sources at the FBI — than about breaking the huge story of J. Edgar Hoover's reprehensible war against Martin Luther King.

With these worries weighing heavily on him, King and the SCLC headed for Selma — from which he predicted some of them would not return alive.

LBJ–MLK: A Quiet Alliance

L YNDON JOHNSON AND MARTIN LUTHER KING had tip-
toed around each other for the fourteen accomplishment-
filled months of the Johnson administration, coolly and politely formal in
their conversations by telephone and in the Oval Office. In their four face-
to-face meetings, each man had prepared carefully for their talks, the
president by reading daily transcripts of the FBI's eavesdropping, the
minister by consulting his advisers, who were all under surveillance. King
carefully strategized with his trusted aides to determine precisely what he
would say to the president — and the FBI told the president exactly what
to expect at the meeting. It was a delicate pas de deux, almost halted by
Johnson's fury at the Mississippi Freedom Democrats' challenge during
the previous summer's Democratic convention — and by King's distress
at the FBI's relentless campaign against him, in which he feared that Johnson himself had a role. Yet each man knew that to reach his own ambitious goals, to achieve momentous change in American society, they
needed each other.

On January 15, 1965, Johnson put in a phone call to King on the occasion of his thirty-sixth birthday. The president found King in Selma, Alabama, where the Nobel Prize winner had just launched a daring voter registration drive. Johnson himself had just challenged the Eighty-ninth
Congress to approve the most far-reaching legislative agenda since Franklin Roosevelt was president in the 1930s.

After complimenting President Johnson on his recent State of the
Union address and exchanging a few pleasantries, King raised his first
point: the civil rights leadership wanted the president to name the first
black American to a Cabinet position. "It would really be a great step for-

ward for the nation, for the Negro, and for the national image," King said. "I am sure it would give a new sense of dignity and self-respect to millions of Negroes." Johnson quickly assured King that he indeed planned to appoint an African American to his Cabinet, and to appoint other blacks to high office as well.*

Johnson then pressed his agenda, urging King to work with him to win historic legislation initiating Medicare, federal aid to education, and poverty relief. Then he surprised King by mentioning the dire need for a voting rights bill. At their White House meeting only a month earlier, the president had told King that voting rights reform would have to wait so as not to alienate southern congressmen, whose support he needed to pass his Great Society programs.

Now, however, buoyed by optimism for the Great Society, Johnson announced that "we have got to come up with [voting rights legislation]. That will answer 70 percent of your problems!" Johnson pledged to support strong legislation to prevent county and state officials from denying the vote to black citizens. Although he hadn't yet thought through the details, Johnson said, he wanted a system in which the only eligibility requirements would be age and the ability to read and write. Poll taxes would be forbidden. So would the tortuous and arbitrary literacy requirements used to keep southern blacks from registering to vote. If state and local officials still wouldn't do the job, the president added, he would consider placing voter registration under federal control: "They [voters] can all go to the Post Office like they buy a stamp," Johnson said.

"There is not going to be anything, Doctor, as effective as all [black citizens] voting," the president continued. "That will give you a message that all the eloquence in the world won't bring," because the candidate or elected official "will be coming to you then, instead of you calling him."

"You're exactly right about that," replied King. "It's very interesting, Mr. President, to notice that the only states that you didn't carry in the South — the five southern states — had less than 40 percent of the Negroes registered to vote," he observed, revealing his own political acumen. "So it demonstrates that it is so important to get Negroes registered to vote in large numbers; it would be this coalition of the Negro vote and the moderate white vote that would really make the New South."

"That is exactly right!" Johnson replied. He cherished just that vision of

---

* Johnson told King that he hoped to appoint Robert Weaver, the federal housing administrator, to be the first secretary of a new Department of Housing and Urban Development. Then, the president said, if the mayors of the nation's largest cities wanted federal help, they would have to come to Weaver, a black man, to seek it.

a political coalition that could give birth to a New South of tolerance and prosperity. Furthermore, Johnson knew, the 1964 election returns carried an ominous political warning — one easily overlooked in the euphoria of the Democratic sweep. The five Deep South states carried by Goldwater were likely to become Republican strongholds, a transformation fueled by white southerners' resentment of Johnson's civil rights advocacy. A solid black vote had saved Johnson from defeat in the border and rim states of Arkansas, Florida, Tennessee, Virginia, and North Carolina. More than ever, it was a question not simply of Democratic policy but of political necessity for Johnson and his party to strengthen the black vote throughout the country. In this the South would be crucial.[1]

"I think you can contribute a great deal by getting your leaders and you, yourself, taking very simple examples of discrimination [in voter registration]," Johnson advised King, "where a man has got to memorize Longfellow, or he has got to quote from the first Ten Amendments, or he has got to tell you what Amendments Fifteen, Sixteen, and Seventeen are. Some people don't have to do that, but when a Negro comes in, he has got to do it.

"If you can find the worst condition that you can run into in Alabama or Mississippi or Louisiana or South Carolina — one of the worst I ever heard of was the president at Tuskegee* . . . being denied the right to cast the vote. If you take that one illustration and get it on radio, get it on television, get it in the pulpits, get it in the meetings — every place you can — then pretty soon the fellow who didn't do anything but drive a tractor would say, 'Well, that is not right — that is not fair.' Then that will help us in what we are going to shove through in the end. . . . I just don't see how anybody can say that a man can fight in Vietnam but he can't vote."

"Yes, you're exactly right about that," King replied with growing enthusiasm.

"I think the greatest achievement of my administration was the passage of the 1964 Civil Rights Act," said Johnson, "but I think this will be bigger because it will do things that even that '64 act couldn't do."[2]

The president and the civil rights leader — the politician and the preacher — were bouncing ideas off each other like two old allies in a campaign strategy huddle, excited about achieving their dreams for a more just society. Here was Johnson, never an admirer of King's direct-action tactics, now advising King about how to put pressure on Congress

---

* The historically black Tuskegee Institute (now Tuskegee University), located in Tuskegee, Alabama, was first established in 1881 under the leadership of Booker T. Washington.

for voting rights. And King, never quite sure of Johnson's motives, was advising Johnson on how to get reelected in 1968. With the Eighty-ninth Congress barely convened, Johnson was so confident that he now seemed willing to risk adding voting rights to his already heavy legislative agenda. But timing was everything, he knew, and both men were masters at sensing when to seize opportunities. Johnson understood that more public pressure was needed before the time would be ripe to pass voting rights. And King was ready to supply the pressure.

The ever-mercurial Lyndon Johnson was in an especially upbeat and optimistic mood. As he embarked on his 1965 legislative agenda with a popular mandate and a friendly Congress, King seemed less of a threat to him — and, he hoped, King would help push the legislation even further. At the same time, Johnson wanted to show King how much the Great Society agenda would help poor black people.

Johnson confided that, for obvious political reasons, he had not publicized the percentage of federal funds in his Great Society initiatives benefiting the black population. He wanted King to realize, though, that $8 billion of new health care, education, and poverty spending would benefit "people who earn less than $2,000 a year."

"You know who earns less than $2,000 a year, don't you?" Johnson asked. The two men chuckled like co-conspirators in a plot to help black America without creating a white backlash that would spoil their plans.[3]

As always, Johnson did most of the talking. As always, King was polite and deferential to the president. But there was a shared sense of new possibilities, new opportunities for cooperation to bring about historic change.

Yet there had been little change in King's relationship with other white officials from the Kennedy and Johnson administrations. With them King remained reticent and formal. Men such as Burke Marshall, Nicholas Katzenbach, and Lee White all felt that they had only glimpsed what lay behind King's stoic exterior. They saw only a man who "made speeches to them." Katzenbach thought he could tell when King was agitated, but only because King began to rock back and forth in his chair. These officials admired King's accomplishments, but they did not really know or like him. They were wary, too, of the FBI reports. As for King, he would have liked a closer relationship with Lyndon Johnson, but he was pragmatic in his dealings with all politicians. King judged presidents and those around them almost totally by their concrete actions to advance the cause of civil rights.

The Alabama Project

Dr. King had launched the Alabama Project with a powerful sermon at the Brown Chapel African Methodist Episcopal Church in Selma on January 2, two weeks before his conversation with the president. Speaking to an enthusiastic audience of seven hundred black citizens who jammed the church, King called Selma a "symbol of bitter-end resistance to the civil rights movement in the Deep South." He excoriated the Dallas County Board of Registrars for preventing black citizens from becoming registered voters by requiring them to pass a literacy test so complex that few government experts could have completed it.

"At the rate they are letting us register now, it will take a hundred and three years to register all of the fifteen thousand Negroes in Dallas County who are qualified to vote," King had declared. "But we don't have that long to wait! . . . Today marks the beginning of a determined, organized, mobilized campaign to get the right to vote everywhere in Alabama. If we are refused, we will appeal to Governor George Wallace. If he refuses to listen, we will appeal to the legislature. If they don't listen, we will appeal to the conscience of the Congress in another dramatic march on Washington.

"We must be ready to march; we must be willing to go to jail by the thousands. . . . Our cry to the state of Alabama is a simple one: GIVE US THE BALLOT!"

The crowd of black Selma and Dallas County residents shouted back, "Amen," "Yes, Lord," and "Give us the ballot!"

Finally, King told the frenzied crowd, "When we get the right to vote, we will send to the statehouse not men who will stand in the doorways of universities to keep Negroes out, but men who will uphold the cause of justice. GIVE US THE BALLOT.

"We're not on our knees begging for the ballot. WE ARE DEMANDING THE BALLOT."

As the audience leaped to a standing ovation, King promised to work in Alabama as long as it took to achieve victory.

In his first address to Selma's black citizens, King was at his oratorical best, mixing religious metaphors and old-time preaching with political and intellectual substance. King's oratory aimed to arouse an apathetic and frightened population to stand up and fight for its rights. But the meticulous planning of the Alabama Project — and the selection of Selma as its focal point — reflected different King skills. At work here was the pragmatist, the direct-action strategist and tactician, the field general willing to draw hostile fire to achieve his aims, the skilled manipulator of the news media, and the man of steely courage who, despite his own deep fears, was willing to risk his own and others' lives to achieve his goals.

Recognizing the enormous personal dangers inherent in the campaign, King instructed his associates that should anything happen to him, his deputy Ralph Abernathy was to take over as SCLC president.[4]

The idea behind the campaign in Alabama was to expose voting rights discrimination so dramatically that it would anger the country and embarrass the federal government into action. The merits of choosing Selma, a city of 27,000 and the government seat of Dallas County, as a civil rights battleground were not immediately obvious. The town was obscure and isolated, with limited transportation service for moving in the civil rights forces — and, just as important, enough reporters and television cameramen to cover the battle. Dallas County lay in the center of the "Yellowhammer State" and in the heart of the Black Belt — so called because of its dark alluvial soil, which stretches in a band across Alabama, Mississippi, and Georgia, an area that once yielded large cotton crops and prosperity thanks also to a plentiful supply of cheap black labor. Cotton was no longer king in the Black Belt. The soils were depleted, most black field hands had been replaced by machines, and poverty was rampant. Nevertheless, civil rights strategists saw a new resource there, ready to be tilled and harvested by men and women with enough courage and ingenuity to seize it. In place of the rich black earth, there lay the potential of black political power: In virtually every Black Belt county, African Americans constituted 40 percent or more of the population. In Selma, they were in the majority. The new cash crop was the power that lay in black votes. That was why white leaders across the Black Belt and the Deep South so intransigently and bitterly resisted giving African Americans what had been guaranteed to them in 1870 by the Fifteenth Amendment to the Constitution.

Selma — a community that had prided itself on being "the friendliest town in Alabama" — had never been a hospitable place for black Americans who desired a life beyond servility as sharecroppers and menial servants. The small black middle class of teachers, ministers, and doctors felt itself powerless to effect change.

Located fifty miles to the west of Montgomery, the state capital, and bisected by the Alabama River, Selma had one of the worst records of black voter registration of any city in Alabama: only 1.9 percent of eligible blacks were registered.* As of April 1961, roughly 15,000 African Americans accounted for over 56 percent of the voting-age population in Selma

---

* Mississippi, in which only 6.7 percent of eligible black voters were registered, ranked last in the nation in giving blacks the right to vote.

and surrounding Dallas County, yet only 156 could vote. Despite tireless efforts to register voters — including constant litigation using the 1957, 1960, and 1964 Civil Rights Acts — only 335 blacks (2.1 percent) were registered to vote in Dallas County by late 1964.[5] Alabama's model voter registration requirements, drawn up by the state's supreme court, were the toughest in the nation. Registrars could quiz applicants about sixty-eight provisions of the Alabama state constitution and other government procedures. Adding still more obstacles to black voting, the county had limited voter registration to just two days a month, and a county judge issued an order forbidding more than three people to gather together in public — virtually banning any legal demonstrations. With the total failure of legal remedies, Selma seemed to King an ideal place to demonstrate that a stronger federal solution was needed.[6]

King knew that for the Southern Christian Leadership Conference to dramatize voter discrimination in Selma successfully, as it had in Birmingham in 1963, he would need a perfect foil: a racist law enforcement figure whose tactics would stand in stark contrast to the nonviolent actions of civil rights demonstrators. In Selma, SCLC leaders knew, their success depended on provoking a hostile response from Sheriff Jim Clark, a veritable Hollywood caricature of a small-town southern lawman. The SCLC hoped that Clark would play the villain role performed so usefully in Birmingham in 1963 by Bull Connor. Having already seen Sheriff Clark in action, including his indiscriminate use of tear gas and cattle prods against peaceful blacks attempting to test the 1964 Civil Rights Act, SCLC and SNCC organizers were confident they had found their man. Pale and heavyset, with a hair-trigger temper, Clark wore tight-fitting uniforms modeled after those of General George Patton, a green combat helmet decorated with the Confederate flag, sunglasses, and a lapel button stating his views on integration. It read simply, "Never."[7]

Clark's power was reinforced by Dallas County judge James A. Hare, a fervent racist with intellectual pretensions. Hare theorized to willing listeners about the genealogical origins of Selma's black citizens. "Your Negro," he asserted, "is a mixture of African types like the Congolite, who has a long heel, and the blue-gummed Ebo whose IQ is about 50 or 55." Behind these southern Gothic figures in Selma stood Governor George Wallace, whose larger ambitions depended on his ability to stir up a racial backlash, and Colonel Al Lingo, commander of Alabama's state troopers. If dramatic confrontation were needed, King and his lieutenants knew they faced a dependably fearsome group of antagonists who regularly suppressed black Alabamans in the course of their daily official business.[8]

A third reason for choosing Selma was the readiness of a highly motivated cadre of local leaders to risk life and limb to win the right to vote. These activists represented the framework of an organization strong enough to produce the waves of demonstrators needed to challenge the system, fill the jails, and maintain the interest of a fickle national news media. As in the Freedom Democrats' action in Mississippi six months earlier, young SNCC organizers had pioneered the civil rights struggle in Selma. The Reverend Bernard Lafayette, already a veteran SNCC organizer at twenty-two, had gone to Selma with his wife, Kate Bulls Lafayette, in 1963 to help mobilize the local black leadership. The Reverend James Bevel and his wife, Diane Nash, both battle-tested civil rights campaigners, followed Lafayette in 1964. After the Klan church bombing in Birmingham in 1963 that killed the four little black girls, Bevel and Nash briefly contemplated taking violent revenge. Instead they rededicated themselves to the nonviolent struggle and conceived the Alabama Project, which Bevel began ceaselessly promoting to Dr. King. In Selma, Lafayette, Bevel, and Nash found a group of extraordinary leaders, including the Reverend Frederick Reese, a tall, eloquent high school science teacher and Baptist pastor, and Amelia Boynton, an elegant veteran of early NAACP efforts and one of Selma's few registered black voters. Reese and Boynton had been leaders in forming the Dallas County Voters' League. Now the local leaders felt that they needed the visibility of Martin Luther King to carry their campaign to the next level. And King needed Selma to sustain the SCLC's own momentum into 1965. The match was made, and King and his lieutenants headed for Alabama.[9]

On January 18 King and his advisers arrived at the Hotel Albert, an ornate antebellum building modeled after the Doge's Palace in Venice. Dr. King signed the guest register and appeared to have succeeded in peacefully integrating Selma's best hotel. Before King left the crowded lobby, however, a young white man named James Robinson asked to speak with him. As King took a step toward him, Robinson twice slugged the SCLC leader in the head and kicked him in the groin. Selma public safety director Wilson Baker quickly arrested Robinson, a member of the National States' Rights Party, an often violent neo-Nazi group. King managed to appear calm as he rode the elevator to his hotel room.[10]

When the SCLC's Dorothy Cotton entered King's room a few minutes later, she found him sitting in a chair in his undershirt and shorts, sweating profusely. He did not wish to file charges, he told her. Usually a nonsmoker, King was puffing nervously on a cigarette and drinking beer from the can. "Did it hurt?" Cotton asked.

"Oh, he packs a pretty good wallop," replied King, managing a smile.

Cotton was struck by the way King managed to maintain grace under pressure, even after he had been severely assaulted. King knew that Robinson could just as easily have attacked him with a knife or a gun.* After a brief rest, the still-shaken SCLC leader put on his white shirt, his dark suit, and his impassive "game face," and headed for the evening's mass meeting.

Much of Selma was trying hard to remain peaceful. As in King's quiet integration of the hotel before he was attacked, decorum prevailed throughout Selma. The city's business leadership sought to checkmate King's efforts to spark confrontation and headlines.

The success of the Selma campaign would rest in part on the outcome of an internal political struggle between Sheriff Clark and Selma's more moderate leadership, led by newly elected mayor Joe Smitherman and the new police chief, Wilson Baker.† Backed by business leaders, Smitherman and Baker were determined to avoid the kind of violent confrontation that would land Selma on the television evening news and ruin the city's efforts to attract new business and industry.‡ To succeed, they had to contain Sheriff Clark and his posse of special deputies.

On January 19 King led hundreds of black citizens from Brown Chapel to the sidewalk in front of the county courthouse. Sheriff Clark immediately ordered the marchers to move to an alley behind the courthouse, where they could line up and wait to register, entering the building one person at a time. The day before, the marchers had complied with an identical command, but this time they stood their ground in front of the courthouse. There would be no more "back alley waiting" for first-class citizens, they said. When the marchers did not respond to a second command to clear the sidewalk, the burly sheriff, his face flaming, grabbed the well-dressed Amelia Boynton by her coat collar and shoved her down the block into a patrol car. Scores of marchers were arrested. At the mass rally that night, Ralph Abernathy pronounced Sheriff Clark an "honorary SCLC member" and "honorary member of the Dallas County Voters' League" for falling into their trap. King stoked the rhetorical fire: Amelia Boynton's arrest was "one of the most brutal and unlawful acts I have seen an officer commit," he said. Front-page news stories and television

---

* In 1958 King nearly died after a woman attending his book signing at a New York department store plunged a knife into his chest, missing his heart by a fraction of an inch.

† As public safety director, Baker served as chief of both the police and fire departments.

‡ Soon after Smitherman was elected in October 1964, he sent Baker to Washington to ask the help of Attorney General Robert Kennedy and Assistant Attorney General Burke Marshall in keeping King out of Selma.

footage of Clark pushing Boynton subsequently dominated the news. The battle was joined, the losers that day being city officials Baker and Smitherman, whose plan to contain Sheriff Clark had not lasted twenty-four hours.[11]

Seeking a Great Society

On January 20, 1965, standing on a platform before the Capitol in the freezing Washington air, Lyndon Baines Johnson raised his right hand to take his second oath of office as president — a very different scene from the one aboard Air Force One only fourteen months earlier. As Chief Justice Earl Warren administered the oath, Lady Bird Johnson stood beside the president, holding the family Bible. Over a million supporters, friends, government officials, and dignitaries filled the Capitol grounds and spread out across the area to hear the president address the nation from the East Front of the Capitol. At a time of "rapid and fantastic change . . . shaking old values and uprooting old ways," Johnson challenged Americans to seek "a Great Society" that would not only provide material benefits to the needy but also improve the quality of life for everyone. On the subject of civil rights, the president declared, "Justice requires us to remember: when any citizen denies his fellow, saying: 'His color is not mine or his beliefs are strange and different,' in that moment, he betrays America, though his forebears created this nation."[12]

Lyndon Johnson's inaugural celebration included greater participation by black Americans than any previous gala. Opera star Leontyne Price, an African American soprano from Mississippi, performed a soaring rendition of "America the Beautiful." Leaders of the Mississippi Freedom Democratic Party, the bane of Johnson's existence only five months earlier in Atlantic City, were official White House guests at the swearing-in ceremony and the inaugural balls. Roy Wilkins of the NAACP, Whitney Young of the National Urban League, and Floyd McKissick, national chairman of CORE, were among a dozen civil rights leaders who watched part of the inaugural parade at Lyndon Johnson's side as honored guests in the presidential reviewing stand. Although he too had been invited by the president, Martin Luther King regretfully declined.* He spent January 20 instead in Selma, directing a new wave of demonstrators, then flew off to

---

* At the inauguration, the FBI continued its campaign to undermine King as J. Edgar Hoover told Atlanta police chief Herbert Jenkins of King's alleged Communist ties and immoral behavior. Eight days later, the FBI learned via its wiretaps that Jenkins, on returning home, had informed King's father of the FBI's information. Martin Luther King Sr. spoke with his son about what Jenkins had told him, renewing the younger King's anxiety and anger about the FBI (FBI King File, 100-106670-780, 1/28/65).

fulfill two days of speaking engagements in Pennsylvania. His top priority was nurturing the still embryonic Selma protest. His next was to raise enough funds through speeches across the country to keep the SCLC in business.[13]

With the arrival of the most liberal, most Democratic Congress since 1940, many of whose members had been elected on his coattails, Lyndon Johnson wasted no time in trying to convert his Great Society vision into a legislative reality. In his State of the Union speech on January 4, Johnson had proposed "a program in education to ensure every American child the fullest development of his mind and skills . . . a massive attack on crippling and killing disease . . . a national effort to make the American city a better and a more stimulating place to live," an effort to "end the poisoning of our rivers and the air we breathe," and the elimination of "every remaining obstacle to the right and the opportunity to vote."[14]

Johnson believed that he had to move quickly. Two months after his historic victory he knew that, the specter of Barry Goldwater having vanished, some of his support had already eroded. "After a fight with Congress," he warned his advisers, "I'll lose another couple of million [supporters]. I could be down to [a margin of] 8 million in a couple of months."[15]

"I've just been elected and right now we'll have a honeymoon with Congress," Johnson told his congressional liaison officers. "But after I make my recommendations, I'm going to start to lose the power and authority I have. . . . Every day that I'm in office and every day I push my program, I'll be losing part of my ability to be influential, because that's in the nature of what the President does. He uses up capital. Something is going to come up . . . something like the Vietnam War or something else where I will begin to lose all that I have now. So," he urged them, "I want you guys to get off your asses and do everything possible to get everything in my program passed as soon as possible, before the aura and the halo that surround me disappear."[16]

Having watched House Rules Committee chairman "Judge" Howard Smith block and delay bill after bill — nearly sinking the 1964 Civil Rights Act — Johnson saw to it that the Eighty-ninth Congress changed House rules to authorize the Speaker to bring to the floor any bill that had sat for three weeks in the Rules Committee. No longer would Smith's absences for "farm renovations" mean the death of progressive legislation. Next the president persuaded congressional leaders to ensure that vacancies on the most important House committees — Appropriations and Ways and Means — were filled with Johnson supporters. Having picked up dozens of House seats, Democrats now held a large enough majority to prevail on some measures despite defections by southerners. The Democrats' advantage over Republicans in the House was 295 to 140, the largest since 1936, and the Senate margin of 68 to 32 was the widest since 1940. For the moment at least, the conservative coalition had been cracked, if not broken altogether. Johnson observed, beaming, that the new Congress "could be better, but not this side of heaven."[17]

The president had prepared well for this rare opportunity to win liberal legislation expanding the role of the federal government. He could move swiftly on his proposals thanks to the work of fourteen task forces he had appointed the previous summer and directed to come up with the best ideas available for each of his priorities: medical care for seniors, aid to elementary and secondary education, an expanded poverty program, and a hundred other initiatives ranging from protecting the environment to providing federal aid to the arts and humanities. The task forces, made up chiefly of noted academics from prestigious universities, were given a free hand. Instead of depending on the federal bureaucracy, Johnson wanted fresh ideas from outside the government. The task forces were sworn to secrecy, allowing Johnson to maintain the element of surprise and avoid exposing his programs to criticism before he was ready to act. In rapid succession, the president delivered his highest-priority legislation to Congress: health care programs on January 7, education assistance on January 12, immigration reform on January 13, foreign aid on January 14, new antipoverty measures on January 17, defense programs on January 18. Even before his inauguration the president had phoned congressional leaders of both parties and committee chairmen with jurisdiction over his ambitious legislative agenda. He reached out to Representative Gerald Ford, the new House minority leader, replacing Charles Halleck. "I don't want to start out fighting with you," he told Ford, "because I'm not running for re-election. I'm just trying to make a good president and I want you to help me. I thought you could support me when you thought it was right and be proud of it."[18]

His message to each committee chairman was, "Get your hearings going!" When a chairman such as Harry Byrd opposed his legislation, the president improvised new twists on the "Johnson treatment." The conservative Byrd, still chairman of the Senate Finance Committee, strongly opposed the president's top priority, medical care for senior citizens. After inviting Byrd and other congressional leaders to the White House for an important meeting, he surprised them by bringing in network television cameras. With the cameras rolling, Johnson repeatedly pressed Byrd for early hearings on Medicare until the courtly Virginian finally gave his consent.

Building a Crisis

On Friday afternoon, January 22, an unexpected formation of fresh recruits to the Selma struggle marched two by two from Brown Chapel to confront a surprised Sheriff Jim Clark at the Dallas County Courthouse. Dressed in their Sunday best, virtually the entire membership of the Selma Negro Teachers Association lined up to demand the right to vote. One hundred and ten teachers started up the courthouse steps. Clark and his forces began to beat them back, wielding nightsticks and electric cattle prods.

"You have one minute to get off these steps!" the sheriff bellowed. The teachers started up the steps again, following their leader, Fred Reese — science teacher, preacher, and head of the Dallas County Voters' League. After three attempts to enter the building, and three attacks by Clark, the teachers marched back to Brown Chapel, where three hundred school-children — their students — gave them a heroes' welcome. The SCLC's Andrew Young called the event "the most significant thing that happened in the racial movement since Birmingham." Literally true or not, the significance was lost on no one. Never before had black schoolteachers marched as a group in a civil rights protest in the Deep South. Subject to instant dismissal by white superintendents and school boards, black teachers had been conservative in the extreme, hanging on to their fragile status in the middle class. But they too had been caught up in the Selma movement, asking how they could teach civics when they were afraid to assert their own right to vote. Now it was Selma officials who blinked. Faced with the prospect of black schools without teachers, the superintendent ordered a furious Clark not to arrest them.

Day after day, the dangerous parry and thrust continued. City officials and moderate business leaders were convinced that if they could prevent violence, the television cameras would go dark and the movement would fizzle. They worked hard to muzzle Sheriff Clark and made enough cosmetic changes in voter registration procedures to defuse the confrontation. Faced with such wily and resourceful officials, King struggled to stay a step ahead — leading wave after wave of would-be registrants to the courthouse, hoping all the while to provoke Clark and create as many confrontations as necessary to prick the nation's conscience. The American citizenry then would demand a voting rights law — one strong enough to stop local officials from beating up black citizens and flouting the Constitution.

On Monday, January 25, King led another group of 250 to the courthouse steps.* Television news cameras captured images of Sheriff Clark beating fifty-three-year-old Annie Lee Cooper with a nightstick as three of his deputies pinned her to the ground after she shouted at Clark, "I wish you would hit me, you scum!"† What the cameras missed was the opening of this scene: when Clark twisted Mrs. Cooper's arm, she retaliated with three solid punches that put him on the ground. She had already been fired from her job at Dunn's Rest Home for attempting to register and felt that she had little left to lose.

King's plan was working, but it was fraught with problems. Maintaining discipline and passive resistance was becoming more difficult. King understood Mrs. Cooper's behavior; self-defense is a natural reaction. Nevertheless, at that night's rally King urged renewed dedication to nonviolence and to loving one's enemies. With several hundred demonstrators already in jail, King was also concerned that he would soon run out of willing foot soldiers. His advisers in Selma decided that it was once again time for their leader to go to jail.[19]

The 264 demonstrators marched out of Brown Chapel on February 1 into a cold drizzle. Dr. King led the march toward the Dallas County Courthouse, defying the city's parade ordinance and courting arrest by Police Chief Baker — a much safer potential opponent than the nightstick-swinging Sheriff Clark, who stood guard at the courthouse. As King had hoped, Baker stopped the group. The chief had ordered them to walk in pairs at intervals of thirty feet.

"This is a deliberate attempt to violate the parade ordinance — which you have followed for three weeks," said the exasperated officer. "If you

---

* King briefly left Selma that day to attend an Atlanta dinner honoring him for his Nobel Prize. The FBI failed in its efforts to sabotage the dinner, but resistance in Atlanta's business community initially slowed ticket sales. One afternoon at Atlanta's Piedmont Driving Club, a popular gathering spot for local bank presidents, Paul Austin, the president of Coca-Cola, walked in and delivered a message from Bob Woodruff, Coke's powerful chairman. "Fellas," Austin said, "the boss says we oughta have the dinner." Because Woodruff controlled stock in their banks, resistance crumbled. The 1,500-person dinner sold out, the attendees evenly divided between blacks and whites. (Taylor Branch, *Pillar of Fire*, pp. 568–569; AI, Eugene Patterson).

† After seeing a front-page picture in the *New York Times* of Clark beating Mrs. Cooper, Eugene Rostow, dean of Yale Law School and a former State Department official, wrote the White House urging President Johnson to set the tone against "the charade we see in Selma." At the same time, the president received letters from the South condemning King.

don't break up the line into small groups, I'll have to arrest you." King replied that the city ordinance violated their constitutional right of peaceable assembly. He signaled the marchers forward. Baker, who desperately wanted to avoid arresting anyone, felt that he now had no choice; Sheriff Clark and his allies were intently watching to see what he would do. Baker arrested all 264 demonstrators — 258 black and 6 white — for holding a parade without a permit. He marched them to the city jail.[20]

Realizing that he had again been outmaneuvered by King, Baker tried to recover by informing King and Ralph Abernathy, King's chosen jail companion, that they were not under arrest and should leave the jail. Outside, King continued his ploy by holding an impromptu news conference virtually under Baker's nose. "I must admit this is a deliberate attempt to dramatize conditions in this city and state," King said. "We're going to turn Selma upside down and inside out in order to make it rightside up." Baker had had enough. He threw King and Abernathy back into jail, where, refusing bail, they conducted a Quaker-style prayer service with the county's other black prisoners. King had achieved his immediate goal: intensified coverage by the news media, including headlines in Tuesday morning's newspapers.[21]

Following the scripted plan, a second formation of nearly five hundred Selma high school students set out for the courthouse, where they were arrested by Sheriff Clark. Chief Baker pleaded with King to send the jailed children back to school "where they belonged." King politely declined. The students were entitled to protest for voting rights, he said, even though they themselves were too young to vote. As planned, more arrests followed on Tuesday and Wednesday, leaving jails in every Black Belt county around Selma overflowing with prisoners.[22]

From his jail cell on February 2, King continued to orchestrate the movement's actions in Alabama — and in Washington and New York. On a sheet of Waldorf-Astoria stationery acquired on a New York trip, he wrote a list of twelve orders to SCLC executive director Andrew Young. "Do the following," he instructed, "to keep national attention focused on Selma":

1. Make a call to Governor [LeRoy] Collins [director of the new Community Relations Service] and urge him to make personal visit to Selma to talk with city and county authorities concerning speedier registration and more days for registering.
2. Follow through on suggestions of having a congressional delegation to come in for personal investigation. They should also make an appearance at mass meeting if they come.

3. Make personal call to President Johnson urging him to intervene in some way (send a personal emissary to Selma; get Justice Department involved; make plea to Dallas County & Selma officials in press conference).
4. Urge lawyers to go to 5th Circuit if Judge [Daniel] Thomas does not issue an immediate injunction against continued arrests and speeding up registration.
5. Keep some activity alive every day this week.
6. Consider a night march to the city jail to protest my arrest (an arrest which must be considered unjust). Have another night march to courthouse to let Clark show true colors.
7. Stretch every point to get teachers to march.
8. Immediately post bond for staff members essential for mobilization who are arrested.
9. Seek to get big name celebrities to come in for moral support.
10. Get Wyatt [Tee Walker] to contact Gov. Rockefeller and other Republican big names to come out with strong statements about the arrests, and right to vote and Selma.
11. Call C. T. [Vivian] and have him return from Cal. In case other staff put out of circulation.
12. Local Selma editor sent telegram to President calling for congressional committee to come and study the true situation in Selma. We should join in calling for this. By all means do not let them get the offensive. . . . They are trying to give the impression that they are an orderly and good community because they integrated public accommodations. We must insist that voting is the issue and here Selma has dirty hands.

Let me hear on all this tomorrow.[23]

J. L. "Ike" Chestnut, a Birmingham lawyer with Selma roots who all but lived in the Dallas County courthouses while representing the jailed marchers, had sat through dozens of contentious strategy meetings and come to view King as "one hell of a field general." After all conflicting arguments had been aired, Chestnut observed, King spent "30 minutes summing up the different points of view, then logically analyzed the pros and cons of each proposal, declared which proposal he favored, and began to lay out the next move." Chestnut concluded that "no one else [but King] could have unified the collection of ministers, gangsters, self-seekers, students, prima donnas, and devoted, high-minded people we had in Selma that winter."[24]

Like the best of military leaders, the celebrated man of peace kept in mind a clear distinction between his strategic objectives and the tactical maneuvers necessary to win both skirmishes and battles. He maintained a broad view of the entire battlefield and measured the relative strengths and capabilities of his own and opposing forces. And as he delegated authority through Andrew Young to half a dozen of his most competent and trusted lieutenants, King understood the critical importance of giving clear, simple orders.

Young passed along King's crisp directives, which produced quick and encouraging results. In Washington, Walter Fauntroy lined up a congressional delegation to visit King in the Selma jail. Wyatt Tee Walker contacted Governor Nelson Rockefeller of New York, who set in motion a statement of support for King from Republican governors, senators, and congressmen, several of whom made airline reservations for a trip to Selma. Clarence Jones in New York began recruiting celebrities; Dick Gregory, the black comedian and activist, was the first to volunteer. Jim Bevel kept up daily demonstrations in Selma, refusing to be deflected by judicial orders that only chipped away at the massive barriers to black voting. Most important, Young spoke with White House special counsel Lee White and conveyed King's requests that the president send an emissary to Selma, speak out against the injustices there, and call for a new voting rights law.*

In a memo to President Johnson on February 3, however, White recommended that the president sidestep all of King's requests and that White report back to Young that the president had already stated his commitment to voting rights. Assistant Attorney General John Doar was closely following the situation in Selma, he said. Furthermore, White assured the president, Attorney General Katzenbach might soon succeed in defusing the crisis. From secret negotiations with federal district judge Daniel Thomas in Alabama, White explained, Katzenbach expected the judge to issue an order that would ease voting restrictions and reduce tensions in Selma.[25]

Employing traditional political tactics, White was seeking to protect President Johnson by shielding him from public involvement in the Selma crisis. Martin Luther King, by contrast, was trying to draw the president in. Remembering their upbeat telephone conversation two weeks earlier, King sought Johnson's public endorsement of the Selma campaign — or at least an acknowledgment of the serious problems there.

---

* As usual, President Johnson was apprised by the FBI of all of King's jailhouse instructions to Young. Even before Young called Lee White at the White House, Deke DeLoach had hand-delivered to Bill Moyers on February 3 a letter from Hoover describing King's plans. The bureau learned about King's instructions as agents listened to Young relate them to Clarence Jones over Jones's wiretapped telephone in New York (FBI, King File, 100-1066 70, 2/3/65).

Despite the efforts of White and Katzenbach to protect him, Johnson stepped into the middle of the controversy. He would not remain silent on a subject about which he felt passionately.

At a press conference in the White House theater on Thursday, February 4, the president read a prepared statement: "I should like to say that all Americans should be indignant when one American is denied the right to vote. The loss of that right to a single citizen undermines the freedom of every citizen. That is why all of us should be concerned with the efforts of our fellow Americans to register to vote in Alabama. . . . I intend to see that the right [to vote] is secured for all our citizens."[26]

Although Johnson did not go beyond pledging to enforce the voting rights provisions contained in the 1964 Civil Rights Act and did not mention new legislation, King was elated. Lyndon Johnson had acknowledged a problem in Selma and had told the nation that he would do something about it.

The political maneuvers in Selma took another turn Thursday afternoon when Judge Thomas issued a wide-ranging order commanding local officials to stop harassing potential registrants, to eliminate use of Alabama's lengthy registration test, to take at least one hundred applications on days when the registrars met, and to clear out the entire backlog of voter registration applicants by July 1. Thomas's order was the product of sustained lobbying by Katzenbach.* Selma officials lobbied Judge Thomas as well, their principal goals being to take away King's headlines and encourage him to leave Selma.[27]

Buoyed by the president's public statement and by the judge's order, King's SCLC lieutenants canceled demonstrations scheduled for Thursday. When news of the cancellation reached King in his jail cell, however, the SCLC leader was not pleased.†

King drafted another message to Young arguing that the marches should continue and that the SCLC should ask its New York lawyer, Jack Greenberg of the NAACP Legal Defense Fund, to press Judge Thomas for stronger, faster relief. Revealing his own tough pragmatism, King wrote: "Please don't be too soft. We have the offensive. It was a mistake not to march today. In a crisis we must have a sense of drama. Don't let Baker

---

* Katzenbach had been acting attorney general since Robert Kennedy resigned in the fall of 1964 to run for the Senate. Although concerned that Katzenbach was "a Kennedy man," Johnson was impressed with his work on the 1964 Civil Rights Act and appointed him attorney general on January 31, 1965.

† Another distraction on February 4, while King was in jail, was the unexpected visit of Black Muslim firebrand Malcolm X. Andrew Young feared that he might incite violence. The organizers were relieved when Malcolm assured Coretta King that he wanted to help Martin, not hinder him. After several hours in Selma, he rushed to make airplane connections to London and never visited King in jail.

control our movement. We may accept the restraining order [against Selma officials] as a partial victory, but we cannot stop."

King's urgency was propelled by another consideration. Instructing Young to redouble his effort to recruit entertainer Sammy Davis Jr. for a benefit concert, King explained, "These fellows respond better when I'm in jail, or [there is] a crisis. You should try to get him tonight."

King won a further payoff from his instructions to Young when a delegation of fifteen Democratic congressmen visited him in jail on Friday, February 5; a separate group, including Republicans Charles Mathias of Maryland and Ogden Reid of New York, reached through the bars of his cell to shake King's hand and promised that they would introduce new voting rights legislation promptly.[28]

The major break of the day came almost by accident as King and his advisers Clarence Jones and Harry Wachtel improvised to recover from a botched plan. Jones and Wachtel had placed a full-page advertisement in that day's *New York Times* under the headline "Letter from the Selma Jail." Patterned after King's famous "Letter from the Birmingham Jail" two years earlier, the letter sought to raise funds and publicize the Selma campaign — including the racism of Sheriff Clark. "She's a nigger woman and she hasn't got a Miss or Mrs. in front of her name," the ad quoted Clark as saying about a protester he had arrested. After spelling out the voting rights abuses in Selma, King's letter declared in bold type: "THIS IS SELMA, ALABAMA. THERE ARE MORE NEGROES IN JAIL WITH ME THAN THERE ARE ON THE VOTING ROLLS."

There was just one problem — a potentially embarrassing one. Unbeknownst to his New York advisers, King was no longer in jail, having posted bond that afternoon. Fearing ridicule about their "Letter from the Selma Jail," King's aides devised an explanation: King had left the jail in order to see President Johnson at the White House on Monday. Now they had another problem: the announcement that King would see the president took the White House by surprise. Improvising again, Wachtel made a series of frantic telephone calls to Lee White at the White House, where White had just been chewed out by the president. "Where the hell does [King] get off inviting himself to the White House?" Johnson had shouted.*[29]

---

* The FBI's tactics in dealing with both President Johnson and King were informed by its wiretap-obtained knowledge. The bureau listened on February 7 as Clarence Jones learned from Wachtel how upset the president was at King's public announcement that he was going to the White House. Discovering via its wiretaps that Wachtel was now King's White House intermediary, the bureau stepped up its efforts to identify Wachtel to the president as a Communist Party member. Earlier the FBI had identified Wachtel only as a onetime member of the left-wing National Lawyers Guild (FBI, King File, 100-1066-70, 2/7/65).

Despite his pique, the president didn't slam the door on an Oval Office visit. He had been following the Selma situation closely, and he saw an opportunity. The dramatic events there might galvanize support for new voting rights legislation. But Johnson saw peril as well: Selma could be engulfed in chaos, precipitating a disastrous clash between federal troops and hidebound segregationists. King, Johnson recognized, was the central player in Selma — one whose cooperation he now needed.

At 3 P.M. Friday, Katzenbach reported to the president that demonstrations were continuing in Selma "despite the court order we got yesterday. . . . About four hundred school kids were arrested a little while ago for singing out in front of the courthouse. They've gotten about everything they wanted, but they're still demonstrating. I suppose they don't want to lose their momentum. They've lost their own judgment." Then the attorney general added hopefully, "King's getting out of jail later in the afternoon — maybe he'll be more reasonable."

"I think we ought to give a chance for [Judge Thomas's court] order to operate," replied the president, "and we ought to be fair and reserved about it, and [King] ought to be told that . . . and told what I said yesterday [that the president would enforce the right to vote]. That is about as strong as a man can say it. King must not ignore . . . these kind of statements. He must help achieve them, and the best way to help achieve them now is to give us a chance. We've been in one court and we'll be in others. . . . This is what he asked for and this is what he's got. And we expect some quid pro quos."[30]

The president and his attorney general hoped that the court order forbidding Selma officials from using blatantly discriminatory tactics to keep blacks off the voter rolls would ease the confrontation there. Johnson needed time to draft and build support for a tough new law. The "quid pro quo" Johnson sought was for King to cut back on his demonstrations and give the president some breathing space.

Johnson and King already had agreed in principle that only a tough law mandating the use of federal voting registrars would break segregationist resistance. Earlier laws had failed because they relied almost exclusively on the federal court system, which southern officials tied up with endless appeals. Furthermore, federal lawyers had to develop and file cases county by county rather than seek an overall solution. In Selma and elsewhere in the South, the segregationists received aid and comfort from sympathetic federal judges like Daniel Thomas. Judge Thomas's rulings had been overturned repeatedly by higher courts, but the cases inevitably were sent back to his court, where he and county officials devised new strategies for delay.*

Although President Johnson welcomed traditional political lobbying on behalf of voting rights, he feared that too much pressure in the streets from King, provoking too much repression from Sheriff Clark and his allies, could result in violence and bloodshed, and the political repercussions would be difficult to predict, much less control. As in earlier battles, however, King would not call a halt to the Selma demonstrations, which he believed were the movement's principal weapon for change. Yet he too monitored the pressure he applied. If he pressed too hard, King feared, he could lose the support of sympathetic Americans or bring serious injury or even death to his own protesters. He was walking on a narrow ledge. But neither negative consequence had happened yet in Selma.

With prisoners now stashed in work camps and makeshift jails around the county, SNCC chairman John Lewis called White House aide Clifford Alexander to complain about inhumane treatment of the prisoners. He described how three hundred young black men had been packed like sardines into a fifty-by-eighteen-foot cell at Camp Selma, where they were forced to stand on a wet concrete floor without any bedding or blankets. Women prisoners had been treated similarly at a facility in Centreville. While Lewis was on the phone with Alexander, the president himself received an urgent request: the fifteen Democratic congressmen who had seen King on Friday wanted to meet with the president to discuss voting rights legislation.

With demands for reform increasing daily, Johnson took another giant step. Late Saturday morning, February 6, he had press secretary George Reedy inform reporters that the president soon planned to make "a strong recommendation" that Congress pass a voting rights act that year. Reedy also announced that Martin Luther King Jr. would meet with Vice President Humphrey and Attorney General Katzenbach on Tuesday, February 9, to discuss voting rights legislation and the situation in Selma. In answer to a reporter's question, Reedy said that the president had not ruled out meeting with Dr. King.[31]

On Sunday, Lee White made King's lawyer Harry Wachtel an offer with strings attached: if King maintained total secrecy, the president would see him briefly after his meeting on Tuesday with Humphrey and Katzenbach, but if King breathed a word about the arrangement, "all bets were

---

* Judge Thomas was reversed on appeal so many times that a provision in the 1964 Civil Rights Act was called the "Thomas rule." It provided that civil rights challenges could be sent to a three-judge panel rather than to a single judge.

off." The presidential visit could not take place on Monday, White told Wachtel, because LBJ would be occupied all day in crisis meetings on Vietnam.

Viet Cong guerrillas had just launched the most devastating attack yet on the limited U.S. military force in Vietnam. At the American air base at Pleiku, eight soldiers had been killed and more than one hundred wounded. Within forty-eight hours the president escalated the American presence in Vietnam. Forty-nine navy jets launched a retaliatory attack against bases in North Vietnam, and a combat battalion of marines was ordered to Vietnam. Military and diplomatic dependents were sent home from what suddenly was perceived to be a dangerous war zone.

Not wanting to see his 1964 reelection chances — or his Great Society initiatives — hurt by the escalating conflict, Johnson had avoided, for more than a year, the inevitable decision about whether to send U.S. combat forces into battle to aid South Vietnam. Now, with the South Vietnamese government in danger of collapse, Johnson could no longer avoid deciding whether to commit troops. He soon would have to make up his mind whether the United States would become more involved or leave South Vietnam to its own fate.

On Tuesday morning King led a demonstration in Montgomery, then flew by chartered plane to keep his appointment in Washington with Katzenbach and Humphrey. Meeting in Humphrey's office in the Executive Office Building, King asked for legislation to eliminate the arbitrary tests used to prevent black citizens from registering to vote. Federal registrars were needed, King said, to ensure that African American citizens could vote not only in federal but also in state and local elections. Throughout the two-hour meeting, King waited expectantly for Humphrey's phone to ring — the signal, he had been told, for the vice president to bring him to see President Johnson. Finally the phone rang, and Humphrey accompanied King to the Oval Office.

The meeting lasted only fifteen minutes, but it accomplished the purpose King had hoped for: President Johnson forcefully committed himself to new voting rights legislation. The president and the preacher reaffirmed and strengthened their pact to work together for voting rights and other Great Society legislation.

Speaking with reporters afterward, King was careful to respect Johnson's confidences and not to put him on the spot about specific issues that the administration was still considering. He called the meeting "very successful" and praised the president's "deep commitment to obtain[ing] the right to vote for all Americans." President Johnson had told him, King said, that he "realizes the pace is far too slow" in ensuring voting rights, and that "very soon" he would send new legislation to Congress. "The President made it very clear to me," King said, "that he was determined during his Administration to see all remaining obstacles removed to the right of Negroes to vote."

King told reporters, as he had told administration officials, that to be effective, the legislation must stop the arbitrary denial of voting rights by state and local officials, forbid the use of literacy tests in areas where blacks historically had received inferior educational opportunities, provide for enrollment of voters by federal registrars, and apply to federal, state, and local elections.

The president and his advisers concurred with King's view that a new law was needed. A constitutional amendment would be less subject to judicial challenge, but it would take too long to enact. Dealing with the civil rights crisis in the South demanded much quicker action. Because the Constitution vested in the states the right to establish voting qualifications, Justice Department lawyers were still struggling with the thorny issue of writing a law that would allow Congress to override the states' authority — and wanted to be certain the law would survive judicial scrutiny.

King did not share with reporters his only disappointment from the meetings: Humphrey's pessimistic assessment of congressional support. But the civil rights leader left no doubt of his own intentions. "We intend to continue this right-to-vote campaign throughout Alabama," he said emphatically.[32]

King's Balancing Act

His spirits lifted by his White House visit, King returned to Alabama to face a serious problem: disunity in the ranks of his forces in Selma. In keeping with the SCLC's pressure tactics, King lieutenant Jim Bevel had thumbed his nose at an innovation by Dallas County officials. The county, hoping to discourage the daily marches to the courthouse, had provided an "appearance book." Would-be voters could sign the book, reserving one of the hundred slots available for the next date on which the registrar would take applications. Contemptuously ignoring the appearance book, Bevel and a group of fifty demonstrators instead demanded immediate access to voter application forms, even though Monday, February 8, was not a designated day for the registration office to be open. For Bevel, the appearance book was one more "white man's trick," another delaying tactic, a meaningless charade. After five weeks of demonstrating in

Selma, not a single black citizen's name had been added to the list of eligible voters.

Sheriff Clark responded to Bevel's disdain for the appearance book as SCLC strategists had expected he would — by first jabbing Bevel in the stomach with his billy club, then pushing him down the steps, shouting, "You're making a mockery out of justice!" When Bevel refused to retreat, the sheriff commanded two deputies, "Lock him up!" In short order, Bevel and all of his companions were in the county jail.* In the five weeks since King launched the campaign, more than three thousand protesters had been jailed in Selma and the surrounding area.[33]

Bevel's tactic of ignoring positive gestures by local officials did not sit well with the leaders of the Dallas County Voters' League. Fred Reese, the group's president, thought that the appearance book innovation offered hope that some of Selma's black citizens might actually become registered voters, not just foot soldiers in the SCLC's daily marches to confront Sheriff Clark at the courthouse.

King arrived back in Selma just in time to witness the Bevel–Reese dispute expose a divergence of motives and goals among the groups taking part in the campaign. Reese's priority was to win Selma's black citizens the vote so they could exert some influence on matters as mundane as paving the streets in their neighborhoods. "This is our movement," he told King. "You are our guests." For King and the SCLC, however, Selma was a stage on which to dramatize how jurisdictions throughout the Deep South had disenfranchised black citizens. Registering another two hundred or three hundred black voters in Selma was not their paramount consideration. Without continued confrontation and resistance by local authorities, King was convinced that the media would lose interest. SCLC leaders acknowledged to officials from the new Federal Conciliation Service that if Selma did open its voter rolls, the campaign would move to a county where officials had not permitted even a handful of blacks to register.[34]

As usual, King listened quietly for more than an hour to the respective arguments as Reese called for using the appearance book and SNCC organizers demanded that the boycott continue. King finally agreed that the boycott should be dropped. The appearance book represented a small step forward, he said. King realized that he could not conduct a campaign in Selma without the cooperation of the city's black citizens. The SNCC organizers bristled at his decision. Once again, they felt that they had per-

---

* After jailers doused Bevel's cell with cold water, he developed viral pneumonia and was transferred to a hospital, where he was shackled to his bed and kept under guard. Only after Bevel's wife, Diane Nash, protested to federal authorities were the shackles removed.

formed the tough pioneering work only to see the SCLC ministers take command and reap the glory, as well as the financial contributions.[35]

Just as it appeared that Police Chief Wilson Baker's brand of polite segregation would prevail in Selma, Sheriff Clark again restored the movement to the front pages. On February 10, 165 students marched to the courthouse. Among the signs they carried was one that read "Jim Clark Is a Cracker." In a new tactic, Clark and several deputies took the students on a two-mile forced march and run through the countryside. "You've been wanting to march. Now let's go!" the deputies shouted as they chased the children and teenagers, pounding laggards with their billy clubs and cattle prods. The next night King told a cheering throng of students, including many who had endured the march, that the problem of "brutality, meanness and terror" in Selma would remain unresolved until "the federal government is willing to do something about it."[36]

Six days later Clark again made front-page news. When SCLC leader C. T. Vivian attempted to lead a group of hopeful registrants out of the rain into the courthouse, the sheriff and his deputies blocked the entrance and began shoving the demonstrators down the courthouse steps. Vivian kept climbing back, taunting Clark as being "like Hitler" and daring the sheriff to hit him. Predictably, Clark lost his composure and slugged Vivian in the face, then jailed the entire group.* Vivian shrugged off the mouth wound, which bled profusely and required stitches to close. The Indiana minister was inured to the perils of the battlefront and proud of his reputation as a practitioner of "active insistence" rather than "passive resistance." Like Jim Bevel and Hosea Williams, Vivian was a tough King lieutenant who believed in nonviolence but dared to provoke southern lawmen when it served their purposes.[37]

At a strategy meeting late Sunday night at Selma's Torch Motel, King decided that sustained pressure for voting rights legislation called for expanding the demonstrations to fresh Alabama battlefields. "How far can Selma take us on the right to vote?" King asked leaders from the SCLC, SNCC, and the Dallas County Voters League. Answering his own question, he mused, "In order to get the voting rights bill passed, we need to make a dramatic appeal through Lowndes and other counties because the people of Selma are tired." In Lowndes County, twelve thousand of whose fifteen thousand residents were black, not a single African American was

---

* Almost forty years later, after studying numerous photographs of the incident, Vivian was still not certain whether it was actually Clark or one of his deputies who hit him, though Clark was quick to take the credit.

registered to vote. Nor were any registered in Perry or Wilcox counties, where they also constituted majorities.

King knew that to hold the attention of the news media — and of officials in Washington — he would have to court even greater risks for the demonstrators and himself. He decided to heighten the intensity of demonstrations in Selma while expanding the protests to surrounding counties, where he expected fresh confrontations with sheriffs and police unaccustomed to dealing with the civil rights movement. At a Brown Chapel meeting on Wednesday, February 17, he challenged five hundred protesters to prepare for more militant actions. Unless Selma's leaders fired Sheriff Clark and eliminated all barriers to voting, King announced, "we will engage in broader forms of civil disobedience. We may have to march out of this church tonight and stand at the courthouse all night long."[38]

The following day, King ordered one of the first night marches since the bloody St. Augustine demonstrations of 1964. In St. Augustine, King and his lieutenants had learned that forays in the dark stretched thin the resources of local law enforcement but also exposed marchers to unseen assailants in the black of night.

After a stirring speech by C. T. Vivian, who had just been bailed out of jail in Dallas County, four hundred protesters launched a night demonstration in Marion, the county seat of Perry County, twenty-three miles northwest of Selma. At 9:30 P.M., the demonstrators began filing two abreast out of the Zion's Chapel Methodist Church across the square from the county courthouse. Their destination was the county jail, their immediate purpose to protest the arrest the previous day of SCLC organizer James Orange. They had walked less than half a block when they were halted by Police Chief T. O. Harris.

"This is an unlawful assembly," Harris announced through a loudspeaker. "You are hereby ordered to disperse or go back to the church." The marchers stopped, with two-thirds of them still trying to file out of the church. When the protesters refused to move, Colonel Al Lingo and fifty of his state troopers waded into the group, shouting and jabbing with their nightsticks. As the demonstrators tried to retreat, the troopers pursued them. Streetlights went out as panicked demonstrators ran for safety in the church and buildings behind it, including the church parsonage and Mack's Café.[39]

Cager Lee, an eighty-two-year-old black man, fled bleeding into the café, seeking his daughter Viola and grandson Jimmie Lee Jackson. State troopers pursued Lee and other frightened marchers into the café, swinging their nightsticks wildly at protesters and customers alike, smashing furniture, lights, and dishes. The troopers attacked Lee again in the kitchen and beat his daughter as she tried to pull them off her father. As Jimmie Lee Jackson tried to protect his mother, one trooper hurled him against a cigarette machine; another raised his pistol and shot him twice in the stomach. The troopers then dragged Jackson outside and left him in the street. By the time the violence ended, ten black men and women were in Good Samaritan Hospital in Selma.* Among them was Jackson, in critical condition as doctors tried to stanch the internal bleeding.[40]

At the height of the rioting, reporters spotted Sheriff Clark among the state troopers, wearing sports clothes and carrying a nightstick. "Don't you have enough trouble of your own in Selma?" someone asked Clark. "Things got a little too quiet for me over in Selma tonight," he replied, "and it made me nervous."[41]

Violence was in the air. The riotous attack by Alabama state police and the shooting of Jimmie Lee Jackson followed by two days the assassination in New York of Black Muslim leader Malcolm X, killed after he split with the sect's founder, Elijah Muhammad. By the time Malcolm was killed, he had begun to moderate his earlier views of separatism — which King had considered a hopeful development.

As King visited the mortally wounded Jackson at Good Samaritan Hospital, Attorney General Katzenbach called to warn him of a plot against his life.† Shaken by Malcolm's assassination and the new threat to him, King instructed Clarence Jones to send telegrams to the president, the attorney general, and the FBI director requesting federal protection for him in Selma. Upon learning of King's request through the FBI's wiretap on Jones, Hoover instructed his assistants that neither King "nor anyone else is to be furnished protection."[42]

That night, speaking to a charged gathering of seven hundred activists at Brown Chapel, King announced plans for a demonstration at the state capitol in Montgomery to protest the denial of voting rights and the brutal treatment of black citizens in Alabama. "We will be going there to tell Governor Wallace that we aren't going to take it anymore!" said King.[43]

Jimmie Lee Jackson died at 8:10 A.M. on Friday, February 26. He was twenty-six years old and had earned six dollars a day as a pulpwood cutter. The youngest deacon at St. James Baptist Church, Jackson was a quietly determined activist who had tried five times to register to vote, begin-

---

* NBC television correspondent Richard Valeriani sustained serious head injuries while covering the melee.

† Colonel Lingo, the Alabama public safety director, had also gone to the hospital — to charge Jackson with assault and battery and intent to murder a highway patrolman.

ning when he was twenty-one. Nurses at Good Samaritan said he might have survived the shooting if it had not taken three hours to get him to the hospital.

Jim Bevel, the SCLC's Alabama project director, walked to Cager Lee's frame home in the woods to offer condolences to Jackson's grandfather, mother, and sister. The family told Bevel that the marches should continue. He asked if they could bear to take part in the next one. "Oh, yeah," replied Cager Lee.[44]

That night at Brown Chapel, Bevel vowed that Jackson's death would be a rallying point. "I tell you the death of that man is pushing me kind of hard," Bevel told the crowd of six hundred. "The blood of Jackson will be on our hands if we don't march. Be prepared to walk to Montgomery. Be prepared to sleep on the highways."[45]

On Wednesday, March 3, as King presided at Jackson's funeral in Marion, he announced that the fifty-four-mile march from Selma to Montgomery would begin on Sunday, March 7. In his sermon, King told the crowd of nearly one thousand where he thought the blame lay for Jimmie Jackson's death:

> He was murdered by every white minister of the gospel who has remained silent behind the safe security of his stained-glass windows.
>
> He was murdered by the irresponsibility of every politician from governors on down who has fed his constituents the stale bread of hatred and the spoiled meat of racism.
>
> He was murdered by the timidity of a federal government that is willing to spend millions of dollars a day to defend freedom in Vietnam, but cannot protect the rights of its citizens at home.
>
> He was murdered by every sheriff who practices lawlessness in the name of the law.
>
> He was murdered by the cowardice of every Negro who passively accepts the evils of segregation and stands on the sidelines in the struggle for justice.[46]

✦ ✦ ✦ ✦ ✦ ✦ ✦

We Shall Overcome

M ARTIN LUTHER KING waited impatiently at Boston's
Logan International Airport. His Friday afternoon
flight to Washington, D.C., was delayed by bad weather, and King was sure
to be late for his 5 P.M. meeting with President Johnson at the White
House. It was their third face-to-face meeting in as many months. In less
than forty-eight hours, King would face the most critical confrontation of
his two-month voting rights campaign. On the following Sunday morning, March 7, he was to lead his demonstrators on a fifty-four-mile march
from Brown Chapel in Selma to the Alabama state capitol in Montgomery. Governor George Wallace had forbidden the march. An apprehensive
King hoped that the president could be persuaded to dispatch federal
marshals to protect the marchers.

Waiting for King in the Oval Office, the president was already aware
that King wanted federal protection for himself and the demonstrators.
Earlier in the day, FBI director J. Edgar Hoover had sent Johnson a secret
report describing King's plan to lobby the White House. In that report to
the president, Hoover quoted from a wiretapped telephone conversation
between two King advisers. "It is a mockery to talk about freedom in
South Vietnam when the one man who is defending [freedom] in Selma
is in jeopardy," the two had agreed.

King was in Boston that Friday, March 5, for a meeting with northern
church leaders supportive of the civil rights movement. Before the meeting, the FBI had told a conference participant about King's sexual activities and alleged Communist ties in hopes of persuading the organizers to
cancel King's invitation, but that effort had failed. Director Hoover had
just reemphasized to his principal assistants that the FBI would not pro-

tect Dr. King, as it had done for several days on presidential orders the previous year in Mississippi. Nor would it inform King when it learned of threats against his life — although the agency would report such threats to federal, state, and local authorities.[1]

President Johnson strongly opposed committing federal marshals or troops to Selma — or anywhere else in the South — except in the most dire circumstances. He was apprehensive that a federal clash with southern segregationists would destroy any chance for peaceful integration under the 1964 Civil Rights Act — not to mention the possibility of passing a new voting rights law. Yet he was eager to meet with King to talk about voting rights and Great Society programs. Johnson needed King's help to reassure Congress and the civil rights movement that he was moving forward on civil rights legislation as fast as he could. More and more Democrats and Republicans were criticizing the president for inaction in Selma — and Johnson wanted to keep King from joining the critics. Rising political pressure for voting rights had prompted liberal Senate Republicans to issue an ultimatum to the White House.

"I see they have given us until Friday [to propose voting rights legislation]," Johnson had told Attorney General Nicholas Katzenbach. "If we don't move, they're going to put in their own bill."

"I like the fact that Republicans are hollering for it," Katzenbach replied. "It takes some of the King pressure off. It makes it look less like we're jumping for King. I don't want to have anyone pressuring, and I know you don't, but I'd rather have [the Republicans] doing it than the civil rights groups."

"That's right," agreed the president. "I wonder why it wouldn't be a good thing to say [to the Republicans] that . . . we welcome their support, and would be glad to have them introduce anything they've got, and we'll make our recommendations just as soon as the lawyers complete their work."

Initially, Johnson had delayed introducing voting rights because he did not think the time was right politically. He wanted first to push Medicare, aid to education, and expansion of his poverty program. Now that King had built up the political pressure, there was another problem: Justice Department lawyers remained conflicted on how to frame the bill constitutionally. Still another factor was that Johnson did not want to appear to be pushed into action. Instead, he decided to let the impact of the events in Selma settle in for a few days.

King finally arrived at the Oval Office at 6:22 that evening. For the next ninety minutes, he and Johnson discussed voting rights and the president's most immediate legislative priority: a historic bill to provide federal aid to elementary and secondary education. Johnson gave King encouraging news: Minority Leader Everett Dirksen had promised to back a strong voting rights bill. Dirksen held the key to Republican Senate support, essential to crack an expected southern filibuster. King was delighted when the president indicated that he favored seeking a voting rights *law* rather than pursuing the much more protracted route of a constitutional amendment. In the proposed legislation, Johnson virtually committed to federalizing voter registration. If southern county officials refused to register African Americans, then federal registrars, responsible to the president, would add the applicants' names to the voter rolls. The president encouraged King to work with Katzenbach on the details.

"We've got work to do on the education bill," he next told King. Presidential aide Lee White, sitting in on the meeting, observed that the president had now moved to his "shooting range." White saw Johnson's problem-solving technique as that of a single-minded marksman, who would hang a target and fire at it until he scored a bull's-eye, then hang the next target. His top target now was the education bill, and Johnson wanted King to lobby members of the House and Senate, especially Adam Clayton Powell, chairman of the House Education and Labor Committee. After an argument with the House leadership, Powell had abruptly abandoned the legislation and left for his hideout in the Bahamas, where King had visited him. In a telephone call, Johnson had just given Powell a tongue-lashing. "Adam, what the hell has been happening in your committee?" Johnson yelled at the congressman. "What the hell! Are you blackmailing me?"[2]

Now Johnson emphasized to King that more than a billion dollars in the education bill was targeted at poor black children. The president believed that with the right to vote, new educational opportunities, and job training through the poverty program, minorities, especially the poor, soon would have a better chance in America.

On March 6, the day after his meeting with King, Johnson would give Vice President Hubert Humphrey an exaggerated replay of what he had told King the day before about the importance of the education bill for black Americans: "Now, by God, they can't work in a filling station and put water in a radiator unless they can read and write. Because they've got to go and punch their cash register, and they don't know which one to punch. They've got to take a check, and they don't know which one to cash. They've got to take a credit card and they can't pull the numbers. . . . Now that's what you damn fellows [King and the civil rights leaders] better be working on."[3]

As King left the Oval Office Friday evening, he spoke diplomatically. "From time to time," he told reporters, "I feel the necessity of exchanging views with the President on vital issues facing the nation. We talked about several today." King described his hopes for a voting rights bill, but — as he and Johnson had agreed — committed the president to nothing.

Questioned about the looming march on Sunday, King was curiously vague. He had informed the president that "Negroes had to continue their demonstrations to dramatize their plight." The president had said nothing to discourage the demonstrations, said King, and did not seem to think that they would result in violence, although "it may be necessary to call on federal marshals before we start," King added. He had not asked the president for such protection, he told reporters, but would discuss the situation further on Saturday with other march leaders. If marshals were needed, he would make the request through the attorney general — not the president. In truth, King was growing even more apprehensive about the Sunday march and was still gauging his options.[4]

Bloody Sunday

King returned to Atlanta on Friday night. He planned to preach at his own Ebenezer Baptist Church on Sunday morning, fly to Montgomery afterward, and then drive the fifty-four miles to Selma. Saturday morning, Governor Wallace threw down the gauntlet: "The march is not conducive to the orderly flow of traffic and commerce within and through the state of Alabama. The additional hazard placed on highway travel by any such actions cannot be countenanced. Such a march cannot and will not be tolerated."[5] When King heard the report, his concerns intensified.

Facing the prospect of Wallace's blocking the march, perhaps with force — as well as death threats — and lacking logistical preparation, federal protection, or a protective court order, King and Ralph Abernathy decided on Saturday to postpone the march. In a conference call with his principal advisers in New York, Atlanta, and Selma, King explained that he had to preach at Ebenezer on Sunday morning in place of his ailing father. He wanted to wait until Monday to return to Selma. All the men approved except Hosea Williams, who insisted that the march must go on.* King went to bed Saturday night still undecided. Early Sunday morning he called Andrew Young, also in Atlanta, and instructed him to go immediately to Selma and cancel the Sunday march.

Young took an 8 A.M. plane to Montgomery and then drove urgently

---

* James Bevel, who disapproved of the delay, avoided participating in the call with King.

toward Selma. As he crossed the Edmund Pettus Bridge spanning the Alabama River at the gateway into Selma, Young was startled by the sight of two hundred law enforcement officers — Governor Wallace's state troopers with Sheriff Clark's deputies and an armed posse — monitoring traffic at the bridge. Arriving at Brown Chapel, Young found a gathering of six hundred protesters busily assembling backpacks and other equipment, eager and ready to march. Hosea Williams and Jim Bevel, the designated leaders, insisted that the march must proceed. To cancel it, as King had decreed, after so many people had assembled "would seriously damage our credibility," Williams argued. Young, Bevel, Williams, and SNCC president John Lewis conferred. The four young leaders agreed that a postponement was impossible.* They called King at the Ebenezer Baptist Church, summoning him from the pulpit. "All these people are here ready to go now, the press is gathering expecting us to go, and we think we've just got to march, even if you aren't here," Young told him. "There'll probably be arrests when we hit the bridge." Reluctantly, King acceded to their request. He would remain in Atlanta.

"Listen," King instructed his deputies, "don't all three of you go. If John Lewis is going, let Bevel or Hosea go with him as a co-leader, and the other two stay behind as a backup in case of emergencies." Bevel, Williams, and Young flipped coins; Hosea Williams was selected to co-lead the march.[6]

After a brief prayer led by Young and a chorus of "God Will Take Care of You," a hymn Williams reserved for dangerous situations, Williams and Lewis set out on a clear and breezy afternoon with nearly six hundred black and white men and women following them. Two by two the marchers began moving silently through Selma's streets toward the Edmund Pettus Bridge. Following them was a small team of doctors and nurses from a group called Medical Committee for Human Rights, who had flown in from New York the day before, arranged for the use of four ambulances, and set up an emergency first aid tent near Brown Chapel. The demonstrators marched down Sylvan, the red clay street that snaked alongside the wooden shacks and red brick housing projects in the black section of town, then down Water Street parallel to the muddy Alabama River. As they turned left on Broad Street to cross the high-arched steel bridge, the marchers passed three dozen members of Sheriff Clark's posse lounging in the shadows of the *Selma Times-Journal* building. The marchers started up the bridge's narrow walkway, which was barely wide enough for their two-abreast formation.

* SNCC, in still another disagreement with the SCLC, decided that its organization would not participate in the march but that Lewis could take part as an individual.

None of the marchers knew what to expect that afternoon. In John Lewis's army backpack were an orange, an apple, toothpaste, a toothbrush, and several books. Lewis didn't expect the marchers to reach Montgomery. Most likely they would be stopped and arrested as they left Selma. Perhaps they would be roughed up a little bit, he thought. Nothing more than that.[7]

As they reached the crest of the bridge, Lewis and Williams stopped. Ahead of them were fifty blue-uniformed, helmeted state troopers, lined up four deep across the highway just beyond the bridge. Behind the troopers were several dozen members of Sheriff Clark's posse dressed in khakis and armed with clubs, bullwhips, and lengths of rubber tubing wrapped in barbed wire. Some of the posse members were on horseback. Along one side of the road, Lewis saw several hundred whites holding Confederate flags, laughing and yelling. On the other side of the road, next to an auto dealership, stood dozens of news reporters.

Williams looked at Lewis and at the water a hundred feet below the bridge. "Can you swim?" he asked his companion. Lewis said he could not. "Well, neither can I. But we might have to." They moved forward.*

After the marchers had ascended the arched roadway and descended on the other side, they were met by a double line of state troopers massed across Highway 80, the road to Montgomery. Williams and Lewis halted the procession. The frontline of troopers stood only fifty feet away.

"This is an unlawful assembly," trooper major John Cloud declared through his bullhorn. "Your march is not conducive to public safety. You are ordered to disperse and go back to your church or your homes."

"May we have a word with [you]?" Hosea Williams asked.

"There is no word to be had," replied Cloud. "You have two minutes to turn around and go back to your church."

Twice more Williams asked to speak to Cloud, but the officer did not reply.

The front rows of marchers knelt in prayer. Exactly one minute later, according to John Lewis's watch, Major Cloud ordered, "Troopers, advance!"[8]

Williams, Lewis, and others in the front ranks of marchers were trapped between the six hundred protesters behind them and the troops who now swept over them, nightsticks flailing. Behind the troopers surged waves of possemen wielding their clubs, whips, and barbed trun-

---

* Williams later playfully accused his friends Andrew Young and Jim Bevel of having rigged the coin toss earlier that day. The next day, after Williams saw the extensive national press coverage of his role in the march, his resentment dissipated (AI, Andrew Young and Hosea Williams).

cheons. The marchers could hear Sheriff Clark urging his men on: "Get those goddamned niggers! And get those goddamned white niggers!"

John Lewis went down under a blow to the left side of his head from a club wielded by a husky trooper, who struck Lewis again as the SNCC leader tried to curl up in a protected position. Lewis felt blood streaming down his head as he lapsed into unconsciousness. Also clubbed unconscious was Amelia Boynton, the stately veteran leader of voter efforts in Selma, who was two rows behind Lewis in the march. Hosea Williams, a special target of Sheriff Clark, managed to vault over the troopers to a sidewalk on the far side of the bridge, where a black woman threw a blanket over Williams's head and pulled him to safety on her front porch.[9]

Roy Reed, a reporter for the *New York Times,* described the first minutes of the attack:

> The troopers rushed forward, their blue uniforms and white helmets blurring into a flying wedge as they moved.
>
> The wedge moved with such force that it seemed almost to pass over the waiting column instead of through it.
>
> The first ten or twenty Negroes were swept to the ground screaming, arms and legs flying, and packs and bags went skittering across the grassy divider strip and onto the pavement on both sides [of the highway].
>
> Those still on their feet retreated.
>
> The troopers continued pushing, using both the force of their bodies and the prodding of their nightsticks.
>
> A cheer went up from the white spectators lining the south side of the highway.
>
> The mounted possemen spurred their horses and rode at a run into the retreating mass. The Negroes cried out as they crowded together for protection, and the whites on the sidelines whooped and cheered.
>
> The Negroes paused in their retreat perhaps for a minute, still screaming and huddling together.
>
> Suddenly there was a report like a gunshot, and a gray cloud spewed over the troopers and Negroes.
>
> "Tear gas!" someone shouted.
>
> The cloud began covering the highway. . . . Before the cloud finally hid it all, there were several seconds of unobstructed view. Fifteen or twenty nightsticks could be seen through the gas, flailing at the heads of the marchers.
>
> The Negroes broke and ran. Scores of them streamed across the parking lot of the Selma Tractor Company. Troopers and possemen, mounted and unmounted, went after them.[10]

Out of Reed's field of vision came yet another attack on the marchers as they staggered across the bridge back into Selma. Sheriff Clark's possemen, whom John Lewis had spotted earlier next to the newspaper building, now came out of the shadows to cut off the marchers' route of retreat. Joined by state troopers and street vigilantes, the sheriff's posse continued to pursue and beat the marchers bloody as they fled back to Brown Chapel and into their homes and those of neighbors. The posse found a black youth in the First Baptist Church and threw him through a stained-glass window depicting Jesus as the Good Shepherd.[11] Back in the comparative safety of their own neighborhood, the black residents of Selma began to fight back, hurling bricks and bottles at the marauding lawmen.

The beatings stopped only when Police Chief Wilson Baker, who had kept his men out of the attack at the Edmund Pettus Bridge, finally reasserted his authority, telling Clark, "All right now, get your cowboys out of here now!"[12]

The emergency tent next to the church resembled a battlefield hospital. Wounded marchers were carried in, to be transported by ambulance to city hospitals, where more than ninety marchers were treated, with forty-one requiring hospitalization. A disoriented John Lewis, bleeding profusely, somehow found his way back over the bridge to Brown Chapel. Before he would go to the hospital, Lewis insisted on speaking to the marchers gathering in the church.

"I don't know how President Johnson can send troops to Vietnam," Lewis thundered, his hair covered in blood. "I don't see how he can send troops to the Congo. I don't see how he can send troops to Africa, AND HE CAN'T SEND TROOPS TO SELMA, ALABAMA!"[13] Lewis then went to the Good Samaritan Hospital, where he was admitted and treated for a skull fracture.

The Second March

ABC television was broadcasting its heavily promoted Sunday night movie premiere of *Judgment at Nuremberg*, a film about the trial of Nazis accused of genocide and other war crimes. The film was interrupted at about 9:30 P.M. Eastern Time by a special bulletin about the confrontation in Selma, including fifteen minutes of footage of the bloody attack. By the time the next morning's newspapers across the country carried front-page stories and pictures of the police riot, much of the nation had witnessed scenes of the event that became known as "Bloody Sunday."

The events in Selma that Sunday afternoon registered shock waves across America that would have a profound impact on national politics and race relations, yet Lyndon Johnson and Martin Luther King were both taken by surprise. Each quickly tried to assess the meaning of Selma and react to its reverberations.

Johnson had spent the weekend at the White House, his attention focused on mounting problems in Vietnam. A coup had taken down another American-backed Vietnamese government. U.S. retaliation for the deadly attack on Pleiku had received broad public support, but Johnson's first small escalations of the American presence in Vietnam were arousing voices of dissent. Protests came from members of Students for a Democratic Society, a radical group that planned to picket the LBJ Ranch over Easter weekend, and from a handful of U.S. senators as well. Most troubling to Johnson, the worsening situation in Vietnam came just as he was hoping to focus the nation's attention on his historic legislation to improve the quality of life for every American.

As he often did, Johnson called Senator Richard Russell Saturday afternoon for his counsel about Vietnam. "Dick," Johnson said, "a man can fight if he can see daylight down the road somewhere. But there ain't no daylight in Vietnam. There's not a bit."

"There's no end to the road," Russell replied. "There's just nothing."

"The more bombs you drop, the more nations you scare, the more people you make mad, the more embassies you get mad," Johnson said sadly.[14]

Two hours later, in a telephone conversation with Defense Secretary Robert McNamara, Johnson made a fateful decision: he would dispatch two battalions of marines to protect the American air base at Danang. Sending the marines "is going to put the flag up," frightening mothers across the country, the president lamented. As he authorized the troops, Johnson told McNamara, "My answer is 'yes,' but my judgment is 'no.'"[15] McNamara promised the president that he would announce the marine deployment late on Saturday evening so that it would get minimum initial news coverage. Johnson knew that he was taking small but decisive steps into what he feared was becoming a quagmire. He attempted to move stealthily, fearing that conservatives in Congress would use Vietnam expenditures as an argument to defeat his ambitious domestic plans. McNamara and other key aides tried to portray escalations in Vietnam as routine movements, not big news.

After a quiet Sunday following services at the National City Christian Church, President Johnson enjoyed a leisurely late dinner in the family quarters with Lady Bird, aide Jack Valenti, adviser Clark Clifford, newspaper columnist William S. White, and Texas congressmen Jack Brooks and Jake Pickle and their wives. Vietnam was still on Johnson's mind. "I can't get out, and I can't finish it with what I've got," the president told his dinner guests. "And I don't know what the hell to do."[16]

The only White House statement released that Sunday evening regarding the news from Alabama was a comment from the press office that the president was "keeping fully informed about the latest developments in Selma." The Department of Justice said only that it had a number of observers on the scene and was keeping "closely informed."[17]

Meanwhile, at the Ebenezer Church in Atlanta, a horrified Martin Luther King learned of the day's events in telephone calls from Bevel, Williams, and Young. The SCLC leaders agreed that they had to attempt to march again and set the date for Tuesday, March 9.

King sent telegrams Sunday night to every sympathetic church leader in the country, calling on them "to join us on Tuesday in our peaceful, non-violent march for freedom."[18] King also decided that the SCLC's lawyers should go into federal court in Montgomery on Monday to seek a temporary restraining order forbidding Alabama and Dallas County officials from interfering with the new march.

In his telegram to the church leaders King declared:

> In the vicious maltreatment of defenseless citizens in Selma, where old women and young children were gassed and clubbed at random, we have witnessed an eruption of the disease of racism which seeks to destroy all America. No American is without responsibility. . . . The people of Selma will struggle on for the soul of the nation, but it is fitting that all Americans help to share the burden. I call therefore on clergy of all faiths to join me in Selma for a ministers' march to Montgomery on Tuesday morning, March ninth.

In Montgomery, Governor George Wallace declined any official comment about the events at the Edmund Pettus Bridge. On his way out of the office at the end of the day, however, he remarked to reporters, "These folks in Selma have made this a seven-day-a-week job, but we can't give in one inch. We're going to enforce state laws."[19]

At 8:30 Monday morning, President Johnson's first call was to Katzenbach. The attorney general briefed the president on Sunday's violence and King's plans for another march Tuesday. Federal authorities had made only two arrests so far, both of men who had assaulted an FBI agent taking pictures of the battle. "I didn't give the arrests any publicity last night," Katzenbach explained, "because . . . that didn't look right to me from a [publicity] viewpoint: all the Negroes beat up — and the only people we arrest are the people who beat up the FBI agents!" But, he added, "there ought to be some more arrests [for the assaults on the marchers], and that ought to help the situation."

"Do you know Wallace very well?" Johnson queried Katzenbach, hoping to open a communications channel to the Alabama governor. "Hardly at all, Mr. President. But I don't know anyone who really does. . . . The [Alabama] senators say they can't get to Wallace at all."

Johnson suggested that Katzenbach talk to former Tennessee governor Buford Ellington, director of the federal Office of Emergency Planning. "This would have to be extremely quiet. . . . It could be that he knows Wallace and could be that he could sit down with you." If Ellington had a good relationship with the Alabaman, Johnson suggested hopefully, "he might be a go-between."

The president also quizzed Katzenbach about the civil rights leaders who were involved in the Bloody Sunday march: "Are they [SNCC] directed by other people?" Katzenbach replied that while SNCC had "more Communists and near Communists" than the other major civil rights groups, John Lewis clearly "is not a Communist."

Johnson pressed. "Do we have any influence with him?"

"Some, not much. He is in the hospital right now. Got cracked on the head yesterday. We have a little. I wouldn't try with Lewis. I would rather work with King . . . through King to Lewis."[20]

Johnson was weighing how to cope with an inflammatory situation that could easily spin further out of control. The keys to establishing peace and order, he decided, were George Wallace and Martin Luther King. The challenge with Wallace was to persuade him to assume responsibility for law and order in Alabama. Johnson feared that the alternative — sending federal troops to protect marchers and maintain the peace — would herald a second poisonous Reconstruction period in the South. To avoid a rising demand for federal intervention, Johnson needed Wallace's help — and perhaps Wallace needed his as well. Johnson saw the "banty-rooster" Alabama governor as a clever and ambitious demagogue. Chaos in Wallace's own state might doom the governor's national ambitions, Johnson surmised. As for the civil rights forces, Johnson knew he had to work with King. Roy Wilkins and Whitney Young could not tame the storm of a citizenry aroused by the official brutality perpetrated at Selma.

On Monday morning Johnson telephoned Ellington, a moderate as governor of Tennessee and a savvy southern politician. "The biggest problem we have in the Alabama situation," Johnson confided, "is communicating with George Wallace. They're [the civil rights protesters] going to have another march tomorrow. As we see it, it's going to go from bad to worse."

"My relationship with George [Wallace] has been very good," Ellington replied, "but you can't trust him."

"You think he'll believe you?" asked Johnson.

"He'll trust me, yes," replied Ellington.

As Johnson coached Ellington on what he might say to Wallace, he echoed John Lewis's impassioned plea the night before from Brown Chapel: "You could say, 'Governor, they're [the civil rights movement] wanting us to send troops in, and they say if we can send them into Vietnam, we can send them in to protect Americans . . . who are being beat up here." Ellington agreed to work with Katzenbach to arrange a conversation with Wallace and to tape-record it.[21]

Lyndon Johnson was not the only leader in a tight spot the day after Bloody Sunday. Martin Luther King also faced conflicting pressures. Predictably, the SNCC organizers, led by James Forman — who had deigned to march with the SCLC on Sunday — now were demanding an immediate march, regardless of the dangers or any other considerations. SNCC leaders once again were sniping at King, suggesting that the SCLC leader's concern for his own safety had led him to avoid the Sunday march.* King's own "wild men," Jim Bevel and Hosea Williams, also were demanding immediate action. King knew that his credibility in the movement was at stake, yet he feared that an ill-prepared, impetuous demonstration would endanger not only the marchers themselves but also his continued ability to work with Lyndon Johnson for a voting rights law.

With these concerns in mind, King called the man who was his most trustworthy channel to the White House — Democratic National Committee deputy chairman Louis Martin. A black former newspaper publisher, "Louie" Martin was the most influential political figure who commanded confidence and respect in both the civil rights movement and the Johnson White House. King saw Martin as a sympathetic, honest broker — one who would represent his interests, as well as those of the president, fairly.

In his conversation with Martin on Monday morning, King asked for the president's help in avoiding another horrendous clash. If Johnson would announce the appointment of a top aide to mediate the confrontation in Selma, King suggested, "such an action would give [him] a reason for calling off the march which is scheduled for Tuesday morning." Without the president's intervention, King "was too deeply committed to call it

---

* Accounts differ about the reasons for King's absence from Selma on Bloody Sunday. King clearly didn't want to be there, partly because of assassination threats, party because he felt he had neglected the pulpit at Ebenezer, and partly because neither he nor his aides expected much more to happen than that officers would stop the marchers before they reached the highway and arrest them. Furthermore, plans for the march were at best hazy and not thoroughly thought through.

off." If the march could not be avoided, King asked that the president at least send federal marshals to prevent more police brutality. Martin quickly passed King's request along to the president.[22]

King's effort to recruit religious leaders from across the country succeeded beyond his most optimistic expectations. The dean of Yale Divinity School, Robert C. Johnson, was among the first to respond to King's call. The wife of Illinois senator Paul Douglas, the widow of the late interior secretary Harold Ickes, CORE director James Farmer, deputy Peace Corps director Harris Wofford, and more than one hundred members of the Church Federation of Greater Chicago were among the hundreds to follow suit. Forty clergy members from Washington, D.C., chartered a plane for the trip, among them Methodist bishop John Wesley Lord, messenger George Gingras of the Roman Catholic Archdiocese of Washington, and Rabbi Richard Hirsch of the Union of American Hebrew Congregations. Hirsch had received a call from the National Council of Churches saying that it had organized a large delegation of Protestant and Catholic leaders but needed a representative of the Jewish community. When Hirsch could not immediately locate anyone else, he drafted himself. After calling his wife and four young children to tell them he was heading for Selma, he arrived at Washington National Airport just in time to board the plane before its dusk departure.[23]

SCLC leaders asked NAACP Legal Defense Fund director Jack Greenberg to seek a restraining order protecting the marchers. To avoid the unsympathetic Judge Daniel Thomas in Mobile, the SCLC lawyers filed the suit in the Montgomery courtroom of federal district judge Frank M. Johnson. An Eisenhower appointee with a decent record in equal protection cases, the no-nonsense Judge Johnson had already been involved with voting rights issues in Selma. Now the civil rights leaders asked him to enjoin the police from blocking Tuesday's Selma-to-Montgomery march.

Down the street from the Montgomery federal courthouse, George Wallace was under fire. Reflecting national outrage, members of Congress took the floor to denounce the Bloody Sunday violence. Democrats and Republicans alike were calling for federal action and passage of a voting rights bill. Senator Ralph Yarborough of Texas intoned, "I abhor this brutality which so smears the good name of one of the fairest sections of our land. Shame on you, George Wallace." House Speaker John McCormack called the attacks "a disgraceful exercise of arbitrary power." Even the usually conservative NAACP chairman Roy Wilkins issued a public statement warning that should similar violence occur in a second march attempt, the demonstrators this time might well shoot back. Referring to the recent landing of 3,500 marines in Vietnam, Wilkins said, "Damn it, they can send somebody to Alabama, and defend the government right here." Wilkins's comments, like those of John Lewis on Bloody Sunday, signaled a new political development: the linking of the federal government's response to the mistreatment of black Americans with its escalating involvement in Vietnam.[24]

For his part, Wallace scoffed at complaints that police had used unnecessary force. "We saved [the marchers'] lives by stopping that march," Wallace claimed, denying the carnage wreaked by billy clubs, horses' hooves, and tear gas. "There's a good possibility that death would have resulted to some of these people if we had not stopped them." As for the prospect of another march the next day, Wallace warned, "It has always been my policy to use the least force possible."[25] Behind the scenes, however, Wallace lectured Colonel Lingo and Sheriff Clark that they had gone too far. He didn't want any more police violence.

Before the hearing scheduled in Judge Johnson's courtroom in Montgomery, the president called Alabama senator Lister Hill to tell him that Buford Ellington had just spoken to Wallace. "It looks like he wants a way out," Johnson said, "because this is getting pretty bad from their standpoint." King also "wants a way out," Johnson added, referring to the information Louis Martin had sent over earlier in the day. "It's getting pretty bad from *his* standpoint. He's concerned about the safety and everything."

Johnson laid out the problem facing his administration: If he were to join King's court petition, it would look as if he were "advocating the goddamn march. If every time [King] wants to march, I go in and tell the judge, 'I want you to enjoin the local officials,' it may look like I'm stirring up these marches. . . . But if you don't, you get a lot of killings, and they say, 'What did you do?'" He paused: "And you didn't do anything."

"You've got a hell of a dilemma," sympathized Senator Hill.

"Yes, I do," replied Johnson.[26]

The president decided that the prudent course was for the Justice Department to join King's lawsuit as a "friend of the court." In a statement read by press secretary George Reedy, Johnson said, "I am certain all Americans everywhere join in deploring the brutality with which a number of Negro citizens of Alabama were treated when they sought to dramatize their deep and sincere interest in obtaining the precious right to vote." Johnson further stated that he expected to have his voting rights law recommendations ready by the weekend. In comments that Reedy explained were directed at both Dr. King and Governor Wallace, the president urged "all who are in positions of leadership and capable of influencing the conduct of others to approach this tense situation with calmness, reasonableness, and respect for law and order."

Late Monday afternoon, Judge Johnson agreed to hold a hearing on the restraining order later in the week but refused to issue an injunction before he could hear from the state of Alabama. In the meantime, the judge ordered King and the SCLC to cancel Tuesday's march. "There will be no irreparable harm if the plaintiffs will await a judicial determination of the matters involved," the judge declared. His message was clear: if King wished to have the situation addressed in court, he would have to wait.[27]

Now it was King who faced a dilemma. Prominent Americans had responded to his call and were arriving by the hundreds, ready to march the next morning in solidarity with the citizens of Selma. On the one hand, canceling the march would embarrass King and the SCLC before both the local and national civil rights forces. The momentum building in Selma also would be lost. On the other hand, the SCLC mantra had always been that local and state segregation statutes were invalid, but that federal laws must be followed. And King had never defied a federal court order.

King's dilemma grew even sharper Monday evening when attorney Jack Greenberg told King that Judge Johnson had warned that he would "put Martin Luther King under the jail" if he disobeyed the restraining order. In a conference call with King and Greenberg, Attorney General Katzenbach emphasized that marching in defiance of the court order would alienate Judge Johnson, not to mention the Johnson in the White House. "Dr. King, you promised you would not march," Katzenbach said several times. Finally, King replied, "Mr. Attorney General, you have not been a black man in America for the past three hundred years."[28]

At 11:25 P.M., Lyndon Johnson picked up the telephone to get the latest report on Selma. Bill Moyers reported that King still was undecided on whether or not to march the next morning. Already in bed in his pajamas, the president told Moyers that he had just watched television news reports showing civil rights protesters being carried out of the Justice Department in Washington. Calling the protesters' sit-in tactics "absolutely disgraceful," Johnson said that a tougher approach might be necessary. "They're going to respect the law," Johnson warned. "[King] better go on behaving himself or all of them are going to get put in jail."[29]

Later Monday night in Montgomery, King and his senior staff met with John Lewis and James Forman of SNCC and CORE leader James Farmer. Despite having opposed the initial march, the young SNCC leaders now demanded that King ignore Judge Johnson's order. Most of the ministers in the SCLC leadership supported King's desire to postpone the march. As the meeting broke up, King told the group that he had decided to accept the judge's conditions. He would postpone the march.

After their contentious meeting, the civil rights leaders left together, just before midnight, for a mass rally at Brown Chapel. Many of Sunday's marchers were there, battered and bruised, along with hundreds of new recruits from all over the country. To the surprise of the leadership, King again reversed himself. He announced to the crowd that the march would go ahead as planned.[30] Looking out at the walking wounded from Selma and at the ministers, priests, and rabbis who had rallied to his cause, King simply could not bring himself to say that he would not march.

With King's announcement that he would march, the White House instructed Assistant Attorney General John Doar to try to change the minister's mind again. Doar told King that the president and Judge Johnson would both endorse a march to Montgomery if he would cancel the Tuesday march. King replied that he could not disappoint the thousands of supporters who believed the march would go on. Finally, Doar warned King that marching in defiance of a court order would seriously hurt the SCLC's relations with the Johnson administration. King would not relent.

Seeking a last-minute solution, the president awakened LeRoy Collins, the newly confirmed director of the Community Relations Service, the race relations agency created by the 1964 Civil Rights Act at the specific urging of President Johnson.* As governor of Florida from 1955 to 1961, Collins had demonstrated courage by urging Florida citizens to obey the 1954 Supreme Court school desegregation decision and to integrate lunch counters and restaurants voluntarily. The president, offering Collins the CRS job in 1964, had said, "It will hurt your political career, but it will help your nation." Now, in the middle of the night, Johnson asked Collins to fly to Selma in a presidential plane. Collins's mission was to broker a compromise between King and Alabama officials to avoid further violence and bloodshed.[31]

Still conflicted about what to do, King and Andrew Young organized a conference call with SCLC attorneys and advisers in New York — Jack Greenberg, Clarence Jones, Bayard Rustin, and Harry Wachtel. King told his confidants that he was very depressed. There was a general feeling of hopelessness in Selma, King said, a sense that "we are engaged in a kind of federal conspiracy, which in substance says . . . the robber can continue to

---

* As Senate majority leader, Johnson had tried unsuccessfully to create a race reconciliation agency as part of the 1957 Civil Rights Act.

rob for three more days and we will give you a hearing on whether the robber was wrong." There was nothing in Judge Johnson's order, King said, that spoke to moral principles.[32]

Around 5 A.M., just before finally going to bed, King made one last call to Attorney General Katzenbach and alerted him that the march would go on. Minutes later, the White House Lockheed Jet Star carrying Collins touched down at Craig Air Force Base outside Selma. Hurrying to the federal building in downtown Selma, Collins huddled with John Doar.[33] The two federal officials brainstormed to come up with a compromise that would satisfy the minimum demands of both sides, allowing each to claim victory. They settled on the idea of an abbreviated march, which President Johnson had suggested the day before. With the outlines of a plan in mind, they headed off to meet Martin Luther King.

Collins and Doar found King at the home of Dr. Sullivan Jackson, a black dentist, and his wife, Jean, his usual hosts in Selma. The pajama-clad King emerged from his bedroom for yet another debate about the march. Collins and Doar urged the minister to obey the court order. The SCLC's Fred Shuttlesworth, summoned to the meeting, insisted that, instead of asking King not to march, the federal officials should instruct the state troopers not to engage in brutality.

Collins laid out his proposal: the demonstrators would walk across the Edmund Pettus Bridge, confront the troopers, kneel in prayer, and then return to Selma. The protesters would have made their point, Collins said, while avoiding another clash with the troopers. "I cannot agree to do anything," replied King, "because I don't know what I can get my people to do. But if you will get Sheriff Clark and [Colonel] Lingo to agree to something like that, I will try."[34]

Collins then raced across town and found Clark and Lingo organizing their forces on the far side of the Pettus Bridge, where they had charged into the marchers on Sunday. This time Lingo had brought five hundred troopers to Selma, more than two-thirds of the state's entire force. Meeting with the lawmen at the nearby Lehman Pontiac dealership, Collins laid out his plan: the demonstrators would cross the bridge, hold a brief prayer service, and then return to Selma. Collins stressed that the state officials would have accomplished their mission of blocking the march. After excusing himself for a telephone call to Governor Wallace, Lingo accepted Collins's proposal. "The state did not want violence," Lingo said, "and there would be none if the marchers turned back at the designated point."[35] Clark sketched out a map of the route he wanted King to follow and handed it to Collins, who rushed back across the bridge to report to King.

King, meanwhile, had roused the fifteen hundred demonstrators with a stirring speech and started the march from Brown Chapel, uncertain of how far they would get or what fate awaited them across the bridge. "I have got to march," King told the marchers. "I do not know what lies ahead of us. There may be beatings, jailings, tear gas. But I would rather die on the highways of Alabama than make a butchery of my soul."

Collins fell into the line of marchers next to King, explained to him the agreement with Clark and Lingo, and handed him Clark's map of the march route. Once again King expressed doubts that he could stop his marchers but said, "I'll do my best to turn them back. I won't promise you, but I'll do my best." Collins pledged that he would stand in the frontline of troopers to try to ensure that they kept their word. "We'll all do the best we can," said Collins. "I think everything will be all right." Collins then hurried back across the bridge to stand with the troopers.

At the foot of the bridge, U.S. deputy marshal H. Stanley Fountain was waiting for King with a copy of Judge Johnson's order. After Fountain read the order, King said, "I am aware of the order," but insisted on proceeding. Fountain stepped aside, saying he would not block King's march.

The marchers sang "Ain't Gonna Let Nobody Turn Me Round" as King led them across the bridge toward a line of one hundred state troopers who blocked Highway 80 beyond the bridge. When the marchers were fifty feet from the troopers, Major John Cloud shouted through his bullhorn, "I am asking you to stop where you are. We are here to see that this march will not continue."

"We have a right to march," King replied. "There is also a right to march to Montgomery."

After Cloud repeated his order, King asked whether his group might stop to pray. "You can have your prayer," replied Cloud, "and then you must return to your church."

King led the marchers in singing one verse of "We Shall Overcome," then asked them to kneel. He called on Bishop Lord, Rabbi Hirsch, and Dr. George Dockery to lead them in prayer. The line of kneeling marchers stretched for a mile back across the bridge into Selma. As King rose to his feet, Major Cloud ordered his troopers to move to the side of the highway. Suddenly, Highway 80 stood wide open, with Montgomery fifty-four miles away.* King paused for a moment, then turned and began walking back toward Selma. Wave after wave of marchers walked to the spot where

---

* Governor Wallace had added a new wrinkle to LeRoy Collins's plan by ordering Lingo's state troopers blocking the road to stand aside, opening Highway 80 to any demonstrator who dared to march further. Wallace had hoped to embarrass King by giving him only two options: to march forward into a possible trap, or to look foolish by turning back.

King had stood, then turned and followed him, singing "We Shall Overcome," the anthem of the movement, and "Ain't Gonna Let Nobody Turn
Me Round."[36]

From a vantage point high in the federal building in Selma, John Doar
gave minute-by-minute reports of the march to Nicholas Katzenbach in
Washington. The attorney general in turn relayed reports to President
Johnson in the Oval Office. On another White House line, Buford Ellington stayed in constant touch with Governor Wallace, urging restraint. On
the Alabama troopers' frontline, LeRoy Collins girded himself, determined to grab the first officer who moved against the marchers. From the
state capitol in Montgomery, Wallace gave orders by telephone to Colonel
Lingo at the blockade on Highway 80. Finally, it was over. The tenuous
agreement had held despite mistrust on all sides. A clash had been
averted, in large part because of the calm leadership and pragmatic flexi-
bility of President Johnson and Dr. King, each firm in his position but ac-
commodating the other's needs. As in Atlantic City, the partnership was
strained but not broken. From the White House to Selma, everyone involved in the tense drama could breathe again. The national concern over
voting rights, however, continued to intensify.

The peace that prevailed during Tuesday's march did not last through
the evening. Three white Unitarian ministers, James Reeb and Orloff
Miller of Boston and Clark Olsen from Berkeley, California, had flown in
for the march. The ministers finished dinner at Walker's, a black café, at
dusk and were making their way to SCLC headquarters when four white
men emerged from the shadows shouting, "Hey, you niggers," and attacked them. One of the assailants struck Reeb's skull with a long club.
The ministers managed to stagger to the SCLC office. Olsen and Miller
were only bruised, but Reeb was critically injured. The thirty-seven-year-
old activist had flown in from Boston, where he worked on housing for
the poor in a black ghetto neighborhood in Dorchester, where he lived
with his own family. After the first ambulance broke down, and with the
sheriff's department refusing to provide an escort, it took four hours before Reeb reached University Medical Center in Birmingham. There
doctors diagnosed a massive skull fracture and listed him in grave condition.

As word of Reeb's injuries reached Brown Chapel, King told the gathering that Selma had shown its true colors: "It was cowardly work done by
night." Tension mounted in the streets as hundreds of demonstrators
tried to hold a prayer service for Reeb at the county courthouse. They

were blocked by Police Chief Baker, who was determined to keep them out of the clutches of Sheriff Clark and his posse.[37]

King's already strained relations with the militant SNCC organizers had been further aggravated Tuesday afternoon when he turned the marchers back toward Selma. SNCC leaders had opposed and boycotted the original Sunday march, then blamed its bloody outcome on King's absence. Now they charged that King had betrayed them on Tuesday by turning back after they had brought in SNCC forces from all over the South to support a continued march. James Forman, SNCC's executive secretary, called King's action "a classic example of trickery against the people."[38]

King faced another dilemma as he prepared to testify on Thursday in Judge Johnson's federal district court. If he insisted — as he had all day Tuesday — that he had made no agreement for a limited march, the judge likely would find King in contempt of court for violating his temporary ban on the march. If King admitted making a deal with law enforcement officers for a limited march, he would face more scorn from SNCC militants, as well as the embarrassment of having to confess that he had misled his followers. On Thursday, King chose the truth and ridicule over defying the federal courts. He admitted, albeit reluctantly, that there had been a "tacit agreement" between the authorities and himself.[39]

The rift with SNCC widened further as King sought to suspend demonstrations until Judge Johnson ruled on the Selma-to-Montgomery march. Thumbing his nose at King, Forman pulled his SNCC staff out of Selma. They would concentrate instead on student demonstrations already planned for Montgomery.

The antagonism between the two groups stemmed from different concepts of leadership, jealousy on the part of the young SNCC leaders, and overreaching for credit by the SCLC ministers. Now, however, the disagreements were becoming more fundamental. King still believed that the American system of government could live up to its founding principles on behalf of all its citizens. He was intent on reforming the political process to include African Americans and other minorities. King's immediate goal was to win a voting rights law with the cooperation and support of President Johnson in Washington and Judge Johnson in Alabama.

Although King's Gandhian tactics were radical at the time, his goals in 1965 were mainstream: inclusion of black citizens in an integrated American democracy. But Forman and other SNCC leaders were disillusioned. For them the system had been exposed as corrupt in Atlantic City. Nor did they believe in King's confrontational tactics, which relied on stirring the conscience of white America. SNCC's leaders were growing even more radical in their ideas and more inflammatory in their rhetoric.

The President Under Fire

From a second-floor window in the White House Tuesday morning, President Johnson saw for the second day a line of seven hundred protesters who were maintaining an around-the-clock vigil along the Pennsylvania Avenue sidewalk in front of the White House. Across the street in Lafayette Park, six hundred more demonstrators chanted, "LBJ, just you wait! See what happens in '68!" At the Justice Department, a SNCC-led group of young people had organized another sit-in, larger than the one the day before. At nightfall police carried 120 protesters out of the building. The demonstrations at the White House and Justice Department were relatively small, however, compared to a weeklong outpouring of protest in other cities across the United States. In Detroit on Tuesday, Governor George Romney, a Republican, and Mayor James Cavanaugh, a Democrat, had led ten thousand marchers five times around the federal building to protest the brutality of Bloody Sunday. They demanded that President Johnson send federal forces to protect the Selma demonstrators — and send civil rights legislation to Congress. Major demonstrations broke out in Chicago, Boston, Cleveland, and Oakland. In New York, hundreds of protesters stalled traffic in front of the Manhattan FBI office.[40]

At the Executive Office Building next to the White House, Vice President Humphrey met Tuesday afternoon with civil rights and church leaders brought together by the Reverend Walter Fauntroy, the SCLC's Washington director. "The dominant mood of the meeting was the expression of deep concern and disappointment that the federal government had not taken more decisive action to protect those persons' petition for the right to vote," Humphrey reported candidly to Johnson. "Several persons expressed the view that the federal government was playing 'politics' with the situation."[41]

Pressure on President Johnson to act was mounting not only from the city streets and churches of America but also from the halls of Congress. Not just liberal Democrats but conservative Republicans as well introduced voting rights legislation, criticizing Johnson for inaction. Senate leaders Everett Dirksen and Mike Mansfield both privately complained that the administration's early drafts of the bill were too complicated and unwieldy. Representative William McCulloch of Ohio, the key House Republican on civil rights, was critical of the president for the delay on voting rights. On Tuesday alone, forty-three House members and seven senators rose in Congress to demand immediate voting rights legislation.[42]

The initial reaction to the police rampage at Selma equaled the nationwide outrage over Bull Connor's use of police dogs and fire hoses against demonstrators in Birmingham two years earlier. The real villains of Selma were Governor George Wallace, the Alabama state troopers, Sheriff Clark, and an entrenched system of segregation and denial of equal rights, but Johnson was a convenient target for critics who demanded immediate action from the federal government. In the week following Bloody Sunday, Johnson faced tough questions: Why hadn't the president immediately sent troops to Selma? Why hadn't he sent voting rights legislation to Capitol Hill? The demonstrators wanted action, not explanations.

The president was wounded by the criticism. Once again, he felt that his southern heritage was being held against him as he dealt with a racial crisis, that, as he told Katzenbach, his actions in dealing with the crisis were being condemned "because of the origins of my antecedents." In a Wednesday morning conversation, as he instructed Katzenbach on how to handle the crisis, Johnson told him, "What I'm anxious to do is not to have the image that you're following a southern president over here who is afraid of [Colonel] Lingo." At bedtime on Wednesday night, Johnson continued to worry about how he was being judged. "Do you find any agitation against Johnson the southerner not acting?" he asked the attorney general. "Not a bit, not a bit," Katzenbach assured him.[43]

Despite his achievements as a national leader, Lyndon Johnson was still sensitive to suggestions by easterners and Ivy League liberals that he was a "hick southerner" with the same prejudices still being defended by members of Congress from the South. Criticism of his handling of Selma was particularly hurtful. Johnson felt that he had already done more for civil rights than any other president since Abraham Lincoln. But Johnson also knew that he needed to ride the wave of indignation and protest, to stay ahead of its powerful currents and turn them to his advantage in achieving voting rights legislation — without plunging the federal government into a new civil war against segregationists in the South. As Johnson would reflect later, "It would probably not take long for those aroused emotions [of Selma] to melt away. It was important to move at once, if we were to achieve anything permanent from this transitory mood."[44]

King and Johnson faced similar challenges to their leadership. Both were being pushed to move faster and harder — no matter what the consequences actually might be in terms of national support for voting rights legislation. For several days both Johnson and King lay low and contemplated their next moves. Each man calculated how best to ride that wave of indignation over Selma without alienating either his core supporters by failing to act or his broad public support by taking actions that might seem excessive or extreme.

The two men were also careful not to embarrass each other. King did not criticize the president for inaction, and Johnson was careful to deny that King had made a deal with federal authorities regarding the Tuesday march. Disclosing the agreement would have caused King even more trouble with the SNCC radicals.

On Wednesday, March 11, Vice President Humphrey reported to President Johnson that the church leaders who had come to him the day before planned to escalate their protests. A continuous prayer vigil would begin at the White House that night, to be followed on Sunday by a massive rally in Lafayette Park. If on Monday the president still had not introduced legislation on voting rights or met with their representatives, the national church groups would call on their members to descend on Washington. The coalition of Protestant, Catholic, and Jewish clergymen that had mobilized to support the 1964 civil rights legislation was back in force, seasoned veterans of the civil rights wars.

Mike Mansfield, normally a mild-mannered and cooperative Senate leader, let the White House's Larry O'Brien know that he would introduce his own voting rights bill. Mansfield was irritated. He felt that the administration was ignoring him, the Democratic majority leader, while dealing instead with Minority Leader Dirksen. Johnson immediately dispatched Attorney General Katzenbach to reassure Mansfield.[45]

On Thursday morning, Jack Valenti reported to the president, "All quiet on the civil rights front. Mostly waiting to see what happens to the beaten minister [James Reeb]. Trouble will erupt when he dies." Johnson had dispatched a presidential jet to fly Reeb's wife and father from Boston to his bedside in Birmingham. When Marie Reeb arrived in Birmingham, she told reporters of her last conversation with her husband before he left for Alabama. "I said that I would prefer that he not go," she said. "But he said that he had to go." The family now faced the painful decision of whether to turn off the life support systems that were keeping Reeb alive.[46]

The protests outside the White House on Thursday morning were augmented by a dramatic new tactic. Twelve young civil rights demonstrators entered the White House on the regular morning visitors' tour and then staged a sit-down in a hallway between the East Wing and the State floor rooms. After Secret Service agent Rufus Youngblood informed Johnson of their presence at 11:20 A.M., the president took personal charge of handling the protest. At an initial strategy session, he rejected Lee White's advice that the youngsters from CORE and SNCC be ejected and arrested. Sensitive to a possible public relations disaster, Johnson sought gentler means of persuasion.

"Let them eat and drink, but don't let them go to the bathroom," Johnson suggested. Lady Bird Johnson directed that the demonstrators be served coffee — a gesture rewarded an hour later when two of the young men rushed out of the White House in search of a restroom. Later in the day, the president dispatched a trio of White House aides to inquire subtly whether the remaining demonstrators would like to meet with him. As the aides engaged the youngsters in conversation, one burly demonstrator blurted out, "We want to see the president!" But he was silenced by fellow protesters terrified at the prospect of having to meet President Johnson. Having failed in their mission to offer a presidential dialogue, the embarrassed aides — Lee White, Bill Moyers, and Clifford Alexander — returned to the Oval Office. "I send three of the supposed smartest guys in the world on a simple assignment, and they can't even get some kids to talk to me," Johnson complained.[47]

Finally, while Johnson was briefly absent from the White House, Secret Service agent Youngblood executed the president's own detailed plan for ejecting the demonstrators. Five teams of guards in civilian attire — one black and one white officer per team — took the remaining ten demonstrators out five different White House exits; once outside, they were quietly arrested.*

Thursday night, as the president was briefing members of Congress on his forthcoming voting rights bill, he learned that James Reeb had died. The president, first lady, and Vice President Humphrey went up to the family quarters to call Reeb's wife and father to offer condolences. As she painfully and helplessly searched for words to console Mrs. Reeb, Lady Bird Johnson could hear the music playing at the congressional reception downstairs and the chanting of civil rights demonstrators in front of the White House. She found the contrast striking.[48]

In Selma, Police Chief Wilson Baker delivered the news of Reeb's death to the hundreds of demonstrators standing in a drizzling rain outside Brown Chapel. The assembled protesters were blocked by Baker's policemen from marching to the courthouse to confront Sheriff Clark. After three hours of singing and speeches, the demonstrators settled into makeshift bedrolls on the gravel of Sylvan Street and on the bare benches of

* The demonstrators were released immediately without posting bail.

Brown Chapel for a third night, determined to stay until they could march to the courthouse for what would now be a memorial service. Tears over James Reeb's death were mixed with fury. The four men charged with his murder were free on minimal bail after only a few hours in jail. Despite Chief Baker's efforts, Selma remained a lawless town of inequality and violence.[49]

By Friday morning, March 12, a beleaguered Lyndon Johnson knew that he had to explain his position to the church leaders and civil rights activists who were calling for even bigger demonstrations demanding action.* Starting at 10 A.M., he met for two hours with Walter Fauntroy and a group of civil rights and church leaders, then for another two hours with an assembly of bishops and other officials representing the National Council of Churches.

Johnson no longer tried to smooth over his handling of the voting rights issue by citing his past accomplishments on civil rights. Instead, he confided how he was trying to deal with the crisis. As he described his frustrated effort the previous day to meet with the young protesters in the White House, he seemed to connect with Fauntroy. Other listeners became less judgmental about Johnson's willingness to provide protection for the marchers after he revealed that he had had two battalions of crack troops on alert less than an hour from Selma throughout Tuesday's march. He stressed that the federal government now had joined the SCLC lawsuit asking the federal court to enjoin Alabama officials from interfering with the march from Selma to Montgomery. He explained the advantages of waiting for Judge Johnson's order authorizing the march and then forcing Governor Wallace to use the Alabama National Guard to implement it and protect the marchers. At the first sign of violence, the president assured them, he would commit the federal troops.

Johnson also complained to the gathering that the around-the-clock demonstrations outside the White House were keeping his daughters, Lynda and Luci, from doing their homework or getting any sleep.[†]

---

* Catholic archbishop Patrick O'Boyle sent a letter to each of the 400,000 parishioners of his Washington diocese urging their participation in the Lafayette Park rally. He also sent a copy to President Johnson. The president promptly responded, thanking O'Boyle for his friendship and efforts on behalf of civil rights.

† Lynda Bird, a student at George Washington University, and Luci Baines, a high school student at National Cathedral School, normally slept in White House bedrooms that overlooked Pennsylvania Avenue and Lafayette Park, sites where the chanting protesters had gathered. To escape the noise, Lynda Bird wrote in her diary, she moved from room to room, finally going to sleep in her mother's bedroom on the south side of the White House. What made the protests so painful, said Lynda, was that "we were on [the protesters'] side" (AI, Lynda Bird Johnson Robb).

Whether the president was seeking sympathy or just being a worried father was of little concern to the veterans of Selma. After the meeting, H. Rap Brown — who later would become head of SNCC and a radical proponent of Black Power — ridiculed Johnson for worrying about his daughters' sleep while demonstrators were being battered and killed in Alabama. Still, Johnson won some breathing room with his pledge to send legislation to Congress by the following Monday or Tuesday.[50]

The President and the Governor

Late Friday afternoon, President Johnson learned from the United Press International news wire about a development he had been waiting for. The UPI story reported that Governor George Wallace of Alabama had sent a telegram to the White House asking for an appointment with the president "at the earliest possible moment" to discuss the three-day-old stalemate in Selma between police and thousands of civil rights demonstrators. "The situation existing in Selma poses some of the greatest internal problems ever faced by the nation," the story quoted Wallace as saying.

Even though the White House hadn't yet received the telegram, Johnson fired back an answer to Wallace: "I want you to know, as well as every other governor to know, I am willing to see you on any matter of mutual interest and concern. I will be available in my office at any time that is convenient to you." With former governor Buford Ellington of Tennessee as his secret emissary, Johnson had been trying for several days to lure Wallace into just such a meeting.[51]

The previous day, Johnson and his advisers had debated yet again whether to send federal troops to Alabama, as prominent citizens across the country were demanding. "If I just send in federal troops with their big black boots," Johnson said, "it will look like Reconstruction all over again. I will lose every moderate, not just in Alabama but all over the South. Most southern people don't like this violence," Johnson asserted. "They know deep in their hearts that things are going to change. They may not like it, but they will accommodate. But not if it looks like the Civil War all over again! That will force them right into the arms of extremists and make a martyr of Wallace. And that's not going to help the Negroes, to have to fight a war — unless we're going to occupy the South all over again. I may have to send in troops, but not until I have to, not until everyone can see I had no other choice."

An aide interjected, "We have to do something!"

"We will," Johnson said. "Keep the pressure on. Make it clear we're not going to yield an inch." He paused, reflecting on his adversary. "Now, that

Wallace, he's a lot more sophisticated than your average southern politician, and it's his ox that's in the ditch. Let's see how he gets him out."[52]

The trap was set. Wallace, a populist demagogue with his sights set on national office, was in a bind. Even as he had preached racism to reach the governor's office and stood in the schoolhouse door to symbolize his opposition to integration, Wallace knew that fostering bloody racial violence would doom his political aspirations. He needed the president's help to de-escalate the crisis in Selma.

The next morning, flying toward Washington in the Alabama state airplane, its nose emblazoned with the state flag's Confederate stars and bars, the governor and his advisers rehearsed their strategy. They hoped to use the "summit conference" with the president to divert attention from Alabama's denial of voting rights to blacks and to turn the spotlight instead on reckless demonstrators they claimed posed a threat to law and order. After the request for a meeting had been sent to the White House, one Wallace aide began to have second thoughts. Why, he wondered, had the president responded so enthusiastically? By then, however, the governor's airplane was landing at Washington National Airport.[53]

President Johnson welcomed the Alabama governor to the White House just before noon on Saturday, March 13 — six days after "Bloody Sunday." As the president led Wallace and his assistant Seymore Trammel into the Oval Office, he joked that the governor and Martin Luther King Jr. had "something in common." They were the only two men, the president said with a grin, who had ever wired him to request an appointment and then released the telegram to the press before he had even received it.[54]

The six-foot-four Johnson took the diminutive Wallace by the arm and steered him to a seat on a low, deep-cushioned couch. Then Johnson pulled up his rocking chair, positioning it so that he sat towering over Wallace. When the president leaned forward, their noses nearly touched. It was an intimidating Johnson maneuver that Hubert Humphrey called a "nostril inspection." The psychological warfare had begun.

"Well, Governor," the president said, "you wanted to see me."[55]

Wallace tried to seize the initiative. He claimed that law and order were disintegrating in Alabama. Communist agitators were stirring up trouble. The president needed to put a stop to the demonstrations.

The real problem, the president responded, was voting rights. The protesters were simply seeking the most basic right of a democracy — the right to cast a ballot. "You can't stop a fever by putting an icepack on your head," Johnson said. "You've got to use antibiotics and get to the *cause* of the fever."[56]

Johnson rather liked the spunky governor, a former college bantam-weight boxing champion who had scratched his way out of rural poverty and started his career as a fiery populist — much as Lyndon Johnson had done. But Johnson quickly demonstrated his own confidence that Wallace was badly overmatched in this bout.

His expression never changing, his hooded eyes focused tightly on Wallace, Johnson listened in silence as the governor made his case about "outside agitators and Communists." Then, for the next two hours, Lyndon Johnson gave George Wallace an extended version of "the treatment."

"Now, Governor, I know that you're like me, not approving of brutality," the president said. After Wallace denied that brutality had been used against the demonstrators, Johnson handed him a newspaper showing an Alabama trooper kicking a black demonstrator who was lying on the ground. After a half-dozen denials and evasions by Wallace and assertions by Johnson, the governor finally acknowledged instances of police brutality in Alabama.[57]

Addressing Wallace's desire to end the demonstrations, the president said, "You know, George, you can turn those off in a minute. Why don't you just desegregate all your schools? You and I go out there in front of those television cameras right now, and you announce you've decided to desegregate every school in Alabama."

"Oh, Mr. President, I can't do that," Wallace protested. "You know, the schools have got school boards. They're locally run. I haven't got the political power to do that."

"Don't you shit me, George Wallace," replied the president.[58] Then he turned the conversation back to the right to vote. "George, why don't you just tell them county registrars to register those Negroes?" Johnson asked.

"I don't have that power, Mr. President, under Alabama law," replied Wallace.

"Don't be modest with me, George," Johnson shot back. "You had the power to keep the president of the United States off the ballot." (Alabama had refused to put Johnson's name on the ballot in the 1964 election.)[59]

Johnson shifted from sarcasm and satire to the most effective part of "the treatment": he appealed to Wallace's sense of patriotism as well as his ego. "George, why are you doing this?" Johnson asked. "You came into office a liberal — you spent all your life trying to do things for the poor. Now, why are you working on this? Why are you off on this Negro thing? You ought to be down there calling for help for Aunt Susie in the nursing home."[60]

Then he told Wallace about all the things he hoped to accomplish as president — from Medicare for the elderly to aid to education for children, and from environmental protection to help of all kinds for the poor. He challenged Wallace to join him: "Now, listen, George, don't think about 1968 [the next presidential election]. Think about 1988. You and me, we'll be dead and gone then, George. . . . What do you want left after you, when you die? Do you want a great big marble monument that reads, 'George Wallace — He Built.' Or do you want a little piece of pine board lying across that harsh caliche soil that reads, 'George Wallace — He Hated.' "[61]

Johnson then stood up and guided Wallace out into a hallway, where three hundred reporters and photographers awaited them. Gut fighter George Wallace, the fiery champion of "segregation forever," the demagogic politician who had terrified the Democrats in three 1964 presidential primaries, seemed totally subdued. The two men's assistants, Trammel with Wallace and Katzenbach, Jack Valenti, and speechwriter Richard Goodwin with Johnson, had watched Wallace almost disappear into the deep-cushioned couch, his initial confidence slowly disintegrating.[62]

"The President was a gentleman, as he always is," Wallace told the reporters, "and I hope I was a gentleman too. We had a frank and friendly discussion. I do appreciate the courtesy of the President." Later Wallace jested gamely, "Hell, if I'd stayed in there much longer, he'd have had me coming out for civil rights."[63]

Wallace had not been converted, but Johnson had made his point. The president would not let Wallace wriggle off the hook: Wallace would protect the rights of the protesters to march from Selma to Montgomery, and the president would hold him responsible for their safety. If Wallace didn't want that responsibility, the president was ready to assume it. But Wallace would have to ask for help.*

At 3:45 P.M. the president walked into the Rose Garden. For the first time since the marchers were routed at the Edmund Pettus Bridge the previous Sunday, after six days of criticism from political, civic, and civil rights leaders, the president spoke out about the issues facing the nation in Selma.

Johnson announced that he would send voting rights legislation to

---

* A few days later, speaking with reporters at his ranch, Johnson had second thoughts about how he had handled the Wallace meeting, especially his own comments to the press and his gleeful retelling of it. Johnson confided that "Lady Bird said I sounded like I was questioning his integrity in my statement, but I don't want to do that and try to ruin a man. It's like a man who wrestles his wife to the ground for an hour and finally pins her shoulders to the ground. As he lifts his 250 pounds up off her, he says, 'I can lick any little hundred-pound woman in the world.' Now, I don't want to do that, say that the President of the United States can lick any man" (Richard Harwood and Haynes Johnson, *Lyndon*, p. 107).

Congress on Monday, March 15. His bill would "strike down all restrictions used to discriminate and deny the right to vote." It would establish "a simple, uniform standard, which cannot be used — however ingenuous the effort — to flout our Constitution." And "if state officials refuse to cooperate, then citizens will be registered by federal officials."

"What happened in Selma was an American tragedy," the president said. "It is wrong to do violence to peaceful citizens in the streets of their town. It is wrong to deny Americans the right to vote. It is *wrong* to deny any person full equality because of the color of his skin."

About his conversation with George Wallace, the president reported, "I told the governor that the brutality in Selma last Sunday just must not be repeated." He had urged the governor "to declare his support for universal suffrage, to assure that the right of peaceful assembly will be permitted in Alabama," and to appoint a biracial commission. To Governor Wallace's concerns "that demonstrations . . . are a threat to the peace and security of the people of Alabama," Johnson replied with his own "concern about the need for remedying the grievances which led to the demonstrations."

Johnson had told Wallace that if state and local governments were unable to protect the right of citizens to vote and to demonstrate, "the federal government will completely meet its responsibilities."[64]

On Sunday afternoon President Johnson asked permission from congressional leaders to address a joint session of Congress at nine o'clock Monday evening. It would be the first time in nineteen years that a president would appear before Congress to present a legislative message.* Ordinarily, the president sends legislative proposals — even important ones — to Congress by messenger. But Johnson sensed that America was at a pivotal moment in its agonizing three hundred–year history of slavery and racial discrimination. He wanted to seize the moment, and do so with all the power at his command. Speechwriters were awakened and summoned. Just before retiring Sunday night, Johnson called Martin Luther King in Chicago to invite him to sit with Mrs. Johnson during Monday night's speech.† King accepted, but then called back Monday morning to convey his regrets and disappointment. He explained that no flight was

---

* President Harry S. Truman last addressed a joint session on May 25, 1946, concerning a crisis caused by a national railroad workers' strike.

† Also invited to sit with Lady Bird and Lynda Bird Johnson in seats reserved for the president's family and guests were several churchmen — Monsignor George Higgins, Rabbi Uri Miller, Reverend Eugene Carson Blake, Reverend Robert Spike — who had protested President Johnson's inaction after Bloody Sunday. Johnson wanted them to be there to hear his answers to their complaints (Lady Bird Johnson, *White House Diary*, p. 252).

available that would get him to Washington in time after he preached at James Reeb's memorial service Monday afternoon in Selma.

Lady Bird Johnson noticed a difference in her husband Sunday night. She had been worried about him for weeks. On Saturday morning, before his meeting with George Wallace, Johnson's longtime doctors and friends Willis Hurst and James Cain had come by at her urging to assess Lyndon Johnson's health. That night, Lady Bird dictated into her diary her thoughts on the doctors' examination and her husband's health: "Essentially, everything is fine — all the basic organs and the functioning thereof. But there is this heavy load of tension and this fog of depression. . . . [The doctors'] prescription is exercise, diet, and a break — to get off to sunshine and rest for a couple of days every two weeks. . . . But Lyndon feels chained right here, and it's having an erosive effect on his personality."

Mrs. Johnson was as concerned as she had been during the 1964 Democratic convention, when Johnson was deeply depressed over his inability to satisfy black leaders and deal with racial issues. Now he again faced uncertainty in a racial crisis. He was despondent about the demonstrators he heard chanting throughout the night. And he was deeply worried about his first commitment of combat troops to Vietnam — a problem to which, he lamented, he saw no answers.

But after Johnson's encounter with Wallace on Saturday afternoon, his strong Rose Garden statement on Selma and voting rights, and his decision Sunday to go before Congress, his mood changed. Lady Bird felt more optimistic about the president's state of mind. Sunday night she noted in her diary that Johnson had missed his afternoon nap to attend a meeting requested by congressional leaders, who "asked him to come address them on the subject of the turmoil in the nation."

"And so," she observed, "with only twenty-four hours' notice, there will be a major speech Monday night at nine o'clock. It's like deciding to climb Mount Everest while you are sitting around a cozy family picnic. . . . I am glad that he is launched, that he is being intensely active. It is the milieu for him. It is his life. He is loosed from the bonds of depression."[65]

An American Problem

The black presidential limousine glided slowly through the White House's northwest gate at 8:30 Monday night, bound for the Capitol. In the back seat, the president silently read over his speech. Johnson didn't speak with his aides or look up as his limousine passed the chanting civil rights protesters still lining the White House sidewalk, demanding that he take action on Selma.[66]

At 9 P.M. William "Fishbait" Miller, the doorkeeper of the House of Representatives, entered the rear door of the chamber. "Mr. Speaker," Miller proclaimed to the joint session of Congress in his distinctive Mississippi accent, "the President of the United States." Lyndon Johnson walked down the center aisle of the House chamber to the loud applause of dozens of old friends with whom he had served in Congress. When Johnson reached the podium, Speaker John McCormack, who had urged Johnson to make this address, again formally introduced "the President of the United States." The 535 members of the Senate and House — and a television audience of 70 million Americans — listened as the president began his speech.[67]

"At times," he said, "history and fate meet in a single place to shape a turning point in man's unending search for freedom. So it was at Lexington and Concord. So it was a century ago at Appomattox. So it was last week in Selma, Alabama."

There was a slight rustling in the room as the members of Congress recognized almost immediately that Johnson's course was set, his intentions clear, and the issues at stake ones that Congress had to face.

"There, long-suffering men and women peacefully protested the denial of their rights as Americans. Many were brutally assaulted. One good man, a man of God, was killed. There is no cause for pride in what has happened in Selma. There is no cause for self-satisfaction in the long denial of equal rights to millions of Americans."

A hush settled over the House chamber as Johnson defined the significance of Selma. "Rarely, in any time does an issue lay bare the heart of America itself. Rarely are we met with a challenge, not to our growth or abundance, our welfare or security, but rather to the values and the purposes and meanings of our beloved nation.

"The issue of equal rights for American Negroes is such an issue. And should we defeat every enemy, should we double our wealth and conquer the stars, and still be unequal to this issue, then we will have failed as a people and a nation."

For the first time, applause rippled through the audience. Johnson paused, letting the applause pass unacknowledged. Then, in a strong, measured voice, his face conveying total seriousness and determination, the president continued to define his theme.

"There is no Negro problem. There is no Southern problem. There is no Northern problem. There is only an *American* problem. And we are met here tonight as Americans — not as Democrats or Republicans — we are met here as Americans to solve that problem."

"The problem," Johnson explained, was "the failure of America to live up to its unique founding purpose — a purpose defined in phrases still found in every American heart . . . 'all men are created equal' — 'government by the consent of the governed' — 'give me liberty or give me death.'

"These words are a promise to every citizen that he shall share in the dignity of man. This dignity . . . really rests on his right to be treated as a man equal in opportunity to all others. It says he shall share in freedom, he shall choose his leaders, educate his children, provide for his family according to his ability and his merits as a human being."

Johnson then detailed the many ways in which state and local officials in the South had denied to millions of African Americans one of the most basic rights of democracy and human freedom: the right to vote. Evasions, rationalization, and complexities aside, Johnson declared, "the harsh fact is that in many places in this country, men and women are kept from voting simply because they are Negroes."

So far as the maze of "literacy tests" confronting voters in Deep South states, Johnson declared flatly, "The fact is that the only way to pass these barriers is to show a white skin."

The president described the failure of three previous civil rights laws — in each of which he acknowledged his own major role — to remedy the problem. He announced that he would send to the Congress on Wednesday a bipartisan bill that would "strike down restrictions to voting in all elections, Federal, State, and local — which have been used to deny Negroes the right to vote." The bill "would establish a simple, uniform standard [of voter registration] which cannot be used, no matter how ingenious the effort, to flout our Constitution." If state and local officials still refused to register Negro voters, the president declared, the new law "will provide for citizens to be registered by officials of the United States government."

Although the president did not detail the formula by which entire states and counties would come under the law because of their massive denial of voting rights, it was understood that the law initially would apply to Alabama, Georgia, Louisiana, Mississippi, South Carolina, and parts of North Carolina and other states.

Johnson then sought to clarify the fundamental simplicity and urgency of the voting rights crisis. "There is no constitutional issue here. The command of the Constitution is plain. There is no moral issue. It is wrong — deadly wrong — to deny any of your fellow Americans the right to vote in this country. There is no issue of states' rights or national rights. There is only the struggle for human rights. . . . This time on this issue, there must be no delay, no hesitation, and no compromise with our purpose. . . . And we ought not and we cannot and we must not wait another eight months before we get a bill. We have already waited a hundred years and more, and the time for waiting is gone."

Whatever Johnson's earlier complaints about the political wisdom of the rising tide of protests in front of the White House and in cities across America; whatever his hurt feelings about those protesting voices directed at him, Johnson now announced that he clearly heard those protests, and embraced the outpouring of emotion from the civil rights revolution.

"From the window where I sit with the problems of our country, I recognize that outside this chamber, is the outraged conscience of a nation, the grave concern of many nations, and the harsh judgment of history on our acts. . . .

"The real hero of this struggle is the American Negro. His actions and protests, his courage to risk safety and even to risk his life, have awakened the conscience of this nation. His demonstrations have been designed to call attention to injustice, designed to provoke change, designed to stir reform. He has called upon us to make good the promise of America. And who among us can say that we would have made the same progress were it not for his persistent bravery and his faith in America."

Scarcely waiting for the ovation to end — the applause coming now in waves after each new point made, each summons to the most cherished American ideals — the president, still serious and unsmiling, moved beyond voting rights to broader themes.

"Even if we pass this bill, the battle will be not over. What happened in Selma is part of a far larger movement which reaches into every section and state of America. It is the effort of American Negroes to secure for themselves the full blessings of American life. Their cause must be our cause too. Because it is not just Negroes, but really it is all of us, who must overcome the crippling legacy of bigotry and injustice."

Pausing for several seconds, Lyndon Baines Johnson continued slowly in a powerful, determined voice, with distinct emphasis on each word.

"And — we — *shall* — overcome!"

After a breathless moment of recognition, most in the audience jumped to their feet, cheering and applauding. Representative Emanuel Celler of New York, chairman of the House Judiciary Committee, and at seventy-seven a veteran — often a losing one — of forty years of civil rights battles, stood shouting with the abandon he once displayed celebrating some monumental feat of the Brooklyn Dodgers. Mike Mansfield, the laconic, dry-witted exemplar of fairness in the Senate, sat with tears running down his face. Members of the diplomatic corps stood and cheered. Generals and admirals, heads of the armed forces, rose and applauded. And most of the august justices of the Supreme Court, led by Chief Justice Earl Warren, also stood smiling and applauding — in violation of the protocol of appearing neutral and evenhanded about great national issues certain to come before the Court.

In Montgomery, Alabama, the Reverend Martin Luther King Jr. was watching the speech on television in the living room of his friends the Jacksons, at whose home he had stayed during the long, difficult weeks of the voting rights campaign. As President Johnson embraced the ringing anthem of the civil rights movement, Dr. King wiped tears from his eyes. John Lewis, sitting beside him, also was moved. He had always dismissed Johnson as a "politician." On that night, however, he felt that the president was "a man who spoke from his heart, a statesman, a poet." Lewis was surprised by King's tears. In his experience King had always been a man in careful control of his emotions — a man of reason, of calm resolution, of compassion, a passionate orator, yes, but not a man of tears.[68]

Reaction in the House chamber was not unanimous acclaim. Democratic senator Allen Ellender of Louisiana, a leader of the southern irreconcilables, slumped in his chair, looking miserable, as did many other of his southern colleagues. And in Alabama, Johnson won little praise from the radical SNCC dissidents. As far as SNCC field secretary James Forman was concerned, the president had "ruined a good song."[69]

Lyndon Johnson had struck a powerful chord, but he had by no means finished what he wanted to tell the Congress and the nation — how he felt about the civil rights of African Americans, and about the problems of all those Americans, black and white, left out of the American dream.

"Let none of us in any section look with prideful righteousness on the troubles in another section, or on the problems of our neighbors. There is really no part of America where the promise of equality has been fully kept. In Buffalo as well as in Birmingham, in Philadelphia as well as in Selma, Americans are struggling for the fruits of freedom."

Johnson then turned to his own personal experiences long ago which had touched a deep nerve, left a lasting effect on the way he viewed himself and his country, and how those experiences underlay his concern that civil rights alone was not enough — that civil rights must lead to broader opportunities for all Americans.

"My first job after college was as a teacher in Cotulla, Texas, in a small Mexican-American school. Few of [the students] could speak English. . . . My children were poor, and they often came to class without breakfast, hungry. They knew even in their youth the pain of prejudice. They never seemed to know why people disliked them. But they knew it was so, because I saw it in their eyes. I often walked home after the classes were finished, wishing there was more that I could do. But all I knew was to teach them the little that I knew, hoping that it might help them against the hardships that lay ahead.

"Somehow, you never forget what poverty and hatred can do when you see its scars on the hopeful face of a young child.

"I never thought then, in 1928, that I would be standing here in 1965. It never occurred to me in my fondest dreams that I might have the chance to help the sons and daughters of those students and to help people like them all over the United States."

Again Johnson paused, and again one heard the big Texan speak with all the determination and passion at his command.

"But now I do have that chance — and I'll let you in on a little secret. *I — mean — to use — it!*"

The audience was on its feet again, with a second standing ovation, and the fortieth interruption of Johnson's speech for applause. He was winding up now, expressing his own philosophy, his own dreams about what he might accomplish, and about how history might view his presidency.

"The might of past empires is little compared to our own. But I do not want to be the President who built empires, or sought grandeur, or extended dominion. I want to be the President who educated young children to the wonders of their world. I want to be the President who helped to feed the hungry . . . who helped the poor to find their own way, who protected the right of every citizen to vote. I want to be the President who helped end hatred among his fellow men and who promoted love among the people of all races and all regions and all parties. I want to be the President who helped end war among the brothers of this earth."*

Beyond any question, President Johnson had struck a powerful chord with a vast number of Americans. In Tuesday's *New York Times,* White House correspondent Tom Wicker commented: "No other American President had so completely identified himself with the cause of the Ne-

---

* Johnson picked White House aide Richard Goodwin to write the speech because, he said, Goodwin as a Jew had experienced and felt discrimination. Johnson told Goodwin to include his experience at Cotulla, and worked on the speech himself. Of the assignment, Goodwin said: "Although I had written the speech, the document was pure Lyndon Johnson. . . . I had talked with him at length, observed him as he dealt with others. . . . I had come to know not merely his views, but his pattern of expression, patterns of reasoning, the natural cadences of his speech." There was not time to put the speech on the TelePrompTer, yet Johnson read the speech as if he had memorized it and had total command of what he said (AI, Horace Busby; Richard Goodwin, *Remembering America,* pp. 338–348).

gro. No other President had made the issue of equality for Negroes so frankly a moral cause for himself and all Americans." The next Gallup Poll showed that Johnson had achieved the highest approval rating ever achieved by a president on the issue of civil rights.* Never before had the civil rights movement received the breadth of support and the strength of federal endorsement that it had during the eight days beginning with Bloody Sunday and culminating in Johnson's speech. Twenty years later David Garrow, the Pulitzer Prize–winning biographer of Dr. King, would write that the week ending with Johnson's speech "was an emotional peak unmatched by anything that had come before, nor by anything that would come later" for the civil rights movement.[70]

Back in the living quarters of the White House, as the telephone calls and telegrams started pouring in, the president sat drinking a Scotch and soda with Lady Bird, Lynda, and several aides, still surging with the energy and optimism that had begun to fill him Saturday afternoon during his charged meeting with George Wallace. From Puerto Rico came congratulations from Senator Richard Russell, Johnson's mentor and leader of the southern segregationists, now recuperating from a serious illness. It was the finest political speech he had ever heard, said Russell.

From Montgomery came the congratulations and heartfelt thanks of Martin Luther King Jr. "It is ironic, Mr. President," said King, "that after a century, a southern white President would help lead the way toward the salvation of the Negro."

"Thank you, Reverend," replied Johnson. "You're the leader who is making it all possible. I'm just following along trying to do what's right."

After the call with King, Johnson, visibly moved by King's words, said to speechwriter Richard Goodwin, "You know Dick, I understand why he's surprised, why a lot of folks are surprised, but I'm going to do it. Hell, we're just halfway up the mountain. Not even half."[71]

---

* Polls taken March 18–23, 1965, showed that the American public favored the Voting Rights Act by a margin of 76 to 16 percent.

12

✦ ✦ ✦ ✦ ✦ ✦ ✦ ✦

Shining Moment

I N THE DAYS FOLLOWING the president's speech to Congress, a surge of support for the civil rights movement was cresting all across America, as was the tempo of the social revolution Lyndon Johnson had dreamed about from the first night of his presidency. Johnson's call for the nation to overcome the stains that marred an idealized democracy was in tune with a buoyant, optimistic national mood, and great social and political changes seemed within reach. A Gallup Poll showed that four out of five Americans supported a voting rights law. Even in the South, a majority of white Americans supported legislation to ensure the right of black Americans to vote. And the Eighty-ninth Congress — perhaps one of the most liberal in the nation's history — was moving at breakneck speed under Lyndon Johnson's insistent leadership to enact legislation that would significantly increase the responsibilities of the federal government toward its citizenry. The benefits of proposed Medicare legislation would lift millions of older Americans out of dire poverty, and new federal education, housing, and job programs promised to expand the possibilities for millions to share more equitably in the American dream.

For the moment at least, the civil rights movement and the three branches of the federal government appeared united in fulfilling the agenda black Americans had pursued with increasing insistence since World War II. And many civil rights activists, ever impatient with the grudging resistance of white America to full rights for black Americans, suddenly felt that the government was on their side. The movement's rising faith in government was reflected in the telegram Martin Luther King sent to Lyndon Johnson on Tuesday, March 16:

Your speech to the Joint Session of Congress last night was the most moving, eloquent, unequivocal and passionate plea for human rights ever made by any President of the nation. You evidenced amazing understanding of the depth and dimensions of the problems we face in our struggle. Your tone was sincere throughout and your persuasive power was never more forceful. We are ready to join with you in a quick passage of the voting bill. Please know that we are deeply encouraged and inspired by your support and leadership.

On Wednesday, more positive news for King came out of the federal courtroom in Montgomery, Alabama. After five days of contentious hearings, U.S. district judge Frank Johnson authorized King's protest march from Selma to Montgomery. Furthermore, the judge not only enjoined Alabama's state and local officials from interfering with the march but also ordered them to protect the marchers from harm on their fifty-four-mile walk from Brown Chapel to the Alabama state capitol.

As he spelled out his findings and ordered his remedies, Frank Johnson, a native son of Alabama's mountains, spoke with the same determination, the same vivid distinctions between right and wrong, that President Johnson had shown the nation two days earlier. Judge Johnson, whose civil rights rulings had subjected him to almost constant death threats from the Ku Klux Klan, was one of a group of outstanding southern Republicans appointed to the federal bench by President Eisenhower in the 1950s. He did not mince words.

"The evidence in this case," he wrote, "reflects that an almost continuous pattern of conduct has existed on the part of the defendants Sheriff Clark, his deputies, and his auxiliary deputies known as 'possemen,' of harassment, intimidation, coercion, threatening conduct, and sometimes brutal mistreatment toward these plaintiffs and other members of their class." The judge ruled that the outrageous mistreatment of protesters on Bloody Sunday had been carried out by state and local lawmen "acting under the instructions of Governor Wallace." The defendants' actions were aimed not at enforcing any valid law, the judge declared, but merely at "preventing and discouraging Negro citizens from exercising their rights of citizenship, particularly the right to register to vote, and the right to demonstrate peacefully for the purpose of protesting discriminatory practices."

He declared that "the constitutional rights to assemble, demonstrate and to march peacefully along public streets and highways" must be measured against the constitutional rights of other citizens to travel freely on those highways. The right to protest should be commensurate with the enormity of the wrongs that are being protested. In this case, the wrongs are enormous."[1]

Johnson approved the Southern Christian Leadership Conference's plans for a five-day, fifty-four-mile march, starting on Sunday, March 21, in Selma and concluding on Thursday, March 25, in Montgomery.

In Washington, D.C., Congress initially moved with the alacrity demanded by the president, who stepped down from the podium at the joint session to demand that House Judiciary Committee chairman Celler begin hearings that very night on the proposed Voting Rights Act. Nearly fulfilling Johnson's wishes, Celler called his subcommittee to order on Wednesday, March 17. "The murder, savage brutality, and violence" perpetrated by Alabama lawmen "have so aroused the nation as to make action by the Congress necessary and speedy," Celler announced. With an increasingly pro–civil rights Congress, more favorable rules governing the legislative process, and even a number of southern Democrats conceding that a voting rights bill was inevitable — and perhaps even desirable — it appeared that this new civil rights battle would proceed more easily and quickly than in the record-setting Senate filibuster in the monumental fight of 1964. And with the leader of the southern forces, Richard Russell, suffering from emphysema and spending most of his time in the hospital, the role of opposition leader was left to the much less powerful Senator Allen Ellender of Louisiana.

Rather than waiting for the House to pass the bill, as it had done in the past, the Senate began deliberations at the same time. With sixty-six sponsors already aboard, the bill was introduced on Wednesday, March 18, and referred to the Judiciary Committee with very strict instructions that it must be reported back to the full Senate by April 9. Only twelve southerners (opposed to the bill) and Senator Margaret Chase Smith, the fiercely independent Maine Republican (opposed to referring the bill to Mississippi senator James Eastland's legislative graveyard), voted against this fast-track consideration. If the Senate failed to pass the bill by April 15, there would be no Easter recess, warned Majority Leader Mansfield.[2]

Although broad bipartisan support emerged for the voting rights concept, differences remained as to how best to achieve it. Most controversial, in the initial legislation, was the formula by which states would be covered by the toughest provisions. The formula called for the law to apply to states that required so-called literacy tests, and in which less than 50 percent of the state's eligible population had voted for president in 1964. This standard, though arbitrary, was designed to reach the Deep South states with the worst abuses. Yet even though the proposed administration bill would eliminate all registration tests and give the federal government the discretionary power to put federal registrars in those states with the lowest overall rates of African American registration, it omitted pockets of discrimination in other southern states. As a result, while the *states* of Alabama, Georgia, Louisiana, Mississippi, South Carolina, and Virginia would be covered, as well as parts of North Carolina, *counties* with significant racial discrimination in Arkansas, Florida, and Texas would be omitted. Republican congressmen John Lindsay of New York and William Cramer of Florida vowed to fix this oversight. Roy Wilkins, in testimony for the bill, endorsed their efforts. Additionally, a group of liberals led by freshman Democratic senator Edward Kennedy of Massachusetts sought to add an amendment to prohibit all state poll taxes.* Attorney General Katzenbach, worried about the constitutionality of Congress's abolishing state and local poll taxes, instead preferred to attack discriminatory taxes in the federal courts.

But those differences over process seemed minor obstacles that surely would be overcome by the broad national support for ending voter discrimination. Indeed, it seemed at that moment that Abraham Lincoln's 1861 summoning of the "better angels of our nature" to resolve racial inequality would finally come to fruition more than one hundred years after the Great Emancipator's first inaugural address.

Yet the road to racial and social justice remained uncertain. In 1960s America, the realities of racism seemed as deeply ingrained as the loftiest national ideals. Whether the turbulence of a truly revolutionary time could be calmed was a question that would test the best intentions of Lyndon Johnson and Martin Luther King.

Reactionaries and Revolutionaries

At a breakfast meeting the day after Johnson's voting rights speech, the Senate's southern irreconcilables gloomily assessed their prospects for stopping yet another piece of civil rights legislation. "Did you hear ol' Lyndon say 'we shall overcome'?" Florida's Spessard Holland asked his colleagues. Alabama's Lister Hill, a moderate man trapped by the politics

---

* Although the poll tax was already banned in federal elections by the Twenty-fourth Amendment to the Constitution, it was otherwise permissible and was used in some state and local elections.

of race, turned to Richard Russell, asking, "Dick, tell me something. You trained that boy. . . . What happened to that boy?"

"I just don't know, Lister," Russell responded. "He's a turncoat if there ever was one."[3]

These southern senators were frightened by the racial turbulence that threatened not just their power in Congress but their very political lives. Alabama's Hill and John Sparkman, both progressive men at heart, faced threats from Governor Wallace, whom they detested. In the temper of the times, Wallace was a politician capable of defeating either of them if he chose to run for the Senate.* Hill and Sparkman also faced threats from the liberal Democratic Senate majority, who resented the power they held as committee chairmen. In Georgia, Russell faced a possible 1966 reelection challenge from Governor Carl Sanders, who would position himself as a paragon of the "New South" to court support from moderate whites as well as the tens of thousands of blacks who would be instantly enfranchised by the proposed voting rights law. Given these political complexities, the southerners were determined to fight the new legislation as long as they could, relying on the filibuster — and hoping for conservative Republican support, dissension among the liberals, and white backlash against the disruptive tactics of the most militant wing of the civil rights movement.

The leaders of the Student Nonviolent Coordinating Committee poured oil on the already hot flame of the civil rights revolution, hoping to incite total rejection of the existing system. At a time when King was desperately trying to avoid further violence in Selma — as he awaited Judge Johnson's decision authorizing the march — James Forman was courting confrontation in Montgomery. A former Chicago schoolteacher, Forman spoke a different, tougher language than King and his fellow southern ministers of the Southern Christian Leadership Conference. After a brutal assault by state troopers against a SNCC-led student demonstration in Montgomery on March 17, an infuriated Forman declared before a mass meeting at a Montgomery church, "If we can't sit at the table of democracy, then we'll knock the fucking legs off."†[4]

---

* Sparkman's concern about being challenged and beaten for reelection by Wallace in 1966 was more than confirmed by a poll the senator commissioned. It showed that only 5 percent of white Alabamans gave Wallace a "poor" rating as governor. Another poll showed that Wallace's popularity encompassed the entire South, with the support of more than 80 percent of white voters (Dan T. Carter, *Politics of Rage*, pp. 261–262).

† The news media did not quote the second part of his statement: "But before we tear it completely down, they will move to build a better one, rather than see this one destroyed."

Even though he was deeply disturbed by SNCC's violent direction and its hostility toward him, King could not afford a break with the young leaders whose militancy was attracting followers not only in the South but also among young black men and women in the North.* After Forman's call to arms, King delivered a fiery message of his own, saying that "we cannot stand idly by and allow" more brutal beatings. "We must get together a peaceful and orderly march on the courthouse in Montgomery." The next morning, March 18, King and Forman together led two thousand marchers, in a driving rainstorm, to the courthouse, where they persuaded Sheriff Mac Sim Butler to apologize to the student demonstrators for the brutality of his possemen. Martin Luther King, like Lyndon Baines Johnson, walked the treacherous path between a white majority whose consent he had to gain and impatient activists unwilling to follow any leader they judged to be too timid.

On Sunday, March 21 — exactly two weeks after Bloody Sunday — Martin Luther King Jr. and 3,200 civil rights demonstrators set forth from Brown Chapel in a third attempt to march across the Edmund Pettus Bridge in Selma. They had vowed not to stop until they had presented their grievances to Governor Wallace at the state capitol in Montgomery. The original march had been conceived to protest the killing of Jimmie Lee Jackson, shot a month earlier by a state trooper. Standing with King in the first row of marchers was Jackson's grandfather, Cager Lee, the eighty-two-year-old son of a slave.

"Yes, it was worth the boy dying," said Lee, as he walked beside King. "He was my daughter's onliest son but she understands. She's taking it good. And he was a sweet boy. Not pushy. Not rowdy. He took me to church every Sunday, he worked hard. But he had to die for something. And thank God it was for this!"[5]

The marchers included white pilgrims from the North and devoutly religious black southerners, national celebrities and anonymous celebrants of freedom, powerful politicians and the foot soldiers of a revolution. Some of these enlistees — without whom there would have been no civil rights movement — had lit a spark of hope when they stubbornly refused, for more than a year in 1955 and 1956, to ride the segregated public buses in Montgomery. But this symbolic rite of passage — the March from Selma to Montgomery — was strikingly different from the two earlier

---

* With the FBI listening via its wiretaps, King dismissed Bayard Rustin's suggestion that the SCLC break with SNCC. Instead, he called on entertainer Harry Belafonte, a major financial supporter of both groups, to mediate the dispute.

thwarted efforts to assert rights long denied. This march bore the imprimatur of a federal judge and of the president of the United States. Their constitutional authority was backed up by the federalized National Guard of Alabama, crack regular army units, U.S. marshals, Justice Department officials, and even the reluctant state troopers and sheriff's deputies.

After Judge Johnson had issued his March 17 order authorizing the march, Governor Wallace lashed out with two more days of demagoguery against what he called "mobs employing the street-warfare tactics of the Communists," while he tried to outwit President Johnson about who would assume responsibility for enforcing a court order and maintaining law and order. In the end, Wallace and his obedient state legislature declared that Alabama could not afford to protect the marchers and asked for the federal government to do the job. As Johnson had guessed, "Wallace's ox was in a ditch,"* and he needed to ask for help to get him out. Johnson's patience and his shrewd handling of Wallace had helped avoid a calamitous clash between federal and state forces. He had federalized the Alabama National Guard only after Wallace requested assistance.[6]

As the 3,200 marchers set out on their journey that cool, sunny Sunday in March, they were accompanied by hundreds of reporters and 1,800 members of the Alabama National Guard. The guardsmen watched warily for potential assassins lurking high in Selma's downtown buildings and along the weed-strewn banks of the muddy Alabama River. Army helicopters circled overhead. Ramsey Clark, the deputy attorney general, representing the president, communicated by radio with FBI agents and U.S. marshals spread out through the crowd. Lest the marchers forget that bigotry still was prevalent in the Deep South, their departure through downtown Montgomery was punctuated by segregationists' loudspeakers blaring "Bye Bye Blackbird," as well as by the jeers and taunts of white citizens lining the sidewalks.

Under Judge Johnson's strict order, the SCLC was permitted a total of 3,200 marchers on four-lane stretches of Highway 80 but only 300 per day on the middle stretch of the journey, where the highway narrowed to two lanes as it meandered through the swamps of Lowndes County. In that county, with a population that was 80 percent black, not a single African American was registered to vote.

On the first day's march, the demonstrators walked six abreast toward Montgomery along the left-hand lanes of the divided highway. Two-way traffic was diverted into the right-hand lanes. A black Volkswagen passed

---

* A reference to a biblical judgment excusing a person from obeying the commandment prohibiting work on the Sabbath in certain emergencies (Luke 14:5).

the marchers several times, its doors and fenders embellished with slogans in whitewash reading "Martin Luther Kink," "Walk Coon," and "Rent Your Priest Suit Here," a derogatory reference to the abundance of clergymen walking in their clerical attire. Several small white children standing at the roadside pointed toy rifles at the marchers and chanted "Nigger lover," "White nigger," and other epithets learned at an early age from their elders. By day's end, the march had covered seven miles. Most of the marchers were driven back to Selma, while the three hundred stalwarts who would continue the next day slept in four tents pitched on the property of David Hall, a black farmer.

At eight o'clock on the second morning, Martin Luther and Coretta Scott King, wearing green caps with earmuffs to protect against the chill, led the marchers on the seventeen-mile trek to the next campsite at Rosa Steele's farm. As darkness fell, Dr. King held a press conference at which he praised the steadfastness of the marchers, whose campaign badges included sunburns and badly blistered feet. On the third day the marchers slogged through the rain to their mud-soaked campsite on the farm of A. G. Gaston, a black entrepreneur from Birmingham. On the last night the marchers reached the outskirts of Montgomery, where their four huge tents were pitched on the grounds of the Catholic City of St. Jude, a compound that included a church, hospital, and school. Spirits soared as the now veteran marchers entered their final campsite, singing "We Shall Overcome" (with two new verses added: "All the way from Selma" and "My feet are soaked").

Renata Adler, who covered the march for *The New Yorker*, listened as the marchers chanted responsively with their welcoming hosts from Montgomery:

"What do you want?" asked the marchers.

"Freedom!" loudly responded their hosts.

"When do you want it?"

"Now!"

"How much of it?"

"All of it!"

And then came gala entertainment arranged by Harry Belafonte, with an all-star cast including Sammy Davis Jr., actors Shelley Winters and Tony Perkins, and singers Nina Simone, Odetta, and Tony Bennett. Laughter relieved tension as the crowd listened to standup comics Dick Gregory and Nipsey Russell and the comedy duo of Mike Nichols and Elaine May.

"I cain't afford to call up the National Guard," said Nichols, imitating Governor Wallace.

"Why not?" asked May, impersonating a telephone operator. "It only costs a dime."

Many of the marchers missed the show, having either collapsed on cots or been taken to the hospital for treatment of foot injuries, dehydration, and total exhaustion.[7]

On Thursday morning the march expanded to more than thirty thousand people, led by the three hundred original marchers. Behind them came the national civil rights leaders — the venerable A. Philip Randolph, Roy Wilkins, James Farmer, John Lewis, and Martin Luther King, as well as Ralph Bunche, the black American Nobel laureate who served as undersecretary-general of the United Nations. There were labor leaders and church officials from most Protestant, Catholic, and Jewish denominations. There were the battle-scarred SCLC, SNCC, and CORE organizers, each of whom had been assaulted and beaten at least once in campaigns from Montgomery in 1955 to the 1960 student sit-ins, the 1961 Freedom Rides, the 1962 defeat in Albany, the victory at Birmingham in 1963, and the relentless violence of St. Augustine in 1964. SCLC lieutenants included the Reverends Ralph David Abernathy, Fred Shuttlesworth, Hosea Williams, Andrew Young, James Bevel, C. T. Vivian, Bernard Lafayette, and James Orange. The SNCC organizers who had dug in with poor blacks in hostile territory included James Forman, John Lewis, Ivanhoe Donaldson, Stokely Carmichael, and Diane Nash.

The triumphant march through the streets of Montgomery blended the pageantry of a national political convention with the solemnity of a religious pilgrimage. King led the way past the Dexter Avenue Baptist Church, where he had been baptized into the struggle nearly ten years earlier at the age of twenty-six.

As the marchers headed toward the square in front of the capitol, they sang out victoriously:

> Keep your eyes on the prize, hold on, hold on.
> I've never been to heaven, but I think I'm right.
> You won't find George Wallace anywhere in sight.
> Oh, keep your eyes on the prize, hold on, hold on.

The fifty-four-mile march reached its final destination at the steps of the Alabama state capitol, a classic white-columned Greek revival building. Standing in front of the capitol, King spoke passionately about the victory of that moment, and of the optimism with which he faced the challenges still ahead. He compared the marchers' spirit with that of Sister Pollard, a seventy-year-old black woman who, during the Montgomery bus boycott of 1955, refused the offer of a ride, saying, "My feets is tired, but my soul is rested."

Referring to the Alabama segregationists who had vowed to prevent the march, King declared: "They told us we wouldn't get here. And there were those who said we would get here only over their dead bodies. But all the world today knows that we are here. And we are standing before the forces of power in the state of Alabama, saying, 'We ain't going to let nobody turn us around!'"

The huge audience began responding to King with spontaneous exclamations of its own.

"Yes, sir!" "Speak!" And then thunderous waves of applause.

"Once more, the method of nonviolent resistance was unsheathed from its scabbard, and once again an entire community was mobilized to confront the adversary. And again the brutality of a dying order shrieks across the land," King proclaimed.

"Yet, Selma, Alabama, became *A Shining Moment in the Conscience of Man.*"

He went on: "If the worst of America lurked in its dark streets, the best of American instincts arose passionately from across the nation to overcome it. There never was a moment in American history more honorable and more inspiring than the pilgrimage of clergymen and laymen of every race and faith pouring into Selma to face danger at the side of its embattled Negroes."

Then, pausing, King properly shared credit for the "shining moment" with Lyndon Baines Johnson. "A President born in the South had the sensitivity to feel the will of the country," declared King. "And in an address that will live in history as one of the most passionate pleas for human rights ever made by a President of our nation, he pledged the might of the federal government to cast off the centuries-old blight. President Johnson praised the courage of the Negro for awakening the conscience of the nation.

"For our part," said King, "we must pay our profound respects to the white Americans who cherish their democratic traditions over the ugly customs and privileges of generations and come forth boldly to join hands with us."[8]

Dr. King, with this speech in Montgomery, and President Johnson, with his own address to Congress and the nation ten days earlier, had sounded the same resonant themes. They stood together as national leaders in summoning "the better angels" of the American conscience. They had carefully modulated their actions and words during the nearly three months of the Selma campaign, pooling their individual efforts to empower millions of black men and women to enter the voting booth for the first time. At that moment, King and Johnson had each reached the zenith of his power to promote the noble ideals of American democracy.

The still immense problem of violent racism in the Deep South jolted the movement hard Thursday night, even as triumphant marchers by the thousands were still streaming away from the Alabama capitol. Helping transport the departing marchers, SCLC volunteer Viola Liuzzo was driving east on Highway 80 toward Montgomery when another car pulled alongside her. As Liuzzo glanced at the car, a blast of gunfire shattered her side window. Liuzzo was killed instantly, a .38-caliber bullet lodged in the base of her brain. As the assassins' vehicle sped away, Liuzzo's car careened into a ditch. Her sole passenger, Leroy Moton, another volunteer, crawled out of the car, unhurt, and ran for help down Highway 80 — so recently the scene of the dramatic and peaceful march.[9]

Martin Luther King received the news that evening after he and his wife, Coretta, had arrived back in Atlanta. King was devastated. Only hours earlier, while extolling the accomplishments of the marchers, the goodwill of white America, and the leadership of President Johnson, King had also pointedly reminded his audience that the struggle was not over — that "a season of suffering" still lay ahead. But he had not expected it so soon.[10]

At 8:10 Friday morning, Lyndon Johnson was on the telephone with FBI director Hoover, demanding information, seeking answers. Hoover was prepared. Mrs. Liuzzo was a thirty-nine-year-old white woman from Detroit, the wife of a Teamsters union official, the mother of five. She had driven to Selma a week earlier to help out with the march. Her passenger, Ben Mouton, was a nineteen-year-old black volunteer from Selma.

Hoover had good news for the president. The FBI was in the process of arresting four Birmingham men, all members of the United Klans of America, Knights of the Ku Klux Klan. They would be charged under a federal statute with interfering with the constitutional rights of Mrs. Liuzzo. The crime had been solved so quickly, Hoover explained, because one of the men in the assassins' car, Gary Thomas Rowe Jr., was a paid FBI informer. He had called the FBI soon after the shooting.[11]

Only four hours later, the president stood in the East Room of the White House, flanked by Hoover and Attorney General Katzenbach, to announce that four suspects had been arrested moments earlier and charged with the dastardly crime.* "Mrs. Liuzzo, who went to Alabama to serve the struggle for justice," the president said, "was murdered by the enemies of justice who for decades have used the rope and the gun and tar and feathers to terrorize their neighbors."

Johnson used the occasion to declare war on the Ku Klux Klan, announcing that he had directed the attorney general "to develop legislation that would bring the Klan under the effective control of the law." What Johnson did not reveal was the role of the FBI informer — a role of surveillance and penetration of the Klan that Johnson had urged on Hoover a year earlier.[12]

No sooner had the Selma march ended than King and his lieutenants again faced the continuing dilemma of how to sustain momentum in the quest for civil rights. Within the organization itself disagreements set in. Some staff members wanted to start a program of interracial dialogue between whites and blacks in southern cities. Others wanted to move the SCLC northward to tackle economic issues. Several wanted to continue the voter registration effort in Alabama. King, however, had another idea — one that he uncharacteristically seized impulsively, without adequate study or consideration of consequences.

King was anxiously focused on how he might keep the pressure on in Alabama following the dramatic events of the previous week. In an interview on NBC's *Meet the Press* on Sunday, March 28, King announced a new phase in the Alabama Project: an economic boycott. While vague on details, King proposed to end a "reign of terror" by asking labor unions, businesses, and the U.S. government to participate in an "economic withdrawal" from Alabama. He called for boycotting goods and withdrawing all investments from Alabama banks, and asked for the people of Alabama to refuse to pay state taxes until the racial situation improved.

"Conditions in Alabama have degenerated to such a low level of social disruption and man's inhumanity to man that the whole conscience of the nation must rise up," King argued. Wallace's refusal to accept the de-

---

* Johnson and King both praised Hoover for the arrests of Rowe, William Orville Easton, Collie Leroy Wilkins Jr., and Eugene Thomas. Even with the fine police work, Hoover could not resist trying to smear the Liuzzo family with his racism, his lurid preoccupation with interracial sex, and intimations that Mrs. Liuzzo used drugs and had served jail time and that her husband was associated with the mob. Hoover's reports to the president stressed how close Liuzzo and Mouton were seated in the car, and what appeared to be hypodermic needle marks on her arm. None of this information proved true; but Hoover seemed determined to show that anyone involved with the civil rights movement was either politically or morally suspect.

mands of the Selma-to-Montgomery march, combined with Viola Liuzzo's murder, had left him deeply pessimistic.[13]

News of King's proposal caught allies off guard and ignited a firestorm of criticism. Alabama's attorney general, Richmond Flowers, a moderate who had spoken out against Wallace's segregation efforts, warned that "a great many people would suffer that were not to blame and probably the greatest suffering would be among the Negroes of the state."[14] Syndicated columnist William S. White blasted King's boycott as "nothing less than the application of the principle of total warfare — against the just as well as the unjust, against the Alabama Negro as well as the Alabama white." Whitney Young expressed "reservations," and the *New York Times* described the general reception to the plan as "cool" in the nation's capital.[15]

When asked about the proposal, President Johnson was careful not to criticize King personally, but he noted that a boycott would hurt black Alabamans as well as whites. Behind the scenes, however, Johnson called for help from Andrew Brimmer, a young African American economist he had just promoted to serve as an assistant secretary of commerce. In an effort to persuade King to drop his boycott plans, Brimmer explained to the minister that steel — the chief export of Alabama — could not be boycotted, as it was virtually impossible to trace its origin. Though bewildered by Brimmer's complicated economic analysis, a disappointed King agreed to consider dropping the idea.[16]

Beyond Brimmer's argument of impracticality, Stanley Levison finally convinced King that he risked losing the vast constituency he had just won in Selma by venturing into very different areas — ones that the American public was unprepared for and would overwhelmingly reject. "The coalition of Selma and Montgomery, with its supporting millions," Levison warned, "is not a coalition with an unrestricted program. It is a coalition around a fairly narrow objective. It is basically a coalition for moderate change, for gradual improvements which are to be attained without excessive upheavals as it gently alters old patterns. It is militant only against shocking violence and gross injustice. It is not for radical change." In conclusion, Levison observed, "the American people are not inclined to change their society in order to free the Negro. They are ready to undertake some, and perhaps major reforms, but not to make a revolution."

For the moment, King accepted Levison's advice, but he worried incessantly about what might come next. He realized that new battlegrounds — questions of economic inequality, war and peace — would indeed be of a different order of magnitude.[17]

A Triumph for Voting Rights

In contrast with the excruciating pace of civil rights legislation in 1963–64, when ominous shadows of defeat were always present, the proposed 1965 Voting Rights Act got off to a fast start in Congress. Just three weeks after President Johnson declared to Congress, "We shall overcome," the bill moved forward in both the House and Senate.

On Friday, April 9, with few modifications made, Manny Celler's House subcommittee and Jim Eastland's Senate Judiciary Committee both completed their markups. The full House Judiciary Committee began its consideration the following Monday, and the entire House of Representatives scheduled action for April 21. The Senate debate began a day later. Majority Leader Mansfield optimistically predicted passage in a fortnight.

As in 1964, however, civil rights advocates faced a southern filibuster in the Senate. Once again, Everett Dirksen, the wily Republican minority leader who had previously expressed general support for a voting rights bill, held the key to defeating the filibuster on the administration's version. President Johnson wasted little time in trying to nail down Dirksen's support. By now, Dirksen and Johnson were like two well-matched boxers who had sparred in the ring together many times. Each knew how to counter the other's best moves. Theirs was a unique relationship — that of opponents, sometime allies, and solid friends. Neither wanted to knock the other out. The political game, properly played, would benefit both.

That game began on March 18, when Dirksen called Johnson to discuss two Republican vacancies on federal regulatory commissions — one at the Federal Trade Commission (FTC) and one at the Federal Power Commission (FPC). As usual, Dirksen wanted to select the Republican appointments, giving him a base of power throughout the executive branch. Yet on this occasion Dirksen's candidate for the FPC, an Illinois attorney named Carl Bagge, had generated considerable opposition.

Johnson and Dirksen began their usual thrust and parry: Dirksen would get his nominees, Johnson would again have his support for a civil rights bill. In another call on April 5, Johnson pushed Dirksen to stop maneuvering and bring the bill to a vote.[18]

During this time Lady Bird Johnson observed them "in earnest conversation in the West Hall, two brother artisans in government, heads close together." Two hours later, when Mrs. Johnson again passed through the West Hall, as she noted in her diary, "to my surprise I found Lyndon and Senator Dirksen in practically the same posture.

"You don't mind if we denounce you once in a while, do you, Lyndon?"

she heard Dirksen intone in his "great organ voice." "You can explain that better than when someone on *your* side of the aisle denounces you," Dirksen had continued. The president responded by telling Dirksen how, as Democratic minority leader during the Eisenhower administration, he had decided that he "was going to be with the President every time I could, when I thought what he was doing was for the best interest of the country." For his part, Dirksen intended to be with this president, at least on voting rights. He was appalled by the brutality in Selma. But in the bargain, Dirksen would try to get his price — and enhance his own power.[19]

Although it should have been easier than in 1964 to break the southerners' filibuster, this one too turned out to be a struggle. The southerners were weakened by their 1964 defeat, and by Senator Russell's absence as he battled emphysema. And even southern segregationists found it hard to explain on the Senate floor why black Americans should be barred from the ballot box. But Dirksen had used up much of his political capital and was having trouble maintaining discipline with his thirty-two Republicans, little more than a corporal's guard. As always, the conservative Republican senators were reluctant to tamper with the Senate's right to unlimited debate. Several of them also were genuinely concerned that the voting rights bill, with its strong assumption of federal power over voting procedures, was a usurpation of the proper balance between federal and states' rights. A battle to control what little power remained available to the Senate's small Republican minority then ensued. After the 1964 civil rights negotiations, when Dirksen had rarely consulted his colleagues, Senator Bourke Hickenlooper of Iowa, chairman of the Senate Republican Policy Committee, was determined to put a brake on Dirksen's unilateral power. Hickenlooper eventually relented, but valuable time was lost as summer began. Johnson and his White House staff feared a repeat of 1964's eruptions in several of the nation's inner cities.

Finally, the president, Dirksen, and Mansfield agreed on a bill. Their coalition defeated the Senate liberals, who wanted to ban the use of state poll taxes by federal law rather than through a constitutional court challenge. The vote on that proposed amendment was 49 to 45. On May 25 the southern filibuster was defeated on a cloture vote of 70 to 30. The following day the Senate passed the 1965 Voting Rights Act by a vote of 77 to 19. Two southern senators, Ross Bass and Albert Gore of Tennessee, took their leave of the Old Confederacy's "say never" philosophy and joined 1964 Civil Rights Act supporter Ralph Yarborough of Texas in voting in favor of the legislation. Three Republican senators who had voted against the 1964 Civil Rights Act — Bourke Hickenlooper of Iowa, Norris Cotton of New Hampshire, and Milward Simpson of Wyoming — now gave their support to the voting rights law, bowing to overwhelming public opinion that denying blacks the right to vote was unconscionable.

In the House, there arose a political rebellion of another sort. Representative Gerald Ford, the new minority leader, and his group of highly partisan young supporters decided that Johnson and the Democrats were getting too much credit for civil rights. In an effort to embarrass Johnson and slow down his legislative juggernaut, Ford and his supporters sought to paint the president as a hypocrite, citing his opposition to civil rights during the first twenty years of his congressional career. Asked at a press conference about his inconsistency on civil rights, Johnson made one of his few confessions of error. "I am going to try to provide all the leadership I can," he told the nation, "notwithstanding the fact that someone may point to a mistake or a hundred mistakes that I made in the past."[20]

The Republicans' efforts to pass their own substitute voting rights bill failed after southern segregationists rushed to support it, as it was weaker than the administration bill. Liberal and moderate Republicans then refused to vote with the segregationists.

On July 9 the Republican alternative was defeated 215 to 166, and the House version of the Voting Rights Act passed 333 to 85. Twenty-one southern Democrats, including Majority Whip Hale Boggs of Louisiana, cast their votes for civil rights.[21]

Still, passage was not assured. The conference committee, made up of six members of each body, struggled to work out language acceptable to all. The principal disagreement was over the House's insistence on abolishing poll taxes through legislation rather than through a court challenge. After two weeks of deliberations, President Johnson and Attorney General Katzenbach sought out the one man with the credibility to get both sides to agree to a compromise.

In a telephone call on July 7, Johnson and King had expressed their mutual concern that the voting rights bill still had not passed Congress. Johnson noted that the liberal coalition that had dominated the Eighty-ninth Congress and passed a record amount of legislation now was weakening. As the president had prophesied in January, he was gradually losing his grip on Congress by expending his political capital gained in the landslide 1964 presidential election. He pointed out to King that his proposal for the government to provide "rent supplements" to help the poor afford better housing had barely squeaked through the House. Partisanship was on the rise, said Johnson. They needed to end the stalemate on voting rights. Even though King had argued strongly in favor of including the repeal of the poll tax in the voting rights bill, he agreed that the time had come to compromise and pass the legislation. Once again, pragmatically working together, Johnson and King had made a mutual decision to advance civil rights.[22]

On July 29, Katzenbach sent the reluctant House liberals — still holding out for a poll tax ban — a letter, saying:

> Late last night, I discussed with Martin Luther King the proposed voting rights bill as it now stands in conference, and particularly the poll tax provision. Dr. King strongly expressed to me his desire that the bill promptly be enacted into law and said that he felt this was an overriding consideration. He expressed his understanding and appreciation of the difficulties in achieving satisfactory compromise in conference.
>
> With respect to the poll tax provision he expressed his view to me thusly: "While I would have preferred that the bill eliminate the poll tax at this time — once and for all — it does contain an express declaration by Congress that the poll tax abridges and denies the right to vote. In addition, Congress directs the Attorney General to 'institute forthwith' suits which will eliminate and prevent the use of the poll tax in the four States where it is still employed. I am confident that the poll tax provision of the bill — with vigorous action by the Attorney General — will operate finally to bury this iniquitous device."

A majority of the conferees agreed and submitted their final conference report. On August 3, 1965, the House voted in favor of the compromise legislation, 328 to 74, with seven more southerners than a month before. A day later, the Senate passed the identical bill by a 79–18 vote. Senator George Smathers, Democrat of Florida, unexpectedly switched and voted in favor, bringing the southern Senate supporters to four.[23]

In addition to working on pushing the Voting Rights Act through Congress, Johnson also was busy trying to push two other major components of his Great Society package: the Medicare and education bills. The Elementary and Secondary Education Act passed the House by a 263–153 margin only after a Johnson legislative full-court press. To avoid a conference committee, he had orchestrated the House version through the Senate with no amendments whatsoever, to pass 73 to 18 on April 9. Johnson had broken a generation-old deadlock on providing federal aid to elementary and secondary education. With Protestants opposed to any aid to parochial schools, and Catholics determined to block any bill that excluded them, there had always been a deadlock. The ingenious solution was for federal school aid to be targeted not at the schools but at the individual poor children who would benefit from added funds to help raise their educational achievement.[24]

Although the bill would benefit children across the nation, Johnson knew that the greatest beneficiaries would be poor minority children. On April 11, Palm Sunday, Johnson returned to the dilapidated one-room Johnson City schoolhouse he had first attended. On the school's front lawn, in the presence of Katie Deadrich, his first teacher, and several of the Mexican American students he had taught in Cotulla, Johnson signed the bill into law. "By passing this bill, we bridge the gap between helplessness and hope for more than 5 million educationally deprived children," Johnson declared. "As a son of a tenant farmer, I know that education is the only valid passport from poverty. . . . As President of the United States, I believe deeply no law I have signed or will ever sign means more to the future of America."[25]

Having already maneuvered committee chairmen Senator Harry Byrd of Virginia and Congressman Wilbur Mills of Arkansas to grant hearings on Medicare, Johnson continued to lobby members of the Senate until Congress finally passed the Medicare bill on July 28, 1965.[26]

President Johnson pointed out that the new Medicare law, under the Social Security system, would provide every American over sixty-five years of age with hospital and medical care.* The legislation also created Medicaid, a joint federal–state program that would provide free medical care to the poor of all ages. These measures, along with a 7 percent increase in Social Security payments, had an immediate combined effect of lifting tens of thousands of older Americans out of poverty.

Two days after passage, Johnson traveled to the Harry S. Truman Presidential Library in Independence, Missouri. There, as Johnson sat with his octogenarian predecessor, the thirty-third president of the United States welcomed the thirty-sixth. Truman, who had proposed a national health insurance program for senior citizens two decades earlier, clutched his

---

* To make sure that the members of the powerful American Medical Association (AMA), which had opposed the bill, would comply, Johnson initiated a meeting with its leaders. On July 30 at the White House, the president asked the assembled medical community to arrange to send American doctors to help serve Vietnamese civilians suffering in the escalating war. The doctors gave their enthusiastic agreement. Then Johnson brought reporters into the room as he praised the AMA members for their patriotic commitment to help in Vietnam. The news media representatives predictably asked whether the AMA would abide by the Medicare bill. "These men are going to get doctors to go to Vietnam where they might be killed. . . . Medicare is the law of the land. Of course they'll support the law of the land," Johnson said, goading the AMA leadership into confirming this for the reporters. "Of course we will," AMA president James Zappel responded. "We are, after all, law-abiding citizens."

cane, saying, "I am glad to have lived this long and to witness today the signing of the Medicare bill which puts this Nation right where it needs to be — to be right."

Johnson praised Truman's "tradition of leadership." But, Johnson added, "there is another tradition that we share today. It calls upon us never to be indifferent towards despair. It commands us never to turn away from helplessness. It directs us never to ignore or to spurn those who suffer untended in a land that is bursting with abundance." As Lyndon Johnson signed the bill, he handed President Truman a pen and an application form, personally enrolling Medicare's first participant. Within months, over 90 percent of the more than 19 million eligible Americans would follow suit.[27]

Freedom Is Not Enough

In passing the 1964 Civil Rights Act and pushing for a Voting Rights Act in 1965, Lyndon Johnson was reacting to a demand for change, stimulated by the brilliant civil rights campaigns executed by Dr. Martin Luther King in Birmingham and Selma. It had required strong leadership skills for the president to shepherd legislation successfully through Congress. But Johnson wanted to do more. He wanted to take the initiative on civil rights. He wanted to lead the civil rights movement in furthering the cause of poor African Americans. In a commencement speech on June 4, 1965, at Howard University, a predominantly black institution, Johnson urged the nation to take a further giant step toward equality.[28]

Sitting in the audience with 933 Howard graduates was twenty-one-year old Lynda Byrd Johnson, the president's elder daughter (herself a student at nearby George Washington University). Wanting her to witness what he viewed as a historic "second emancipation," he had brought her to the ceremony. On her father's face she noted a "camaraderie and shared sense of purpose" with Howard University president James Nabrit. Johnson began his address by talking about legal equality. He said that the 1957, 1960, and 1964 Civil Rights Acts and the 1965 Voting Rights Act would establish a solid basis of legal equality for black Americans. As proud as he was to have participated in the approval of each of these four civil rights laws, Johnson said, they were not enough.

"As Winston Churchill said of another triumph for freedom," he continued, the civil rights laws were not the end. "'It is not even the beginning of the end. But it is, perhaps, the end of the beginning.' That beginning is freedom; and the barriers to that freedom are tumbling down."

Then Johnson moved into very new territory. He began to talk about a new concept, which soon would become known as "affirmative action." "Freedom is not enough," said the president.

> You do not wipe away the scars of centuries by saying: Now you are free to go where you want, and do as you desire, and choose the leaders you please.
>
> You do not take a person who, for years, has been hobbled by chains and liberate him, bring him up to the starting line of a race and then say, "you are free to compete with all the others," and still justly believe that you have been completely fair. Thus it is not enough just to open the gates of opportunity. All our citizens must have the ability to walk through those gates.
>
> This is the next and the more profound stage of the battle for civil rights. We seek not just freedom but opportunity. We seek not just legal equity but human ability, not just equality as a right and a theory but equality as a fact and equality as a result. For the task is to give 20 million Negroes the same chance as every other American to learn and grow, to work and share in society, to develop their abilities — physical, mental and spiritual, and to pursue their individual happiness.
>
> To this end equal opportunity is essential, but not enough, not enough. Men and women of all races are born with the same range of abilities. But ability is not just the product of birth. Ability is stretched or stunted by the family that you live with, and the neighborhood you live in — by the school you go to and the poverty or the richness of your surroundings. It is the product of a hundred unseen forces playing upon the little infant, the child, and finally the man.

Johnson sounded a note of warning and of promise. He cautioned that one problem needing immediate attention was that of the decline of the black family:

> Only a minority — less than half — of all Negro children reach the age of 18 having lived all their lives with both of their parents. At this moment, tonight, little less than two-thirds are at home with both of their parents. Probably a majority of all Negro children receive federally-aided public assistance sometime during their childhood. . . .
>
> So, unless we work to strengthen the family, to create conditions under which most parents will stay together — all the rest: schools, and playgrounds, and public assistance, and private concern, will never be enough to cut completely the circle of despair and deprivation.[29]

Johnson finished by pledging a White House conference with the title and theme "To Fulfill These Rights." President Truman had organized a task force called "To Secure These Rights." Now that legal rights had been secured, it was time to get to work in fulfilling these new promises of equal rights for all, regardless of race.[30]

Johnson had offered the speech to King and to Roy Wilkins in advance and each had enthusiastically endorsed it. As a young Texas congressman, Johnson had opposed even the most modest civil rights efforts. Now he was working with the nation's preeminent African American leaders to venture beyond even their efforts to level the racial playing field, economically as well as legally.[31]

On August 4, the day the Voting Rights Act passed the Senate and was sent on to the president for his signature, Martin Luther King arrived for a three-day visit in Washington, D.C., the final stop in his tour of four northern cities, a tour that had started in Chicago, then moved on to Cleveland and Philadelphia. During his first day and a half in Washington, he visited many neighborhoods throughout the District of Columbia, meeting with residents and interested members of Congress to discuss the need for D.C. home rule.*

On his second day in Washington, King met for an hour with President Johnson in a conversation he would later describe to reporters as "fruitful and meaningful." Along with the SCLC's Walter Fauntroy and Ralph Abernathy, King listened as the president discussed his hopes for an upcoming White House Conference on Civil Rights. At that conference, the president said, he hoped that he and the participants would discuss how to advance some of the ideas for affirmative action for black Americans which he had set forth in the Howard University speech. For his part, King related his observations in visiting the black ghettoes of the northern cities. He feared especially that the northern ghetto was becoming "more intensified than dispersed" despite the Civil Rights Act of 1964. He told the president that "economic insecurity is very real in the Negro community," in both the South and the North. Johnson then asked King to submit a detailed report. King pledged to provide the president with a comprehensive set of recommendations.[32]

King wrapped up his day by leading a rally of five thousand in Lafayette Park in favor of home rule. He pledged to do whatever it took to "make justice a reality" by allowing District residents to elect their own local government. "We know Negroes can run this city as well as any white man,"

---

* Article 1, section 8, of the United States Constitution uniquely grants Congress the right to "exercise exclusive legislation" over "the Seat of the Government of the United States," so the ability of the residents of the predominantly black District of Columbia to govern themselves is entirely dependent on congressional legislation that no resident can vote on.

he told the cheering crowds. King was also careful to make clear that the purpose of the rally was not only to encourage support for self-government but also "to thank the great President of our nation for his stand" in favor of the effort.[33]

Nearly ninety years after the 1876 Hayes–Tilden compromise had ended southern Reconstruction and with it the guarantee of voting rights for black Americans, approximately seven months after King and the SCLC had kicked off their Selma drive, and exactly 104 years to the day after Abraham Lincoln had sat in the same room, signing legislation that freed all slaves who had served in the Confederate Army, Lyndon Johnson entered the President's Room, just off the Senate floor in the United States Capitol.[34]

It was just after noon on August 6, 1965. Moments earlier, the president had spoken in front of the two towering statues of Lincoln in the Capitol Rotunda, to an audience of hundreds. Dr. Martin Luther King Jr., Rosa Parks, Roy Wilkins, James Farmer, and other civil rights leaders sat in seats of honor. Vice President Hubert Humphrey and members of the United States Senate, House of Representatives, Cabinet, Joint Chiefs of Staff, and diplomatic corps took their places. While only a handful of congressional southerners were in the room, the Senate leader of the southern opposition to the bill, Louisiana's Allen J. Ellender, displayed his statesmanship by attending what he called a "good political speech" by his president.[35]

Beginning a forceful address, Johnson told the assembled guests and, through television and radio, the entire nation:

> Today is a triumph for freedom as huge as any victory that has ever been won on any battlefield. Yet to seize the meaning of this day, we must recall darker times.
>
> Three and a half centuries ago the first Negroes arrived at Jamestown. They did not arrive in brave ships in search of a home for freedom. They did not mingle fear and joy, in expectation that in this New World anything would be possible to a man strong enough to reach for it. They came in darkness and they came in chains.
>
> And today we strike away the last major shackle of those fierce and ancient bonds. Today the Negro story and the American story fuse and blend.

To his fellow southerners, Johnson made a special plea:

> It is difficult to fight for freedom. But I also know how difficult it can be to bend long years of habit and custom to grant it. There is no room for in-

justice anywhere in the American mansion. But there is always room for understanding toward those who see the old ways crumbling. And to them today I say simply this: It must come. It is right that it should come. And when it has, you will find that a burden has been lifted from your shoulders too.

It is not just a question of guilt, although there is that. It is that men cannot live with a lie and not be stained by it.[36]

The first president since Herbert Hoover, three decades earlier, to sign a piece of legislation in the Capitol building, Johnson grabbed one of the scores of fountain pens awaiting him. In this small room, with a hundred dignitaries looking on, sitting at the very desk he had used as Senate majority leader, Lyndon Baines Johnson began to sign the Voting Rights Act. Following presidential tradition, he signed his name, curve by curve, using as many different pens as possible. The souvenir pens were then distributed to the onlookers. Dr. King received one. So did Detective Sergeant Everett L. Cooper, the Metropolitan Police officer assigned to protect King.[37]

Next, Johnson made his way into the Senate chamber, as he had so many times throughout his twelve years as a senator and nearly three years as vice president. Majority Leader Mansfield greeted him as he reached the door: "We'll invite you in, Mr. President, if you want us to." Johnson joked, "I'm sorry, I forgot [that I no longer work here]." The Senate recessed to welcome the president, and Johnson moved to the front-row majority leader's seat that had been his for six years.

Senator Wayne Morse of Oregon, sitting in the presiding officer's seat, played along. "The Chair recognizes the Senator from Texas, the Majority Leader." Johnson gave Mansfield's chair back, quipping, "This seat is too hot for me."[38]

Self-deprecation aside, Lyndon Johnson, considered by historians to have been the most powerful majority leader in the history of the Senate, had just accomplished something few had ever imagined — signing not one but two groundbreaking civil rights laws in just over a year.

After the ceremony, King praised President Johnson for an "eloquent and persuasive speech," telling reporters that the new voting rights laws would "go a long way toward removing all the obstacles to the right to vote." Through King's dramatic Selma campaign and Johnson's legislative efforts, the two men had helped to achieve legal equality for all voting-age adults, at last fulfilling the promise made to America by the Fifteenth Amendment nearly a century before. It was, for two giants of the 1960s, as King had said, a "shining moment."[39]

13

✦ ✦ ✦ ✦ ✦ ✦ ✦

This Time the Fire

"General, be advised; He comes to bad intent."
— Iago, from William Shakespeare's *Othello*, act 1, scene 2

MARQUETTE FRYE, a twenty-one-year-old unemployed African American, was driving through his own neighborhood in South Central Los Angeles on a hot August night when his car was pulled over by a white California highway patrolman named Lee Minikus. Believing that Frye was intoxicated, Minikus gave him a sobriety test, which Frye failed. A disagreement developed after police officers refused to permit Frye's twenty-two-year-old brother, Ronald, to drive the car to their home, even though they lived only two blocks away; the officer insisted that only their mother could drive the vehicle. As the Frye brothers argued with the police, a crowd of neighbors began to gather in this predominantly black neighborhood just outside the Watts section of Los Angeles.

When their mother, Rena Frye, arrived on the scene, tempers flared. More officers were summoned as Mrs. Frye jumped on an officer's back and tore his shirt. After a scuffle in which police officers wielding batons subdued the two brothers, they and their mother were arrested. As California highway patrolmen and Los Angeles police officers departed with the Frye family in custody and their car attached to a tow truck, the growing crowd of onlookers — estimated at over one thousand people — erupted in anger, throwing stones at the departing police cars.

One of the deadliest race riots in American history was under way — only five days after Lyndon Johnson had signed the historic 1965 Voting Rights Act and handed one of the first pens to a beaming Dr. Martin Luther King Jr.

The violence in Watts flared quickly. As word of the arrests spread to surrounding neighborhoods, hundreds of irate black residents began stoning and overturning cars, assaulting white drivers, setting fire to white-owned businesses, looting and vandalizing the city. Twenty-nine arrests were made that first night, Wednesday, August 11. The next day, the Los Angeles Human Rights Commission held a mass meeting in an effort to calm tensions. This intervention failed, and the riots spread to other neighborhoods. Looting continued into Friday morning, August 13, when Mayor Sam Yorty, a gravelly voiced conservative Democrat, asked the office of Governor Pat Brown to call in the National Guard.*

Despite the increased police and new military presence, the rioting intensified. Soon, entire blocks were on fire. Firefighters attempting to combat the blazes were pelted with missiles. Gunfire sprayed the streets. On Friday night the fires and looting spread across fifty square miles of southeast Los Angeles, and the death toll began to mount. Watts had become a war zone.[1]

The Watts uprising delivered a jolt to Lyndon Johnson and Martin Luther King. Neither government officials nor civil rights leaders had expected or were prepared to cope with a massive urban uprising, especially in sunny southern California, where many in the black population lived in tree-lined neighborhoods with rows of neat bungalows and small, well-tended lawns, so different in appearance — at least on the surface — from the crowded tenements of eastern ghettoes. California had been seen as a promised land of freedom and opportunity for tens of thousands of blacks who had fled the segregated South during World War II for jobs in the West Coast defense industry. That opportunity had been realized by some African Americans, but too little attention had been paid, either by the government or by national civil rights leaders, as the industrial jobs disappeared from their cities, and new ghettoes developed with problems not unlike those in the East.

As the riot began, both Johnson and King were leaving on brief escapes from the unrelenting pressures of their jobs — Johnson to his Texas ranch for a long weekend, King to a resort hotel in Puerto Rico. At first, they both were slow to comprehend fully the gathering fury of the black storm rising in Los Angeles. Johnson had just signed the second monumental civil rights law approved by Congress in thirteen months. The riots in Los Angeles seemed to mock the triumph that Johnson and King had shared — and barely had time to savor.

In the privacy of the LBJ Ranch, Johnson's aides and family found the

---

* Governor Brown was in Europe when the riot began on August 11 and did not get back to California until August 14.

president depressed and withdrawn, so much so that he refused to accept urgent telephone calls about the situation in Watts. At the White House, Joseph Califano, Johnson's new assistant for domestic programs, tried unsuccessfully for two days to get the president to respond to a plea for federal help from California state officials. In the governor's absence, Lieutenant Governor Glenn Anderson desperately wanted the president to authorize the use of air force C-130 transport planes to move California National Guardsmen from northern California to Los Angeles, and to provide the California Guard with needed vehicles, tear gas, and other supplies. When Califano could not give him an answer, Anderson bluntly warned him, "If you don't provide support, the violence will rest on the White House's head."

After Defense Secretary McNamara and General Creighton Abrams, deputy chief of staff of the U.S. Army, strongly recommended approval of the California Guard's request, Califano finally dared to issue the order himself. After the president learned what Califano had done, only a timely appeal from White House aide Jack Valenti saved Califano's job.[2]

At the LBJ Ranch, Valenti watched a distressed Lyndon Johnson retreat to the comforting company of his family and a few close Texas friends. The president took long walks with Lady Bird, drove his car alone on inspection tours around his ranch, and took family and friends out for a long boat ride on Lake Lyndon Baines Johnson. After his bold, politically risky efforts to improve life for black Americans, Johnson reacted to the Watts riot as a personal insult, a slap in the face. "How is it possible?" Johnson wondered. "After all we've accomplished. How could it be?"

"You can't go by this," Valenti tried to console him. "It's not a referendum on you. Just poor people being upset."

"Why couldn't the police and firemen bring this under control?" Johnson lamented to Valenti. "Didn't anyone plan? Didn't anyone understand this undercurrent of dissatisfaction and these desperate feelings?"[3]

On Saturday, August 14, the fourth day of the riots, Johnson finally authorized White House press secretary Bill Moyers to issue a statement that sought to balance a call for law and order with a willingness to listen to grievances from Watts: "The events of the past two days in Los Angeles are tragic and shocking. . . . I urge every person in a position of leadership to make every effort to restore order in Los Angeles. Killing, rioting and looting are contrary to the best traditions of this country.

"We are deeply committed to the fulfillment of every American's constitutional rights. We have worked hard to protect those rights but rights will not be won with violence. Equal rights carry equal responsibilities."

The *New York Times* described the tone of the president's message as "disturbed and chagrined."[4]

When President Johnson finally spoke with Califano that Saturday, his tone had turned from one of anger and self-pity to a deep sadness and fear that his dreams for the Great Society would be doomed by nihilistic rioters and an angry white backlash against civil rights and poverty programs. Johnson wanted white America to understand the plight of blacks in Watts, "out of work, living in filth, homes torn up." And he fretted to Califano that black Americans could lose their recent hard-won gains by repeating the excesses that marked the era of Reconstruction — as he put it, that "Negroes will end up pissing in the aisles of the Senate" and "will once again take unwise actions out of frustration, impatience, and anger."*

President Johnson finally snapped out of his despondence on Sunday afternoon and energetically took command. If California needed military aid, including the use of regular army troops, Johnson told Califano, "I'll approve it so quick, it will make your head spin." As for programs to help the citizens of Watts, Johnson said, "Let's move in money, marbles, and chalk!"[5]

Three days later, Johnson called former CIA director John McCone, urging him to head a commission that Governor Brown was organizing to investigate the Watts uprising. "We are on a powder keg in a dozen places," the president told McCone. "You have no idea of the depth of feeling of these people. I see some of the boys that have worked for me, have two thousand years of persecution, and now they suffer from it. They have absolutely nothing to live for; 40 percent of them are unemployed. These youngsters live with rats and have no place to sleep, and they all start from broken homes and illegitimate families. . . . And we have isolated them, and they are all in one area, and when they move in, why we move out. . . . We have just got to find some way to wipe out these ghettoes and find some housing and put them to work!"

The governor's commission on the Los Angeles riots, known as the McCone Commission, as well as a report to Johnson from federal officials, would paint a stark picture basically confirming the problems that he had so vividly described in the days after the riot: high unemployment, overcrowded housing, failing schools, high crime rates, alcoholism and

---

* During the decade of Reconstruction after the Civil War, freed southern blacks, many with little or no formal education, briefly held many elective and appointed government offices, including seats in the U.S. Senate.

narcotics addiction, isolation from the rest of the city, a sense of hopelessness, police brutality and insensitivity, and lack of health care.[6]

Martin Luther King and his personal assistant Bernard Lee were passing through the Miami airport on their way to a vacation in Puerto Rico when reports reached King that the riot in Watts was spreading. Black ministers in Los Angeles were asking that he come to help them restore order and negotiate for relief with the mayor and police department. After consulting Bayard Rustin, King determined that there was little he could accomplish in Los Angeles. As in Harlem a year earlier, he feared that he would wind up again trapped in the political crossfire, criticized by both blacks and whites. Like Lyndon Johnson, King was finding it difficult to confront the nightmare now threatening the realization of his bright dreams. On his second day in San Juan, however, after more urgent requests for help, King suddenly decided that he must indeed go to Los Angeles.

King met Rustin and SCLC executive director Andrew Young in Los Angeles on Tuesday, August 17, just as the six-day riot was finally subsiding. Passing through block after block of devastation, King was shaken by the destruction wrought by the rioters and appalled that angry young black youths were shouting claims of victory — boasting that they finally had got the attention of city officials and the nation. King lamented to Young that the destruction evidenced his own personal failure to get across his message of nonviolence. Young replied that King must not take it "so personally," but should realize that violence ran through the fabric of American history, an elemental force not easily tamed even by the exhortations of a Martin Luther King.[7]

As with Lyndon Johnson, hubris had led King to grand assumptions about how much his message and accomplishments had meant to African Americans across the country. In the glowing optimism of the early 1960s, with the economy booming, then with King and Johnson scoring hard-won but significant victories, it was easy to overestimate those accomplishments while naïvely underestimating the intractability of the problems of race and poverty in America. Like Johnson, King was quickly awakening to a deepening realization of just how much more needed to be done to bring racial justice and harmony to the nation. For Johnson and King, and for their countrymen, Watts was a defining moment — an ominous one.

King was rattled as well by the depth of alienation and despair he discovered among African Americans there. As he addressed hundreds of local residents at the Westminster Community Center, he was greeted by boos from hecklers, including one Black Muslim who yelled, "Get out of here, Dr. King! We don't want you!" Another young man shouted, "We don't need your dreams; we need jobs!"

While some local black leaders embraced King's visit, others publicly charged that he was more of a distraction than a help. With Watts, King came to a fuller awareness that the two great civil rights laws of 1964 and 1965 basically addressed the evils of *southern* segregation but had barely touched the ghetto's problems of poverty, joblessness, isolation, family disintegration, and hopelessness.

"I worked to get these people the right to eat hamburgers," he told Rustin that night in Watts, "and now I've got to do something . . . to help them get the money to buy it."

A day later King looked into the face of California's white hostility and racism. He met for three futile hours with Mayor Yorty and Los Angeles chief of police William Parker. To King's chagrin, Chief Parker belligerently denied any claims of police brutality or discrimination against black people — people whom Parker had publicly demeaned as "monkeys." Incensed by Parker's rude denials and Yorty's unwillingness "to grant just a few concessions to bring about a new sense of hope," King emerged from the meeting to demand Parker's immediate dismissal. Beneath the thinnest veneer of civility, King concluded, Parker and Yorty were cut from the same cloth as Police Commissioner Bull Connor in Birmingham and Sheriff Jim Clark in Selma.*[8]

King told reporters that the riots had been "a class revolt of underprivileged against privileged," explaining that "the main issue is economic."[9] Watts confirmed his earlier conclusion that the SCLC's next campaign must venture out of the South to focus on poverty and despair in the urban ghettoes of the North. Even in his brief visit, King recognized the same desperate problems he had seen earlier in Chicago, Cleveland, and Philadelphia. With Watts, Martin Luther King began moving toward a far more radical critique of what ailed American society.

By the time the 14,000 National Guardsmen and 1,500 local officers had restored order, the six-day riot had claimed the lives of 34 people, with another thousand reported injured. Arrests totaled 3,438 adults and 514 youths.† More than 600 buildings were burned or looted, with more than $40 million in damage. In steamy Los Angeles, all of King's and Johnson's

* The president's high-ranking team of federal officials encountered similar hostility from Parker and Yorty when they visited the city officials. Andrew Brimmer, a young black assistant secretary of commerce, detected a crude slur even in their introduction. After shaking Brimmer's hand, Yorty wiped off his own hand with his handkerchief (AI, Andrew Brimmer).

† In the midst of the riot, Marquette Frye, whose arrest had triggered the racial explosion, quietly pled guilty and paid a fine for driving while intoxicated.

optimistic political formulations for achieving racial and social justice in America had been severely challenged.[10]

Before King left California on August 20, the civil rights leader called President Johnson to report on the crisis. In their Oval Office conversation only two weeks earlier, they had agreed on the importance of tackling the problems of urban poverty. But Watts now added a new urgency and political complexity to determining what could be done to help the inner-city ghettoes.

"What is frightening," King told the president, "is to hear all of these tones of violence from [black] people out there in Watts. . . . And the minute that happens, there will be retaliation from the white community. People have bought up guns. . . . I'm fearful that if something isn't done to give a new sense of hope to people in that area, [a] full-scale race war can develop. . . . I'm not optimistic about the outcome."

"Well, now, what should we do about it?" asked the president. "What is your recommendation?"

"If they could get, in the next few days, this poverty program going in Los Angeles, I believe that it would help us," replied King.[11]

Johnson assured King that federal agencies were preparing an emergency $25 million aid package with programs ranging from Head Start for preschool children to job training. But both men knew that the Watts aid package represented only a small symbolic beginning — and even that initial effort had earlier been rejected by Mayor Yorty.

Johnson warned King that the successful political calculus that had produced their earlier victories for civil rights and poverty programs had been jarred not only by a white backlash — further fueled by the Watts riot — but also by telltale signs of a decline in the president's own political power. As an example, Johnson noted that his proposal for nearly doubling the 1966 budget for the poverty programs had barely prevailed by a 44–43 vote in the Senate* — and that only after Johnson had lobbied relentlessly and persuaded the governors of Indiana and Nevada to ask their senators to support the bill.

Johnson explained that he had already spent much of the political capital he had won in the 1964 presidential landslide. As the election receded, he admitted, "that crowd is not supporting me anymore." Governors and mayors were "just raising the dickens." His opponents in Congress, Johnson complained, were "determined to destroy, to scandalize" his poverty programs.

---

* The Senate was divided not only on the level of spending but also on a provision that would give governors the right to veto poverty programs. Johnson resisted, but eventually had to concede limited veto powers to the states.

The opposition stemmed from a variety of sources. State and local officials were becoming wary of federal antipoverty programs, seeing them as transferring their own power to federal bureaucrats allied with radical advocates for the poor. Even staunch liberal allies in Congress such as Senator Abraham Ribicoff of Connecticut were complaining to the president about confusion and lack of coordination in the new programs. In those earlier heady moments of passing Great Society and War on Poverty legislation, there was little immediate reflection by either President Johnson or civil rights leaders — including King — that the rhetorical claims for the poverty programs far exceeded any proven knowledge of what they might accomplish. But Johnson had consciously moved ahead at lightning speed — "shoving in his stack of chips" — to accomplish what he could while his mandate held and he could capitalize on his vast experience and skills at passing legislation. Implementing the programs, getting adequate funds, the trial-and-error process of discovering what would work best — all that would be dealt with later. A full realization of the complexity and difficulty of changing the lives of the poor in urban and rural ghettoes was still years away. For the moment, the growing opposition in Congress consisted mainly of southerners who equated antipoverty programs with civil rights and Republicans who saw a partisan opportunity to stop the Johnson juggernaut.

Johnson also wanted King to know that the white backlash, fueled by the Watts riot, demanded a different kind of presidential rhetoric. He did not want King to misunderstand his tough statement, several days earlier, that "a rioter with a Molotov cocktail was no different than a Klansman with a bomb." If he were to sustain and build the poverty programs, the president could not appear to be rewarding rioters.* Yet he wanted King to know that he was still passionately committed — that he had combined his tough call for law and order with a plea for the nation to "find a cure, and go in and correct these conditions in the ghetto — housing, rats eating the children, hunger, unemployment. We are all God's children and we better get at it."

Johnson, King, and Vietnam

Before their conversation ended, Johnson raised another sensitive issue with King. The president edged into the subject by noting that members of Congress had "the impression that you are against me in Vietnam."

"You better not leave that impression," Johnson told King. "I want

* To avoid criticism that he was appeasing rioters, Johnson demanded that the Watts emergency aid package be prepared in total secrecy.

peace as much as you do, and more so, because I am the fellow that wakes up in the morning with a report that fifty of our boys died last night. These [North Vietnam] folks just will not come to the conference table."

Johnson wanted King to discuss Vietnam with Arthur Goldberg, the former Supreme Court justice who had recently been named U.S. ambassador to the United Nations. Goldberg would explain to King "what he is trying to do behind the scenes" to achieve a settlement, Johnson said, "if we have enough strength out there to hold on and not get discouraged, and we can ever get [the North Vietnamese] to the conference table. We just have to get them to the table because there is no use in shooting when you can talk. . . . Let's not let this country get divided."[12]

Although King readily agreed to meet with Goldberg, the president and the civil rights leader were shadowboxing, avoiding a frank discussion of how each felt about the other's position on the war. King knew full well that if he followed his moral inclination to speak out against the president's foreign policy, it would seriously risk his ability to influence Johnson on poverty and civil rights. As he ramped up the war, Johnson became far more sensitive to outside criticism, particularly from trusted national figures who could influence public opinion. After Watts, and facing a more conservative climate in Congress, Johnson and King had never needed each other's support more to sustain the drive for civil rights and the war on poverty. And so they politely dissembled — King saying that he supported the president's position on the necessary conditions for a negotiated peace settlement, and Johnson pretending that he knew little about King's emerging views on Vietnam. Yet Johnson, in fact, was in the midst of secretly committing the United States to a major land war in Vietnam, a war that King's conscience now impelled him to oppose.

As Watts burned, Lyndon Johnson and Martin Luther King were making their own fateful decisions about the war in Vietnam, the flames from which would scar the American experience just as painfully as the urban riots that engulfed the nation's cities. Ironically, Johnson made his most fateful plunge into the Vietnam quagmire at precisely the triumphal moment when he succeeded in leading the nation's quest to fulfill its founders' ideal for a just society.

That a profound American commitment had just been made to the Vietnam conflict was not readily apparent from President Johnson's subdued remarks at a press conference in the East Room of the White House at 12:30 P.M. on Wednesday, July 28.

"I have asked General [William] Westmoreland [the U.S. commander in Vietnam] what more he needs to meet this mounting aggression," the president began. "He has told me. We shall meet his needs. . . . I have to-day ordered to Vietnam . . . forces that will increase our fighting strength from 75,000 to 125,000 men." He conceded, "Additional forces will be needed later, and they will be sent as requested."

When a reporter asked whether the dispatch of more troops implied any change in U.S. policy, the president replied, "It does not imply any change in policy whatever."[13]

Johnson had now reached the point where the war in Vietnam was affecting the War on Poverty and his other programs. He worried that the battle in Asia would consume both the attention and the funds needed to fulfill his ambitious plans to create a "Great Society." At this point, however, he refused to face the reality that it was probably impossible to have both guns and butter on a national scale. He was determined to win both wars, at any cost. Johnson dissembled about the war in Vietnam to put off a judgment day — handling it badly, in part, to protect his bold domestic agenda. He was trapped by his fear that withdrawal from Vietnam without an honorable settlement would destroy his presidency, the Democratic Party, and the domestic reforms he wanted as his legacy.

Johnson's announcement came after an agonizing month-long debate in which the president and his national defense advisers considered options in Vietnam ranging from withdrawing, to standing pat, to a major expansion of forces. The third course was chosen, but its announcement was veiled in deception by a tormented president unwilling to tell the American public that he was leading the country into a major land war — one that would cost thousands of American lives.[14]

What Johnson actually had committed the nation to was an increase of American forces by 200,000 troops — not the 50,000 he had just announced — and an additional expenditure of billions of dollars to support them, not the $700 million supplemental appropriation he had requested from Congress. The clear mission of those troops would be ground combat against the Viet Cong and North Vietnamese troops, *not* the earlier job of protecting U.S. air bases while the South Vietnamese did the ground fighting. Furthermore, Johnson took those profoundly grave steps without calling up reserve forces, as his advisers unanimously recommended.

Johnson's pessimism about Vietnam had existed from the very beginning. On only his third day as president, after receiving a grim report on the continuing disintegration of the South Vietnamese government and its armed forces, Johnson had told Bill Moyers that the situation in Vietnam was hopeless. He never changed that view. With the escalation that he announced in July 1965, the best result the president could hope for was finally to persuade the North Vietnamese to agree to a negotiated settlement. And the odds of that happening, the president told Senator Richard Russell at the time, were only a meager 5 percent.[15]

Johnson persisted for many reasons, which he offered to Moyers, other close aides, his friends, and national defense officials. For one thing, he did not intend to be the first American president to lose a war. As he put it in his Texas vernacular, "I do not intend to cut and run." He firmly believed in the Cold War thinking that had guided American defense and foreign policy since the end of World War II. Namely, he believed that a defeat in South Vietnam would lead to further losses to Communism in Southeast Asia and elsewhere in the world. Cold War orthodoxy, subscribed to by every American president since Harry Truman, held that Communism was a unified force in which the Soviet Union, China, and other countries such as North Vietnam relentlessly pursued a common agenda of world domination. The American commitment began in 1954, as the Eisenhower administration came to the aid of South Vietnam after the Communists had driven out the French colonial rulers. From then on, American presidents had subscribed unquestioningly to the doctrine that the loss of South Vietnam would trigger a "domino effect," toppling other Asian countries in its wake.

In the White House deliberations preceding the July 28 escalations, Johnson ignored his advisers' strong recommendation that he level with Congress and the American public about the breadth and possible costs of the new commitment.* Without full support from Congress and the public, defense officials argued, it was questionable whether the nation could long sustain the cost in lives and in dollars. Johnson's stated reason for stealth was to avoid encouraging North Vietnam and its Soviet and Chinese allies to match the U.S. escalation. But other reasons guided the president's dissembling. As an essential part of his modus operandi, secrecy had always been a means of keeping his options open, of maintaining an element of surprise. As he later explained, "I was determined to keep the war from shattering that dream [of a Great Society], which meant I simply had no choice but to keep my foreign policy in the wings. I knew the Congress as well as I knew Lady Bird, and I knew that the day

---

* In stark contrast with his Voting Rights Act speech, made to a joint session of Congress and national television audience in evening prime time, Johnson purposefully made his troop announcement in early afternoon, hoping that it would receive far less public attention and scrutiny.

that it exploded into a major debate on the war, that day would be the beginning of the end of the Great Society."[16]

As one after another of his major legislative initiatives passed through critical congressional hurdles that July, Johnson grew increasingly sensitive about revealing any Vietnam developments that might hurt his domestic programs. He stalled release of news, for example, that Chinese MIG fighters had shot down a U.S. plane over the South China Sea just as the Senate faced a critical vote on the administration's education bill. "I just hope we don't get too much information too quick up at the Senate before they pass that education bill," Johnson cautioned Undersecretary of State George Ball.[17] Johnson's overriding worry was to forestall the ominous argument over whether the nation could afford both guns and butter.

At the July 28 press conference the president plaintively revealed just how concerned he was that Vietnam should not derail the plans he cared about most:

> When I was young, poverty was so common that it didn't have a name. Education was something you had to fight for, and water was life itself. I have now been in public life 35 years — and in each of those years I have seen good men struggle to bring the blessings of this land to all of our people.
>
> And now I am the President. It is now my opportunity to help every child get an education, to help every Negro and every American citizen have an equal opportunity, to have every family get a decent home, and to help bring healing to the sick and dignity to the old.
>
> As I have said before, that is what I have lived for, that is what I have wanted all my life since I was a little boy. And I do not want to see all those hopes and all those dreams of so many people for so many years now drowned in the wasteful ravages of cruel wars.[18]

Martin Luther King's initiative to influence public opinion about the Vietnam War had grown out of his December 1964 trip to Oslo to receive the Nobel Peace Prize. Wrapped in the Nobel mantle, King saw for himself both an opportunity and a responsibility to speak out on issues that were broader than that of American civil rights. He advocated nonviolent resistance as a means to further human rights in South Africa and other countries, and to advance the cause of world peace. As American involvement in Vietnam deepened in the spring and summer of 1965, King began, in his public statements, to question the U.S. role there. He saw the war not only as morally questionable but also as a growing commitment likely to divert resources needed to solve problems of poverty at home.

At the annual convention of the Southern Christian Leadership Conference in Birmingham on August 12, 1965, Dr. King purposefully staked out his role as a peacemaker. He announced that he planned to write to the Vietnam combatants, calling on them to reach a negotiated settlement. He would appeal to both President Johnson and President Ho Chi Minh of North Vietnam, as well as to leaders of South Vietnam, the Viet Cong insurgents in South Vietnam, the Soviet Union, and China.

"What is required is a small first step that may establish a new spirit of mutual confidence and respect — a step capable of breaking the cycle of mistrust, violence and war," King declared. He called on President Johnson to make "unconditional and unambiguous statements" of his willingness to negotiate with the Viet Cong and to consider halting the bombing of North Vietnam. To appear evenhanded, King acknowledged "that President Johnson has demonstrated a greater desire to negotiate than the Hanoi and Beijing governments."[19]

To King's surprise, his publicized venture into foreign policy drew immediate criticism from within his own SCLC. "I question whether it is wise for us to go too far in the international arena," said board member Benjamin Hooks, a Memphis minister. Hooks and other civil rights leaders believed that it was a mistake to dilute the focus and resources of the civil rights movement — especially in opposition to a president who was at the peak of his power as a champion for the cause for black equality. The board affirmed King's right to express his own views but stressed that "the primary function of our organization is to secure full citizenship rights for the Negro citizens of this country."[20]

On Vietnam as on other issues, King was buffeted by conflicting pressures. Militant peace groups were urging him to take a stand on Vietnam, as were several of his most influential lieutenants. James Bevel, who had been a driving force in both the Birmingham and Selma campaigns, publicly pushed King to add a peace initiative to the SCLC agenda. Similar pressure came from SNCC — an outright opponent of the war, as well as a challenger to King for the allegiance of youths in the urban ghettoes. Yet King also knew that a majority of stalwart black leaders agreed with Hooks that the civil rights movement should stick to its own mission, which was difficult enough. And King was ever mindful of the risky consequences of crossing the powerful Lyndon Johnson.

When King spoke out about the president's conduct of the war, he predictably aroused Johnson's ire. But the manner in which Johnson learned about King's activities had still another powerful effect: it fed the president's paranoia.

By virtue of FBI wiretaps, Johnson had a week's notice of what King would say about Vietnam at the SCLC convention. Although J. Edgar Hoover's efforts to stop Johnson from working with King had been thus far unsuccessful, Johnson had continued to read the FBI's frequent reports and wiretap summaries. The president was kept well informed not just about King's Vietnam plans but about King's private conversations, too, including ones in which he discussed his feelings about LBJ. The information was delivered eagerly by Hoover from wiretaps not only on King's phones but also on those of King's chief strategic advisers in New York — Stanley Levison, Bayard Rustin, and attorney Clarence Jones. When those members of what King called his "research committee" met with him in his hotel rooms, the FBI was often able to place electronic microphones as well.[21]

As King ventured deeper into the politics of Vietnam, Johnson and Hoover, each for his own reasons, paid renewed attention to the relationship between King and his "research committee," particularly Levison. For obvious reasons, the president did not want the nation's most respected civil rights leader to emerge as a powerful voice against his Vietnam policy. Meanwhile, for Hoover, King's involvement with Vietnam presented a new opportunity to achieve his stated objective of destroying King. During the previous year, Hoover had failed in his relentless campaign to disgrace King by exposing him as an adulterer. Despite its many efforts, the FBI could not enlist either public figures or reporters to help carry out Hoover's attempt at character assassination. Now, Hoover returned to his original argument: Martin Luther King was a menace to American national security because he was influenced by Stanley Levison.

In Hoover's memos to the president, the FBI's boilerplate description of Levison as "a long-time communist" with "secret membership in the Communist Party, USA" now included the added phrase "who has been influencing Martin Luther King, Jr., concerning the Vietnam situation."* In the five weeks before King finally fulfilled the president's request to meet with U.N. ambassador Arthur Goldberg, Hoover bombarded John-

---

* The FBI also used standard descriptions of King's other advisers. Bayard Rustin was always described as a member of the Young Communist League in the early 1940s who had served three years in prison as a conscientious objector during World War II and served jail time in 1948 and 1953 after pleading guilty to illegal homosexual activities. Jones was identified as "having held a position of leadership during the mid-1950's in the Labor Youth League, an organization which has been designated subversive." Harry Wachtel, another close adviser, was identified as having been "in the late 1940s a member of the National Lawyers Guild, an organization which has been cited a communist front by the House Committee on Un-American Activities."

son with memos providing details to show that Levison was indeed playing a major role in advising King on Vietnam, as well as in writing his speeches and magazine articles.[22]

King and Goldberg met on September 10 in the ambassador's office in New York. The president had hoped that Goldberg, one of the nation's most skilled labor negotiators, would convince King that the United States was doing everything possible to bring the North Vietnamese to the bargaining table. Instead, King left the ambassador's office to issue an already prepared statement — which the president took as a stinging rebuke to his foreign policy. King had used his U.N. platform again to call on the United States to include the Viet Cong in peace negotiations, to stop bombing North Vietnam, to advocate a seat for Communist China in the United Nations, and to reassess American foreign policy.[23]

A day later, Senator Thomas Dodd of Connecticut — a reliable Johnson ally often used by the president as his unofficial spokesman for attacking critics — excoriated King for meddling. "King has absolutely no competence to speak about complex matters of foreign policy," Dodd told reporters. "And it is nothing short of arrogant when Dr. King takes it upon himself to thus undermine the policies of the United States and to enter into personal negotiations with the heads of hostile governments." He added: "When Dr. Martin Luther King takes advantage of his pulpit as a prime leader of the civil rights movement to call for Red China's admission into the United Nations, he ventures into dangerous waters. But when he advocates that the United States reorient its foreign policy along lines of accommodation with the Communists then I can only regret that such intemperate alignment with the forces of appeasement has alienated much of the support he has enjoyed in Congress." Furthermore, Dodd suggested that King, in his plan to communicate with foreign leaders about Vietnam, might have violated the Logan Act, which forbids private citizens from interfering with foreign policy.[24]

A chorus of voices joined in criticizing King. His friend Whitney Young, director of the National Urban League, stated that King did "the cause of civil rights a disservice" by linking it with the Vietnam issue.[25] An editorial in the Washington Evening Star ridiculed King as a "home-made foreign policy expert" who, if he chose to venture into fields other than civil rights, might choose for criticism "the Broadway stage" or "the rising hemline on women's dresses," among "a hundred fields of human endeavor in which he can do less harm and in which he is at least as well qualified as in foreign policy." Criticism came as well from longtime liberal supporters. Syndicated editorial cartoonist Bill Mauldin portrayed a baffled-looking King stuck on a horse labeled "civil rights" in the midst of a Vietnamese rice paddy.[26]

Stung by the public outcry, King quickly retreated from his foreign policy venture, while President Johnson closely observed King's agony through the prism of the FBI wiretaps. As Deke DeLoach hand-delivered to the White House the latest inside information on King's retreat, Johnson aide Marvin Watson relayed it to the Oval Office with his own telling summaries.* Watson's cover sheet on a Hoover memo to Johnson read: "Martin Luther King is convinced that you persuaded Senator Dodd to criticize his public stand after his conference with Ambassador Goldberg. King said that he is not strong enough to carry on two struggles at the same time, the civil rights battle and the Vietnam peace struggle. He says that he had to conceive some graceful means whereby he can withdraw since he is convinced that his plea would be rebuffed by Ho Chi Minh."

The accompanying two-page memo quoted King as saying that he "must forget the peace issue and get back to civil rights" since he had concluded that he "cannot battle these forces who are out to defeat my influence. They will take the Communist China thing and what Dodd said and use it to say that I am under the influence of the Communists which may confuse some of our supporters and contributors." King told his advisers that the growing amount of time devoted to Vietnam had left him "emotionally fatigued."†

The White House campaign had succeeded. King dropped his idea about writing to Ho Chi Minh and other international leaders, and for the time being at least, he stopped criticizing the president. King was shaken by criticism coming, for the first time, not from right-wing segregationists but from mainstream public figures and news media that regularly praised him. His discomfort was heightened by the fear that President Johnson could pick up the telephone and unleash the critics. King also recognized two other sobering realities: American public opinion, white and black, still strongly supported the president on the war; and most

---

* King, following the counsel of advisers on good terms with the FBI, had sent DeLoach a congratulatory telegram on his promotion to assistant director of the FBI, the third-most-powerful position in the agency.

† In the FBI transcript of a conversation between Stanley Levison and Clarence Jones on September 13, 1965, Levison says of King's U.N. press conference performance, "I think the idea of [King's] coming out for the admission of Red China at this time is insane, after taking a position on Vietnam." Always pragmatic and politically savvy, Levison was conservative in trying to keep King from being portrayed as an irresponsible "bomb thrower" and to avoid being associated with others stereotyped as dangerous radicals. He strove for King's acceptance as a responsible mainstream leader.

Americans still trusted the judgments of their national leaders about Vietnam and did not recognize the competence of celebrities — or civil rights leaders — to make those judgments.

Lyndon Johnson gained little satisfaction from muzzling King. Instead, he grew increasingly agitated about King and anyone else who questioned his Vietnam policy — even though it was a policy in which Johnson himself had little faith. Making the decision to escalate the war had left him so depressed that his wife and closest aides feared for his mental health. As he weighed the Vietnam decision on July 8, he told Lady Bird: "Things are not going well here. Vietnam is getting worse every day. I have the choice to go in with great casualty lists or to get out with disgrace. It's like being in an airplane and I have to choose between crashing the plane or jumping out. I don't have a parachute." The first lady concluded her diary entry with, "It's a bad time all around."[27]

Press secretary Bill Moyers worried that Johnson was showing signs of "paranoia," a tendency that at times could affect the president's critical judgment on affairs of state. Lady Bird was also deeply concerned about her husband's erratic mood swings and behavior under pressure of the dilemma of what to do about Vietnam.[28]

To Johnson's aides, the most troubling problem was that the president had begun to perceive opponents of his war plans as guided by sinister designs or forces — particularly the Communists, or anyone associated with the Kennedy family. Bill Moyers, speechwriter Richard Goodwin, and White House counsel Harry McPherson were deeply concerned. Each had been exposed to new Johnson tirades. Moyers and Goodwin read medical texts and consulted with psychiatrists. They even considered taking their concerns to high administration officials, but never did.

"You know, Dick," Johnson told Goodwin on July 5, 1965, "the communists are taking over the country." Lifting a manila folder from his desk, the president said, "Look here. It's Teddy White's FBI file and he's a communist sympathizer."*[29]

If Johnson suspected that he was surrounded by enemies, J. Edgar Hoover was eager to supply proof. He inundated the president with FBI intelligence reports on dozens of people involved in some way with discussions of foreign policy, especially Vietnam. Like Iago to Shakespeare's *Othello,* Hoover appeared to be running his own smear campaign, with

---

* White, a former *Life* magazine correspondent, was author of the series of election histories called *The Making of the President.* In another conversation, Johnson told his staff that "the Communists already control the three major networks and the forty major outlets of communications" (Robert Dallek, *Flawed Giant,* p. 281).

Lyndon Johnson as his principal customer. And like Iago, Hoover knew his man's biases and weaknesses, and nourished them with his own brand of poison. The reports that poured out of Hoover's office onto Johnson's desk were characterized by accusations often based on the skimpiest of evidence, on information from unreliable sources or rumors or just plain conjecture. The FBI files gave the president a convenient rationale for accusing anyone who opposed him — whether Martin Luther King Jr. or members of the U.S. Congress such as Senator William Fulbright of Arkansas, chairman of the Foreign Relations Committee — of being "Communist-inspired."*

Harry McPherson, a soft-spoken lawyer with Texas roots, a skilled speechwriter with a literary bent, and a "moderate liberal" in White House debates, tried to reason with the president about his growing fears that his closest national defense advisers were disloyal to him. In a memorandum to the president, McPherson attempted to reassure Johnson that Secretary of Defense McNamara and other former aides to President John F. Kennedy were loyally serving him — rather than trying to further the interests of Robert Kennedy.

Normally, Lyndon Johnson was a shrewd judge of human nature, of people's abilities, motives, intelligence, and reliability. He understood Hoover's biases and personal agenda, as he did those of other men with whom he dealt. And, like Hoover, the president used his knowledge of other people to achieve his aims. What now most concerned Lady Bird Johnson and aides such as Moyers and Goodwin, however, was at times the president's anxiety about his actions in Vietnam was causing him to suspend his sharpest critical judgments.

Passion for Equality

In the darkest days of Vietnam decision making in 1965, Lady Bird Johnson noticed that her husband's spirits lifted whenever he turned his powerful energies to Great Society legislation. With the Vietnam decisions settled — at least for a few months — Johnson focused on his continuing agenda to help racial minorities and poor Americans.

Three days after making his decision to escalate the war in Vietnam, Lyndon Johnson summoned Joseph Califano, a young lawyer from Brooklyn and a Harvard Law School graduate, who would spearhead the 1966 legislative initiative. Johnson told him that "there are three big [jobs]

---

* The "witch-hunts," which supposedly had ended with the McCarthy era more than a decade earlier, continued in the raw files of the FBI.

I want you to make sure you do." First, the president wanted "to straighten out the transportation mess" with a new Cabinet-level Department of Transportation. Second, he was determined "to rebuild the nation's cities" by launching new initiatives such as the Model Cities program. Finally, he wanted Congress to approve yet another civil rights law — the third in as many years.

"I want a fair housing bill," Johnson told Califano, whom he had summoned to the Texas ranch. "We've got to end this God-damn discrimination against Negroes. Until people — whether they're purple, brown, yellow, red, green, or whatever — live together, they'll never know that they have the same hopes for their children, the same fears, troubles, woes, ambitions. I want a bill that makes it possible for anybody to buy a house anywhere they can afford to. Now, can you do that? Can you do all those things?"

"Yes, sir, Mr. President," stammered Califano. By the time the overwhelmed aide went to bed that night at the ranch, he was certain of one thing: Johnson was determined to have both guns and butter.[30]

In another civil rights initiative, Johnson stepped up his effort to promote talented black Americans to top government positions. With each new appointment, the president made an intentional, well-publicized political statement. The time and energy he devoted to searching for minority talent, then to nurturing the careers of those he appointed, suggests a dedicated and determined personal effort to break down barriers and to create a racially diverse government and society.

A case in point was Johnson's carefully mapped plan to appoint Thurgood Marshall as the first African American justice of the U.S. Supreme Court. A brilliant and courageous lawyer, Marshall had won twenty-nine cases before the Court, including the NAACP's historic 1954 school desegregation victory. In July 1965 Johnson asked Marshall to give up a lifetime appointment on the U.S. court of appeals to become his solicitor general. In this way Johnson hoped to prepare Marshall for appointment to the highest court. "I want to do this job that Lincoln started, and I want to do it the right way," Johnson told Marshall. Less than two years later Marshall was named to the Supreme Court.[31]

Johnson next named Robert Weaver to head the new Department of Housing and Urban Development, the first black member of a president's Cabinet, and Constance Baker Motley as a U.S. district court judge, the first African American woman ever appointed to the federal bench.[32] In March 1966 Johnson appointed Andrew Brimmer, a Ph.D. economist and assistant secretary of commerce, the first African American to serve on the Federal Reserve Board of Governors.* "If you have abilities, you should be able to reach the highest levels," Johnson told Brimmer. "It's necessary not only to speak in support of equality — you have to *act* and you have to be *seen acting.*" Furthermore, Johnson wanted to show that a black man could be trusted with money — and he wanted white bankers to have to go to a black man to borrow it.[33]

As Johnson won one confirmation battle after another, southern resistance to his appointments was weakening. At one level, the country was changing, and whites were getting used to the idea of seeing black faces in important positions of power and trust. Seeking to nurture the career of talented young black men and women, in the same way that he mentored young white men on his staff, Johnson named Roger Wilkins, age thirty-three, assistant attorney general; Clifford Alexander, a thirty-three-year-old White House aide, chairman of the Equal Opportunity Commission; and Major Hugh Robinson to serve as his White House army aide.†

President Johnson also pushed hard to implement the 1964 and 1965 civil rights acts. Title VI of the 1964 act gave the U.S. government the power to deny federal funds to any state or local government programs that practiced discrimination. With enactment of Medicare in 1965, the nation's hospitals — including the segregated ones in the Deep South — would become eligible to receive billions of dollars in federal funds. Johnson saw a civil rights opportunity with Medicare and eagerly seized it. "We're not going to lock the barn door after the horse has been stolen," the president told policymakers. "We're going to desegregate first." The president had decided that hospitals would not receive a single penny

---

* When Senator Russell Long of Louisiana suggested a candidate for the Federal Reserve vacancy, Johnson told him he had a more qualified candidate — and a Louisianan — in mind. After sharing Brimmer's impressive résumé with Long, Johnson pulled out a picture of the economist. A stunned Long pledged to tell his constituents, "I couldn't get a white man from Louisiana — but I got a black man from Louisiana" (AI, Andrew Brimmer).

† Roy Wilkins and Whitney Young urged Johnson to champion the promotion of black military officers. In one instance, Young told Johnson that General Benjamin O. Davis Jr. had followed in the footsteps of his father as the army's only black general, but since the younger Davis had no children, the army would soon be out of black generals unless the president started appointing some. He did. In another case, Johnson, personally conspiring with Wilkins, sent him out of the Oval Office to criticize the U.S. Naval Academy for its lack of black midshipmen. Johnson then called on the Defense Department to take action in response to Wilkins's complaint. Hugh Robinson eventually retired from the army as a major general. As secretary of the army in the Carter administration (1977–1981), Clifford Alexander appointed thirty black generals.

of Medicare funds until *after* they had desegregated.* His plan worked. Within nine months, all but a handful of southern hospitals had desegregated their patient rooms and staffs. Title VI enforcement also helped to desegregate southern schools. Enforcement of the 1965 Voting Rights Act, too, brought swift initial results. Within two years, several hundred thousand black citizens had been added to the voter rolls in the six southern states.

Efforts were less successful, however, in the North, where segregation resulted not from Jim Crow laws but from housing patterns and manipulation of school district borders. In dealing with this more subtle de facto segregation, Johnson was not about to run roughshod over the powerful local political establishment. When federal officials cut off education funds to Chicago's schools for violating the 1964 Civil Rights Act, Mayor Daley called President Johnson, and the order was pulled back.

To Fulfill These Rights

In June 1966 the Johnson administration convened the long-promised civil rights conference, "To Fulfill These Rights." All of the major civil rights groups were represented, except for SNCC — which was now being led by the radical Stokely Carmichael. The young men and women of SNCC boycotted the event,† citing a "tragic gulf between promise and fulfillment" of the civil rights and antipoverty initiatives in light of the enormous spending on Vietnam.[34]

When White House aides first asked the president what he wanted out of the conference, he had told them: "Have you been to the Pedernales in the spring?‡ The sun comes up early. You can see the grass beginning to turn green. You can feel the sap in the trees. You know it's time to let the

---

* As the hospital desegregation fight began, Johnson watched a CBS television news program in which a Mississippi hospital administrator vowed to bar black patients even if they arrived in an ambulance. At Johnson's direction, F. Peter Libassi, a health official overseeing civil rights compliance, was sent to do a CBS interview and assure the nation that the law would be fully enforced. The president interrupted a Cabinet-level meeting to monitor Libassi's performance (AI, F. Peter Libassi).

† Later that summer SNCC organized an antiwar rally at Luci Johnson's wedding in Washington. The SCLC, the NAACP, and the National Urban League criticized the action as "in extremely poor taste." SNCC fired back that their critics had "displayed more backbone in defending Luci" than they had shown on behalf of "the millions of black people being brutalized every day in the United States" and "our black soldiers being exterminated in Viet Nam today."

‡ The LBJ Ranch is located along the Pedernales River in the hill country of south central Texas.

bull out. And you let the bull out, and as the bull hits those cows — the cows' assholes start quivering." Johnson paused, before finishing. "I want this to be an asshole-quivering conference!" The president's crudity gave the conference its internal nickname.[35]

In his initial enthusiasm, Johnson had expected to gather from the conference concrete ideas and support for the affirmative action effort that he saw as the next phase in fulfilling the rights long denied black Americans. But the president's enthusiasm cooled after the young black radicals from SNCC and CORE aroused a growing controversy about one of the conference's proposed subjects for study: the weakness of the black family. The president's 1965 Howard University speech, though acclaimed by most of the nation's civil rights leaders, contained a section calling for strengthening the "Negro family structure" written by Assistant Secretary of Labor Daniel Patrick Moynihan. Moynihan had noted that an increasing percentage of African American families with children were headed by single women — a result of jobless black men leaving home or not marrying in the first place. The black protesters charged that giving priority to a study of problems of the black family amounted to "blaming the victim" at a point when society had barely started to address the problems of massive racial discrimination.

Disheartened by growing disarray in the movement, and fearing disruptive protests from the black radicals, Johnson told conference organizer Beryl Bernhard to make certain that Moynihan was not at the conference. The president's advisers also limited the role of Dr. King, fearing that he would dominate the conference and overwhelm the other participants — especially Lyndon Johnson. Invited to speak at only one session, King complained to Andrew Young that Johnson had snubbed him. In fact, the president was now struggling with the question of how to move ahead with a fractious civil rights movement at a time when he was seeing a growing sentiment across the nation that blacks now wanted too much, too soon. Polls reported that white public opinion — so strongly in favor of civil rights during Johnson's first eighteen months, the peak of the civil rights movement — now showed the same level of resentment that similar surveys had registered just before President Kennedy's assassination.*

Despite concerns about protests against him, President Johnson came to Washington's Shoreham Hotel to deliver the conference's final speech. As Thurgood Marshall, the nation's first black solicitor general, rose to in-

---

* Gallup Polls in September 1966 showed that 52 percent of Americans felt the administration was pushing too fast on integration, well in excess of the 30 percent who had expressed that view in February 1964 (George H. Gallup, *Gallup Poll*, 3: 2030–31).

troduce the president, Lyndon Johnson changed the script. After asking Marshall to sit down, Johnson announced, "Thurgood Marshall is one of the greatest Americans of our times. Thurgood Marshall is not introducing anyone. I am honored to introduce *him*." Johnson delivered his speech, emphasizing concrete achievements and his historic black appointees, then turned the microphone over to Marshall, as the audience wildly cheered both men.[36]

But the night of goodwill between those who had fought together successfully for civil rights legislation could not obscure the deepening schisms in the movement — or the continuing danger of speaking out for civil rights in the Deep South.

Black Power Rising

James Meredith, the first African American student to attend the University of Mississippi, embarked June 5, 1966, on a sixteen-day march from Memphis, Tennessee, to the Mississippi state capitol in Jackson to demonstrate that blacks could overcome their fear of white violence. Two days into Meredith's journey, an unemployed white Memphis resident named Aubrey James Norvell fired three shots into him. On learning of the attack, Martin Luther King immediately denounced the "dastardly" shooting and the "reign of terror [that] still exists in the South." Within hours, CORE chairman Floyd McKissick had recruited King, Stokely Carmichael of SNCC, Mississippi NAACP leader Charles Evers (brother of the slain Medgar Evers), Roy Wilkins, Whitney Young, and others to complete the remaining portion of the hospitalized Meredith's march. As the march got under way, King announced, "We are going to put President Johnson on the spot. We are demanding immediate action by the federal government. We need help and we need it now." Once again, King and his friends were in the midst of a long trek, on foot, to a southern capital.[37]

In Philadelphia, Mississippi, King confronted the unrepentant and unrestrained face of racist violence as the marchers paused at the Neshoba County Courthouse to commemorate the murders exactly two years earlier of the three CORE workers. "I believe in my heart that the murderers are somewhere around me at this moment," King declared. Standing only a few feet away, Deputy Sheriff Cecil Price muttered, "You're damn right; they're right behind you right now."*[38]

---

* Price and his co-conspirators in the murders finally were convicted of violating the civil rights of Michael Schwerner, James Chaney, and Andrew Goodman. Price served four years in prison.

In Washington, President Johnson was trying to respond to King's call for action by pressing the House of Representatives to pass his 1966 civil rights bill. Two key provisions of the legislation were pertinent to the Meredith attack: the proposed law would make it a federal crime to harm anyone while he or she demonstrated for civil rights. A second provision would prohibit racial discrimination in the selection of both federal and local juries. Demand for these legal protections for civil rights protesters arose as one all-white southern jury after another refused to convict Klansmen who had attacked — even murdered — civil rights workers.

McKissick and Carmichael represented a new breed within the civil rights community. Less committed to the concepts of nonviolence and cooperation with white allies than James Farmer and John Lewis had been, they were far more radical than the centrist King and the more cautious Roy Wilkins and Whitney Young. King spent a substantial portion of the march trying to calm Carmichael, who complained bitterly about the lack of progress on dealing with issues of poverty, hunger, and segregation. "Is it really *that* bad?" King pressed.

A few days into the march through the Mississippi Delta, the several hundred marchers set up camp at a Greenwood public school. When local police informed the campers that they would have to move, Carmichael refused and was promptly arrested. Upon his release several hours later, a furious Carmichael rose to tell hundreds of people assembled for an evening rally, "Every courthouse in Mississippi should be [burned] down tomorrow so we can get rid of the dirt." Livid, he continued, "This is the 27th time [I've been arrested]. We've been saying 'Freedom' for six years. . . . What we are going to start saying now is 'Black Power'!"

The audience began to chant, "We want Black Power. We want Black Power."

At the next evening's mass meeting, Carmichael repeated the refrain. King, hearing the "We want Black Power" chants for the first time, looked stricken. He knew that the words represented a repudiation of both his message of nonviolence and his moderate leadership. King's initial public response was a statement that the term was "unfortunate because it tends to give [an] impression of black nationalism." King was very concerned that the "Black Power" slogan would divide the movement even further and scare the white community.[39]

King issued his most forceful response indirectly, in a passionate speech a few days later. "I am not interested," he told his audience, "in power for power's sake, but I'm interested in power that is moral, that is right and that is good. That is what we are trying to do in America." He cautioned against turning to violence, warning, "The minute we start, we will end up getting many people killed unnecessarily. . . . We can't win violently. We have neither the instruments nor the techniques at our disposal, and it would be totally absurd for us to believe we could do it." Carmichael and the SNCC members, however, had already settled on the inflammatory Black Power slogan — and the philosophy.[40]

The movement had broken apart at a critical turning point. With the signal victories against official southern segregation and denial of black voting rights behind them, the mainstream movement of the NAACP, the National Urban League, and King's SCLC turned to attack even tougher issues preventing blacks from sharing more equitably in the affluent American economy. At the same time, SNCC and CORE and newer groups were capturing the imagination of many black Americans, especially the young, with the "Black Power" slogan. It had many different meanings to different people. Clearly, it was a call for pride in black identity, self-respect, and self-reliance, demonstrated in various ways from adoption of African tribal clothing to formation of all-black political, business, and social enterprises. The political controversy heightened when the concept of Black Power centered on black separatism — including rejection of King's dream of an integrated society in which men and women, white and black, would unite in brotherhood. As Black Power advocates rejected King's practice of nonviolent resistance and substituted armed black self-defense, or called for armed resistance, they not only split the movement but also further polarized American politics. Whether truly frightened by the most militant implications of Black Power or merely looking for a rationale to change their allegiances, whites formerly supportive of civil rights either moved to the sidelines or actively opposed further advances.

Clearly troubled by the polarizing issue of Black Power, Lyndon Johnson told Whitney Young that he was "not for black power or white power." He explained, "I am for American power and democracy with a small d, the fellow armed with the right to vote or armed with a job, a fellow armed with a house to live in, armed against discrimination."

As always, the Reverend Martin Luther King Jr. was the man in the middle. The SCLC had thrived because of its courageous nonviolent militancy combined with goals of inclusion according to the highest ideals of a society based on the values of the Constitution and Judeo-Christian teachings. Without the militancy, the SCLC would be another NAACP. But now various interpretations of Black Power were used to advocate philosophies and actions that were inimical to King's core beliefs and goals. As the disagreements sharpened, King finally found a new battle-ground.

Showdown in Chicago

In 1966 Martin Luther King chose a daunting new challenge. He moved the battle for civil rights to the North, where he faced an unfamiliar opposition and different issues. In Chicago there were no official segregation laws to shatter or voting booths to open to black voters. The issues were economic: the distribution of jobs, housing, and wealth. And there was no enlightened national consensus, as there had been in the case of southern segregation, to back King's demands that black Americans share more fully in the nation's abundance.

The movement's new opponent was Chicago mayor Richard Daley, a liberal champion of the civil rights laws — and an old-time boss with a sophisticated political machine. Whereas Sheriff Jim Clark had met King in Selma with a vigilante posse wielding cattle prods, Richard Daley sent the director of the Chicago Commission on Human Relations to greet King at O'Hare Airport with promises of full cooperation. Fighting a Mayor Daley would be a very different challenge from any the SCLC had faced before.

Martin Luther and Coretta Scott King also prepared for a temporary change of residence. As part of the kickoff of the new Chicago Freedom Movement, the now combined SCLC and Coordinating Council of Community Organizations (CCCO) project, King had decided to rent a small flat in the heart of Chicago's West Side ghetto. He would reside there for several days each week. Vowing to "bring about the unconditional surrender of forces dedicated to the creation and maintenance of slums and ultimately to make slums a moral and financial liability upon the whole community," King launched an effort to dramatize the housing inequalities in America's northern cities in general, and in Chicago in particular. "Our work will be aimed at Washington," King said. At the least, he hoped that the revelations of discrimination in Chicago would result in Congress's passing an open housing law and sharply raising appropriations for the antipoverty programs.[41]

In early March 1966 King and Ralph Abernathy took reporters to visit a rat-infested apartment near King's. They saw broken hot water lines and a broken heating system at the home of a black family living in abject poverty. "We've got to do more in terms of organizing people into permanent units, rather than on a temporary basis just for demonstrations," King said. He proposed "rent strikes," an effort that would be led by King's firebrand SCLC colleague Jim Bevel. Additionally, a young newcomer, the Reverend Jesse Jackson, would lead "Operation Breadbasket," in which a coalition of ministers would seek to increase black hiring by local businesses. Their weapon would be boycotts. If a firm would not share its jobs, the black community would not buy its products.

One of King's first actions in Chicago was to take over a neglected apartment building in the middle of the urban ghetto. Showing up in work clothes with his wife, Coretta, King announced that the SCLC would collect the rent instead of having the tenants pay their landlord. The money, he said, would be used for building repairs. When asked how they could do this legally, King replied, "The moral question is far more important than the legal one." The local media lambasted the move, warning that it could lead to anarchy.

Although King denied that his efforts were aimed at Mayor Daley, the popular perception was otherwise. The white majority did not react with great enthusiasm when King told audiences, "A stage has been reached in which the reality of equality will require extensive adjustments in the way of life of some of the white majority."

King complained that the mayor had chosen to "play tricks with [the civil rights movement] — to say he's going to end slums but not doing concrete things."[42] King was frustrated by his inability to confront Daley squarely — to pin him down, to get results. In the North, King was learning rapidly, he faced a far more complex opponent, and issues perhaps even more difficult to solve than official segregation in the South. Political labels were deceptive. Daley was a card-carrying liberal Democrat. The city of Chicago *did* have an open housing ordinance and a state law forbidding employment discrimination. Daley insisted that the congressmen in his Chicago political machine supported every civil rights law, poverty program, and new federal program to rebuild the cities.

But Daley's rule over Chicago depended on his weaving together and maintaining a coalition that included Lake Shore Drive liberals, downtown businessmen, ethnic enclaves of more than a dozen different nationalities from Italians to eastern Europeans, and black neighborhoods on the South and West sides. He could not tolerate actions that would upset the balance in his coalition. And what King proposed would do nothing less than undermine "the arrangement" by which Daley ruled and Chicago functioned smoothly — even receiving plaudits as the best-run city in America.[43]

King pleaded and he threatened. He cautioned that Daley "fails to understand that if gains are not made, and made in a hurry through responsible civil rights organizations, it will open the door to militant groups to gain a foothold." Seeing little alternative, King announced plans to step up his efforts — in a nonviolent but disruptive way.

On July 10 King led an SCLC rally at Chicago's Soldier Field. Organizers had hoped for 100,000 participants, but the attendance fell far short of that. Hoping to capture the energy of the "Black Power" enthusiasm, King called out: "We must be appreciative of our great heritage. We must be proud of our race. We must not be ashamed of being black. We must believe with all of our hearts that black is as beautiful as any other color. . . . Freedom is never voluntarily granted by the oppressor; it must be demanded by the oppressed . . . [but] I do not see the answer to our problems in violence."

King then led five thousand of the protesters to City Hall, two miles away. There, following a historic precedent,* he taped a list of demands to the outer door of the mayor's office: nondiscriminatory real estate listings of properties, nondiscriminatory bank loan practices, a civilian review board for the Chicago Police Department, improved low-cost public housing, school desegregation, and tenant protections.

A meeting with the mayor the next day to discuss these demands was fruitless. Daley rejected King's demands but kept up the rhetoric of a progressive politician — vowing to eliminate slums, persuade Realtors to agree to open housing, and work with local civil rights leaders — some of whom were functionaries in Daley's political machine. These black leaders no more wanted King in Chicago than Adam Clayton Powell had welcomed his presence in Harlem.

Just days later, a riot swept through Chicago. It was precipitated by the city's shutting off a fire hydrant where African American youths were trying to cool themselves in the intense summer heat. As in Harlem in 1964 and Watts in 1965, a single event provided enough sparks to release enormous pent-up anger in an American inner city. "I told Mayor Daley something like this would happen," commented King.[44]

The governor of Illinois, Otto Kerner, dispatched National Guardsmen to restore the peace, and President Johnson sent Assistant Attorney General John Doar and Community Relations Service director Roger Wilkins to Chicago to investigate. Wilkins found the same litany of complaints they had heard in Watts a year earlier: joblessness, overcrowded housing, poor schools, lack of health care, a powerless black population locked in

---

* In 1517 another Martin Luther had nailed his historic Reformation movement's Ninety-five Theses to the door of All Saints Church in Wittenberg, Germany.

their ghetto neighborhoods. King, too, was powerless to change the complex dynamics that governed people's lives in the metropolis. Poor blacks were trying to survive in the depleted urban core, surrounded by working-class and affluent whites who blocked entry to their suburban enclaves.

Before Wilkins and Doar returned to Washington, they went to see King at his rented slum apartment in Chicago's Lawndale neighborhood. As the riot still simmered outside, the Justice Department officials stood inside King's apartment doorway while the civil rights leader sat on the floor surrounded by several dozen members of Chicago's notorious black gangs. Wilkins was amazed as he watched King quietly holding a "seminar in nonviolence, trying to convince these kids that rioting was destructive and suicidal; and that the way to change a society was to approach it with love of yourself and of mankind, and dignity in your own heart." The hours-long dialogue, Wilkins thought, "would have tested the patience of a saint. . . . There was no glory in it. It was just the most bone-racking kind of drudgery. He dealt with those kids with a reverence for their humanity, dignity, belief in their importance that he communicated to them, and with the patience of a saint." By the time the youths left, King had convinced many that rioting would gain them nothing. And he had won the respect of Doar and Wilkins, who, like many officials in the Kennedy and Johnson administrations, had mixed feelings about him.[45]

Desperate for a victory, King now pushed his demonstrations in Chicago deep into hostile white neighborhoods, hoping for a dramatic showdown that would expose racism as it was practiced in the Windy City — imprisoning nearly 1 million blacks in their overcrowded ghettoes. King was tackling the most rigidly segregated city in America. In the previous ten years, efforts by individual black families to move into all-white neighborhoods had ignited arson, bombings, and more than a dozen riots. The living "arrangement" was maintained by the Chicago Board of Realtors, whose members refused to show houses in white neighborhoods to black buyers or renters. Demonstrations against individual Realtors and against the Board of Realtors were rewarded only with attacks by white mobs. In the face of irrefutable evidence that the city maintained a rigidly enforced dual housing market, Mayor Daley insisted that there were no ghettoes in Chicago. People lived where they wanted to live.

King and his lieutenants led successive marches out of the ghetto into bordering all-white neighborhoods. Each march produced larger white mobs, who pelted the marchers with stones, bottles, and other missiles. When Jim Bevel led a march into all-white Belmont-Cragin on August 2, 1966, 140 policemen battled 1,000 whites in an effort to protect the marchers. On August 5, King led 800 marchers into Gage Park. The presence of 1,000 police officers did not stop the 4,000 whites from bombarding the marchers with rocks, bottles, cherry bombs, and eggs. A rock struck King in the side of the head, dropping him to his knees. Shaking off the pain, King continued the walk. Afterward, King said that the venomous hatred expressed in Chicago was as bad as — or worse than — anything the movement had encountered in the South.

The escalating racial clashes and violence brought Mayor Daley forward to negotiate. He wanted "law and order" in Chicago. After a summit conference between civil rights leaders, church leaders, and the business community, King agreed to a settlement on August 26, 1966 — a toothless set of pledges to try to end discrimination. King had given up on Chicago. He had determined that the battle must move elsewhere. Yet he still nursed hope that out of the violent turmoil in Chicago, the president and Congress might see the urgent need to approve open housing legislation.

Harsh New Realities

Against the judgment of all his advisers, President Johnson insisted in 1966 on trying to pass a major civil rights law for the third consecutive year. Twice in the spring Johnson had summoned Martin Luther King Jr. and other civil rights leaders to the White House to launch the proposed 1966 Civil Rights Act. The new law would make discrimination in the sale or rental of housing illegal; it would criminalize violent acts against persons seeking their civil rights; and it would forbid discrimination in selecting juries. Attorney General Katzenbach cautioned King and the other assembled leaders that passage would be difficult — and that Minority Leader Dirksen would be unlikely to support any housing provision. Johnson vowed to try his best.[46]

In sending the legislation to Congress, the president had declared: "Once more this year I am asking the Congress to join in an attack on the discrimination that still afflicts our land." He stressed the same issues that Martin Luther King had been fighting for in Chicago:

> Negro ghettos indict our cities North and South, from coast to coast. Hope of cutting back the severe unemployment rate among Negroes is tied directly to the expansion of our national economy. And the ultimate need in human terms — of a more generous idea of brotherhood and a more responsible conception of equality — are part of the unfinished business of every state. . . .
>
> The ghettos of our major cities — North and South, from coast to coast, represent fully as severe a denial of freedom and the fruits of American cit-

izenship as more obvious injustices. As long as the color of a man's skin determines his choice of housing, no investment in the physical rebuilding of our cities will free the men and women living there.

Despite dwindling white support for civil rights, President Johnson, like Martin Luther King, continued to call for an end to both urban riots and the conditions that caused them. After riots in 1966 had rocked Chicago, Cleveland, Baltimore, Brooklyn, South Bend, and several other cities, Johnson, speaking at an Indianapolis civic event, declared:

> What we must do is no less than to correct the injustices of two centuries which give men their reasons to protest. But there are ways of protesting that any civilized society can tolerate. There are also ways of protesting that are unacceptable. The ballot box, the neighborhood committees, the political and civil rights organizations — these are the means by which Americans express their resentment against intolerable conditions, their design to reform society, but not to rip it apart.[47]

A month later, the House of Representatives passed the Civil Rights Act of 1966. In a televised address from the White House theater, the president lauded this "important new milestone on the nation's journey toward equality of justice and of opportunity for all our citizens."[48] But the legislative triumphs of 1964 and 1965 were not to be repeated. Despite numerous overtures by the president to Senator Dirksen, the Republican leader refused to support the open housing portions of the bill. Other Republicans, including Roman Hruska of Nebraska, opposed the jury selection provisions.[49] Valiant efforts by Johnson and Majority Leader Mansfield notwithstanding, the bill was blocked for more than two months by a Senate filibuster and died when supporters failed by ten votes to secure cloture. King blasted Dirksen for "sheer hypocrisy."[50] The law that might have justified King's futile effort in Chicago was now dead.

The successful filibuster against the 1966 civil rights bill was only one sign that Johnson's mastery of the Eighty-ninth Congress was weakening. He still was able to influence an impressive batch of legislation — winning approval for his new Department of Transportation, coal mine safety legislation, a child nutrition law, a clean water restoration bill, the Endangered Species Preservation Act, and a Model Cities program aimed at halting urban decline. But Congress stopped expanding the War on Poverty programs to spending levels that would better test their effectiveness. The civil rights leaders criticized Johnson for not asking for enough money, while Johnson complained that Congress would not even approve the levels of spending he had requested. The cost of the war in Vietnam had soared, with 325,000 troops there as 1966 ended and peace nowhere in sight. Inflation was on the rise, and Congress would not grant the president's request for a tax increase. Congress had chosen guns over butter.[51]

Tackling discrimination and hard-core ghetto poverty had proven much tougher than either Johnson or King had initially anticipated. Reflecting the buoyant optimism of the times, both men had thought the passage of social programs and laws ending discrimination would produce a sea change in American society. Now, they began to see how naïve they had been — about how much change white Americans would tolerate and about how difficult it would be to improve people's lives. Attempting change of this magnitude was unprecedented, and the efficacy of untested programs was being thrown into greater doubt as their funding was drastically curtailed to fight a war.

Once again, King felt that his hold on leadership was tenuous. His failure in Chicago to raise the nation's conscience, and the Johnson administration's inability — or unwillingness — to escalate its War on Poverty as it had escalated the war in Vietnam, disturbed him greatly. His disappointment was compounded by the failure of Congress to pass the new civil rights bill, with its provision against housing discrimination. The concepts and practices of nonviolent demonstrations that had moved the conscience of white America in Birmingham and Selma had failed to work in Chicago. King had followed his southern formula — summoning forth the visible hatred of the white residents, demonstrating the patent injustice of segregated housing, bringing his passion play into the nation's homes with television images every bit as vivid and frightening as the fire hoses and police dogs in Birmingham and the vigilantes of Selma. This time, however, the response of Congress was deadlock. From the public came only indifference, or a sense that black Americans and their white liberal allies, including Lyndon Johnson, were pushing too hard.

Furthermore, Chicago convinced King that white America, North as well as South, was not ready to share the goods of an affluent society — the jobs, the nice neighborhoods, the brotherhood of man he had so eloquently preached and dreamed about. King emerged from the failure in Chicago further radicalized in his politics, much less the pragmatic moderate ready to work with government for incremental victories. Now he called for a guaranteed annual income for families — a redistribution of wealth not likely to draw support from old allies who were ready to oppose overt segregation and discrimination. "Something is wrong with the economic system of our country," King declared. "Something is wrong with capitalism."[52]

King now indicted the government and American society with a fierce new rhetoric. At the SCLC convention in Jackson, Mississippi, on August 11, he proclaimed, "The majority of the people in our society are now powerless, and in no way able to participate in the decision making. . . . I am afraid that the cries of warning and the shouts of desperation of our ghettos now fall on deaf ears."* The SCLC board approved resolutions criticizing the Johnson administration for "inadequate enforcement" of the 1964 and 1965 laws — and for the "relentless escalation" in Vietnam. After almost three years of hope and collaboration, Martin Luther King had given up on Lyndon Johnson.[53]

With Vietnam and racial tensions continuing to escalate simultaneously, Johnson's popularity had begun to wane. Polls at the end of 1966 showed his once sky-high approval ratings sliding down to 48 percent. Johnson and the Democratic Party took a beating in the 1966 midterm elections.[54] Many of the freshman House Democrats, elected in the 1964 landslide, were defeated by Republican opponents. In all, the Republicans gained forty-seven House seats (nine more than the Democrats had gained two years before) and four Senate seats. Georgia elected as its new governor segregationist businessman Lester Maddox, who had closed down his restaurant rather than comply with the 1964 Civil Rights Act. A new Republican South continued to emerge as hard-line Republican conservatives replaced the old-style segregationist Democrats. The fruits of the 1965 Voting Rights Act — thousands of southern blacks registering to vote — came too late to show immediate results in statewide elections, although black candidates scored a few signal victories in local races where the black population represented a majority of the electorate. For civil rights advocates, though, one bright note was the election to the Senate of Edward Brooke, one of the new Republicans. The Massachusetts attorney general became the first black United States senator since Reconstruction.

Days after the election, a frustrated King met with his top aides in a two-room hotel suite in New York City. He complained about the Johnson administration's increasing efforts in Vietnam — and the toll it was taking on social programs at home. King accused his colleagues, "You always want to rationalize sin. You ought to call sin, sin." In other words, King felt that the Vietnam War was immoral and they should say so.

His staffers goaded him, saying, "We agree with you. Why don't you call someone who can do something about it? Why don't you tell the president?" King replied that he would, if only the president would sit down

---

* King, in bed with a fever and unable to speak because of laryngitis, asked Andrew Young to read the speech for him.

and listen to him. His personal assistant, Bernard Lee, placed a call to the White House. Thirty minutes later the phone rang. "Well, Doc," Lee announced, "you got your wish. The president is on the phone."

King assured President Johnson that his desire for negotiations leading to peace was based on moral grounds. Then he listened patiently as Johnson lamented the Vietnam situation. Explaining that the "doves" wanted him to "turn tail and walk away from Vietnam," while the military wanted him to escalate the war, the president told King that he was trying to follow a middle road, which he hoped would lead to negotiations. King politely allowed Johnson to speak and then let the president know that he sympathized with his plight.

As King hung up the phone, his aides goaded him again about "all this big talk about what you were going to tell the president."

King responded, "There is a time to be a prophet and a time to be a pastor. A good prophet can also be a good pastor. The president needed someone to hear him out. This was not an occasion to preach to him."[55] It would be the last private conversation between Martin Luther King and Lyndon Baines Johnson.

"Lay Down My Sword and Shield"

On January 14, 1967, King flew to Jamaica for a month's vacation in the sun, hoping to restore his depleted energy and to contemplate how he might revive the floundering cause of civil rights. In the airport he bought a copy of *Ramparts* magazine. It featured a story and pictures showing Vietnamese children who had been horribly maimed or killed by the chemical agent napalm, dropped by U.S. planes. King had kept a low profile on the Vietnam War since September 1965, when critics, some inspired by President Johnson, had challenged his competence as a war critic. Since then, he had spoken on occasion about Vietnam, but never in a forum designed to attract national attention. King had stepped back at a time when he still had great hopes that a partnership with Johnson would yield further progress on civil rights and poverty. Now, sickened and conscience-stricken by what he had read, King resolved to speak out against the war.[56]

By the outset of 1967, the political landscape had changed dramatically. Soaring military costs blocked expansion of the poverty programs. Opposition to the Vietnam War now had a larger constituency, many drawn away from the civil rights rank and file. With open housing defeated, with little to lose by breaking with Johnson, and with no plan for his next campaign, King spent his time in Jamaica thinking about what his role might be in the antiwar movement.

On his return from vacation, King told Stanley Levison and Andrew Young that he had decided that he must forthrightly oppose the war; he could no longer stand on the sidelines. King had just about concluded that "we are marking time in the battle in the ghetto with the war in Vietnam going on" and believed that the civil rights movement could gain strength only by joining forces with the rapidly growing peace movement. "Lyndon can't stand this constant bombardment," said King, urging that the SCLC help build the pressure on the president to end the war.[57] At a conference sponsored by the *Nation* magazine, King said that American foreign policy "was supporting a new form of colonialism . . . moving down a dead end road that can only lead to national disaster."[58]

Soon afterward, the depth of disagreement among black leaders over Vietnam surfaced in a heated argument between King and Whitney Young at a private fundraising event in Great Neck, Long Island. After King criticized the war, Young responded that King's Vietnam opposition would so alienate President Johnson that it would be impossible to maintain his support for programs benefiting black Americans. "Whitney, what you're saying may get you a foundation grant," King replied, "but it won't get you into the kingdom of truth." Young fired back that he *did* care about the ghettoes while King didn't. "You're eating well," Young cracked at King, who constantly battled a bulging waistline. Later that evening a mortified Martin Luther King called his friend to apologize.*
Even when provoked, King had always remained calm, ever the gentleman, the understanding minister. But these were unusual times, in which friendships were strained or broken over the Vietnam issue. In retrospect, the war may be seen as an unmitigated disaster. In early 1967, however, most Americans — including an overwhelming percentage of black Americans — still supported the war effort.[59]

Another factor moving King toward outright opposition to the war was his mounting concern that black youths from the ghettoes were providing the "cannon fodder" for Vietnam. He sent Clarence Jones to Washington to see a Pentagon general, who provided him with statistics on black battlefield casualties. "That's enough!" King said, after he examined the information. Blacks were being drafted to serve in Vietnam in disproportionate numbers to their percentage in the nation's population. And the black casualty rate was even higher.[60]

* After King's death, Young told an oral historian at the LBJ Library that in hindsight, King's position on Vietnam had perhaps been "more right" than his own.

King decided to make his stand; he would speak at the Riverside Church in Manhattan, home of the prestigious National Council of Churches. His sponsor would be Clergymen and Laymen Concerned About Vietnam, an organization that included top officials of the major religious denominations.

Until the last moment, the content of the address itself was unresolved. King was dissatisfied with the speechwriting efforts of Levison and Clarence Jones, the most influential advisers on his research committee. "You've gotten conservative on me," he told Jones. "You're supposed to be my 'take no prisoners, guy!' This [speech] is too wishy-washy. I can't equivocate when we're bombing innocent women and children. And it's destroying the moral fabric of our country. Clarence, I love you like a brother. But you should know I'm a minister of God before I'm a civil rights leader. This is about morality, not politics!" The final draft was pieced together by Andrew Young from material prepared by two theologians, Vincent Harding, a black professor at Spelman College in Georgia, and John Maguire, a white professor at Wesleyan University in Connecticut. The provenance of the speech would later become significant, since the FBI insisted that Levison, whom the bureau called "the secret Communist," wrote all of King's "suspect" speeches and articles.[61]

At the White House, an embattled Lyndon Johnson was still trying to reason with his most prominent critics — or to intimidate them. Learning that King would be in town for a discussion of urban development on March 12 and 13, Johnson asked his assistant James Jones and Louis Martin, deputy national chairman of the Democratic National Committee, to set up an off-the-record meeting with King. A White House meeting was scheduled for March 13 at 5:30 P.M., but King canceled at the last minute. Hurt and bewildered, Johnson sent a memo to his aides: "Ask Louis Martin why he hasn't brought [King] in. He's canceled two engagements with me, and I don't understand it." At this point King was avoiding Johnson, not wanting to be "used" by the president. Never confrontational by nature, King was nevertheless ready to speak his piece. His mind was made up.[62]

For more than three years, Martin Luther King had worked pragmatically with Johnson and members of Congress toward the goal of winning passage of civil rights legislation. At times he had carefully modulated his direct-action protests and moderated his rhetoric to synchronize with the president's efforts. Now he decided that he must follow his own conscience, whatever the political consequences.

On April 4, 1967, the Riverside Church was packed with an overflow audience of three thousand and a small army of journalists who came to hear the Nobel laureate explain why he opposed the U.S. role in Vietnam. They got his explanation and more as King condemned the country's role in world affairs.

He began by describing the inseparable connection between the battle for civil rights and antipoverty programs at home and the war in Vietnam — a connection his critics insisted King should not make. "A few years ago," he said, "there was a shining moment in [our] struggle. It seemed as if there was a real promise of hope for the poor — both black and white — through the poverty program. There were experiments, hopes, new beginnings. Then came the buildup in Vietnam and I watched the program broken and eviscerated as if it were some idle political plaything of a society gone mad on war."

King deplored the effect of the war on the black men sent to fight it. Young African Americans "already crippled by our society" were being sent to Southeast Asia to fight for liberties "which were denied them at home." Furthermore, King said, the war defied the philosophy of nonviolence he had preached as he spoke with "desperate, rejected, angry young men" in the ghetto, seeking to defuse their violence and to deter them from igniting urban riots. He had finally realized that "I could never again raise my voice against the violence of the oppressed in the ghettos without having first spoken clearly to the *greatest purveyor of violence in the world today — my own government.* For the sake of those boys, for the sake of this government, for the sake of hundreds of thousands trembling under our violence, I cannot be silent."

His calling the United States "the greatest purveyor of violence in the world" would command headlines the next morning, as would his declaration that the United States was "on the wrong side of the world revolution." King described the death and devastation that the U.S. war effort had brought to the citizens of Vietnam. Then, expanding his theme beyond Vietnam, King indicted his country for being aligned with dictators and the wealthy rather than liberation movements in Central America and elsewhere in the world:

> I am convinced that if we are to get on the right side of the world revolution, we as a nation must undergo a radical revolution of values. We must rapidly begin the shift from a "thing-oriented" society to a "person-oriented" society. When machines and computers, profit motives and property rights are considered more important than people, the giant triplets of racism, materialism, and militarism are incapable of being conquered. . . . A nation that continues year after year to spend more money on military

defense than on programs of social uplift is approaching spiritual death. Somehow this madness must cease, [and Americans must] begin the long and difficult process of extricating ourselves from this nightmarish conflict.

The United States should end all bombing of North and South Vietnam, King said, declare a unilateral cease-fire (in the hope that such action would create the atmosphere for negotiation), and "remove all foreign troops from Vietnam."

In his last controversial recommendation, King advised that young men facing the military draft should consider becoming conscientious objectors against the war. Ministers, he said, should give up their automatic draft exemptions and also assume the status of conscientious objectors. "These are the times for real choices and not false ones," concluded King. "We are at the moment when our lives must be placed on the line if our nation is to survive its own folly."[63]

A Serious Tactical Mistake?

King's speech provoked a firestorm of criticism among some of his former supporters. A *Washington Post* editorial called his remarks "bitter and damaging allegations that he did not and could not document . . . sheer inventions of unsupported fantasy." It defended Johnson, highlighting the irony that "the Government which has labored the hardest to right [historic] wrongs, is the object of the most savage denunciation . . . and the most unfair blame. . . . King has diminished his usefulness to his cause, to his country, and to his people."[64] The *New York Times* criticized King for his "fusing of two public problems [racial inequality and the war] that are distinct and separate," for "by drawing them together, he has done a disservice to both."[65]

The Jewish War Veterans of America, sports hero Jackie Robinson, and liberal Republican senator Jacob Javits of New York also criticized the speech. Whitney Young did so as well, suggesting that African American citizens were more "concerned about the rat tonight and the job tomorrow. The limited resources and personnel available to civil rights agencies should not be diverted into other channels."[66] The NAACP's board of directors unanimously adopted a resolution condemning King's "serious tactical mistake." It firmly stated the view that "civil rights battles will have to be fought and won on their own merits, irrespective of the state of war or peace in the world."[67]

Lyndon Johnson was crushed. Having worked passionately for civil rights, he was devastated to see King turn his back on him. Already aware that the cost of the war was killing his Great Society "baby," and now forfeiting the support of the allies most dedicated to his vision, Johnson lamented that "he was losing both ways."[68]

Johnson's sorrow, however, quickly turned to what his new press secretary, George Christian, saw as "cold anger." He was now "coldly contemptuous of Martin Luther King." Johnson told Christian that King had committed "an act of disloyalty to the country." If Johnson retained any skepticism about Hoover's reports on King's Communist ties, the Riverside speech convinced him. Concerned that the attack by the nation's most respected civil rights figure would undermine his ability to lead, Johnson decided to strike back.[69]

Johnson asked Christian to start quietly contacting "reliable" reporters and columnists to supply them with information about King's ties with the alleged "secret Communist" Stanley Levison. In particular, the president wanted to encourage a column by Carl Rowan, his former director of the United States Information Agency and the nation's best-known black syndicated columnist. When Christian approached Rowan, he found him agreeable. Rowan, too, thought that King had "hurt the civil rights movement with his statements."[70] A few days later, Rowan wrote a column criticizing "the transformation of King from the . . . boycott leader with an uncanny knack for saying the right things, into the King of today who has very little sense of, or concern for, public relations, or tactical skill."* Rowan then accused King of "listening most to one man who is clearly more interested in embarrassing the United States than in the plight of either the Negro or the war-weary people of Vietnam."[71]

To J. Edgar Hoover, the King speech was a gift. It provided the final proof he needed to convince the president that King was being manipulated by Communists. On April 7 Hoover sent Johnson a memo informing him that after an eight-hour conference with "long-time communist" Stanley Levison, King had delivered a "highly critical" speech that had included a set of five recommendations "similar in concept to the conditions imposed by Hanoi as a prerequisite to negotiations." He further compared King's proposals to the "propaganda line which the Communist Party USA" has been projecting regarding the war in Vietnam."[72]

* Rowan later expanded on the column in 1967 article in *Reader's Digest* magazine. As USIA director, Rowan had received many of the FBI memos on the King–Levison connection. Later in life, in writing his own autobiography, *Breaking Barriers*, Rowan had a more favorable view of King and a less favorable view of Lyndon Johnson's Vietnam policy.

Hoover contended that Levison had written the speech, when in fact the FBI's own wiretaps revealed that Levison was highly critical of the speech, viewing it as intemperate.*

On April 15, King, singer Harry Belafonte, and noted pediatrician Dr. Benjamin Spock led 100,000 anti-Vietnam protesters from Central Park in Manhattan to the United Nations building, where King delivered the principal speech for the Spring Mobilization, calling for an end to the bombing of North Vietnam. Later, however, King disassociated himself from demonstrators who had chanted, "Hey, hey, LBJ, how many kids did you kill today!" or had waved Viet Cong flags or burned the American flag.†

Hoover's April 19 memo to Johnson reported that "King's recent activities and public utterances" made clear that "he is an instrument in the hands of subversive forces seeking to undermine our nation." Hoover referred the president to his recent report "Communist Influence in Racial Matters," which, he claimed, "makes it possible to understand more readily why [King] . . . willingly played a key role in the anti-war rally on April 15, 1967, where such government leaders as the President, Secretary of State Dean Rusk, and Secretary of Defense Robert S. McNamara were viciously attacked as 'buffoons,' 'fools,' and 'racists.'"[73]

Despite the burning criticism, King was relieved that he had finally expressed his deepest thoughts, his own theology, and his moral point of view. He told his aides that "his conscience [didn't] bother him, since he [was] speaking out on the war like he should." On April 8 he told Levison, "I was probably politically unwise but will not agree that I was morally unwise. . . . I think I have a role to play which may be unpopular."[74]

Although King realized that his new antiwar militancy would cost him constituents and contributions to the SCLC, he hoped that those losses would be offset, at least in part, by new supporters. Many of King's affluent liberal contributors had turned their efforts from civil rights to the antiwar movement, and he perhaps hoped to retain their allegiance with his antiwar stance. Furthermore, King saw his opposition to the war as a

* Hoover did not always forward to the president intelligence that he found inimical to his thesis about Levison. In this case the FBI wiretaps on Levison's telephones show that Levison not only found the speech intemperate but also told King so. More significantly, Hoover did not share with the president FBI reports indicating that Levison might have broken with the Communist Party.

† At the next combined meeting of the civil rights leadership, Roy Wilkins disdainfully said to King, "Well, Martin, I see you were out there demonstrating yesterday." King drawled back, "Yehhhs . . . where were *you*, Roy?" (AI, Leslie Dunbar).

means to regain support from the radical black youths who had dismissed him as an "Uncle Tom."

King followed up the Riverside speech with a Sunday sermon at his Ebenezer Baptist Church in Atlanta, making a special point of inviting SNCC chairman Stokely Carmichael to attend. "I really want you to come tomorrow," King told him, "because tomorrow, I'm going to make my statement against the war in Vietnam." King wanted to reach out to the young Black Power advocates with whom he had disagreed and who had denounced the war long before he did. In his sermon King focused on the notion that "there is a point where caution can become cowardice." Along with the rest of the congregation, Carmichael joined in a standing ovation. The Black Power advocate praised King's "beautiful" speech and noted that King, like a "true teacher," had helped his entire congregation understand his rationale.[75]

While King's gambit paid off with both his Atlanta congregation and Carmichael,* the rest of the nation was not as receptive. A May 22 Harris Poll showed that 73 percent of Americans disagreed with King's stand on Vietnam (compared to 9 percent who agreed), and 48 percent of African Americans opposed King's view (compared to only 25 percent support). Sixty percent of the nation, according to the same poll, believed that King's antiwar stance would harm the civil rights movement. Only 3 percent felt that it would not hurt the cause.

King's popularity, like Johnson's, was sinking. As 1967 drew to a close, Lyndon Johnson and Martin Luther King, now avowed political enemies, faced identical dilemmas: how to end an escalating war, with mounting casualties, which was siphoning funds from the dream they still shared of a more just society — and how to deal with increasing hostility from each other as well as from their own hard-won constituencies.[76]

---

* Andrew Young remarked in an April conference call that within the civil rights community, "the best friend we have right now is Stokely" (SDLTAP, 4/12/67).

14

✦ ✦ ✦ ✦ ✦ ✦ ✦

Another Martyr

L YNDON BAINES JOHNSON and Martin Luther King Jr. had shared their shining moment with enactment of the Civil Rights Act of 1964, the Voting Rights Act of 1965, and other historic social justice legislation, including Medicare and federal aid to education. But as 1968 began, Johnson and King each faced critical decisions. Johnson had to determine whether to escalate the American presence in Vietnam even further — an issue on which his advisers were now deeply divided and to which King was powerfully opposed.

Another pressing question, known only to those closest to the president, was whether Johnson would seek reelection, a virtual certainty only a year earlier. But now Senators Robert Kennedy and Eugene McCarthy were fiercely challenging Johnson's right to be the Democratic Party's nominee. If Johnson wanted to continue as president, he would have to battle his opponents for delegates to the Democratic Convention. The president's advisers, closest friends, and family were disagreeing about what he should do. Johnson was exhausted, physically and emotionally — and undecided.

Meanwhile, as he grappled with his next move, King envisioned a last-ditch effort to arouse the nation's conscience once again. He had proposed to bring a large contingent of poor people from across the country to the steps of the Capitol to demand that the government address the problem of poverty in America. But King was filled with grave doubts about his plan for a "Poor People's Campaign." Recruitment efforts had been slow, his organization was in chaotic disarray, funds were meager, and King's key lieutenants were balking at what they believed would be an ill-fated venture. Other, more conservative civil rights leaders such as Roy

Wilkins of the NAACP opposed the campaign — as did SNCC and CORE Black Power advocates, who believed that the notion of petitioning the government for a redress of grievances was irrelevant. Furthermore, King's threat of civil disobedience, which would tie up the federal government, stirred LBJ to implement countermeasures.

King's timetable called for his caravan of the poor to arrive in Washington in early spring. The Washington campaign was King's desperate effort to revitalize a faction-ridden civil rights movement that had been crumbling ever since the victory at Selma in 1965. As emotionally and physically exhausted as the president, King longed for a respite from nearly thirteen years of battle, yet he could not quit.

The distance separating Johnson and King on poverty issues was cast in sharp relief by King's reaction to the president's 1968 State of the Union address.* Johnson, offering more than a dozen major new programs, had thought that he was reaching boldly beyond what Congress was likely to approve. A day later, however, Martin Luther King, at a gathering of students at Georgia State College in Atlanta, called the president's speech "dispiriting." He hadn't heard anything that would "begin to grapple" with the enormous problems facing the nation's cities and its poor citizens. If the nation could provide jobs for the unemployed through the Works Progress Administration during the depths of the Great Depression, said King, then it "can certainly do it now when we are sick with wealth."

"We're going to Washington," King promised, "and nothing will stop us from going. . . . And we won't be run out either!"[1]

The Poor People's Campaign was conceived in the autumn of 1967 out of King's own desperation to find an effective means of confronting the still wide disparity between the ideals of the civil rights revolution and the glaring needs of the nation's black poor. A third consecutive summer of race riots had driven home the plight of millions of African Americans in the nation's inner-city ghettoes. In Newark, six days of rioting in July 1967 had resulted in 26 deaths, 1,500 injuries, and the destruction of much of

---

* Disagreements between the president and the civil rights leader were escalating rapidly. A year earlier, after King had criticized the 1967 State of the Union address, Johnson had sent his African American aide Clifford Alexander to smooth over the disagreement and explain that it was Congress that had slashed his spending requests for poverty programs. In 1968, however, Johnson did not bother to send an emissary. The president and the preacher were talking past each other from irreconcilable conceptions of what was politically possible (LBJL, Clifford Alexander memo to LBJ, 1/11/67).

the inner city. Several days later, the Detroit riot claimed 37 lives and re-sulted in 337 injuries, 3,374 arrests, and 1,397 fires.² Order was restored only after President Johnson dispatched federal troops.

Speaking with Supreme Court justice Abe Fortas, President Johnson bemoaned the impact of the riots on his domestic programs as well as his own political standing. "It's knocked our polls down 15 percent — more than Vietnam [and] inflation. . . . Every white man says he doesn't want his car turned over, [he] doesn't want his neighbor throwing bricks at him."

With blacks facing huge problems of unemployment and inadequate education, job training, housing, and health care, King had concluded that only a massive federal program for the cities — on the scale of the U.S. Marshall Plan to rebuild Europe after World War II — would make a difference in improving life for the teeming millions trapped in the ghettoes.

The campaign represented a radical departure from King's earlier civil rights efforts. Previously, the SCLC had organized its troops to march and pray on behalf of ending segregation in the South. Now that civil rights goals had evolved into class and economic issues, King was trying to put together a populist coalition in which poor blacks, whites, Mexican Americans, and Native Americans would seek to transform the economy. And the proposed tactics of disrupting the nation's capital were far more radical than the orderly marches of Selma and Birmingham. King's hope was to jolt the president and Congress into granting major concessions to the poor. He was not confident that the plan would work, but he saw it as an alternative to another season of riots. He felt that his leadership must be saved from passing to the militant voices preaching separatism and revolution in the name of Black Power. He remained fervently committed to nonviolent protest. King knew that blacks, a 10 percent minority in America, were only inviting their own repression — or slaughter — by de-claring war on the white majority.

Their vastly different reactions to the summer riots of 1967 had com-pounded the continuing bitter disagreements between President Johnson and Dr. King about the proper American course in Vietnam. The presi-dent had responded to the unrest first by condemning the rioters of New-ark and Detroit. He then appointed a National Advisory Commission on Civil Disorders to study the causes. King fired back a stinging message to the president, saying, "Only drastic changes in the life of the poor will provide the kind of order and stability you desire." Protesting congres-sional cutbacks in social programs, King asserted that "the suicidal and irrational acts which plague our streets daily are being sowed by and watered by the irrational, irrelevant equally suicidal debate and delay in Congress." He then boldly proposed that the government provide a job for every person who needed work.[3]

Both men had realized the profound differences between the earlier challenges to civil rights — as monumentally difficult as they were — and the problems they now sought to solve. "It didn't cost the nation one penny to integrate lunch counters," King said in January 1968. "It didn't cost the nation one penny to guarantee the right to vote. But now, we are dealing with issues that cannot be solved without the nation spending billions of dollars — and undergoing a radical redistribution of economic power."[4]

In the context of contemporary American politics, Lyndon Johnson and Martin Luther King were both proposing revolutionary action. Both men hoped to effect profound changes in the nation's distribution of political and economic power — with minorities and the poor gaining more of each. Johnson believed that those goals could be achieved peacefully within the existing political and economic system — *if* only enough effort and money were spent to increase opportunity for the have-nots, and *if* the powerful American economy continued to thrive and grow fast enough to support the transformation. The president had assumed that the world's most affluent society could share its prosperity with the poor without undue hardship for better-off Americans. King had started out with similar views. But by 1967, both men had been disabused of their earlier, perhaps naïve optimism. A deeper understanding of the multiple layers of calamitous problems created by three centuries of racism and deprivation — not to mention the limits of the affluent society's willingness to pay for both a war in Asia and a war against poverty at home — awoke the president and the preacher to far more pessimistic realities.

King's frustrating failures in Chicago, and the devastation of the riots, had changed his mind not just about the difficulty of the struggle but about its very nature. As the leader of a mostly middle-class southern movement led by ministers, King was truly shocked when he came face to face with hard-core urban poverty. He became convinced that racism in white America was more deeply embedded than he had first assumed. White Americans, particularly those who felt most threatened and insecure, would not easily give up either political or economic power. As a committed believer in nonviolence, he could conceive no positive answer other than a form of democratic socialism. Given the political realities of 1968, however, King knew that openly advocating socialism would drive away support — black as well as white — and give J. Edgar Hoover more ammunition to charge that he was controlled by Communists. So King instead called for a transformation of values and demanded "guaranteed jobs or guaranteed income," a "Marshall Plan for the cities." Neither Lyndon Johnson nor Congress nor any other powerful American institution was prepared even to begin such a sweeping transformation.

The idea of bringing an army of poor people to Washington had sprung from several sources. Stanley Levison had been reminded of the depression era Bonus Marchers — World War I veterans demanding benefits, who camped out in Washington until they were driven out of the city by army forces commanded by General Douglas MacArthur. An encampment of the poor also had been suggested by Senator Robert Kennedy, who passed the idea on to Dr. King via Marian Wright, an NAACP lawyer.*

By 1968, the divisions separating Lyndon Johnson and Martin Luther King — indeed, those fissures splitting the entire country — were not just about levels of spending for federal programs, but were raw emotional disagreements over everything from the war in Vietnam, to the urban riots, to the rhetoric and actions of Black Power advocates who spoke of violent revolution. H. Rap Brown, who succeeded Stokely Carmichael as head of SNCC, shouted the slogan "Burn, Baby, Burn" to characterize his remedy for inequality in America. On the day after the president's State of the Union speech to Congress, the depth of political anger was dramatized at the White House. Invited to a seminar on combating youth crime and delinquency, singer Eartha Kitt turned to Lady Bird Johnson and, in front of an audience including television reporters, condemned the first lady and the nation's leaders: "You send the best of this country off to be shot and maimed. They rebel in the street. . . . They don't go to school because they're going to be snatched off from their mothers to be shot in Vietnam." Pale, in a trembling voice, Mrs. Johnson replied that, the war notwithstanding, "that still does not give us a free ticket not to try to work for better things, such as against crime in the streets, for better education and better health for our people." The personal gulf between Lyndon

---

* Kennedy, who was becoming more involved in poverty issues as he considered challenging Johnson for the presidency, told Wright that the plan would dramatize the issues of poverty — and, incidentally, would give President Johnson trouble, a possibility Kennedy viewed with some relish. Later in 1968 Wright married Peter Edelman, who had been Robert Kennedy's legislative assistant (AI, Marian Wright Edelman).

Johnson and Martin Luther King was further widened when King praised Kitt for speaking her mind.[5]

Iago's Opportunity

As the country's divisions hardened over the Vietnam War, riots in the cities, and militant black demands, FBI director J. Edgar Hoover took these disturbances of public tranquillity as a new opportunity to pursue his campaign to destroy Martin Luther King as an American political leader. After King's April 1967 condemnation of America's role in Vietnam, Hoover moved into high gear. President Johnson had become appreciably more receptive to the FBI's contention that King was being manipulated by the "secret Communist" Stanley Levison. In July 1967 King's stinging criticism of the president's response to the riots in Detroit and Newark provided Hoover with a new opportunity to engage Johnson in the FBI's campaign against King.

Hoover told the president that King's telegram criticizing him after the riots actually had been written by Stanley Levison. In a teletype message Hoover provided further details: "Both Levison and [Harry] Wachtel advised King to rebut the statements concerning the racial situation in the United States made by President Johnson on July 24. Levison told King that King has more to gain nationally by agreeing with the violence and not making statements against it, because the President is afraid at this time, and it will be easy to get concessions from him."[6]

The president was infuriated by King's criticisms. He spoke to FBI White House liaison Deke DeLoach about publicly exposing King's relationship with Levison, in the hope of damaging King's credibility as a presidential critic. After a conversation with Johnson, DeLoach reported back to Hoover: "The President asked how much information could get out [about King's relationship with Levison]. I told him that handling the information with newspapers was perhaps the best way." DeLoach also told the president that Attorney General Ramsey Clark, Hoover's nominal superior, was opposed to leaking negative information about King to members of Congress and the news media.[7]

In fact, Clark was concerned that the FBI's relentless campaign to poison the president's mind against King was harmful not only to King but also to the federal government and to the nation's best interests. Doubts about King, some stronger than others, had run through the White House staff, including Walter Jenkins, Bill Moyers, and Marvin Watson. The FBI's constant presence at the White House had a chilling effect as well on

White House aides, who assumed that their telephone lines were being tapped and that they too could become unsuspecting targets of the bureau. Within the White House and the Justice Department, few officials were willing to challenge the FBI's power and its dubious counterintelligence campaigns. Ramsey Clark, the Texas-bred son of former Supreme Court associate justice Tom Clark, who had been a close Johnson friend and political ally, was the rare exception.* In January 1968, when Hoover sought to renew wiretaps on King's home telephones, Clark turned him down flat.[8]

As President Johnson grew increasingly incensed by King's criticisms, he explored with the FBI other means to thwart the civil rights leader. Hoover was delighted to respond. In November 1967 Hoover sent the president a copy of an SCLC fundraising letter signed by King, which was highly critical of the administration. At the bottom Johnson scrawled a note to his assistant Marvin Watson: "Show this to Abe F and to Carol and then to Sheldon and report to me." In his shorthand, Johnson was telling Watson to find out from Supreme Court associate justice Abe Fortas, his wife, Carol Fortas (a tax lawyer), and Internal Revenue commissioner Sheldon Cohen whether King might have run afoul of the tax laws in raising and spending funds.† Watson reported back that the IRS had audited King's personal tax return and the SCLC's returns for the previous several years and had found that "they have been pretty meticulous in keeping their records."[9]

In another Johnson initiative, the FBI, CIA, and IRS engaged in a continuing investigation to discover whether King and the SCLC were being financed with Communist funds, an assumption based on Hoover's obsession — often shared by the president — that Communists were behind the militant civil rights and antiwar protest movements. The exercise revealed only that the SCLC was perpetually broke and that King and his family scraped by on a modest salary from his Atlanta church.[10]

* Frustrated by Clark's reluctance to prosecute militant Black Power activists, Johnson told Clark that he had thought he "was appointing Tom Clark's son as attorney general." Ramsey Clark replied that he was sorry to disappoint the president by not being more like his more conservative father. Hoover and DeLoach derisively called Ramsey Clark the "bull butterfly" (AI, Ramsey Clark and Cartha "Deke" DeLoach).

† King's fundraising letter offered contributors the option of getting a tax deduction by making their gifts to the SCLC's foundation. Contributions to the foundation could not be used by the SCLC for political purposes, though government officials considered it a likely possibility that they had been. Ironically, the FBI overheard Stanley Levison and King discussing an audit by an IRS agent whom Levison described as very helpful in making suggestions so that the SCLC's record keeping would be proper (see FBI Levison wiretaps). Abe Fortas, a Johnson lawyer, confidant, and friend for many years, continued to advise the president after Johnson named him to the Supreme Court. Fortas's continuing service to the president was a factor in the Senate's later refusal to confirm him as chief justice.

When the president learned from the FBI on November 30, 1967, that the SCLC was in line to receive a $250,000 grant from the Ford Foundation, he instructed Marvin Watson to find out from the FBI whether the grant might be stopped. A day later, Johnson's confidential secretary Mildred Stegall reported back that the FBI had already sabotaged the SCLC at the Ford Foundation.* In her note to the president Stegall reported: "Deke [DeLoach] says the [initial recommendation was] to give this organization four million dollars. When Deke got word of it, he talked to one of the Ford Motor Company people, a former FBI agent, and after the talk, the Company cut it down to a quarter million dollars."[11]

Literally hundreds of FBI communications to the White House and to other government agencies clearly captured Hoover's animus toward King and his desire to destroy King's public standing and influence. These communications also show that President Johnson was at times sympathetic to Hoover's schemes. At the very least, Lyndon Johnson and John Kennedy before him did virtually nothing to restrain Hoover. Whether they knew all the details of the FBI's official machinations is doubtful — or at least unclear.†

Spurred by the 1967 riots, the FBI initiated a new counterintelligence program, which it captioned "Black Nationalist — Hate Groups." The document initiating the program stated: "The purpose of this new counterintelligence endeavor is to expose, disrupt, misdirect, discredit, or otherwise neutralize the activities of black-nationalist, hate-type organizations and groupings, their leadership, spokesmen, membership and supporters, and to counter their propensity for violence and civil disorder." The original targets were listed as SNCC, CORE, the Nation of Islam, the Revolutionary Action Movement (RAM), the Deacons for Defense and Justice — and, surprisingly, the Southern Christian Leadership Conference, which under King's direction was neither a black hate group nor a proponent of black nationalism.[12]

In February 1968 the Domestic Intelligence Division of the FBI ex-

---

* The easy exchange of favors between the White House and FBI was typified by a Johnson request to DeLoach that Stegall be placed on the FBI payroll at a salary and rank higher than she could earn on the White House payroll. In return, the president approved Hoover's request of White House support for a new FBI Academy building at Quantico, Virginia. In an atmosphere of mutual trust, the FBI carried out sensitive assignments for the president and felt emboldened to pursue its own schemes against King (AI, Deke DeLoach; Cartha "Deke" DeLoach, *Hoover's FBI*).

† The author obtained several thousand previously closed White House and FBI documents by filing Freedom of Information requests with the Lyndon Baines Johnson Library, the National Archives, and the FBI. There is very little record that the FBI's detailed internal communications planning and executing various counterintelligence programs against King were shared in writing with the presidents or their attorneys general.

panded the "Black Nationalist — Hate Groups" department procedures, naming Martin Luther King himself as a "target." The instructions from Hoover to FBI field offices gave as a "goal" to "prevent the rise of a 'messiah' who could unify and electrify the militant black nationalist movement. Malcolm X might have been such a 'messiah'; he is the martyr of the movement today.* Martin Luther King, Stokely Carmichael, and Elijah Muhammad all aspire to this position. Elijah Muhammad is less of a threat because of his age. King could be a real contender for this position should he abandon his supposed 'obedience' to 'white liberal doctrines' (non-violence) and embrace black nationalism."[13]

The 1967 riots had led President Johnson to create a gigantic intelligence-gathering network in the nation's inner cities. Led by the FBI, this spy network included the Justice Department, Defense Department, Central Intelligence Agency, intelligence branches of each of the armed services, and local law enforcement agencies. The objective was to gather information about potential ghetto troublemakers in order to forecast and prevent riots before they began. To help achieve this objective, the FBI recruited three thousand informers in the ghettoes through a program it called GIP — for Ghetto Informant Program. The forthcoming Poor People's Campaign led by Dr. King provided the first major opportunity for the FBI to mobilize and test its intelligence network. What may have started as a reasonable effort soon mushroomed into an immense dragnet in which the nation's intelligence agencies swept up information on thousands of Americans who had been identified — often with little evidence — as black troublemakers or activist opponents of the Vietnam War. Hoover even devised a rating system — called the "Rabble Rouser Index" — to characterize the level of threat posed by specific individuals.

But the FBI did not stop here. In the case of the Poor People's Campaign, Hoover ordered an active counterintelligence program (COINTELPRO) to sabotage King's campaign. The goal was to prevent the caravans of poor people from ever reaching Washington. The FBI plan, code-named POCAM, was launched on January 4, 1968, with a directive sent to FBI offices in twenty-one cities. Destroying the Poor People's Campaign became a companion enterprise to the FBI's six-year-old counterintelligence drive to destroy King as a political leader.[14]

In early March the FBI held a "racial conference" in Washington to discuss means of disrupting the Poor People's Campaign. Techniques included spreading lies and rumors that would discourage people from joining the campaign. FBI agents frightened off potential recruits in Bir-

---

* Malcolm X was assassinated in a power struggle within the Black Muslim organization in 1965.

mingham with warnings of violence and by inciting fears that they would lose welfare benefits if they joined King. In Georgia the bureau planted stories in the news media that SCLC leader Hosea Williams planned to take gullible blacks to Washington and then strand them there without funds. In Richmond and other Virginia cities the FBI dispatched a black undercover operative to make speeches accusing King's Washington campaign of being part of a Communist conspiracy.[15]

The FBI's assault received timely help from James Harrison, a bookkeeper in the SCLC Atlanta office. Acting as a paid informer for the FBI, Harrison was able to keep the bureau well informed about recruitment efforts around the country. The King campaign suffered from its own lack of organization and resources, but the FBI counterintelligence effort compounded the SCLC's own weaknesses. On March 12 the FBI distributed an updated profile of King to the White House and other government agencies "to again remind top-level officials in government of the wholly disreputable character of King" before the Poor People's Campaign arrived in Washington.[16]

By late March, FBI officials were judging their COINTELPRO a success after they eavesdropped on King and his lieutenants bemoaning a lack of funds and failure to recruit more than a few dozen poor people for the trip to Washington.[17]

"Don't Ask Me What I Had to Give Him"

President Johnson's animosity toward King and his concern about the Poor People's Campaign failed to deter his advocacy of new civil rights legislation. Even though the administration's open housing bill had failed in Congress in both 1966 and 1967, Johnson now directed that the legislation banning housing discrimination be presented again to Congress in 1968. One week after his State of the Union speech, he followed it up with a special message to Congress on civil rights.[18]

The message, delivered to both houses of Congress by courier, highlighted the progress in racial equality the nation had made in the preceding five years. Nevertheless, the president emphasized, "one out of three nonwhite families still lives below the poverty level, the infant mortality rate for non-white children is nearly double that of whites . . . the nonwhite unemployment rate, while declining, is nearly double that of whites . . . [and] living conditions in some of the most depressed slum areas have actually worsened in the past decade."

President Johnson again called on Congress to "complete the task it [had] begun" by passing laws to protect the exercise of civil rights, to ban discrimination in selecting juries, and "to make equal opportunity in housing a reality for all Americans." In a special plea for the most controversial aspect of his proposal, he asserted:

> Segregation in housing compounds the Nation's social and economic problems. When those who have the means to move out of the central city are denied the chance to do so, the result is a compression of population in the center. In that crowded ghetto, human tragedies — and crime — increase and multiply. Unemployment and education problems are compounded — because isolation in the central city prevents minority groups from reaching schools and available jobs in other areas. . . . Nothing can justify the continued denial of equal justice and opportunity to every American.[19]

Johnson's push to revive the failed open housing legislation from the previous Congress ran counter to the advice of nearly all of his advisers. Attorney General Clark, like Nicholas Katzenbach before him, warned the president that fair housing had no chance of passing. Pressing the issue would only waste the administration's valuable and rapidly dwindling influence with Congress. Dorothy Height of the National Council of Negro Women was struck by the fact that the only two people really willing to push for the 1968 bill were Clarence Mitchell of the NAACP and President Johnson himself. "We must go on, deal with housing," the president had told her. He urged White House assistant Lawrence Levinson, "Go ahead and write the best and toughest bill you can."[20]

By the time Congress received the president's new civil rights message on January 24, the Senate had already taken up a very different bill, to protect the rights of civil rights workers, passed by the House of Representatives the previous August. The House had refused to include fair housing in that bill. After their efforts had failed to ban housing discrimination in 1966 and 1967, House Democratic leaders concluded that such a law would never pass the more conservative Congress in 1968.

In the Senate the outlook for fair housing was equally bleak. Unlike the 1964 and 1965 civil rights acts, housing had become a politically charged national issue that even liberal northern members of Congress approached warily. The urban riots of the three previous years had reinforced the resistance of northern whites to opening their neighborhoods to black citizens. Many feared that the arrival of even a few black neighbors would panic whites, causing them to flee the neighborhood. They feared a calamitous impact on property values. The violent white resistance to King's efforts to integrate Chicago's white neighborhoods frightened northern congressmen, particularly those whose districts contained attractive and affordable housing alternatives nearby for blacks seeking to escape the inner city.

Almost by default, Walter "Fritz" Mondale, a freshman Democratic senator from Minnesota, became his party's champion for open housing in the Senate. Mondale found an ally in another freshman, Republican Edward Brooke of Massachusetts, a former state attorney general who had seen firsthand that "many social problems stem from poor housing." On February 6, 1968, Mondale and Brooke sprang a surprise. They added a nearly verbatim version of President Johnson's proposed open housing legislation to the House civil rights bill already pending on the Senate floor — legislation that made it a federal crime to interfere with or injure civil rights workers, who still faced beatings and even death as they continued to pursue the movement's cause in the South. With only the support of the president and the skeptical encouragement of Attorney General Clark, the two young senators pursued vigorously, and perhaps naïvely, a task most Washington veterans considered impossible. As expected, the southerners filibustered.

Two weeks later, on February 20, the Senate took its first key vote on the legislation — an attempt to cut off the filibuster. Although the motion garnered a surprising fifty-five votes (with thirty-seven against), it fell seven votes shy of the two-thirds requirement.* The Republican vote was evenly split, 18 to 18, with Minority Leader Dirksen opposing cloture and open housing. By the time the Senate took its second cloture vote (which failed 56 to 36), however, Dirksen had changed his mind. Should the bill fail, Dirksen feared that the Republican Party would be blamed for any resulting racial unrest.[21]

Ever the effective bargainer, Dirksen began working quietly with Attorney General Clark, Vice President Humphrey, and, most important, with his friend Lyndon Johnson. After meeting with Dirksen, Johnson cryptically told several of his surprised aides, "We are going to get the Civil Rights bill! Dirksen is going to come out in support . . . and don't ask me what I had to give him."†[22]

Despite the renewed Johnson–Dirksen alliance, however, a third attempt to cut off the Senate filibuster again failed on March 1, still four

---

* The cloture rule required the votes of two-thirds of those senators present and voting to cut off debate.

† Johnson assistant Jim Gaither noticed that "a lot of things [happened] in Illinois in 1968" as a result of Dirksen's support of fair housing. Johnson enhanced Dirksen's power by placing his candidates on several more federal regulatory commissions, and by trying to reassure him that the national Democratic Party would give minimal support to Dirksen's Democratic opponent in 1968. President Kennedy had fulfilled a similar promise to Dirksen in the 1962 election (AI, James Gaither).

votes short of the necessary two-thirds needed to invoke cloture. With other urgent administration legislation piling up in the congressional pipeline, an exasperated Mike Mansfield called Mondale in. "You're holding up the Senate's business," cautioned the majority leader. "I'll give you one more vote, and then I'm pulling it down."

Johnson, Dirksen, Mondale, and Brooke all went back to work. At the president's urging, Democrat Howard Cannon of Nevada, moved by the injustice of black soldiers coming home to a country in which their color barred them from living where they chose, signed on.

On Monday, March 4, as time for the "last chance" drew near, Mondale realized that he still needed at least one more Democratic vote to invoke cloture. From the Democratic cloakroom off the Senate floor, he urgently called the White House. In less than an hour, Mondale received a return call from President Johnson, who was on board Air Force One, traveling through the Southwest and to Puerto Rico.

"We're *real* close, Mr. President," said Mondale. "We need one vote."

Mondale told the president that there were only two possibilities, Lee Metcalf of Montana and E. L. "Bob" Bartlett of Alaska, both Democrats from small western states — and therefore traditionally averse to voting for cloture. Metcalf seemed a lost cause. Concerning Senator Bartlett, however, Mondale had gathered interesting intelligence. Bartlett had let it be known that he wanted an $18 million federal housing project for Anchorage. Mondale believed that approval of the housing grant was Bartlett's price to vote for cloture. "Thank you for the information, Senator," said Johnson, quickly concluding the conversation.

As the Senate clerk began to call the roll, Mondale waited tensely, recording the votes on his own tally sheet. Finally, Bartlett emerged from the Democratic cloakroom and quietly said "aye" — casting the deciding vote. By a vote of 65 to 32, cloture was invoked for the third time in the Johnson presidency — all three times for civil rights laws.[23] And with appropriate political fanfare in his home state, Bartlett later announced federal approval of an $18 million housing grant for Anchorage.[24]

On March 11 the Senate version of HR 2516, amended to include the Open Housing Act, passed on a 71–20 vote. President Johnson immediately called on the House to ensure that all Americans "be protected in the exercise of their basic rights." Two days later the president urged all the members of his Cabinet to lobby their contacts in the House of Representatives to vote for open housing: "If any Cabinet member has a 'deposit in the bank' with any House member — particularly Republicans or southern Democrats — now is the time to use it."[25]

✳   ✳   ✳

Johnson focused on the 1968 civil rights legislation as a sliver of hope in a bleak picture of reverses at home and abroad. The March 15 Cabinet meeting revealed a president with his back against the wall, still trying to avoid defeat in Vietnam, to fight a war against poverty, to avoid another summer of riots, and to cope with the upcoming arrival of Martin Luther King's Poor People's Campaign — a venture that Johnson referred to as "our April visitors." He was trying to improvise answers by marshaling limited resources. With temporary remedies, he felt that he might at least ease, if not solve, huge problems. He called on each Cabinet officer to "go up the hill and back down" analyzing the feasibility and the cost of responding to the recommendations of the National Advisory Commission on Civil Disorders.[26]

The commission, chaired by Governor Otto Kerner of Illinois, had stunned the nation when it issued its report on March 1, 1968, indicting white America for the ills of the ghetto. The commission charged that "white racism is essentially responsible for the explosive mixture [of pervasive discrimination and segregation] that has been accumulating in our cities since the end of World War II." Failure to take massive action to remedy "economic and social decay" in the urban ghetto and the "resulting discontent and disruption threaten democratic values fundamental to our progress as a free society," the commission declared. Its provocative conclusion was that "our nation is moving toward two societies, one black, one white — separate and unequal."[27]

Martin Luther King immediately seized on the Kerner Commission report, declaring at a press conference that the commission had made "an important confession of a harsh truth." The only way he would be dissuaded from the Poor People's Campaign, King said, would be if the president and Congress adopted the commission's recommendations for massive government spending to aid the ghettoes and their citizens.[28]

President Johnson was devastated by the report. He felt that the commission had failed to give him credit for five years of historic accomplishments in achieving civil rights and advancing social justice. He believed that the commission was indulging in an empty gesture — though one embarrassing to him — by calling for massive spending programs that they knew Congress would never approve. He sulked, refusing to meet with the commission members. As in the case of the Watts riots more than two years earlier, however, Johnson quickly got over his hurt feelings. He tried to come up with answers — not what King and the Kerner Commission wanted, but whatever he realistically could wangle from Congress while still getting a tax increase.

After the stunning victories of his first years in office, the president was now merely trying to hang on. The sweeping Tet offensive in February, in which North Vietnamese forces had temporarily overrun thirty-eight cities in the south, had convinced many Americans that the battle to save South Vietnam was a lost cause.* Senator Eugene McCarthy had nearly defeated Johnson in the New Hampshire Democratic primary, and Senator Robert Kennedy entered the race four days later. Johnson would now have to fight for the party's nomination. Another blow to the president was his inability to travel freely and to appear in public forums around the nation. Constantly hounded by hostile, chanting antiwar protesters, the president went to few places — except to military bases, where he was protected by high fences and sentries on duty at the gates. At historic Bruton Parish in Williamsburg, Virginia, the president sat captive with his family through a Sunday service during which the minister excoriated Johnson's Vietnam policy. Even going to church had become a humiliating ordeal.†[29]

As a growing number of members of Congress from both parties — including both Senator Ted Kennedy of Massachusetts and his brother, Senator Robert Kennedy of New York — publicly expressed their opposition to the administration's Vietnam policy, Johnson decided to make a last-ditch effort to bring them back into the fold. He invited dozens of his congressional critics to the White House for a 4 P.M. meeting in the Cabinet Room. There, alongside Secretaries McNamara and Rusk, Johnson asked each of them how they would solve the Vietnam crisis.

The president kept his visitors there for seven hours, trying mightily to answer their questions and criticisms. He did not even break to offer food or drink. Late that evening as they left the White House, Ted Kennedy and several colleagues reflected that they had just witnessed a Johnsonian "tour de force." Although he marveled at a performance "like none we'd ever seen," Kennedy noted that Johnson had not changed a single mind. Not even "the Johnson treatment" could unite a divided Congress.[30]

---

* The American military steadfastly claimed that they had "won" the Tet offensive, retaking the cities and inflicting terrible casualties on the enemy — and for a while the president and civilian defense officials shared the military's view. Finally, however, it dawned on them that Tet was the definitive statement to the American public that the South Vietnamese would not defend themselves and the war could not be won.

† Before Johnson attended the Williamsburg church service, White House assistant Sherwin Markman had visited the church, spoken with the minister, and read his prepared sermon. The minister, however, switched to a sermon critical of the president. After that experience, Johnson asked the Reverend William Baxter, pastor of St. Mark's Episcopal Church near the Capitol and a friend of the Johnson family, to speak on his behalf with a high Episcopal Church official in Washington who had relentlessly attacked the president's Vietnam policy.

In the turmoil of the late 1960s, with Lyndon Johnson under attack from many quarters, his occasional tirades against those who opposed or had forsaken him touched many groups — including black Americans and their leaders. With the first black riots, Johnson had been hurt, angry, and uncomprehending about the nature of the riots and rioters. "Don't they know that I'm their friend?" Johnson plaintively asked his aide Larry Temple. "I'm trying to help them. After all I've done, don't they understand?" At that point, Johnson and most other Americans knew little about the nature and depth of complaints from the black poor.

From vastly different perspectives, President Johnson and SCLC leader King saw the ugly hand of racism shaping attitudes toward the struggle in Vietnam and the role of black American troops there. For Johnson, there was a white racist bias against helping yellow people fight for their freedom against Communist oppression — unlike the national support for America's vigorous rescue of white western Europe after World War II. Johnson dreamed of creating prosperity in a free Southeast Asia by building mighty dams,* as he had done for his native Texas hill country. For King, the struggle in Vietnam was between nationalist freedom fighters, led by Ho Chi Minh, and white westerners — first France, now the United States — determined to maintain colonial control. King saw poor African American youths being used as cannon fodder against their equally oppressed Asian brothers, while Johnson saw black Americans finding work and training in the military — which he was determined to make into the country's best equal opportunity employer. Johnson's viewpoint received strong support from the NAACP's Roy Wilkins and the Urban League's Whitney Young.

Despite the turmoil of the civil rights revolution, Johnson's approval ratings among black Americans remained consistently high.† Nevertheless, he was rock hard in his contempt for the radical Black Power leaders who called for revolution, and for antiwar protesters who ducked the draft or burned their draft cards. He wanted them stopped, and was impatient when Attorney General Clark hesitated to prosecute SNCC leader Rap Brown and others without firm evidence that they had broken a federal statute. Though reluctant to welcome the Poor People's Campaigners to Washington and assist them in asserting their rights of free speech and

---

* Johnson wished that he could persuade North Vietnamese leader Ho Chi Minh to "accept a dam on the Mekong River instead of a residence in Saigon" (Lloyd Gardner, *Pay Any Price*, p. 23).

† A Gallup Poll on September 6, 1967, showed that 67 percent of nonwhite Americans supported Johnson, compared to only 38 percent of white Americans (George H. Gallup, *Gallup Poll*, 3:2078).

assembly, Johnson acceded to Clark's judgment that federal cooperation would provide more promise for peaceful assembly.

Martin Luther King Jr. was a special case. Johnson saw King, as the best-known and most highly respected civil rights leader, at first as a rival, albeit in the same cause, but later as the adversary whose criticism could most deeply hurt his presidency. There was a belief among King's aides that the president had told associates, "That goddamn Nigger preacher [is ruining me]." Whether he made the statement or not, it was the kind of thing that Johnson — at his crudest — might have said; but it did not fairly characterize his evolving understanding of race in America or his steady commitment to civil rights.

Trying to understand the causes of inner-city riots, Johnson asked his White House aides to go anonymously into the ghettoes and report their findings.* At the same time, Johnson's private comments began to reflect a more empathetic understanding of the black American revolution. Speaking with a group of reporters after the Newark and Detroit riots, the president said, "When someone is kept as a slave, there is a minimum of trouble. As suppressed people begin to rise from prejudice and discrimination, there [are] naturally going to be more problems." In conversations with young White House aides Jim Jones and Tom Johnson, the president explained his evolving views of the civil rights revolution. After Jones sympathized with the president about the ingratitude of black protesters in front of the White House, the president said that he understood their impatience. "They're like wild stallions," he said. "All I did was open the inner fence." And he told Tom Johnson that he had learned from reading Alexis de Tocqueville that the leaders of revolutions often become their victims.[31] Johnson saw himself as such a victim. Indeed, the president was besieged by blacks who felt that he was moving too slowly, and by the backlash forces of the new counterrevolution, who blamed him for advocating and pushing through the civil rights laws.

At a time when everything seemed to be going badly for Lyndon Johnson, he seized on the open housing legislation, focusing his attention on one more concrete opportunity to advance the cause of civil rights. Johnson's practical sense of the politically possible made it highly unrealistic in

---

* After living in a Chicago ghetto for three days and nights, White House aide Sherwin Markman reported "that the key to the problem [is] alienation of the ghetto poor from the rest of society. They felt cut off. They do not look on government as either 'friendly' or 'theirs.' " A militant black leader described the ghetto to Markman as "a 'jail' that must be destroyed." Johnson read Markman's eight-page report at a Cabinet meeting, then encouraged his Cabinet to fight for their urban programs in Congress (AI, Sherwin Markman; LBJL, Sherwin Markman to LBJ, 8/5/67).

his mind even to propose a Marshall Plan for the cities — such as Martin Luther King and other liberals were advocating. But outlawing discrimination in housing was a safe alternative, one that would not require spending billions of dollars. It required only the political will, effort, and leadership to overcome deeply embedded racial prejudice and the political power of major financial interests.

On March 14 the House of Representatives sent the Senate's version of the 1968 civil rights bill to the Rules Committee, now chaired by Mississippi Democrat William Colmer. At their meeting five days later, as expected, Colmer and two other Democrats joined with the committee's five Republicans to "delay consideration" of HR 2516 until April 9. Reasserting its power, the old alliance of southern Democrats and conservative Republicans set out to defeat open housing by creating a deadlock between the House and the Senate. By the time Congress returned from its Easter recess, opponents figured, King would have arrived in town, and reaction to his threatening hordes would finish off open housing. "I couldn't have drafted a better resolution myself," exulted John C. Williamson, lobbyist for the National Association of Real Estate Boards, the bill's most powerful opponent.[32]

On March 27 President Johnson signed into law the Jury Selection and Service Act, banning racial discrimination in federal jury selection. He used the ceremony as an opportunity to blast the delay by the House of Representatives on the fair housing bill:

> I am shocked to even think that the boys I put on a plane at the 82nd Airborne — most of whom were Negro boys going back to Vietnam the second time to protect that flag and to preserve our freedom — that they can't live near the base where they have to train in this country; they must drive 15, 20, or 30 miles sometimes to get to their homes.* . . . I think the conscience of America calls on the Congress to quit *fiddling and piddling* and take action on this civil rights bill. The time for excuses has ended. The time for action is here.[33]

Most northern Democrats would vote for open housing if the legislation reached the House floor, but dozens told White House lobbyists that there was no political capital to be gained in voting for a measure so unpopular with many white northerners. Even House Judiciary chairman Emanuel Celler, longtime godfather of civil rights legislation, was hesi-

---

* In mid-February, Johnson had visited elite airborne troops at Fort Bragg as they headed off on their second tour to Vietnam. At the base, the president learned that black troops and their families were not welcome in most suitable housing near the base outside Fayetteville, North Carolina.

tant. As blacks began moving into Crown Heights, a neighborhood in Celler's Brooklyn district, Jews and Italian Americans were starting to flee. At the end of March, despite the president's support, the outlook for the bill was problematic in the House. Nationally, public opinion ran strongly against open housing legislation. Polls showed that most whites would not welcome blacks to their neighborhoods.[34]

During this month of relentless pressure for civil rights, Johnson was inundated with devastating reports from Vietnam. After years of claiming that victory was just around the next escalation, the generals had turned pessimistic — and perhaps more realistic. The president wrestled with how he should respond to a startling new request from General William Westmoreland, the commander of U.S. forces in Vietnam. To avoid defeat, Westmoreland reported, he needed another 200,000 men — and needed them quickly. Even more jarring to the president, Westmoreland and the other generals made it clear that raising troop levels from the current 500,000 to 700,000 would only maintain a tenuous stalemate. The North Vietnamese could be expected to match any U.S. expansion with one of their own. Furthermore, still another 200,000 troops might be needed the following year. In any case, 300,000 reservists now must be called to active duty. The South Vietnamese army would not fight. And the North Vietnamese and Viet Cong would not quit. Johnson had finally reached his limit with regard to the escalation in Vietnam. He saw ever more clearly that there was no end in sight. The cost of war was rising prohibitively — not only in dollars but in the spilled blood of American soldiers as well. Since the Tet offensive had begun the previous month, five hundred American soldiers were dying every week.[35] Often, late at night, the president would go down to the White House Situation Room to check on casualty reports. At times, when Johnson sat with visitors in the Oval Office, he would weep openly as he read from the previous day's casualty lists.[36]

As the agonizing review continued, Johnson's hawkish advisers were changing their minds. "We simply have to end this thing," a sobbing Secretary of Defense Robert McNamara said at one meeting, his last before turning the job over to Clark Clifford (who had advised every Democratic president since Harry Truman). "It is out of control!" McNamara was near the breaking point. After serving as Johnson's closest military adviser for five years, McNamara was now privately counseling Senator Robert Kennedy to run for president.

Clifford soon echoed his predecessor. "This is madness," said the new defense secretary, who balked at sending hundreds of thousands of additional troops "with no end in sight." Clifford appointed a task force, which reported that increasing troop levels was futile. "We can only attain our objective in Vietnam by a negotiation that brings the Viet Cong into the political process," the report concluded.[37]

A further political reality with huge consequences hit hard. Public opinion finally had turned against the war. Governor William Guy of North Dakota, a Johnson loyalist, told the president, "The public will vote for those candidates or that party in which they have the most confidence that a plan will be followed to get us out of this costly Vietnam War and back coping with some gigantic domestic problems. Unless the Administration develops very soon a plan of disengagement . . . I would have to rate Democratic chances in North Dakota — and perhaps in the nation — very poor."[38]

Ironically, President Johnson now was hearing from his most trusted associates practically the same advice he had considered disloyal — if not treasonous and Communist-inspired — when coming from the lips of Dr. King during the previous twelve months. Namely, he had to get out of Vietnam and turn his attention to the domestic needs of the United States.

The president dispatched Lawrence O'Brien, now postmaster general, to Wisconsin to gather information about that state's Democratic presidential primary. "What do you think will happen?" asked the president. "I think you are going to be badly defeated," replied O'Brien, a wise and loyal political operative for both the Kennedy and Johnson administrations. Martin Luther King threw his own political influence into the Democratic race, announcing that Senators McCarthy and Kennedy were equally worthy of support. He could not support Lyndon Johnson.*[39]

The president had to make some critical decisions. On March 23 he sent General Earle Wheeler on a secret mission to the Philippines to tell General Westmoreland that he would receive only thirteen thousand troops and, moreover, that the president was "promoting" Westmoreland to become army chief of staff. President Johnson wanted a different kind of general in Vietnam.[40]

Three days later, on March 26, the president poured out his frustration to General Creighton Abrams, his newly appointed military commander for Vietnam, and to civilian officials including Defense Secretary Clifford:

---

* Privately, King told Stanley Levison that Kennedy would be the stronger candidate to defeat Johnson because he would draw some black support away from Johnson but McCarthy would not. He hoped that either McCarthy or Kennedy eventually would withdraw so that their forces would combine against the president (SDLTAP, 3/26/68).

What will happen if we cut housing, education, poverty programs? I don't give a damn about the election. I will be happy to just keep on doing what's right and lose the election. . . . I will have overwhelming disapproval in the polls. I will go down the drain. . . . How can we get this job done? We need more money — in an election year. We need more troops in an election year. And we need cuts in the domestic budget in an election year. And yet I cannot tell the people what they will get in Vietnam in return for these cuts. We have no support for the war.[41]

In despair, the president was seeking a way to save what he could from the ashes of a losing war in Vietnam and the smoldering cities in which he had tried to erect a Great Society. After nearly a month of debate and agonized study, the president scheduled a national address for March 31 to tell the American public his next steps in Vietnam. Meanwhile, Johnson pondered his own political future.

While Lyndon Johnson wrestled with his Vietnam conundrum, Martin Luther King was crisscrossing the South, with occasional forays into the North, recruiting for the Poor People's Campaign. As time drew near for the encampment in Washington, King grew increasingly troubled. His rhetoric became more provocative, describing a doomsday that threatened an unresponsive white America. At Grosse Point High School on March 14, King told a Michigan audience that Americans either "will live together as brothers or perish as fools." In Los Angeles two days later, King warned that "there aren't enough white people in the country who are willing to cherish democratic principles over privilege." In Eutaw, Alabama, on March 22, King reiterated his ominous threat that "we will so tie up [Washington] that it won't be able to function."

King was still learning about the depths and degradation of hard-core black poverty. In the Mississippi Delta town of Marks, in the poorest county in the nation, he saw children without shoes, visited a daycare center where four hungry children shared a single apple. "Johnson said when he come in he was going to wipe out poverty, ignorance, and disease," cried one black woman. "Now, where's our money?" With tears in his eyes, King replied, "It's criminal for people to have to live in these conditions. God does not want you to live like you are living." He urged Delta families to join his campaign "to plague Congress and the President until they do something." And he vowed to start the caravan to Washington from Marks.[42]

King was sounding increasingly more radical now, calling for a major reshuffle of economic and political power by guaranteeing everyone either a job or an assured annual income. Still, he tried to remain the pragmatic political leader. He used threats to focus attention on the movement's plans, but when criticism of his disruptive tactics grew too severe, he pulled back, explaining that "disruption" of Washington was only an extreme last resort.

At most stops, King also ventured for the first time into the swirling political waters of the developing presidential campaign. King favored either Kennedy or McCarthy as the 1968 Democratic nominee, and Governor Nelson Rockefeller of New York to carry the Republican standard. He was definitely opposed to Richard Nixon, and Lyndon Johnson was unacceptable unless he were to make peace in Vietnam. In the internal councils of the SCLC, however, King revealed that he still retained hopes for — and perhaps an understanding of — Johnson's underlying passion for civil rights. He told his lieutenants that they should not demonize the president; their target should be Congress. With enough pressure on Congress, he hoped that Johnson would not only act but also once again lead the way.

In the midst of his nonstop journey in late March to rally participants and raise funds, King felt so neglectful of his sons, Marty, age ten, and Dexter, seven, that he impulsively took them with him one Saturday on an exhausting all-day recruiting tour through Georgia. By Sunday night, March 24, however, King had flown on to New York for three backbreaking days of speeches, recruiting, and mournful arguments with key supporters who believed that the Poor People's Campaign was a profound mistake. First, he tried out on a conference of friendly rabbis a new message: his own less threatening version of Black Power. Integration, said King, must mean "power sharing, not just adding color."[43]

While in New York, King stayed at the apartment of Marian Logan, the SCLC's assistant board secretary, and her husband, Arthur. Until almost daybreak, King tried to persuade Logan to withdraw her strong objections to the Poor People's Campaign and her warnings to the SCLC board that the project was a disastrous miscalculation. Marian Logan argued that its most likely outcome would be another summer of riots, followed by the election of a more reactionary and repressive Congress. The Logans, who shared a reciprocated love and respect for King, thought that he was "losing hold." His periodic "escapes" no longer refreshed him. Earlier in the month, King had flown with Ralph Abernathy to Acapulco for a doctor-ordered rest, but he had been unable to sleep. It had been the same at a meeting in Miami a month earlier. Yet King kept going.

With only two hours' sleep, King traveled through New Jersey all day

Wednesday, March 27, giving speeches in Newark, Paterson, Orange, and Jersey City, trying to build his small grassroots army of the poor. Like an apocalyptic prophet, he warned that President Johnson's Vietnam policy "risks destruction of mankind." By nightfall, King was too tired to fly home to Atlanta. Instead, he spent the night in New York before heading south to Memphis, Tennessee, early the following morning.[44]

"I Am a Man"

A telephone call from an old friend had started the chain of events that brought Martin Luther King Jr. to Memphis. He had detoured from his Poor People's Campaign travels to help the Reverend James Lawson, a pioneer civil rights veteran and advocate of nonviolent protest. Lawson was the embattled leader of a Memphis citizens' group, Community On the Move for Equality (COME), formed to support Memphis's black sanitation workers, who had gone on strike. What had started as a wildcat walkout in February quickly developed into a full-fledged civil rights battle, in which Lawson's group was backing the workers' demands for a union, for decent working conditions, and for better than their poverty wages. Displayed on their picket signs was the strikers' slogan "I Am a Man."

When Memphis city officials fired the striking workers, flatly refusing any concessions, the confrontation turned nasty. Police used force to break up a peaceful demonstration. King first responded to Lawson's summons by speaking at a March 18 rally of fifteen thousand strike supporters at the huge Mason Temple in Memphis. Moved by the enthusiasm of the crowd, King impulsively pledged to return later in the month to lead a one-day citywide strike. What excited King about Memphis was the massive black community support for poor workers fighting against the kind of economic oppression that was now his principal target. "You're doing in Memphis what we are hoping to do" with the Poor People's Campaign, King told Lawson. "The plight of the Negro and of the underpaid worker is one situation in the United States. They go hand in hand. One won't advance without the other advancing."[45]

King's flight from New York to Memphis arrived late, just before 10:30 A.M. Lawson hustled King to the Clyburn Temple, where more than five thousand demonstrators had been waiting restlessly for almost two hours for the march to begin. After King was shoved through the crowd to the head of the line, the protest marchers headed north on Hernando, turned west on Beale Street and then north onto Main Street toward their destination at City Hall. Within fifteen minutes, however, the march was disrupted by some unruly black youths walking in the march. They tore their protest signs off the two-by-two-inch wooden handles and hurled the sticks like javelins through the plate glass windows of several shops. In a matter of minutes, a mini-riot exploded as the youths were joined by street idlers and hoodlums, who began to loot the stores. Several hundred policemen responded immediately with tear gas, Mace, and billy clubs.

At the head of the march, King and Lawson could hear behind them the shattering of glass and cries from the crowd as police waded in. Grabbing a bullhorn, Lawson shouted to the marchers to turn around and return to Clyburn Temple. But his warning came too late. Although the vandalism was perpetrated by about a hundred gang members and petty criminals, several thousand peaceful marchers were caught in a pincers movement between two formations of policemen who indiscriminately attacked the orderly demonstrators as well as the looters.

Lawson and King's aides were immediately concerned for King's safety. "I have to get out of here," King agreed. His lieutenant Bernard Lee flagged down a car, asking for an emergency ride for Dr. King. Quickly acquiring an escort of two police officers on motorcycles, King was led to the formerly segregated Holiday Inn Rivermont, where the officers requested a room for him. The policemen thought that it would be unsafe to take King to other hotels (including the Lorraine, where he had stayed before), as that would require driving back through the riot corridor.

Once in the hotel, a clearly shaken King, surrounded by his lieutenants, lay under the bedcovers, fully dressed, nervously puffing on a cigarette. For the first time in his career, King had led a march in which peaceful protests had turned violent. His chagrin and bewilderment only increased when the Memphis leaders explained that the instigators of the violence were a small group of militant young blacks who called themselves the "Invaders," or the Black Organizing Project (BOP). Lawson's COME group had denied the Invaders a role in the organization's leadership. Perhaps in retaliation, they had contributed to the disruption that morning — which attracted others unrelated to the civil rights movement. King's aides were incensed by the failure of the Memphis march leaders to warn them about the potential for trouble.[46] By the time order was restored by the police and 3,500 members of the Tennessee National Guard, four blacks had been shot, eighteen-year-old Larry Payne fatally, 150 fires set, and 300 persons arrested.[47]

From his motel room, King called Stanley Levison in New York to describe what he considered a catastrophic defeat. He was so depressed by the violence in Memphis, he said, that he was thinking about calling off the Poor People's Campaign. Levison replied that King's depression un-doubtedly was compounded by physical exhaustion. He urged King, in-stead of being on the defensive about the Memphis march, to stress the positive news: that the vast majority of marchers were peaceful. King was not reassured. He lamented to Ralph Abernathy, "Maybe we just have to admit that the day of violence is here, and maybe we just have to give up, and let violence take its course." He finally fell asleep at 4 A.M.[48]

The next day, resuming his long-distance telephone conversation with Levison, King expressed certainty that the disrupted Memphis march would be interpreted as a sign "that Martin Luther King is at the end of his rope." To reaffirm his own deep belief in the practice of nonviolent passive resistance, King said, he would begin a fast (as Gandhi had done). "Let's face it," he told Levison, predicting that critics of the Poor People's Campaign, including Roy Wilkins and Bayard Rustin, would now feel vindicated in saying, "Martin Luther King is dead! He's finished! His non-violence is nothing. No one is listening to it."[49]

Iago Whispers

King's prediction proved accurate. Newspapers branded the Memphis march a failure of King's reliance on nonviolence. A *New York Times* edi-torial cited the Memphis riot as one more reason why King should call off the planned encampment of poor people in Washington. The FBI imme-diately seized on the Memphis incident to deploy still another barrage in its war against King. With Hoover driving his agents hard, the FBI had not only stepped up its COINTELPRO campaign against King and the SCLC but also targeted the sanitation workers and their supporters in Memphis as another "Black Hate Group" with a potential for violence. The Invaders also were targeted, the gang's activities closely reported by a Memphis Police Department undercover agent who had joined the group.* With information about King in Memphis flowing in from multiple sources, the FBI now aimed to humiliate him for the disastrous Memphis march. The same afternoon that King, in his motel room, was lamenting the vio-lence, William Sullivan, assistant FBI director for domestic intelligence, acting with Hoover's approval, instructed FBI agents to write two "edito-rials" or "stories" to be offered immediately to friendly newspaper editors and reporters in an effort to damage King's reputation. The two themes of

---

* Andrew Young and other King aides believed that a government undercover agent had in-stigated the window-breaking. Later, Senate and House investigators looked into this allega-tion but dismissed it as unconfirmed (AI, Andrew Young).

the FBI's propaganda offensive were that King had acted in a cowardly and hypocritical manner by leaving the scene, and that the Memphis march was a prelude to violence in Washington. One suggested article read, in part: "Like Judas leading lambs to slaughter, King led the marchers to violence, and when the violence broke out, King disappeared. The fine Hotel Lorraine in Memphis is owned and patronized exclusively by Negroes but King didn't go there for his hasty exit. Instead, King decided [that] the plush [Rivermont] Holiday Inn Motel, white owned, operated, and almost exclusively patronized, was the place to 'cool it.' There will be no boycotts of white merchants for King, only for his followers."[50]

The following day's *St. Louis Globe Democrat* and *Memphis Commercial Appeal* contained articles inspired by — if not copied from — the FBI's prose.* "Dr. King's pose as a leader of a nonviolent movement has been shattered," the *Commercial Appeal* wrote. The newspaper also ran an editorial cartoon of the civil rights leader fleeing the scene of the march. The cartoon was captioned "Chicken à la King."

As the date of the Poor People's Campaign approached, the volume of FBI messages about King to the president and to various other high government officials multiplied. In the administration, Marvin Watson, the president's regular White House liaison with the FBI, passed on the Hoover memos to Johnson with an apparent and grave appreciation of the importance of the material, and with little or no critical analysis. In contrast, on April 2, 1968, Attorney General Clark again turned down Hoover's request to renew wiretaps on King. As he had in January, Hoover cited dangers to national security from the Poor People's Campaign as the reason for eavesdropping. Clark's disapproval came with rejection of any claimed "national security threat." Clark favored having the federal government assist King in holding a peaceful protest in Washington. An opposing opinion came from White House lawyer Larry Temple, a conservative Texan. "We have permitted the Stokely Carmichaels, the Rap Browns, and the Martin Luther Kings to cloak themselves in an aura of respectability to which they are not entitled," Temple advised the president. "When Martin Luther King talks about violating the law by obstructing the flow of traffic in Washington or stopping operations of the government, he is talking about criminal disobedience. 'Civil disobedience' is a complete misnomer. There is no such thing. . . . As the time nears for Dr. King's April activities, I hope the President will publicly unmask this type of conduct for what it really is."[51]

* Such was the opinion reported by congressional investigators for the Senate Select Committee on Intelligence in 1975 and the House Select Committee on Assassinations in 1976.

As President Johnson grew increasingly incensed by King's criticisms, he explored with the FBI other means of thwarting the civil rights leader. Hoover was delighted. As for Johnson himself, the deeper his frustrations with the Vietnam War and with the protesters who appeared not just at the White House but wherever he went, the more he complained that Communists were behind the domestic protests and unrest — and the more attention he paid to Hoover's flurry of memos. Observing the dynamic between Hoover, King, and Johnson, White House aide Joseph Califano noted, "Hoover would push the button and the president would get angry."[52]

The day after the aborted Memphis march, President Johnson sent out a brief public statement noting "the grave peril rioting poses" and stressing that the "nation must seek change within the rule of law in an environment of social order." In his March 30 press conference the president was asked, "How do you feel about the proposed Poor People's March on Washington next month, in light of the events in Memphis?"

"I would hope," he replied, "if there is a march, that it will be in keeping with the law, that the law will be obeyed, that the individual rights of all will be respected, and that no violence will flow from it."[53]

The Last Supper

King and Abernathy flew home to Atlanta Friday afternoon. Martin Luther and Coretta Scott King then bought several pounds of catfish, which they took to the home of Ralph and Juanita Abernathy. While the women fried two heaping plates of fish, King and Abernathy sat in the family room devouring Juanita Abernathy's special annual dish, a casserole of pig's feet, ears, and tails. The two inseparable friends, closest of civil rights partners for thirteen years, reminisced about old times and all they had come through together. At dinner King returned to his worries. "They're saying I led a violent march," he lamented. "How can you say something like this is destroying you?" asked Juanita Abernathy. "Anyone with any intelligence knows it was a plant." Replied King, "Who's going to know those weren't our people?" The two men, both exhausted, fell asleep after dinner on their favorite couches in the Abernathy family room. They awoke at 8 A.M. to face another crucial day. They had to decide whether to go back to Memphis, and whether to continue with their Washington crusade.[54]

At King's request, Stanley Levison had flown in from New York, Walter Fauntroy from Washington, James Bevel, Jesse Jackson, and attorney

Chauncey Eskridge from Chicago, and other lieutenants from around the country, where they were struggling to raise the Poor People's Army. King believed that the SCLC simply had to return to Memphis to reestablish the credibility of nonviolent resistance. Then he definitely wanted to carry out the campaign in Washington. But he was powerless without the dedication of his disciples to such dangerous missions, with no guarantee of success.

King arrived late in the third-floor conference room at his father's Ebenezer Baptist Church to find the men already arguing vigorously against his now desperate wishes. Bevel believed that resistance to the war in Vietnam should be the movement's first priority. Jackson wanted to nationalize Operation Breadbasket, his Chicago-based campaign to persuade corporate America to provide jobs to black workers, who were important consumers. Hosea Williams, the SCLC's director of political action, wanted to focus on voter registration and running black candidates for public office. These three men were the SCLC's mainstay organizers — and all were exhausted, burned out from that difficult work. Joined by Andrew Young, Bevel, Jackson, and Williams argued further that the Washington campaign was doomed to failure. Young added that Congress would be in recess — a poor time to lobby its members. He disagreed with Levison's example of the depression era Bonus Marchers as a model for success.

Backing King were C. T. Vivian, Randolph Blackwell, and Bernard Lafayette. They were prepared to carry out the Washington campaign, but they opposed the return to Memphis as an expensive, wasteful diversion of resources. "Why take us to Memphis, as broke as we are?" they questioned.[55]

Seated at an old wooden Sunday school chair and desk, King listened silently, then finally spoke out: "Now that I want you to come back to Memphis to help me, everyone is too busy." With an anger he rarely displayed, King barked, "Everyone here wants to drag me into your particular projects. I've always supported what you wanted to do, even when I disagreed. You wanted to go raise hell — but they were going to blame me. You have all these brilliant ideas. But I'm the one that's going to get killed."

After he had finished speaking, the argument resumed. King stalked out. Abernathy and Jackson ran after him. As King was going down the stairs, Jackson called out, "Doc!" Glancing back over his shoulder at Jackson, King snapped, "Jesse, it may be necessary for you to carve out your own niche in society, but don't you bother me!"[56]

King headed for the apartment of Dorothy Cotton, the SCLC's director of education, a powerful organizer and member of the small group of

SCLC staff with whom King felt he could truly relax. After explaining to Cotton what had happened at the meeting, King began to smile sheepishly. "They don't know where I am," he said. Cotton realized that King was deeply wounded by the failure of his men to support him. But after years of observing King's style of leadership in contentious situations, she assumed that he had left the meeting so "they could come to their senses."[57]

King later returned to the ten-hour meeting at the church after Abernathy found him talking with his father in the senior King's study downstairs. In his absence, the twelve staff members, urged by Abernathy to support their troubled leader, had resolved not only to return to Memphis the following week but also to proceed to Washington. They assured King that they would prove that nonviolent direct action was still possible — that it still could bring change. "The Holy Spirit is in this room," concluded the Reverend Joseph Lowry. Relieved but still emotionally drained, King went home to pack. He was flying to Washington early the next morning — scheduled to preach at the Washington National Cathedral.[58]

As King and Walter Fauntroy boarded the plane for Washington, Fauntroy thought about how much King had endured since they had stood together on the sidewalk at John F. Kennedy's funeral four and a half years earlier, with King wondering whether America could ever focus its attention and conscience for more than ten days at a time. Not only the nation's short attention span, Fauntroy thought, but also the incessant scheming of the FBI, the brutal, never-ending schedule, the constant death threats had all worn his friend down. King was a "spent force," Fauntroy observed sadly.[59]

The President's Men

While Martin Luther King was being jostled in the aborted Memphis march on Thursday, March 28, Lyndon Johnson was meeting with his advisers to decide what he would tell the nation Sunday night about the war — and about his own future. The president sat down to a late lunch in the White House Rose Garden with his assistants Harry McPherson and Joe Califano. Johnson had already settled one issue: the military escalation of troops was over. But the battle for the president's mind over the course of the war continued. Secretary of Defense Clifford, with White House counsel McPherson as his ally, wanted the speech to signal a major change of policy. Along with a pause in bombing, they wanted the president "to point toward peace, not toward more of the same," as McPherson argued. But the remaining civilian hawks, led by Secretary of State Rusk and Walt Rostow, who had succeeded McGeorge Bundy as national security adviser, urged a militant speech signaling renewed American determination to succeed in Vietnam. As the speech went through draft after draft, so did the president's still undecided views.

With McPherson and Califano, Johnson reiterated the arguments about Vietnam and then suddenly changed the subject. "What do you think about my not running for reelection?" he asked. He *had* to run, both men replied. He was "the only guy who can get anything done! No one else knows how to get anything through Congress."

But the president demurred. He and Congress were "like an old married couple," he said. "We're tired of each other." Any of the other candidates would have the traditional honeymoon with Congress, he continued, but "I'd be the same old Johnson, coming back to the well again, beggin' and pushin' 'em to give me a better bill than last year." Later in the Oval Office, Califano again expressed concern that "the legislative program would go down the tubes in Congress" if Johnson announced that he was not running for reelection. Again, Johnson disagreed. Perhaps, he said, if he chose not to run, he could be "above politics" — and might gain more leverage with both the North Vietnamese and Congress.[60]

On Friday, Johnson sought the counsel of a second group of White House aides, Marvin Watson, Jim Jones, and White House press secretary George Christian. Watson and Jones strongly urged Johnson to run — saying that it was too late for him to withdraw from the battle. They pointed to a recent poll which showed that he would handily defeat any of the other aspirants for the presidency — Democrat or Republican. Christian, however, agreeing with advice Johnson had received from Governor John Connally of Texas, thought that the president had already borne as much of a burden as any person should have to carry. He was entitled, said Christian, to return to his ranch and to enjoy life with his children and grandchildren. Furthermore, both Christian and Connally believed, although Johnson *could* win, it would be a hollow victory. The country was too divided for him to govern effectively. Those sentiments were shared by Horace Busby, Johnson's longtime speechwriter and adviser. The president had already summoned him to start working on an "I shall not run" statement to end his speech. These Texas allies, who had lived for decades with Johnson's soaring ambition and his deep inner doubts, also took heed of concerns that the president had been expressing about his own mortality. He often mentioned the fact that "Johnson men" — his father and grandfather included, did not live past their early sixties. In the fourth year of a second full term, Johnson would be sixty-two years old.

All day Saturday the president worked on the speech, surrounded by his key defense and White House advisers. The speech would call for a halt in bombing over 90 percent of North Vietnam, and would offer peace, as Clifford and McPherson had urged. As for the ending, the president continued to ask questions and to mull over his decision.

Washington National Cathedral was packed Sunday morning, March 31, with an integrated audience of peace and civil rights activists who had joined parishioners to hear the Reverend Martin Luther King Jr. offer advice and inspiration for their causes. What they heard was the Nobel peacemaker prophesying that the fate of America could end in redemption or in doom. Dressed in a black clerical robe, King thundered from the pulpit that the United States was waging "one of the most unjust wars in the history of the world." Referring directly to President Johnson, King said, "A real leader does not rely on consensus. He *builds* consensus."

Nothing less than full adoption of the Kerner Commission's recommendations for massive spending to bring about social justice could redeem the soul of America, Dr. King insisted. "Ultimately, a great nation is a compassionate nation," he stated from the pulpit, "but America has not met its obligations to the poor."

Later, at a press conference, King declared that he could not support President Johnson for reelection. "I see an alternative in Senator McCarthy and Senator Kennedy," he said. "They are both very competent. They understand urban problems."

King forecast that a "right-wing takeover and a fascist state" would arise in America by 1970 if the nation did not do more for its poor. "I don't like to predict violence," he added, "but if nothing is done between now and June to raise ghetto hope, I feel this summer will be not only as bad, but worse, than last year."

King then pledged that he was going ahead with his "poor people's crusade," that he would bring thousands of the destitute to Washington, where they would camp out for weeks, or even months, until their demands were met. If Congress failed to act by August, King promised, "there will be a real awakening," with demonstrations at the Democratic National Convention in Chicago. But first, King said, he had to return to Memphis on Tuesday, April 2, to attend to unfinished business there. He would prove that nonviolent direct-action protest still could raise public support and change America.[61]

"I Shall Not Seek, and I Will Not Accept"

Lyndon and Lady Bird Johnson woke at 7 A.M. Sunday morning to greet their daughter Lynda Johnson Robb at the Diplomatic Reception entrance. She had arrived home on the red-eye flight from San Francisco, where she had said good-bye to Marine Corps captain Charles Robb, her husband, as he left for combat in Vietnam. To her mother, Lynda "looked like a ghost . . . like a wraith from another world."

"Mother, it was so awful," Lynda said, describing reporters pushing and shoving, almost running over a child to get through a crowd of other wives to reach the president's daughter and her husband. As the Johnsons went back to their bedroom, Lady Bird thought that her husband's "face was sagging and there was such pain in his eyes that I had not seen since his mother died."

In the early afternoon, Lady Bird Johnson told her daughters Lynda and Luci that their father would announce that night that he would not be a candidate for reelection. Both young women protested mightily, crying uncontrollably. Both soon would have husbands fighting on Vietnam battlefields. Chuck Robb and Pat Nugent were serving there, at least in part, to stand tall with their father-in-law the president.

"No, this is wrong!" cried Lynda. "What does this do to the servicemen?" both daughters questioned. "What will they think? 'What have I been sent out here for?'" Lynda worried. "Chuck will hear this on his way to Vietnam."

Later, Lady Bird described their daughters' concerns to her husband. He thought he had examined all the many possible repercussions of his decision. He had asked General Westmoreland whether his withdrawal would affect the morale of the soldiers. The general had told him that it "would not matter appreciably."[62] But now, as he faced the raw emotions of his two daughters, it was simply too late for still one more reconsideration. His mind was made up. He told Horace Busby to put the end of the speech on the TelePrompTer.

At 9 P.M., with his family and closest advisers present, the president addressed the nation from the Oval Office.

"Tonight, I want to speak to you of peace in Vietnam and Southeast Asia," he began, setting the tone for the diplomatic opening that he hoped might follow and somehow end the Vietnam nightmare.

Coming to the end of his speech, Johnson paraphrased Lincoln: "A house divided against itself by the spirit of faction, of party, of region, of religion, of race, is a house that cannot stand." He urged Americans to end their divisiveness, with "its peril to the progress of the American people and the hope and the prospect of peace for all peoples."

Finally, he announced to a stunned nation the decision that had tormented him in various moments of doubt during his four and one-half years as president: "With America's sons in the fields far away, with America's future under challenge right here at home, with our hopes and the world's hopes for peace in the balance every day, I do not believe that I should devote an hour or a day to any personal partisan causes or to any duties other than the awesome duties of this office — the Presidency of your country.

"Accordingly, I shall not seek, and I will not accept, the nomination of my party for another term as your President."

A relieved Lyndon Johnson joined his family and friends for a dinner interrupted by a barrage of congratulatory telephone calls from leaders who praised his statesmanship and self-sacrifice. In the following days, standing ovations greeted the president wherever he went, including trips to Chicago and to St. Patrick's Cathedral in New York. For the moment, his political stock rose as well. The public had expressed disapproval of his handling of the presidency by a margin of 52 to 36 percent earlier on the day of his speech. Four days later, in a reversal of fortune, 49 percent approved of his presidency, with 40 percent disapproving, according to a Gallup Poll. But Johnson was not elated at the upswing. He knew the fickleness of American public opinion.

As he watched the president's speech on his living room television set in Atlanta, Martin Luther King's spirits lifted. His first reaction was renewed hope — for an end to the Vietnam War, and for the prospect that America would face its responsibilities to the country's minorities and its poor. A victory by a new Democratic president — whether McCarthy, Kennedy, or Humphrey — surely would lead to a national rededication to the causes and ideals King cared about, he told his aides. The next morning, King decided to postpone the Poor People's Campaign. Perhaps it would not be needed. By Wednesday morning, King was headed back to Memphis to prove that nonviolence could indeed overcome injustice.[63]

"I've Been to the Mountaintop"

That Wednesday morning, April 3, began so inauspiciously that Martin Luther King had to shake his head and laugh. Along with Abernathy, Cotton, Young, and Lee, King was buckled into his seat as his American Airlines flight prepared to take off from Atlanta bound for Memphis. Instead, there was an interminable delay. Finally, the pilot announced that Dr. King was on board, a threat had been received, and all the bags had to be examined. For King, it was just one more bomb scare — one more threat about which the FBI had informed the airline, the police department, in fact, everyone in authority except the intended victim. Not letting King know about threats against his life had been J. Edgar Hoover's official policy for five years.

Arriving in Memphis at 10:33 A.M., King and his party checked in to the Lorraine Motel, a three-story structure with balconies overlooking a courtyard and parking lot. The Lorraine was located in a black neighborhood on Memphis's west side. King had stayed there before, as well as at upscale hotels including the Peabody and the Holiday Inn Rivermont, where police had spirited him away from the riot five days earlier.

Just after noon, King attended a meeting of Jim Lawson's Community On the Move for Equality to discuss plans for a renewed "orderly" march the following Monday. Back at the Lorraine, he was served with a restraining order issued by U.S. district court judge Bailey Brown forbidding a protest march for ten days. With King's concurrence, his lawyers decided to go to court the next morning to seek a modified order — one that would permit a small, tightly disciplined march. Despite King's expansive rhetoric about "not being stopped by injunctions," it would be much better, he believed, to obey a court order than to violate one, and to use the court order pragmatically to help enforce a peaceful march.[64]

Back at the Lorraine, King and his staff met for several hours with Charles Cubbage and other leaders of the Invaders, whose members had participated in the vandalism that disrupted the earlier march. The Invaders now wanted King to help them find funding for their Black Organizing Project. In return, King wanted their guarantee to help conduct a peaceful march. King's aides were infuriated by what they considered a blatant shakedown. But King, as always, was willing to listen — and to listen patiently — even to those whose motives appeared suspect. Finally, they reached an agreement. The Invaders would serve as parade marshals to help maintain order, and King would try to help them raise money.[65]

That night, in a heavy rainstorm, Ralph Abernathy went in King's place to the COME rally in the cavernous Mason Temple. King would take the night off and rest his sore throat, they agreed. But the crowd of two thousand had come to hear King, and so Abernathy sent for him.

As rain thundered down on the sheet-metal roof, Dr. King spoke as if possessed. He told about his brushes with death as a civil rights leader. He dwelled at length on the day in 1958 when a woman jammed a letter opener into his chest as he was signing books in a Harlem department store. If he had even "sneezed," King said the doctors told him, he would have died. In story after story, King talked about all the great moments in the movement that he would have missed had he sneezed that day: the student sit-ins of 1960; the Albany campaign of 1962; the Birmingham confrontation of 1963, which led to the 1964 Civil Rights Act; the 1963 March on Washington when he had spoken about his "dream for America"; the Selma march of 1965, which led to the Voting Rights Act; and now the Memphis march "to see a community rally around those brothers and sisters who are suffering. . . . I am so glad that I didn't sneeze," he echoed. He talked about the bomb threat that very morning, and rumors that he would be killed in Memphis. "I am a happy man," King said, "to have had the opportunity to have experienced life and given service at a time of great struggles — including the struggle of black people throughout the world, from South Africa to Memphis, crying out, 'We want to be free.'"

"If something isn't done in a hurry to bring the colored peoples of the world out of their poverty, these long years of hurt and neglect," he warned, "the whole world is doomed." But, he added, "I'm just happy that God has allowed me to live in this period to see what is unfolding."

"Another reason I'm happy to live in this period," King continued, "[is that] we're going to have to grapple with problems that men have been trying to grapple with throughout history. . . . Men, for years now, have been talking about war and peace. But now, no longer can they just talk about it. It is no longer a choice between violence and nonviolence in this world. It's nonviolence or nonexistence."

Drenched in sweat, his eyes gleaming, King finally came to the mighty climax of his peroration:

Well, I don't know what will happen now. We've got some difficult days ahead. It doesn't matter what happens with me now. Because I've been to the mountaintop. And I don't mind. Like anybody, I would like to live a long life. Longevity has its place. But I'm not concerned about that now. I just want to do God's will. And he's allowed me to go up to the mountain. And I've looked over. And I've seen the promised land. I may not get there with you. But I want you to know tonight that we, as a people, will get to the promised land. And I'm happy tonight. I'm not worried about anything. I'm not fearing any man. Mine eyes have seen the glory of the coming of the Lord. His truth is marching on.[66]

His listeners jumped to their feet, applauding, many crying openly. King sat down as if dazed, surrounded by his fellow ministers. Out of his deepest exhaustion, he had summoned the energy to deliver an inspiring call to celebrate life by participating in the joyous — peaceful — struggle for human dignity and justice.

King, Abernathy, and Bernard Lee went to a friend's home for dinner, returning to the Lorraine early in the morning. King then visited for several hours with A. D. King, his older brother, and other friends who had driven in together from Louisville to stand by his side in Memphis. Finally, he slept until noon.

Early Thursday afternoon, April 4, King and his staff again met with the Invaders. This time, his seemingly infinite tolerance grew thin. The group kept upping the ante of their demands, flatly refusing to commit themselves to nonviolence. He could abide someone not accepting nonviolence as a philosophy of life, King said, but he could not and would not permit anyone into the SCLC who did not at least accept nonviolence as a necessary tactic. King had drawn a line. Even though his vision of a new America had become more radical, he would not tolerate violence. For Martin Luther King, nonviolence was a reverent way of life. It was his way as a minister of God, and as a leader for the cause of justice.

At 5 P.M., after spending the day in federal court, Andrew Young returned to the Lorraine with good news. It appeared that Judge Brown was going to permit the march to take place after all, on the following Monday, April 8. Young found King, along with other SCLC staff, in his brother A.D.'s motel room. In contrast to the tension of the previous few days, Young was pleased to see King in the kind of "playful, clowning around, happy-go-lucky" mood that he could enjoy with his closest friends.

"L'il nigger, just where you been?" King yelled at Young in mock horror, fully enjoying the pretense of being angry. "You're always running off doing something without me knowing about it." King then leaped from the bed, and along with Abernathy began beating Young with pillows. Young grabbed a pillow of his own and the three men roared with laughter throughout their pillow fight. Then they went to their rooms to dress for dinner. The Reverend Billy Kyles, an old friend and stalwart SCLC supporter in Memphis, had invited King and his entourage to his home, where Mrs. Kyles had prepared a special soul food dinner for Dr. King. He told his friends that he was looking forward to it.

At 6 P.M., Martin Luther King Jr. stepped out onto the balcony of room 306, which he was sharing with Abernathy. Below stood his lieutenants, and Ben Branch, a Chicago trumpet player, waiting to go with him to dinner. "I want him to play my favorite song, 'Precious Lord, Take My Hand,'" King called down. King chatted for a moment about the weather with Solomon Jones, the limousine driver, who stood looking up from the parking lot below.

"Dr. King, it's going to be cool tonight," Jones said. "Be sure to carry your coat."

At that moment, Jones and King's aides, who were standing in the courtyard, heard a loud noise. Some thought it was a firecracker. Then they realized that King was no longer standing on the balcony. He was flat on his back on the concrete balcony floor. A rifle shot had penetrated his jaw and shattered his spinal column. Abernathy cradled his friend's head in his arms.

"Martin," said Abernathy. "It's all right. This is Ralph. Martin, can you hear me?"

"Oh my God, my God, it's all over," said Andrew Young, weeping at the sight of King lying on the balcony.[67]

An ambulance took Dr. King to St. Joseph's Hospital, where he was pronounced dead at 7:05 P.M. He was thirty-nine years old.

Commemoration

President Johnson was in the Oval Office when he received word that Martin Luther King had been shot. The president's evening schedule called for him to attend a Democratic Party dinner at the Washington Hilton Hotel, then fly to Hawaii to consult with American military commanders from Vietnam. For the first time, the North Vietnamese had agreed to peace talks.

At 8:20 P.M., press secretary George Christian confirmed to the president that Dr. King was dead. Johnson canceled plans for the dinner and for the trip to Hawaii. Instead, he began to monitor reports of immediate and spontaneous rioting in cities around the country. He could hear fire engines racing to buildings already burning only blocks from the White House. Black America had erupted in rage and sorrow.

On the night of King's killing, Johnson acted with the same steely calm that he had summoned after John F. Kennedy's murder. He called Coretta King to express his and the nation's sorrow at her family's great loss. He dispatched Attorney General Ramsey Clark to Memphis with orders to bring the assassin to justice. With Defense Secretary Clifford, he assessed the need for federal help as the rioting spread from city to city. And he quickly invited an array of the nation's most prominent black and white leaders to meet with him the next morning to reason together about how to restore a torn, divided America.

For Lyndon Johnson, there were somber memories. Less than five years earlier he had assumed the presidency in the crisis of Kennedy's murder. Now, as he had on that earlier day of tragedy, Johnson sought to comfort the bereaved, to reassure and lead the nation. And, as in November 1963, Johnson quickly resolved on a course to honor a martyred hero — a lasting legislative memorial to the cause King had championed. The ground-work already was in place: it was to be open housing.

In 1966 in Chicago, Martin Luther King had fought to establish the rights of black Americans to escape their teeming inner-city ghettoes and live in neighborhoods of their own choosing. In Chicago, when King was stoned and his disciples attacked, the response was only silence. As in earlier battles, King's resolute nonviolent warriors had marched out of those ghettoes to face the ugly racism, anger, and fears of white Americans, cowering in the fortresses of their all-white neighborhoods. The American conscience had been stirred by black Americans walking for miles as they united to boycott the segregated buses of Montgomery. Deep feelings of compassion and justice were touched by the old black lady in Montgomery who proclaimed softly, "My feets is tired, but my soul is rested." The better nature of the republic's citizens had been stirred again by the peaceful march of 100,000 black and white Americans to hear Martin Luther King's dream of an America worthy of its founding ideals, and responded yet again to King's prayerful armies facing fire hoses in Birmingham and mounted vigilantes at the Edmund Pettus Bridge in Selma.

Now, as cities burned, as black Americans raged and wept, as his own presidency lay in ruins, its lustrous accomplishments tarnished by cruel fate and by America's unwillingness to respond generously to the least among its number, tormented by his own flagrant flaws, weaknesses, and doubts, Lyndon Johnson sought again to rouse the spirit of brotherhood in the land. Out of the ashes of King's death and of cities now in flames, Johnson would try to forge a final victory.

At 11 A.M. Friday morning, April 5, the president walked into the Cabinet Room, next to the Oval Office, to greet the cream of the nation's leadership, both old and new. Gathered there were Chief Justice Earl Warren, who had led his Court to strike down school desegregation; Mike Mansfield, Hubert Humphrey, Everett Dirksen, and William McCulloch, who had led Congress to enact two epic civil rights acts; Whitney Young, Roy Wilkins, Clarence Mitchell, and Dorothy Height, who had steadily advanced the cause of justice from their venerable civil rights organizations. And there were the new leaders, including several who had been recognized and appointed to high office by Johnson himself: Supreme Court associate justice Thurgood Marshall and federal district court judge Leon Higginbotham; Robert Weaver, secretary of the Department of Housing and Urban Development; Mayor Walter Washington of Washington, D.C.; King's SCLC lieutenant Walter Fauntroy, vice chairman of the Washington City Council. As they met in the Cabinet Room, Mayor

Washington informed the president that federal troops would be needed immediately to quell the riot in the streets outside. His police department had been overwhelmed. Firemen were under assault by rioters as they tried to fight blazes along Seventh Street, Fourteenth Street, and in northeast Washington. Johnson signed an order declaring martial law in the nation's capital.

The group then heard the young mayor of Gary, Indiana, Richard Hatcher, the first elected black mayor of a large American city, as he decried the still virulent racism of white America — racism further incited by inchoate black rage in the streets. President Johnson warned that society must not succumb to the violence that some blacks and whites now embraced to confront racial problems in America. If the prophets of violence prevailed, Johnson said, "that would be a catastrophe for the country." He asked the congressional leaders seated around the table to enact the legislation that he earlier had proposed to help root out racism in America. "It's been sitting too long in the Congress," he told them. Then President Johnson led these men and women to Washington National Cathedral, where they prayed together for the soul of the Reverend Martin Luther King Jr. and for the nation.[68]

Back in the White House, the president summoned Joseph Califano, his director of legislation. "We've got to show the nation," said Johnson, speaking particularly of its grieving black population, "that we can get something done." With Califano at his side, Johnson wrote an urgent message to Speaker John McCormack and Minority Leader Gerald Ford: "Last night, America was shocked by a senseless act of violence. A man who devoted his life to the nonviolent achievement of rights that most Americans take for granted was killed by an assassin's bullet. This tragedy has caused all good men to look deeply into their hearts. When the Nation so urgently needs the healing balm of unity, a brutal wound on our conscience forces upon us all this question: What more can I do to achieve brotherhood and equality among all Americans?"

The most immediate action that Congress could take, the president wrote, was to pass the fair housing law, which still loomed in the House Rules Committee. "I urge the members of the House of Representatives to rise to this challenge," Johnson said. "In your hands lies the power to renew for all Americans the great promise of opportunity and justice under law. . . . The time for action is now."[69]

Following the president's instructions, J. Edgar Hoover immediately directed the FBI to conduct a full investigation of the assassination. Their probe of the killing moved quickly. In an April 6 memo Hoover assured the president that "every effort is being made to identify the individual or individuals responsible for this murder." Hoover's daily reports to the president now focused on investigating King's assassination rather than on exposing King's associations and indiscretions.

The president declared Sunday, April 7, a national day of mourning for Dr. King and issued a proclamation declaring that "the dream of Dr. Martin Luther King Jr. has not died with him. We must move with urgency, with resolve, and with new energy in the Congress, in the courts, in the White House — wherever there is leadership — until we do overcome."[70]

Then Johnson set about the work at which he had always been a master — shepherding legislation through Congress. He told Barefoot Sanders (White House director of congressional relations) and Califano to enlist every available member of the White House staff to speak with members of Congress in behalf of the open housing bill. Where presidential influence might help, Johnson asked Sanders to give him the names of members to call.

Speaker McCormack immediately pledged his cooperation, but Ford was not swayed by the president's appeal. The House Republican leadership, influenced in part by the National Board of Realtors, remained opposed to accepting the strong Senate-approved open housing bill. A group of twenty-one moderate Republican House members, however, including the venerable William McCulloch, ranking Republican on the House Judiciary Committee, rebelled against their own leaders. Citing the "dastardly" murder of Dr. King, they called for immediate acceptance of the Senate bill. When the House Republicans caucused together three days later, McCulloch challenged his colleagues to remain the party of Abraham Lincoln.

On Monday, April 8, as members of Congress returned from their Easter recess, George Christian went to the president's bedroom to report that rioting was subsiding, but not yet over, in more than one hundred cities. Washington, D.C., was still under martial law, with curfews being enforced by police and elite U.S. Army troops. The president had also ordered federal troops to nearby Baltimore, where rioting was still rampant. Christian shook his head over the violence: 46 dead and 2,600 injured, 21,000 arrested by week's end.[71] The president replied, "What did you expect? I don't know why we're so surprised. When you put your foot on a man's neck and hold him down for three hundred years, and then you let him up, what's he going to do? He's going to knock your block off."[72]

Later in the day, Barefoot Sanders reported to the president that the open housing bill was still in trouble in both the House Rules Committee and the full House of Representatives. He urged the president to call Hale Boggs, the House Democratic whip, or assistant majority leader, and former Republican House leader Charles Halleck, both of whom were still undecided about the critical vote.

With army troops now surrounding Capitol Hill, Speaker McCormack met in his office that afternoon with open housing advocates. "I'm not sure we are going to accomplish anything," McCormack began pessimistically. But he was willing to try. Gathered around the Speaker's conference table, Democratic House leaders and their allies from the White House and the Leadership Conference on Civil Rights read through the entire list of 435 House members. They needed to find another 15 to 20 votes. As they checked off names and made assignments, the officials looked out McCormack's tall office windows at the clouds of smoke still billowing from fires burning in downtown Washington. Sanders now hoped for a favorable vote from Jake Pickle, the Democrat who represented Lyndon Johnson's old congressional district; the White House had just approved a $1.4 million housing grant that Pickle wanted for his district. A leader had been slain, the nation's cities were in flames, but the give-and-take of Washington politics continued.[73]

As the House Rules Committee met for its critical vote on Tuesday morning, April 9, the body of the Reverend Martin Luther King Jr. was borne on a farm wagon pulled by two prison mules on a four-mile journey from his father's Ebenezer Baptist Church to his alma mater, Morehouse College. Behind the wagon walked Dr. King's family and the fellow leaders of his movement. Following them came the politicians aspiring to the presidency — Vice President Humphrey, Senators Robert Kennedy and Eugene McCarthy, and former vice president Richard Nixon. In the cortege of fifty thousand walkers were lawmakers, athletes, entertainers, construction workers, milkmen, housekeepers, and one thousand black sanitation workers from Memphis for whose cause he had died fighting. At Morehouse, there were speeches. Mahalia Jackson sang "Precious Lord, Take My Hand" — the song King had requested seconds before the assassin's bullet brought him down. Finally, there was a mighty chorus of the movement's anthem, "We Shall Overcome."[74]

In Washington, the Rules Committee was preparing to vote. Chairman William Colmer of Mississippi decried holding a vote in an atmosphere of riots. Fourteen committee members, divided equally for and against, remained firm in their votes of three weeks earlier. John Anderson, a Republican from Rockford, Illinois, cast the decisive vote. Switching from his earlier opposition, Anderson turned the 8–7 majority against the bill into an 8–7 majority in favor. This defeated Colmer's attempt to force a Joint House–Senate conference committee, with all its delays and uncertainties. The assassination of Dr. King had changed Anderson's position.[75]

The full House of Representatives took up the bill the next day, April 10, 1968 — six days after Dr. King's assassination. Expressing the sentiment of numerous colleagues, Congressman William Fitts Ryan, a New York Democrat, called on Congress to "respond to the Poor People's Campaign that [King] did not live to lead. We must pass the bill which is before us to guarantee open housing and the free exercise of civil rights. But that is a barest beginning."[76]

Other representatives reflected the attitudes of a still divided nation. William Tuck of Virginia argued that King's nonviolent direct-action protests were designed to incite violence.* "Violence followed in [King's] wake wherever he went, North or South, until he himself fell a victim to violence."[77]

At the conclusion of the debate, the House accepted the Senate's version of the legislation. On the critical vote, 152 Democrats and 77 Republicans supported open housing, while 89 Democrats and 106 Republicans were opposed. The final roll call vote, 250 to 172, was a formality. Remorse over King's assassination — and concern about the riots — contributed significantly to the bill's passage.

Despite the angry frenzy of rioters, the unending nightmare of Vietnam, and the derision of antiwar protesters, Lyndon Johnson had remained focused on the day-to-day business of a presidential and congressional democracy. In the first twenty-four hours after King was slain, Johnson decided that he would try to raise one momentous, passionate last hurrah for life's underdogs. He had announced that he would speak to the nation on Monday night, April 8. Perhaps, he thought, he could rouse the country again as he had done with his determined "And we *shall* overcome" challenge after Bloody Sunday in Selma. Humphrey, Califano, and others who had forged the shining moments with him urged Johnson to reach higher — to again inspire the nation to expand his War on Poverty far beyond its opening salvos. But Lyndon Johnson decided not to make that speech. He was too tired, too enmeshed in the Vietnam War, too con-

---

* New Jersey Democrat Charles Joelson articulated the opposite view: "I did not attend the funeral of the Reverend Dr. Martin Luther King . . . but I intend to place a rose on his grave by voting for the pending civil rights resolution. I have not had the opportunity to deliver a funeral oration, but I hope to speak very eloquently in one word, in fact, in one syllable, when I say 'aye' for the resolution" (*Cong Rec,* 4/10/68, p. 9537).

sumed in coping with the petty tyrants of Congress, who would slash his beloved Great Society programs even further if he did not bend to their wishes. He was sadly but stolidly resigned to the political mathematics of the United States and its elected representatives. And they mirrored the voices of a divided people.

Civil rights leaders put the fair housing victory in sober perspective. King's successor as SCLC president, Ralph Abernathy, called the law "a step in the right direction" but said its provisions would be meaningless unless enforced. Whitney Young added his own historical context: "Those whites who feel that they have been purged of the national guilt and shame caused by Dr. King's assassination are dead wrong. The law is only one step toward a national resurgence of decency."[78]

The day after House passage, one week after Dr. King's death, President Johnson signed the 1968 Civil Rights Act in the East Room of the White House.

"The proudest moments of my Presidency," Johnson said, "have been times such as this when I have signed into law the promises of a century. . . . With this bill, the voice of justice speaks again. It proclaims that fair housing for all — all human beings who live in this country — is now a part of the American way of life. We all know that the roots of injustice run deep. But violence cannot redress a solitary wrong, or remedy a single unfairness.

"I think we can take some heart that democracy's work is being done. In the Civil Rights Act of 1968, America does move forward and the bell of freedom rings a little louder. We have come some of the way, not near all of it. There is much yet to do."[79]

Out of the sorrow of John F. Kennedy's assassination and the passion, determination, and skill of President Lyndon Baines Johnson and the Reverend Martin Luther King Jr. had emerged the 1964 Civil Rights Act. Out of courage and horror on the Edmund Pettus Bridge and in fiery protests throughout the nation, the two men had again ignited the nation's passion for justice in passing the 1965 Civil Rights Act. And out of the ashes of burning cities following Dr. King's assassination and Johnson's decision not to seek reelection had come one final declaration for justice written powerfully into the fabric of American law.

Epilogue: The Legacy

I N THE AMERICAN SUMMER of 1968, with the nation awash in sorrow and strife, the Reverend Ralph David Abernathy led a racially diverse cadre of poverty-stricken Americans to the nation's capital, where they set up camp on the National Mall and called their shantytown "Resurrection City." Plagued by rain and mud throughout its six-week stay on the Mall, the effort was widely considered a failure. The SCLC's executive director, Bill Rutherford, dubbed the campaign the Little Bighorn of the civil rights movement.* The movement was fractured and spent.

On June 5, minutes after winning the 1968 presidential primary in California, Senator Robert F. Kennedy was assassinated while leaving a Los Angeles victory celebration. In tribute to Dr. King's memory, Kennedy's funeral procession passed through Resurrection City on its way to Arlington National Cemetery. He was buried down the hillside from his brother, the murdered President John F. Kennedy. (At the moment of Robert Kennedy's burial, J. Edgar Hoover announced that James Earl Ray, an escaped convict from Missouri, had been arrested in London and charged with King's assassination. He pleaded guilty.†)

In the final months of his presidency, Lyndon Johnson desperately sought peace negotiations with the North Vietnamese. He was haunted now by the ghosts of the two Kennedys and King — each hallowed in

---

* A reference to Custer's failed efforts against Chief Sitting Bull and his forces in Montana in 1876.

† Ray later recanted his plea and gained sympathy from King's family, but he died in prison on April 23, 1998 — thirty years into his ninety-nine-year sentence.

martyrdom for his contributions to civil rights, while Johnson was vilified for the war in Vietnam.

In August, at the Democratic National Convention in Chicago, the Democrats tore one another apart over Vietnam as they nominated Hubert Humphrey for president. Barely noticed during violent clashes between police and antiwar demonstrators, the proud integrated delegation from the Mississippi Freedom Democratic Party was seated in place of the Mississippi regulars. Fannie Lou Hamer, now an official delegate at last, received a standing ovation from the convention as she took her seat. The integration reforms that President Johnson had promised four years earlier now governed the Democratic Party.* At his ranch, the president himself watched the convention on television. He was waiting for an invitation to address the convention; the call never came. In November, former vice president Richard Nixon defeated Humphrey by a 1 percent margin of the popular vote.

As Lyndon Baines Johnson prepared to leave office, he was asked at his final press conference what his proudest moment had been as president of the United States. Without hesitation Johnson replied, "I expect the thing that has pleased me as much as any other thing that has come to me is the response that the Congress made to my Voting Rights Act."[1]

In the Hill Country, 1972

The old movement warriors bundled up against a South Texas ice storm as their bus inched its way from the San Antonio airport toward a last hurrah in Austin. They were headed for a reunion with the flawed giant who had helped them seize historic victories for civil rights.† Together, these men and women had propelled the nation out of a shameful past: former chief justice Earl Warren, Associate Justice Thurgood Marshall, former vice president Hubert Humphrey, Clarence Mitchell, Roy Wilkins, Dorothy Height — a pantheon of civil rights leaders. There were younger

---

* The Democratic Party delegate selection process now includes specific diversity goals. The number of African American delegates, 65 in 1964, more than tripled to 209 in 1968. At the 2000 Democratic National Convention, 872 of the 4,338 delegates were African Americans, over 20 percent of the convention. The Republican National Conventions have been far less successful at increasing racial diversity. At the 2000 convention, only 85 of the 2,066 delegates (4.1 percent) were black (Joint Center for Political and Economic Studies, "Blacks and the 2000 Republican National Convention" and "Blacks and the 2000 Democratic National Convention").

† *Flawed Giant* is the title of the second volume of Robert Dallek's acclaimed biography of Lyndon Johnson.

faces as well: Julian Bond of SNCC, now a Georgia state senator; Reynaldo J. Garza, the first Mexican American appointed to the federal courts; and U.S. Representative–elect Barbara Jordan from Houston, the youngest and last of the former president's protégés and, as of a few weeks before, the first African American member elected to Congress in Texas history. Among those sadly missing was the eloquent minister, prophet, and dreamer, already enshrined in American history.

Despite the forbidding weather, these distinguished Americans had come to honor former president Lyndon Baines Johnson, now an outcast from his nation's — and even his own party's — councils. In the niches of statuary halls, real and imagined, Johnson's rightful place remained vacant. Politicians — even former Democratic allies — found it inconvenient to remind themselves of the president inextricably linked with the tragedy of Vietnam. Ignoring Johnson and his immense accomplishments for social justice was a phenomenon that Martin Luther King Jr. would have understood: another example of the nation's "ten-day attention span."

Johnson's physicians and his wife, Lady Bird, insisted that the ailing former president stay home at his LBJ Ranch that Monday morning, December 11, 1972. He should watch the proceedings on television, they urged. But Johnson would have none of it. Impatiently taking the wheel for part of the way, Johnson traveled seventy miles over icy roads through his beloved hill country to the auditorium at the Lyndon Baines Johnson Library. The occasion was the official opening of his civil rights papers at the National Archives.[2]

As Johnson slowly mounted the speaker's podium, old friends and allies were shocked at his appearance — his hair grown long and streaked with gray, his huge frame bent with too much weight. Pausing several times as he began to speak, the former president slipped nitroglycerin tablets under his tongue to ease the pain of an enlarged and broken heart.

Yet Johnson's voice strengthened as he began to speak about the challenges remaining to achieve a just society. For those who had shared the journey, his talk rekindled memories of those battle cries with which he had roused a nation to action — his steadfast "Let us continue!" and his ringing "We shall overcome!" But Johnson was not resting on past glory.

"I [don't] want this symposium to spend two days talking about what we've done," Johnson said. "The progress has been much too small. I'm kind of ashamed of myself that I had six years and couldn't do more. So let no one delude himself that his work is done. To be black or brown in a white society is not to stand on equal ground. We must overcome unequal history before we overcome unequal opportunity."

"We've proved that great progress is possible," Johnson concluded. "We know how much remains to be done. And if our efforts continue, and if our will is strong, and if our hearts are right, and if courage remains our constant companion — then I am confident we shall overcome."

As Johnson stepped down from the podium, two black militants, Roy Innis, the chairman of CORE, and the Reverend Kendall Smith from the National Council of Churches, startled the audience when they rose to demand that the conference not adjourn without first protesting the rollback of civil rights efforts by President Richard M. Nixon. In an instant, the NAACP's Clarence Mitchell was on his feet, physically shielding Lyndon Johnson "from demagogues whether white or black." But Johnson needed neither surrogates nor bodyguards.

The former president almost bounded back up to the microphone. He gracefully acknowledged the protesters' arguments, and suddenly sounded like the campaigner of old, working a courthouse square. He told homespun stories about the county judge and the town drunk — the judge too had suffered hard times — and reminisced about his distress forty years earlier when he had watched the Bonus Marchers being driven out of Washington.

"Let's try to get our folks reasoning together and reasoning with Congress and with the Cabinet!" Johnson told the protesters. "Reason with the leadership and with the President! There's not a thing in the world wrong — as a matter of fact, there is everything right — about a group saying, 'Mr. President, we would like you to set aside an hour to let us talk.' And you don't need to start off by saying he is terrible — because *he* doesn't think he's terrible. Start talking about how you believe that he wants to do what's right and how you believe *this* is right, and you'll be surprised how many who want to do what's right will try to help you."

Here was the old Lyndon Johnson, still urging people of very different viewpoints "to come reason together," still recommending the balm of friendly persuasion as a vital part of his own special "Johnson treatment."

"While I can't provide much go-go at this stage of my life, I can provide a lot of hope and dreams and encouragement, and I'll sell a few wormy cows now and then and contribute," he offered. "Let's watch what's been done, and see that it is preserved, but let's say we have just begun, and let's go on. Until every boy and girl born in this land, whatever state, whatever color, can stand on the same level ground, our job will not be done."[3]

Six weeks later, Lyndon Johnson was seized by one final heart attack as he took an afternoon nap in his bedroom at the ranch. He was sixty-four years old. As his body lay in state in the U.S. Capitol, thousands passed his casket to pay their respects. Many of them were not dignitaries but ordinary black citizens who remembered the president whose white southern voice rang with unmistakable righteous passion when he spoke of the rights of the least Americans. On January 25, 1973, he was buried in the Johnson family cemetery at the Stonewall Ranch.

Forty Years Later

In the more than forty years since President Lyndon Johnson met with Martin Luther King Jr. in the White House in the first days of his presidency, black citizens have made historic gains toward fulfilling the promise of America. The most dramatic change has been in the South, with total dismantling of the cruel legal structures of segregation and discrimination. Gone are the laws and practices that deprived black citizens of access to public accommodations, to equal educational opportunity, and to all but the most menial jobs. The pernicious system that denied African Americans the sacred democratic rights of political participation no longer exists. From city halls to state legislatures to the U.S. Congress, thousands of African American officials from the South now participate in governing their communities and their country. And as Lyndon Johnson had hoped, access to the ballot box has not only empowered the South's black citizens but also freed the region from the stigmatized isolation of its accursed racist past.

Throughout the nation, black people have realized better jobs and greater income, higher levels of educational achievement, and improved housing, with more freedom to live in neighborhoods of their own choosing. Yet progress has been highly uneven. Racism, bigotry, and the insidious legacy of past discrimination still haunt the South — and every other section of America. While millions of black citizens have benefited from wider opportunities, their growing prosperity has barely touched the lives of a large black underclass still mired in poverty in the inner cities. The much faster growing Hispanic minority has also experienced uneven gains.*

The stark problems of poverty still facing many black Americans today leads some critics to dismiss the decade of the 1960s as one in which little meaningful change actually occurred. Others, increasingly vocal, would like to roll back the "affirmative action" programs that most presidents from Lyndon Johnson onward, along with Congress and the courts, have

* The 2000 U.S. Census reported an African American population of 36.4 million, 12.9 percent of the total U.S. population. The reported Hispanic population in 2000 was 35.3 million, 12.3 percent of the total (U.S. Census, Racial and Ethnic Residential Segregation in the U.S.).

preserved as means to help African Americans overcome the legacy of hundreds of years of slavery and discrimination.

In the more than three decades since adoption of the 1964, 1965, and 1968 civil rights acts, Congress has strengthened all three laws and defended them against attacks. A 1982 law extended and strengthened the Voting Rights Act.* A 1988 law increased enforcement and broadened coverage of the Fair Housing Act. In 1987 and 1991 Congress defended and reinforced the 1964 law against employment discrimination.

Major institutions in American society also support the civil rights laws in Congress and the courts. As a lonely band of lawyers up against the might of the American legal establishment, Thurgood Marshall and his NAACP associates won the 1954 Supreme Court decision outlawing school segregation. In 2003, however, before the Supreme Court, the NAACP defended affirmative action programs at the University of Michigan with strong support from a wide array of institutions, including the American Bar Association, the nation's law schools and medical schools, major universities, and leaders from corporate America and organized labor. However, the Supreme Court has been equivocal in its support of civil rights efforts for the past two decades.

What Congress and presidents since Lyndon Johnson still have *not* done is launch initiatives of a large enough magnitude to address poverty in the inner cities. Nevertheless, whether one views the glass as half full or half empty is a matter of perspective, but the United States is a very different society today than it was in 1963 — thanks in large part to the sweeping power of the grassroots civil rights movement, the Johnson presidency, and the most liberal Congress since the Great Depression.[4] The civil rights revolution was not a mere passing event along an endless continuum of routine political change. It was an exceptional, defining moment in American history.

Two Americas

The Kerner Commission's 1968 report forecasting an America split into two societies — one black and one white, separate and unequal — has to some extent proved true. The split has also occurred along economic lines — a divide that is starkly visible within the African American community itself, as well as within society at large. National Urban League president Marc Morial acknowledges that "things have gotten better for some." He points out, on the one hand, that the past forty years have been a period

* The Voting Rights Act is up for renewal by Congress in 2007.

of increased prosperity for a growing black middle class, which has benefited from the elimination of discriminatory barriers. But millions of
black Americans, Hispanic Americans, and poor whites continue to live
in the iron grip of poverty and chaos in the urban ghettoes and barrios, as
well as in isolated rural areas.[5] For many black and Hispanic Americans in
the inner cities, conditions have actually worsened, with hundreds of
thousands of blue-collar jobs vanishing. As middle- and working-class
blacks have seized new opportunities to improve their education, income,
jobs, and housing, they have migrated out of the inner cities. Those people left behind are further handicapped by the exodus of the workers,
shopkeepers, professionals, and institutions that once provided some
measure of stability in the central city. The interwoven problems of broken families, teenage pregnancy, crime, drugs, inadequate schools, and
lack of jobs combine to sustain a continuing American tragedy in the
midst of plenty. One stark statistic is telling: black families in the bottom
20 percent of the income scale have *not* improved their economic well-being in more than three decades.* For many of the inner-city poor, perhaps
the most debilitating problem is the loss of hope.

In contrast, a large black middle class is growing and prospering. African Americans have achieved success in careers from which they earlier
were excluded. In 2001 the mean annual income of intact black families —
those with both a mother and father in the home — nearly equaled the income of all similar families. More than 40 percent of black families in
2001 earned middle-class incomes or higher — a twofold rise since 1960.[6]

Nationally, the rise of black Americans to positions of prominent leadership in virtually every profession and business is no longer only a token
phenomenon. Black leaders direct major universities, large corporations,
departments of medicine in leading hospitals. In a Republican presidential administration, America has been served by a black secretary of state
and a black national security adviser. And African Americans are employed alongside whites throughout the ranks of public and private institutions. When Lyndon Johnson was president, there was only one black
general in the armed services. In 2004 there were forty-six African American generals and admirals — still only 5 percent of the total, but a visible
inspiration for the many blacks who have found career opportunities in
the military.[7]

The gap, however, between blacks and whites on virtually every eco-

---

* The mean family income for the bottom 20 percent of black families in 2001 was $7,140.
The comparable figure, adjusted for inflation, was $7,051 in 1969 (U.S. Census, Historic Fam-
ily Income).

nomic measure — income and accumulated wealth, including home ownership — remains significant. Even though the black poverty rate has been more than cut in half since the advent of the civil rights era — from 55 percent in 1959 to less than 25 percent in 2003 — it still persistently remains more than twice that of white families. Even though unemployment among blacks reached historic lows during the 1990s boom, it stubbornly remains twice the rate of white unemployment.[8] The only time those gaps have closed — and then closed only slightly — has been during periods of extraordinary sustained economic growth such as in the 1960s and the 1990s. Even those black middle-income families who have achieved the greatest gains still earn less than equally successful white American families. The biggest impediment to future black economic progress relative to that of white America is the vast disparity in accumulated wealth. While black family income had grown to average two-thirds of white family income in 2001, the gap in accumulated wealth between blacks and whites remained a staggering fourfold. Seventy percent of white families owned their homes, while fewer than 50 percent of black families owned theirs. The amount of accumulated wealth — or the lack of it — affects families' ability to withstand periods of unemployment, to help children complete higher education, and to invest in and build business ownership.[9]

Return to the Battlefields

When Martin Luther King marched in Selma, Alabama, to push for a voting rights law, most African Americans in the Deep South could not vote, let alone hold public office. With the 1965 Voting Rights Act, those barriers rapidly fell. In the U.S. House of Representatives, the number of black members has risen from only five in 1964 to thirty-seven in 2004 — with fifteen of the black members elected from southern states.* Major cities across the South, including Atlanta, Birmingham, Jackson, New Orleans, and Durham, have elected majority-black city councils and mayors. Blacks are strongly represented in southern state legislatures.† In addi-

---

* Including one Alabaman, one Mississippian, one South Carolinian, one Tennessean, one Texan, one Virginian, two North Carolinians, three Floridians, and four Georgians.

† In Alabama as of 2004, 27 African Americans served in the state house of representatives (out of 105) and 8 in the state senate (out of 35). In Mississippi, 36 (of 122) state representatives and 11 (of 52) state senators were African American. Twenty-five blacks served in the South Carolina house (out of 123) and 7 in the state senate (46). Georgia had 39 (of 180) black state representatives and 10 (of 56) black state senators. In Georgia, 6 black Americans held statewide office, as did others in Louisiana and North Carolina.

tion, the increased African American voting base has led many previously ardent segregationists publicly to change their tune. With the rise of the southern black vote, the worst of racist politics has disappeared almost completely, although more subtle forms of discrimination persist.

Women, too, have made great strides. Between 1964 and 2004, the number of female senators has increased from two to fourteen, while the number of congresswomen has risen from eleven to sixty-one.

As President Johnson predicted, however, the backlash against his party's civil rights advocacy cost the Democrats their hold on the South. Conservative Republicans gained a majority of congressional seats from what once was the solid Democratic South, and Republicans have gerry-mandered congressional districts in efforts to limit the influence of the new black vote. Nevertheless, African Americans combined with moderate whites to deliver the electoral votes of several southern states to Democratic presidential candidates Jimmy Carter in 1976 and Bill Clinton in 1992 and 1996. Virtually all of the African American elected officials in the South are Democrats.

Forty years ago, J. L. "Ike" Chestnut was the only black lawyer in Selma, Alabama. Today there are several dozen. In Selma, Montgomery, and Birmingham — Martin Luther King's battlegrounds — the visible signs of change are everywhere. The streets along the route of the Selma march are paved now; the houses have plumbing and running water. The courthouses and city halls are governed by black elected officials, who have replaced the tyrannical Sheriff Clarks and Bull Connors of the 1960s. The shops along the main streets and in the suburbs are staffed by black clerks as well as whites. Black men and women serve in the police and fire departments. The hospitals of Selma are now open to all, with patients cared for by both black and white doctors.[10]

In southern communities, police brutality against blacks decreased almost in direct proportion to the rise in the number of black voters, as Vernon Jordan, former president of the National Urban League, observed.[11] Provisions of the 1968 civil rights laws ensuring fair jury selection and protection of civil rights workers have greatly reduced vigilante injustice. In acts of redemption, southern prosecutors and juries finally brought to justice over thirty years later some of the most notorious perpetrators of the hate crimes of the 1960s.* The day has passed when all-white juries routinely dismiss charges against whites blatantly guilty of murdering black civil rights activists.

---

* The murderer of Mississippi NAACP leader Medgar Evers in 1963 was convicted by an integrated jury in 1994. Two of the infamous bombers who killed four African American girls at Birmingham's Sixteenth Street Baptist Church in 1963 were convicted in 2001 and 2002.

Artur Davis, the congressman for the district that includes both Selma and Birmingham, was born in West Montgomery in 1967. An honors graduate of Harvard University and Harvard Law School, Davis was elected in 2002 as only the second African American member of Congress from Alabama since Reconstruction. He sees the civil rights movement as having "opened up a new flow of talent" with "black and Hispanic leaders [increasing] the talent pool for American civic leadership." Unfortunately, he also sees a region that has not yet addressed the problems of those who have not shared in the economic gains. The West Montgomery neighborhood where Davis was born remains deeply impoverished. "It looks exactly like in 1967," he notes, with the roads still unpaved. Poverty is still rampant across the rural "Black Belt" section of his district. Although he represents pockets of wealth and prosperity, five of the twelve counties in Congressman Davis's district ranked among the one hundred poorest counties in the country in the 2000 census. "With the political progress and the economic progress of middle-class African Americans," Davis explains, "we have gotten a little bit complacent; we've convinced ourselves that [poverty] is a tolerable thing. The basic problem is the sense of resignation about poverty in our society."[12]

Selma's mayor, James Perkins, was a twelve-year-old civil rights protester at the time of the Selma march. He was less interested in gaining voting rights than in being able to buy a hot dog at the segregated Thirsty Boy fast food restaurant. After college and jobs with Fortune 500 companies, Perkins returned to Selma to build a large computer software business. Although he has had some success in recruiting industry to Selma, he is frustrated by the persistence of black poverty and by the difficulty of obtaining investment capital for black-owned businesses.[13]

In Atlanta, too, things have changed. Since 1974, four African Americans have served as mayor, including King's trusted colleague Andrew Young. The city is home to the Martin Luther King Jr. Center, under the leadership of his widow. Coretta Scott King has continued to advocate peace and equality. Her home, in Georgia's Fifth Congressional District in Atlanta, was represented in 2004 by John Lewis, the former SNCC chairman. A nine-term veteran, Lewis is the third-ranking member of the Democratic leadership in the House. He continues to push for a national effort to address the massive problems of the inner cities and their poor inhabitants. Despite his pride in black progress, however, Lewis is not optimistic. "During the 1960s we had a coalition of conscience," says Lewis. "We had it in the American community at large, and we had a bipartisan group in Congress dedicated to justice. Today, we no longer have that powerful coalition."[14]

From his office on the forty-fourth floor, Andrew Young looks down on a city that barely resembles the Atlanta where he led demonstrations forty years ago. Now retired from public service after fourteen years as a member of Congress, U.S. ambassador to the United Nations, and mayor of Atlanta, Young reflects on changes there. A rigidly segregated city has been transformed into a bustling metropolis with an integrated work-force and a prospering and growing black middle class. Young notes that white and black families sit together at football games at the Atlanta Fal-cons' stadium, integrated and equally represented in every section, cheer-ing for their team. On a flight to New York City in the spring of 2004, he observed with interest that "in the first-class section of the plane, half of the passengers were African Americans . . . young businesspeople, work-ing on their laptop computers and talking with the other passengers." He feels an enormous sense of pride and optimism about these everyday ex-amples of progress. Yet he remains painfully aware of those at the bottom, in what Martin Luther King called "a lonely island of poverty in an ocean of material wealth and affluence."[15]

At the University of Mississippi, where a white mob fomented a deadly riot in 1962 to protest James Meredith's enrollment as the first black stu-dent, the student body is now 18 percent African American, as is 12 per-cent of the faculty. Joseph Meredith, son of the civil rights pioneer, re-ceived his Ph.D. in business administration from the university in 2003 and was honored as the outstanding graduate student. That same year the president of the student body, the editor of the university newspaper, and the quarterback of the football team all were African Americans, as was assistant university provost Donald Cole. After being expelled from the university in the late 1960s for civil rights activism, Cole had vowed never to return to his native state. Yet after earning a Ph.D. in mathematics from the University of Michigan and rising in the business world as a corporate executive, Cole came back to help lead the university.[16]

In the town of Marks, however, deep in the Mississippi Delta, results from the 1960s are less encouraging. When Martin Luther King visited Marks in 1968 to recruit for the Poor People's Campaign, he wept at the abject poverty of black people he met there. As a twenty-year-old activist, James Figgs rode the mule train from Marks to Washington, but eventu-ally returned home discouraged by the protesters' failure to move either the government or the nation. Figgs has remained an activist, serving seven years as the first black member of the Mississippi State Parole Board, where he helped institute reforms in the prison system. In 2004 blacks held most elected offices in Marks and in Quitman County. Figgs's son, Dwight Barfield, is mayor of Marks. Yet both father and son are disappointed, as Figgs puts it, that "blacks have not been fair to themselves." In a comment echoing those of other movement veterans, Figgs complains that not enough successful blacks help those left behind. "The saddest thing I see is that nobody's reaching back to work in major efforts with these young black boys," says Figgs. "They are lost. They don't have any understanding of what the movement did." Others point out that too few successful African Americans today realize that their achievements rest, in part, on the backs of both the Martin Luther Kings and the faceless thousands of heroes who changed a nation. Barfield feels that what his town and state are most in need of is competent public officials, "whether black or white." Quitman remains the poorest county in the nation, with 44 percent of its population living in poverty in 2000.[17]

The Power of Education

For several decades after President Johnson signed the 1965 Elementary and Secondary Education Act, the educational attainment of black Americans under the age of twenty-five rose rapidly. In the 1970s and 1980s, spurred in part by the higher income of their parents, as well as by Johnson's federal programs to help poor students, these young people virtually closed the gap between blacks and whites in attaining a high school diploma. Black and white high school graduates also were enrolling in college at approximately the same rate.

A crucial truth, however, is that even as blacks rapidly gained further education, they still could not keep pace with the rising educational demands necessary for success in the twenty-first-century workplace. Only one out of six blacks who begins college graduates, one-half the completion rate of white students.

The most integrated public schools in the United States in 2003 were located in the South — an irony of the fifty-year experience with school integration. School integration, like housing integration, has succeeded best in areas where blacks represent a relatively small minority of the population. The open housing provisions of the 1968 Civil Rights Act have offered many black citizens a passport out of the inner city — although their new suburban neighborhoods often re-segregate, as do their schools. The pace of housing integration grew in the 1990s as a burgeoning economy gave black families enough income to leave the central cities. The greatest increase in integration of neighborhoods took place in booming areas of the South, Southwest, and West. New communities there were more amenable to blacks and whites living in the same neighborhoods. The greatest residential integration of the last twenty years occurred in California, Texas, and Florida, the least in the old industrial cities of the Midwest and the East. Public opinion polls show that both whites and blacks have increasingly accepted living in integrated neighborhoods.

Uncertain Future

The struggle of African Americans and Hispanic Americans to share more equitably in American democracy grew more difficult as the fight shifted in large part from winning legal rights to achieving equality in fact. In Lyndon Johnson's and Martin Luther King's views, the passage of civil rights laws against discrimination was far from sufficient to overcome four hundred years of inequality and deeply ingrained racial prejudice. The favorable political climate for major change in the mid-1960s was brief. It had largely dissipated even before Dr. King's assassination and the end of the Johnson presidency. The revolution lost its political force after scoring its extraordinary initial victories. Yet the civil rights movement directly inspired and led to successful protest movements against the Vietnam War, and on behalf of women's rights, the rights of older workers, rights for the handicapped, and struggles overseas for human rights.

Since the 1960s there has been no comparable organized movement or political leadership that has dared to seek the massive change required to remake the inner cities and help their poor residents. Nor has there been the kind of research into bold solutions that excited policymakers in the 1960s. Also missing at the outset of the twenty-first century is the strong bipartisan coalition in Congress of liberal Democrats and liberal-to-moderate Republicans who passed the reforms of the 1960s.

As Detroit and Newark burned during July 1967, President Johnson told the nation what it would take to change the conditions that had led to four years of rage and rioting: "The only genuine, long-range solution for what has happened lies in an attack — mounted at every level — upon the conditions that breed despair and violence. All of us know what those conditions are: ignorance, discrimination, slums, poverty, disease, not enough jobs. We should attack these conditions not because we are frightened by conflict, but because we are fired by conscience. We should attack them because there is simply no other way to achieve a decent and orderly society in America."[18]

Johnson's and King's challenges remain to be answered.

ACKNOWLEDGMENTS

My first debt is to the journalists and historians who pioneered the research and the telling of this American story. Their extraordinary work includes contemporary news reports, thoughtfully written articles, and scholarly studies. My hope is to add useful new information and insights to their body of work. The contributions of many talented writers are acknowledged in the Author's Note on Sources, and in the endnotes and bibliography.

Another debt of gratitude is to the more than 150 persons I interviewed, each of whom spoke on the record, with candor and interest in accurately portraying the events in which they were participants or observers. I owe special thanks to Lady Bird Johnson, President Lyndon Johnson's gracious widow, who spent the better part of a day answering my questions, and to the president's daughter Lynda Johnson Robb, who was equally generous with her time and frank insights. The names of all persons interviewed are noted in the interview list.

I am grateful to the many archivists and librarians who assisted me in locating valuable primary source materials on this complex period of American history. Their knowledge, patience, and courtesy immeasurably helped this project. At the Lyndon Baines Johnson Library in Austin, Texas, those archivists included library director Harry Middleton and his successor, Betty Sue Flowers. The library, part of the National Archives and Records Administration, made available several thousand pages of White House documents not previously released, as well as more than a dozen of Lyndon Johnson's tape-recorded telephone conversations that previously had been expurgated. The LBJ Library archivists who assisted my work included Tina Houston, Regina Greenwell, Linda Seelke, Claudia Anderson, Jacqueline Thornburg, Allen Fisher, Ted Gittinger, Will Clements, Jennifer Cuddeback, Laura Harmon, Shannon Jarrett, Mary Knill, Charlaine McCauley, Philip Scott, Robert Tissing, John Wilson, and Kyla Wilson.

I also wish to thank, at the Martin Luther King Library in Atlanta, Georgia, Cynthia Patterson Lewis, Elaine Hall, Steve Klein, and Robert Vickers. At the National Archives in Washington, D.C., Michael Gillette, Kristen Wilhelm, and Charles Schamel. At the Freedom of Information office of the FBI in Washington, D.C., Marcia Daniel, Deborah Beatty, Kirk Cromer, Harry Kuntz, Nicole Lee, Anna Mae Mitchell, Nancy Stuart, Rex Tomb, Josie Walker, Ethel Willis, and Luann Wilkins. At the John F. Kennedy Library in Boston, Massachusetts, Megan Desnoyers and Jim Cedrone. At the Richard B. Russell Library in Athens, Georgia, Jill Severn. At the George Smathers Library manuscript collection in Gainesville, Florida, Frank Orser. At the Moorland-Spingarn Research Center at Howard University, Robin Van Fleet. At the Everett Dirksen Library in Pekin, Illinois, Frank Mackaman and Lynn Kasinger. At the Minnesota State Historical Society's manuscript collection, Steve Nielsen, as well as Philip Byrne and Linda Pederson, assistant to former vice president Walter Mondale. At the Stanford University Martin Luther King Jr. Papers Project, Clayborne Carson.

I owe special thanks to Robert Dallek, biographer of Lyndon Johnson, and David Garrow, biographer of Martin Luther King Jr., both of whom generously encouraged and aided my project, making available material from their personal papers. Historian Gerald McKnight provided me with his insight, as well as his extensive files of FBI documents on the Poor People's Campaign. Others who kindly helped me obtain material for the book include David Busby, Elizabeth Carpenter, Cartha "Deke" DeLoach, Finlay Lewis, Charles Maguire, Walter Naegle, and David Shreve at the University of Virginia.

The following generously made available material from their personal papers: former senator Edward Brooke, Faythe Canson (access to the diaries of her mother, Verna Canson), Mary Cooper and James Hamilton (access to National Council of Churches papers), former representative Steve Horn, Clarence Jones, former representative James Jones, Gertrude Martin (access to the unpublished autobiography of her late husband, Louis), Matthew Nimetz, Arthur Schlesinger Jr., and Jean Stein.

Among the journalist friends who encouraged me to write this book and contributed their own recollections and other assistance were Kenneth DeCell, James Dickinson, Ernest B. Furgurson, James Lehrer, Roger Mudd, Tom Wicker, and Roger Wilkins. Ken DeCell, an extraordinary editor at the *Washingtonian* magazine, read and edited the book manuscript, as he had a half-dozen major pieces I wrote for the magazine.

Attorney David Wauken helped review the book contract. Esther Campbell and her team at the Rail Stop provided both good cheer and fine food.

I owe special thanks to a series of research assistants who made it possible for me to review far more material than I ever could have covered alone. James Mokhiber, now a history professor, helped obtain, examine, and analyze thousands of FBI documents. Bill Pugsley conducted research over several years at the LBJ Library, of which he has exceptional knowledge. Britt Krivicich listened to several hundred hours of Lyndon Johnson's tape-recorded telephone conversations. Erin Ashwell, working as a summer intern, gathered material on the 1965 Civil Rights Act. Nathan Means helped with research. Diana Claitor did photo research at the LBJ Library. Erick Powell did research at the Russell Library, and Benjamin Houston at the George Smathers manuscript collection.

Two exceptional young men successively worked full-time with me on every aspect of the book during the final three years of research and writing: Marc Borbely, now editor of a community newspaper, and Joshua Israel, a rising Democratic political activist. Marc and Josh both brought intelligence, dedication, and their own ideals to the book. They, as well as all the other Washington-based researchers, assisted me on many interviews. Each assistant helped make this five-year project a less lonely journey and a more joyful pursuit to understand our past.

Anton Mueller, my editor at Houghton Mifflin, believed in the value of this book, commissioned its writing, and provided perceptive counsel and editing along the way. His questions and insights helped me to probe and try to understand the complexities of Lyndon Johnson and Martin Luther King. His assistant Erica Avery helped in many ways, as did Gracie Doyle. Amanda Heller copyedited the manuscript for Houghton Mifflin with a scholar's eye and sensitive attention to grammar and language.

My literary agent and friend, Timothy Seldes, president of Russell and Volkening, encouraged me to write this history, guided the book proposal, presented the book to Houghton Mifflin, and has provided wise counsel at every step of the journey.

Finally, I express my appreciation and love to my family for their extraordinary support and help: my daughter-in-law, Mary Ann Bennett, a calm and reassuring voice at all times; Nathan Bennett Kotz, a grandson whose wit, intelligence, and energy always put book writing in proper perspective; my son, Jack Mitchell Kotz, a talented photographer who contributed the author's photo for this book and has an exceptional ability to help his father sort out problems, whether about writing, business, or life — a steady companion with whom to climb mountains of all kinds.

My beloved wife, Mary Lynn Kotz, an exceptional writer and biographer, edited this book with sensitive skill, as she has edited every other major piece of writing I have attempted since we were young journalists in Des Moines, Iowa. Whenever I hesitated, Mary Lynn insisted that it was important that I write this story. We are full partners in all of our endeavors, and it is to her that I lovingly dedicate this book. Lyndon Johnson and Martin Luther King Jr. had their shining moment together. My life has been brighter since the day on which I was lucky enough to meet Mary Lynn Booth.

Nick Kotz
Broad Run, Virginia

AUTHOR'S NOTE ON SOURCES

In writing this book, I had the privilege of drawing from a rich historical record. Important holders of primary source material that I used included the Lyndon Baines Johnson Library, part of the National Archives and Records Administration, in Austin, Texas; the Martin Luther King Jr. Library in Atlanta, Georgia; and the Freedom of Information office of the FBI. At the LBJ Library, President Johnson's tape-recorded telephone conversations offered unique information about the president's actions and insights into his personality and character. The Johnson White House files, oral histories conducted by the library, and documents from and concerning the FBI were valuable. Responding to my Freedom of Information Act (FOIA) requests, the FBI and the LBJ Library released for the first time several thousand documents from the library's so-called "Stegall files" (after Mildred Stegall, a confidential secretary to Lyndon Johnson). Historians should pursue for release other important material still withheld in the Johnson files. The LBJ Library has a deserved reputation for openness of its files, but is in need of additional resources to complete the job of making President Johnson's files fully available to the nation.

In this brief author's note I can mention only a few of the several hundred authors whose valuable work I drew from. (I have tried to cite carefully all my sources of information, and to list them as well in the bibliography.)

On Lyndon Johnson and the Johnson presidency, Robert Dallek's two-volume biography (*Lone Star Rising* and *Flawed Giant*) is the most complete and fair account to date. Ronnie Dugger's biography *The Politician* is insightful on Johnson's early life and career. Doris Kearns Goodwin, in *Lyndon Johnson and the American Dream,* makes highly effective and wise use of the unparalleled personal access she had as a historian to Lyndon Johnson after his presidency.

Lady Bird Johnson's *White House Diary* is filled with candid thoughts and observations about her husband. In some ways her diary is more revealing and useful than the president's own memoir, *The Vantage Point*. Robert Caro's four-part biography *The Years of Lyndon Johnson* (*The Path to Power, Means of Ascent,* and *Master of the Senate* are the three volumes published thus far) offers exceptional detail on the Johnson years. Vaughn Davis Bornet's study *The Presidency of Lyndon Johnson* is a solid history and biography, as are half a dozen others.

Of the inside accounts of the Johnson presidency, there are eight books by former Johnson White House aides, each of which provides important information and insights: *The Triumph and Tragedy of Lyndon Johnson* by Joseph Califano, *Ruffles and Flourishes* by Liz Carpenter, *Remembering America* by Richard Goodwin, *A Political Education* by Harry McPherson, *The Tragedy of Lyndon Johnson* by Eric Goodman, *Lyndon B. Johnson* by George Reedy, *The President Steps Down* by George Christian, and *A Very Human President* by Jack Valenti. Merle Miller's oral biography *Lyndon* also provides a portrait of Johnson as told by those who knew him best. Michael Beschloss has contributed the first two volumes of his three-volume collection of well-annotated excerpts (*Taking Charge* and *Reaching for Glory*) from the LBJ telephone tapes. The Miller Center at the University of Virginia is in the early stages of what will be an ambitious effort of publishing material from the Johnson tapes, as well as recorded telephone calls and meetings from other presidencies.

Of the many good contemporaneous books by journalists on Lyndon Johnson, three I found especially useful were *JFK and LBJ* by Tom Wicker, *Lyndon B. Johnson: The Exercise of Power* by Rowland Evans and Robert Novak, and *A Very Personal Presidency* by Hugh Sidey. Of many useful books concerning Lyndon Johnson and the Vietnam War, I most often consulted *Pay Any Price* by Lloyd C. Gardner and *Into the Quagmire* by Brian Van-DeMark. Michael L. Gillette's *Launching the War on Poverty* is excellent on the origins of the poverty program. Other helpful information on Johnson came from Robert A. Divine's *Johnson Years* trilogy; Bernard J. Firestone and Robert C. Vogt's *Lyndon Baines Johnson and the Uses of Power;* Jeff Shesol's *Mutual Contempt: Lyndon B. Johnson, Robert Kennedy, and the Feud That Defined a Decade;* Mark Stern's *Calculating Visions: Kennedy, Johnson, and Civil Rights;* and *Lyndon Johnson Remembered,* edited by Thomas W. Cowger and Sherwin J. Markman.

There will be countless more studies about Lyndon Johnson, one of the nation's most fascinating presidents. At this point, the Johnson literature is sparser than it should be because for several decades Johnson was "out of style" for historians and publishers. That situation is now changing with release of the Johnson tapes and with the beginning of serious revisionist thinking about Johnson's place in history.

The most complete biographical study of the Reverend Martin Luther King Jr. to date comes from the work of David Garrow, with his three books (*Bearing the Cross, Protest at Selma,* and *The FBI and Martin Luther King Jr.*), as well as his work as editor of and contributor to several major anthologies on King. Taylor Branch's *Parting the Waters* and *Pillar of Fire* are the first two volumes of his excellent work on King and the movement. Among the many other books on King from which I benefited are David Levering Lewis, *King: A Biography;* Stephen B. Oates, *Let the Trumpet Sound;* Michael Eric Dyson, *I May Not Get There with You;* Ralph Abernathy, *And the Walls Came Tumbling Down;* John J. Ansbro, *Martin Luther King Jr.;* Clayborne Carson, *The Autobiography of Martin Luther King Jr.;* James H. Cone, *Martin and Malcolm and America;* Adam Fairclough, *To Redeem the Soul of America;* Vincent Harding, *Martin Luther King;* C. Eric Lincoln, *Martin Luther King Jr.: A Profile;* L. D. Reddick, *Crusader Without Violence: A Biography of Martin Luther King Jr.;* and Andrew Young, *An Easy Burden: The Civil Rights Movement and the Transformation of America.* King's own words were found in *Why We Can't Wait; The Measure of a Man; A Testament of Hope: The Essential Writings and Speeches of Martin Luther King Jr.,* edited by James Washington; *A Call to Conscience,* edited by Clayborne Carson; and *The Martin Luther King Jr. Companion,* edited by Coretta Scott King.

To understand the history of the civil rights movement, I relied particularly on Seth Cagin and Philip Dray, *We Are Not Afraid: The Story of Goodman, Schwerner, and Chaney and the Civil Rights Campaign for Mississippi;* Clayborne Carson, *In Struggle: SNCC and the Black Awakening of the 1960s* and *The Eyes on the Prize: Civil Rights Reader;* J. L. Chestnut and Julia Cass, *Black in Selma;* David R. Colburn, *Racial Change and Community Crisis: St. Augustine, Florida, 1877–1980;* John Dittmer, *Local People: The Struggle for Civil Rights;* Charles Fager, *Selma, 1965: The March That Changed the South;* James Farmer, *Lay Bare the Heart;* James Forman, *The Making of Black Revolutionaries;* David Halberstam, *The Children;* John Lewis, *Walking with the Wind: A Memoir of the Movement;* Gerald McKnight, *The Last Crusade: Martin Luther King Jr. and the Poor People's Campaign;* Fred Powledge, *Free at Last?;* Howell Raines, *My Soul Is Rested;* Cleveland Sellers, *The River of No Return: The Autobiography of a Black Militant;* Milton Viorst, *Fire in the Streets: America in the 1960s;* and Juan Williams, *Eyes on the Prize: America's Civil Rights Years, 1954–1965.*

Several books offered special insight on the civil rights laws of the 1960s.

They included Daniel Berman, *A Bill Becomes a Law: Congress Enacts Civil Rights Laws;* James F. Findlay Jr., *Church People in the Struggle;* Hugh Davis Graham, *The Civil Rights Era: Origins and Development of National Policy;* Robert D. Loevy, *To End All Segregation: The Politics of the Passage of the Civil Rights Act of 1964;* Robert Mann, *The Walls of Jericho;* and Charles and Barbara Whalen, *The Longest Debate: A Legislative History.*

To understand the role of the FBI in this story, the most useful works were Cartha "Deke" DeLoach, *Hoover's FBI: The Inside Story by Hoover's Trusted Lieutenant;* Curt Gentry, *J. Edgar Hoover: The Man and the Secrets;* Kenneth O'Reilly, *Racial Matters: The FBI's Secret File on Black America;* Richard Gid Powers, *Secrecy and Power: The Life of J. Edgar Hoover;* Athan G. Theoharis and John Stuart Cox, *The Boss: J. Edgar Hoover and the Great Inquisition;* and David Wise, *The American Police State: The Government Against the People.*

My interest in Lyndon Johnson goes back to Texas in the 1930s and 1940s, when my grandfather Nathan Kallison and my uncles Perry and Morris Kallison ran a farm and ranch store in San Antonio and raised registered Hereford cattle on the Kallison Ranch in the Texas hill country, not too far from where Johnson grew up. Congressman — then Senator — Johnson was highly regarded by my family, in part because he helped bring electric power and other benefits to a needy, sparsely settled region. Uncles Perry and Morris, along with many other Texans, took credit for helping put LBJ over the top in his eighty-seven-vote Senate victory in 1948. They were Franklin Roosevelt New Dealers, as was my mother, Tybe Kallison Kotz, a dedicated liberal who admired Johnson's advocacy of civil rights and his War on Poverty. Out of that rich heritage came my own ideals, a passion for history, and an interest in the career of Lyndon Johnson, whose actions I followed as a newspaper reporter in Washington, D.C., for the *Des Moines Register, Minneapolis Tribune,* and *Washington Post.*

NOTES

ABBREVIATIONS

AI	Author's interview
ASINT	Arthur Schlesinger Jr. Interviews (John F. Kennedy Library)
Church	Senate Select Committee to Study Government Operations with Respect to Intelligence Activities ("Church Committee")
Cong Rec	*Congressional Record*
DD	Lyndon Johnson Daily Diary (LBJ Library)
DDB	Lyndon Johnson Daily Diary Backup (LBJ Library)
Ervin	Senate Select Committee on Presidential Campaign Activities ("Ervin Committee")
FBIMLK	FBI King Main File (100-106670) (FBI Archives)
FBISDL	FBI Stanley David Levison File (FBI Archives)
Horn Log	Steve Horn's Log (Manuscript Division, Library of Congress)
HUOH	Howard University Oral History (Moorland-Spingarn Research Center)
JFKL	John F. Kennedy Library — Other Files
JFKOH	John F. Kennedy Library Oral History
LBJL	LBJ Library — Other Files
LBJOH	LBJ Library Oral History
McCone	Governor's Commission on the Los Angeles Riots ("McCone Commission")
NYT	*New York Times*
O&C	FBI J. Edgar Hoover Official and Confidential File (FBI Archives)
PitC	*Pittsburgh Courier*
Pottinger	Report of the Department of Justice Task Force to Review the FBI Martin Luther King Jr. Security and Assassination Investigations ("Pottinger Report")
PPP	Lyndon Baines Johnson, *Public Papers of the President of the United States* (Washington, D.C.: Government Printing Office, 1964–1970)
Romaine	Anne Romaine, "The Mississippi Freedom Democratic Party" (Master's thesis, University of Virginia, 1970)
Russell	Richard B. Russell Collection (University of Georgia Library)
SCLC	Southern Christian Leadership Conference Papers (Manuscript Division, Library of Congress)
SDLTAP	FBI Wiretaps and Recordings of Stanley David Levison (100-111180) (FBI Archives)
Stegall	LBJ Library, Mildred Stegall Files (FBI)
Stokes	House Select Committee on Assassinations ("Stokes Committee")
TKC	Martin Luther King Papers (The King Center)
TT	Lyndon Johnson Telephone Tape (LBJ Library)
UPI	United Press International Wire
WAA	*Washington Afro-American*
Warren	President's Commission on the Assassination of President Kennedy ("Warren Commission")
WHCF	LBJ Library White House Central Files
WP	*Washington Post*

Introduction

1. Robert Parker, *Capitol Hill in Black and White*, p. 79.
2. Robert Dallek, *Flawed Giant*, p. 282; Lady Bird Johnson, *White House Diary*, p. 567.
3. Doris Kearns Goodwin, *Lyndon Johnson and the American Dream*, p. 1.

1. The Cataclysm

1. Warren, 4:147.
2. Ibid., pp. 129–149.
3. Cliff Carter, LBJOH; DD, 11/22/63, 11:30 A.M.
4. Robert Dallek, *Flawed Giant*, pp. 47–49.
5. Coretta Scott King, Mayerson interview, 16:60–62 (from the Smathers Library, Gainesville, Fla.); Coretta Scott King, *My Life*, p. 244.
6. Michael Beschloss, *Taking Charge*, p. 14.
7. Merle Miller, *Lyndon: An Oral Biography*, p. 315.
8. Ibid., p. 319.
9. Ibid., p. 318.
10. Marie Fehmer, LBJOH, 2:52; Merle Miller, *Lyndon: An Oral Biography*, p. 320.
11. Cliff Carter, LBJOH.
12. AI, Willard Wirtz.
13. Merle Miller, *Lyndon: An Oral Biography*, p. 322.
14. Ibid., p. 323.
15. Robert Mann, *The Walls of Jericho*, p. 381; Frank Cormier, *LBJ the Way He Was*, p. 6; Arthur Schlesinger Jr., *Robert Kennedy*, p. 655.
16. Merle Miller, *Lyndon: An Oral Biography*, p. 324.
17. TT, LBJ and Richard Maguire, 11/23/63, 9:10 P.M., K6311.01 PNO 2.
18. Merle Miller, *Lyndon: An Oral Biography*, p. 324; TT, LBJ and Dwight Eisenhower, 11/22/63, 7:10 P.M., conversation 2.
19. TT, LBJ and J. Edgar Hoover, 11/23/63, 10:01 A.M., K6311.01 PNO 3.
20. "Warren Commission Born Out of Fear; Washington Wanted to Stop Speculation," *WP*, 11/14/93, p. A1; AI, Horace Busby.
21. William Colmer, LBJOH.
22. www.usdoj.gov/kidspage/crt/edu.htm, accessed 4/8/03.
23. Gilbert C. Fite, *Richard B. Russell Jr.*, pp. 402–404.
24. AI, Jerry H. Booth.
25. "Racial Hostility Ignored by South," *NYT*, 11/23/63, p. 6.
26. AI, Leslie Dunbar.
27. AI, Ramsey Clark and John Douglas.
28. AI, Walter Fauntroy.
29. AI, Julian Bond.
30. Coretta Scott King, *My Life*, p. 244.
31. Andrew Young, *An Easy Burden*, pp. 278–279.
32. AI, C. T. Vivian.
33. AI, Clarence Jones; TKC, "Statement of Dr. Martin Luther King Jr.," 11/22/1963.
34. Merle Miller, *Lyndon: An Oral Biography*, pp. 319–320.
35. Lawrence O'Brien, *No Final Victories*, p. 163.

36. Jack Brooks, LBJOH.
37. John Connally, *In History's Shadow*, p. 194.
38. Cliff Carter, LBJOH.
39. Merle Miller, *Lyndon: An Oral Biography*, p. 323.
40. George Reedy, LBJOH, 3:25.
41. Lady Bird Johnson, *White House Diary*, p. 6.
42. Ibid., p. 10; LBJL, "Diary of Lady Bird Johnson," 12/24/63.
43. AI, Elizabeth Carpenter.
44. AI, John Riley and Charles Whaley.
45. AI, Harry McPherson; Harry McPherson, *A Political Education*, pp. 191–192, 200.
46. Inaugural Address of President John F. Kennedy, 1/20/61, www.presidency .ucsb.edu/docs/inaugurals/kennedy.php, accessed 6/8/04.
47. Taylor Branch, *Parting the Waters*, p. 901.
48. Robert Dallek, *Flawed Giant*, p. 114; George H. Gallup, *Gallup Poll*, 3:1838.
49. David Garrow, *Bearing the Cross*, p. 303.
50. Merle Miller, *Lyndon: An Oral Biography*, p. 324.
51. AI, Horace Busby.
52. Merle Miller, *Lyndon: An Oral Biography*, p. 324.
53. Ibid.
54. Jack Valenti, LBJOH, 2:22; AI, Jack Valenti.
55. Merle Miller, *Lyndon: An Oral Biography*, p. 325.
56. Cliff Carter, LBJOH, 4:14.
57. Ibid.
58. TT, LBJ and Arthur Goldberg, 11/22/63, 9:06 P.M., K6311.01A PNO 1.
59. AI, Jack Valenti; Jack Valenti, *A Very Human President*, pp. 152–153.
60. AI, Jack Valenti.
61. Ibid.; Jack Valenti, *A Very Human President*, pp. 152–153.

2. Let Us Continue

1. Roy Young, "Presidential Leadership and Civil Rights Legislation," p. 303; *Chicago Daily News*, 11/27/63, p. 5.
2. Robert Dallek, *Flawed Giant*, p. 54.
3. Cliff Carter, LBJOH.
4. Taylor Branch, *Pillar of Fire*, p. 183; David Garrow, *Bearing the Cross*, pp. 307–308.
5. "King Statement on the Assassination of President Kennedy," 12/23/63, King Center Archives.
6. AI, Walter Fauntroy.
7. David Garrow, *Bearing the Cross*, p. 307.
8. Mark Stern, *Calculating Visions*, p. 115.
9. TT, LBJ and Martin Luther King, 11/25/63, 9:20 P.M., K6311.02 PNO 22.
10. Robert Mann, *The Walls of Jericho*, p. 370.
11. AI, Jack Valenti.
12. Taylor Branch, *Pillar of Fire*, p. 182.
13. Donald H. Smith, interview with Martin Luther King, 11/29/63, State Historical Society of Wisconsin.

14. David Garrow, *Bearing the Cross*, p. 306.

15. Ibid., p. 279.

16. Andrew Young, LBJOH, p. 3.

17. Robert Dallek, *Flawed Giant*, pp. 99–100; Lloyd C. Gardner, *Pay Any Price*, pp. 86–95.

18. TT, LBJ and George Smathers, 11/23/63, 2:10 P.M., K6311.01A PNO 12 and 13.

19. Merle Miller, *Lyndon: An Oral Biography*, p. 337.

20. AI, James Farmer.

21. William E. Leuchtenburg, "The Old Cowhand from Dixie," *Atlantic Monthly* (December 1992): 94.

22. Roy Wilkins, *Standing Fast*, p. 262.

23. www.multied.com/Bio/people/Wilkins.html, accessed 3/18/03.

24. Roy Wilkins, *Standing Fast*, p. 276.

25. DD, 11/29/63; Robert Mann, *The Walls of Jericho*, p. 382; Roy Young, "Presidential Leadership and Civil Rights Legislation," p. 303; *WP*, 11/30/63, p. A8.

26. *NYT*, 12/2/63, p. 41.

27. Roy Wilkins, *Standing Fast*, p. 296.

28. AI, Dorothy Height.

29. AI, Horace Busby; Robert Caro, *Master of the Senate*, pp. 725–737; Robert Caro, *The Path to Power*, pp. 512–515.

30. AI, Horace Busby.

31. Ibid.; LBJL, T. Harry Williams, "Huey, Lyndon, and Southern Radicalism," *Journal of American History*, pp. 267–293.

32. AI, Horace Busby.

33. Merle Miller, *Lyndon: An Oral Biography*, p. 361; Robert Dallek, *Flawed Giant*, p. 61.

34. Nicholas Lemann, *The Promised Land*, p. 142; Elizabeth Wickendon Goldschmidt, LBJOH, tape 2.

35. Robert Dallek, *Flawed Giant*, p. 61; Nicholas Lemann, "The Unfinished War," *Atlantic Monthly* (December 1988): 37–56.

36. Robert Dallek, *Flawed Giant*, p. 413; Joseph Califano, *Triumph and Tragedy of Lyndon Johnson*, p. 211.

37. Bourke Hickenlooper, LBJOH, p. 2.

38. Helen Gahagan Douglas, LBJOH, p. 15.

39. Rowland Evans and Robert Novak, *Lyndon B. Johnson*, p. 352.

40. TT, LBJ and Ralph Yarborough, 11/23/63, 1:44 P.M., K6311.01 PNO 8.

41. Rowland Evans and Robert Novak, *Lyndon B. Johnson*, p. 353.

42. Taylor Branch, *Pillar of Fire*, p. 187; AI, Harry McPherson.

43. AI, Harry McPherson; Harry McPherson, *A Political Education*, p. 216.

44. Robert Mann, *The Walls of Jericho*, p. 385.

45. Mark Stern, *Calculating Visions*, p. 166.

46. Paul Douglas, LBJOH.

47. Ibid.

48. Ibid.

49. Ibid.

50. AI, Lady Bird Johnson; Rowland Evans and Robert Novak, *Lyndon B. Johnson*, p. 352.

51. Jan Jarboe Russell, *Lady Bird*, pp. 15–18.

52. AI, Lynda Bird Johnson Robb.

53. PPP, 1963–64, bk. 1, pp. 8–11.

54. *California Eagle*, 12/5/63, p. 1; SCLC, pt. 3, reel 3, 584 (statement).

55. Merle Miller, *Lyndon: An Oral Biography*, p. 340.

56. PPP, 1963–64, bk. 1, pp. 8–11.

57. Hubert Humphrey, LBJOH, 3:7.

58. Stuart Symington, LBJOH, 2:16.

59. UPI, 12/4/63; Charles and Barbara Whalen, *The Longest Debate*, p. 82.

60. Mark Stern, *Calculating Visions*, p. 168.

61. TT, LBJ and John McClellan, 12/3/63, 3:47 P.M., K6312.02 PNO 2; LBJ and Robert McNamara, 12/10/63, 11:50 A.M., K6312.06 PNO 17; LBJ and Richard Russell, 12/7/63, 5:00 P.M., K6312.05 PNO 2.

62. Robert Dallek, *Flawed Giant*, pp. 72–73; Gardner Ackley, LBJOH, 1:6; JFKL, "Troika Meeting with LBJ," 11/25/63, Heller Papers.

63. Jack Valenti, LBJOH, 2:31.

64. DD, 12/3/63; Mark Stern, *Calculating Visions*, p. 172; Charles and Barbara Whalen, *The Longest Debate*, p. 81.

65. Charles and Barbara Whalen, *The Longest Debate*, p. 90.

66. Joseph Rauh, LBJOH; Clarence Mitchell, LBJOH.

67. Taylor Branch, *Pillar of Fire*, p. 187.

68. Rowland Evans and Robert Novak, *Lyndon B. Johnson*, p. 380.

69. Gilbert C. Fite, *Richard B. Russell Jr.*, p. 410.

70. Kenneth O'Donnell, LBJOH, p. 70.

71. Ibid., p. 71.

72. TT, LBJ and Richard Daley, 12/3/63, 10:00 A.M., K6312.02 PNO 14.

73. TT, LBJ and Harry Provence, 12/25/63, 8:07 P.M., K6312.18 PNO 1.

74. TT, LBJ and Robert Anderson, 11/30/63, 1:30 P.M., K6311.06 PNO 20.

75. TT, LBJ and Katharine Graham, 12/2/63, 11:10 A.M., K6312.01 PNO 19.

76. *WP*, editorials, 12/3/63, p. A16; 12/4/63, p. A20; 12/5/63, p. A23.

77. David Garrow, *Bearing the Cross*, p. 308; *NYT*, 12/4/63, p. 1.

3. *"A Fellow Southerner in the White House"*

1. FBISDL, 100-1111 80-9, 367a.

2. AI, Clarence Jones.

3. DDB, 12/1/63.

4. Taylor Branch, *Parting the Waters*, p. 809.

5. Philip A. Klinkner and Rogers M. Smith, *The Unsteady March*, p. 155.

6. Ibid., p. 159.

7. Ibid., p. 217.

8. Robert Mann, *The Walls of Jericho*, p. 20.

9. www.presidentelect.org/e1948.html#map, accessed 3/18/03.

10. *Brown v. Board of Education*, 347 U.S. 483 (1954).

11. *Brown v. Board of Education*, 349 U.S. 294 (1955).

12. Philip A. Klinkner and Rogers M. Smith, *The Unsteady March*, p. 246.

13. Ibid., p. 245.

14. David Garrow, *Bearing the Cross*, pp. 12–82.

15. *Gayle v. Browder*, 352 U.S. 903 (1956) (per curiam).

16. David Garrow, *Bearing the Cross*, pp. 32, 48–50.

17. Ibid., pp. 49–50, 51.
18. Ibid., p. 35; Rev. M. L. King Sr., *Daddy King*, pp. 107–108.
19. David Garrow, *Bearing the Cross*, p. 37; Rev. Charles Morton, HUOH.
20. David Garrow, *Bearing the Cross*, p. 37.
21. Ibid., p. 39.
22. Stephen B. Oates, *Let the Trumpet Sound*, pp. 36–41, 47.
23. Ibid., pp. 33–34, 42–45.
24. David Garrow, *Bearing the Cross*, p. 45; Martin Luther King Jr., *Autobiography*, pp. 34–35.
25. David Garrow, *Bearing the Cross*, pp.57–58; Martin Luther King Jr., *Autobiography*, pp. 76–78.
26. Taylor Branch, *Parting the Waters*, p. 146.
27. David Garrow, *Bearing the Cross*, p. 68.
28. Martin Luther King Jr., *Autobiography*, p. 26.
29. David Garrow, *Bearing the Cross*, pp. 85–86, 90.
30. Robert Mann, *The Walls of Jericho*, pp. 178–179, 180–181; AI, Harry McPherson.
31. David Garrow, *Bearing the Cross*, pp. 127–133.
32. Ella Baker, HUOH, p. 39.
33. David Garrow, *Bearing the Cross*, pp. 122–123, 143–144; John Lewis, *Walking with the Wind*, pp. 125–126; AI, Julian Bond.
34. David Garrow, *Bearing the Cross*, pp. 142–149; John Lewis, *Walking with the Wind*, p. 126.
35. David Garrow, *Bearing the Cross*, pp.154–155; AI, James Farmer; James Farmer, *Lay Bare the Heart*, pp. 196–197.
36. David Garrow, *Bearing the Cross*, pp. 156–158; John Lewis, *Walking with the Wind*, pp. 160; AI, John Lewis.
37. David Garrow, *Bearing the Cross*, pp. 158; James Farmer, *Lay Bare the Heart*, pp. 204–205.
38. James Farmer, *Lay Bare the Heart*, pp. 204–205; AI, James Farmer; Robert Dallek, *Flawed Giant*, p. 30; Herbert S. Parmet, *JFK*, pp. 249–262.
39. James Farmer, *Lay Bare the Heart*, p. 197.
40. David Garrow, *Bearing the Cross*, p. 159.
41. AI, James Farmer; David Garrow, *Bearing the Cross*, p. 159; James Farmer, *Lay Bare the Heart*, pp. 206–207.
42. Taylor Branch, *Parting the Waters*, p. 690.
43. David Garrow, *Bearing the Cross*; Taylor Branch, *Pillar of Fire.*
44. Taylor Branch, *Parting the Waters*, p. 690; David Garrow, *Bearing the Cross*, p. 229.
45. "Letter from Birmingham Jail," www.stanford.edu/group/King/popular_requests/frequentdocs/birmingham.pdf, accessed 4/1/04.
46. James Forman, *Making of Black Revolutionaries*, pp. 312–313.
47. Taylor Branch, *Parting the Waters*, pp. 763–764; Roy Young, "Presidential Leadership and Civil Rights Legislation," p. 103.
48. Robert Dallek, *Flawed Giant*, p. 36; AI, Horace Busby.
49. AI, Horace Busby; *WP*, 5/31/63, p. 1; Taylor Branch, *Pillar of Fire*, pp. 91–92.
50. Norbert Schlei, LBJOH; Norbert Schlei, JFKOH.
51. Hugh Davis Graham, *Civil Rights Era*, p. 78; Charles and Barbara Whalen,

The Longest Debate, p. 77; LBJL, "Transcript of LBJ conversation with Ted Sorensen," 6/3/63, Vice Presidential Papers.

52. JFK Library, telephone tapes, 7/9/63, audiotape 96.6; Taylor Branch, *Parting the Waters,* pp. 863–864.

53. *NYT,* 6/10/63.

54. Robert D. Loevy, ed., *Civil Rights Act of 1964,* p. 353; Hugh Davis Graham, *Civil Rights Era,* p. 74.

55. David Garrow, *Bearing the Cross,* p. 269; JFKL, King to Kennedy, 6/12/63, White House Central Files 1478.

56. www.arlingtoncemetery.com/mwevers.htm, accessed 3/20/03.

57. AI, Eugene McCarthy.

58. AI, Harry McPherson; Harry McPherson, LBJOH, pt. 1, pp. 8–10.

59. Roy Young, "Presidential Leadership and Civil Rights Legislation," p. 285; LBJL, "Speech to National Governor's Conference," 7/23/63, Vice Presidential Papers, box 83.

60. Roy Young, "Presidential Leadership and Civil Rights Legislation," p. 285; Rowland Evans and Robert Novak, "Inside Report: Lyndon Leaves the South," *WP,* 8/27/63, p. A15.

61. Robert Kennedy, JFKOH.

62. Martin Luther King Jr., *A Testament of Hope,* pp. 217–220.

63. Karl Fleming, "Not Even Safe in Church," *Newsweek,* 9/30/63; Advisory Board, *Reporting Civil Rights,* pt. 2, p. 28.

64. Taylor Branch, *Pillar of Fire,* p. 145; Taylor Branch, *Parting the Waters,* p. 901.

65. AI, Clarence Jones.

66. Ibid.

67. LBJL, Lee White to LBJ, 12/3/63.

68. David Garrow, *Bearing the Cross,* p. 308; *NYT,* 12/4/64, p. 1; *NYT,* 12/4/63, p. 39; *PitC,* 12/14/63, p. 1; UPI, 12/4/63.

69. TT, LBJ and David McDonald, 12/3/63, 12:10 P.M., K6312.02 PNO 18.

70. UPI, 12/4/63.

71. *NYT,* 12/4/63, p. A2.

72. AI, Clarence Jones.

73. AI, Clarence Jones and Andrew Young.

4. Hoover, King, and Two Presidents

1. Robert Kennedy, JFKOH, pp. 446–447; Church, bk. 3, "Andrew Young Testimony," 2/19/76, p. 97; O&C, file 24, Burke Marshall to J. Edgar Hoover, 9/20/63; Richard Reeves, *President Kennedy,* pp. 530–531, 737.

2. Taylor Branch, *Parting the Waters,* pp. 835–838; Richard Reeves, *President Kennedy,* pp. 530–531.

3. Andrew Young, *An Easy Burden,* pp. 264–266.

4. The Kennedys had passed earlier warnings to King through Harry Belafonte, John Seigenthaler, and Harris Wofford. In a cloak-and-dagger episode that followed the walk in the Rose Garden with President Kennedy, Burke Marshall met Andrew Young in New Orleans to make the case that Levison was a secret Soviet agent. Despite the drama of the rendezvous, Young was not convinced and requested hard evidence, which Marshall was unwilling or unable to pro-

vide. See Arthur Schlesinger Jr., *Robert Kennedy and His Times,* pp. 369–373; Andrew Young, *An Easy Burden,* p. 267; AI, Harris Wofford; Garrow, *The FBI and Martin Luther King Jr.,* p. 44.

5. For a copy of O'Dell's eventual dismissal letter, see FBIMLK, Dora McDonald to Robert Kennedy, 7/3/63, 100-106670-3656.

6. For a detailed discussion, see the 105-page FBI report "Stanley David Levison," 2/21/63, FBI file, 100-111180 and 100-392452.

7. David Garrow, *The FBI and Martin Luther King Jr.,* p. 28.

8. Andrew Young, *An Easy Burden,* p. 131; David Garrow, *The FBI and Martin Luther King Jr.,* p. 28.

9. Coretta Scott King, *My Life,* p. 338; Andrew Young, *An Easy Burden,* pp. 200–201; David Garrow, *The FBI and Martin Luther King Jr.,* pp. 26–27.

10. Andrew Young, *An Easy Burden,* p. 266.

11. Director, FBI, to Chicago, New York, 3/18/77, FBI file, 100-428091-10340, vol. 144; David Garrow, "The FBI and Martin Luther King," *Atlantic Monthly* (July–August 2002): 86.

12. David Garrow uncovered the connections between "Solo," Levison, and King in 1981 with the publication of *The FBI and Martin Luther King Jr.* For a closer look at "Solo" itself, see John Barron, *Operation Solo.*

13. SAC (special agent in charge), Chicago, to Director, FBI, 10/6/52, 61-7665-209.

14. John Barron, *Operation Solo,* pp. 150–154.

15. SAC, New York, to Director, FBI, 5/13/55, 100-340711-162, sec. 2, p. 6.

16. "Stanley David Levison," 2/21/63, 100-111180 and 100-392452-190.

17. Jack Childs reported that Levison had agreed to give Lem Harris $5,000 in November 1962, though it was unclear if the contribution was ever made. See the review of the Stanley Levison file from SAC, New York, to Director, FBI, 8/15/66, FBI file, 100-392452, p. 14.

18. See the later reports of these signs of dissatisfaction in SAC, New York, to Director, FBI, 8/15/66, FBI file, 100-392452.

19. David Garrow, "The FBI and Martin Luther King," p. 86; David Garrow, *The FBI and Martin Luther King Jr.,* p. 42.

20. David Garrow, *The FBI and Martin Luther King Jr.,* p. 26.

21. Director, FBI, to Attorney General, 1/8/62, FBI file, 100-392452-131.

22. For a report of this statement, see "Stanley David Levison," 2/21/63, FBI file, 100-111180 and 100-392452, p. 97. For examples of the repetition of this characterization, see Bland to Sullivan, 3/6/62, FBI file, 100-392452; O&C, file 24, Baumgardner to Sullivan, 7/22/63, FBI file, 100-106670; O&C, file 24, J. E. Hoover, Memorandum for the Attorney General, 7/23/63, FBI file, 100-106670; O&C, file 24, Hoover to SAC, New York, 10/7/63, FBI file, 100-3-116-349; O&C, file 24, Hoover to Attorney General, 10/7/63, FBI file, 100-106670 — ill.; and, as posthumous justification for wiretapping, O&C, file 24, Hoover to Attorney General, 5/13/69, FBI file, 100-106670-NR.

23. David Garrow, *The FBI and Martin Luther King Jr.,* p. 46.

24. See the index and microfilmed logs of the wiretap and office bugs published as "The Martin Luther King Jr. File. Part II: The King–Levison File," ed. David Garrow (Frederick, Md.: University Publishing of America, 1984).

25. David Garrow, *The FBI and Martin Luther King Jr.,* pp. 49–50.

26. Baumgardner to Sullivan, 10/22/62, FBI file, 100-438794, in Stokes, 6:136; Director, FBI, to SAC, Atlanta, 10/23/62, FBI file, 100-438794, in Stokes, 6:137–138; Church, bk. 3, pp. 86–87; David Garrow, *The FBI and Martin Luther King Jr.*, pp. 51–53.

27. See the retrospective account in SAC, New York, to Director, FBI, 8/15/66, FBI file, 100-392452, p. 14.

28. Noted in SAC, New York, to Director, FBI, 8/15/66, FBI file, 100-3-104-34, pp. 14–25.

29. Ibid.

30. Hall apparently shared this perspective, calling Levison "a dirty son of a bitch" in late 1963. SAC, New York, to Director, FBI, 11/26/63, FBI file, 100-3-116-573. Hall criticized the Levison brothers in April 1964 as "no good," and as having stolen party funds and real estate. Hall believed that they were "opportunists" and "ultra-left-wingers," Jack Childs reported, who disagreed with the party line on civil rights and were out to use Martin Luther King for their own gain. Childs noted, however, that Levison had never been formally "drummed out" of the party and might still be an "ideological Communist." SAC, New York, to Director, FBI, 8/15/66, FBI file, 100-392452, pp. 20, 22–23.

31. David Garrow, *The FBI and Martin Luther King Jr.*, pp. 61–62.

32. SAC, New York, to Director, FBI, 9/11/63, FBI file, 100-106670-225, 100-3-116.

33. Church, bk. 3, p. 99.

34. Ibid.

35. O&C, file 24, Evans to Belmont, 7/25/63, FBI file, 100-106670.

36. FBI to White House, 7/15/63, FBI file, 100-3-75-1896.

37. Baumgardner to Sullivan, "March on Washington, August 28, 1963, Possible Subversive Influence," 8/22/63, FBI file, 100-3-116-230; Baumgardner to Sullivan, 8/23/63, FBI file, 100-3-116-253X.

38. Baumgardner to Sullivan, 8/23/63, FBI file, 100-3-116-253X.

39. Sullivan to Belmont, 8/30/63, FBI file, 100-3-116-253X and 100-106670-NR, sec. 7.

40. Director, FBI, to SAC, Detroit, 11/29/63, FBI file, 100-106670-NR, sec. 6; Taylor Branch, *Pillar of Fire*, pp. 197–198.

41. The Church Committee described the "extreme personal vindictiveness" of the campaign against Martin Luther King Jr. See Church, bk. 3, pp. 82–83.

42. On Hoover's background, see especially Richard Gid Powers, *Secrecy and Power;* Kenneth O'Reilly, *Racial Matters;* Athan G. Theoharis and John Stuart Cox, *The Boss;* David Wise, *The American Police State;* William C. Sullivan, *The Bureau;* Curt Gentry, *J. Edgar Hoover;* Cartha "Deke" DeLoach, *Hoover's FBI;* Ray Wannall, *The Real J. Edgar Hoover.*

43. Several authors have discussed the possibility that Hoover and Tolson shared a homosexual relationship. Hoover's aides, including DeLoach, say the story is false. See, for example, Athan G. Theoharis and John Stuart Cox, *The Boss,* p. 108; Kenneth O'Reilly, *Racial Matters,* p. 149; Cartha "Deke" DeLoach, *Hoover's FBI,* pp. 61–81.

44. www.fbi.gov/libref/historic/history/newdeal.htm, accessed 3/28/03.

45. Richard Gid Powers, *Secrecy and Power,* pp. 56, 228–230.

46. Bland to Sullivan, 2/3/62, FBI file, 100-392452-135, in Stokes, 6:131–132.

47. Church, bk. 3, p. 83; Kenneth O'Reilly, *Racial Matters*, p. 136.

48. Richard Gid Powers, *Secrecy and Power*, p. 411.

49. Ibid., p. 324.

50. Church, bk. 3, pp. 89–91. For FBI officials' perspectives on Hoover's anger at King's criticism, see William Sullivan, *The Bureau*, pp. 135–140, and Cartha "Deke" DeLoach, *Hoover's FBI*, pp. 200–203.

51. Taylor Branch, *Pillar of Fire*, p. 28.

52. Taylor Branch, *Parting the Waters*, p. 861; David Garrow, *The FBI and Martin Luther King Jr.*, p. 67.

53. O&C, file 24, Bland to Sullivan, 9/6/63, FBI file, 100-106670-207.

54. O&C, file 24, Evans to Belmont, 10/10/63; Evans to Belmont, 10/21/63, FBI file, 100-106670-259, "June" file.

55. ASINT, Stanley Levison, 8/3/76, box W-56; SDLTAP, 6/10/63 and 6/12/63.

56. Robert Kennedy, JFKOH, pp. 447–448.

57. Taylor Branch, *Parting the Waters*, p. 861; David Garrow, *The FBI and Martin Luther King Jr.*, p. 67.

58. Evan Thomas, *Robert F. Kennedy*, pp. 262–263.

59. Stegall, "Communism and the Negro Movement: A Current Analysis," 10/16/63. Also see Pottinger, Belmont to Tolson, 10/17/63, FBI file, 100-3-116-145, exhibit 13

60. O&C, file 24, Director, FBI, to Attorney General, 10/25/63; O&C, file 24, Hoover to Tolson, Belmont, Mohr, DeLoach, Rosen, and Sullivan, 10/25/63; O&C, file 24, Office of Director, 10/28/63.

61. Richard Gid Powers, *Secrecy and Power*, p. 360.

62. Taylor Branch, *Parting the Waters*, pp. 912–915; Seymour Hersh, *The Dark Side of Camelot*, pp. 398–400.

63. TT, LBJ and J. Edgar Hoover, 11/29/63, 1:40 P.M., K6311.04 PNO 15.

64. Hoover to Attorney General and Kenneth O'Donnell, 11/27/63, FBI file, 100-3-116-539.

65. Stegall, Hoover to Jenkins, 12/3/63, King file; SAC, New York, to Director, FBI, 12/2/63, FBI file, 100-106670, sec. 7; Domestic Intelligence Division, "Informative Note," 12/2/63, FBI file, 100-106670, sec. 7.

66. David Garrow, *Bearing the Cross*, p. 308; *Long Island Press*, 11/25/63, p. 9.

67. Richard Gid Powers, *Secrecy and Power*, p. 394.

68. TT, LBJ and J. Edgar Hoover, 11/29/63, 1:40 P.M., K6311.04 PNO 15; Cartha "Deke" DeLoach, LBJOH, p. 6.

69. Cartha "Deke" DeLoach, LBJOH, pp. 1–3; AI, Cartha "Deke" DeLoach.

70. Cartha "Deke" DeLoach, LBJOH, pp. 3–4; Robert Dallek, *Flawed Giant*, p. 30; AI, Cartha "Deke" DeLoach.

71. Victor S. Navasky, *Kennedy Justice*, p. 812.

72. O&C, file 92, DeLoach to Hoover, 1/15/64.

73. FBIMLK, Baumgardner to Sullivan, 12/19/63, sec. 7.

74. FBIMLK, Sullivan to Belmont, 12/24/63, sec. 7.

75. "Questions to Be Explored at Conference 12/23/63 re Communist Influence in Racial Matters," Stokes, 6:159–161.

76. FBIMLK, Sullivan to Belmont, 12/24/63, sec. 7.

77. Ibid.

78. FBIMLK, Baumgardner to Sullivan, 1/8/64, sec. 7; FBIMLK, "Martin Luther King Jr.," 1/9/64, sec. 7.

79. O&C, file 24, Sullivan to Belmont, 1/6/64, FBI file, 100-3-116-714; David Garrow, *Bearing the Cross*, p. 310.

80. Taylor Branch, *Pillar of Fire*, p. 207.

81. David Garrow, *Bearing the Cross*, p. 312; Taylor Branch, *Pillar of Fire*, pp. 207–208; David Garrow, *The FBI and Martin Luther King Jr*, pp. 106–107; O&C, file 24, Sullivan to Belmont, 1/8/64, FBI file, 77-56944-19, and 1/27/64, FBI file, 100-3-116-792.

82. David Garrow, *The FBI and Martin Luther King Jr.*, p. 106.

83. O&C, file 24, Sullivan to Belmont, 1/27/64, FBI file, 100-3-116-792.

84. Stokes, vol. 6, Sullivan to Belmont, 1/8/64, pp. 164–166.

85. Church, bk. 3, sec. 2, p. 121; Taylor Branch, *Pillar of Fire*, p. 209; David Garrow, *The FBI and Martin Luther King Jr.*, p. 106.

86. Cartha "Deke" DeLoach, *Hoover's FBI*.

87. AI, Cartha "Deke" DeLoach; Cartha "Deke" DeLoach, LBJOH.

88. Church, bk. 3, DeLoach to Hoover, 1/14/64, sec. 2, pp. 121–122.

89. Stokes, vol. 6, Sullivan to Belmont, 1/13/64, FBI file, 100-3-116, pp. 193–194.

5. A Fire That No Water Could Put Out

1. AI, E. Ernest Goldstein and Peggy Goldstein; Merle Miller, *Lyndon: An Oral Biography*, p. 366.

2. AI, Harry Middleton.

3. George H. Gallup, *Gallup Poll*, 3:1859.

4. Ibid., 3:1857.

5. PPP, 1963–64, bk. 1, pp. 112–118.

6. Thurgood Marshall Oral History (Columbia University); George Tames Oral History 1:18 (U.S. Senate Historical Office).

7. John Kenneth Galbraith, *The Affluent Society*.

8. Michael Harrington, *The Other America*.

9. *WP*, 1/12/64, p. 1.

10. TT, LBJ and Larry O'Brien, 3/11/64, 2:20 P.M., WH6403.09 PNO 6.

11. Claude Desautels, LBJOH.

12. TT, LBJ and Larry O'Brien, 3/11/64, 2:20 P.M., WH6403.09 PNO 6; J. B. West and Mary Lynn Kotz, *Upstairs at the White House*, pp. 190–384.

13. Charles and Barbara Whalen, *The Longest Debate*, p. 90; Alfred Steinberg, *Sam Rayburn*, p. 313.

14. TT, LBJ and Larry O'Brien, 1/18/64, 11:50 A.M., WH6401.16 PNO 13.

15. *Los Angeles Times*, 1/19/64.

16. *WAA*, 1/19/64, p. 16.

17. *Sunday (Washington) Star*, 1/19/64, p. A15.

18. *Los Angeles Times*, 1/19/64.

19. *WP*, 1/19/64.

20. *NYT*, 1/19/64, p. 42.

21. Ibid.

22. *New York World*, 2/7/64.

23. SCLC Newsletter (January 1964), Leadership Conference on Civil Rights Collection, Library of Congress, Manuscript Division.

24. *NYT,* 1/19/64, p. 1.

25. TT, LBJ and Walker Stone, 1/6/64, 3:48 P.M., WH6401.06 PNO 4.

26. TT, LBJ and Whitney Young, 1/6/64, 3:55 P.M., WH6401.06 PNO 5.

27. TT, LBJ and Richard Russell, 1/20/64, 7:20 P.M., WH6401.17 PNO 12–13.

28. TT, LBJ and John McClellan, 1/16/64, 4:20 P.M., WH6401.15 PNO 6.

29. TT, LBJ and Thomas Mann, 1/25/64, 12:20 P.M., WH6401.21 PNO 8.

30. TT, LBJ and Robert McNamara, 2/3/64, 6:20 P.M., WH6402.03 PNO 14.

31. PPP, 1963–64, bk. 2, p. 839.

32. AI, Elizabeth Carpenter; Liz Carpenter, *Ruffles and Flourishes,* pp. 35–36; DD, 1/17/64.

33. TT, LBJ and John Macy, 1/6/64, 3:30 P.M., WH6401.06 PNO 2.

34. Martin Luther King Jr., *Why We Can't Wait,* p. 146.

35. *NYT,* 1/12/64, sec. 4, p. 3.

36. *WAA,* 1/19/64, p. 17.

37. TT, LBJ and Robert McNamara, 1/25/64, 11:50 A.M., WH6401.21 PNO 2.

38. Charles and Barbara Whalen, *The Longest Debate,* pp. 96–97; Joseph Rauh, LBJOH, "Rauh Manuscript"; Robert D. Loevy, ed., *Civil Rights Act of 1964,* p. 66.

39. Denton L. Watson, *Lion in the Lobby,* pp. 587–588.

40. Ibid., p. 586.

41. Ibid., p. 597.

42. Ibid., p. 585.

43. PPP, 1963–64, bk. 1, p. 113.

44. *NYT,* 1/23/64.

45. PPP, 1963–64, bk. 1, p. 228.

46. *NYT,* 1/31/64.

47. Rowland Evans and Robert Novak, *Lyndon B. Johnson,* pp. 374–376.

48. TT, LBJ and Vance Hartke, 1/23/64, 1:11 P.M., WH6401.19 PNO 17.

49. TT, LBJ and Abraham Ribicoff, 1/23/64, 1:14 P.M., WH6401.19 PNO 18.

50. David Garrow, *Bearing the Cross,* pp. 312–313.

51. Taylor Branch, *Pillar of Fire,* p. 196; Church, "Dr. Martin Luther King Jr. Case Study."

52. Stegall, "Hoover to Jenkins," series of fifteen memos, 1/9/64–6/10/64, King file.

53. Stegall, "Communism and the Negro Movement: A Current Analysis," 10/16/63, NLJ 02–86.

54. Ibid.; AI, Robert McNamara.

55. *WP,* 4/22/64, p. A10.

56. Carl Rowan, *Breaking Barriers,* pp. 254–255. Rowan writes that in a January 1964 meeting, Rooney told him that Hoover had played tapes of the party for members of his subcommittee and described King as "the most dangerous man in America" and a "moral degenerate."

57. David Garrow, *The FBI and Martin Luther King Jr.,* pp. 110–111.

58. AI, Clarence Jones.

59. AI, Charles Mathias and James Bromwell.

60. *Cong Rec,* House proceedings, 1/31/64, 2:1511–38, and 2/1/64, 2:1582–1647; Charles and Barbara Whalen, *The Longest Debate,* p. 102.

61. *Cong Rec,* House proceedings, 1/31/64, 2:1511–38, and 2/1/64, 2:1582–1647; Charles and Barbara Whalen, *The Longest Debate,* p. 105.
62. TT, LBJ and Robert Kennedy, 2/4/64, 12:43 P.M., WH 6402.05 PNO 8.
63. *Cong Rec,* House proceedings, 2/4/64, 2:1917–27.
64. Smith's comments, not included in *Cong Rec,* come from Charles and Barbara Whalen, *The Longest Debate,* p. 110.
65. *Cong Rec,* House proceedings, 2/4/64, 2:1932–33.
66. AI, Clark MacGregor.
67. *Cong Rec,* House proceedings, 2/5/64, 2:1972–75.
68. Ibid., 2/7/64, 2:2465.
69. TT, LBJ and Orville Freeman, 2/5/64, 10:00 A.M., WH6402.05 PNO 13.
70. Bruce J. Dierenfield, *Keeper of the Rules,* p. 9; Charles and Barbara Whalen, *The Longest Debate,* pp. 114, 116.
71. www.factmonster.com/ipka/A0801429.html and www.senate.gov/reference/resources/pdf/RL30261.pdf, both accessed 4/23/03.
72. Robert D. Loevy, *To End All Segregation,* p. 100; *Time,* 1/17/64, p. 12.
73. AI, Willard Wirtz.
74. *Cong Rec,* House proceedings, 2/8/64, 2:2496–99.
75. Clarence Mitchell, LBJOH, p. 30.
76. AI, Jake Pickle; Jake Pickle, LBJOH, 4:6–7.

6. An Idea Whose Time Has Come

1. Robert D. Loevy, *To End All Segregation,* p. 136.
2. AI, Nicholas Katzenbach; Nicholas Katzenbach, LBJOH; Nicholas Katzenbach, "Toward a More Just America for All," in Thomas W. Cowger and Sherwin J. Markman, eds., *Lyndon Johnson Remembered,* pp. 125–138; Charles and Barbara Whalen, *The Longest Debate,* pp. 125–127.
3. Nicholas Katzenbach, "Toward a More Just America for All," pp. 125–138.
4. Charles and Barbara Whalen, *The Longest Debate,* p. 148.
5. Neil MacNeil, *Dirksen,* p. 228.
6. LBJL, Dirksen to O'Brien, 12/6/63, Office Files of Larry O'Brien, box 27.
7. TT, LBJ and Everett Dirksen, 12/20/63, 1:35 P.M., K6312.10 PNO 25.
8. AI, Jack Valenti.
9. Neil MacNeil, *Dirksen,* p. 229.
10. TT, LBJ and Roy Wilkins, 1/6/64, 5:15 P.M., WH6401.06 PNO 8.
11. Martin Luther King Jr., "Hammer on Civil Rights," in *A Testament of Hope,* p. 170.
12. TT, LBJ and Mike Mansfield, 2/11/64, 5:32 P.M., WH6402.15 PNO 2.
13. *Cong Rec,* 2/17/64; *Washington Star,* 2/17/64, p. A2.
14. *NYT,* 2/28/64, p. 1.
15. PPP, speech, 2/29/64, p. 328.
16. TT, LBJ and Larry O'Brien, 3/6/64, 7:20 P.M., WH6403.03 PNO 25–26.
17. Neil MacNeil, *Dirksen,* p. 231.
18. Charles and Barbara Whalen, *The Longest Debate,* p. 129; Horn Log, p. 6; "Report from Rabbi Richard Hirsch," 2/5/64, Leadership Conference on Civil Rights Collection, Library of Congress, Manuscript Division.
19. *NYT,* 3/22/64, p. 52.
20. Gilbert C. Fite, *Richard B. Russell Jr.,* pp. 408–409.

21. Horn Log, pp. 24–26.

22. Charles and Barbara Whalen, *The Longest Debate*, p. 140.

23. Hubert Humphrey, *Education of a Public Man*, p. 275.

24. AI, John Stewart.

25. AI, Walter Fauntroy.

26. Ibid.

27. Horn Log, pp. 92–95.

28. *NYT*, 4/16/64, p. 1.

29. *NYT*, 4/17/64, p. 1.

30. Taylor Branch, *Pillar of Fire*, p. 291; TKC, MLK to Wilkins, 4/21/64.

31. David Garrow, *Bearing the Cross*, p. 320.

32. Ibid., p. 321; TKC, "Meeting Minutes," 4/16/64 and 4/17/64.

33. David Garrow, *Bearing the Cross*, pp. 319–20; FBI, SAC, New York, to Hoover, 4/2/64, Communist Party USA, Negro Question File 100–3–116–1322; *Detroit Free Press*, 3/20/64.

34. LBJL, William Taylor, U.S. Commission on Civil Rights, to Lee White, 5/19/64, HU2.

35. David Colburn, *Racial Change and Community Crisis*, pp. 41–42.

36. AI, C. T. Vivian.

37. David Colburn, *Racial Change and Community Crisis*, pp. 64–70; AI, Hosea Williams.

38. LBJL, Lee White to LBJ, 3/24/64.

39. David Colburn, *Racial Change and Community Crisis*, pp. 65–67.

40. Ibid., pp. 64–67; AI, Hosea Williams, Malcolm Peabody Jr., and C. T. Vivian; *NYT*, 4/1/64, p. 1.

41. Stegall, Hoover to Jenkins, 2/5/64, 2/10/64, 2/13/64, 2/11/64, 2/28/64, 3/5/64, 3/6/64, 3/9/64, 3/17/64, 3/27/64, King file; David Garrow, *The FBI and Martin Luther King Jr.*, pp. 110, 162.

42. FBI file, Baumgardner to Sullivan, 3/4/64, FK-312.

43. David Garrow, *The FBI and Martin Luther King Jr.*, p. 109.

44. Taylor Branch, *Pillar of Fire*, pp. 246–247; TT, LBJ and Cartha "Deke" DeLoach, 3/12/64, 2:15 P.M., WH6403.09 PNO 16; TT, LBJ and J. Edgar Hoover, 3/9/64, 4:31 P.M., WH6403.06 PNO 9.

45. Bill Moyers, "LBJ and the FBI," *Newsweek*, 3/10/75, p. 84.

46. AI, Cartha "Deke" DeLoach.

47. AI, Harry McPherson.

48. Lady Bird Johnson, *White House Diary*, p. 294.

49. FBI, DeLoach to Mohr, 3/10/64, J. Edgar Hoover Official and Confidential File no. 92.

50. AI, Cartha "Deke" DeLoach.

51. *WP*, 4/15/64.

52. *NYT*, 3/18/64, p. 28.

53. FBI King file, 100–10666, 4/27/64.

54. David Garrow, *Bearing the Cross*, p. 322; *San Francisco Chronicle*, 4/24/64; SCLC, pt. 3, reel 3, 642, Library of Congress, Manuscript Division.

55. "Rauh Manuscript," in Robert D. Loevy, ed., *Civil Rights Act of 1964*, p. 55.

56. Taylor Branch, *Pillar of Fire*, p. 268; E. W. Kensworthy, "Rights Bill Wins 2 Tests in Senate by Wide Margin," *NYT*, 3/27/64, p. 10.

57. Robert D. Loevy, *To End All Segregation,* p. 162.

58. Ibid., pp. 184–185.

59. Robert Mann, *The Walls of Jericho,* p. 413.

60. Horn Log, "Cloture List."

61. Bishop Newell S. Booth, sermon, 5/20/64, National Council of Churches Archives, Washington, D.C.; AI, Steve Horn.

62. AI, Steve Horn; Robert Mann, *The Walls of Jericho,* p. 413.

63. PPP, 1963–64, pp. 418–421; *NYT,* 3/26/64, pp. 1, 16.

64. *NYT,* 3/26/64, p. 13.

65. PPP, 1963–64, p. 318.

66. Ibid., pp. 645–651.

67. Robert Mann, *The Walls of Jericho,* pp. 413–414; *Congressional Quarterly 1964 Almanac,* p. 381.

68. Horn Log, pp. 96–97.

69. Robert Mann, *The Walls of Jericho,* p. 403; *Cong Rec,* Senate proceedings, 3/21/64, p. 5865.

70. *NYT,* 4/12/64, p. 41.

71. Robert Mann, *The Walls of Jericho,* p. 402.

72. Ibid., p. 403; *Cong Rec,* Senate proceedings, 4/20/64, p. 8443.

73. Charles and Barbara Whalen, *The Longest Debate,* pp. 162–163.

74. TT, LBJ and John McCormack, 3/10/64, 7:35 P.M., WH6403.08 PNO 20.

75. AI, Gaylord Nelson.

76. Horn Log, p. 104.

77. TT, LBJ and Richard Russell, 4/9/64, 5:01 P.M., WH6404.06 PNO 12.

78. Horn Log, pp. 47–48.

79. Ibid., pp. 139–144.

80. Ibid., p. 41.

81. Transcript, CBS News, *Face the Nation,* 5/10/64.

82. TT, LBJ and Mike Mansfield, 4/29/64, 11:32 A.M., WH6404.15 PNO 4.

83. Robert Mann, *The Walls of Jericho,* p. 417.

84. TT, LBJ and Robert Kennedy, 4/29/64, 10:50 P.M., WH6404.12 PNO 6; Charles and Barbara Whalen, *The Longest Debate,* p. 169.

85. Robert Kennedy, JFKOH.

86. TT, LBJ and Hubert Humphrey, 4/30/64, 12:11 P.M., WH6404.15 PNO 22.

87. TT, LBJ and Hubert Humphrey, 5/2/64, 2:14 P.M., WH6405.01 PNO 23.

88. *NYT,* 5/8/64, p. 1.

89. "Thoughts on the Civil Rights Bill," in Robert D. Loevy, ed., *Civil Rights Act of 1964,* p. 95.

90. Charles and Barbara Whalen, *The Longest Debate,* p. 185; *NYT,* 5/20/64, p. 34; Neil MacNeil, *Dirksen,* pp. 234–235.

91. AI, Charles Ferris.

92. TT, LBJ and Hubert Humphrey, 5/13/64, 7:25 P.M., WH6405.06 PNO 18; TT, LBJ and Everett Dirksen, 5/13/64, 4:30 P.M., WH6405.06 PNO 5.

93. SCLC, pt. 3, reel 3, 643 (statement); *NYT,* 5/20/64, p. 1; Charles and Barbara Whalen, *The Longest Debate,* pp. 169, 176, 237.

94. Robert D. Loevy, *To End All Segregation,* pp. 265–266.

95. TT, LBJ and Hubert Humphrey, 5/13/64, 7:25 P.M., WH6405.06 PNO 18.

96. TT, LBJ and Hubert Humphrey, 5/2/64, 2:14 P.M., WH6405.01 PNO 23.

97. Robert D. Loevy, *To End All Segregation,* pp. 265–266; *NYT,* 5/21/64, pp. 1, 26; James F. Findlay Jr., *Church People in the Struggle,* pp. 52–55.

98. PPP, pp. 588–589.

99. LBJL, LBJ to Theological Students Vigil, 5/20/64, Main Files, LE/HU2.

100. AI, James Hamilton.

101. James F. Findlay Jr., *Church People in the Struggle,* pp. 53–56; AI, James Bromwell, Charles and Barbara Whalen, *The Longest Debate,* pp. 190–191.

102. TT, LBJ and Mike Manatos, 5/20/64, 6:11 P.M., WH6405.08 PNO 13.

103. TT, LBJ and William Fulbright, 4/29/64, 11:55 A.M., WH6404.15 PNO 7.

104. TT, LBJ and Robert Byrd, 4/9/64, 4:55 P.M., WH6404.08.

105. LBJL, Mike Manatos to Larry O'Brien, 5/11/64, Ex/HU2; LBJL, Stewart Udall to LBJ, 5/7/64, LE/HU2.

106. David Colburn, *Racial Change and Community Crisis,* p. 83.

107. AI, C. T. Vivian, Hosea Williams, Andrew Young, and Fred Shuttlesworth; David Colburn, *Racial Change and Community Crisis,* chaps. 1–4.

108. David Colburn, *Racial Change and Community Crisis.*

109. AI, C. T. Vivian, Hosea Williams, Andrew Young, and Fred Shuttlesworth; Andrew Young, *An Easy Burden,* pp. 289–296.

110. LBJL, Martin Luther King telegram to LBJ, 5/29/64, King name file.

111. TT, LBJ and George Smathers, 6/1/64, 2:48 P.M., WH6406.01 PNO 3–4.

112. FBI, Director, FBI to SAC, Jacksonville, 6/1/64; C. L. McGowan to Rosen, 5/30/64; SAC, Jacksonville, to Director, 5/28/64, Racial Situation, St. Augustine, Florida, file.

113. Taylor Branch, *Pillar of Fire,* p. 333.

114. AI, Fred Shuttlesworth and C. T. Vivian.

115. Taylor Branch, *Pillar of Fire,* p. 325.

116. Ibid.

117. Stegall, Hoover to Stegall, 6/1/64, King file.

118. Charles and Barbara Whalen, *The Longest Debate,* p. 170.

119. Ibid., pp. 187–188.

120. Ibid., pp. 190–191; AI, James Hamilton and James Bromwell.

121. Charles and Barbara Whalen, *The Longest Debate,* pp. 187–192.

122. TT, LBJ and Karl Mundt, 6/5/64, 4:55 P.M., WH6406.04 PNO 13; TT, LBJ and Robert Kennedy, 6/9/64, 12:25 P.M., WH6406.03 PNO 16.

123. Charles and Barbara Whalen, *The Longest Debate,* p. 199.

124. Taylor Branch, *Pillar of Fire,* pp. 338–345.

125. Ibid., pp. 356–357; AI, James Bromwell.

126. TT, LBJ and Charles Halleck, 6/22/64, 6:24 P.M., WH6406.12 PNO 13; *NYT,* 7/3/64, p. 1.

127. Bill Moyers, "What a Real President Was Like" *WP,* 11/13/88, p. C5.

128. TT, LBJ and Robert Kennedy, 7/4/64, 7:15 P.M., WH6407.04 PNO 1.

7. Lyndon Johnson and the Ku Klux Klan

1. Douglas O. Linder, "Bending Toward Justice: John Doar and the Mississippi Burning Trial," p. 2, www.law.umkc.edu/faculty/projects/ftrials/trialheroes/doaressay.html, accessed 8/4/03.

2. Seth Cagin and Philip Dray, *We Are Not Afraid,* p. 2.

3. Taylor Branch, *Pillar of Fire* p. 363.
4. Seth Cagin and Philip Dray, *We Are Not Afraid*, p. 30.
5. John Lewis, *Walking with the Wind*, p. 258.
6. Clayborne Carson, *In Struggle*, pp. 48–49.
7. PPP, 6/23/64, p. 808.
8. LBJL, Lee White to LBJ, 6/17/64, Ex/HU2/ST 24.
9. LBJL, Justice Department report to John Doar, Civil Rights Division, 4/64.
10. TT, LBJ and Lee White, 6/23/64, 12:35 P.M., WH6406.13 PNO 5.
11. TT, LBJ and John McCormack, 6/23/64, 12:45 P.M., WH6406.13 PNO 7–8.
12. TT, LBJ, Jack Valenti, and Robert Kennedy, 6/23/64, 3:11 P.M., WH6406.13 PNO 18.
13. TT, LBJ and Nicholas Katzenbach, 6/23/64, 4:16 P.M., WH6406.14 PNO 7.
14. TT, LBJ and J. Edgar Hoover, 6/23/64, 4:05 P.M., WH6406.14 PNO 4.
15. TT, LBJ and J. Edgar Hoover, 6/23/64, 6:15 P.M., WH6406.14 PNO 24.
16. TT, LBJ and James Eastland, 6/23/64, 4:25 P.M., WH6406.14 PNO 12.
17. TT, LBJ and J. Edgar Hoover, 6/23/64, 5:35 P.M., WH6406.14 PNO 20.
18. Seth Cagin and Philip Dray, *We Are Not Afraid*, pp. 331–332; Bernard Asbell, "My Son Didn't Die in Vain!" *Good Housekeeping* (May 1965).
19. LBJL, Kennedy memo to LBJ, 5/5/64, Ex/HU2/St 24; Seth Cagin and Philip Dray, *We Are Not Afraid*, p. 327.
20. Burke Marshall, LBJOH.
21. TT, LBJ and J. Edgar Hoover, 6/24/64, 5:30 P.M., WH6406.16 PNO 14–16.
22. Seth Cagin and Philip Dray, *We Are Not Afraid*, p. 324.
23. TT, LBJ and James Eastland, 6/23/64, 3:59 P.M., WH6406.14 PNO 3.
24. TT, LBJ and James Eastland, 6/23/64, 4:25 P.M., WH6406.14 PNO 12.
25. Taylor Branch, *Pillar of Fire*, p. 368.
26. TT, LBJ and Allen Dulles, 6/23/64, 7:05 P.M., WH6406.15 PNO 11.
27. TT, LBJ and Paul Johnson, 6/23/64, 8:21 P.M., WH606.16 PNO 1.
28. TT, LBJ and J. Edgar Hoover, 6/24/64, 5:30 P.M., WH6406.16 PNO 14–16; Taylor Branch, *Pillar of Fire*, p. 370.
29. AI, Burke Marshall.
30. Seth Cagin and Philip Dray, *We Are Not Afraid*, p. 357.
31. TT, LBJ, Allen Dulles, and Paul Johnson, 6/26/64, 1:05 P.M., WH6406.17 PNO 20.
32. TT, LBJ, Allen Dulles, and J. Edgar Hoover, 6/26/64, 1:17 P.M., WH6406.17 PNO 22–23.
33. TT, LBJ and J. Edgar Hoover, 7/2/64, 5:02 P.M., WH6407.02 PNO 16; AI, Nicholas Katzenbach and Burke Marshall; Nicholas Katzenbach and Burke Marshall, LBJOH.
34. Seth Cagin and Philip Dray, *We Are Not Afraid*, p. 369.
35. Ibid., p. 340.
36. John Dittmer, *Local People*, p. 248; Taylor Branch, *Pillar of Fire*, p. 399.
37. Sally Belfrage, *Freedom Summer*, pp. 32–33.
38. John Dittmer, *Local People*, pp. 202–207.
39. David Garrow, *Bearing the Cross*, p. 341; Taylor Branch, *Pillar of Fire*, p. 408; John Gibson, HUOH.
40. Harold DeWolf, HUOH.

41. TT, LBJ and Robert Kennedy, 7/21/64, 12:25 P.M., WH6407.11 PNO 3.
42. TT, LBJ and J. Edgar Hoover, 7/21/64, 12:40 P.M., WH6407.11 PNO 7; TT, LBJ and George Reedy, 7/4/64, 7:25 P.M., WH6407.04 PNO 3–4.
43. *NYT,* 7/22/64, p. 20.
44. *NYT,* 7/23/64, p. 15.
45. Ibid.; UPI-22, 7/24/64.
46. Andrew Young, *An Easy Burden,* pp. 305–306.
47. *NYT,* 7/25/64, p. 9.
48. Taylor Branch, *Pillar of Fire,* p. 414; Paul Good, *The Trouble I've Seen,* p. 127.
49. Taylor Branch, *Pillar of Fire,* pp. 417–418.
50. TT, LBJ and Charles Halleck, 6/22/64, 6:24 P.M., WH6406.12 PNO 13.
51. TT, LBJ and George Meany, 7/28/64, 10:15 A.M., WH6407.15 PNO 18.
52. TT, LBJ and Walter Reuther, 8/5/64, 2:54 P.M., WH6408.07 PNO 6.
53. TT, LBJ and George Mahon, 8/5/64, 3:05 P.M., WH6408.07 PNO 11.
54. TT, LBJ and Harold Cooley, 8/5/64, 4:15 P.M., WH6408.08 PNO 7.
55. TT, LBJ and Don Fuqua, 8/5/64, 4:09 P.M., WH6408.08 PNO 2–3.
56. TT, LBJ and Robert Jones, 8/5/64, 2:45 P.M., WH6408.07 PNO 3–4.
57. James Farmer, *Lay Bare the Heart,* pp. 298–300; John Lewis, *Walking with the Wind,* pp. 275–276; Roy Wilkins, *Standing Fast,* pp. 303–304.
58. "Text of Statements by Negro Leaders," *NYT,* 7/30/64, p. 12.
59. "Rights Protest Curb Favored by Johnson," *NYT,* 7/31/64, pp. 1, 11.
60. "FBI Prosecutive Summary of the Investigation of the Abduction and Murder of James Earl Chaney, Andrew Goodman, and Michael Henry Schwerner on June 21, 1964," 12/19/64, foia.fbi.gov/miburn.htm, accessed 5/13/04.
61. Douglas Linder, "The Mississippi Burning Trial," p. 7, www.law.umkc.edu/faculty/projects/ftrials/price&bowers/account.html, accessed 8/25/03.
62. Seth Cagin and Philip Dray, *We Are Not Afraid,* pp. 408–410; Juan Williams, *Eyes on the Prize,* pp. 238–239; Nick Kotz and Mary Lynn Kotz, *A Passion for Equality,* p. 124.

8. A Political Revolution

1. Romaine, pp. 29–30; John Dittmer, *Local People,* pp. 280–283; Mary King, *Freedom Song,* pp. 340–342.
2. United States Census, 1960, www.census.gov, accessed 5/13/04.
3. Sally Belfrage, *Freedom Summer,* pp. 198–199.
4. Romaine, p. 29.
5. Jack Valenti, *A Very Human President,* pp. 201–203.
6. *Newsweek,* 8/7/64.
7. Rowland Evans and Robert Novak, *Lyndon B. Johnson,* p. 453.
8. *NYT,* editorial, 8/19/64.
9. Milton Viorst, *Fire in the Streets,* pp. 255–262.
10. LBJL, MLK telegram to the President, 8/19/64.
11. "Communist Influence in Racial Matters," FBI Bufile 100–3–116.
12. John Dittmer, *Local People,* p. 290.
13. TT, LBJ and Roy Wilkins, 8/15/64, 9:50 A.M., WH6408.21 PNO 2–3.
14. Taylor Branch, *Pillar of Fire,* pp. 403–404.
15. TT, LBJ and James Eastland, 8/17/64, 12:13 P.M., WH6408.26 PNO 1–2.
16. TT, LBJ and Hale Boggs, 8/15/64, 2:25 P.M., WH6408.22 PNO 2–3.

17. TT, LBJ and John Connally, 8/9/64, 9:45 A.M., WH6408.15 PNO 6–7.

18. TT, LBJ and Walter Reuther, 8/1/64, 7:06 P.M., WH6408.03 PNO 1–2.

19. www.archives.gov/federal_register/electoral_college/votes_1965_1969.html, accessed 11/17/03.

20. AI, Sherwin Markman, Cartha "Deke" DeLoach, and others.

21. TT, LBJ and Willard Wirtz, 8/20/64, 11:19 A.M., WH6408.25 PNO 5.

22. TT, LBJ and Roy Wilkins, 8/15/64, 9:50 A.M., WH6408.21 PNO 2 and 3.

23. TT, LBJ and Willard Wirtz, 8/20/64, 11:19 A.M., WH6408.25 PNO 5.

24. TT, LBJ and Richard Daley, 8/17/64, 9:26 A.M., WH6408.25 PNO 2.

25. TT, LBJ and Walter Reuther, 8/17/64, 6:14 P.M., WH6408.27 PNO 2.

26. TT, LBJ and Hubert Humphrey, 8/14/64, 8:25 P.M., WH6408.20 PNO 17.

27. TT, LBJ and Roy Wilkins, 8/15/64, 9:50 A.M., WH6408.21 PNO 2 and 3.

28. "Communist Influence in Racial Matters: Mohr to DeLoach," 8/25/64, FBI file.

29. "Communist Influence in Racial Matters," FBI Bufile 100–3–116, 8/13/64.

30. AI, Andrew Young.

31. TT, LBJ and John McCormack, 7/13/64, 9:20 A.M.?, WH6407.08 PNO 2.

32. TT, LBJ and Hale Boggs, 7/28/64, 8:17 P.M., WH6407.16 PNO 17.

33. Cartha "Deke" DeLoach, *Hoover's FBI*, pp. 3–5.

34. Ibid.; Verna Canson diary of 1964 Democratic Convention (courtesy of Faythe Canson); AI, Victorine Adams.

35. Russell, "Handwritten notes of Richard Russell," 8/20/64.

36. TT, LBJ and Walter Reuther, 8/9/64, 8:51 A.M., WH6408.15 PNO 1–2.

37. TT, LBJ and Walter Reuther, 8/17/64, 6:14 P.M., WH6408.27 PNO 1–2.

38. TT, LBJ and Hubert Humphrey, 8/20/64, 9:20 A.M., WH6408.29 PNO 2–3.

39. TT, LBJ and Walter Reuther, 8/21/64, 8:56 P.M., WH6408.32 PNO 8–9.

40. TT, LBJ and James Eastland, 8/22/64, 11:00 A.M., WH6408.32 PNO 13.

41. TT, LBJ and Walter Reuther, 8/21/64, 8:56 P.M., WH6408.32 PNO 8–9.

42. Joseph Rauh, LBJOH; Romaine, interview with Joseph Rauh, pp. 301–353.

43. *NYT*, 8/22/64, p. 6.

44. TT, LBJ and James Rowe, 8/14/64, 6:35 P.M., WH6408.20 PNO 14.

45. Thomas R. West and James W. Mooney, eds., *To Redeem a Nation*, pp. 236–238.

46. Ibid.

47. LBJL, Paul Popple to LBJ, 8/22/64.

48. John Dittmer, *Local People*, p. 288; Taylor Branch, *Pillar of Fire*, p. 460.

49. John Dittmer, *Local People*, p. 286; Charles Marsh, *God's Long Summer*, p. 36.

50. Kenneth O'Reilly, *Racial Matters*, pp. 186–189; Ervin, Don Sanders to Fred Thompson, 9/6/73; Verna Canson diary of 1964 Democratic Convention (courtesy of Faythe Canson); TT, LBJ and Walter Reuther, 8/17/64, 6:14 P.M., WH6408.27 PNO 1–2.

51. TT, LBJ and Walter Jenkins, 8/24/64, 3:58 P.M., WH6408.34 PNO 1–2.

52. TT, LBJ and Joseph Barr, 8/26/64, 6:10 P.M., WH6408.40 PNO 9; TT, LBJ and James Eastland, 8/23/64, 3:35 P.M., WH6408.33 PNO 16; TT, LBJ and James Eastland, 8/23/64, 3:55 P.M., WH6408.33 PNO 17.

53. LBJL, King telegram to LBJ, Ex. Pl. St. 24.

54. Stegall, "Current Racial Developments," 8/24/64, NLJ 02–81; TT, LBJ and Richard Russell, 8/24/64, 11:10 A.M., WH6408.34 PNO 8; Romaine, interview with Edwin King, p. 271.

55. Verna Canson diary; Romaine, interview with Joseph Rauh, p. 332; AI, Robert

Moses; Romaine, interview with Fannie Lou Hamer, p. 215; Taylor Branch, *Pillar of Fire*, p. 465.

56. TT, LBJ, Hubert Humphrey, and Walter Reuther, 8/25/64, 2:31 P.M., WH6408.36 PNO 7.

57. TT, LBJ and Palmer Hoyt, 8/24/64, 12:56 P.M., WH6408.34 PNO 11.

58. TT, LBJ, Hubert Humphrey, and Walter Reuther, 8/25/64, 2:31 P.M., WH6408.36 PNO 7.

59. Tom Wicker, "Keynoter Is Fiery," *NYT*, 8/25/64, p. 1; TT, LBJ and Walter Reuther, 8/24/64, 8:25 P.M., WH6408.35 PNO 8.

60. Russell, "Handwritten notes of Richard Russell," 8/25/64.

61. Lyndon Johnson, *Vantage Point*, pp. 96–97; TT, LBJ and A. W. Moursund, 8/25/64, 12 P.M., WH6408.36 PNO 6; TT, LBJ and George Reedy, 8/25/64, 11:06 A.M., WH6408.36 PNO 2; TT, LBJ and Walter Jenkins, 8/25/64, 11:23 A.M., WH6408.36 PNO 3.

62. Lady Bird Johnson, *White House Diary*, p. 192.

63. Robert Dallek, *Flawed Giant*, p. 123.

64. Romaine, interview with Joseph Rauh, pp. 341–343.

65. AI, Robert Moses; Taylor Branch, *Pillar of Fire*, p. 469.

66. Romaine, interview with Edwin King, p. 276.

67. Ibid., p. 269.

68. Ibid., pp. 268–270.

69. Romaine, interview with Joseph Rauh, p. 344; AI, Sherwin Markman.

70. Romaine, interview with Joseph Rauh, p. 339.

71. Church, Hearings, vol. 3, pp. 714–715; TT, LBJ and Carl Sanders, 8/25/64, 4:32 P.M., WH6408.37 PNO 1–2; Romaine, interview with Joseph Rauh, pp. 339–352; TT, LBJ and Douglas Wynn, 8/25/64, 9:33 P.M.?, WH6408.38 PNO 17.

72. Cartha "Deke" DeLoach, *Hoover's FBI*, p. 9; LBJL, Walter Adams to Walter Jenkins, 9/1/64, PL1/St 24, box 81.

73. AI, Robert Moses; Romaine, interviews with Fannie Lou Hamer and Edwin King, pp. 213–233, 251–279.

74. Romaine, interview with Joseph Rauh, p. 351.

75. Taylor Branch, *Pillar of Fire*, p. 474.

76. Romaine, interview with Edwin King, p. 261; David Garrow, *Bearing the Cross*, p. 349; AI, Edwin King.

77. AI, Victoria Gray Adams.

78. Cleveland Sellers, *The River of No Return*, p. 111.

79. PPP, "Remarks Before the Democratic National Convention upon Accepting the Nomination," 8/27/64.

80. Robert Dallek, *Flawed Giant*, p. 166.

81. LBJL, LBJ to Hoover, 8/31/64, handwriting file.

82. Liz Carpenter, *Ruffles and Flourishes*, pp. 143–171.

83. LBJL, Moyers memo to Valenti, 10/9/64; LBJL, Frank Gibney memo, 10/9/64.

84. PPP, 10/9/64, pp. 1281–88.

85. LBJL, Horace Busby to LBJ, 10/10/64.

86. *Washington Evening Star*, 10/12/64.

87. *The Worker*, 10/11/64.

88. Washington Capital News Service, Cleveland, 10/23/64.

89. Stegall, Hoover to Moyers, 10/20/64, Martin Luther King folder, item 60.
90. *Baltimore Evening Sun,* 10/31/64.
91. M. S. Handler, "Dr. King Demands Goldwater Rout," *NYT,* 10/14/64.
92. AI, Lawrence Guyot and Robert Moses; Clayborne Carson, *In Struggle,* p. 128.
93. clerk.house.gov/histHigh/Congressional_History/partyDiv.php, accessed 10/28/03.
94. TT, LBJ and Martin Luther King, 11/5/64, 3:20 P.M., WH6411.09 PNO 2.

9. Hoover Attacks

1. David Garrow, *The FBI and Martin Luther King Jr.*, p. 121; Church, Final Report, bk. 3, p. 143; *New York Herald Tribune,* 10/19/64.
2. *WP,* 11/19/64, pp. 1 and 3; *NYT,* 11/19/64, p. 1; *NYT,* 11/20/64, p. 1; Taylor Branch, *Pillar of Fire,* pp. 525–526; *U.S. News & World Report,* 11/10/64, pp. 56–58.
3. FBIMLK, sec. 20, King telegram to Hoover.
4. *Washington Evening Star,* 11/19/64, p. 1.
5. *NYT,* 11/20/64, p. 1.
6. FBIMLK, sec. 19, 11/19/64, Baumgardner memo to Sullivan.
7. TT, LBJ and Cartha "Deke" DeLoach, 11/20/64, 4:23 P.M., WH6411.25 PNO 12.
8. *New York Herald Tribune,* 11/20/64, p. 1.
9. *NYT,* 11/20/64, p. 18; *Washington Evening Star,* 11/29/64, p. A5.
10. Taylor Branch, *Pillar of Fire,* pp. 529–530.
11. TT, LBJ and Cartha "Deke" DeLoach, 11/20/64, 4:23 P.M., WH6411.25 PNO 12.
12. TT, LBJ and Nicholas Katzenbach, 11/11/64, 7:38 P.M., WH6411.16 PNO 1–4.
13. *NYT,* 11/19/64, p. 1; AI, Nicholas Katzenbach.
14. *NYT,* 12/2/64, p. 1; *WP,* 12/2/02, p. 1; Kenneth O'Reilly, *Racial Matters,* p. 146; FBIMLK, DeLoach to Mohr, 12/2/64, sec. 21; Stegall, Hoover to Moyers, 11/6/64, Race Relations and Related Matters, September–December 1964.
15. Stegall, Hoover to LBJ and "Moyers Note for the Record," 12/1/64; "Communism and the Negro Movement — A Current Analysis," NLJ-086; FBIMLK, DeLoach to Mohr, 12/7/64; Church, Final Report, bk. 3, pp. 146–152.
16. David Garrow, *The FBI and Martin Luther King Jr.* p. 74; Pottinger, Belmont to Tolson, 10/17/63 (exhibit 13); Church, Final Report, bk. 3, p. 81.
17. Hugh Sidey, "L.B.J., Hoover, and Domestic Spying," *Time,* 2/10/75, p. 16.
18. AI, Burke Marshall.
19. The best analysis of the FBI's dealings with King and Levison is David Garrow, *The FBI and Martin Luther King Jr.*
20. *San Francisco Chronicle,* 4/4/64; Taylor Branch, *Parting the Waters,* p. 148.
21. Church, Final Report, bk. 3, p. 85.
22. Richard Goodwin, *Remembering America,* p. 248; AI, Nicholas Katzenbach.
23. Jan Jarboe Russell, *Lady Bird,* p. 127.
24. AI, Harry McPherson.
25. Ibid.
26. AI, Nicholas Katzenbach, Burke Marshall, and Lee White; LBJL, White and Reedy memos to the president.
27. *The Quill* (February 1976): 12–18.
28. Ibid.; Howell Raines, *My Soul Is Rested,* pp. 368–370; AI, Eugene Patterson; Church, Final Report, bk. 3, p. 161.
29. David Wise, *The American Police State,* pp. 303–306; David Garrow, *The FBI and Martin Luther King Jr.,* pp. 127–128; FBIMLK, DeLoach to John Mohr,

12/1/64, sec. 21; Church, Final Report, bk. 3, pp. 150–153; AI, Ben Bradlee, Nicholas Katzenbach, and Burke Marshall.

30. AI, Nicholas Katzenbach.

31. AI, James Farmer; James Farmer, LBJOH; James Farmer, *Lay Bare the Heart*, pp. 278–282; Taylor Branch, *Pillar of Fire*, p. 535; Church, bk. 3, pp. 168–169.

32. Church, bk. 3, pp. 162–163.

33. David Garrow, *The FBI and Martin Luther King Jr.*, p. 132; WHCF, Confidential File FG 135–6.

34. AI, John Maguire; David Garrow, *Bearing the Cross*, pp. 374–376.

35. AI, Rabbi Richard Hirsch; David Garrow, *Bearing the Cross*, pp. 374–375.

36. David Garrow, *Bearing the Cross*, p. 129.

37. Ibid., pp. 357, 368.

38. Martin Luther King Jr., *A Testament of Hope*, pp. 224–226; David Garrow, *Bearing the Cross*, pp. 364–365.

39. David Garrow, *Bearing the Cross*, p. 368; Taylor Branch, *Pillar of Fire*, p. 547; DD and DDB, 12/18/64; LBJL, Lee White memo to LBJ, 12/18/64; DDB, Juanita Roberts note, 12/18/64.

40. Martin Luther King Jr., *Autobiography*, pp. 270–271; David Garrow, *Bearing the Cross*, p. 368; *NYT*, 12/19/64, p. 32; *WP*, 12/19/64, p. A2; AI, Andrew Young, Walter Fauntroy, and Lee White.

41. TT, LBJ and Nicholas Katzenbach, 12/14/64, 11:30 A.M., WH6412.02 PNO 2–4.

42. Church, Final Report, bk. 3, pp. 157–158; FBIMLK, Rosen to Belmont, 11/20/64, sec. 20, p. 4.

43. Church, Final Report, bk. 3, pp. 158–159.

44. Ralph David Abernathy, *And the Walls Came Tumbling Down*, pp. 309–310.

45. Taylor Branch, *Pillar of Fire*, pp. 556–557; David Garrow, *The FBI and Martin Luther King Jr.*, pp. 133–134; Ralph David Abernathy, *And the Walls Came Tumbling Down*, pp. 308–310; Andrew Young, *An Easy Burden*, pp. 328–329.

46. David Garrow, *The FBI and Martin Luther King Jr.*, pp. 133–134.

47. Ibid.; Andrew Young, *An Easy Burden*, p. 329.

48. David Garrow, *The FBI and Martin Luther King Jr.*, pp. 134–135; AI, Andrew Young; Andrew Young, LBJOH; Andrew Young, *An Easy Burden*, pp. 330–332; Ralph David Abernathy, *And the Walls Came Tumbling Down*, pp. 309–312.

49. AI, Fred Graham, John Herbers, and Andrew Young; Andrew Young, *An Easy Burden*, p. 316.

10. LBJ–MLK: A Quiet Alliance

1. Hugh Davis Graham, *The Civil Rights Era*, pp. 162–163.

2. TT, LBJ and Martin Luther King, 1/15/65, 12:06 P.M., WH6501.04 PNO 1.

3. Ibid.

4. Charles Fager, *Selma, 1965*, pp. 9–10; David Garrow, *Bearing the Cross*, pp. 371–372; Taylor Branch, *Pillar of Fire*, p. 552.

5. J. L. Chestnut Jr. and Julia Cass, *Black in Selma*, p. 3; David Garrow, *Protest at Selma*, pp. 31–34.

6. Hugh Davis Graham, *The Civil Rights Era*, p. 165.

7. David Garrow, *Protest at Selma*, p. 34; Taylor Branch, *Pillar of Fire*, p. 391; Charles Fager, *Selma, 1965*, pp. 4–5.

8. Steven Lawson, *Running for Freedom,* pp. 103–104.

9. AI, C. T. Vivian. For background on Selma and civil rights, see Taylor Branch, *Pillar of Fire;* David Garrow, *Bearing the Cross* and *Protest at Selma;* Charles Fager, *Selma, 1965;* and Ralph David Abernathy, *And the Walls Came Tumbling Down.*

10. *WP,* 1/19/65, p. A1; *NYT,* 1/19/65, p. 1; Charles Fager, *Selma, 1965,* p. 2.

11. AI, Dorothy Cotton; David Garrow, *Bearing the Cross,* p. 379.

12. PPP, 1/20/65, pp. 71–74.

13. Taylor Branch, *Pillar of Fire,* pp. 562–563; David Garrow, *Bearing the Cross,* pp. 379–380; Mary King, *Freedom Song,* p. 353.

14. PPP, 1/4/65, pp. 1–9.

15. Robert Dallek, *Flawed Giant,* p. 190.

16. Merle Miller, *Lyndon: An Oral Biography,* pp. 407–408.

17. Robert Dallek, *Flawed Giant,* p. 194; Hugh Davis Graham, *The Civil Rights Era,* p. 166.

18. Sidney Milkis, *The President and the Parties,* p. 187.

19. David Garrow, *Bearing the Cross,* p. 381; Charles Fager, *Selma, 1965,* pp. 44–45.

20. *WP,* 2/2/65, p. A1; *NYT,* 2/2/65, p. 1; *NYT,* 2/6/65, p. 10.

21. Charles Fager, *Selma, 1965,* pp. 48–50; David Garrow, *Bearing the Cross,* pp. 381–382; Taylor Branch, *Pillar of Fire,* p. 576; *Washington Evening Star,* 2/2/65, p. A1; *WP,* 2/2/65, p. A1.

22. Taylor Branch, *Pillar of Fire,* p. 576; Charles Fager, *Selma, 1965,* p. 53.

23. TKC, King to Young, Selma jail notes, 2/1/65–2/5/65, pp. 22–26.

24. J. L. Chestnut Jr. and Julia Cass, *Black in Selma,* pp. 191–192.

25. WHCF, Lee White to LBJ, 2/3/65, Hu 2/St. 1.

26. PPP, WH press conference, 2/4/64, pp. 131–139; *NYT,* 2/5/65, p. 17.

27. *NYT,* 2/5/65, p. 1.

28. AI, Charles Mathias; *NYT,* 2/6/65, p. 10.

29. Taylor Branch, *Pillar of Fire,* p. 581; *NYT,* 2/6/65, p. 1.

30. TT, LBJ and Nicholas Katzenbach, 2/5/65, 3:00 P.M., WH6502.01 PNO 3–4.

31. WHCF, Reedy press briefing, 2/6/65; *NYT,* 2/7/65, p. 1; *WP,* 2/7/65, p. 1.

32. Steven Lawson, *Black Ballots,* p. 309; *NYT,* 2/10/65, p. 1.

33. Charles Fager, *Selma, 1965,* pp. 63–65; *NYT,* 2/9/65, p. 17.

34. David Garrow, *Bearing the Cross,* p. 390.

35. TKC, SNCC files, box 7, notes on Torch Motel meeting, 2/10/64; J. L. Chestnut Jr. and Julia Cass, *Black in Selma,* pp. 193–194; David Garrow, *Bearing the Cross,* pp. 388–389.

36. *NYT,* 2/11/65, p. 1; *New York Post,* 2/11/65, p. 5.

37. AI, C. T. Vivian; *NYT,* 2/17/65, p. 1.

38. *NYT,* 2/18/65, p. 17.

39. *NYT,* 2/19/65, p. 1.

40. Taylor Branch, *Pillar of Fire,* p. 593.

41. *NYT,* 2/19/65, p. 1.

42. FBIMLK, Branigan to Sullivan, 2/28/65, sec. 25.

43. *NYT,* 2/23/65, p. 16.

44. Taylor Branch, *Pillar of Fire,* p. 599; *NYT,* 2/27/65, p. 1; *NYT,* 3/1/65.

45. *NYT,* 2/27/65, p. 1.

46. Charles Fager, *Selma, 1965,* p. 85.

11. We Shall Overcome

1. Stegall, Hoover to Watson, 3/5/65, King folder, item 31.
2. TT, LBJ and Nicholas Katzenbach, 2/24/65, 9:28 A.M., WH6502.05 PNO 7; TT, LBJ and Adam Clayton Powell, 3/1/65, 9:32 P.M., WH6503.01 PNO 7; *NYT*, 3/6/65, p. 9; *WP*, 3/6/65, p. 2; AI, Lee White.
3. TT, LBJ and Hubert Humphrey, 3/6/65, 11:25 A.M., WH6503.02 PNO 8–9.
4. *NYT*, 3/6/65, p. 9; *WP*, 3/6/65, p. 2; AI, Lee White.
5. Charles Fager, *Selma, 1965*, p. 65.
6. Andrew Young, *An Easy Burden*, pp. 354–355.
7. John Lewis, *Walking with the Wind*, pp. 324–325.
8. AI, Hosea Williams.
9. AI, John Lewis and Hosea Williams; *NYT*, 3/8/65, p. 1; Charles Fager, *Selma, 1965*, pp. 92–95.
10. *NYT*, 3/8/65, p. 1.
11. Charles Fager, *Selma, 1965*, pp. 94–95.
12. Howell Raines, *My Soul Is Rested*, p. 203.
13. John Lewis, *Walking with the Wind*, pp. 325–331; "525 in Selma Defy Ban of Governor," *NYT*, 3/8/65, p. 20.
14. TT, LBJ and Richard Russell, 3/6/65, 12:05 P.M., WH6503.03 PNO 1–2.
15. TT, LBJ and Robert McNamara, 3/6/65, 2:32 P.M., WH6503.03 PNO 3.
16. LBJL, "Diary of Lady Bird Johnson," 3/7/65.
17. "Johnson Kept Informed," *NYT*, 3/8/65, p. 20.
18. "Dr. King Announces Plan for New Walk and Assails Attack," *NYT*, 3/8/65, p. 20.
19. Ibid.; Andrew Young, *An Easy Burden*, p. 357.
20. TT, LBJ and Nicholas Katzenbach, 3/8/65, 8:38 A.M., WH6503.03 PNO 8.
21. TT, LBJ and Buford Ellington, 3/8/65, 8:29 A.M., WH6503.03 PNO6–7.
22. DDB, 3/8/65, Louis Martin memo to Marvin Watson.
23. "Hundreds on Way to Join March," *NYT*, 3/9/65, p. 23: AI, Rabbi Richard Hirsch.
24. *NYT*, 3/9/65, pp. 23–24.
25. "Wallace Says Police Saved Negro Lives," *NYT*, 3/9/65, pp. 1, 23.
26. TT, LBJ and Lister Hill, 3/8/65, 4:24 P.M., WH6503.04 PNO 1.
27. Andrew Young, *An Easy Burden*, p. 357; *NYT*, 3/10/65, p. 23; Jack Bass, *Taming the Storm*, p. 238.
28. Jack Greenberg, *Crusaders in the Courts*, p. 356.
29. TT, LBJ and Bill Moyers, 3/8/65, time unspecified, WH6503.04 PNO 6.
30. Andrew Young, *An Easy Burden*, pp. 359–360; David Garrow, *Protest at Selma*, pp. 84–85.
31. *Where He Stood*, television documentary on LeRoy Collins, WFSU-TV, Tallahassee, Fla., 1990.
32. Jack Greenberg, *Crusaders in the Courts*, pp. 356–357; AI, Jack Greenberg; David Garrow, *Bearing the Cross*, p. 402.
33. David Garrow, *Protest at Selma*, pp. 85–86; Thomas R. Wagy, "Governor LeRoy Collins of Florida and the Selma Crisis of 1965," *Florida Historical Quarterly* 57, no. 4 (April 1979): 404–421.

34. Thomas R. Wagy, "Governor LeRoy Collins of Florida," p. 410.
35. *NYT,* 3/10/65, p. 1; Thomas R. Wagy, "Governor LeRoy Collins of Florida," p. 411.
36. *NYT,* 3/12/65; Thomas R. Wagy, "Governor LeRoy Collins of Florida," p. 412; Charles Fager, *Selma, 1965,* pp. 103–104; David Garrow, *Bearing the Cross,* p. 403.
37. *NYT,* 3/10/65, p. 1.
38. David Garrow, *Bearing the Cross,* p. 405.
39. Jack Bass, *Taming the Storm,* pp. 241–242.
40. *NYT,* 3/10/65, p. 1.
41. LBJL, Vice President to the President, 3/10/65, Marvin Watson, aides file, box 31.
42. Adam Fairclough, *To Redeem the Soul of America,* p. 247; David Garrow, *Protest at Selma,* pp. 87–103.
43. TT, LBJ and Nicholas Katzenbach, 3/11/65, 10:35 A.M., WH6503.06 PNO3–4; TT, LBJ and Nicholas Katzenbach, 3/10/65, 9:32 P.M.?, WH6503.05 PNO 5–6.
44. Lyndon Baines Johnson, *Vantage Point,* p. 162.
45. LBJL, Vice President to the President, Followup, 3/10/65, Marvin Watson, aides file, box 31; DDB, Larry O'Brien to LBJ, 3/10/65, 11:10 A.M.
46. DDB, Jack Valenti Report to the President, 3/11/65, box 14; Charles Fager, *Selma, 1965,* p. 117.
47. DD, 3/11/65; AI, Lee White and Jack Valenti.
48. Lady Bird Johnson, *White House Diary,* p. 251.
49. Charles Fager, *Selma, 1965,* p. 116.
50. DD and DDB, 3/11/65; AI, Walter Fauntroy; UPI-90, 3/12/65; H. Rap Brown, *Die Nigger Die!,* pp. 52–53.
51. DDB, 3/12/65; UPI-202, 3/12/65; LBJL, LBJ telegram to George Wallace, 3/12/65, HU 2/St 1.
52. Richard Goodwin, *Remembering America,* pp. 320–321.
53. Dan T. Carter, *The Politics of Rage,* pp. 251–252.
54. Ibid., p. 252.
55. Richard Goodwin, *Remembering America,* p. 351.
56. Dan T. Carter, *The Politics of Rage,* p. 252.
57. Richard Goodwin, *Remembering America,* pp. 321–323.
58. Howell Raines, *My Soul Is Rested,* pp. 332–333.
59. Richard Goodwin, *Remembering America,* pp. 332–333.
60. Dan T. Carter, *The Politics of Rage,* p. 253.
61. Richard Goodwin, *Remembering America,* p. 323.
62. AI, Nicholas Katzenbach, Richard Goodwin, and Jack Valenti.
63. *New York Herald Tribune,* 3/14/65.
64. PPP, 3/13/65, pp. 274–281.
65. Michael Beschloss, ed., *Reaching for Glory,* pp. 227–228.
66. Richard Goodwin, *Remembering America,* p. 330.
67. PPP, 3/15/65, pp. 281–287.
68. John Lewis, *Walking with the Wind,* p. 340; AI, John Lewis and Andrew Young.
69. John Lewis, *Walking with the Wind,* p. 340; AI, James Forman.
70. David Garrow, *Bearing the Cross,* p. 409; George H. Gallup, *Gallup Poll,* 3:1933.
71. Richard Goodwin, *Remembering America,* p. 310.

12. Shining Moment

1. LBJL, King telegram to the President, 3/16/64; David Garrow, *Protest at Selma*, p. 111; Dan T. Carter, *The Politics of Rage*, pp. 255–256; Jack Bass, *Taming the Storm*, p. 249.
2. David Garrow, *Protest at Selma*, p. 113.
3. Robert Dallek, *Flawed Giant*, p. 221; William Leuchtenburg, "The Old Farmhand from Dixie," *Atlantic Monthly* (December 1992): p. 97.
4. James Forman, *Sammy Younge Jr.*, p. 100; Clayborne Carson, *In Struggle*, pp. 159–162.
5. *WP*, 3/22/65, p. 1.
6. *NYT*, 3/19/65, p. 20; Robert Dallek, *Flawed Giant*, p. 216.
7. *The New Yorker*, 4/10/65, from Advisory Board, *Reporting Civil Rights*, pt. 2, pp. 367–394.
8. Harris Wofford, *Of Kennedys and Kings*, p. 193; www.stanford.edu/group/ King/publications/speeches/Our_God_Is_Marching_On.html, accessed 6/10/04.
9. Stegall, Hoover to Marvin Watson, 3/26/65, "Communist Influence in Racial Matters."
10. www.stanford.edu/group/King/publications/speeches/Our_God_is_marching _on.html, accessed 6/10/04.
11. Stegall, Hoover to Marvin Watson, 3/26/65, "Communist Influence in Racial Matters."
12. PPP, 3/26/65, pp. 332–333.
13. Laurence Stern, "King Urges National Boycott of Alabama, U.S. Funds Removal," *WP*, 3/29/65, p. A1.
14. "King to Seek Boycott of Alabama Products," *Washington Evening Star*, 3/29/65.
15. William White, "King's Boycott, A Shocking Demand" *WP*, 3/31/65; "Washington Is Cool to Alabama Boycott," *NYT*, 3/30/65, pp. 1, 28.
16. David Garrow, *Protest at Selma*, p. 120; AI, Andrew Brimmer.
17. TKC, Levison to King, 4/7/65.
18. TT, LBJ and Everett Dirksen, 3/18/65, 9:30 A.M., WH6503.07 PNO 9; TT, LBJ and Everett Dirksen, 4/5/65, 12:34 P.M., WH6504.02 PNO 5.
19. Lady Bird Johnson, *White House Diary*, p. 237.
20. PPP, p. 742.
21. David Garrow, *Protest at Selma*, pp. 128–129.
22. TT, LBJ and Martin Luther King, 7/7/65, 8:05 P.M., WH6507.02 PNO 1–3.
23. David Garrow, *Protest at Selma*, pp. 130–131; *Cong Rec* 111, 8/4/65, p. 19444.
24. Robert Dallek, *Flawed Giant*, p. 200.
25. PPP, p. 407.
26. Robert Dallek, *Flawed Giant*, p. 210.
27. www.ssa.gov/history/ssa/lbjmedicare3.html and www.ssa.gov/history/sounds/ med8.ram, accessed 1/12/04; PPP, pp. 811–815.
28. Office of Enrollment Management, Howard University, 1965 class records.
29. AI, Lynda Bird Johnson Robb; PPP, "Commencement Speech at Howard University," 6/4/65, pp. 635–640.

30. Harry McPherson, LBJOH, 4:5.
31. Robert Dallek, *Flawed Giant,* p. 222.
32. David Garrow, *Bearing the Cross,* p. 436; John Herbers, "Dr. King to Fight Bias in the North," *NYT,* 8/6/65.
33. Donald Pfarrer, "King Gives Warning on D.C. Home Rule," *Washington Star,* 8/6/65.
34. Robert E. Baker, "Johnson Today Signs Voting Bill at Capitol," *WP,* 8/6/65, p. A1.
35. Carroll Kilpatrick, "Voting Rights Bill Signed by Johnson," *WP,* 8/7/65, pp. A1, 5.
36. PPP, pp. 840–843.
37. Richard L. Lyons, "Johnson 'Forgets,' Heads for Old Senate Seat," *WP,* 8/7/65, p. A4; LBJL, Lawrence O'Brien to Martin Luther King, 8/6/65, PR13–1/K.
38. Richard L. Lyons, "Johnson 'Forgets,' Heads for Old Senate Seat," p. A4.
39. Carroll Kilpatrick, "Voting Rights Bill Signed by Johnson," *WP,* 8/7/65, p. A5; PPP, p. 842.

13. This Time the Fire

1. McCone, www.usc.edu/isd/archives/cityinstress/mccone/part4.html, accessed 1/17/04; "Case That Sparked Riot Brings a Plea of Guilty," *NYT,* 8/14/65, p. 8.
2. Robert Dallek, *Flawed Giant,* p. 223; Joseph Califano, *Triumph and Tragedy,* pp. 59–65.
3. AI, Jack Valenti; DD, 8/13/65 and 8/14/65.
4. Robert Semple Jr., "Johnson Shocked," *NYT,* 8/15/65, pp. 1, 77.
5. Joseph Califano, *Triumph and Tragedy,* pp. 59–62; TT, LBJ and Joseph Califano, 8/14/65, 6:25 P.M., WH6508.04 PNO 1–2; TT, LBJ and Joseph Califano, 8/14/65, 8:09 P.M., WH6508.04 PNO 3–4.
6. TT, LBJ and John McCone, 8/18/65, 12:10 P.M., WH6508.05 PNO 9; LBJL, "Report of the President's Task Force on the Los Angeles Riots," 9/17/65.
7. Andrew Young, *An Easy Burden,* p. 378.
8. TT, LBJ and Martin Luther King, 8/20/65, 5:10 P.M., WH6508.07 PNO 12; AI, Andrew Brimmer and Roger Wilkins; Peter Bart, "Negro Leaders Reassess Views," *NYT,* 8/18/65, p. 20; "Coast Riot Area Gets Cleanup Aid," *NYT,* 8/19/65, p. 16; David Garrow, *Bearing the Cross,* p. 439.
9. David Garrow, *Bearing the Cross,* p. 440.
10. McCone, www.usc.edu/isd/archives/cityinstress/mccone/part4.html, accessed 1/17/04.
11. TT, LBJ and Martin Luther King, 8/20/65, 5:10 P.M., WH6508.07 PNO 12.
12. Ibid.; TT, LBJ and Russell Long, 8/17/65, 6:05 P.M., WH6508.05 PNO 4; TT, LBJ and Grant Sawyer, 8/17/65, 6:39 P.M., WH6508.05 PNO 6; TT, LBJ and Roger Branigan, 8/17/65, 6:36 P.M., WH6508.05 PNO 5.
13. PPP, 7/28/65, pp. 794–803.
14. Brian VanDeMark, *Into the Quagmire,* pp. 184–214; Lloyd C. Gardner, *Pay Any Price,* pp. 258–264.
15. Bill Moyers, "Flashbacks," *Newsweek,* 2/10/75, p. 76; TT, LBJ and Richard Russell, 7/19/65, 6:07 P.M., WH6507.04 PNO 12–13.

16. Doris Kearns Goodwin, *Lyndon Johnson and the American Dream*, pp. 282–283.
17. TT, LBJ and George Ball, 4/9/65, 9:30 A.M., WH6504.03 PNO 12.
18. PPP, "LBJ Press Conference," vol. 2, 1965, pp. 794–803.
19. *NYT,* 8/13/65, p. 1.
20. Ibid.; David Garrow, *Bearing the Cross,* p. 438.
21. Stegall, J. Edgar Hoover to Marvin Watson, 8/5/65, King file.
22. Stegall, J. Edgar Hoover to Marvin Watson, 8/16/65, King file.
23. *NYT,* 9/12/65.
24. *New York Daily News,* 9/12/65.
25. *WP,* 9/12/65, p. A3.
26. *Washington Evening Star,* 9/20/65.
27. Michael Beschloss, ed., *Reaching for Glory,* p. 390.
28. Robert Dallek, *Flawed Giant,* p. 282.
29. Richard Goodwin, *Remembering America,* pp. 392–405.
30. Joseph Califano, *Triumph and Tragedy,* pp. 51–52.
31. TT, LBJ and Thurgood Marshall, 7/7/65, 1:30 P.M., WH6507.01 PNO 7.
32. Constance Baker Motley, *Equal Justice Under Law,* pp. 212–216.
33. AI, Andrew Brimmer; LBJL, Brimmer appointment file.
34. David Garrow, *Bearing the Cross,* pp. 472–473.
35. AI, Beryl Bernhard.
36. WHCF, Cliff Alexander to the president, 6/22/66, 12:45; AI, Clifford Alexander; AI, Beryl Bernhard.
37. David Garrow, *Bearing the Cross,* pp. 475–476.
38. Ibid., p. 483.
39. Ibid., pp. 481–482; AI, Marian Wright Edelman; Michael T. Kaufman, "Stokely Carmichael, Rights Leader Who Coined 'Black Power,' Dies at 57," *NYT,* 11/16/98. Also see Clayborne Carson, *In Struggle,* and John Lewis, *Walking with the Wind.*
40. David Garrow, *Bearing the Cross,* pp. 483–487.
41. TT, LBJ and Whitney Young, 7/5/66, 3:48 P.M., WH6607.01 PNO 6; Adam Fairclough, *To Redeem the Soul of America.* p. 286.
42. David Garrow, *Bearing the Cross,* pp. 457, 460–466.
43. Adam Fairclough, *To Redeem the Soul of America,* pp. 279–307.
44. David Garrow, *Bearing the Cross,* pp. 490–496.
45. AI, Roger Wilkins; Roger Wilkins, LBJOH, 3:13–17; Roger Wilkins, *A Man's Life,* pp. 208–209.
46. David Garrow, *Bearing the Cross,* p. 467.
47. PPP, "Special Message to the Congress Proposing Further Legislation to Strengthen Civil Rights," 4/28/66; PPP, "Remarks in Indianapolis at a Luncheon with Indiana Business, Labor, and Professional Leaders," 7/23/66.
48. PPP, "Statement by the President Following House Approval of the Civil Rights Bill," 8/10/66.
49. WHCF, Katzenbach memorandum to the President, 9/9/66.
50. David Garrow, *Bearing the Cross,* p. 531; *NYT,* 9/20/66, p. 35.
51. Lloyd C. Gardner, *Pay Any Price,* p. 312.
52. SDLTAP, 12/6/65.

53. David Garrow, *Bearing the Cross*, p. 502.
54. Robert Dallek, *Flawed Giant*, p. 386.
55. AI, Andrew Young.
56. SDLTAP, 2/18/67.
57. Ibid.
58. *NYT*, 2/26/67.
59. Nancy J. Weiss, *Whitney M. Young Jr. and the Struggle for Civil Rights*, p. 159.
60. AI, Clarence Jones.
61. AI, Clarence Jones, Andrew Young, and John Maguire.
62. LBJL, Marvin Watson memo, 2/24/67, King file; LBJL, Marvin Watson to the President, 3/13/67, King file; LBJL, "President's Memo to Staff," 3/13/67, King file; Andrew Young, LBJOH, p. 18.
63. Martin Luther King Jr., 4/4/67 speech at Riverside Church, in *A Testament of Hope*, pp. 231–243.
64. "A Tragedy," *WP*, editorial, 4/6/67, p. A20.
65. "Dr. King's Error," *NYT*, editorial, 4/7/67, p. 36.
66. "Jewish Veterans Attack Dr. King's Stand on the War," *NYT*, 4/6/67, p. 10; "Javits Criticizes Dr. King," *NYT*, 4/10/67, p. 2.
67. "N.A.A.C.P. Decries Stand of Dr. King on Vietnam," *NYT*, 4/11/67, p. 1.
68. AI, Lynda Bird Johnson Robb.
69. AI, George Christian and Larry Temple.
70. LBJL, George Christian to the President, 4/8/67, HU2; AI, George Christian.
71. David Garrow, *Bearing the Cross*, pp. 554–555; Carl Rowan, column, *Cleveland Plain Dealer*, 4/14/67.
72. Stegall, "Martin Luther King," 4/7/67, memo from Hoover.
73. Stegall, "Martin Luther King," 4/19/67, memo from Hoover.
74. SDLTAP, 4/5/67 and 4/8/67.
75. Henry Hampton and Steve Fayer, *Voices of Freedom*, pp. 346–348.
76. LBJL, Fred Panzer to the President, 5/20/67, King file.

14. Another Martyr

1. *Atlanta Constitution*, 1/19/68, p. 16.
2. Stegall, Hoover to Mildred Stegall, 7/27/67, "Race Relations and Related Matters."
3. TT, LBJ and Abe Fortas, 10/3/66, 8:16 A.M., K66.03 PNO 1; David Garrow, *Bearing the Cross*, p. 570; LBJL, King to Johnson, 7/25/67, King name file; *NYT*, 7/27/67, p. 1.
4. Henry Hampton, *Eyes on the Prize: The Promised Land*, video.
5. *WP*, 1/19/68, p. A1; *WP*, 1/20/68, p. A1.
6. Stegall, Hoover to LBJ and Marvin Watson to LBJ, 7/25/68.
7. David Garrow, *Bearing the Cross*, p. 570.
8. Ibid.; AI, Ramsey Clark and Larry Temple; Ramsey Clark, LBJOH.
9. LBJL, Temple memo to LBJ, 2/14/68, HU2 Exec; Stegall, Marvin Watson to LBJ, 11/20/67, MLK folder.
10. AI, Sheldon Cohen.
11. Stegall, Hoover to Stegall, 11/30/67, MLK file; Stegall, Stegall to LBJ, 12/1/67, MLK file.

12. Church, Final Report, bk. 3, pp. 179–180.
13. Ibid., p. 180.
14. Gerald McKnight, *The Last Crusade*, pp. 20–28; FBI, Poor People's Campaign (POCAM) File 154–8428–1.
15. Gerald McKnight, *The Last Crusade*, pp. 25–27.
16. Church, Final Report, bk. 3, p. 174.
17. Gerald McKnight, *The Last Crusade*, pp. 25–26.
18. PPP, 1/17/68, "State of the Union."
19. PPP, 1/24/68, "Special Message to Congress on Civil Rights."
20. AI, Dorothy Height, Ramsey Clark, Nicholas Katzenbach, Lawrence Levinson, and Barefoot Sanders.
21. Neil MacNeil, *Dirksen*, pp. 321–323; David Broder, "Dirksen Influence with GOP Colleagues Wanes," *WP*, 2/28/68, p. A7.
22. AI, Jim Gaither.
23. *Congressional Quarterly 1968 Almanac*, pp. 159–160; Neil MacNeil, *Dirksen*, pp. 324–327; AI, Walter Mondale; Robert Albright, "Cloture Fails in 3d Test," *WP*, 3/2/68, p. A1.
24. AI, Phil Byrne.
25. PPP, 3/11/68, "Statement by the President on the Senate's Action in Passing the Civil Rights Bill."
26. LBJL, "Cabinet Meeting Notes," 3/13/68.
27. *Report of the National Advisory Commission on Civil Disorders*, pp. 1–2, 410–412.
28. David Garrow, *Bearing the Cross*, p. 600; *NYT*, 3/5/68, p. 28.
29. AI, Sherwin Markman, James Jones, William Baxter, and Lynda Bird Johnson Robb.
30. AI, Edward Kennedy.
31. LBJL, "Meeting Notes," 7/28/67, files of George Christian; AI, George Christian, James Jones, and Tom Johnson; Andrew Young, *An Easy Burden*, p. 472.
32. *Congressional Quarterly 1968 Almanac*, p. 165; *WP*, 3/20/68, p. A7.
33. PPP, 3/27/68, "Remarks upon Signing the Jury Selection and Service Act of 1968."
34. AI, Joseph Califano, Robert Hardesty, and Larry Levinson; George H. Gallup, *Gallup Poll*, 3:2022, 2057, 2076; Robert Dallek, *Flawed Giant*, pp. 532–533.
35. Clark Clifford, *Counsel to the President*, pp. 492–494.
36. AI, Cartha "Deke" DeLoach.
37. Lloyd C. Gardner, *Pay Any Price*, p. 439.
38. LBJL, William Guy to Marvin Watson, 3/5/68, Marvin Watson office files.
39. Lawrence F. O'Brien, *No Final Victories*, p. 229; SDLTAP, 3/26/68.
40. Lloyd C. Gardner, *Pay Any Price*, p. 451; LBJL, "Tom Johnson Meeting Notes," 3/22/68.
41. Clark Clifford, *Counsel to the President*, pp. 515–516.
42. Stewart Burns, *To the Mountain Top*, p. 418; Henry Hampton and Steve Fayer, *Voices of Freedom*, pp. 451–456.
43. David Garrow, *Bearing the Cross*, pp. 606–609; *Pontiac (Mich.) Press*, 3/15/68, p. A11; *L.A. Times*, 3/17/68, p. 3.
44. Henry Hampton and Steve Fayer, *Voices of Freedom*, p. 455; David Garrow, *Bearing the Cross*, p. 609.

45. AI, James Lawson; Ralph David Abernathy, *And the Walls Came Tumbling Down*, pp. 417–420.

46. David Garrow, *Bearing the Cross*, pp. 611–612; David Garrow, *The FBI and Martin Luther King Jr.*, p. 194.

47. Pottinger, p. 18.

48. SDLTAP, 3/28/68; David Garrow, *The FBI and Martin Luther King Jr.*, p. 194; Ralph David Abernathy, *And the Walls Came Tumbling Down*, p. 420.

49. SDLTAP, 3/29/68.

50. Church, Final Report, bk. 3, pp. 181–182; Stokes, Final Report, II.E, pp. 414, 439–441.

51. David Garrow, *Bearing the Cross*, p. 570; AI, Ramsey Clark; Ramsey Clark, LBJOH; AI, Larry Temple.

52. AI, Joseph Califano.

53. PPP, "The President's News Conference of March 30, 1968," 3/30/68.

54. AI, Juanita Abernathy; Ralph David Abernathy, *And the Walls Came Tumbling Down*, pp. 423–424.

55. AI, Andrew Young, Hosea Williams, Dorothy Cotton, and Walter Fauntroy.

56. Ralph David Abernathy, *And the Walls Came Tumbling Down*, pp. 424–426; Andrew Young, *An Easy Burden*, 457–459; AI, Andrew Young, Hosea Williams, and Walter Fauntroy.

57. AI, Dorothy Cotton.

58. AI, Andrew Young, Hosea Williams, Dorothy Cotton, and Walter Fauntroy; SDLTAP, 4/1/68.

59. AI, Walter Fauntroy.

60. Joseph Califano, *Triumph and Tragedy*, pp. 265–268; Harry McPherson, *A Political Education*, pp. 427–428.

61. UPI-212A, 3/31/68.

62. Lady Bird Johnson, *White House Diary*, pp. 642–644; AI, Lynda Bird Johnson Robb.

63. PPP, "The President's Address to the Nation," 3/31/68; George H. Gallup, *Gallup Poll*, 3:2113, 2121.

64. Adam Fairclough, *To Redeem the Soul of America*, pp. 379–380; Pottinger, pp. 16–19; David Garrow, *Bearing the Cross*, pp. 619–620.

65. Pottinger, p. 20; Adam Fairclough, *To Redeem the Soul of America*, p. 230.

66. Martin Luther King Jr., *A Testament of Hope*, pp. 279–286; Adam Fairclough, *To Redeem the Soul of America*, p. 381.

67. Andrew Young, *An Easy Burden*, pp. 463–465; Ralph David Abernathy, *And the Walls Came Tumbling Down*, pp. 440–441; David Garrow, *Bearing the Cross*, pp. 623–624; Pottinger, pp. 21–23.

68. Joseph Califano, *Triumph and Tragedy*, pp. 274–275.

69. AI, Joseph Califano; PPP, "Letter to the Speaker of the House Urging Enactment of the Fair Housing Bill," 4/5/68.

70. PPP, "Address to the Nation Proclaiming a Day of Mourning Following the Death of Dr. King," 4/5/68; Stegall, 4/6/68, MLK file.

71. Alex Poinsett, *Walking with Presidents*, p. 165.

72. AI, George Christian.

73. AI, Ken Young and Larry Levinson; LBJL, Markman to Sanders, 4/9/68.

74. UPI-5, 4/9/68.
75. AI, Larry Levinson and John Anderson.
76. *Cong Rec,* 4/10/68, p. 9527.
77. Ibid., pp. 9534–35.
78. Richard L. Lyons,"House Passes Civil Rights Bill," *WP,* 4/11/68, pp. A1, 6.
79. PPP, "Remarks upon Signing the Civil Rights Act," 4/11/68; Carroll Kilpatrick, "President Signs Rights Bill," *WP,* 4/12/68, p. A1.

Epilogue: The Legacy

1. PPP, "The President's News Conference at the National Press Club," 1/17/69.
2. Author as reporter for *WP.*
3. Author observations at ceremony, *WP,* 12/12/72, p. 1.
4. Hugh Davis Graham, *The Civil Rights Era,* pp. 450–452.
5. AI, Marc Morial.
6. U.S. Census statistics, 2000.
7. Department of Defense Statistics, 1/31/04.
8. U.S. Census, 2001, Historic Family Income Tables; U.S. Census, 2003, Income, Poverty, and Health Insurance in the U.S.
9. National Urban League, *The Complexity of Black Progress* (2004), pp. 53–68.
10. AI, J. L. "Ike" Chestnut.
11. AI, Vernon Jordan.
12. AI, Artur Davis.
13. AI, James Perkins.
14. AI, John Lewis.
15. Andrew Young, *An Easy Burden,* p. 523.
16. AI, Jeff Alford.
17. AI, James Figgs and Dwight Barfield; U.S. Census, 2000.
18. PPP, "President's Address to the Nation on Civil Disorders," 7/27/67.

INTERVIEW LIST

The author interviewed more than 150 persons for this book in the period from 1999 to 2004. Research assistants who participated in some of the interviews include Joshua Israel, Marc Borbely, Erin Ashwell, Britt Krivicich, and Nathan Means.

Juanita Abernathy (widow of Rev. Ralph Abernathy)
Victoria Gray Adams (MFDP)
Victorine Adams (1964 DNC Convention Credentials Committee)
Clifford Alexander Jr. (Johnson White House and Equal Employment
    Opportunity Commission)
Jeff Alford (University of Mississippi)
Hon. John Anderson (Congressman, Republican of Illinois)
Hon. William Anderson (Congressman, Democrat of Tennessee)
Bobby Baker (Secretary of the Senate)
Richard Baker (Senate Historian)
Hon. Dwight Barfield (Mayor of Marks, Mississippi)
John Barron (*Washington Evening Star*)
Rev. William Baxter (Episcopal minister)
Hon. Birch Bayh (Senator, Democrat of Indiana)
Beryl Bernhard (Civil Rights Commission)
Hon. Julian Bond (SNCC and NAACP)
Simeon Booker (*Ebony* and *Jet*)
Jerry H. Booth (student, Mississippi State)
Ben Bradlee (*Newsweek, Washington Post*)
Rev. James Breeden (National Council of Churches)
Hon. Daniel Brewster (Senator, Democrat of Maryland)

Dr. Andrew Brimmer (Federal Reserve Board of Governors)

Hon. James Bromwell (Congressman, Republican of Iowa)

Hon. Edward Brooke (Senator, Republican of Massachusetts)

Charlotte Burrows (staff to Senator Edward Kennedy)

Horace Busby (Johnson White House)

Phil Byrne (staff to Senator Walter Mondale)

Joseph Califano Jr. (Johnson White House)

Clarence and Faythe Canson (children of Verna Canson, 1964 DNC Convention
Credentials Committee)

Elizabeth Carpenter (Johnson White House)

Lisle Carter Jr. (Department of Health, Education and Welfare)

Rev. George Chancey (National Council of Churches)

J. L. "Ike" Chestnut (attorney, Selma, Alabama)

George Christian (Johnson White House)

Hon. Warren Christopher (Department of Justice)

Hon. Ramsey Clark (Attorney General)

Charles Cobb (SNCC)

Sheldon Cohen (Commissioner of Internal Revenue Service)

Dorothy Cotton (SCLC)

Wayne Cowan (*Christianity in Crisis*)

Courtland Cox (SNCC)

Hon. John Culver (Senator, Democrat of Iowa)

Hon. Artur Davis (Congressman, Democrat of Alabama)

Cartha "Deke" DeLoach (FBI Assistant Director)

Ivanhoe Donaldson (SNCC)

John Douglas (Department of Justice)

Leslie Dunbar (Field Foundation)

Marian Wright Edelman (NAACP Legal Defense Fund)

Peter Edelman (staff to Senator Robert F. Kennedy)

James Farmer (CORE)

Reynolds Farley (sociologist)

Rev. Walter Fauntroy (SCLC)

Charles Ferris (Chief Counsel to the U.S. Senate Majority)

James Figgs (Poor People's Campaign)

Hon. Hiram Fong (Senator, Republican of Hawaii)

James Forman (SNCC)

Douglas Fraser (United Auto Workers)

James Gaither (Johnson White House)

David Garrow (historian)

Michael Gillette (National Archives)

E. Ernest Goldstein and Peggy Goldstein (Johnson White House)

Doris Kearns Goodwin (Johnson White House)

Richard Goodwin (Johnson White House)

Fred Graham (*New York Times)*

Jack Greenberg (NAACP Legal Defense Fund)

Lawrence Guyot (SNCC)

James Hamilton (National Council of Churches)

Bruce Hanson (National Council of Churches)

Robert Hardesty (Johnson White House)

Hon. Fred Harris (Senator, Democrat of Oklahoma)

Dr. Roderick Harrison (National Urban League)

Dr. Dorothy Height (National Council of Negro Women)

John Herbers (*New York Times*)

Rabbi Richard "Asher" Hirsch (Religious Action Center)

Hon. Stephen Horn (staff to Senator Thomas Kuchel)

Lady Bird Johnson (widow of President Lyndon Johnson)

Tom Johnson (Johnson White House)

Clarence Jones (SCLC)

Hon. James Jones (Johnson White House)

Vernon Jordan Jr. (National Urban League)

Hon. Robert Kastenmeier (Congressman, Democrat of Wisconsin)

Hon. Nicholas Katzenbach (Attorney General)

Hon. Edward Kennedy (Senator, Democrat of Massachusetts)

Rev. Edwin King (MFDP)

Steve Klein (The King Center)

Joe Laitin (Johnson White House)

Edward Lashman (Department of Housing and Urban Development)

Delbert Latta (Congressman, Republican of Ohio)

Rev. James Lawson (SCLC and COME)

Lawrence Levinson (Johnson White House)

Andrew Levison (son of Stanley David Levison)

Hon. John Lewis (SNCC)

F. Peter Libassi (Department of Health, Education and Welfare)

Hon. Clark MacGregor (Congressman, Republican of Minnesota)

Charles Maguire (Johnson White House)

John Maguire (Professor, Wesleyan University)

Sherwin Markman (Johnson White House)

Burke Marshall (Department of Justice)

Hon. Charles Mathias (Congressman, Republican of Maryland)

Margaret Mayer (*Austin American Statesman*)

Hon. Eugene McCarthy (Senator, Democrat of Minnesota)

Hon. George McGovern (Senator, Democrat of South Dakota)

Hon. Robert McNamara (Secretary of Defense)

Harry McPherson (Johnson White House)

Hon. Edwin Mechem (Senator, Republican of New Mexico)

Seymour Melman (Professor, Columbia University)

Harry Middleton (Johnson White House)

Grant Midgley (staff to Senator Frank Moss)

J. Irwin Miller (Chairman, Cummins Engine, Inc.)

Vice President Walter Mondale (Senator, Democrat of Minnesota)

Hon. Marc Morial (National Urban League)

Robert Moses (SNCC and MFDP)

Garrison Nelson (historian)

Hon. Gaylord Nelson (Senator, Democrat of Wisconsin)

Matthew Nimetz (Johnson White House)

Jane O'Grady (Amalgamated Clothing Workers)

Eugene Patterson (*Atlanta Journal and Constitution*)

Malcolm Peabody Jr. (son of Mrs. Malcolm Peabody)

Hon. James Pearson (Senator, Republican of Kansas)

Hon. James Perkins (Mayor, Selma, Alabama)

Hon. J. J. "Jake" Pickle (Congressman, Democrat of Texas)

W. DeVier Pierson (Johnson White House)

Stanley Pottinger (Department of Justice)

Jack Pratt (National Council of Churches)

Hon. Albert Quie (Congressman, Republican of Minnesota)

Hon. George Rawlings (Virginia State Delegate, Democratic nominee for
    Congress)

Lisa Rice (Toledo Fair Housing Center)

John Riley (Federal Trade Commission)

Lynda Bird Johnson Robb (daughter of President Johnson)

Gen. Hugh Robinson (Johnson White House)

Herbert Rommerstein (House Un-American Activities Committee)

Judge Barefoot Sanders (Johnson White House)

Norman Sherman (staff to Vice President Hubert Humphrey)

Hon. Sargent Shriver (Office of Economic Opportunity and Peace Corps)

Stephen Shulman (Equal Employment Opportunity Commission)

Howard Shuman (staff to Senators Paul Douglas and William Proxmire)

Rev. Fred Shuttlesworth (SCLC)

John Simon (Taconic Foundation)

Shanna Smith (National Fair Housing Alliance)

Mildred Stegall (Johnson White House)

John Stewart (staff to Senator and Vice President Hubert Humphrey)

William Taylor (Civil Rights Commission)

Larry Temple (Johnson White House)

Jack Valenti (Johnson White House)

Rev. Cordy "C. T." Vivian (SCLC)

Frank Wallick (United Auto Workers)

William Welch (staff to Senator Philip Hart and Vice President Hubert
    Humphrey)

Charles Whaley (*Louisville Courier-Journal*)

Lee White (Johnson White House)

Hon. Roger Wilkins (Department of Justice and Community Relations Service)

Hosea Williams (SCLC)

Hon. W. Willard Wirtz (Secretary of Labor)

Hon. Harris Wofford (Peace Corps)

Rev. Andrew Young (SCLC)

Kenneth Young (AFL-CIO)

Ben Zelenka (staff to House Judiciary Committee)

BIBLIOGRAPHY

Abernathy, Ralph David. *And the Walls Came Tumbling Down*. New York: Harper-Perennial, 1990.

Adamson, Madeleine, and Seth Borgos. *This Mighty Dream*. Boston: Routledge & Kegan Paul, 1984.

Adelson, Bruce. *Brushing Back Jim Crow: The Integration of Minor League Baseball in the American South*. Charlottesville: University Press of Virginia, 1999.

Advisory Board. *Reporting Civil Rights*. Parts 1 and 2. New York: Library of America, 2003.

Andrew, John A. III. *Lyndon Johnson and the Great Society*. Chicago: Ivan R. Dee, 1998.

Ansbro, John J. *Martin Luther King Jr*. Lanham, Md.: Madison Books, 2000.

Baker, Bobby. *Wheeling and Dealing: Confessions of a Capitol Hill Operator*. New York: W. W. Norton & Company, 1978.

Baker, Leonard. *The Johnson Eclipse*. New York: Macmillan, 1966.

Baldwin, James. *The Fire Next Time*. New York: Dell Publishing, 1963.

Banner-Haley, Charles T. *The Fruits of Integration*. Jackson: University Press of Mississippi, 1994.

Barone, Michael. *Our Country: The Shaping of America from Roosevelt to Reagan*. New York: Free Press, 1990.

Barr, Alwyn. *Black Leaders: Texans for Their Time*. Austin: Texas State Historical Association, 1981.

Barron, John. *Operation Solo: The FBI's Man in the Kremlin*. Washington, D.C.: Regnery Publishing, 1996.

Bartley, Numan B. *The New South, 1945–1980*. Baton Rouge: Louisiana State University Press, 1995.

Bass, Jack. *Taming the Storm: The Life and Times of Judge Frank M. Johnson Jr. and the South's Fight over Civil Rights*. New York: Doubleday, 1993.

Belfrage, Sally. *Freedom Summer*. New York: Viking, 1965.

Belin, David W., Esq. *November 22, 1963: You Are the Jury*. New York: Quadrangle, 1973.

Bell, Derrick. *And We Are Not Saved*. New York: Basic Books, 1989.

———. *Silent Covenants: Brown v. Board of Education and the Unfulfilled Hopes for Racial Reform*. New York: Oxford University Press, 2004.

Bell, Jack. *The Johnson Treatment.* New York: Harper & Row, 1965.

Bennett, Lerone. *What Manner of Man.* New York: Pocket Books, 1964.

Berlin, Ira. *Many Thousands Gone.* Cambridge, Mass.: Belknap Press, 1998.

Berman, Daniel M. *A Bill Becomes a Law: Congress Enacts Civil Rights Laws.* New York: Macmillan, 1966.

Bernstein, Irving. *Guns or Butter: The Presidency of Lyndon Johnson.* New York: Oxford University Press, 1994.

Beschloss, Michael R., ed. *Taking Charge: The Johnson White House Tapes, 1963–1964.* New York: Simon & Schuster, 1997.

———. *Reaching for Glory.* New York: Simon & Schuster, 2001.

Billingsley, Andrew. *Climbing Jacob's Ladder.* New York: Touchstone, 1992.

Bishop, Jim. *The Days of Martin Luther King Jr.* New York: Barnes & Noble Books, 1971.

Blum, John Morton. *Years of Discord.* New York: W. W. Norton & Company, 1991.

Bornet, Vaughn Davis. *The Presidency of Lyndon B. Johnson.* Lawrence: University Press of Kansas, 1983.

Bradlee, Ben. *A Good Life.* New York: Simon & Schuster, 1995.

Brammer, Billy Lee. *The Gay Place.* Austin: University of Texas Press, 1995.

Branch, Taylor. *Parting the Waters: America in the King Years, 1954–63.* New York: Simon & Schuster, 1989.

———. *Pillar of Fire: America in the King Years, 1963–65.* New York: Simon & Schuster, 1998.

Brands, H. W., ed. *Beyond Vietnam: The Foreign Policies of Lyndon Johnson.* College Station: Texas A&M University Press, 1999.

Brauer, Carl M. *John F. Kennedy and the Second Reconstruction.* New York: Columbia University Press, 1977.

Brooke, Edward W. *The Challenge of Change.* Boston: Little, Brown and Company, 1966.

Brown, H. Rap. *Die Nigger Die!* New York: Dial Press, 1969.

Burner, Eric. *And Gently He Shall Lead Them: Robert Parris Moses and Civil Rights in Mississippi.* New York: New York University Press, 1994.

Burns, James MacGregor. *To Heal and to Build: The Programs of President Lyndon Johnson.* New York: McGraw-Hill, 1968.

———. *Edward Kennedy and the Camelot Legacy.* New York: W. W. Norton & Company, 1976.

Burns, Stewart. *To the Mountain Top.* San Francisco: HarperSanFrancisco, 2004.

Cagin, Seth, and Philip Dray. *We Are Not Afraid: The Story of Goodman, Schwerner, and Chaney and the Civil Rights Campaign for Mississippi.* New York: Bantam Books, 1991.

Califano, Joseph A. Jr. *Governing America.* New York: Simon & Schuster, 1981.

———. *The Triumph and Tragedy of Lyndon Johnson: The White House Years.* New York: Simon & Schuster, 1991.

Campbell, Clarice T. *Civil Rights Chronicle: Letters from the South.* Jackson: University Press of Mississippi, 1997.

Caplan, Marvin. *Farther Along: A Civil Rights Memoir.* Baton Rouge: Louisiana State University Press, 1999.

Caro, Robert A. *The Years of Lyndon Johnson: The Path to Power.* New York: Alfred A. Knopf, 1982.

———. *The Years of Lyndon Johnson: Means of Ascent.* New York: Alfred A. Knopf, 1990.

———. *The Years of Lyndon Johnson: Master of the Senate.* New York: Alfred A. Knopf, 2002.

Carpenter, Liz. *Ruffles and Flourishes: The Warm and Tender Story of a Simple Girl Who Found Adventure in the White House.* New York: Pocket Books, 1969.

Carson, Clayborne. *Malcolm X: The FBI File.* New York: Ballantine Books, 1995.

———. *In Struggle: SNCC and the Black Awakening of the 1960s.* Cambridge, Mass.: Harvard University Press, 1996.

Carson, Clayborne, et al. *The Eyes on the Prize: Civil Rights Reader: Documents, Speeches, and Firsthand Accounts from the Black Freedom Struggle, 1954–1990.* New York: Penguin Books, 1991.

Carter, Dan T. *The Politics of Rage: George Wallace, the Origins of the New Conservatism, and the Transformation of American Politics.* New York: Simon & Schuster, 1995.

Cash, W. J. *The Mind of the South.* New York: Vintage Books, 1991.

Chester, Lewis, Godfrey Hodgson, and Bruce Paige. *An American Melodrama: The Presidential Campaign of 1968.* New York: Viking, 1969.

Chestnut, J. L. Jr., and Julia Cass. *Black in Selma.* New York: Farrar, Straus and Giroux, 1990.

Christian, George. *The President Steps Down.* New York: Macmillan, 1970.

Christopher, Warren. *Chances of a Lifetime.* New York: Scribner, 2001.

Clark, Ramsey. *Crime in America.* New York: Pocket Books, 1970.

Clark, Roy Peter, and Raymond Arsenault, eds. *The Changing South of Gene Patterson: Journalism and Civil Rights.* Gainesville: University Press of Florida, 2002.

Clifford, Clark. *Counsel to the President: A Memoir.* New York: Anchor Books, 1992.

Clymer, Adam. *Edward M. Kennedy.* New York: William Morrow and Company, 1999.

Colburn, David R. *Racial Change and Community Crisis: St. Augustine, Florida, 1877–1980.* Gainesville: University of Florida Press, 1991.

Coleman, Jonathan. *Long Way to Go.* New York: Atlantic Monthly Press, 1997.

Collier-Thomas, Bettye, and V. P. Franklin. *My Soul Is a Witness: A Chronology of the Civil Rights Era 1954–1965.* New York: Henry Holt and Company, 2000.

Cone, James H. *Martin and Malcolm and America.* Maryknoll, N.Y.: Orbis Books, 1998.

Congressional Quarterly Almanac. Washington, D.C.: Congressional Quarterly Service, 1964, 1967, 1968.

Conklin, Paul K. *Big Daddy from the Pedernales: Lyndon Baines Johnson.* Boston: Twayne Publishers, 1986.

Connally, John. *In History's Shadow.* New York: Hyperion, 1990.

Cormier, Frank. *LBJ the Way He Was.* Garden City, N.Y.: Doubleday & Company, 1977.

Cose, Ellis. *The Rage of a Privileged Class.* New York: HarperPerennial, 1993.

Cowger, Thomas W., and Sherwin J. Markman, eds. *Lyndon Johnson Remembered.* Lanham, Md.: Rowman & Littlefield, 2003.

Cox, Patrick. *Ralph W. Yarborough, the People's Senator.* Austin: University of Texas Press, 2001.

Cummings, Milton C. Jr., ed. *The National Election of 1964.* Washington, D.C.: Brookings Institution, 1966.

Dallek, Robert. *Hail to the Chief.* New York: Hyperion, 1996.

———. *Flawed Giant: Lyndon B. Johnson, 1960–1973.* New York: Oxford University Press, 1998.

———. *Lone Star Rising: Lyndon Johnson and His Times, 1908–1960.* New York: Oxford University Press, 1998.

———. *An Unfinished Fire: John F. Kennedy, 1917–1963.* New York: Little, Brown and Company, 2003.

Daniels, Lee, ed. *The Complexity of Black Progress.* New York: National Urban League, 2004.

Davis, James Kirkpatrick. *Assault on the Left: The FBI and the Sixties Antiwar Movement.* Westport, Conn.: Praeger Publishers, 1997.

DeLoach, Cartha D. "Deke." *Hoover's FBI: The Inside Story by Hoover's Trusted Lieutenant.* Washington, D.C.: Regnery Publishing, 1995.

Demaris, Ovid. *The Director: An Oral Biography of J. Edgar Hoover.* New York: Harper's Magazine Press, 1975.

D'Emilio, John. *Lost Prophet: The Life and Times of Bayard Rustin.* New York: Free Press, 2003.

DeWolf, L. Harold. *A Hard Rain and a Cross: Fair for a Church Under Fire.* Nashville: Abingdon Press, 1966.

Dickerson, Dennis C. *Militant Mediator: Whitney M. Young Jr.* Lexington: University Press of Kentucky, 1998.

Dierenfield, Bruce J. *Keeper of the Rules: Congressman Howard W. Smith of Virginia.* Charlottesville: University Press of Virginia, 1987.

Dietz, Terry. *Republicans and Vietnam, 1961–1968.* Westport, Conn.: Greenwood Press, 1986.

Dittmer, John. *Local People: The Struggle for Civil Rights.* Urbana: University of Illinois Press, 1995.

Divine, Robert A. *The Johnson Years.* Volume 2. Lawrence: University Press of Kansas, 1987.

———. *The Johnson Years.* Volume 3. Lawrence: University Press of Kansas, 1994.

Divine, Robert A., ed. *Exploring the Johnson Years.* Lawrence: University Press of Kansas, 1987.

Douglas, Paul H. *In the Fullness of Time.* New York: Harcourt Brace Jovanovich, 1972.

Dugger, Ronnie. *The Politician: The Life and Times of Lyndon Johnson: The Drive for Power — From the Frontier to Master of the Senate.* New York: W. W. Norton & Company, 1982.

Dulles, Foster Rhea. *The Civil Rights Commission: 1957–1965.* East Lansing: Michigan State University Press, 1968.

Dunbar, Leslie W. *Minority Report.* New York: Pantheon Books, 1984.

Durr, Virginia Foster. *Outside the Magic Circle: The Autobiography of Virginia Durr.* Ed. Hollings F. Barnard. Tuscaloosa: University of Alabama Press, 1985.

Dyson, Michael Eric. *I May Not Get There with You: The True Martin Luther King Jr.* New York: Free Press, 2000.

Edelman, Marian Wright. *Lanterns: A Memoir of Mentors.* Boston: Beacon Press, 1999.

Edelman, Peter. *Searching for America's Heart: RFK and the Renewal of Hope.* Boston: Houghton Mifflin, 2001.

Eisele, Albert. *Almost to the Presidency: A Biography of Two American Politicians.* San Francisco: Piper Company, 1972.

Ellison, Ralph. *The Collected Essays of Ralph Ellison.* New York: Modern Library, 1995.

Erenrich, Susie, ed. *Freedom Is a Constant Struggle: An Anthology of the Mississippi Civil Rights Movement.* Montgomery: Black Belt Press, 1999.

Evans, Rowland, and Robert Novak. *Lyndon B. Johnson: The Exercise of Power: A Political Biography.* New York: New American Library, 1966.

Fager, Charles. *Uncertain Resurrection: The Poor People's Washington Campaign.* Grand Rapids: William B. Eerdmans Publishing Company, 1969.

———. *Selma, 1965: The March That Changed the South.* New York: Charles Scribner's Sons, 1974.

Fairclough, Adam. *To Redeem the Soul of America.* Athens: University of Georgia Press, 1987.

Farley, Reynolds. *The New American Reality.* New York: Russell Sage Foundation, 1996.

Farley, Reynolds, ed. *State of the Union: America in the 1990s.* New York: Russell Sage Foundation, 1995.

Farmer, James. *Lay Bare the Heart.* Fort Worth: Texas Christian University Press, 1998.

Felt, Mark. *The FBI Pyramid.* New York: G. P. Putnam's Sons, 1979.

Findlay, James F. Jr. *Church People in the Struggle.* New York: Oxford University Press, 1993.

Firestone, Bernard J., and Robert C. Vogt. *Lyndon Baines Johnson and the Uses of Power.* Westport, Conn.: Greenwood Press, 1988.

Fite, Gilbert C. *Richard B. Russell Jr.: Senator from Georgia.* Chapel Hill: University of North Carolina Press, 1991.

Forman, James. *Sammy Younge Jr.* Washington, D.C.: Open Hand Publishing, 1986.

———. *The High Tide of Black Resistance.* Seattle: Open Hand Publishing, 1994.

———. *The Making of Black Revolutionaries.* Seattle: University of Washington Press, 1997.

Frady, Marshall. *Wallace.* New York: World Publishing Company, 1968.

———. *Martin Luther King Jr.* New York: Viking Books, 2002.

Franklin, John Hope. *From Slavery to Freedom.* New York: Vintage Books, 1969.

Freedman, Jonathan. *From Cradle to Grave: The Human Face of Poverty in America.* New York: Atheneum, 1993.

Galbraith, John Kenneth. *The Affluent Society.* Boston: Houghton Mifflin, 1998.

Gallup, George H. *The Gallup Poll: Public Opinion, 1933–1971.* Volumes 1–3. New York: Random House, 1972.

Gardner, Lloyd C. *Pay Any Price: Lyndon Johnson and the Wars for Vietnam.* Chicago: Ivan R. Dee, 1995.

Garrow, David J. *Protest at Selma: Martin Luther King Jr. and the Voting Rights Act of 1965.* New Haven: Yale University Press, 1978.

———. *The FBI and Martin Luther King Jr.: From Solo to Memphis.* New York: W. W. Norton & Company, 1981.

———. *Bearing the Cross: Martin Luther King Jr. and the Southern Christian Leadership Conference.* New York: William Morrow and Company, 1999.

Gentry, Curt. *J. Edgar Hoover: The Man and the Secrets.* New York: W. W. Norton & Company, 1991.

Gillette, Michael L. *Launching the War on Poverty: An Oral History.* New York: Twayne Publishers, 1996.

Ginzberg, Eli, and Robert M. Solow, eds. *The Great Society.* New York: Basic Books, 1974.

Gittinger, Ted, ed. *The Johnson Years: A Vietnam Roundtable.* Austin: Lyndon Baines Johnson Library, 1993.

Goldman, Eric F. *The Tragedy of Lyndon Johnson.* New York: Alfred A. Knopf, 1969.

Good, Paul. *The Trouble I've Seen: White Journalist, Black Movement.* Washington, D.C.: Howard University Press, 1974.

Goodwin, Doris Kearns. *Lyndon Johnson and the American Dream.* New York: St. Martin's Press, 1991.

Goodwin, Richard N. *Remembering America.* New York: Harper & Row, 1988.

Graff, Henry F. *The Tuesday Cabinet: Deliberation and Decision on Peace and War Under Lyndon B. Johnson.* Englewood Cliffs, N.J.: Prentice-Hall, 1970.

Graham, Hugh Davis. *The Uncertain Triumph: Federal Education Policy in the Kennedy and Johnson Years.* Chapel Hill: University of North Carolina Press, 1984.

———. *The Civil Rights Era: Origins and Development of National Policy.* New York: Oxford University Press, 1990.

Graham, Katharine. *Personal History.* New York: Vintage Books, 1997.

Green, George Norris. *The Establishment in Texas Politics: The Primitive Years, 1938–1957.* Norman: University of Oklahoma Press, 1979.

Greenberg, Jack. *Crusaders in the Courts.* New York: Basic Books, 1994.

Halberstam, David. *The Best and the Brightest.* New York: Random House, 1969.

———. *The Children.* New York: Fawcett Books, 1999.

Haley, J. Evetts. *A Texan Looks at Lyndon.* Canyon, Tex.: Palo Duro Press, 1964.

Hampton, Henry, and Steve Fayer. *Voices of Freedom: An Oral History of the Civil Rights Movement from the 1950s Through the 1980s.* New York: Bantam Books, 1990.

Hardeman, D. B., and Donald A. Bacon. *Rayburn: A Biography.* Austin: Texas Monthly Press, 1987.

Hardesty, Robert L., ed. *The Johnson Years: The Difference He Made.* Austin: Lyndon Baines Johnson Library, 1993.

Harding, Vincent. *There Is a River: The Black Struggle for Freedom in America.* New York: Harcourt Brace & Company, 1981.

———. *Martin Luther King: The Inconvenient Hero.* Maryknoll, N.Y.: Orbis Books, 1996.

Harrington, Michael. *The Other America: Poverty in the United States.* New York: Macmillan, 1962.

———. *Decade of Decision: The Crisis of the American System.* New York: Simon & Schuster, 1980.

Harris, Richard. *Justice.* New York: E. P. Dutton and Company, 1970.

———. *Freedom Spent.* Boston: Little, Brown and Company, 1974.

Harwood, Richard, and Haynes Johnson. *Lyndon.* New York: Praeger Publishers, 1973.

Heifetz, Ronald A. *Leadership Without Easy Answers*. Cambridge, Mass.: Harvard University Press, 1994.

Height, Dorothy. *Open Wide the Freedom Gates*. New York: Public Affairs, 2003.

Henderson, Richard B. *Maury Maverick*. Austin: University of Texas Press, 1970.

Hersh, Seymour M. *The Dark Side of Camelot*. Boston: Little, Brown and Company, 1997.

Hesburgh, Theodore M. *God, Country, Notre Dame*. New York: Doubleday, 1990.

Hirsch, Richard G. *From the Hill to the Mount*. Jerusalem: Gefen Publishing House, 2000.

Humphrey, Hubert. *Beyond Civil Rights: A New Day of Equality*. New York: Random House, 1968.

———. *The Education of a Public Man: My Life and Politics*. Ed. Norman Sherman. New York: Doubleday & Company, 1992.

Hunt, Michael H. *Lyndon Johnson's War*. New York: Hill and Wang, 1996.

Hurst, J. Willis, and James C. Cain. *LBJ: To Know Him Better*. Austin: Lyndon Baines Johnson Library, 1995.

Johnson, Charles S. *Growing Up in the Black Belt*. New York: Schocken Books, 1941.

Johnson, Lady Bird. *A White House Diary*. New York: Holt, Rinehart and Winston, 1970.

Johnson, Lyndon Baines. *The Vantage Point: Perspectives on the Presidency, 1963–1969*. New York: Popular Library, 1971.

Johnson, Paul. *A History of the American People*. New York: HarperCollins Publishers, 1998.

Johnson, Sam Houston. *My Brother Lyndon*. New York: Cowles Book Company, 1970.

Jones, Bill. *The Wallace Story*. Northport, Ala.: American Southern Publishing Company, 1966.

Kahin, George McT. *Intervention: How America Became Involved in Vietnam*. Garden City, N.Y.: Anchor Books, 1987.

Kennedy, Robert. *Robert Kennedy in His Own Words*. New York: Bantam Books, 1988.

King, Coretta Scott. *My Life with Martin Luther King Jr*. New York: Holt, Rinehart and Winston, 1969.

King, Rev. M. L. Sr. *Daddy King: An Autobiography*. New York: William Morrow and Company, 1980.

King, Martin Luther Jr. *Why We Can't Wait*. New York: Signet Classic, New American Library, 1964.

———. *A Testament of Hope: The Essential Writings and Speeches of Martin Luther King Jr*. Ed. James M. Washington. New York: HarperCollins Publishers, 1986.

———. *The Words of Martin Luther King Jr*. Ed. Coretta Scott King. New York: Newmarket Press, 1987.

———. *The Measure of a Man*. Philadelphia: Fortress Press, 1988.

———. *The Papers of Martin Luther King Jr*. Volume 1. *Called to Serve, January 1929–June 1951*. Ed. Clayborne Carson. Berkeley: University of California Press, 1992.

———. *The Martin Luther King Jr. Companion*. Ed. Coretta Scott King. New York: St. Martin's Press, 1993.

———. *The Papers of Martin Luther King Jr*. Volume 2. *Rediscovering Precious Values*,

July 1951–November 1955. Ed. Clayborne Carson. Berkeley: University of California Press, 1994.

———. *The Autobiography of Martin Luther King Jr*. Ed. Clayborne Carson. New York: Warner Books, 1998.

———. *A Knock at Midnight*. Ed. Clayborne Carson and Patter Holloran. New York: Warner Books, 1998.

———. *A Call to Conscience*. Ed. Clayborne Carson. New York: Warner Books, 2001.

King, Mary. *Freedom Song*. New York: William Morrow and Company, 1987.

Klarman, Michael J. *From Jim Crow to Civil Rights: The Supreme Court and the Struggle for Racial Equality*. New York: Oxford University Press, 2004.

Klehr, Harvey. *The Heyday of American Communism*. New York: Basic Books, 1984.

Klinkner, Philip A., and Rogers M. Smith. *The Unsteady March: The Rise and Decline of Racial Equality in America*. Chicago: University of Chicago Press, 1999.

Kluger, Richard. *Simple Justice*. New York: Vintage Books, 2004.

Kotlowski, Dean J. *Nixon's Civil Rights*. Cambridge, Mass.: Harvard University Press, 2001.

Kotz, Nick. *Let Them Eat Promises*. Englewood Cliffs, N.J.: Prentice-Hall, 1969.

Kotz, Nick, and Mary Lynn Kotz. *A Passion for Equality*. New York: W. W. Norton & Company, 1977.

Kull, Andrew. *The Color-Blind Constitution*. Cambridge, Mass.: Harvard University Press, 1992.

Lawson, Steven F. *Black Ballots: Voting Rights in the South, 1944–1969*. New York: Columbia University Press, 1976.

———. *In Pursuit of Power: Southern Blacks and Electoral Politics, 1965–1982*. New York: Columbia University Press, 1985.

———. *Running for Freedom: Civil Rights and Black Politics in America Since 1941*. New York: McGraw-Hill, 1997.

Lawson, Steven F., and Charles Payne. *Debating the Civil Rights Movement, 1945–1968*. Lanham, Md.: Rowman & Littlefield, 1998.

Lee, Chana Kai. *For Freedom's Sake: The Life of Fannie Lou Hamer*. Urbana: University of Illinois Press, 1999.

Lemann, Nicholas. *The Promised Land: The Great Black Migration and How It Changed America*. New York: Alfred A. Knopf, 1991.

Lesher, Stephen. *George Wallace: American Populist*. Reading, Mass.: Addison-Wesley, 1994.

Leuchtenburg, William E. *In the Shadow of FDR*. Ithaca: Cornell University Press, 1983.

Levison, Andrew. *The Working Class Majority*. New York: Coward, McCann & Geoghegan, 1974.

Lewis, Anthony. *Portrait of a Decade*. New York: Bantam Books, 1962.

Lewis, David Levering. *King: A Biography*. Urbana: University of Illinois Press, 1978.

Lewis, John. *Walking with the Wind: A Memoir of the Movement*. New York: Simon & Schuster, 1998.

Lincoln, C. Eric, ed. *Martin Luther King Jr.: A Profile*. New York: Hill and Wang, 1970.

Livingston, William S., Lawrence C. Dodd, and Richard L. Schott, eds. *The Presidency and the Congress*. Austin: Lyndon Baines Johnson Library, 1979.

Loevy, Robert D. *To End All Segregation: The Politics of the Passage of the Civil Rights Act of 1964*. Lanham, Md.: University Press of America, 1990.

Loevy, Robert D., ed. *The Civil Rights Act of 1964: The Passage of the Law That Ended Racial Segregation*. Albany: State University of New York, 1997.

Lyndon Baines Johnson: Late President of the United States — Memorial Tributes Delivered in Congress. Washington, D.C.: Government Printing Office, 1973.

MacNeil, Neil. *Dirksen: Portrait of a Public Man*. New York: World Publishing Company, 1970.

Manchester, William. *The Death of a President: November 1963*. New York: Harper & Row, 1967.

———. *The Glory and the Dream: 1932–1972*. Boston: Little, Brown and Company, 1973.

Mann, Robert. *The Walls of Jericho: Lyndon Johnson, Hubert Humphrey, Richard Russell, and the Struggle for Civil Rights*. New York: Harcourt Brace & Company, 1996.

———. *A Grand Delusion: America's Descent into Vietnam*. New York: Basic Books, 2002.

Marable, Manning. *Race, Reform, and Rebellion: The Second Reconstruction in Black America, 1945–1982*. Jackson: University Press of Mississippi, 1984.

Mars, Florence. *Witness in Philadelphia*. Baton Rouge: Louisiana State University Press, 1977.

Marsh, Charles. *God's Long Summer*. Princeton: Princeton University Press, 1997.

Marshall, Burke. *Federalism and Civil Rights*. New York: Columbia University Press, 1964.

Martin, Larry L., chief ed. *African Americans and Civil Rights: A Reappraisal*. Washington, D.C.: Associated Publishers, 1997.

Matusow, Allen J. *The Unraveling of America: A History of Liberalism in the 1960s*. New York: Harper Torchbooks, 1984.

Mayer, Jeremy D. *Running on Race: Racial Politics in Presidential Campaigns, 1960–2000*. New York: Random House, 2002.

McKnight, Gerald D. *The Last Crusade: Martin Luther King Jr. and the Poor People's Campaign*. Boulder, Colo.: Westview Press, 1998.

McPherson, Harry. *A Political Education: A Washington Memoir*. Austin: University of Texas Press, 1995.

McWhorter, Diane. *Carry Me Home*. New York: Simon & Schuster, 2001.

Milkis, Sidney M. *The President and the Parties*. New York: Oxford University Press, 1993.

Milkis, Sidney M., and Michael Nelson. *The American Presidency: Origins and Developments, 1776–1993*. Washington, D.C.: CQ Press, 1994.

Miller, Merle. *Lyndon: An Oral Biography*. New York: G. P. Putnam's Sons, 1980.

Mills, Nicolaus. *Like a Holy Crusade: Mississippi, 1964 . . .* Chicago: Ivan R. Dee, 1992.

Morris, Aldon D. *The Origins of the Civil Rights Movement*. New York: Free Press, 1984.

Moses, Robert P., and Charles E. Cobb Jr. *Racial Equations: Math, Literacy, and Civil Rights*. Boston: Beacon Press, 2001.

Motley, Constance Baker. *Equal Justice Under Law*. New York: Farrar, Straus and Giroux, 1998.

Navasky, Victor S. *Kennedy Justice.* New York: Atheneum, 1971.

Nevin, David, and Robert E. Bills. *The Schools That Fear Built: Segregationist Academies in the South.* Washington, D.C.: Acropolis Books, 1976.

Oates, Stephen B. *Let the Trumpet Sound: A Life of Martin Luther King Jr.* New York: HarperPerrenial, 1994.

Oberdorfer, Don. *Senator Mansfield.* Washington, D.C.: Smithsonian Books, 2003.

O'Brien, Lawrence F. *No Final Victories.* New York: Doubleday & Company, 1974.

Ogletree, Charles J. Jr. *All Deliberate Speed.* New York: W. W. Norton & Company, 2004.

Olson, Lynne. *Freedom's Daughters: The Unsung Heroines of the Civil Rights Movement from 1830 to 1970.* New York: Simon & Schuster, 2001.

O'Neill, Tip. *Man of the House: Life and Political Memoirs of Tip O'Neill.* New York: Random House, 1987.

O'Reilly, Kenneth. *Black Americans: The FBI Files.* New York: Carroll & Graf, 1994.

———. *Racial Matters: The FBI's Secret File on Black America.* Ed. David Gallen. New York: Free Press, 1994.

Orfield, Gary. *The Reconstruction of Southern Education: The Schools and the 1964 Civil Rights Act.* New York: Wiley-Interscience, 1969.

Orfield, Gary, Susan E. Eaton, et al. *Dismantling Desegregation.* New York: New Press, 1996.

Parker, Frank R. *Black Votes Count: Political Empowerment in Mississippi After 1965.* Chapel Hill: University of North Carolina Press, 1990.

Parker, Robert. *Capitol Hill in Black and White.* New York: Dodd, Mead & Company, 1986.

Parmet, Herbert S. *JFK: The Presidency of John F. Kennedy.* New York: Penguin Books, 1983.

Patterson, Orlando. *The Ordeal of Integration.* Washington, D.C.: Civitas/Counterpoint, 1997.

Peabody, Robert L. *Leadership in Congress.* Boston: Little, Brown and Company, 1976.

Peck, James. *Freedom Ride.* New York: Grove Press, 1962.

Phillips, Donald T. *Martin Luther King Jr. on Leadership.* New York: Warner Books, 1998.

Platts, Amelia, and Boynton Robinson. *Bridge Across Jordan.* Washington, D.C.: Schiller Institute, 1991.

Poinsett, Alex. *Walking with Presidents: Louis Martin and the Rise of Black Political Power.* Lanham, Md.: Madison Books, 1997.

Polsby, Nelson W., ed. *Congressional Behavior.* New York: Random House, 1971.

Posner, Gerald. *Killing the Dream: James Earl Ray and the Assassination of Martin Luther King Jr.* San Diego: Harcourt Brace & Company, 1998.

Powers, Georgia Davis. *I Shared the Dream: The Pride, Passion, and Politics . . .* Far Hills, N.J.: New Horizon Press, 1995.

Powers, Richard Gid. *Secrecy and Power: The Life of J. Edgar Hoover.* New York: Free Press, 1987.

Powers, Thomas E. *Vietnam: The War at Home.* Boston: G. K. Hall & Company, 1973.

Powledge, Fred. *Free At Last?* New York: HarperPerennial, 1991.

Raines, Howell. *My Soul Is Rested.* New York: G. P. Putnam's Sons, 1977.

Reddick, L. D. *Crusader Without Violence: A Biography of Martin Luther King Jr.* New York: Harper & Brothers, 1959.

Redding, Saunders. *They Came in Chains: Americans from Africa.* Philadelphia: J. B. Lippincott Company, 1973.

Reed, Roy. *Faubus: The Life and Times of an American Prodigal.* Fayetteville: University of Arkansas Press, 1997.

Reedy, George E. *The Twilight of the Presidency: An Examination of Power and Isolation in the White House.* New York: World Publishing Company, 1970.

———. *Lyndon B. Johnson: A Memoir.* New York: Andrews and McMeel, 1982.

Reeves, Richard. *President Kennedy: Profile of Power.* New York: Simon & Schuster, 1993.

Report of the National Advisory Commission on Civil Disorders. New York: Bantam Books, 1968.

Reston, James. *Deadline: A Memoir.* New York: Times Books, 1992.

Reynolds, Barbara A. *Jesse Jackson.* Chicago: Nelson-Hall, 1975.

Roberts, Chalmers M. *First Rough Draft: A Journalist's Journal of Our Times.* New York: Praeger Publishers, 1973.

Rooney, Robert C., ed. *Equal Opportunity in the United States: A Symposium on Civil Rights.* Austin: Lyndon Baines Johnson Library, 1973.

Rosenberg, Jonathan, and Zachary Karabell. *Kennedy, Johnson, and the Quest for Justice: The Civil Rights Tapes.* New York: W. W. Norton & Company, 2003.

Rowan, Carl. *Breaking Barriers.* Boston: Little, Brown and Company, 1991.

Russell, Jan Jarboe. *Lady Bird: A Biography of Mrs. Johnson.* New York: Scribner, 1999.

Rustin, Bayard. *Down the Line: The Collected Writings of Bayard Rustin.* Chicago: Quadrangle Books, 1971.

———. *Strategies for Freedom.* New York: Columbia University Press, 1976.

Ryan, William. *Equality.* New York: Pantheon Books, 1981.

Safer, Morley. *Flashbacks.* New York: St. Martin's Paperbacks, 1990.

Schlesinger, Arthur Jr. *Robert Kennedy and His Times.* Volumes 1 and 2. Boston: Houghton Mifflin, 1978.

———. *The Disuniting of America.* New York: W. W. Norton & Company, 1993.

Schneier, Rabbi Marc. *Shared Dreams: MLK and the Jewish Community.* Woodstock, Vt.: Jewish Lights Publishing, 1999.

Schott, Richard L., and Dagmar S. Hamilton. *People, Positions, and Power: The Political Appointments of Lyndon Johnson.* Chicago: University of Chicago Press, 1983.

Schulke, Flip, ed. *Martin Luther King Jr.: A Documentary . . . Montgomery to Memphis.* New York: W. W. Norton & Company, 1976.

Schulke, Flip, and Penelope McPhee. *King Remembered.* New York: Pocket Books, 1986.

Schulman, Bruce J. *Lyndon B. Johnson and American Liberalism.* Boston: Bedford Books, 1995.

Sellers, Cleveland. *The River of No Return: The Autobiography of a Black Militant.* Jackson: University Press of Mississippi, 1990.

Shapley, Deborah. *Promise and Power: The Life and Times of Robert McNamara.* Boston: Little, Brown and Company, 1993.

Sherrill, Robert, et al. *Investigating the FBI*. New York: Doubleday & Company, 1971.

Shesol, Jeff. *Mutual Contempt: Lyndon B. Johnson, Robert Kennedy, and the Feud That Defined a Decade*. New York: W. W. Norton & Company, 1997.

Shipler, David K. *The Working Poor: Invisible in America*. New York: Alfred A. Knopf, 2004.

Sidey, Hugh. *A Very Personal Presidency: Lyndon Johnson in the White House*. New York: Atheneum, 1968.

Silver, James W. *Mississippi: The Closed Society*. New York: Harcourt, Brace & World, 1964.

Skrentny, John David. *The Ironies of Affirmative Action*. Chicago: University of Chicago Press, 1996.

Smith, Charles U., ed. *The Civil Rights Movement in Florida and the United States*. Tallahassee, Fla.: Father and Son Publishing, 1989.

Sorensen, Theodore C. *Kennedy*. New York: Harper & Row, 1965.

Sowell, Thomas. *Race and Economics*. New York: David McKay, 1976.

Spike, Robert. *The Freedom Revolution and the Churches*. New York: Association Press, 1965.

Steel, Ronald. *In Love with Night*. New York: Simon & Schuster, 2000.

Stein, Jean. *American Journey: The Times of Robert Kennedy*. Ed. George Plimpton. New York: New American Library, 1970.

Steinberg, Alfred. *Sam Johnson's Boy*. New York: Macmillan, 1968.

———. *Sam Rayburn: A Biography*. New York: Hawthorn Books, 1975.

Stern, Mark. *Calculating Visions: Kennedy, Johnson, and Civil Rights*. New Brunswick, N.J.: Rutgers University Press, 1992.

Stuart, John G. "Independence and Control: The Challenge of Senatorial Party Leadership." Ph.D. diss., University of Chicago, 1968.

Sullivan, William C. *The Bureau: My Thirty Years in the FBI*. New York: W. W. Norton & Company, 1979.

Sunnemark, Fredrik. *Ring Out Freedom: The Voice of Martin Luther King Jr. and the Making of the Civil Rights Movement*. Bloomington: Indiana University Press, 2004.

Theoharis, Athan, ed. *From the Secret Files of J. Edgar Hoover*. Chicago: Ivan R. Dee, 1991.

Theoharis, Athan G., and John Stuart Cox. *The Boss: J. Edgar Hoover and the Great Inquisition*. Philadelphia: Temple University Press, 1988.

Thernstrom, Stephan, and Abigail Thernstrom. *America in Black and White*. New York: Simon & Schuster, 1997.

Thomas, Evan. *Robert F. Kennedy*. New York: Simon & Schuster, 2000.

Thomas, Helen. *Dateline: White House*. New York: Macmillan, 1975.

Thurber, Timothy N. *The Politics of Equality: Hubert H. Humphrey and the African American Freedom Struggle*. New York: Columbia University Press, 1999.

Tressolini, Rocco J., and Richard T. Frost, eds. *Cases in American National Government and Politics*. Englewood Cliffs, N.J.: Prentice-Hall, 1966.

Ture, Kwame, and Charles Hamilton. *Black Power*. New York: Vintage Books, 1992.

Turner, Kathleen J. *Lyndon Johnson's Dual War*. Chicago: University of Chicago Press, 1985.

Ungar, Sanford J. *FBI*. Boston: Little, Brown, 1976.

Unger, Irwin, and Debi Unger. *LBJ: A Life.* New York: John Wiley & Sons, 1999.

Valenti, Jack. *A Very Human President.* New York: W. W. Norton & Company, 1975.

VanDeMark, Brian. *Into the Quagmire: Lyndon Johnson.* New York: Oxford University Press, 1991.

Viorst, Milton. *Fire in the Streets: America in the 1960s.* New York: Simon & Schuster, 1979.

Wannall, Ray. *The Real J. Edgar Hoover: For the Record.* Paducah, Ky.: Turner Publishing Company, 2000.

Warren, Robert Penn. *Segregation: The Inner Conflict in the South.* New York: Vintage Books, 1956.

———. *Who Speaks for the Negro?* New York: Random House, 1965.

Watson, Denton. *Lion in the Lobby: Clarence Mitchell Jr.'s Struggle for the Passage of Civil Rights Laws.* New York: William Morrow & Company, 1990.

Watters, Pat, and Reese Cleghorn. *Climbing Jacob's Ladder.* New York: Harcourt, Brace & World, 1967.

Weisbrot, Robert. *Freedom Bound: A History of America's Civil Rights Movement.* New York: Plume Books, 1991.

Weiss, Nancy J. *Whitney M. Young Jr. and the Struggle for Civil Rights.* Princeton: Princeton University Press, 1989.

West, J. B., and Mary Lynn Kotz. *Upstairs at the White House.* New York: Warner Books, 1974.

West, Thomas R., and James W. Mooney, eds. *To Redeem a Nation.* New York: Brandywine Press, 1993.

Wexler, Stanford. *The Civil Rights Movement.* New York: Facts on File, 1993.

Whalen, Charles, and Barbara Whalen. *The Longest Debate: A Legislative History.* Cabin John, Md.: Seven Locks Press, 1985.

White, Theodore. *The Making of the President, 1964.* New York: Atheneum, 1965.

White, William S. *Citadel.* New York: Harper & Brothers, 1956.

Whitehead, Don. *The FBI Story: A Report to the People.* New York: Random House, 1956.

———. *Attack on Terror: The FBI Against the Ku Klux Klan in Mississippi.* New York: Funk & Wagnalls, 1970.

Wicker, Tom. *JFK and LBJ: The Influence of Personality upon Politics.* New York: William Morrow & Company, 1969.

Wilkins, Roger. *A Man's Life: An Autobiography.* New York: Simon & Schuster, 1982.

Wilkins, Roy. *Standing Fast: The Autobiography of Roy Wilkins.* New York: Penguin Books, 1982.

Williams, Juan. *Eyes on the Prize: America's Civil Rights Years, 1954–1965.* New York: Penguin Books, 1988.

———. *Thurgood Marshall: American Revolutionary.* New York: Times Books, 1998.

Wilson, William Julius. *When Work Disappears: The World of the New Urban Poor.* New York: Vintage Books, 1996.

Windle, Janice Woods. *Hill Country.* Marietta, Ga.: Longstreet Press, 1998.

Wise, David. *The Politics of Lying.* New York: Vintage Books, 1973.

———. *The American Police State: The Government Against the People.* New York: Random House, 1976.

Witcover, Jules. *The Year the Dream Died: Revisiting 1968 in America.* New York: Warner Books, 1997.

Wofford, Harris. *Of Kennedys and Kings: Making Sense of the Sixties.* Pittsburgh: University of Pittsburgh Press, 1980.

Woods, Randall Bennett. *Fulbright: A Biography.* New York: Cambridge University Press, 1995.

Woodward, C. Vann. *The Strange Career of Jim Crow.* New York: Oxford University Press, 1974.

Young, Andrew. *A Way Out of No Way.* Nashville: Thomas Nelson Publishers, 1994.

———. *An Easy Burden: The Civil Rights Movement and the Transformation of America.* New York: HarperCollins, 1996.

Young, Roy. "Presidential Leadership and Civil Rights Legislation." Ph.D. diss., University of Texas at Austin, 1979.

Zinn, Howard. *SNCC: The New Abolitionists.* Boston: Beacon Press, 1964.

INDEX